ABOUT THE COVER ART

Parmigianino (Francesco Mazzola), *Portrait of a Young Man*

Renaissance painters introduced the genre of the individual portrait, such as this sixteenth-century painting of a young man (possibly a self-portrait) attributed to Francesco Mazzola. Renaissance portraits depicted their subjects in a realistic and recognizable manner, replacing the stiffness and artifice of medieval images of the body. This young man's self-confident gaze reflects the bustling urban culture of the Renaissance and its worldly values.

THE CONTEMPORARY WORLD

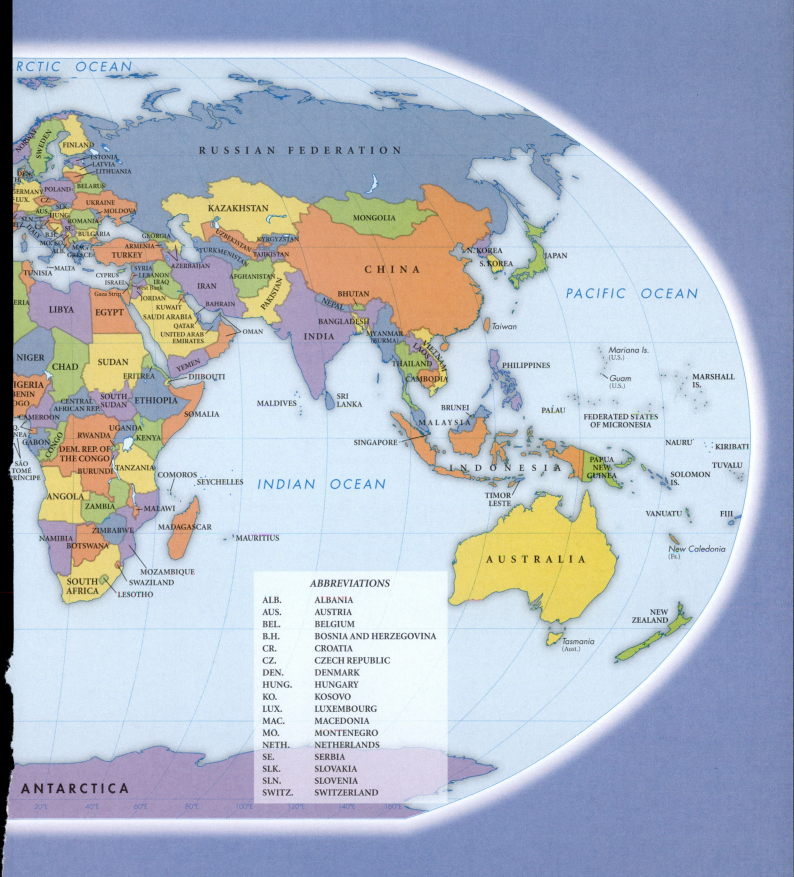

ARCTIC OCEAN

RUSSIAN FEDERATION

NORWAY
SWEDEN
FINLAND
ESTONIA
LATVIA
LITHUANIA
BELARUS
GERMANY
POLAND
LUX.
CZ.
SLK.
UKRAINE
MOLDOVA
SLN.
AUS.
HUNG.
ROMANIA
SWITZ.
CR.
B.H.
BULGARIA
ITALY
MO. KO.
SE.
ALB.
MAC.
GREECE
TUNISIA
MALTA
CYPRUS
ISRAEL
LEBANON
SYRIA
GEORGIA
ARMENIA
AZERBAIJAN
TURKEY
IBERIA
LIBYA
EGYPT
Gaza Strip
West Bank
JORDAN
IRAQ
KUWAIT
BAHRAIN
QATAR
SAUDI ARABIA
UNITED ARAB
EMIRATES
OMAN
YEMEN
IRAN
AFGHANISTAN
TURKMENISTAN
UZBEKISTAN
KAZAKHSTAN
KYRGYZSTAN
TAJIKISTAN
PAKISTAN
NIGER
CHAD
SUDAN
ERITREA
DJIBOUTI
NIGERIA
BENIN
TOGO
CENTRAL
AFRICAN REP.
SOUTH
SUDAN
ETHIOPIA
SOMALIA
CAMEROON
EQ.
GUINEA
GABON
CONGO
DEM. REP. OF
THE CONGO
RWANDA
BURUNDI
UGANDA
KENYA
TANZANIA
SÃO
TOMÉ
PRÍNCIPE
ANGOLA
ZAMBIA
MALAWI
ZIMBABWE
NAMIBIA
BOTSWANA
MOZAMBIQUE
SWAZILAND
SOUTH
AFRICA
LESOTHO
MADAGASCAR
COMOROS
SEYCHELLES
MAURITIUS

MALDIVES
SRI
LANKA
INDIA
NEPAL
BHUTAN
BANGLADESH
MYANMAR
(BURMA)
THAILAND
LAOS
VIETNAM
CAMBODIA
CHINA
MONGOLIA
N. KOREA
S. KOREA
JAPAN
Taiwan

PACIFIC OCEAN

INDIAN OCEAN

PHILIPPINES
BRUNEI
MALAYSIA
SINGAPORE
INDONESIA
TIMOR
LESTE
Mariana Is.
(U.S.)
Guam
(U.S.)
PALAU
FEDERATED STATES
OF MICRONESIA
PAPUA
NEW
GUINEA
MARSHALL
IS.
NAURU
KIRIBATI
TUVALU
SOLOMON
IS.
VANUATU
FIJI
New Caledonia
(Fr.)

AUSTRALIA

NEW
ZEALAND
Tasmania
(Aust.)

ANTARCTICA

20°E 40°E 60°E 80°E 100°E 120°E 140°E 160°E

ABBREVIATIONS

ALB.	ALBANIA
AUS.	AUSTRIA
BEL.	BELGIUM
B.H.	BOSNIA AND HERZEGOVINA
CR.	CROATIA
CZ.	CZECH REPUBLIC
DEN.	DENMARK
HUNG.	HUNGARY
KO.	KOSOVO
LUX.	LUXEMBOURG
MAC.	MACEDONIA
MO.	MONTENEGRO
NETH.	NETHERLANDS
SE.	SERBIA
SLK.	SLOVAKIA
SLN.	SLOVENIA
SWITZ.	SWITZERLAND

A History of Western Society

A History of Western Society

Eleventh Edition

VOLUME B
From the Later Middle Ages to 1815

John P. McKay
University of Illinois at Urbana-Champaign

Bennett D. Hill
Late of Georgetown University

John Buckler
Late of University of Illinois at Urbana-Champaign

Clare Haru Crowston
University of Illinois at Urbana-Champaign

Merry E. Wiesner-Hanks
University of Wisconsin–Milwaukee

Joe Perry
Georgia State University

BEDFORD/ST. MARTIN'S

Boston • New York

FOR BEDFORD/ST. MARTIN'S

Publisher for History: Mary V. Dougherty
Executive Editor for History: Traci M. Crowell
Director of Development for History: Jane Knetzger
Developmental Editor: Annette Fantasia
Senior Production Editor: Christina M. Horn
Senior Production Supervisor: Dennis J. Conroy
Executive Marketing Manager: Sandra McGuire
Editorial Assistant: Emily DiPietro
Production Assistant: Elise Keller
Copy Editor: Jennifer Brett Greenstein
Indexer: Leoni Z. McVey
Cartography: Mapping Specialists, Ltd.
Photo Researcher: Carole Frohlich and Elisa Gallagher, The Visual
  Connection Image Research, Inc.

Senior Art Director: Anna Palchik
Text Designer: Jonathon Nix
Page Layout: Boynton Hue Studio
Cover Designer: Billy Boardman
Cover Art: Parmigianino (Francesco Mazzola) (1503–1540), *Portrait of a Young Man* (oil on panel). Louvre, Paris/Peter Willi/The Bridgeman Art Library.
Composition: Jouve
Printing and Binding: RR Donnelley and Sons

President, Bedford/St. Martin's: Denise B. Wydra
Director of Marketing: Karen R. Soeltz
Production Director: Susan W. Brown
Director of Rights and Permissions: Hilary Newman

Manufactured in the United States of America.

1 2 3 4 5 6   17 16 15 14 13

For information, write: Bedford/St. Martin's, 75 Arlington Street, Boston, MA 02116   (617-399-4000)

ISBN 978-1-4576-1513-9 (Combined Edition)
ISBN 978-1-4576-5270-7 (Loose-leaf Edition)
ISBN 978-1-4576-4222-7 (Volume 1)
ISBN 978-1-4576-5272-1 (Loose-leaf Edition, Volume 1)
ISBN 978-1-4576-4219-7 (Volume 2)

ISBN 978-1-4576-5271-4 (Loose-leaf Edition, Volume 2)
ISBN 978-1-4576-4216-6 (Volume A)
ISBN 978-1-4576-4220-3 (Volume B)
ISBN 978-1-4576-4217-3 (Volume C)
ISBN 978-1-4576-4218-0 (Since 1300)

A History of Western Society grew out of the initial three authors' desire to infuse new life into the study of Western Civilization. With this eleventh edition, we three new authors, Clare Haru Crowston, Merry E. Wiesner-Hanks, and Joe Perry—who first used the book as students or teachers—have assumed full responsibility for the revision and continue to incorporate the latest and best scholarship in the field. All three of us regularly teach introductory history courses and thus bring insights from the classroom, as well as from new secondary works and our own research in archives and libraries, into the text.

In this new edition we aimed to enhance the distinctive attention to daily life that sparks students' interest while also providing a number of innovative tools—both print and digital—designed to help students think historically and master the material. In response to the growing emphasis on historical thinking skills in the teaching of history at all levels, as well as to requests from our colleagues and current adopters, we have significantly expanded the book's primary source program to offer **more sources in more ways**. Every chapter now has at least five primary sources, both written and visual, and additional document sets online. Indeed, as the digital world continues to transform teaching and learning, this edition is integrated with exciting new online resources—automatically available when students purchase a new copy of the book—consisting of **Online Document Assignments** tied closely to each chapter that allow students to practice analysis and synthesis of fascinating document sets, as well as **LearningCurve**, an adaptive learning tool that helps students master the content. Finally, this edition introduces **LaunchPad**, a robust new interactive e-book built into its own course space that makes customizing and assigning the book and its resources simpler than ever. To learn more about the benefits of LearningCurve and LaunchPad, see the "Versions and Supplements" section on page xvii.

The Story of *A History of Western Society*: Bringing the Past to Life for Students

At the point when *A History of Western Society* was first conceptualized, social history was dramatically changing the ways we understood the past, and the original authors decided to create a book that would re-create the lives of ordinary people in appealing human terms, while also giving major economic, political, cultural, and intellectual developments the attention they unquestionably deserve. We three new authors remain committed to advancing this vision for today's classroom, with a broader definition of social history that brings the original idea into the twenty-first century.

History as a discipline never stands still, and over the last several decades cultural history has joined social history as a source of dynamism. Because of its emphasis on the ways people made sense of their lives, *A History of Western Society* has always included a large amount of cultural history, ranging from foundational works of philosophy and literature to popular songs and stories. The focus on cultural history has been heightened in this eleventh edition in a way that highlights the interplay between men's and women's lived experiences and the ways men and women reflect on these experiences to create meaning. The joint social and cultural perspective requires—fortunately, in our opinion—the inclusion of objects as well as texts as important sources for studying history, which has allowed us to incorporate the growing emphasis on material culture in the work of many historians. We know that engaging students' interest in the past is often a challenge, but we also know that the text's hallmark approach—the emphasis on daily life and individual experience in its social and cultural dimensions—connects with students and makes the past vivid and accessible.

Additional "Life" Chapters

Although social and cultural history can be found in every chapter, they are particularly emphasized in the acclaimed "Life" chapters that have always distinguished this book. In response to popular demand by reviewers of the previous edition, these have been increased to five in this edition and now include Chapter 4: Life in the Hellenistic World, 336–30 B.C.E., and Chapter 30: Life in an Age of Globalization, 1990 to the Present, which join Chapter 10: Life in Villages and Cities of the High Middle Ages, 1000–1300; Chapter 18: Life in the Era of Expansion, 1650–1800; and Chapter 22: Life in the Emerging Urban Society, 1840–1914.

We are delighted to incorporate additional "Life" chapters into this edition, as many instructors have told us that it is these distinctive chapters that spark student interest by making the past palpable and approachable in human terms. And because we know that a key challenge of teaching history—and Western Civilization in particular—is encouraging students to appreciate the relevance of the past to our lives today, these five "Life" chapters each include a **NEW feature called "The Past Living Now"** that examines an aspect of life today with origins in the period covered in that chapter. Featuring engaging topics such as the development of the modern university

(Chapter 10) and the dawn of commercialized sports (Chapter 18), these essays were conceived with student interest in mind. These "Life" chapters are also enhanced with **NEW Online Document Assignments**, rich and carefully crafted sets of primary sources that allow students to delve further into a key development from each chapter while they analyze and synthesize the evidence. See the "More Sources More Ways" section below for more details.

More Sources More Ways

Because understanding the past requires that students engage directly with sources on their own, this edition features an exciting **NEW** and expansive primary source program. Each chapter now includes at least five sources, both written and visual, and each source opens with a headnote and closes with questions for analysis that invite students to evaluate the evidence as historians would. Selected for their interest and carefully integrated into their historical context, these sources provide students with firsthand encounters with people of the past along with the means and tools for building historical skills.

To give students abundant opportunities to hone their textual and visual analysis skills as well as a sense of the variety of sources on which historians rely, the primary source program includes a mix of canonical and lesser-known sources; a diversity of perspectives representing ordinary and prominent individuals alike; and a wide variety of source types, from tomb inscriptions, diaries, sermons, letters, poetry, and drama to artifacts, architecture, and propaganda posters. In addition, we have quoted extensively from a wide range of primary sources in the narrative, demonstrating that such quotations are the "stuff" of history. We believe that our extensive use of primary source extracts as an integral part of the narrative as well as in extended form in the primary source boxes will give students ample practice in thinking critically and historically.

This edition also breaks new ground by offering additional document sets online—called **Online Document Assignments**—tied closely to each chapter of the text and available with the purchase of a new textbook via the code printed on the inside front cover. Each assignment, based on either the "Individuals in Society" feature or key developments from the "Life" chapters (Chapters 4, 10, 18, 22, and 30), prompts students to explore a key question through analysis of multiple sources. Chapter 14, for example, asks students to analyze documents on the complexities of race, identity, and slavery in the early modern era to shed light on the conditions that made Juan de Pareja's story possible. The assignments feature a wealth of textual and visual sources as well as video and audio. Assignments based on the "Individuals in Society" feature include three to four documents in each assignment, while those based on the "Life" chapters include six to

eight documents. These Online Document Assignments provide instructors with a rich variety of assignment options that encourage students to draw their own conclusions, with the help of short-answer questions, multiple-choice questions that provide instant feedback, and a final essay assignment that asks students to use the sources in creative ways.

Finally, the thoroughly revised companion reader, *Sources for Western Society*, Third Edition, provides a rich selection of documents to complement each chapter of the text and is **FREE** when packaged with the textbook.

Distinctive Essay Features

In addition to the new primary source program, we are proud of the two unique boxed essay features in each chapter—"**Individuals in Society**" and "**Living in the Past**"—that personalize larger developments and make them tangible.

To give students a chance to see the past through ordinary people's lives, each chapter includes one of the popular "**Individuals in Society**" biographical essays, which offer brief studies of individuals or groups, informing students about the societies in which they lived. We have found that readers empathize with these human beings as they themselves seek to define their own identities. The spotlighting of individuals, both famous and obscure, perpetuates the book's continued attention to cultural and intellectual developments, highlights human agency, and reflects changing interests within the historical profession as well as the development of "microhistory." **NEW** features include essays on Anna Jansz of Rotterdam, an Anabaptist martyr; Hürrem, a concubine who became a powerful figure in the Ottoman Empire during the sixteenth century; and Rebecca Protten, a former slave and leader in the Moravian missionary movement. As mentioned previously, the majority of these features are tied to **NEW Online Document Assignments** that allow students to further explore the historical conditions in which these individuals lived.

To introduce students to the study of material culture, "**Living in the Past**" essays use social and cultural history to show how life in the past was both similar to and different from our lives today. As authors, we found it both a challenge and a pleasure to focus on relatively narrow aspects of social and cultural history in order to write compelling stories that would encourage students to think about the way the past informs the present. These features are richly illustrated with images and artifacts and include a short essay and questions for analysis. We use these essays to explore the deeper ramifications of things students might otherwise take for granted, such as consumer goods, factories, and even currency. Students connect to the people of the past through a diverse range of topics such as "Assyrian Palace Life and Power," "Roman Table Manners," "Foods of the Columbian Exchange," "Coffeehouse

Culture," "The Immigrant Experience," "A Model Social-ist Steel Town," and "The Supermarket Revolution."

Updated Organization and Coverage

To meet the demands of the evolving course, we took a close and critical look at the book's structure and have made changes in the organization of chapters to reflect the way the course is taught today. Most notably, in addi-tion to consolidating some coverage in the two new "Life" chapters described previously, we have combined the three chapters on the High Middle Ages in the previous edition into two (Chapters 9 and 10), restructuring and in some cases shortening sections but retaining all key con-cepts and topics, resulting in one fewer chapter overall. Chapter 9 now focuses more tightly on political, legal, and institutional developments in church and state, and Chapter 10 on the life of both villagers and city folk.

This edition is also enhanced by the incorporation of a wealth of new scholarship and subject areas that immerse students in the dynamic and ongoing work of history. Chapters 1–6 have been intensively revised to incorpo-rate the exciting cross-disciplinary scholarship that has emerged over the last several decades on the Paleolithic and Neolithic eras, river valley civilizations, and the ancient Mediterranean. For example, archaeologists working at Göbekli Tepe in present-day Turkey have unearthed rings of massive, multiton, elaborately carved limestone pillars built around 9000 B.C.E. by groups of foragers, which has led to a rethinking of the links between culture, religion, and the initial development of agriculture. Similarly, new research on the peoples of Mesopotamia, based on cunei-form writing along with other sources, has led scholars to revise the view that they were fatalistic and to emphasize instead that Mesopotamians generally anticipated being well treated by the gods if they behaved morally. Through-out these chapters, new material on cross-cultural connec-tions, the impact of technologies, and changing social relationships has been added, particularly in Chapter 4, which has been recast as Life in the Hellenistic World. Other additions include an expanded discussion of the historiography of the fall of the Roman Empire (Chap-ter 7); new material on the reconquista (Chapter 9); recent ideas on the impact of empire on the Scientific Revolu-tion (Chapter 16); more on the experiences of African Americans, Native Americans, and women in the revolu-tionary era (Chapter 19); significant updates to the Indus-trial Revolution coverage, including increased attention to the global context (Chapter 20); revised treatment of ideologies and romanticism (Chapter 21); new coverage of the popular appeal of nationalism (Chapter 23); new material on Orientalism and European imperialism (Chapter 24); extensive updates on the Cold War (Chap-ter 28); and up-to-date coverage of contemporary events in the final chapter, now called Life in an Age of Global-ization, including the euro crisis, issues surrounding im-

migration and Muslims in Europe, and the Arab Spring (Chapter 30).

Improved Learning Aids

We know firsthand and take seriously the challenges stu-dents face in understanding, retaining, and mastering so much material that is often unfamiliar. With the goal of making this the most student-centered edition yet, we continued to enhance the book's pedagogy on many fronts. As mentioned earlier, the **NEW LearningCurve online adaptive tool** allows students to rehearse the con-tent and come to class prepared. In addition, to focus stu-dents' reading, each chapter opens with a **chapter preview with focus questions** keyed to the main chapter head-ings. These questions are repeated within the chapter and again in the **NEW "Review and Explore" section** at the end of each chapter that provides helpful guidance for reviewing key topics. In addition, **NEW "Make Con-nections" questions** prompt students to assess larger de-velopments across chapters, thus allowing them to develop skills in evaluating change and continuity, making com-parisons, and analyzing context and causation.

Each "Review and Explore" section concludes with a **NEW "Suggested Reading and Media Resources"** list-ing that includes up-to-date readings on the vast amount of new work being done in many fields, as well as recom-mended documentaries, feature films, television, and Web sites.

To help students understand the material and prepare for exams, each chapter includes **"Looking Back, Look-ing Ahead" conclusions** that provide an insightful synthe-sis of the chapter's main developments, while connecting to events that students will encounter in the chapters to come. In this way students are introduced to history as an ongoing process of interrelated events.

To promote clarity and comprehension, boldface **key terms** in the text are defined in the margins and listed in the chapter review. **Phonetic spellings** are located directly after terms that readers are likely to find hard to pro-nounce. The **chapter chronologies**, which review major developments discussed in each chapter, mirror the key events of the chapter, and the topic-specific **thematic chronologies** that appear in many chapters provide a more focused timeline of certain developments. Once again we also provide a **unified timeline** at the end of the text. Comprehensive and easy to locate, this useful time-line allows students to compare developments over the centuries.

The high-quality art and map program has been thor-oughly revised and features hundreds of **contemporane-ous illustrations**. To make the past tangible, and as an extension of our attention to cultural history, we include numerous **artifacts**—from swords and fans to playing cards and record players. As in earlier editions, all illustra-tions have been carefully selected to complement the text, and all include captions that inform students while encouraging them to read the text more deeply. High-quality **full-size maps** illustrate major developments in the narrative, and helpful **spot maps** are embedded in the narrative to show areas under discussion.

We recognize students' difficulties with geography, and the new edition includes the popular "**Mapping the Past**" **map activities**. Included in each chapter, these activities give students valuable skills in reading and interpreting maps by asking them to analyze the maps and make connections to the larger processes discussed in the narrative.

These new directions have not changed the central mission of the book, which is to introduce students to the broad sweep of Western Civilization in a fresh yet balanced manner. Every edition has incorporated new research to keep the book up-to-date and respond to the changing needs of readers and instructors, and we have continued to do this in the eleventh edition. As we have made these changes, large and small, we have sought to give students and teachers an integrated perspective so that they could pursue—on their own or in the classroom—the historical questions that they find particularly exciting and significant.

Acknowledgments

It is a pleasure to thank the many instructors who read and critiqued the manuscript through its development:

William M. Abbott, Fairfield University
Joseph Avitable, Quinnipiac University
Dudley Belcher, Tri-County Technical College
Amy Bix, Iowa State University
Nancy Bjorklund, Fullerton College
Robert Blackey, California State University, San Bernardino
Stephen Blumm, Montgomery County Community College
Robert Brennan, Cape Fear Community College
Daniel Bubb, Gonzaga University
Jeff Burson, Georgia Southern University
George Carson, Central Bible College
Michael Cavey, Northern Virginia Community College
Marie Therese Champagne, University of West Florida
Mark W. Chavalas, University of Wisconsin–LaCrosse
David Cherry, Montana State University, Bozeman
Benzion Chinn, Ohio State University
Thomas Colbert, Marshalltown Community College
Elizabeth Collins, Triton College
Amy Colon, Sullivan County Community College
Kristen Cornelis, Community Colleges of Spokane, Institute for Extended Learning
Michael H. Creswell, Florida State University

Andrea DeKoter, State University of New York at Cortland
Donna Donald, Liberty University
Kurt J. Eberly, Tidewater Community College
John Ebley, Anne Arundel Community College
Christopher Ferguson, Auburn University
Robert Figueira, Lander University
Paula Findlen, Stanford University
Jennifer Foray, Purdue University
Laura Gathagan, State University of New York at Cortland
Stephen Gibson, Allegany College of Maryland
Gregory Golden, Rhode Island College
Jack Goldstone, George Mason University
Chuck Goodwin, Illinois Valley Community College
Dolores Grapsas, New River Community College
Robert Grasso, Monmouth University
Robert H. Greene, University of Montana
Edward Gutierrez, University of Hartford
David Halahmy, Cypress College
Michael Harkins, Harper College
David M. Head, John Tyler Community College
Jeff Horn, Manhattan College
Barry Jordan, Cape Fear Community College
Cheryl L. Kajs, Pellissippi State Community College
Michael Kennedy, High Point University
Michele Kinney, Strayer University
Willem Klooster, Clark University
Pamela Koenig, Seminole State College
Roy G. Koepp, University of Nebraska at Kearney
James Krapfl, McGill University
Andrew E. Larsen, Marquette University
Kenneth Loiselle, Rice University
Susan Mattern, The University of Georgia
Maureen A. McCormick, Florida State College at Jacksonville
James McIntyre, Moraine Valley Community College
Deena McKinney, East Georgia College
Linda A. McMillin, Susquehanna University
Jennifer McNabb, Western Illinois University
Michael Meng, Clemson University
Scott Merriman, Troy University
Ryan Messenger, Monroe Community College/Genesee Community College
Byron J. Nakamura, Southern Connecticut State University
Jeannine Olson, Rhode Island College
Lisa Ossian, Des Moines Area Community College
Jotham Parsons, Duquesne University
Margaret Peacock, The University of Alabama
Kathy L. Pearson, Old Dominion University
Amanda Podany, California State Polytechnic University, Pomona
Ann Pond, Bishop State Community College

Matthew Restall, Pennsylvania State University

Michael D. Richards, Northern Virginia Community College

Jason Ripper, Everett Community College

Russell J. Rockefeller, Anne Arundel Community College

Leonard N. Rosenband, Utah State University

Mark Edward Ruff, Saint Louis University

Ernest Rugenstein, Hudson Valley Community College

Anne Ruszkiewicz, Sullivan County Community College

Wendy A. Sarti, Oakton Community College

Linda Scherr, Mercer County Community College

Elise Shelton, Trident Technical College

Chris Shepard, Trident Technical College

Robert Shipley, Widener University

Sherri Singer, Alamance Community College

Daniel Snell, University of Oklahoma

Steven Soper, The University of Georgia

Susan Souza-Mort, Bristol Community College

James Taw, Valdosta State University

Alfred T. Terrell, Yuba College

Timothy Thibodeau, Nazareth College

Karl Valois, University of Connecticut, Torrington

Liana Vardi, University at Buffalo, The State University of New York

Joseph Villano, Indian River State College

Gregory Vitarbo, Meredith College

David Weiland, Collin County Community College

Scott White, Scottsdale Community College

Pamela Wolfe, Yeshiva of Greater Washington

James Wright, Triton College

Sergei Zhuk, Ball State University

It is also a pleasure to thank the many editors who have assisted us over the years, first at Houghton Mifflin and now at Bedford/St. Martin's. At Bedford/St. Martin's, these include development editor Annette Fantasia; free-lance development editors Michelle McSweeney and Dale Anderson; associate editor Jack Cashman and editorial assistant Emily DiPietro; executive editor Traci Mueller Crowell; director of development Jane Knetzger; publisher for history Mary Dougherty; photo researcher Carole Frohlich; text permissions editor Eve Lehmann; and Christina Horn, senior production editor, with the assistance of Elise Keller and the guidance of managing editor Michael Granger and assistant managing editor John Amburg. Other key contributors were designer Jonathon Nix, page makeup artist Cia Boynton, copy editor Jennifer Brett Greenstein, proofreaders Andrea Martin and Angela Morrison, indexer Leoni McVey, and cover designer Billy Boardman. We would also like to thank president Denise Wydra and copresident of Macmillan Higher Education Joan E. Feinberg.

Many of our colleagues at the University of Illinois, the University of Wisconsin–Milwaukee, and Georgia State University continue to provide information and stimulation, often without even knowing it. We thank them for it. We also thank the many students over the years with whom we have used earlier editions of this book. Their reactions and opinions helped shape the revisions to this edition, and we hope it remains worthy of the ultimate praise that they bestowed on it: that it's "not boring like most textbooks." Merry Wiesner-Hanks would, as always, also like to thank her husband, Neil, without whom work on this project would not be possible. Clare Haru Crowston thanks her husband, Ali, and her children, Lili, Reza, and Kian, who are a joyous reminder of the vitality of life that we try to showcase in this book. Joe Perry thanks his colleagues and students at Georgia State for their intellectual stimulation and is grateful to Joyce de Vries for her unstinting support and encouragement.

Each of us has benefited from the criticism of our co-authors, although each of us assumes responsibility for what he or she has written. Merry Wiesner-Hanks has intensively reworked and revised John Buckler's Chapters 1–6 and has revised Chapters 7–13; Clare Crowston has written and revised Chapters 14–19 and took responsibility for John McKay's Chapter 20; and Joe Perry took responsibility for John McKay's Chapters 21–24 and has written and revised Chapters 25–30.

We'd especially like to thank the founding authors, John P. McKay, Bennett D. Hill, and John Buckler, for their enduring contributions and for their faith in each of us to carry on their legacy.

Clare Haru Crowston
Merry E. Wiesner-Hanks
Joe Perry

Versions and Supplements

Adopters of *A History of Western Society* and their students have access to abundant extra resources, including documents, presentation and testing materials, the acclaimed Bedford Series in History and Culture volumes, and much more. See below for more information, visit the book's catalog site at **bedfordstmartins .com/mckaywest/catalog**, or contact your local Bedford/ St. Martin's sales representative.

Get the Right Version for Your Class

To accommodate different course lengths and course budgets, *A History of Western Society* is available in several different formats, including three-hole-punched loose-leaf Budget Books versions and e-books, which are available at a substantial discount.

- Combined edition (Chapters 1–30): available in paperback, loose-leaf, and e-book formats
- Volume 1, From Antiquity to the Enlightenment (Chapters 1–16): available in paperback, loose-leaf, and e-book formats
- Volume 2, From the Age of Exploration to the Present (Chapters 14–30): available in paperback, loose-leaf, and e-book formats
- Volume A, From Antiquity to 1500 (Chapters 1–12): available in paperback and e-book formats
- Volume B, From the Later Middle Ages to 1815 (Chapters 11–19): available in paperback and e-book formats
- Volume C, From the Revolutionary Era to the Present (Chapters 19–30): available in paperback and e-book formats
- Since 1300 (Chapters 11–30): available in paperback and e-book formats

Any of these volumes can be packaged with additional books for a discount. To get ISBNs for discount packages, see the online catalog at **bedfordstmartins.com /mckaywest/catalog** or contact your Bedford/St. Martin's representative.

NEW Assign LaunchPad — the Online, Interactive e-Book in a Course Space Enriched with Integrated Assets. The new standard in digital history, LaunchPad course tools are so intuitive to use that online, hybrid, and face-to-face courses can be set up in minutes. Even novices will find it's easy to create assignments, track students' work, and access a wealth of relevant learning and teaching resources. It is the ideal learning environment for students to work with the text, maps, documents, and assessment. LaunchPad is loaded with the full interactive e-book and the *Sources for Western Society* documents collection — plus LearningCurve, the Online Document Assignments, additional primary sources, guided reading exercises designed to help students read actively for key concepts, boxed feature reading quizzes, chapter summative quizzes, and more. LaunchPad can be used as is or customized, and it easily integrates with course management systems. And with fast ways to build assignments, rearrange chapters, and add pages, sections, or links, it lets teachers build the course materials they need and hold students accountable.

Let Students Choose Their e-Book Format. In addition to the LaunchPad e-book, students can purchase the downloadable *Bedford e-Book to Go for A History of Western Society* from our Web site or find other PDF versions of the e-book at our publishing partners' sites: Course-Smart, Barnes & Noble NookStudy, Kno, CafeScribe, or Chegg.

NEW Go Beyond the Printed Page with Bedford Integrated Media

As described in the preface and on the inside front cover, students purchasing new books receive access to LearningCurve and Online Document Assignments for *A History of Western Society.*

☑ **Assign LearningCurve so You Know What Your Students Know and They Come to Class Prepared.** Assigning LearningCurve in place of reading quizzes is easy for instructors, and the reporting features help instructors track overall class trends and spot topics that are giving students trouble so they can adjust their lectures and class activities. This online learning tool is popular with students because it was designed to help them rehearse content at their own pace in a nonthreatening, gamelike environment. The feedback for wrong answers provides instructional coaching and sends students back to the book for review. Students answer as many questions as necessary to reach a target score, with repeated chances to revisit material they haven't mastered. When LearningCurve is assigned, students come to class better prepared.

🇪 **Assign the Online Document Assignments so that Students Put Interpretation into Practice.** In addition to the five primary sources embedded in each chapter, this text comes with brand-new, ready-made assignable document sets based either on the five "Life" chapters (Chapters 4, 10, 18, 22, and 30) or on the popular "Individuals in Society" feature. Callouts to these assignments appear in each chapter and prompt students to go online to explore a key question through analysis of the document set. The Online Document Assignments provide a helpful framework for working with the sources. Each assignment comes with an introduction that sets the specific context for the document set, as well as pre-reading questions that ask students to recall the related developments in the textbook. Individual documents are accompanied by a brief headnote and a set of questions. In addition, multiple-choice questions help students analyze the sources by providing instant feedback, and each assignment culminates in a one- to two-page essay prompt that encourages students to use the sources in creative ways. With Online Document Assignments, students draw their own conclusions about the past while practicing critical thinking and synthesis skills.

Send Students to Free Online Resources

The book's Student Site at **bedfordstmartins.com /mckaywest** gives students a way to read, write, and study by providing plentiful quizzes and activities, study aids, and history research and writing help.

FREE   Online Study Guide. Available at the Student Site, this popular resource provides students with quizzes and activities for each chapter, including multiple-choice self-tests that focus on important concepts; flash cards that test students' knowledge of key terms; timeline activities that emphasize causal relationships; and map quizzes intended to strengthen students' geography skills. Instructors can monitor students' progress through an online Quiz Gradebook or receive e-mail updates.

FREE   Research, Writing, and Anti-plagiarism Advice. Available at the Student Site, Bedford's **History Research and Writing Help** includes **History Research and Reference Sources**, with links to history-related databases, indexes, and journals; **Build a Bibliography**, a simple Web-based tool known as The Bedford Bibliographer that generates bibliographies in four commonly used documentation styles; and **Tips on Avoiding Plagiarism**, an online tutorial that reviews the consequences of plagiarism and features exercises to help students practice integrating sources and recognize acceptable summaries.

Take Advantage of Instructor Resources

Bedford/St. Martin's has developed a wide range of teaching resources for this book and for this course. They range from lecture and presentation materials and assessment tools to course management options. Most can be downloaded or ordered at **bedfordstmartins.com/mckaywest /catalog**.

Instructor's Resource Manual. The instructor's manual offers both experienced and first-time instructors tools for preparing lectures and running discussions. It includes chapter-review material, teaching strategies, and a guide to chapter-specific supplements available for the text, plus suggestions on how to get the most out of LearningCurve and a survival guide for first-time teaching assistants.

Guide to Changing Editions. Designed to facilitate an instructor's transition from the previous edition of *A History of Western Society* to the current edition, this guide presents an overview of major changes as well as of changes in each chapter.

Computerized Test Bank. The test bank includes a mix of fresh, carefully crafted multiple-choice, short-answer, and essay questions for each chapter. It also contains brand-new primary source and map-based questions. All questions appear in Microsoft Word format and in easy-to-use test bank software that allows instructors to add, edit, resequence, and print questions and answers. Instructors can also export questions into a variety of formats, including Blackboard, Desire2Learn, and Moodle.

The Bedford Lecture Kit: **PowerPoint Maps, Images, Lecture Outlines, and i>clicker Content.** Look good and save time with The Bedford Lecture Kit. These presentation materials are downloadable individually from the Instructor Resources tab at **bedfordstmartins.com /mckaywest/catalog** and are available on The Bedford Lecture Kit **Instructor's Resource CD-ROM**. They provide ready-made and fully customizable PowerPoint multimedia presentations that include lecture outlines with embedded maps, figures, and selected images from the textbook and extra background for instructors. Also available are maps and selected images in JPEG and PowerPoint formats; content for i>clicker, a classroom response system, in Microsoft Word and PowerPoint formats; the Instructor's Resource Manual in Microsoft Word format; and outline maps in PDF format for quizzing or handing out. All files are suitable for copying onto transparency acetates.

Videos and Multimedia. A wide assortment of videos and multimedia CD-ROMs on various topics in Western Civilization is available to qualified adopters through your Bedford/St. Martin's sales representative.

Package and Save Your Students Money

For information on free packages and discounts up to 50 percent, visit **bedfordstmartins.com/mckaywest /catalog**, or contact your local Bedford/St. Martin's sales representative. The products that follow all qualify for discount packaging.

Sources for Western Society, **Third Edition.** This primary source collection—available in Volume 1, Volume 2, and

Since 1300 versions—provides a revised and expanded selection of sources to accompany *A History of Western Society*, Eleventh Edition. Each chapter features five or six written and visual sources by well-known figures and ordinary individuals alike. With over fifty new selections—including a dozen new visual sources—and enhanced pedagogy throughout, students are given the tools to engage critically with canonical and lesser-known sources and prominent and ordinary voices. Each chapter includes a "Sources in Conversation" feature that presents differing views on key topics. This companion reader is an exceptional value for students and offers plenty of assignment options for instructors. Available free when packaged with the print text and included in the LaunchPad e-book. Also available on its own as a downloadable PDF e-book or with the main text's e-Book to Go.

The Bedford Series in History and Culture. More than one hundred titles in this highly praised series combine first-rate scholarship, historical narrative, and important primary documents for undergraduate courses. Each book is brief, inexpensive, and focused on a specific topic or period. For a complete list of titles, visit **bedfordstmartins .com/history/series**. Package discounts are available.

Rand McNally Atlas of Western Civilization. This collection of over fifty full-color maps highlights social, political, and cross-cultural change and interaction from classical Greece and Rome to the postindustrial Western world. Each map is thoroughly indexed for fast reference. Available for $5.00 when packaged with the text.

The Bedford Glossary for European History. This handy supplement for the survey course gives students historically contextualized definitions for hundreds of terms—from *Abbasids* to *Zionism*—that they will encounter in lectures, reading, and exams. Available free when packaged with the text.

Trade Books. Titles published by sister companies Hill and Wang; Farrar, Straus and Giroux; Henry Holt and Company; St. Martin's Press; Picador; and Palgrave Macmillan are available at a 50 percent discount when packaged with Bedford/St. Martin's textbooks. For more information, visit **bedfordstmartins.com/tradeup**.

A Pocket Guide to Writing in History. This portable and affordable reference tool by Mary Lynn Rampolla provides reading, writing, and research advice useful to students in all history courses. Concise yet comprehensive advice on approaching typical history assignments, developing critical reading skills, writing effective history papers, conducting research, using and documenting sources, and avoiding plagiarism—enhanced by practical tips and examples throughout—has made this slim reference a bestseller. Package discounts are available.

A Student's Guide to History. This complete guide provides the practical help students need to be successful in any history course. In addition to introducing students to the nature of the discipline, author Jules Benjamin teaches a wide range of skills from preparing for exams to approaching common writing assignments and explains the research and documentation process with plentiful examples. Package discounts are available.

The Social Dimension of Western Civilization. Combining current scholarship with classic pieces, this reader's forty-eight secondary sources, compiled by Richard M. Golden, hook students with the fascinating and often surprising details of how everyday Western people worked, ate, played, celebrated, worshipped, married, procreated, fought, persecuted, and died. Package discounts are available.

The West in the Wider World: Sources and Perspectives. Edited by Richard Lim and David Kammerling Smith, the first college reader to focus on the central historical question "How did the West become the West?" offers a wealth of written and visual source materials that reveal the influence of non-European regions on the origins and development of Western Civilization. Package discounts are available.

Brief Contents

11 The Later Middle Ages, 1300–1450 322

12 European Society in the Age of the Renaissance, 1350–1550 356

13 Reformations and Religious Wars, 1500–1600 390

14 European Exploration and Conquest, 1450–1650 426

15 Absolutism and Constitutionalism, ca. 1589–1725 462

16 Toward a New Worldview, 1540–1789 502

17 The Expansion of Europe, 1650–1800 540

18 *Life* in the Era of Expansion, 1650–1800 574

19 Revolutions in Politics, 1775–1815 610

Glossary G-1
Index I-1
Timeline A History of Western Society: An Overview I-24
About the Authors I-36

Contents

Preface   xi

Versions and Supplements   xvii

Maps, Figures, and Tables   xxix

Special Features   xxxi

11 The Later Middle Ages
1300–1450   322

Prelude to Disaster   324
Climate Change and Famine   •   Social Consequences

The Black Death   325
Pathology   •   Spread of the Disease   •   Care of the
Sick   •   Economic, Religious, and Cultural Effects
Primary Source 11.1 Dance of Death   331

The Hundred Years' War   332
Causes   •   English Successes   •   Joan of Arc and France's
Victory   •   Aftermath
Primary Source 11.2 The Trial of Joan of Arc   337

Challenges to the Church   338
The Babylonian Captivity and Great Schism   •   Critiques,
Divisions, and Councils   •   Lay Piety and Mysticism
Primary Source 11.3 Raimon de Cornet on the
Avignon Papacy   339

Social Unrest in a Changing Society   343
Peasant Revolts   •   Urban Conflicts   •   Sex in the
City   •   Fur-Collar Crime   •   Ethnic Tensions and
Restrictions   •   Literacy and Vernacular Literature
Primary Source 11.4 The Statute of Laborers   345
Primary Source 11.5 Christine de Pizan, Advice to
the Wives of Artisans   347

REVIEW and EXPLORE   354   ☑ **LearningCurve**

Individuals in Society Meister Eckhart   342
🄴 **ONLINE DOCUMENT ASSIGNMENT**

Mapping the Past The Course of the Black Death in
Fourteenth-Century Europe   327
Living in the Past Treating the Plague   328

12 European Society in the Age of the Renaissance
1350–1550   356

Wealth and Power in Renaissance Italy   358
Trade and Prosperity   •   Communes and Republics of
Northern Italy   •   City-States and the Balance of Power
Primary Source 12.1   A Sermon of Savonarola   362

Intellectual Change   362
Humanism   •   Education   •   Political Thought   •
Christian Humanism   •   The Printed Word
Primary Source 12.2   Cassandra Fedele on Humanist
Learning   364
Primary Source 12.3   Pico della Mirandola, "On the
Dignity of Man"   366
Primary Source 12.4   Thomas More, *Utopia*   370

Art and the Artist   373
Patronage and Power   •   Changing Artistic Styles   •
The Renaissance Artist

Social Hierarchies   379
Race and Slavery   •   Wealth and the Nobility   •
Gender Roles

Politics and the State in Western Europe   383
France   •   England   •   Spain
Primary Source 12.5   Tax Collectors   386

REVIEW and EXPLORE   388   ☑ LearningCurve

Individuals in Society   Leonardo da Vinci   368
e ONLINE DOCUMENT ASSIGNMENT

Mapping the Past   The Growth of Printing in Europe,
1448–1552   372

Living in the Past   Male Clothing and Masculinity   382

13 Reformations and Religious Wars
1500–1600   390

The Early Reformation   392
The Christian Church in the Early Sixteenth Century   •
Martin Luther   •   Protestant Thought   •   The Appeal
of Protestant Ideas   •   The Radical Reformation and the
German Peasants' War   •   Marriage, Sexuality, and the
Role of Women
Primary Source 13.1   Martin Luther, *On Christian
Liberty*   396
Primary Source 13.2   Domestic Scene   403

The Reformation and German Politics   404
The Rise of the Habsburg Dynasty   •   Religious Wars
in Switzerland and Germany

The Spread of Protestant Ideas   407
Scandinavia   •   Henry VIII and the Reformation in
England   •   Upholding Protestantism in England   •
Calvinism   •   The Reformation in Eastern Europe
Primary Source 13.3   Elizabethan Injunctions
About Religion   411
Primary Source 13.4   1547 Ordinances in Calvin's
Geneva   412

The Catholic Reformation   414
Papal Reform and the Council of Trent   •   New and
Reformed Religious Orders
Primary Source 13.5   Saint Teresa of Ávila,
The Life   418

Religious Violence   417
French Religious Wars   •   The Netherlands Under
Charles V   •   The Great European Witch-Hunt

REVIEW and EXPLORE   423   ☑ LearningCurve

Individuals in Society   Anna Jansz of Rotterdam   401
e ONLINE DOCUMENT ASSIGNMENT

Living in the Past   Uses of Art in the Reformation   398

Mapping the Past   Religious Divisions in Europe,
ca. 1555   415

14 European Exploration and Conquest

1450–1650   426

World Contacts Before Columbus   428
The Trade World of the Indian Ocean • The Trading States of Africa • The Ottoman and Persian Empires • Genoese and Venetian Middlemen

The European Voyages of Discovery   432
Causes of European Expansion • Technology and the Rise of Exploration • The Portuguese Overseas Empire • The Problem of Christopher Columbus • Later Explorers • Spanish Conquest in the New World • Early French and English Settlement in the New World
Primary Source 14.1 A Portuguese Traveler Describes Swahili City-States of East Africa   437
Primary Source 14.2 Columbus Describes His First Voyage   438
Primary Source 14.3 Doña Marina Translating for Hernando Cortés During His Meeting with Montezuma   442
Primary Source 14.4 Interpreting the Spread of Disease Among Natives   444

The Impact of Conquest   445
Colonial Administration • Impact of European Settlement on Indigenous Peoples • Life in the Colonies • The Columbian Exchange
Primary Source 14.5 Tenochtitlán Leaders Respond to Spanish Missionaries   447

Europe and the World After Columbus   449
Sugar and Slavery • Spanish Silver and Its Economic Effects • The Birth of the Global Economy

Changing Attitudes and Beliefs   456
New Ideas About Race • Michel de Montaigne and Cultural Curiosity • William Shakespeare and His Influence

REVIEW and EXPLORE   460   ✔ LearningCurve
Individuals in Society Juan de Pareja   453
e ONLINE DOCUMENT ASSIGNMENT

Mapping the Past Overseas Exploration and Conquest in the Fifteenth and Sixteenth Centuries   436
Living in the Past Foods of the Columbian Exchange   450

15 Absolutism and Constitutionalism

ca. 1589–1725   462

Seventeenth-Century Crisis and Rebuilding   464
The Social Order and Peasant Life • Famine and Economic Crisis • The Thirty Years' War • Achievements in State-Building • Warfare and the Growth of Army Size • Popular Political Action

Absolutism in France and Spain   469
The Foundations of Absolutism • Louis XIV and Absolutism • Life at Versailles • French Financial Management Under Colbert • Louis XIV's Wars • The Decline of Absolutist Spain in the Seventeenth Century
Primary Source 15.1 Louis XIV, King of France and Navarre, 1701   471
Primary Source 15.2 Letter from Versailles   475

Absolutism in Austria and Prussia   478
The Return of Serfdom in the East • The Austrian Habsburgs • Prussia in the Seventeenth Century • The Consolidation of Prussian Absolutism

The Development of Russia and the Ottoman Empire   482
The Mongol Yoke and the Rise of Moscow • The Tsar and His People • The Reforms of Peter the Great • The Growth of the Ottoman Empire
Primary Source 15.3 A German Account of Russian Life   484

Alternatives to Absolutism in England and the Dutch Republic   489
Absolutist Claims in England • Religious Divides and the English Civil War • Cromwell and Puritanical Absolutism in England • The Restoration of the English Monarchy • Constitutional Monarchy and Cabinet Government • The Dutch Republic in the Seventeenth Century
Primary Source 15.4 Diary of an English Villager   493
Primary Source 15.5 John Locke, Two Treatises of Government   495

Baroque Art and Music   498

REVIEW and EXPLORE   500   ✔ LearningCurve
Individuals in Society Hürrem   488
e ONLINE DOCUMENT ASSIGNMENT

Living in the Past The Absolutist Palace   472
Mapping the Past Europe After the Peace of Utrecht, 1715   477

16 Toward a New Worldview

1540–1789   502

Major Breakthroughs of the Scientific Revolution   504
Scientific Thought in 1500 • Origins of the Scientific Revolution • The Copernican Hypothesis • Brahe, Kepler, and Galileo: Proving Copernicus Right • Newton's Synthesis
Primary Source 16.1 Galileo Galilei, *The Sidereal Messenger*   509

Important Changes in Scientific Thinking   511
Bacon, Descartes, and the Scientific Method • Medicine, the Body, and Chemistry • Empire and Natural History • Science and Society
Primary Source 16.2 "An Account of a Particular Species of Cocoon"   514

The Enlightenment   516
The Emergence of the Enlightenment • The Influence of the Philosophes • Jean-Jacques Rousseau • The International Enlightenment • Urban Culture and Life in the Public Sphere • Race and the Enlightenment
Primary Source 16.3 Du Châtelet, *Foundations of Physics*   519
Primary Source 16.4 Enlightenment Culture   523
Primary Source 16.5 Denis Diderot, "Supplement to Bougainville's Voyage"   528

Enlightened Absolutism   529
Frederick the Great of Prussia • Catherine the Great of Russia • The Austrian Habsburgs • Jewish Life and the Limits of Enlightened Absolutism

REVIEW and EXPLORE   538   ✔ LearningCurve
Individuals in Society Moses Mendelssohn and the Jewish Enlightenment   534
🅔 ONLINE DOCUMENT ASSIGNMENT

Living in the Past Coffeehouse Culture   526
Mapping the Past The Partition of Poland, 1772–1795   532

17 The Expansion of Europe

1650–1800   540

Working the Land   542
The Legacy of the Open-Field System • New Methods of Agriculture • The Leadership of the Low Countries and England
Primary Source 17.1 Arthur Young on the Benefits of Enclosure   545

The Beginning of the Population Explosion   546
Long-Standing Obstacles to Population Growth • The New Pattern of the Eighteenth Century

The Growth of Rural Industry   549
The Putting-Out System • The Lives of Rural Textile Workers • The Industrious Revolution
Primary Source 17.2 Contrasting Views on the Effects of Rural Industry   552

The Debate over Urban Guilds   554
Urban Guilds • Adam Smith and Economic Liberalism
Primary Source 17.3 Adam Smith on the Division of Labor   556

The Atlantic World and Global Trade   557
Mercantilism and Colonial Competition • The Atlantic Economy • The Atlantic Slave Trade • Identities and Communities of the Atlantic World • The Colonial Enlightenment • Trade and Empire in Asia and the Pacific
Primary Source 17.4 Olaudah Equiano's Economic Arguments for Ending Slavery   565
Primary Source 17.5 Mulatto Painting   566

REVIEW and EXPLORE   572   ✔ LearningCurve
Individuals in Society Rebecca Protten   568
🅔 ONLINE DOCUMENT ASSIGNMENT

Mapping the Past Industry and Population in Eighteenth-Century Europe   550
Living in the Past The Remaking of London   560

18 *Life* in the Era of Expansion
1650–1800   574

Marriage and the Family   576
Late Marriage and Nuclear Families   •   Work Away from Home   •   Premarital Sex and Community Controls   •   New Patterns of Marriage and Illegitimacy   •   Sex on the Margins of Society

Children and Education   580
Child Care and Nursing   •   Foundlings and Infanticide   •   Attitudes Toward Children   •   The Spread of Elementary Schools
Primary Source 18.1   Parisian Boyhood   583
Primary Source 18.2   The Catechism of Health   584

Popular Culture and Consumerism   586
Popular Literature   •   Leisure and Recreation   •   New Foods and Appetites   •   Toward a Consumer Society
Primary Source 18.3   A Day in the Life of Paris   590
Primary Source 18.4   The Fashion Merchant   593

Religious Authority and Beliefs   596
Church Hierarchy   •   Protestant Revival   •   Catholic Piety   •   Marginal Beliefs and Practices
Primary Source 18.5   Advice to Methodists   599

Medical Practice   601
Faith Healing and General Practice   •   Improvements in Surgery   •   Midwifery   •   The Conquest of Smallpox

REVIEW and EXPLORE   607   ✔ LearningCurve
The Inner Life of the Individual   608
e ONLINE DOCUMENT ASSIGNMENT

Mapping the Past Literacy in France, ca. 1789   587
The Past Living Now The Commercialization of Sports   588
Individuals in Society Rose Bertin, "Minister of Fashion"   595
Living in the Past Improvements in Childbirth   602

19 Revolutions in Politics
1775–1815   610

Background to Revolution   612
Social Change   •   Growing Demands for Liberty and Equality   •   The Seven Years' War

The American Revolutionary Era, 1775–1789   615
The Origins of the Revolution   •   Independence from Britain   •   Framing the Constitution   •   Limitations of Liberty and Equality
Primary Source 19.1   Abigail Adams, "Remember the Ladies"   618

Revolution in France, 1789–1791   619
Breakdown of the Old Order   •   The Formation of the National Assembly   •   Popular Uprising and the Rights of Man   •   A Constitutional Monarchy and Its Challenges
Primary Source 19.2   Abbé Sieyès, *What Is the Third Estate?*   622
Primary Source 19.3   Petition of the French Jews   626

World War and Republican France, 1791–1799   626
The International Response   •   The Second Revolution and the New Republic   •   Total War and the Terror   •   The Thermidorian Reaction and the Directory
Primary Source 19.4   Contrasting Visions of the Sans-Culottes   629

The Napoleonic Era, 1799–1815   634
Napoleon's Rule of France   •   Napoleon's Expansion in Europe   •   The Grand Empire and Its End
Primary Source 19.5   Napoleon's Proclamation to the French People   635

The Haitian Revolution, 1791–1804   640
Revolutionary Aspirations in Saint-Domingue   •   The Outbreak of Revolt   •   The War of Haitian Independence

REVIEW and EXPLORE   646   ✔ LearningCurve
Individuals in Society   Toussaint L'Ouverture   644
e ONLINE DOCUMENT ASSIGNMENT

Living in the Past A Revolution of Culture and Daily Life   632
Mapping the Past Napoleonic Europe in 1812   638

Glossary   G-1

Index   I-1

**Timeline   A History of Western Society:
An Overview**   I-24

About the Authors   I-36

Maps, Figures, and Tables

Maps

Chapter 11
Map 11.1 The Course of the Black Death in Fourteenth-Century Europe   327
Map 11.2 The Hundred Years' War, 1337–1453   334
Map 11.3 Fourteenth-Century Revolts   344
Spot Map The Great Schism, 1378–1417   340
Spot Map The Hussite Revolution, 1415–1436   341

Chapter 12
Map 12.1 The Italian City-States, ca. 1494   361
Map 12.2 The Growth of Printing in Europe, 1448–1552   372
Map 12.3 The Unification of Spain and the Expulsion of the Jews, Fifteenth Century   385
Spot Map The Expansion of France, 1475–1500   384

Chapter 13
Map 13.1 The Global Empire of Charles V, ca. 1556   405
Map 13.2 Religious Divisions in Europe, ca. 1555   415
Spot Map The Route of the Spanish Armada, 1588   410
Spot Map The Netherlands, 1609   420

Chapter 14
Map 14.1 The Fifteenth-Century Afroeurasian Trading World   430
Map 14.2 Overseas Exploration and Conquest in the Fifteenth and Sixteenth Centuries   436
Map 14.3 Seaborne Trading Empires in the Sixteenth and Seventeenth Centuries   452
Spot Map Columbus's First Voyage to the New World, 1492–1493   439
Spot Map Invasion of Tenochtitlán, 1519–1521   441

Chapter 15
Map 15.1 Europe After the Thirty Years' War   467
Map 15.2 Europe After the Peace of Utrecht, 1715   477

Map 15.3 The Growth of Austria and Brandenburg-Prussia to 1748   480
Map 15.4 The Ottoman Empire at Its Height, 1566   487
Spot Map The Acquisitions of Louis XIV, 1668–1713   476
Spot Map The Expansion of Russia to 1725   483
Spot Map The English Civil War, 1642–1649   492

Chapter 16
Map 16.1 The Partition of Poland, 1772–1795   532
Spot Map The War of the Austrian Succession, 1740–1748   530
Spot Map The Pale of Settlement, 1791   535

Chapter 17
Map 17.1 Industry and Population in Eighteenth-Century Europe   550
Map 17.2 The Atlantic Economy in 1701   559
Spot Map Plantation Zones, ca. 1700   562
Spot Map India, 1805   570

Chapter 18
Map 18.1 Literacy in France, ca. 1789   587

Chapter 19
Map 19.1 European Claims in North America and India Before and After the Seven Years' War, 1755–1763   614
Map 19.2 Napoleonic Europe in 1812   638
Map 19.3 The War of Haitian Independence, 1791–1804   643
Spot Map The Great Fear, 1789   623
Spot Map Areas of Insurrection, 1793   628
Spot Map German Confederation of the Rhine, 1806   636

Figures and Tables

Thematic Chronology The Hundred Years' War   333

Thematic Chronology Major Contributors to the Scientific Revolution   512

Thematic Chronology Major Figures of the Enlightenment   521

Figure 17.1 The Growth of Population in England, 1550–1850   546

Figure 17.2 The Increase of Population in Europe, 1650–1850   547

Figure 17.3 Exports of English Manufactured Goods, 1700–1774   562

Thematic Chronology The American Revolution   617

Thematic Chronology The French Revolution   631

Thematic Chronology The Napoleonic Era   637

Thematic Chronology The Haitian Revolution   645

Special Features

The Past Living Now

Exclusive to the "Life" chapters

Chapter 18 The Commercialization of Sports 588

Primary Sources

Chapter 11

11.1 Dance of Death 331
11.2 The Trial of Joan of Arc 337
11.3 Raimon de Cornet on the Avignon Papacy 339
11.4 The Statute of Laborers 345
11.5 Christine de Pizan, Advice to the Wives of Artisans 347
 e **ONLINE DOCUMENT ASSIGNMENT**
 Meister Eckhart

Chapter 12

12.1 A Sermon of Savonarola 362
12.2 Cassandra Fedele on Humanist Learning 364
12.3 Pico della Mirandola, "On the Dignity of Man" 366
12.4 Thomas More, *Utopia* 370
12.5 Tax Collectors 386
 e **ONLINE DOCUMENT ASSIGNMENT**
 Leonardo da Vinci

Chapter 13

13.1 Martin Luther, *On Christian Liberty* 396
13.2 Domestic Scene 403
13.3 Elizabethan Injunctions About Religion 411
13.4 1547 Ordinances in Calvin's Geneva 412
13.5 Saint Teresa of Ávila, *The Life* 418
 e **ONLINE DOCUMENT ASSIGNMENT**
 Anna Jansz of Rotterdam

Chapter 14

14.1 A Portuguese Traveler Describes Swahili City-States of East Africa 437
14.2 Columbus Describes His First Voyage 438
14.3 Doña Marina Translating for Hernando Cortés During His Meeting with Montezuma 442
14.4 Interpreting the Spread of Disease Among Natives 444
14.5 Tenochtitlán Leaders Respond to Spanish Missionaries 447
 e **ONLINE DOCUMENT ASSIGNMENT**
 Juan de Pareja

Chapter 15

15.1 *Louis XIV, King of France and Navarre*, 1701 471
15.2 Letter from Versailles 475
15.3 A German Account of Russian Life 484
15.4 Diary of an English Villager 493
15.5 John Locke, *Two Treatises of Government* 495
 e **ONLINE DOCUMENT ASSIGNMENT**
 Hürrem

Chapter 16

16.1 Galileo Galilei, *The Sidereal Messenger* 509
16.2 "An Account of a Particular Species of Cocoon" 514
16.3 Du Châtelet, *Foundations of Physics* 519
16.4 Enlightenment Culture 523
16.5 Denis Diderot, "Supplement to Bougainville's Voyage" 528
 e **ONLINE DOCUMENT ASSIGNMENT**
 Moses Mendelssohn and the Jewish Enlightenment

Chapter 17

17.1 Arthur Young on the Benefits of Enclosure 545
17.2 Contrasting Views on the Effects of Rural Industry 552
17.3 Adam Smith on the Division of Labor 556
17.4 Olaudah Equiano's Economic Arguments for Ending Slavery 565
17.5 Mulatto Painting 566
 e **ONLINE DOCUMENT ASSIGNMENT**
 Rebecca Protten

Chapter 18

18.1 Parisian Boyhood 583
18.2 The Catechism of Health 584
18.3 A Day in the Life of Paris 590
18.4 The Fashion Merchant 593
18.5 Advice to Methodists 599
 e **ONLINE DOCUMENT ASSIGNMENT**
 The Inner Life of the Individual

Chapter 19

19.1 Abigail Adams, "Remember the Ladies" 618
19.2 Abbé Sieyès, *What Is the Third Estate?* 622
19.3 Petition of the French Jews 626
19.4 Contrasting Visions of the Sans-Culottes 629
19.5 Napoleon's Proclamation to the French People 635
 e **ONLINE DOCUMENT ASSIGNMENT**
 Toussaint L'Ouverture

Living in the Past

Treating the Plague   328
Male Clothing and Masculinity   382
Uses of Art in the Reformation   398
Foods of the Columbian Exchange   450
The Absolutist Palace   472
Coffeehouse Culture   526
The Remaking of London   560
Improvements in Childbirth   602
A Revolution of Culture and Daily Life   632

Individuals in Society

Meister Eckhart   342
Leonardo da Vinci   368
Anna Jansz of Rotterdam   401
Juan de Pareja   453
Hürrem   488
Moses Mendelssohn and the Jewish Enlightenment   534

Rebecca Protten   568
Rose Bertin, "Minister of Fashion"   595
Toussaint L'Ouverture   644

Mapping the Past

Map 11.1 The Course of the Black Death in Fourteenth-Century Europe   327
Map 12.2 The Growth of Printing in Europe, 1448–1552   372
Map 13.2 Religious Divisions in Europe, ca. 1555   415
Map 14.2 Overseas Exploration and Conquest in the Fifteenth and Sixteenth Centuries   436
Map 15.2 Europe After the Peace of Utrecht, 1715   477
Map 16.1 The Partition of Poland, 1772–1795   532
Map 17.1 Industry and Population in Eighteenth-Century Europe   550
Map 18.1 Literacy in France, ca. 1789   587
Map 19.2 Napoleonic Europe in 1812   638

11
The Later Middle Ages

1300–1450

During the later Middle Ages the last book of the New Testament, the Book of Revelation, inspired thousands of sermons and hundreds of religious tracts. The Book of Revelation deals with visions of the end of the world, with disease, war, famine, and death—often called the "Four Horsemen of the Apocalypse"—triumphing everywhere. It is no wonder this part of the Bible was so popular in this period, for between 1300 and 1450 Europeans experienced a frightful series of shocks. The climate turned colder and wetter, leading to poor harvests and famine. People weakened by hunger were more susceptible to disease, and in the middle of the fourteenth century a new disease, probably the bubonic plague, spread throughout Europe. With no effective treatment, the plague killed millions of people. War devastated the countryside, especially in France, leading to widespread discontent and peasant revolts. Workers in cities also revolted against dismal working conditions, and violent crime and ethnic tensions increased as well. Massive deaths and preoccupation with death make the fourteenth century one of the most wrenching periods of Western civilization. Yet, in spite of the pessimism and crises, important institutions and cultural forms, including representative assemblies and national literatures, emerged. Even institutions that experienced severe crisis, such as the Christian Church, saw new types of vitality. ■

Life and Death in the Late Middle Ages. In this French manuscript illumination from 1465, armored knights kill peasants while they work in the fields or take refuge in a castle. Aristocratic violence was a common feature of late medieval life, although nobles would generally not have bothered to put on their armor to harass villagers. (Musée Condé, Chantilly, France/The Bridgeman Art Library)

CHAPTER PREVIEW

 LearningCurve
After reading the chapter, go online and use LearningCurve to retain what you've read.

Prelude to Disaster
How did climate change shape the late Middle Ages?

The Black Death
How did the plague reshape European society?

The Hundred Years' War
What were the causes, course, and consequences of the Hundred Years' War?

Challenges to the Church
Why did the church come under increasing criticism?

Social Unrest in a Changing Society
What explains the social unrest of the late Middle Ages?

Toward the end of the thirteenth century the expanding European economy began to slow down, and in the first half of the fourteenth century Europe experienced ongoing climate change that led to lower levels of food production, which had dramatic and disastrous ripple effects. Rulers attempted to find solutions but were unable to deal with the economic and social problems that resulted.

Climate Change and Famine

The period from about 1000 to about 1300 saw a warmer-than-usual climate in Europe, which underlay all the changes and vitality of the High Middle Ages. Around 1300, however, the climate changed for the worse, becoming colder and wetter. Historical geographers refer to the period from 1300 to 1450 as a "little ice age," which they can trace through both natural and human records.

Evidence from nature emerges through the study of Alpine and polar glaciers, tree rings, and pollen left in bogs. Human-produced sources include written reports of rivers freezing and crops never ripening, as well as archaeological evidence such as the collapsed houses and emptied villages of Greenland, where ice floes cut off contact with the rest of the world and the harshening climate meant that the few hardy crops grown in earlier times could no longer survive. The Viking colony on Greenland died out completely, though Inuit people who relied on hunting sea mammals continued to live in the far north, as they had before the arrival of Viking colonists.

Across Europe, an unusual number of storms brought torrential rains, ruining the wheat, oat, and hay crops on which people and animals almost everywhere depended. Since long-distance transportation of food was expensive and difficult, most urban areas depended for grain, produce, and meat on areas no more than a day's journey away. Poor harvests—and one in four was likely to be poor—led to scarcity and starvation. Almost all of northern Europe suffered a **Great Famine** in the years 1315 to 1322, which contemporaries interpreted as a recurrence of the biblical "seven lean years" that afflicted Egypt.

Even in non-famine years, the cost of grain, livestock, and dairy products rose sharply, in part because diseases hit cattle and sheep. Increasing prices meant that fewer people could afford to buy food. Reduced

Death from Famine   In this fifteenth-century painting, dead bodies lie in the middle of a path, while a funeral procession at the right includes a man with an adult's coffin and a woman with the coffin of an infant under her arm. People did not simply allow the dead to lie in the street in medieval Europe, though during famines and epidemics it was sometimes difficult to maintain normal burial procedures. (Erich Lessing/Art Resource, NY)

caloric intake meant increased susceptibility to disease, especially for infants, children, and the elderly. Workers on reduced diets had less energy, which meant lower productivity, lower output, and higher grain prices.

Social Consequences

The changing climate and resulting agrarian crisis of the fourteenth century had grave social consequences. Poor harvests and famine led to the abandonment of homesteads. In parts of the Low Countries and in the Scottish-English borderlands, entire villages were deserted, and many people became vagabonds, wandering in search of food and work. In Flanders and eastern England, some peasants were forced to mortgage, sublease, or sell their holdings to richer farmers in order to buy food. Throughout the affected areas, young men and women sought work in the towns, delaying marriage. Overall, the population declined because of the deaths caused by famine and disease, though the postponement of marriages and resulting decline in offspring may have also played a part.

As the subsistence crisis deepened, starving people focused their anger on the rich, speculators, and the Jews, who were often targeted as creditors fleecing the poor through pawnbroking. (As explained in Chapter 10, Jews often became moneylenders because Christian authorities restricted their ownership of land and opportunities to engage in other trades.) Rumors spread of a plot by Jews and their agents, the lepers, to kill Christians by poisoning wells. Based on "evidence" collected by torture, many lepers and Jews were killed, beaten, or heavily fined.

Meanwhile, the international character of trade and commerce meant that a disaster in one country had serious implications elsewhere. For example, the infection that attacked English sheep in 1318 caused a sharp decline in wool exports in the following years. Without wool, Flemish weavers could not work, and thousands were laid off. Without woolen cloth, the businesses of Flemish, Hanseatic, and Italian merchants suffered. Unemployment encouraged people to turn to crime.

Government responses to these crises were ineffectual. The three sons of Philip the Fair who sat on the French throne between 1314 and 1328 condemned speculators who held stocks of grain back until conditions were desperate and prices high, and they forbade the sale of grain abroad. These measures had few actual results, however. In England, Edward II (r. 1307–1327) also condemned speculators after his attempts

to set price controls on livestock and ale proved futile. He did try to buy grain abroad, but little was available, and such grain as reached southern English ports was stolen by looters and sold on the black market. The king's efforts at famine relief failed.

Chronology

1300–1450	Little ice age
1309–1376	Babylonian Captivity; papacy in Avignon
1310–1320	Dante writes *Divine Comedy*
1315–1322	Great Famine in northern Europe
1320s	First large-scale peasant rebellion in Flanders
1337–1453	Hundred Years' War
1347	Black Death arrives in Europe
1358	Jacquerie peasant uprising in France
1366	Statute of Kilkenny
1378–1417	Great Schism
1381	English Peasants' Revolt
1387–1400	Chaucer writes *Canterbury Tales*

The Black Death

How did the plague reshape European society?

Colder weather, failed harvests, and resulting malnourishment left Europe's population susceptible to disease, and unfortunately for the continent, a virulent one appeared in the mid-fourteenth century. Around 1300 improvements in ship design had allowed year-round shipping for the first time. European merchants took advantage of these advances, and ships continually at sea carried all types of cargo. They also carried vermin of all types, especially insects and rats, both of which often harbored pathogens. Rats, fleas, and cockroaches could live for months on the cargo carried along the coasts, disembarking at ports with the grain, cloth, or other merchandise. Just as modern air travel has allowed diseases such as AIDS and the H1N1 virus to spread quickly over very long distances, medieval shipping allowed the diseases of the time to do the same. The most frightful of these diseases, carried on Genoese ships, first emerged in western Europe in 1347; the disease was later called the **Black Death**.

Great Famine A terrible famine in 1315–1322 that hit much of Europe after a period of climate change.

Black Death Plague that first struck Europe in 1347 and killed perhaps one-third of the population.

Pathology

Most historians and microbiologists identify the disease that spread in the fourteenth century as the bubonic plague, which is caused by the bacillus *Yersinia pestis*. The disease normally afflicts rats. Fleas living on the infected rats drink their blood and then pass the bacteria that cause the plague on to the next rat they bite. Usually the disease is limited to rats and other rodents, but at certain points in history—perhaps when most rats have been killed off—the fleas have jumped from their rodent hosts to humans and other animals. One of these instances appears to have occurred in the Eastern Roman Empire in the sixth century, when a plague killed millions of people. Another was in China and India in the 1890s, when millions again died. Doctors and epidemiologists closely studied this outbreak, identified the bacillus as bubonic plague, and learned about the exact cycle of infection for the first time.

The fourteenth-century outbreak showed many similarities to the nineteenth-century one, but also some differences. There are no reports of massive rat die-offs in fourteenth-century records. The medieval plague was often transmitted directly from one person to another through coughing and sneezing (what epidemiologists term *pneumonic* transmission) as well as through fleabites. The fourteenth-century outbreak spread much faster than the nineteenth-century epidemic and was much more deadly, killing as much as one-third of the population when it first reached an area. These differences have led a few historians to question whether the Black Death was actually not the bubonic plague but a different disease, perhaps something like the Ebola virus. Other scholars counter that the differences could be explained by variant strains of the disease or improvements in sanitation and public health that would have significantly limited the mortality rate of later outbreaks, even in poor countries such as India. These debates fuel continued study of medical aspects of the plague, with scientists using innovative techniques such as studying the tooth pulp of bodies in medieval cemeteries to see if it contains DNA from plague-causing agents.

Though there is some disagreement about exactly what kind of disease the plague was, there is no dispute about its dreadful effects on the body. The classic symptom of the bubonic plague was a growth the size of a nut or an apple in the armpit, in the groin, or on the neck. This was the boil, or *bubo*, that gave the disease its name and caused agonizing pain. If the bubo was lanced and the pus thoroughly drained, the victim had a chance of recovery. If the boil was not lanced, however—and in the fourteenth century, it rarely was—the next stage was the appearance of black spots or blotches caused by bleeding under the skin. (This syndrome did not give the disease its common name; contemporaries did not call the plague the Black Death. Sometime in the fifteenth century the Latin phrase *atra mors*, meaning "dreadful death," was translated as "black death," and the phrase stuck.) Finally, the victim began to cough violently and spit blood. This stage, indicating the presence of millions of bacilli in the bloodstream, signaled the end, and death followed in two or three days. The coughing also released those pathogens into the air, infecting others when they were breathed in and beginning the deadly cycle again on new victims.

Spread of the Disease

Plague symptoms were first described in 1331 in southwestern China, then part of the Mongol Empire. Plague-infested rats accompanied Mongol armies and merchant caravans carrying silk, spices, and gold across Central Asia in the 1330s. The rats then stowed away on ships, carrying the disease to the ports of the Black Sea by the 1340s. One Italian chronicler told of more dramatic means of spreading the disease as well: Mongol armies besieging the city of Kaffa on the shores of the Black Sea catapulted plague-infected corpses over the walls to infect those inside. The city's residents dumped the corpses into the sea as fast as they could, but they were already infected.

In October 1347 Genoese ships brought the plague from Kaffa to Messina, from which it spread across Sicily. Venice and Genoa were hit in January 1348, and from the port of Pisa the disease spread south to Rome and east to Florence and all of Tuscany. By late spring southern Germany was attacked. Frightened French authorities chased a galley bearing plague victims away from the port of Marseilles, but not before plague had infected the city, from which it spread to southern France and Spain. In June 1348 two ships entered the Bristol Channel and introduced it into England, and from there it traveled northeast into Scandinavia. The plague seems to have entered Poland through the Baltic seaports and spread eastward from there (Map 11.1).

Medieval urban conditions were ideal for the spread of disease. Narrow streets were filled with refuse, human excrement, and dead animals. Houses whose upper stories projected over the lower ones blocked light and air. Houses were beginning to be constructed of brick, but many wood, clay, and mud houses remained. A determined rat had little trouble entering such a house. In addition, people were already weakened by famine, standards of personal hygiene remained frightfully low, and the urban populace was crowded together. Fleas and body lice were universal afflictions: everyone from peasants to archbishops had them. One more bite did not cause much alarm, and the associa-

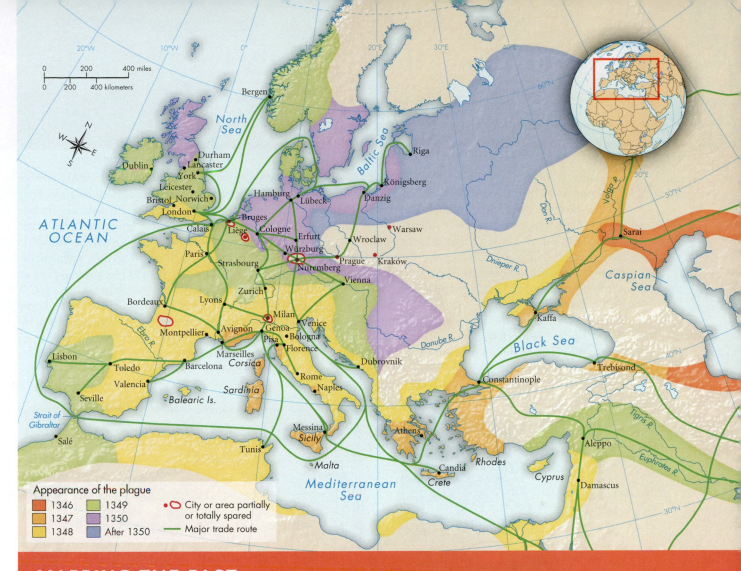

Map 11.1 The Course of the Black Death in Fourteenth-Century Europe

The bubonic plague spread across Europe after beginning in the mid-1340s, with the first cases of disease reported in Black Sea ports.

ANALYZING THE MAP When did the plague reach Paris? How much time passed before it spread to the rest of northern France and southern Germany? Which cities and regions were spared?

CONNECTIONS How did the expansion of trade contribute to the spread of the Black Death?

tion between rats, fleas, and the plague was unknown. Mortality rates can be only educated guesses because population figures for the period before the arrival of the plague do not exist for most countries and cities. Of a total English population of perhaps 4.2 million, probably 1.4 million died of the Black Death. Densely populated Italian cities endured incredible losses. Florence lost between one-half and two-thirds of its population when the plague visited in 1348. Islamic parts of Europe were not spared, nor was the rest of the Muslim world. The most widely accepted estimate for western Europe and the Mediterranean is that the plague killed about one-third of the population in the first wave of infection. (Some areas, including such cities as Milan, Liege, and Nuremberg, were largely spared, primarily because city authorities closed the gates to all outsiders when plague was in the area, and enough food had been stored to sustain the city until the danger had passed.)

Nor did central and eastern Europe escape the ravages of the disease. One chronicler records that, in the summer and autumn of 1349, between five hundred and six hundred died every day in Vienna. As the Black Death took its toll on the Holy Roman Empire, waves of emigrants fled to Poland, Bohemia, and Hungary, taking the plague with them. In the Byzantine Empire

Treating the Plague

Medieval physicians based treatments for the plague on their understanding of how the body worked, as do doctors in any era. Fourteenth-century people—lay, scholarly, and medical—attributed the disease to "poisons" in the air that caused the fluids in the body to become unbalanced. The imbalance in fluids led to illness, an idea that had been the core of Western ideas about the primary cause of disease since the ancient Greeks. Certain symptoms of the plague, such as boils that oozed and blood-filled coughing, were believed to be the body's natural reaction to too much fluid.

Doctors thus recommended preventive measures that would block the poisoned air from entering the body, such as burning incense or holding strong-smelling herbs or other substances, like rosemary, juniper, or sulfur, in front of the nose. Treatment concentrated on ridding the body of poisons and bringing the fluids into balance. As one fifteenth-century treatise put it, "everyone over seven should be made to vomit daily" and twice a week wrap up in sheets to "sweat copiously." The best way to regain health, however, was to let blood: "as soon as [the patient] feels an itch or pricking in his flesh [the physician] must use a goblet or cupping horn to let blood and draw down the blood from his heart, and this should be done two or three times at intervals of one or two days at the most." Letting blood was considered the most effective way to rebalance the fluids and to flush the body of poisons.

From ancient times to the nineteenth century, physicians often used cups such as this (above) to aid in bloodletting. The cup was heated to create a vacuum and then placed on the skin, where it would draw blood to the surface before a vein was cut. (doctor: Private Collection/Archives Charmet/The Bridgeman Art Library; cup: Courtesy of the Trustees of the British Museum)

the plague ravaged the population. The youngest son of Emperor John VI Kantakouzenos died just as his father took over the throne in 1347. "So incurable was the evil," wrote John later in his history of the Byzantine Empire, "that neither any regularity of life, nor any bodily strength could resist it. Strong and weak bodies were all similarly carried away, and those best cared for died in the same manner as the poor."[1]

Across Europe the Black Death recurred intermittently from the 1360s to 1400. It reappeared from time to time over the following centuries as well, though never with the same virulence because by then Europe-

A plague doctor is depicted in a seventeenth-century German engraving published during a later outbreak of the dreaded disease. The doctor is fully covered, with a coat waxed smooth so that poisons just slide off. The beaked mask contains strong-smelling herbs, and the stick, beaten on the ground as he walks along, warns people away. (akg-images)

QUESTIONS FOR ANALYSIS

1. In the background of the plague doctor engraving, the artist shows a group of children running away as the plague doctor approaches. What aspects of his appearance or treatment methods contributed to this reaction?
2. Many people who lived through the plague reported that it created a sense of hopeless despair. Do the quotations from medical treatises and the objects depicted here support this idea? Why or why not?

Source: Quotations from Rosemary Horrox, *The Black Death* (Manchester: Manchester University Press, 1994), p. 194.

ans now had some resistance. Improved standards of hygiene and strictly enforced quarantine measures also lessened the plague's toll, but only in 1721 did it make its last appearance in Europe, in the French port of Marseilles. And only in 1947, six centuries after the arrival of the plague in Europe, did the American mi-

crobiologist Selman Waksman discover an effective treatment, streptomycin. Plague continues to infect rodent and human populations sporadically today.

Care of the Sick

Fourteenth-century medical literature indicates that physicians tried many different methods to prevent and treat the plague. People understood that plague and other diseases could be transmitted person to person, and they observed that crowded cities had high death rates, especially when the weather was warm and moist. We now understand that warm, moist conditions make it easier for germs to grow and spread, but fourteenth-century people thought in terms of "poisons" in the air or "corrupted air" coming from swamps, unburied animals, or the positions of the stars. Their treatments thus focused on ridding the air and the body of these poisons and on rebalancing bodily fluids. (See "Living in the Past: Treating the Plague," at left.)

People tried anything they thought might help. Perhaps loud sounds like ringing church bells or firing the newly invented cannon would clean poisoned air. Medicines made from plants that were bumpy or that oozed liquid might work, keeping the more dangerous swelling and oozing of the plague away. Magical letter and number combinations, called cryptograms, were especially popular in Muslim areas. They were often the first letters of words in prayers or religious sayings, and they gave people a sense of order when faced with the randomness with which the plague seemed to strike.

It is noteworthy that, in an age of mounting criticism of clerical wealth (see page 341), the behavior of the clergy during the plague was often exemplary. Priests, monks, and nuns cared for the sick and buried the dead. In places like Venice, from which even physicians fled, priests remained to give what ministrations they could. Consequently, their mortality rate was phenomenally high. The German clergy, especially, suffered a severe decline in personnel in the years after 1350.

There were limits to care, however. The Italian writer Giovanni Boccaccio (1313–1375), describing the course of the disease in Florence in the preface to his book of tales, *The Decameron*, identified what many knew—that the disease passed from person to person:

This pestilence was so powerful that it was transmitted to the healthy by contact with the sick, the way a fire close to dry or oily things will set them aflame. And the evil of the plague went even further: not only did talking to or being around the sick bring infection and a common death, but also touching the clothes of the sick or anything touched or used by them seemed to communicate this very disease to the person involved.[2]

To avoid contagion, wealthier people often fled cities for the countryside, though sometimes this simply spread the plague faster. Some cities tried shutting their gates to prevent infected people and animals from coming in, which worked in a few cities. They also walled up houses in which there was plague, trying to isolate those who were sick from those who were still healthy. In Boccaccio's words, "Almost no one cared for his neighbor . . . brother abandoned brother . . . and—even worse, almost unbelievable—fathers and mothers neglected to tend and care for their children."[3]

Economic, Religious, and Cultural Effects

Economic historians and demographers sharply dispute the impact of the plague on the economy in the late fourteenth century. The traditional view that the plague had a disastrous effect has been greatly modified. By the mid-1300s the population of Europe had grown somewhat beyond what could easily be supported by available agricultural technology, and the dramatic drop in population allowed less fertile land to be abandoned. People turned to more specialized types of agriculture, such as raising sheep or wine grapes, which in the long run proved to be a better use of the land.

The Black Death did bring on a general European inflation. High mortality produced a fall in production, shortages of goods, and a general rise in prices. The price of wheat in most of Europe increased, as did the costs of meat, sausage, and cheese. This inflation continued to the end of the fourteenth century. But labor shortages resulting from the high mortality caused by the plague meant that workers could demand better wages, and the broad mass of people who survived enjoyed a higher standard of living. The greater demand for labor also meant greater mobility for peasants in rural areas and for artisans in towns and cities.

The plague also had effects on religious practices. Despite Boccaccio's comments about family members' coldness, people were saddened by the loss of their loved ones, especially their children. Not surprisingly, some people sought release from the devastating affliction in wild living, but more became more deeply pious. Rather than seeing the plague as a medical issue, they interpreted it as the result of an evil within themselves. God must be punishing them for terrible sins, they thought, so the best remedies were religious ones: asking for forgiveness, praying, trusting in God, making donations to churches, and trying to live better lives. John VI Kantakouzenos reported that in Constantinople, "many of the sick

Flagellants   In this manuscript illumination from 1349, shirtless flagellants scourge themselves with whips as they walk through the streets of the Flemish city of Tournai. The text notes that they are asking for God's grace to return to the city after it had been struck with the "most grave" illness. (Private Collection/The Bridgeman Art Library)

Dance of Death

In this fifteenth-century fresco from a tiny church in Croatia, skeletons lead people from all social classes in a procession.

(Vladimir Bugarin, photographer)

EVALUATE THE EVIDENCE

1. Based on their clothing and the objects they are carrying, who are the people shown in the fresco? What does this suggest was the artist's message about death?
2. Paintings such as this clearly provide evidence of the preoccupation with death in this era, but does this work highlight other social issues as well? If so, what are they?

turned to better things in their minds . . . they abstained from all vice during that time and they lived virtuously; many divided their property among the poor, even before they were attacked by the disease."[4] In Muslim areas, religious leaders urged virtuous living in the face of death: give to the poor, reconcile with your enemies, free your slaves, and say a proper good-bye to your friends and family.

Believing that the Black Death was God's punishment for humanity's wickedness, some Christians turned to the severest forms of asceticism and frenzied religious fervor, joining groups of **flagellants** (FLA-juh-luhnts), who whipped and scourged themselves as penance for their and society's sins. Groups of flagellants traveled from town to town, often growing into unruly mobs. Officials worried that they would provoke violence and riots, and ordered groups to disband or forbade them to enter cities.

flagellants People who believed that the plague was God's punishment for sin and sought to do penance by flagellating (whipping) themselves.

Along with seeing the plague as a call to reform their own behavior, however, people also searched for scapegoats, and savage cruelty sometimes resulted. As in the decades before the plague, many people believed that the Jews had poisoned the wells of Christian communities and thereby infected the drinking water. Others thought that killing Jews would prevent the plague from spreading to their town, a belief encouraged by flagellant groups. These charges led to the murder of thousands of Jews across Europe, especially in the cities of France and Germany. In Strasbourg, for example, several hundred Jews were publicly burned alive. Their houses were looted, their property was confiscated, and the remaining Jews were expelled from the city.

Hundred Years' War A war between England and France from 1337 to 1453, with political and economic causes and consequences.

The literature and art of the late Middle Ages reveal a people gripped by morbid concern with death. One highly popular literary and artistic motif, the Dance of Death, depicted a dancing skeleton leading away living people, often in order of their rank. (See "Primary Source 11.1: Dance of Death," page 331.) In the words of one early-fifteenth-century English poem:

> Death spareth not low nor high degree
> Popes, Kings, nor worthy Emperors
> When they shine most in felicity
> He can abate the freshness of their flowers
> Eclipse their bright suns with his showers . . .
> Sir Emperor, lord of all the ground,
> Sovereign Prince, and highest of nobles
> You must forsake your round apples of gold
> Leave behind your treasure and riches
> And with others to my dance obey.[5]

The years of the Black Death witnessed the foundation of new colleges at old universities and of entirely new universities. The foundation charters explain the shortage of priests and the decay of learning as the reasons for their establishment. Whereas older universities such as those at Bologna and Paris had international student bodies, these new institutions established in the wake of the Black Death had more national or local constituencies. Thus the international character of medieval culture weakened, paving the way for schism (SKIH-zuhm) in the Catholic Church even before the Reformation.

As is often true with devastating events, the plague highlighted central qualities of medieval society: deep religious feeling, suspicion of those who were different, and a view of the world shaped largely by oral tradition, with a bit of classical knowledge mixed in among the educated elite.

The Hundred Years' War

What were the causes, course, and consequences of the Hundred Years' War?

The plague ravaged populations in Asia, North Africa, and Europe; in western Europe a long international war that began a decade or so before the plague struck and lasted well into the next century added further misery. England and France had engaged in sporadic military hostilities from the time of the Norman conquest in 1066, and in the middle of the fourteenth century these became more intense. From 1337 to 1453 the two countries intermittently fought one another in what was the longest war in European history, ultimately dubbed the **Hundred Years' War**, though it actually lasted 116 years.

Causes

The Hundred Years' War had a number of causes, including disagreements over rights to land, a dispute over the succession to the French throne, and economic conflicts. Many of these revolved around the duchy of Aquitaine, a province in southern France that became part of the holdings of the English crown when Eleanor of Aquitaine married King Henry II of England in 1152 (see Chapter 9; a duchy is a territory ruled by a duke). In 1259 Henry III of England had signed the Treaty of Paris with Louis IX of France, affirming English claims to Aquitaine in return for becoming a vassal of the French crown. French policy in the fourteenth century was strongly expansionist, however, and the French kings resolved to absorb the duchy into the kingdom of France. Aquitaine therefore became a disputed territory.

The immediate political cause of the war was a disagreement over who would inherit the French throne after Charles IV of France, the last surviving son of Philip the Fair, died childless in 1328. With him ended the Capetian dynasty of France. Charles IV had a sister—Isabella—but her son was Edward III, king of England. An assembly of French high nobles, meaning to exclude Isabella and Edward from the French throne, proclaimed that "no woman nor her son could succeed to the [French] monarchy." French lawyers defended the position with the claim that the exclusion of women from ruling or passing down the right to rule was part of Salic law, a sixth-century law code of the Franks (see Chapter 7), and that Salic law itself was part of the fundamental law of France. They used this invented tradition to argue that Edward should be barred from the French throne. (The ban on female succession became part of French legal tradition until the end of the monarchy in 1789.) The nobles passed the crown to Philip VI of Valois (r. 1328–1350), a nephew of Philip the Fair.

In 1329 Edward III formally recognized Philip VI's lordship over Aquitaine. Eight years later, Philip, eager to exercise full French jurisdiction there, confiscated the duchy. Edward III interpreted this action as a gross violation of the treaty of 1259 and as a cause for war. Moreover, Edward argued, as the eldest directly surviving male descendant of Philip the Fair, he deserved the title of king of France. Edward III's dynastic argument upset the feudal order in France: to increase their independent power, many French nobles abandoned Philip VI, using the excuse that they had to transfer their loyalty to a different overlord, Edward III. One reason the war lasted so long was that it became a French civil war, with some French nobles, most importantly the dukes of Burgundy, supporting English monarchs in order to thwart the centralizing goals of the French kings. On the other side, Scotland—resisting English efforts of assimilation—often allied with France; the French supported Scottish raids in northern England, and Scottish troops joined with French armies on the continent.

The governments of both England and France manipulated public opinion to support the war. The English public was convinced that the war was waged for one reason: to secure for King Edward the French crown he had been unjustly denied. Edward III issued letters to the sheriffs describing the evil deeds of the French in graphic terms and listing royal needs. Philip VI sent agents to warn communities about the dangers of invasion. Kings in both countries instructed the clergy to deliver sermons filled with patriotic sentiment. Royal propaganda on both sides fostered a kind of early nationalism, and both sides developed a deep hatred of the other.

Economic factors involving the wool trade and the control of Flemish towns were linked to these political issues. The wool trade between England and Flanders served as the cornerstone of both countries' economies; they were closely interdependent. Flanders technically belonged to the French crown, and the Flemish aristocracy was highly sympathetic to that monarchy. But the wealth of Flemish merchants and cloth manufacturers depended on English wool, and Flemish burghers strongly supported the claims of Edward III. The disruption of commerce with England threatened their prosperity.

The Hundred Years' War

1337	Philip VI of France confiscates Aquitaine; war begins
1346	English longbowmen defeat French knights at Crécy
1356	English defeat French at Poitiers
1370s–1380s	French recover some territory
1415	English defeat the French at Agincourt
1429	French victory at Orléans; Charles VII crowned king
1431	Joan of Arc declared a heretic and burned at the stake
1440s	French reconquer Normandy and Aquitaine
1453	War ends
1456	Joan cleared of charges of heresy and declared a martyr

The war also presented opportunities for wealth and advancement. Poor and idle knights were promised regular wages. Criminals who enlisted were granted pardons. The great nobles expected to be rewarded with estates. Royal exhortations to the troops before battles repeatedly stressed that, if victorious, the men might keep whatever they seized.

English Successes

The war began with a series of French sea raids on English coastal towns in 1337, but the French fleet was almost completely destroyed when it attempted to land soldiers on English soil, and from that point on the war was fought almost entirely in France and the Low Countries (Map 11.2). It consisted mainly of a series of random sieges and cavalry raids, fought in fits and starts, with treaties along the way to halt hostilities.

During the war's early stages, England was highly successful. At Crécy in northern France in 1346, English longbowmen scored a great victory over French knights and crossbowmen. Although the aim of longbowmen was not very accurate, the weapon allowed for rapid reloading, and an English archer could send off three arrows to the French crossbowman's one. The result was a blinding shower of arrows that unhorsed the French knights and caused mass confusion. The roar of English cannon—probably the first use of artillery in the Western world—created further panic. This was not war according to the chivalric rules that Edward III would have preferred. Nevertheless, his son, Edward the Black Prince, used the same tactics ten years later to smash the French at Poitiers, where he captured the French king and held him for ransom.

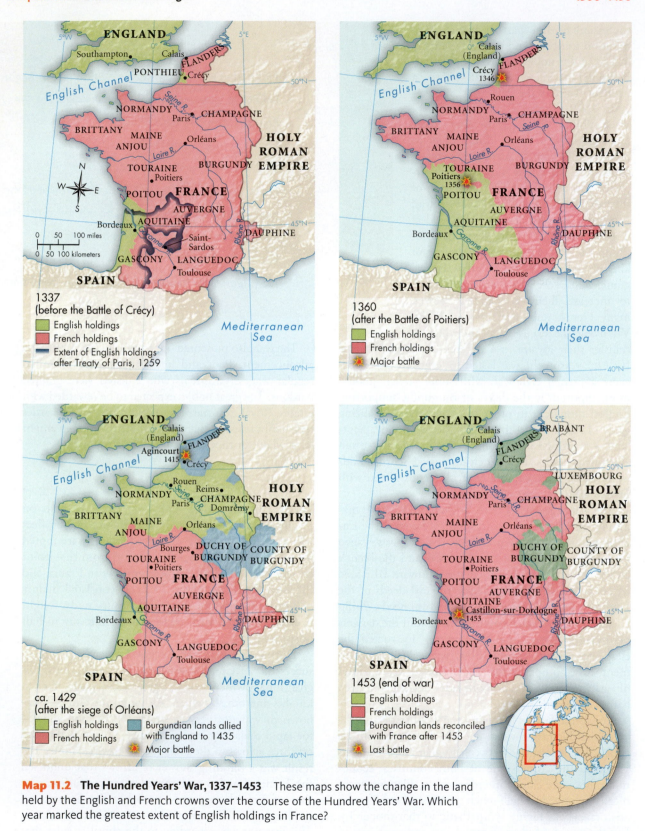

Map 11.2   The Hundred Years' War, 1337–1453   These maps show the change in the land held by the English and French crowns over the course of the Hundred Years' War. Which year marked the greatest extent of English holdings in France?

Edward was not able to take all of France, but the English held Aquitaine and other provinces, and allied themselves with many of France's nobles. After a brief peace, the French fought back and recovered some territory during the 1370s and 1380s, and then a treaty again halted hostilities as both sides concentrated on conflicts over power at home.

War began again in 1415 when the able English soldier-king Henry V (r. 1413–1422) invaded France. At Agincourt (AH-jihn-kort), Henry's army defeated a much larger French force, again primarily through the skill of English longbowmen. Henry followed up his triumph at Agincourt with the reconquest of Normandy, and by 1419 the English had advanced to the walls of Paris (see Map 11.2). Henry married the daughter of the French king, and a treaty made Henry and any sons the couple would have heir to the French throne. It appeared as if Henry would indeed rule both England and France, but he died unexpectedly in 1422, leaving an infant son as heir. The English continued their victories, however, and besieged the city of Orléans (or-lay-AHN), the only major city in northern France not under their control. But the French cause was not lost.

Joan of Arc and France's Victory

The ultimate French success rests heavily on the actions of Joan, an obscure French peasant girl whose vision and military leadership revived French fortunes and led to victory. (Over the centuries, she acquired the name "of Arc"—*d'Arc* in French—based on her father's name; she never used this name for herself, but called herself "the maiden"—*la Pucelle* in French.) Born in 1412 to well-to-do peasants in the village of Domrémy in Champagne, Joan grew up in a religious household. During adolescence she began to hear voices, which she later said belonged to Saint Michael, Saint Catherine, and Saint Margaret. In 1428 these voices spoke to her with great urgency, telling her that the dauphin (DOH-fuhn), the uncrowned King Charles VII, had to be crowned and the English expelled from France. Joan traveled to the French court wearing male cloth-

ing. She had an audience with Charles, who had her questioned about her angelic visions and examined to make sure she was the virgin she said she was. She secured his support to travel with the French army to Orléans dressed as a knight—with borrowed armor

Suit of Armor This fifteenth-century suit of Italian armor protected its wearer, but its weight made movement difficult. Both English and French mounted knights wore full armor at the beginning of the Hundred Years' War, but by the end they wore only breastplates and helmets, which protected their vital organs but allowed greater mobility. This particular suit has been so well preserved that it was most likely never used in battle; it may have been made for ceremonial purposes. (Image copyright © The Metropolitan Museum of Art/Art Resource, NY)

Siege of the Castle of Mortagne Medieval warfare usually consisted of small skirmishes and attacks on castles. This miniature shows the French besieging an English-held castle near Bordeaux in 1377 that held out for six months. Most of the soldiers use longbows, although at the left two men shoot primitive muskets above a pair of cannon. Painted in the late fifteenth century, the scene reflects the military technology available at the time it was painted, not at the time of the actual siege. (© British Library Board, MS Royal 14 e. IV f. 23)

and sword. There she dictated a letter to the English ordering them to surrender:

> King of England . . . , do right in the King of Heaven's sight. Surrender to The Maid sent hither by God the King of Heaven, the keys of all the good towns you have taken and laid waste in France. She comes in God's name to establish the Blood Royal, ready to make peace if you agree to abandon France and repay what you have taken. And you, archers, comrades in arms, gentles and others, who are before the town of Orléans, retire in God's name to your own country.[6]

Such words coming from a teenage girl—even one inspired by God—were laughable given the recent course of the conflict, but Joan was amazingly successful. She inspired and led French attacks, forcing the

English to retreat from Orléans. The king made Joan co-commander of the entire army, and she led it to a string of victories; other cities simply surrendered without a fight and returned their allegiance to France. In July 1429, two months after the end of the siege of Orléans, Charles VII was crowned king at Reims.

Joan and the French army continued their fight against the English and their Burgundian allies. In 1430 the Burgundians captured Joan. Charles refused to ransom her, and she was sold to the English. A church court headed by a pro-English bishop tried her for heresy, and though nothing she had done was heretical by church doctrine, she was found guilty and burned at the stake in the marketplace at Rouen. (See "Primary Source 11.2: The Trial of Joan of Arc," at right.)

The French army continued its victories without her. Sensing a shift in the balance of power, the Bur-

The Trial of Joan of Arc

Joan's interrogation was organized and led by Bishop Pierre Cauchon, one of many French clergy who supported the English. In a number of sessions that took place over several months, she was repeatedly asked about her voices, her decision to wear men's clothing, and other issues. This extract is from the fourth session, on Tuesday, February 27, 1431; Joan is here referred to with the French spelling of her name, Jeanne.

❝ In their presence Jeanne was required by my lord the Bishop of Beauvais to swear and take the oath concerning what touched her trial. To which she answered that she would willingly swear as to what touched her trial, but not as to everything she knew. . . .

Asked whether she had heard her voice since Saturday, she answered: "Yes, indeed, many times." . . . Asked what it said to her when she was back in her room, she replied: "That I should answer you boldly." . . . Questioned as to whether it were the voice of an angel, or of a saint, or directly from God, she answered that the voices were those of Saint Catherine and of Saint Margaret. And their heads are crowned with beautiful crowns, most richly and preciously. And [she said] for [telling you] this I have leave from our Lord. . . .

Asked if the voice ordered her to wear a man's dress, she answered that the dress is but a small matter; and that she had not taken it by the advice of any living man; and that she did not take this dress nor do anything at all save by the command of Our Lord and the angels.

Questioned as to whether it seemed to her that this command to take male dress was a lawful one, she answered that everything she had done was at Our Lord's command, and if He had ordered Jeanne to take a different dress, she would have done so, since it would have been at God's command. . . .

Asked if she had her sword when she was taken prisoner, she said no, but that she had one which was taken from a Burgundian. . . . Asked whether, when she was before the city of Orleans, she had a standard, and of what colour it was, she replied that it had a field sown with fleurs-de-lis, and showed a world with an angel on either side, white in colour, of linen or *boucassin* [a type of fabric], and she thought that the names JESUS MARIA were written on it; and it had a silk fringe. . . . Asked which she preferred, her sword or her standard, she replied that she was forty times fonder of her standard than she was of her sword. . . . She said moreover that she herself bore her standard during an attack, in order to avoid killing anyone. And she added that she had never killed anyone at all. . . .

She also said that during the attack on the fort at the bridge she was wounded in the neck by an arrow, but she was greatly comforted by Saint Catherine, and was well again in a fortnight. . . . Asked whether she knew beforehand that she would be wounded, she said that she well knew it, and had informed her king of it; but that notwithstanding she would not give up her work. ❞

EVALUATE THE EVIDENCE

1. How does Joan explain the way that she chose to answer the interrogators' questions, and her decisions about clothing and actions in battle?
2. Thinking about the structures of power and authority in fifteenth-century France, how do you believe the interrogators would have regarded Joan's answers?

Source: *The Trial of Joan of Arc*, translated with an introduction by W. S. Scott (Westport, Conn.: Associated Booksellers, 1956), 76, 77, 79–80, 82, 83. © 1956, The Folio Society.

gundians switched their allegiance to the French, who reconquered Normandy and, finally, ejected the English from Aquitaine in the 1440s. As the war dragged on, loss of life mounted, and money appeared to be flowing into a bottomless pit, demands for an end increased in England. Parliamentary opposition to additional war grants stiffened, fewer soldiers were sent, and more territory passed into French hands. At the war's end in 1453, only the town of Calais (KA-lay) remained in English hands.

What of Joan? A new trial in 1456—requested by Charles VII, who either had second thoughts about his abandonment of Joan or did not wish to be associated with a condemned heretic—was held by the pope. It cleared her of all charges and declared her a martyr. She became a political symbol of France from that point on, and sometimes also a symbol of the Catholic Church in opposition to the government of France. In 1920, for example, she was canonized as a saint shortly after the French government declared separation of church and state in France. Similarly, Joan has been (and continues to be) a symbol of deep religious piety to some, of conservative nationalism to others, and of gender-bending cross-dressing to others. Beneath the pious and popular legends is a teenage girl who saved the French monarchy, the embodiment of France.

Aftermath

In France thousands of soldiers and civilians had been slaughtered and hundreds of thousands of acres of rich farmland ruined, leaving the rural economy of many areas a shambles. These losses exacerbated the dreadful losses caused by the plague. The war had disrupted trade and the great trade fairs, resulting in the drastic reduction of French participation in international commerce. Defeat in battle and heavy taxation contributed to widespread dissatisfaction and aggravated peasant grievances.

The war had wreaked havoc in England as well, even though only the southern coastal ports saw actual battle. England spent the huge sum of over £5 million on the war effort, and despite the money raised by some victories, the net result was an enormous financial loss. The government attempted to finance the war by raising taxes on the wool crop, which priced wool out of the export market.

In both England and France, men of all social classes had volunteered to serve in the war in the hope of acquiring booty and becoming rich, and some were successful in the early years of the war. As time went on, however, most fortunes seem to have been squandered as fast as they were made. In addition, the social order was disrupted because the knights who ordinarily served as sheriffs, coroners, jurymen, and justices of the peace were abroad.

The war stimulated technological experimentation, especially with artillery. Cannon revolutionized warfare, making the stone castle no longer impregnable. Because only central governments, not private nobles, could afford cannon, their use strengthened the military power of national states.

The long war also had a profound impact on the political and cultural lives of the two countries. Most notably, it stimulated the development of the English Parliament. Between 1250 and 1450 **representative assemblies** flourished in many European countries. In the English Parliament, German *diets*, and Spanish *cortes*, deliberative practices developed that laid the foundations for the representative institutions of modern democratic nations. While representative assemblies declined in most countries after the fifteenth century, the English Parliament endured. Edward III's constant need for money to pay for the war compelled him to summon not only the great barons and bishops, but knights of the shires and citizens from the towns as well. Parliament met in thirty-seven of the fifty years of Edward's reign.

The frequency of the meetings is significant. Representative assemblies were becoming a habit. Knights and wealthy urban residents—or the "Commons," as they came to be called—recognized their mutual interests and began to meet apart from the great lords. The Commons gradually realized that they held the country's purse strings, and a parliamentary statute of 1341 required parliamentary approval of most new taxes. By signing the law, Edward III acknowledged that the king of England could not tax without Parliament's consent.

In England, theoretical consent to taxation and legislation was given in one assembly for the entire country. France had no such single assembly; instead, there were many regional or provincial assemblies. Why did a national representative assembly fail to develop in France? Linguistic, geographical, economic, legal, and political differences remained very strong. People tended to think of themselves as Breton, Norman, Burgundian, and so on, rather than French. In addition, provincial assemblies, highly jealous of their independence, did not want a national assembly. The costs of sending delegates to it would be high, and the result was likely to be increased taxation and a lessening of their own power. Finally, the initiative for convening assemblies rested with the king, but some monarchs lacked the power to call them, and others, including Charles VI, found the very idea of representative assemblies thoroughly distasteful.

In both countries, however, the war did promote the growth of nationalism—the feeling of unity and identity that binds together a people. After victories, each country experienced a surge of pride in its military strength. Just as English patriotism ran strong after Crécy and Poitiers, so French national confidence rose after Orléans. French national feeling demanded the expulsion of the enemy not merely from Normandy and Aquitaine but from all French soil. Perhaps no one expressed this national consciousness better than Joan when she exulted that the enemy had been "driven out of *France*."

representative assemblies
Deliberative meetings of lords and wealthy urban residents that flourished in many European countries between 1250 and 1450.

Challenges to the Church
Why did the church come under increasing criticism?

In times of crisis or disaster, people of all faiths have sought the consolation of religion. In the fourteenth century, however, the official Christian Church offered little solace. Many priests and friars helped the sick and the hungry, but others paid more attention to worldly matters, and the leaders of the church added to the sorrow and misery of the times. In response to this lack of leadership, members of the clergy challenged the power of the pope, and laypeople challenged the authority of

Raimon de Cornet on the Avignon Papacy

Criticism of the church during the period of the Avignon papacy included learned treatises, but also works written for a more popular audience. In this poem, probably written in the 1330s, Raimon de Cornet, a troubadour poet from southern France who was himself a priest, criticizes the entire church hierarchy: pope, cardinals, and bishops.

" I see the pope his sacred trust betray,
For while the rich his grace can gain alway,
His favors from the poor are aye withholden.
He strives to gather wealth as best he may,
Forcing Christ's people blindly to obey,
So that he may repose in garments golden.
The vilest traffickers in souls are all
His chapmen, and for gold a prebend's stall
He'll sell them, or an abbacy or miter [the hat of a bishop].
And to us he sends clowns and tramps who crawl
Vending his pardon briefs from cot to hall —
Letters and pardons worthy of the writer,
Which leaves our pokes [money-pouches], if not our
    souls, the lighter.

No better is each honored cardinal.
From early morning's dawn to evening's fall,
Their time is passed in eagerly contriving
To drive some bargain foul with each and all.
So if you feel a want, or great or small,
Or if for some preferment [church position] you are
    striving,
The more you please to give the more 't will bring,
Be it a purple cap or bishop's ring.

And it need ne'er in any way alarm you
That you are ignorant of everything
To which a minister of Christ should cling,
You will have revenue enough to warm you —
And, bear in mind, the lesser gifts won't harm you.

Our bishops, too, are plunged in similar sin,
For pitilessly they flay the very skin
From all their priests who chance to have fat livings.
For gold their seal official you can win
To any writ, no matter what's therein.
Sure God alone can make them stop their thievings.
'T were hard, in full, their evil works to tell,
As when, for a few pence, they greedily sell
The tonsure [the haircut of a monk or priest] to some
    mountebank or jester,
Whereby the temporal courts are wronged as well,
For then these tonsured rogues they cannot quell,
Howe'er their scampish doings may us pester,
While round the church still growing evils fester. "

EVALUATE THE EVIDENCE

1. What actions of the church hierarchy does Raimon de Cornet view as particularly worthy of criticism?
2. How did popular poems such as this one both reflect and shape attitudes toward the church in the fourteenth century?

Source: James Harvey Robinson, *Readings in European History*, vol. 1 (Boston: Ginn and Company, 1904), pp. 375–376.

the church itself. Women and men increasingly relied on direct approaches to God, often through mystical encounters, rather than on the institutional church.

The Babylonian Captivity and Great Schism

Conflicts between the secular rulers of Europe and the popes were common throughout the High Middle Ages, and in the early fourteenth century the dispute between King Philip the Fair of France and Pope Boniface VIII became particularly bitter (see Chapter 9). After Boniface's death, in order to control the church and its policies, Philip pressured the new pope, Clement V, to settle permanently in Avignon in southeastern France. The popes lived in Avignon from 1309 to 1376, a period in church history often called the Babylonian Captivity (referring to the seventy years the ancient Hebrews were held captive in Mesopotamian Babylon).

The Babylonian Captivity badly damaged papal prestige. The seven popes at Avignon concentrated on bureaucratic and financial matters to the exclusion of spiritual objectives, and the general atmosphere was one of luxury and extravagance, which was also the case at many bishops' courts. (See "Primary Source 11.3: Raimon de Cornet on the Avignon Papacy," above.) The leadership of the church was cut off from its historic roots and the source of its ancient authority, the city of Rome. In 1377 Pope Gregory XI brought the papal court back to Rome but died shortly

Babylonian Captivity The period from 1309 to 1376 when the popes resided in Avignon rather than in Rome. The phrase refers to the seventy years when the Hebrews were held captive in Babylon.

afterward. Roman citizens pressured the cardinals to elect an Italian, and they chose a distinguished administrator, the archbishop of Bari, Bartolomeo Prignano, who took the name Urban VI.

Urban VI (pontificate 1378–1389) had excellent intentions for church reform, but he went about it in a tactless manner. He attacked clerical luxury, denouncing individual cardinals and bishops by name, and even threatened to excommunicate some of them. The cardinals slipped away from Rome and met at Anagni. They declared Urban's election invalid because it had come about under threats from the Roman mob, and excommunicated the pope. The cardinals then elected Cardinal Robert of Geneva, the cousin of King Charles V of France, as pope. Cardinal Robert took the name Clement VII. There were thus two popes in 1378—Urban at Rome and Clement VII (pontificate 1378–1394) at Avignon. So began the **Great Schism**, which divided Western Christendom until 1417.

The powers of Europe aligned themselves with Urban or Clement along strictly political lines. France naturally recognized the French pope, Clement. England, France's long-time enemy, recognized the Italian pope, Urban. Scotland, an ally of France, supported Clement. Aragon, Castile, and Portugal hesitated before deciding for Clement as well. The German emperor, hostile to France, recognized Urban. At first the Italian city-states recognized Urban; later they opted for Clement.

John of Spoleto, a professor at the law school at Bologna, eloquently summed up intellectual opinion of the schism: "The longer this schism lasts, the more it appears to be costing, and the more harm it does; scandal, massacres, ruination, agitations, troubles and disturbances."[7] The schism weakened the religious faith of many Christians and brought church leadership into serious disrepute.

Great Schism The division, or split, in church leadership from 1378 to 1417 when there were two, then three, popes.

conciliarists People who believed that the authority in the Roman Church should rest in a general council composed of clergy, theologians, and laypeople, rather than in the pope alone.

Allegiance to Rome
Allegiance to Avignon
Official allegiance to Rome but with shifting local allegiances

The Great Schism, 1378–1417

Critiques, Divisions, and Councils

Criticism of the church during the Avignon papacy and the Great Schism often came from the ranks of highly learned clergy and lay professionals. One of these was William of Occam (1289?–1347?), a Franciscan friar and philosopher who predated the Great Schism but saw the papal court at Avignon during the Babylonian Captivity. Occam argued vigorously against the papacy and also wrote philosophical works in which he questioned the connection between reason and faith that had been developed by Thomas Aquinas (see Chapter 10). All governments should have limited powers and be accountable to those they govern, according to Occam, and church and state should be separate.

The Italian lawyer and university official Marsiglio of Padua (ca. 1275–1342) agreed with Occam. In his *Defensor Pacis* (The Defender of the Peace), Marsiglio argued against the medieval idea of a society governed by both church and state, with church supreme. Instead, Marsiglio claimed, the state was the great unifying power in society, and the church should be subordinate to it. Church leadership should rest in a general council made up of laymen as well as priests and superior to the pope. Marsiglio was excommunicated for these radical ideas, and his work was condemned as heresy—as was Occam's—but in the later part of the fourteenth century many thinkers agreed with these two critics of the papacy. They believed that reform of the church could best be achieved through periodic assemblies, or councils, representing all the Christian people. Those who argued this position were called **conciliarists**.

The English scholar and theologian John Wyclif (WIH-klihf) (ca. 1330–1384) went further than the conciliarists in his argument against medieval church structure. He wrote that Scripture alone should be the standard of Christian belief and practice and that papal claims of secular power had no foundation in the Scriptures. He urged that the church be stripped of its property. He also wanted Christians to read the Bible for themselves and produced the first complete translation of the Bible into English. Wyclif's followers, dubbed Lollards, from a Dutch word for "mumble" by those who ridiculed them, spread his ideas and made many copies of his Bible. Lollard teaching allowed women to preach, and women played a significant role in the movement. Lollards were persecuted in the fifteenth century; some were executed, some recanted, and others continued to meet secretly in houses, barns, and fields to read and discuss the Bible and other religious texts in English. Bohemian students returning from study at the University of Oxford around 1400 brought Wyclif's ideas with them to Prague, the capital of what was then Bohemia and is now the Czech Republic. There another university theologian, Jan Hus (ca. 1372–1415), built on them. He also denied papal authority, called for translations of the Bible into the local Czech language, and declared indulgences—papal offers of remission of penance—useless. Hus gained many followers, who linked his theological ideas with their opposition to the church's wealth and power and with a growing sense of Czech nationalism in opposition to the pope's international power. Hus's followers were successful at defeating the combined armies of the pope and the emperor many times. In the 1430s the emperor finally agreed to recognize the Hussite Church in Bohemia, which survived into the Reformation and then merged with other Protestant churches.

The ongoing schism threatened the church, and in response to continued calls throughout Europe for a council, the cardinals of Rome and Avignon summoned a council at Pisa in 1409. That gathering of prelates and theologians deposed both popes and selected another. Neither the Avignon pope nor the Roman pope

The Hussite Revolution, 1415–1436

would resign, however, and the appalling result was the creation of a threefold schism.

Finally, under pressure from the German emperor Sigismund, a great council met at the imperial city of Constance (1414–1418). It had three objectives: to wipe out heresy, to end the schism, and to reform the church. Members included cardinals, bishops, abbots, and professors of theology and canon law from across Europe. The council moved first on the last point: despite being granted a safe-conduct to go to Constance by the emperor, Jan Hus was tried, condemned, and burned at the stake as a heretic in 1415. The council also eventually healed the schism. It deposed both the Roman pope and the successor of the pope chosen at Pisa, and it isolated the Avignon pope. A conclave elected a new leader, the Roman cardinal Colonna, who took the name Martin V (pontificate 1417–1431).

Martin proceeded to dissolve the council. Nothing was done about reform, the third objective of the council. In the later part of the fifteenth century the

The Execution of Jan Hus   This fifteenth-century manuscript illustration shows men placing logs around Hus at the Council of Constance, while soldiers, officials, a priest, and a cardinal look on. Hus became an important symbol of Czech independence, and in 1990 the Czech Republic declared July 6, the date of his execution in 1415, a national holiday. (The Art Archive at Art Resource)

INDIVIDUALS IN SOCIETY
Meister Eckhart

Mysticism—the direct experience of the divine—is an aspect of many world religions and has been part of Christianity throughout its history. During the late Middle Ages, however, the pursuit of mystical union became an important part of the piety of many laypeople, especially in the Rhineland area of Germany. In this they were guided by the sermons of the churchman generally known as Meister Eckhart. Born into a German noble family, Eckhart (1260–1329?) joined the Dominican order and studied theology at Paris and Cologne, attaining the academic title of "master" (*Meister* in German). The leaders of the Dominican order appointed him to a series of administrative and teaching positions, and he wrote learned treatises in Latin that reflected his Scholastic training and deep understanding of classical philosophy.

He also began to preach in German, attracting many listeners through his beautiful language and mystical insights. God, he said, was "an oversoaring being and an overbeing nothingness," whose essence was beyond the ability of humans to express: "if the soul is to know God, it must know Him outside time and place, since God is neither in this or that, but One and above them." Only through "unknowing," emptying oneself, could one come to experience the divine. Yet God was also present in individual human souls, and to a degree in every creature, all of which God had called into being before the beginning of time. Within each human soul there was what Eckhart called a "little spark," an innermost essence that allows the soul—with God's grace and Christ's redemptive action—to come to God. "Our salvation depends upon our knowing and recognizing the Chief Good which is God Himself," preached Eckhart; "the Eye with which I see God is the same Eye with which God sees me." "I have a capacity in my soul for taking in God entirely," he went on, a capacity that was shared by all humans, not only members of the clergy or those with special spiritual gifts. Although Eckhart did not reject church sacraments or the hierarchy, he frequently stressed that union with God was best accomplished through quiet detachment and simple prayer rather than pilgrimages, extensive fasts, or other activities: "If the only prayer you said in your whole life was 'thank you,' that would suffice."*

Eckhart's unusual teachings led to charges of heresy in 1327, which he denied. The pope—who was at this point in Avignon—presided over a trial condemning him, but Eckhart appears to have died during the course of the proceedings or shortly thereafter. His writings were ordered destroyed, but his followers preserved many and spread his teachings.

In the last few decades, Meister Eckhart's ideas have been explored and utilized by philosophers and mystics in Bud-

A sixteenth-century woodcut of Meister Eckhart teaching.
(Visual Connection Archive)

dhism, Hinduism, and neo-paganism, as well as by Christians. His writings sell widely for their spiritual insights, and quotations from them—including the one above about thank-you prayers—can be found on coffee mugs, tote bags, and T-shirts.

QUESTIONS FOR ANALYSIS

1. Why might Meister Eckhart's preaching have been viewed as threatening by the leaders of the church?
2. Given the situation of the church in the late Middle Ages, why might mysticism have been attractive to pious Christians?

ONLINE DOCUMENT ASSIGNMENT
What does Meister Eckhart's life tell us about the religious climate of the early fourteenth century?
Go to the Integrated Media and examine a selection of Eckhart's writings and those of his critics. Then complete a writing assignment based on the evidence and details from this chapter.

*Meister Eckhart's Sermons, trans. Claud Field (London: n.p., 1909).

papacy concentrated on Italian problems to the exclusion of universal Christian interests. But the schism and the conciliar movement had exposed the crying need for ecclesiastical reform, thus laying the foundation for the great reform efforts of the sixteenth century.

Lay Piety and Mysticism

The failings of the Avignon papacy followed by the scandal of the Great Schism did much to weaken the spiritual mystique of the clergy in the popular mind. Laypeople had already begun to develop their own forms of piety somewhat separate from the authority of priests and bishops, and these forms of piety became more prominent in the fourteenth century.

In the thirteenth century lay Christian men and women had formed **confraternities**, voluntary lay groups organized by occupation, devotional preference, neighborhood, or charitable activity. Some confraternities specialized in praying for souls in purgatory, either for specific individuals or for the anonymous mass of all souls. In England they held dances, church festivals, and collections to raise money to clean and repair church buildings and to supply churches with candles and other liturgical objects. Like craft guilds, most confraternities were groups of men, but separate women's confraternities were formed in some towns, often to oversee the production of vestments, altar cloths, and other items made of fabric. All confraternities carried out special devotional practices such as prayers or processions, often without the leadership of a priest. Famine, plague, war, and other crises led to an expansion of confraternities in larger cities and many villages.

In Holland beginning in the late fourteenth century, a group of pious laypeople called the Brethren and Sisters of the Common Life lived in stark simplicity while daily carrying out the Gospel teaching of feeding the hungry, clothing the naked, and visiting the sick. They sought to both ease social problems and make religion a personal inner experience. The spirituality of the Brethren and Sisters of the Common Life found its finest expression in the classic *The Imitation of Christ* by the Dutch monk Thomas à Kempis (1380?–1471), which gained wide appeal among laypeople. It urges Christians to take Christ as their model, seek perfection in a simple way of life, and look to the Scriptures for guidance in living a spiritual life. In the mid-fifteenth century the movement had founded houses in the Netherlands, in central Germany, and in the Rhineland.

For some individuals, both laypeople and clerics, religious devotion included mystical experiences. (See "Individuals in Society: Meister Eckhart," at left.) Bridget of Sweden (1303–1373) was a noblewoman who journeyed to Rome after her husband's death. She began to see visions and gave advice based on these visions to both laypeople and church officials. At the end of her life Bridget made a pilgrimage to Jerusalem, where she saw visions of the Virgin Mary, who described to her exactly how she was standing "with my knees bent" when she gave birth to Jesus, and how she "showed to the shepherds the nature and male sex of the child."[8] Bridget's visions provide evidence of the ways in which laypeople used their own experiences to enhance their religious understanding; Bridget's own experiences of childbirth shaped the way she viewed the birth of Jesus, and she related to the Virgin Mary in part as one mother to another.

> **confraternities** Voluntary lay groups organized by occupation, devotional preference, neighborhood, or charitable activity.

The confraternities and mystics were generally not considered heretical unless they began to challenge the authority of the papacy the way Wyclif, Hus, and some conciliarists did. However, the movement of lay piety did alter many people's perceptions of their own spiritual power.

Social Unrest in a Changing Society

What explains the social unrest of the late Middle Ages?

At the beginning of the fourteenth century famine and disease profoundly affected the lives of European peoples. As the century wore on, decades of slaughter and destruction, punctuated by the decimating visits of the Black Death, added further woes. In many parts of France and the Low Countries, fields lay in ruin or untilled for lack of labor. In England, as taxes increased, criticisms of government policy and mismanagement multiplied. Crime and new forms of business organization aggravated economic troubles, and throughout Europe the frustrations of the common people erupted into widespread revolts.

Peasant Revolts

Nobles and clergy lived on the food produced by peasant labor, thinking little of adding taxes to the burden of peasant life. While peasants had endured centuries of exploitation, the difficult conditions of the fourteenth and fifteenth centuries spurred a wave of peasant revolts across Europe. Peasants were sometimes joined by those low on the urban social ladder, resulting in a wider revolution of poor against rich.

The first large-scale rebellion was in the Flanders region of present-day Belgium in the 1320s (Map 11.3). In order to satisfy peace agreements, Flemish peasants were forced to pay taxes to the French, who claimed fiscal rights over the county of Flanders. Monasteries also pressed peasants for additional money above their customary tithes. In retaliation, peasants burned and pillaged castles and aristocratic country houses. A French army crushed the peasant forces, however, and savage repression and the confiscation of peasant property followed in the 1330s.

In the following decades, revolts broke out in many other places. In 1358, when French taxation for the Hundred Years' War fell heavily on the poor, the frustrations of the French peasantry exploded in a massive uprising called the **Jacquerie** (zhah-kuh-REE), after a mythical agricultural laborer, Jacques Bonhomme (Good Fellow). Peasants blamed the nobility for oppressive taxes, for the criminal banditry of the countryside, for losses on the battlefield, and for the general misery. Crowds swept through the countryside, slashing the throats of nobles, burning their castles, raping their wives and daughters, and killing or maiming their horses and cattle. Artisans and small merchants in cities and parish priests joined the peasants. Rebels committed terrible destruction, and for several weeks the nobles were on the defensive. Then the upper class united to repress the revolt with merciless ferocity.

Jacquerie A massive uprising by French peasants in 1358 protesting heavy taxation.

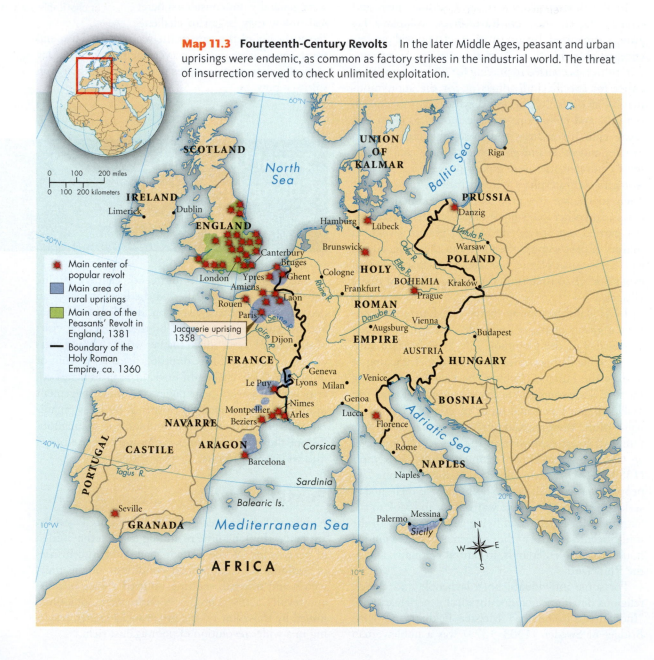

Map 11.3 Fourteenth-Century Revolts   In the later Middle Ages, peasant and urban uprisings were endemic, as common as factory strikes in the industrial world. The threat of insurrection served to check unlimited exploitation.

The Statute of Laborers

The English population had declined by about one-third because of the Black Death, and rural and urban workers responded by demanding higher wages. In 1351 the English Parliament and King Edward III passed a law ordering wages to be set at their pre-plague levels, and attempting to force people to work.

❝ Because a great part of the people and especially of the workmen and servants has now died in that pestilence, some, seeing the straights of the masters and the scarcity of servants, are not willing to serve unless they receive excessive wages, and others, rather than through labour to gain their living, prefer to beg in idleness: We, considering the grave inconveniences which might come from the lack especially of ploughmen and such labourers . . . have seen fit to ordain: that every man and woman of our kingdom of England, of whatever condition, whether bond or free, who is able bodied and below the age of sixty years, . . . if he, considering his station, be sought after to serve in a suitable service, he shall be bound to serve him who has seen fit so to seek after him; and he shall take only the wages . . . or salary which, in the places where he sought to serve, were accustomed to be paid in the twentieth year of our reign of England [1346], . . . and if any man or woman, being thus sought after in service, will not do this, the fact being proven by two faithful men before the sheriffs or the bailiffs of our lord the king, or the constables of the town where this happens to be done, — straightway through them, or some one of them, he shall be taken and sent to the next jail, and there he shall remain in strict custody until he shall find surety for serving in the aforesaid form.

And if a reaper or mower, or other workman or servant, of whatever standing or condition he be, who is retained in the service of any one, do depart from the said service before the end of the term agreed, without permission or reasonable cause, he shall undergo the penalty of imprisonment. . . .

Likewise saddlers, skinners, white-tawers, cordwainers, tailors, smiths, carpenters, masons, tilers, shipwrights, carters and all other artisans and labourers shall not take for their labour and handiwork more than what, in the places where they happen to labour, was customarily paid to such persons in [1346]; and if any man take more, he shall be committed to the nearest jail in the manner aforesaid. . . .

And because many sound beggars do refuse to labour so long as they can live from begging alms, giving themselves up to idleness and sins, and, at times, to robbery and other crimes — let no one, under the aforesaid pain of imprisonment presume, under colour of piety or alms to give anything to such as can very well labour, or to cherish them in their sloth, — so that thus they may be compelled to labour for the necessaries of life. ❞

EVALUATE THE EVIDENCE

1. What does the law require rural laborers, urban artisans, and the poor to do, and what penalties does it provide if they do not?
2. Why were measures such as this most likely ineffective, and how did they contribute to growing social tensions?

Source: Ernest F. Henderson, trans. and ed., *Select Historical Documents of the Middle Ages* (London: George Bell and Sons, 1892).

Thousands of the "Jacques," innocent as well as guilty, were cut down. That forcible suppression of social rebellion, without any effort to alleviate its underlying causes, served to drive protest underground.

In England the Black Death drastically cut the labor supply, and as a result peasants demanded higher wages and fewer manorial obligations. Their lords countered in 1351 with the Statute of Laborers, a law issued by the king that froze wages and bound workers to their manors. (See "Primary Source 11.4: The Statute of Laborers," above.) This attempt to freeze wages could not be enforced, but a huge gap remained between peasants and their lords, and the peasants sought release for their economic frustrations in revolt. Other factors combined with these economic grievances to fuel the rebellion. The south of England, where the revolt broke out, had been subjected to destructive French raids during the Hundred Years' War. The English government did little to protect the region, and villagers grew increasingly frightened and insecure. Moreover, decades of aristocratic violence against the weak peasantry had bred hostility and bitterness. Social and religious agitation by the popular preacher John Ball fanned the embers of discontent. Ball's famous couplet calling for a return to the social equality that had existed in the Garden of Eden ("When Adam delved and Eve span; / Who was then the gentleman?") reflected real revolutionary sentiment.

The English revolt was ignited by the reimposition of a tax on all adult males. Despite widespread opposition to the tax in 1380, the royal council ordered the sheriffs to collect it again in 1381. This led to a major uprising known as the **English Peasants' Revolt**, which involved thousands of people. Beginning with assaults on the tax collectors, the revolt in England followed a course similar to that of the Jacquerie in France. Castles and manors were sacked. Manorial records were destroyed. Many nobles, including the archbishop of Canterbury who had ordered the collection of the tax, were murdered. The center of the revolt lay in the highly populated and economically advanced south and east, but sections of the north also witnessed rebellions (see Map 11.3).

English Peasants' Revolt
Revolt by English peasants in 1381 in response to changing economic conditions.

The boy-king Richard II (r. 1377–1399) met the leaders of the revolt, agreed to charters ensuring peasants' freedom, tricked them with false promises, and then crushed the uprising with terrible ferocity. In the aftermath of the revolt, the nobility tried to restore the labor obligations of serfdom, but they were not successful, and the conversion to money rents continued. The English Peasants' Revolt did not bring social equality to England, but rural serfdom continued to decline, disappearing in England by 1550.

Urban Conflicts

In Flanders, France, and England, peasant revolts often blended with conflicts involving workers in cities. Unrest also occurred in Italian, Spanish, and German cities. The urban revolts had their roots in the changing conditions of work. In the thirteenth century craft guilds had organized the production of most goods, with masters, journeymen, and apprentices working side by side. In the fourteenth century a new system evolved to make products on a larger scale. Capitalist investors hired many households, with each household performing only one step of the process. Initially these investors were wealthy bankers and merchants, but eventually shop masters themselves embraced the system. This promoted a greater division within guilds between wealthier masters and the poorer masters and journeymen they hired. Some masters became so wealthy from the profits of their workers that they no longer had to work in a shop themselves, nor did their wives and family members, though they still generally belonged to the craft guild.

While capitalism provided opportunities for some artisans to become investors and entrepreneurs, especially in cloth production, for many it led to a decrease in income and status. Guilds sometimes responded to crises by opening up membership, as they did in some places immediately after the Black Death, but they more often responded to competition by limiting membership to existing guild families, which meant that journeymen who were not master's sons or who could not find a master's widow or daughter to marry could never become masters themselves. Remaining journeymen their entire lives, they lost their sense of solidarity with the masters of their craft. Resentment led to rebellion.

Urban uprisings were also sparked by issues involving honor, such as employers' requiring workers to do tasks they regarded as beneath them. As their actual status and economic prospects declined and their work became basically wage labor, journeymen and poorer masters emphasized skill and honor as qualities that set them apart from less-skilled workers.

Guilds increasingly came to view the honor of their work as tied to an all-male workplace. When urban economies were expanding in the High Middle Ages, the master's wife and daughters worked alongside him, and female domestic servants also carried out productive tasks. (See "Primary Source 11.5: Christine de Pizan, Advice to the Wives of Artisans," at right.) Masters' widows ran shops after the death of their husbands. But in the fourteenth century women's participation in guilds declined, despite labor shortages caused by the plague. First, masters' widows were limited in the amount of time they could keep operating a shop or were prohibited from hiring journeymen; later, female domestic servants were excluded from any productive tasks; finally, the number of daughters a master craftsman could employ was limited. When women were allowed to work, it was viewed as a substitute for charity.

Sex in the City

Peasant and urban revolts and riots had clear economic bases, but some historians have suggested that late medieval marital patterns may have also played a role. In northwestern Europe, people believed that couples should be economically independent before they married. Thus not only during times of crisis such as the Great Famine, but also in more general circumstances, men and women spent long periods as servants or workers in other households, saving money for married life and learning skills, or they waited until their own parents had died and the family property was distributed.

The most unusual feature of this pattern was the late age of marriage for women. Unlike in earlier time periods and in most other parts of the world, a woman in late medieval northern and western Europe generally entered marriage as an adult in her twenties and took charge of running a household immediately. She was thus not as dependent on her husband or mother-in-law as was a woman who married at a younger age.

Christine de Pizan, Advice to the Wives of Artisans

Christine de Pizan (1364?–1430) was the daughter and wife of highly educated men who held positions at the court of the king of France. She was widowed at twenty-five with young children and an elderly mother to care for, and she decided to support her family through writing, an unusual choice for anyone in this era and unheard of for a woman. She began to write prose works and poetry, and gained commissions to write a biography of the French king Charles V, several histories, a long poem celebrating Joan of Arc's victory, and a book of military tactics. She became the first woman in Europe to make her living as a writer.

Among Christine's many works were several in which she considered women's nature and proper role in society, a topic of debate since ancient times. Among these was The Treasure of the City of Ladies *(1405, also called* The Book of Three Virtues*), which provides moral suggestions and practical advice on behavior and household management for women of all social classes. Most of the book is directed toward princesses and court ladies, but she also includes shorter sections for more ordinary women. Excerpted here is her advice to the wives of artisans, whose husbands were generally members of urban craft guilds, such as blacksmiths, bakers, or shoemakers.*

" All wives of artisans should be very painstaking and diligent if they wish to have the necessities of life. They should encourage their husbands or their workmen to get to work early in the morning and work until late, for mark our words, there is no trade so good that if you neglect your work you will not have difficulty putting bread on the table. And besides encouraging the others, the wife herself should be involved in the work to the extent that she knows all about it, so that she may know how to oversee his workers if her husband is absent, and to reprove them if they do not do well. She ought to oversee them to keep them from idleness, for through careless workers the master is sometimes ruined. And when customers come to her husband and try to drive a hard bargain, she ought to warn him solicitously to take care that he does not make a bad deal. She should advise him to be chary of giving too much credit if he does not know precisely where and to whom it is going, for in this way many come to poverty, although sometimes the greed to earn more or to accept a tempting proposition makes them do it.

In addition, she ought to keep her husband's love as much as she can, to this end: that he will stay at home more willingly and that he may not have any reason to join the foolish crowds of other young men in taverns and indulge in unnecessary and extravagant expense, as many tradesmen do, especially in Paris. By treating him kindly she should protect him as well as she can from this. It is said that three things drive a man from his home: a quarrelsome wife, a smoking fireplace and a leaking roof. She too ought to stay at home gladly and not go every day traipsing hither and yon gossiping with the neighbours and visiting her chums to find out what everyone is doing. That is done by slovenly housewives roaming about the town in groups. Nor should she go off on these pilgrimages got up for no good reason and involving a lot of needless expense. Furthermore, she ought to remind her husband that they should live so frugally that their expenditure does not exceed their income, so that at the end of the year they do not find themselves in debt.

If she has children, she should have them instructed and taught first at school by educated people so that they may know how better to serve God. Afterwards they may be put to some trade by which they may earn a living, for whoever gives a trade or business training to her child gives a great possession. The children should be kept from wantonness and from voluptuousness above all else, for truly it is something that most shames the children of good towns and is a great sin of mothers and fathers, who ought to be the cause of the virtue and good behavior of their children, but they are sometimes the reason (because of bringing them up to be finicky and indulging them too much) for their wickedness and ruin. "

EVALUATE THE EVIDENCE

1. How would you describe Christine's view of the ideal artisan's wife?
2. The regulations of craft guilds often required that masters who ran workshops be married. What evidence does Christine's advice provide for why guilds would have stipulated this?
3. How are economic and moral virtues linked for Christine?

Source: Excerpts from pp. 167–168 in Christine de Pisan, *The Treasure of the City of Ladies*, translated with an Introduction by Sarah Lawson (Penguin Classics, 1985). This translation copyright © 1985 by Sarah Lawson. Reproduced by permission of Penguin Books Ltd. For more on Christine, see C. C. Willard, *Christine de Pisan: Her Life and Works* (1984), and S. Bell, *The Lost Tapestries of the City of Ladies: Christine de Pizan's Renaissance Legacy* (2004).

She also had fewer pregnancies than a woman who married earlier, though not necessarily fewer surviving children.

Men of all social groups had long tended to be older than women when they married. In general, men were in their middle or late twenties at first marriage, with wealthier urban merchants often much older. Journeymen and apprentices were often explicitly prohibited from marrying, as were the students at universities, who were understood to be in "minor orders" and thus like clergy, even if they were not intending to have careers in the church.

The prohibitions on marriage for certain groups of men and the late age of marriage for most men meant that cities and villages were filled with large numbers of young adult men with no family responsibilities who often formed the core of riots and unrest. Not surprisingly, this situation also contributed to a steady market for sexual services outside of marriage, services that in later centuries were termed prostitution. Research on the southern French province of Languedoc in the fourteenth and fifteenth centuries has revealed the establishment of legal houses of prostitution in many cities. Municipal authorities set up houses or districts for prostitution either outside the city walls or away from respectable neighborhoods. For example, authorities in Montpellier set aside Hot Street for prostitution, required women who sold sex to live there, and forbade anyone to molest them. Prostitution thus passed from being a private concern to a social matter requiring public supervision. The towns of Languedoc were not unique. Public authorities in Amiens, Dijon, Paris, Venice, Genoa, London, Florence, Rome, most of the larger German towns, and the English port of Sandwich set up brothels.

Young men associated visiting brothels with achieving manhood; for the women themselves, of course, their activities were work. Some women had no choice, for they had been traded to the brothel manager by their parents or some other person as payment for debt, or had quickly become indebted to the manager (most of whom were men) for the clothes and other finery regarded as essential to their occupation. The small amount they received from their customers did not equal what they had to pay for their upkeep in a brothel. Poor women—and men—also sold sex illegally outside of city brothels, combining this with other sorts of part-time work such as laundering or sewing. Prostitution was an urban phenomenon because only populous towns had large numbers of unmarried young men, communities of transient merchants, and a culture accustomed to a cash exchange.

Though selling sex for money was legal in the Middle Ages, the position of women who did so was always marginal. In the late fifteenth century cities began to limit brothel residents' freedom of movement and choice of clothing, requiring them to wear distinctive head coverings or bands on their clothing so that they would not be mistaken for "honorable" women. Cities also began to impose harsher penalties on women who did not live in the designated house or section of town. A few women who sold sex did earn enough to donate money to charity or buy property, but most were very poor.

Along with buying sex, young men also took it by force. Unmarried women often found it difficult to avoid sexual contact. Many worked as domestic servants, where their employers or employers' sons or male relatives could easily coerce them, or they worked in proximity to men. Notions of female honor kept upper-class women secluded in their homes, particularly in southern and eastern Europe, but there was little attempt anywhere to protect female servants or day laborers from the risk of seduction or rape. Rape was a capital crime in many parts of Europe, but the actual sentences handed out were more likely to be fines and brief imprisonment, with the severity of the sentence dependent on the social status of the victim and the perpetrator.

According to laws regarding rape in most parts of Europe, the victim had to prove that she had cried out and had attempted to repel the attacker, and she had to bring the charge within a short period of time after the attack had happened. Women bringing rape charges were often more interested in getting their own honorable reputations back than in punishing the perpetrators. For this reason, they sometimes asked the judge to force their rapists to marry them.

Same-sex relations—what in the late nineteenth century would be termed "homosexuality"—were another feature of medieval urban life (and of village life, though there are very few sources relating to sexual relations of any type in the rural context). Same-sex relations were of relatively little concern to church or state authorities in the early Middle Ages, but this attitude changed beginning in the late twelfth century. By 1300 most areas had defined such actions as "crimes against nature," with authorities seeing them as particularly reprehensible because they thought they did not occur anywhere else in creation. Same-sex relations, usually termed "sodomy," became a capital crime in most of Europe, with adult offenders threatened with execution by fire. The Italian cities of Venice, Florence, and Lucca created special courts to deal with sodomy, which saw thousands of investigations.

How prevalent were same-sex relations? This is difficult to answer, even in modern society, but the city of Florence provides a provocative case study. In 1432 Florence set up a special board of adult men, the Office of the Night, to "root out . . . the abominable vice of

City Brothel In this rather fanciful scene of a medieval brothel, two couples share baths and wine, while a third is in bed in the back, and two nobles peer in from a window across the street. Most brothels were not this elaborate, although some did have baths. Many cities also had commercial bathhouses where people paid a small fee to take a hot bath, a luxury otherwise unavailable. Bathhouses did sometimes offer sex, but their main attraction was hot water. (Bibliothèque nationale de France)

sodomy."[9] Between 1432 and the abolition of the board in 1502, about seventeen thousand men came to its attention, which, even over a seventy-year period, represents a great number in a population of about forty thousand. The men came from all classes of society, but almost all cases involved an adult man and an adolescent boy; they ranged from sex exchanged for money or gifts to long-term affectionate relationships. Florentines believed in a generational model in which different roles were appropriate to different stages in life. In a socially and sexually hierarchical world, the boy in the passive role was identified as subordinate, dependent, and mercenary, words usually applied to women. Florentines, however, never described the dominant

partner in feminine terms, for he had not compromised his masculine identity or violated a gender ideal; in fact, the adult partner might be married or have female sexual partners as well as male. Only if an adult male assumed the passive role was his masculinity jeopardized.

Thus in Florence, and no doubt elsewhere in Europe, sodomy was not a marginal practice, which may account for the fact that, despite harsh laws and special courts, actual executions for sodomy were rare. Same-sex relations often developed within the context of all-male environments, such as the army, the craft shop, and the artistic workshop, and were part of the collective male experience. Homoerotic relationships played

Same-Sex Relations This illustration, from a thirteenth-century French book of morals, interprets female and male same-sex relations as the work of devils. The illustration was painted at the time that religious and political authorities were increasingly criminalizing same-sex relations. (ONB/Vienna, Picture Archives, Cod. 2554, fol. 2r)

important roles in defining stages of life, expressing distinctions of status, and shaping masculine gender identity. Same-sex relations involving women almost never came to the attention of legal authorities, so it is difficult to find out how common they were. However, female-female desire was expressed in songs, plays, and stories, as was male-male desire, offering evidence of the way people understood same-sex relations.

Fur-Collar Crime

The Hundred Years' War had provided employment and opportunity for thousands of idle and fortune-seeking knights. But during periods of truce and after the war finally ended, many nobles once again had little to do. Inflation hurt them. Although many were living on fixed incomes, their chivalric code demanded lavish generosity and an aristocratic lifestyle. Many nobles thus turned to crime as a way of raising money. The fourteenth and fifteenth centuries witnessed a great deal of what we might term "fur-collar crime," a medieval version of today's white-collar crime in which those higher up the social scale prey on those who are less well-off.

This "fur-collar crime" involved both violence and fraud. Groups of noble bandits roamed the English countryside, stealing from both rich and poor. Operating like modern urban racketeers, knightly gangs demanded that peasants pay protection money or else have their hovels burned and their fields destroyed. They seized wealthy travelers and held them for ransom. Corrupt landowners, including some churchmen, pushed peasants to pay higher taxes and extra fees. When accused of wrongdoing, fur-collar criminals intimidated witnesses, threatened jurors, and used their influence to persuade judges to support them—or used cash to bribe them outright.

Aristocratic violence led to revolt, and it also shaped popular culture. The ballads of Robin Hood, a collection of folk legends from late medieval England, describe the adventures of the outlaw hero and his merry men as they avenge the common people against fur-collar criminals—grasping landlords, wicked sheriffs, and mercenary churchmen. Robin Hood was a popular figure because he symbolized the deep resentment of aristocratic corruption and abuse; he represented the struggle against tyranny and oppression.

Ethnic Tensions and Restrictions

Large numbers of people in the twelfth and thirteenth centuries migrated from one part of Europe to another in search of land, food, and work: the English into Scotland and Ireland; Germans, French, and Flemings into Poland, Bohemia, and Hungary; Christians into Muslim Spain. Everywhere in Europe, towns recruited people from the countryside as well (see Chapter 10). In frontier regions, townspeople were usually long-distance immigrants and, in eastern Europe, Ireland, and Scotland, ethnically different from the surrounding rural population. In eastern Europe, German was the language of the towns; in Irish towns, French, the tongue of Norman or English settlers, predominated. As a result of this colonization and movement to towns, peoples of different ethnic backgrounds lived side by side.

In the early periods of conquest and colonization, and in all regions with extensive migrations, a legal dualism existed: native peoples remained subject to their traditional laws; newcomers brought and were subject to the laws of the countries from which they came. On the Prussian and Polish frontier, for example, the law was that "men who come there . . . should be judged on account of any crime or contract engaged in there according to Polish custom if they are Poles and according to German custom if they are Germans."[10] Likewise, the conquered Muslim subjects of Christian kings in Spain had the right to be judged under Muslim law by Muslim judges.

The great exception to this broad pattern of legal pluralism was Ireland. From the start, the English practiced an extreme form of discrimination toward the native Irish. The English distinguished between the free and the unfree, and the entire Irish population, simply by the fact of Irish birth, was unfree. When English legal structures were established beginning in 1210, the Irish were denied access to the common-law courts. In civil (property) disputes, an English defendant did not need to respond to an Irish plaintiff; no Irish person could make a will. In criminal procedures, the murder of an Irishman was not considered a felony. Other than in Ireland, although native peoples commonly held humbler positions, both immigrant and native townspeople prospered during the expanding economy of the thirteenth century. But with the economic turmoil of the fourteenth century, ethnic tensions multiplied.

The later Middle Ages witnessed a movement away from legal pluralism or dualism and toward legal homogeneity and an emphasis on blood descent. The dominant ethnic group in an area tried to bar others from positions of church leadership and guild membership. Marriage laws were instituted that attempted to maintain ethnic purity by prohibiting intermarriage, and some church leaders actively promoted ethnic discrimination. As Germans moved eastward, for example, German bishops refused to appoint non-Germans to any church office, while Czech bishops closed monasteries to Germans.

The most extensive attempt to prevent intermarriage and protect ethnic purity is embodied in the **Statute of Kilkenny** (1366), a law the ruling English

imposed on Ireland, which states that "there were to be no marriages between those of immigrant and native stock; that the English inhabitants of Ireland must employ the English language and bear English names; that they must ride in the English way [that is, with saddles] and have English apparel; that no Irishmen were to be granted ecclesiastical benefices or admitted to monasteries in the English parts of Ireland."[11]

Late medieval chroniclers used words such as *gens* (race or clan) and *natio* (NAH-tee-oh; species, stock, or kind) to refer to different groups. They held that peoples differed according to language, traditions, customs, and laws. None of these were unchangeable, however, and commentators increasingly also described ethnic differences in terms of "blood," which made ethnicity heritable. As national consciousness grew with the Hundred Years' War, for example, people began to speak of "French blood" and "English blood." Religious beliefs came to be conceptualized in terms of blood as well, with people regarded as having Jewish blood, Muslim blood, or Christian blood. The most dramatic expression of this was in Spain, where "purity of blood"—having no Muslim or Jewish ancestors—became an obsession. Blood also came to be used as a way to talk about social differences, especially for nobles. Just as the Irish and English were prohibited from marrying each other, those of "noble blood" were prohibited from marrying commoners in many parts of Europe. As Europeans increasingly came into contact with people from Africa and Asia, and particularly as they developed colonial empires, these notions of blood also became a way of conceptualizing racial categories.

Literacy and Vernacular Literature

The development of ethnic identities had many negative consequences, but a more positive effect was the increasing use of the vernacular, that is, the local language that people actually spoke, rather than Latin (see Chapter 10). Two masterpieces of European culture, Dante's *Divine Comedy* (1310–1320) and Chaucer's *Canterbury Tales* (1387–1400), illustrate a sophisticated use of the rhythms and rhymes of the vernacular.

The *Divine Comedy* of Dante Alighieri (DAHN-tay ah-luh-GYEHR-ee) (1265–1321) is an epic poem of one hundred cantos (verses), each of whose three equal parts describes one of the realms of the next world: Hell, Purgatory, and Paradise. The Roman poet Virgil, representing reason, leads Dante through Hell, where Dante observes the torments of the damned and denounces the disorders of his own time. Passing up into

Statute of Kilkenny
Law issued in 1366 that discriminated against the Irish, forbidding marriage between the English and the Irish, requiring the use of the English language, and denying the Irish access to ecclesiastical offices.

Purgatory, Virgil shows the poet how souls are purified of their disordered inclinations. From Purgatory, Beatrice, a woman Dante once loved and who serves as the symbol of divine revelation in the poem, leads him to Paradise.

The *Divine Comedy* portrays contemporary and historical figures, comments on secular and ecclesiastical affairs, and draws on the Scholastic philosophy of uniting faith and reason. Within the framework of a symbolic pilgrimage, the *Divine Comedy* embodies the psychological tensions of the age. A profoundly Christian poem, it also contains bitter criticism of some church authorities. In its symmetrical structure and use of figures from the ancient world such as Virgil, the poem perpetuates the classical tradition, but as the first major work of literature in the Italian vernacular, it is distinctly modern.

Geoffrey Chaucer (1342–1400) was an official in the administrations of the English kings Edward III and Richard II and wrote poetry as an avocation. His *Canterbury Tales* is a collection of stories in lengthy rhymed narrative. On a pilgrimage to the shrine of Saint Thomas Becket at Canterbury (see Chapter 9), thirty people of various social backgrounds tell tales. In depicting the interests and behavior of all types of people, Chaucer presents a rich panorama of English social life in the fourteenth century. Like the *Divine Comedy*, the *Canterbury Tales* reflects the cultural tensions of the times. Ostensibly Christian, many of the pilgrims are also materialistic, sensual, and worldly, suggesting the ambivalence of the broader society's concern for the next world and frank enjoyment of this one.

Beginning in the fourteenth century, a variety of evidence attests to the increasing literacy of laypeople. Wills and inventories reveal that many people, not just nobles, possessed books—mainly devotional texts, but also romances, manuals on manners and etiquette, histories, and sometimes legal and philosophical texts. In England the number of schools in the diocese of York quadrupled between 1350 and 1500. Information

Chaucer's Wife of Bath   Chaucer's *Canterbury Tales* were filled with memorable characters, including the often-married Wife of Bath, shown here in a fifteenth-century manuscript. In the prologue that details her life, she denies the value of virginity and criticizes her young and handsome fifth husband for reading a book about "wicked wives." "By God, if women had but written stories, . . . " she comments, "They would have written of men more wickedness / Than all the race of Adam could redress." (Private Collection/The Bridgeman Art Library)

from Flemish and German towns is similar: children were sent to schools and were taught the fundamentals of reading, writing, and arithmetic. Laymen increasingly served as managers or stewards of estates and as clerks to guilds and town governments; such positions obviously required the ability to keep administrative and financial records.

The penetration of laymen into the higher positions of governmental administration, long the preserve of clerics, also illustrates rising lay literacy. With growing frequency, the upper classes sent their daughters to convent schools, where, in addition to instruction in singing, religion, needlework, deportment, and household management, they gained the rudiments of reading and sometimes writing.

The spread of literacy represents a response to the needs of an increasingly complex society. Trade, commerce, and expanding government bureaucracies required an increasing number of literate people. Late medieval culture remained a decidedly oral culture. But by the fifteenth century the evolution toward a more literate culture was already perceptible, and craftsmen would develop the new technology of the printing press in response to the increased demand for reading materials.

Notes

1. Christos S. Bartsocas, "Two Fourteenth Century Descriptions of the 'Black Death,'" *Journal of the History of Medicine* (October 1966): 395.
2. Giovanni Boccaccio, *The Decameron*, trans. Mark Musa and Peter Bondanella (New York: W. W. Norton, 1982), p. 7.
3. Ibid., p. 9.
4. Bartsocas, "Two Fourteenth Century Descriptions," p. 397.
5. Florence Warren, ed., *The Dance of Death* (Oxford: Early English Text Society, 1931), 10 lines from p. 8. Spelling modernized. Used by permission of Oxford University Press and the Council of the Early English Text Society.
6. W. P. Barrett, trans., *The Trial of Jeanne d'Arc* (London: George Routledge, 1931), pp. 165–166.
7. Quoted in J. H. Smith, *The Great Schism, 1378: The Disintegration of the Medieval Papacy* (New York: Weybright & Talley, 1970), p. 15.
8. Quoted in Katharina M. Wilson, ed., *Medieval Women Writers* (Athens: University of Georgia Press, 1984), p. 245.
9. Michael Rocke, *Forbidden Friendships: Homosexuality and Male Culture in Renaissance Florence* (New York: Oxford University Press, 1996), p. 45.
10. Quoted in R. Bartlett, *The Making of Europe: Conquest, Colonization and Cultural Change, 950–1350* (Princeton, N.J.: Princeton University Press, 1993), p. 205.
11. Quoted ibid., p. 239.

LOOKING BACK LOOKING AHEAD

The fourteenth and early fifteenth centuries were certainly times of crisis in western Europe, meriting the label "calamitous" given to them by one popular historian. Famine, disease, and war decimated the European population, and traditional institutions, including secular governments and the church, did little or nothing or, in some cases, made things worse. Trading connections that had been reinvigorated in the High Middle Ages spread the most deadly epidemic ever experienced through western Asia, North Africa, and almost all of Europe. No wonder survivors experienced a sort of shell shock and a fascination with death.

The plague did not destroy the prosperity of the medieval population, however, and it may in fact have indirectly improved the European economy. Wealthy merchants had plenty of money to spend on luxuries and talent. In the century after the plague, Italian artists began to create new styles of painting, writers to pen new literary forms, educators to found new types of schools, and philosophers to develop new ideas about the purpose of human life. These cultural changes eventually spread to the rest of Europe, following the same paths that the plague had traveled.

REVIEW and EXPLORE

MAKE IT STICK

> ✓ **LearningCurve**
> After reading the chapter, go online and use LearningCurve to retain what you've read.

Identify Key Terms

Identify and explain the significance of each item below.

Great Famine (p. 324)

Black Death (p. 325)

flagellants (p. 331)

Hundred Years' War (p. 332)

representative assemblies (p. 338)

Babylonian Captivity (p. 339)

Great Schism (p. 340)

conciliarists (p. 340)

confraternities (p. 343)

Jacquerie (p. 344)

English Peasants' Revolt (p. 346)

Statute of Kilkenny (p. 351)

Review the Main Ideas

Answer the focus questions from each section of the chapter.

◆ How did climate change shape the late Middle Ages? (p. 324)

◆ How did the plague reshape European society? (p. 325)

◆ What were the causes, course, and consequences of the Hundred Years' War? (p. 332)

◆ Why did the church come under increasing criticism? (p. 338)

◆ What explains the social unrest of the late Middle Ages? (p. 343)

Make Connections

Think about the larger developments and continuities within and across chapters.

1. The Black Death has often been compared with later pandemics, including the global spread of HIV/AIDS, which began in the 1980s. It is easy to note the differences between these two, but what similarities do you see in the course of the two diseases and their social and cultural consequences?

2. Beginning with Chapter 7, every chapter in this book has discussed the development of the papacy and relations between popes and secular rulers. How were the problems facing the papacy in the fourteenth century the outgrowth of long-term issues? Why had attempts to solve these issues not been successful?

3. In Chapter 3 you learned about the Bronze Age Collapse, and in Chapter 7 about the end of the Roman Empire in the West, both of which have also been seen as "calamitous." What similarities and differences do you see in these earlier times of turmoil and those of the late Middle Ages?

ONLINE DOCUMENT ASSIGNMENT
Meister Eckhart

What does Meister Eckhart's life tell us about the religious climate of the early fourteenth century?

You encountered Meister Eckhart's story on page 342. Keeping the question above in mind, go to the Integrated Media and examine a selection of Eckhart's writings and those of his critics. Think about why he appealed to lay audiences and what compelled church leaders to condemn his teachings. Then complete a writing assignment based on the evidence and details from this chapter.

Suggested Reading and Media Resources

BOOKS

• Allmand, Christopher. *The Hundred Years War: England and France at War, ca. 1300–1450*, rev. ed. 2005. Designed for students; examines the war from political, military, social, and economic perspectives, and compares the way England and France reacted to the conflict.

• Cohn, Samuel K. *Lust for Liberty: The Politics of Social Revolt in Medieval Europe.* 2006. Analyzes a number of revolts from across Europe in terms of the aims of their leaders and participants.

• Dunn, Alastair. *The Peasants' Revolt: England's Failed Revolution of 1381.* 2004. Offers new interpretations of the causes and consequences of the English Peasants' Revolt.

• Dyer, Christopher. *Standards of Living in the Later Middle Ages.* 1989. Examines economic realities and social conditions more generally.

• Herlihy, David. *The Black Death and the Transformation of the West*, 2d ed. 1997. A fine treatment of the causes and cultural consequences of the Black Death; the best starting point for study of the great epidemic.

• Jordan, William Chester. *The Great Famine: Northern Europe in the Early Fourteenth Century.* 1996. Discusses catastrophic weather, soil exhaustion, and other factors that led to the Great Famine and the impact of the famine on community life.

• Karras, Ruth M. *Sexuality in Medieval Europe: Doing unto Others.* 2005. A brief overview designed for undergraduates that incorporates the newest scholarship.

• Keen, Maurice. *Medieval Warfare: A History.* 1999. Traces actual battles and the art of warfare from Charlemagne to 1500.

• Kieckhefer, Richard. *Unquiet Souls: Fourteenth-Century Saints and Their Religious Milieu.* 1984. Sets the ideas of the mystics in their social and intellectual contexts.

• Lehfeldt, Elizabeth, ed. *The Black Death.* 2005. Includes excerpts from scholarly articles about many aspects of the Black Death.

• Swanson, R. N. *Religion and Devotion in Europe, c. 1215–c. 1515.* 2004. Explores many aspects of spirituality.

• Tanner, Norman. *The Church in the Later Middle Ages.* 2008. A concise survey of institutional and intellectual issues and developments.

• Tuchman, Barbara. *A Distant Mirror: The Calamitous Fourteenth Century.* 1978. Written for a general audience, it remains a vivid description of this tumultuous time.

DOCUMENTARIES

• *The Hundred Years' War* (BBC, 2012). This three-part series examines the military, political, and cultural aspects of the Hundred Years' War.

• *Michael Wood's Story of England* (BBC, 2010). This series focuses on the village of Kibworth in central England, for which extensive archives survive that give insight into daily life. Episode 3 examines the Great Famine and the Black Death, and episode 4 the Hundred Years' War and economic change.

• *The Plague* (History Channel, 2005). A documentary examining the path and impact of the plague in Europe, with first-hand accounts taken from diaries and journals.

FEATURE FILMS

• *Henry V* (Kenneth Branagh, 1989). A widely acclaimed film adaptation of Shakespeare's play about the English king and the Battle of Agincourt, with nearly every well-known English actor.

• *The Name of the Rose* (Jean-Jacques Annaud, 1986). Based on the novel by Umberto Eco about a fourteenth-century monk (played by Sean Connery), this is both a murder mystery and a commentary on issues facing the church.

• *The Reckoning* (Paul McGuigan, 2003). The story of a troupe of actors who perform a morality play for the villagers of a fourteenth-century English town, combined with a murder mystery about the death of a child.

• *The Seventh Seal* (Ingmar Bergman, 1957). A classic film about a knight who comes home from war to find plague and religious suspicion, and engages in a chess game with Death.

WEB SITES

• *Brought to Life.* A fascinating Web site on the history of medicine sponsored by the Science Museum, London, featuring thousands of objects from their medical collections. Provides multimedia introductions to topics and themes in medical history, including one on the Black Death.
www.sciencemuseum.org.uk/broughttolife/themes/diseases/black_death.aspx

12

European Society in the Age of the Renaissance

1350–1550

While the Hundred Years' War gripped northern Europe, a new culture emerged in southern Europe. The fourteenth century witnessed remarkable changes in Italian intellectual, artistic, and cultural life. Artists and writers thought that they were living in a new golden age, but not until the sixteenth century was this change given the label we use today — the *Renaissance*, derived from the French word for "rebirth." That word was first used by art historian Giorgio Vasari (1511–1574) to describe the art of "rare men of genius" such as his contemporary Michelangelo. Through their works, Vasari judged, the glory of the classical past had been reborn after centuries of darkness. Over time, the word's meaning was broadened to include many aspects of life during that period. The new attitude had a slow diffusion out of Italy, so that the Renaissance "happened" at different times in different parts of Europe. The Renaissance was a movement, not a time period.

Later scholars increasingly saw the cultural and political changes of the Renaissance, along with the religious changes of the Reformation (see Chapter 13) and the European voyages of exploration (see Chapter 14), as ushering in the "modern" world. Some historians view the Renaissance as a bridge between the medieval and modern eras because it corresponded chronologically with the late medieval period and because there were many continuities with that period along with the changes that suggested aspects of the modern world. Others have questioned whether the word *Renaissance* should be used at all to describe an era in which many social groups saw decline rather than advance. The debates remind us that these labels — medieval, Renaissance, modern — are intellectual constructs devised after the fact, and all contain value judgments. ■

Life in the Renaissance. In this detail from a fresco, Italian painter Lorenzo Lotto captures the mixing of social groups in a Renaissance Italian city. Wealthy merchants, soldiers, and boys intermingle, while at the right women sell vegetables and bread, a common sight at any city marketplace. (Scala/Art Resource, NY)

CHAPTER PREVIEW

 LearningCurve
After reading the chapter, go online and use LearningCurve to retain what you've read.

Wealth and Power in Renaissance Italy
How did politics and economics shape the Renaissance?

Intellectual Change
What new ideas were associated with the Renaissance?

Art and the Artist
How did art reflect new Renaissance ideals?

Social Hierarchies
What were the key social hierarchies in Renaissance Europe?

Politics and the State in Western Europe
How did nation-states develop in this period?

The magnificent art and new ways of thinking in the **Renaissance** rested on economic and political developments in the city-states of northern Italy. Economic growth laid the material basis for the Italian Renaissance, and ambitious merchants gained political power to match their economic power. They then used their money and power to buy luxuries and hire talent in a system of **patronage**, through which cities, groups, and individuals commissioned writers and artists to produce specific works. Political leaders in Italian cities admired the traditions and power of ancient Rome, and this esteem shaped their commissions. Thus economics, politics, and culture were interconnected.

Renaissance A French word meaning "rebirth," used to describe the rebirth of the culture of classical antiquity in Italy during the fourteenth to sixteenth centuries.

patronage Financial support of writers and artists by cities, groups, and individuals, often to produce specific works or works in specific styles.

Trade and Prosperity

Northern Italian cities led the way in the great commercial revival of the eleventh century (see Chapter 10). By the middle of the twelfth century Venice, supported by a huge merchant marine, had grown enormously rich through overseas trade, as had Genoa and Milan, which had their own sizable fleets. These cities made important strides in shipbuilding that allowed their ships to sail all year long at accelerated speeds and carrying ever more merchandise.

Another commercial leader, and the city where the Renaissance began, was Florence, situated on fertile soil along the Arno River. Its favorable location on the main road northward from Rome made Florence a commercial hub, and the city grew wealthy buying and selling all types of goods throughout Europe and the Mediterranean — grain, cloth, wool, weapons, armor, spices, glass, and wine.

Florentine merchants also loaned and invested money, and they acquired control of papal banking toward the end of the thirteenth century. Florentine mercantile families began to dominate European banking on both sides of the Alps, setting up

communes Sworn associations of free men in Italian cities led by merchant guilds that sought political and economic independence from local nobles.

popolo Disenfranchised common people in Italian cities who resented their exclusion from power.

offices in major European and North African cities. The profits from loans, investments, and money exchanges that poured back to Florence were pumped into urban industries such as clothmaking, and by the early fourteenth century the city had about eighty thousand people, about twice the population of London at that time. Profits contributed to the city's economic vitality and allowed banking families to control the city's politics and culture.

By the first quarter of the fourteenth century, the economic foundations of Florence were so strong that even severe crises could not destroy the city. In 1344 King Edward III of England repudiated his huge debts to Florentine bankers, forcing some of them into bankruptcy. Soon after, Florence suffered frightfully from the Black Death, losing at least half its population, and serious labor unrest shook the political establishment (see Chapter 11). Nevertheless, the basic Florentine economic structure remained stable, and the city grew again. In the fifteenth century the Florentine merchant and historian Benedetto Dei (DAY-ee) boasted proudly of his city in a letter to an acquaintance from Venice:

> Our beautiful Florence contains within the city in this present year two hundred seventy shops belonging to the wool merchants' guild . . . eighty-three rich and splendid warehouses of the silk merchants' guild. . . . The number of banks amounts to thirty-three; the shops of the cabinet-makers, whose business is carving and inlaid work, to eighty-four . . . there are forty-four goldsmiths' and jewellers' shops.[1]

In Florence and other thriving Italian cities, wealth allowed many people greater material pleasures, a more comfortable life, and leisure time to appreciate and patronize the arts. Merchants and bankers commissioned public and private buildings from architects, and hired sculptors and painters to decorate their homes and churches. The rich, social-climbing residents of Venice, Florence, Genoa, and Rome came to see life more as an opportunity to be enjoyed than as a painful pilgrimage to the City of God.

Communes and Republics of Northern Italy

The northern Italian cities were **communes**, sworn associations of free men who, like other town residents, began in the twelfth century to seek political and economic independence from local nobles. The merchant guilds that formed the communes built and maintained the city walls and regulated trade, collected taxes, and kept civil order within them. The local nobles frequently moved into the cities, marrying the daughters of rich commercial families and starting their own businesses, often with money they had gained through the dowries provided by their wives. This merger of the northern Italian nobility and the commercial elite created a powerful oligarchy, a small group that ruled the city and surrounding countryside. Yet because of rivalries among competing powerful families within this oligarchy, Italian communes were often politically unstable.

Unrest from below exacerbated the instability. Merchant elites made citizenship in the communes dependent on a property qualification, years of residence within the city, and social connections. Only a tiny percentage of the male population possessed these qualifications and thus could hold political office. The common people, called the **popolo**, were disenfranchised and heavily taxed, and they bitterly resented their exclusion from power. Throughout most of the thirteenth century, in city after city, the popolo used armed force to take over the city governments. At times republican government—in which political power theoretically resides in the people and is exercised by their chosen representatives—was established in numerous Italian cities, including Bologna, Siena, Parma, Florence, Genoa, and other cities. These victories of the popolo proved temporary, however, because they could not establish civil

Chronology

ca. 1350	Petrarch develops ideas of humanism
1434–1737	Medici family in power in Florence
1440s	Invention of movable metal type
1447–1535	Sforza family in power in Milan
1455–1471	Wars of the Roses in England
1469	Marriage of Isabella of Castile and Ferdinand of Aragon
1477	Louis XI conquers Burgundy
1478	Establishment of the Inquisition in Spain
1492	Spain conquers Granada, ending reconquista; practicing Jews expelled from Spain
1494	Invasion of Italy by Charles VIII of France
1508–1512	Michelangelo paints ceiling of Sistine Chapel
1513	Machiavelli writes *The Prince*
1563	Establishment of first formal academy for artistic training in Florence

A Florentine Bank Scene
Originally a "bank" was just a counter; money changers who sat behind the counter became "bankers," exchanging different currencies and holding deposits for merchants and business people. In this scene from fifteenth-century Florence, the bank is covered with an imported Ottoman geometric rug, one of many imported luxury items handled by Florentine merchants. Most cities issued their own coins, but the gold coins of Florence, known as florins (above), were accepted throughout Europe as a standard currency. (bank scene: Prato, San Francesco/Scala/Art Resource, NY; coins: Scala/Art Resource, NY)

order within their cities. Merchant oligarchies reasserted their power and sometimes brought in powerful military leaders to establish order. These military leaders, called *condottieri* (kahn-duh-TYER-ee; singular *condottiero*), had their own mercenary armies, and in many cities they took over political power once they had supplanted the existing government.

Many cities in Italy became **signori** (seen-YOHR-ee), in which one man—whether condottiero, merchant, or noble—ruled and handed down the right to rule to his son. Some signori (the word is plural in Italian and is used for both persons and forms of government) kept the institutions of communal government in place, but these had no actual power. As a practical matter, there wasn't much difference between oligarchic regimes and signori. Oligarchies maintained a façade of republican government, but the judicial, executive, and legislative functions of government were restricted to a small class of wealthy merchants.

In the fifteenth and sixteenth centuries the signori in many cities and the most powerful merchant oligarchs in others transformed their households into **courts**. Courtly culture afforded signori and oligarchs the opportunity to display and assert their wealth and power. They built magnificent palaces in the centers of cities and required all political business to be done there. Ceremonies connected with family births, baptisms, marriages, and funerals offered occasions for magnificent pageantry and elaborate ritual. Cities welcomed rulers who were visiting with magnificent entrance parades that often included fireworks, colorful banners, mock naval battles, decorated wagons filled with people in costume, and temporary triumphal arches modeled on those of ancient Rome. Rulers of nation-states later copied and adapted all these aspects of Italian courts.

signori Government by one-man rule in Italian cities such as Milan; also refers to these rulers.

courts Magnificent households and palaces where signori and other rulers lived, conducted business, and supported the arts.

City-States and the Balance of Power

Renaissance Italians had a passionate attachment to their individual city-states: political loyalty and feeling centered on the city. This intensity of local feeling perpetuated the dozens of small states and hindered the development of one unified state.

In the fifteenth century five powers dominated the Italian peninsula: Venice, Milan, Florence, the Papal States, and the kingdom of Naples (Map 12.1). The major Italian powers controlled the smaller city-states, such as Siena, Mantua, Ferrara, and Modena, and competed furiously among themselves for territory. While the states of northern Europe were moving toward centralization and consolidation, the world of Italian politics resembled a jungle where the powerful dominated the weak. Venice, with its enormous trade empire, ranked as an international power. Though Venice was a republic in name, an oligarchy of merchant-aristocrats actually ran the city. Milan was also called a republic, but the condottieri-turned-signori of the Sforza (SFORT-sah) family ruled harshly and dominated Milan and several smaller cities in the north from 1447 to 1535. Likewise, in Florence the form of government was republican, with authority vested in several councils of state, but the city was effectively ruled by the great Medici (MEH-duh-chee) banking family for three centuries, beginning in 1434. Though not public officials, Cosimo, his son Piero, and his grandson Lorenzo ruled from behind the scenes from 1434 to 1492. The Medici were then in and out of power for several decades, and in 1569 Florence became no longer a republic, but the hereditary Grand Duchy of Tuscany, with the Medici as the Grand Dukes until 1737. The Medici family produced three popes, and most other Renaissance popes were also members of powerful Italian families, selected for their political skills, not their piety. Along with the Italians was one Spaniard, Pope Alexander VI (pontificate 1492–1503), who was the most ruthless; aided militarily and politically by his illegitimate son Cesare Borgia, he reasserted papal authority in the papal lands. South of the Papal States, the kingdom of Naples was under the control of the king of Aragon.

In one significant respect, however, the Italian city-states anticipated future relations among competing European states after 1500. Whenever one Italian state appeared to gain a predominant position within the peninsula, other states combined against it to establish a balance of power. In the formation of these alliances, Renaissance Italians invented the machinery of modern diplomacy: permanent embassies with resident ambassadors in capitals where political relations and commercial ties needed continual monitoring. The resident ambassador was one of the great political achievements of the Italian Renaissance.

At the end of the fifteenth century Venice, Florence, Milan, and the papacy possessed great wealth and represented high cultural achievement. Wealthy and divided, however, they were also an inviting target for invasion. When Florence and Naples entered into an agreement to acquire Milanese territories, Milan called on France for support, and the French king Charles VIII (r. 1483–1498) invaded Italy in 1494.

Prior to this invasion, the Dominican friar Girolamo Savonarola (1452–1498) had preached in Florence a number of fiery sermons attended by large crowds predicting that God would punish Italy for its moral vice and corrupt leadership. Florentines interpreted the French invasion as the fulfillment of this prophecy

Map 12.1 The Italian City-States, ca. 1494 In the fifteenth century the Italian city-states represented great wealth and cultural sophistication, though the many political divisions throughout the peninsula invited foreign intervention.

Minor city-state

→ Invasion of Charles VIII of France, 1494

and expelled the Medici dynasty. Savonarola became the political and religious leader of a new Florentine republic and promised Florentines even greater glory in the future if they would reform their ways. (See "Primary Source 12.1: A Sermon of Savonarola," page 362.) He reorganized the government; convinced it to pass laws against same-sex relations, adultery, and drunkenness; and organized groups of young men to patrol the streets looking for immoral dress and behavior. He held religious processions and what became known as "bonfires of the vanities," huge fires on the main square of Florence in which fancy clothing, cosmetics, pagan books, musical instruments, paintings, and poetry that celebrated human beauty were gathered together and burned.

For a time Savonarola was wildly popular, but eventually people tired of his moral denunciations, and he

was excommunicated by the pope, tortured, and burned at the very spot where he had overseen the bonfires. The Medici returned as the rulers of Florence.

The French invasion inaugurated a new period in Italian and European power politics. Italy became the focus of international ambitions and the battleground of foreign armies, particularly those of the Holy Roman Empire and France in a series of conflicts called the Habsburg-Valois wars (named for the German and French dynasties). The Italian cities suffered severely from continual warfare, especially in the frightful sack of Rome in 1527 by imperial forces under the emperor Charles V. Thus the failure of the city-states to consolidate, or at least to establish a common foreign policy, led to centuries of subjection by outside invaders. Italy was not to achieve unification until 1870.

A Sermon of Savonarola

In the autumn of 1494 French armies under Charles VIII surrounded Florence. The Dominican friar Girolamo Savonarola met with the French king and convinced him to spare the city and keep moving his huge army southward. He preached a series of sermons that winter saying that God had chosen Florence to achieve even greater heights under his leadership than it had in the past, provided that it followed his instructions.

" O Florence . . . I tell you, do first those two things I told you another time, that is, that everyone go to confession and be purified of sins, and let everyone attend to the common good of the city; and if you will do this, your city will be glorious because in this way she will be reformed spiritually as well as temporally, that is, with regard to her people, and from you will issue the reform of all Italy. Florence will become richer and more powerful than she has ever been, and her empire will expand into many places. But if you will not do what I tell you, God will elect those who, as I said, want to see you divided, and this will be your final destruction. If you would do what I have told you, here is the fire and here is the water: now do it! . . .

But, Florence, if you want your government to be stable and strong and to endure a long time, you must return to God and to living uprightly; otherwise, you will come to ruin. . . . *Furthermore*, it is necessary that the Magnificent Signory [the government of the city] ordain that all those things contrary to godly religion be removed from the city, and in the first place, to act and ordain that the clergy must be good, because priests have to be a mirror to the people wherein everyone beholds and learns righteous living. But let the bad priests and religious be expelled. . . . They should not puff themselves up with so much material wealth, but give it to the very poor for God's sake. . . .

It is necessary that the Signory pass laws against that accursed vice of sodomy [same-sex relations], for which you know that Florence is infamous throughout the whole of Italy; this infamy arises perhaps from your talking and chattering about it so much, so that there is not so much in deeds, perhaps, as in words. Pass a law, I say, and let it be without mercy; that is, let these people be stoned and burned. On the other hand, it is necessary that you remove from among yourselves these poems and games and taverns and the evil fashion of women's clothes, and, likewise, we must throw out everything that is noxious to the health of the soul. Let everyone live for God and not for the world. . . .

The second [resolution]: attend to the common good. O citizens, if you band together and with a good will attend to the common welfare, each shall have more temporal and spiritual goods than if he alone attended to his own particular case. Attend, I say, to the common good of the city, and if anyone would elevate himself, let him be deprived of all his goods. "

EVALUATE THE EVIDENCE

1. What does Savonarola tell Florentines they must do, and what will be their reward if they follow his instructions?
2. Savonarola initially had many followers, including well-known writers and artists. Why might his words have found such a ready audience in Florence at that time?

Source: *Selected Writings of Girolamo Savonarola: Religion and Politics, 1490–1498*, trans. and ed. Anne Borelli and Maria Pastore Passaro (New Haven: Yale University Press, 2006), pp. 153, 157, 158. Copyright © 2006 Yale University. All rights reserved. Used by permission of Yale University Press.

Intellectual Change

What new ideas were associated with the Renaissance?

The Renaissance was characterized by self-conscious conviction among educated Italians that they were living in a new era. Somewhat ironically, this idea rested on a deep interest in ancient Latin and Greek literature and philosophy. Through reflecting on the classics, Renaissance thinkers developed new notions of human nature, new plans for education, and new concepts of political rule. The advent of the printing press with movable type would greatly accelerate the spread of these ideas throughout Europe.

Humanism

Giorgio Vasari was the first to use the word *Renaissance* in print, but he was not the first to feel that something was being reborn. Two centuries earlier the Florentine poet and scholar Francesco Petrarch (1304–1374) spent long hours searching for classical Latin manuscripts in dusty monastery libraries and wandering around the many ruins of the Roman Empire remaining in Italy.

He became obsessed with the classical past and felt that the writers and artists of ancient Rome had reached a level of perfection in their work that had not since been duplicated. Writers of his own day should follow these ancient models, thought Petrarch, and ignore the thousand-year period between his own time and that of Rome, which he called the "dark ages" ushered in by the barbarian invasions. Petrarch believed that the recovery of classical texts would bring about a new golden age of intellectual achievement, an idea that many others came to share.

Petrarch clearly thought he was witnessing the dawning of a new era in which writers and artists would recapture the glory of the Roman Republic. Around 1350 he proposed a new kind of education to help them do this, in which young men would study the works of ancient Roman authors, using them as models of how to write clearly, argue effectively, and speak persuasively. The study of Latin classics became known as the *studia humanitates* (STOO-dee-uh oo-mahn-ee-TAH-tayz), usually translated as "liberal studies" or the "liberal arts." People who advocated it were known as *humanists* and their program as **humanism**. Humanism was the main intellectual component of the Renaissance. Like all programs of study, humanism contained an implicit philosophy: that human nature and achievements, evident in the classics, were worthy of contemplation. (See "Primary Source 12.2: Cassandra Fedele on Humanist Learning," page 364.)

The glory of Rome had been brightest, in the opinion of the humanists, in the works of the Roman author and statesman Cicero (106–43 B.C.E.). Cicero had lived during the turbulent era when Julius Caesar and other powerful generals transformed the Roman Republic into an empire (see Chapter 5). In forceful and elegantly worded speeches, letters, and treatises, Cicero supported a return to republican government. Petrarch and other humanists admired Cicero's use of language, literary style, and political ideas. Many humanists saw Caesar's transformation of Rome as a betrayal of the great society, marking the beginning of a long period of decay that the barbarian migrations then accelerated. In his history of Florence written in 1436, the humanist historian and Florentine city official Leonardo Bruni (1374–1444) closely linked the decline of the Latin language after the death of Cicero to the decline of the Roman Republic: "After the liberty of the Roman people had been lost through the rule of the emperors . . . the flourishing condition of studies and of letters perished, together with the welfare of the city of Rome."[2] In this same book, Bruni was also very clear that by the time of his writing, the period of decay had ended and a new era had begun. He was the first to divide history into three eras—ancient, medieval, and modern—though it was another humanist historian who actually invented the term "Middle Ages."

In the fifteenth century Florentine humanists became increasingly interested in Greek philosophy as well as Roman literature, especially in the ideas of Plato. Under the patronage of Cosimo de' Medici (1389–1464), the scholar Marsilio Ficino (1433–1499) began to lecture to an informal group of Florence's cultural elite; his lectures became known as the Platonic Academy, but they were not really a school. Ficino regarded Plato as a divinely inspired precursor to Christ. He translated Plato's dialogues into Latin and wrote commentaries attempting to synthesize Christian and Platonic teachings. Plato's emphasis on the spiritual and eternal over the material and transient fit well with Christian teachings about the immortality of the soul. The Platonic idea that the highest form of love was spiritual desire for pure, perfect beauty uncorrupted by bodily desires could easily be interpreted as Christian desire for the perfection of God.

For Ficino and his most gifted student, Giovanni Pico della Mirandola (1463–1494), both Christian and classical texts taught that the universe was a hierarchy of beings from God down through spiritual beings to material beings, with humanity, right in the middle, as the crucial link that possessed both material and spiritual natures. (See "Primary Source 12.3: Pico della Mirandola, 'On the Dignity of Man,'" page 366.)

Man's divinely bestowed nature meant there were no limits to what he could accomplish. Families, religious brotherhoods, neighborhoods, workers' organizations, and other groups continued to have meaning in peoples' lives, but Renaissance thinkers increasingly viewed these groups as springboards to far greater individual achievement. They were especially interested in individuals who had risen above their background to become brilliant, powerful, or unique. (See "Individuals in Society: Leonardo da Vinci," page 368.) Such individuals had the admirable quality of **virtù** (vihr-TOO), which is not virtue in the sense of moral goodness, but their ability to shape the world around them according to their will. Bruni and other historians included biographies of individuals with virtù in their histories of cities and nations, describing ways in which these people had affected the course of history. Through the quality of their works and their influence on others, artists could also exhibit virtù, an idea that Vasari captures in the title of his major work, *The Lives of the Most Excellent Painters, Sculptors, and Architects*. His subjects had achieved not simply excellence but the pinnacle of excellence.

The last artist included in Vasari's book is Vasari himself, for Renaissance thinkers did not exclude them-

> **humanism** A program of study designed by Italians that emphasized the critical study of Latin and Greek literature with the goal of understanding human nature.
>
> **virtù** The quality of being able to shape the world according to one's own will.

Cassandra Fedele on Humanist Learning

Italian humanists detailed the type of education that they regarded as ideal and promoted its value to society and the individual. Several women from the bustling cities of northern Italy became excited by the new style of learning and through tutors or self-study became extremely well educated. One of these was the Venetian Cassandra Fedele (1465–1558), who became the best-known female scholar in her time, corresponding with humanist writers, church officials, university professors, nobles, and even the rulers of Europe. She gave this oration in Latin at the University of Padua in honor of her (male) cousin's graduation.

❝ I shall speak very briefly on the study of the liberal arts, which for humans is useful and honorable, pleasurable and enlightening since everyone, not only philosophers but also the most ignorant man, knows and admits that it is by reason that man is separated from beasts. For what is it that so greatly helps both the learned and the ignorant? What so enlarges and enlightens men's minds the way that an education in and knowledge of literature and the liberal arts do? . . . But erudite men who are filled with the knowledge of divine and human things turn all their thoughts and considerations toward reason as though toward a target, and free their minds from all pain, though plagued by many anxieties. These men are scarcely subjected to fortune's innumerable arrows and they prepare themselves to live well and in happiness. They follow reason as their leader in all things; nor do they consider themselves only, but they are also accustomed to assisting others with their energy and advice in matters public and private.

And so Plato, a man almost divine, wrote that those states would be fortunate in which the men who were heads of state were philosophers or in which philosophers took on the duty of administration. . . . The study of literature refines men's minds, forms and makes bright the power of reason, and washes away all stains from the mind, or at any rate, greatly cleanses it. It perfects the gifts and adds much beauty and elegance to the physical and material advantages that one has received by nature. States, however, and their princes who foster and cultivate these studies become more humane, more gracious, and more noble. For this reason, these studies have won for themselves the sweet appellation, "humanities." . . . Just as places that lie unused and uncultivated become fertile and rich in fruits and vegetables with men's labor and hard work and are always made beautiful, so are our natures cultivated, enhanced, and enlightened by the liberal arts. . . .

But enough on the utility of literature since it produces not only an outcome that is rich, precious, and sublime, but also provides one with advantages that are extremely pleasurable, fruitful, and lasting—benefits that I myself have enjoyed. And when I meditate on the idea of marching forth in life with the lowly and execrable weapons of the little woman—the needle and the distaff [the rod onto which yarn is wound after spinning]—even if the study of literature offers women no rewards or honors, I believe women must nonetheless pursue and embrace such studies alone for the pleasure and enjoyment they contain. ❞

EVALUATE THE EVIDENCE

1. What does Fedele see as the best course of study and the purposes of study?
2. Compare Fedele's oration to Pico della Mirandola's essay "On the Dignity of Man" (see page 366). In what ways does gender appear to shape the two authors' ideas about humanist learning?

Source: Excerpt from Cassandra Fedele, *Letters and Orations*, pp. 159–162, ed. and trans. Diana Robin. Copyright © 2000 by The University of Chicago Press. Used with permission of the publisher.

selves when they searched for models of talent and achievement. Vasari begins his discussion of his own works modestly, saying that these might "not lay claim to excellence and perfection" when compared with those of other artists, but he then goes on for more than thirty pages, clearly feeling he has achieved some level of excellence.

Leon Battista Alberti (1404–1472) had similar views of his own achievements. He had much to be proud of: he wrote novels, plays, legal treatises, a study of the family, and the first scientific analysis of perspective; he designed churches, palaces, and fortifications effective against cannon; he invented codes for sending messages secretly and a machine that could cipher and decipher them. In his autobiography—written late in his life, and in the third person, so that he calls himself "he" instead of "I"—Alberti described his personal qualities and accomplishments:

> Assiduous in the science and skill of dealing with arms and horses and musical instruments, as well as in the pursuit of letters and the fine arts, he was devoted to the knowledge of the most strange and difficult things. . . . He played ball, hurled the javelin, ran, leaped, wrestled. . . . He learned music without teachers . . . and then turned to physics and the mathematical arts. . . . Ambition was alien to him. . . . When his favorite dog died he wrote a funeral oration for him.[3]

His achievements in many fields did make Alberti a "Renaissance man," as we use the term, though it may be hard to believe his assertion that "ambition was alien to him."

Biographies and autobiographies presented individuals that humanist authors thought were worthy models, but sometimes people needed more direct instruction. The ancient Greek philosopher Plato, whom humanists greatly admired, taught that the best way to learn something was to think about its perfect, ideal form. If you wanted to learn about justice, for example, you should imagine what ideal justice would be, rather than look at actual examples of justice in the world around you, for these would never be perfect. Following Plato's ideas, Renaissance authors speculated about perfect examples of many things. Alberti wrote about the ideal country house, which was to be useful, convenient, and elegant. The English humanist Thomas More described a perfect society, which he called Utopia (see page 370).

Education

Humanists thought that their recommended course of study in the classics would provide essential skills for future politicians, diplomats, lawyers, military leaders, and businessmen, as well as writers and artists. It would provide a much broader and more practical type of training than that offered at universities, which at the time focused on theology and philosophy or on theoretical training for lawyers and physicians. Humanists poured out treatises, often in the form of letters, on the structure and goals of education and the training of rulers and leaders. They taught that a life active in the world should be the aim of all educated individuals and that education was not simply for private or religious purposes but also for the public good.

Humanists put their ideas into practice. Beginning in the early fifteenth century, they opened schools and academies in Italian cities and courts in which pupils began with Latin grammar and rhetoric, went on to study Roman history and political philosophy, and then learned Greek in order to study Greek literature and

philosophy. Gradually, humanist education became the basis for intermediate and advanced education for well-to-do urban boys and men. Humanist schools were established in Florence, Venice, and other Italian cities, and by the early sixteenth century across the Alps in Germany, France, and England.

Humanists disagreed about education for women. Many saw the value of exposing women to classical models of moral behavior and reasoning, but they also wondered whether a program of study that emphasized eloquence and action was proper for women, whose sphere was generally understood to be private and domestic. In his book on the family, Alberti stressed that a wife's role should be restricted to the orderliness of the household, food preparation and the serving of meals, the education of children, and the supervision of servants. (Alberti never married, so he never put his ideas into practice in his own household.) Women themselves were bolder in their claims about the value

Portrait of Baldassare Castiglione In this portrait by Raphael, the most sought-after portrait painter of the Renaissance, Castiglione is shown dressed exactly as he advised courtiers to dress, in elegant but subdued clothing that would enhance the splendor of the court, but never outshine the ruler. (akg-images/André Held)

Pico della Mirandola, "On the Dignity of Man"

Giovanni Pico della Mirandola, the son of an Italian count, was a brilliant student who studied Hebrew and Arabic along with the standard Latin and Greek. Based on his reading, Pico developed 900 theses, or points of argumentation, regarding philosophical, religious, magical, and other subjects, and he offered to defend them against anyone who wanted to come to Rome to debate him. The pope declared some of the theses heretical, blocked the debate, and had Pico arrested. Through the influence of Lorenzo de' Medici, his friend and patron, Pico was freed, and he settled near Florence. At the death of Lorenzo in 1492, Pico came under the influence of Savonarola (see page 360), gave away all his money, and renounced his former ideas and writings. He died unexpectedly shortly afterward. Forensic tests on his remains done in 2008 indicate he died of arsenic poisoning, and the suspicion is that the Medici family, which had just been ousted from Florence through the French invasion and the rise of Savonarola, had had him poisoned. Pico's life and death were full of drama, and so is his writing. As an introduction to his 900 theses, he wrote the essay "On the Dignity of Man," an impassioned and eloquent summary of humanist ideas about human capacities.

❝ Now the Highest Father, God the Architect, according to the laws of His secret wisdom, built this house of the world, this world which we see, the most sacred temple of His divinity. He adorned the region beyond the heavens with Intelligences, He animated the celestial spheres with eternal souls, and He filled the excrementary and filthy parts of the lower world with a multitude of animals of all kinds. But when His work was finished, the Artisan longed for someone to reflect on the plan of so great a creation, to love its beauty, and to admire its magnitude. When, therefore, everything was completed as Moses and the *Timaeus* [Plato's dialogue] testify, He began at last to consider the creation of man. But among His archetypes there was none from which He could form a new offspring, nor in His treasure houses was there any inheritance which He might bestow upon His new son, nor in the tribunal seats of the whole world was there a place where this contemplator of the universe might sit. All was now filled out; everything had been apportioned to the highest, the middle, and the lowest orders. But it was not in keeping with the paternal power to fail, as though exhausted, in the last act of creation; it was not in keeping with His wisdom to waver in a matter of necessity through lack of a design; it was not in keeping with His beneficent love that the creature who was to praise the divine liberality with regard to others should be forced to condemn it with respect to himself. Finally the Great Artisan ordained that man, to whom He could give nothing belonging only to himself, should share in common whatever properties had been peculiar to each of the other creatures. He received man, therefore, as a creature of undetermined nature, and placing him in the middle of the universe, said this to him: "Neither an established place, nor a form belonging to you alone, nor any special function have We given to you, O Adam, and for this reason, that you may have and possess, according to your desire and judgment, whatever place, whatever form, and whatever functions you shall desire. The nature of other creatures, which has been determined, is confined within the bounds prescribed by Us. You, who are confined by no limits, shall determine for yourself your own nature, in accordance with your own free will, in whose hand I have placed you. I have set you at the centre of the world, so that from there you may more easily survey whatever is in the world. We have made you neither heavenly nor earthly, neither mortal nor immortal, so that, more freely and more honourably the moulder and maker of yourself, you may fashion yourself in whatever form you shall prefer. You shall be able to descend among the lower forms of being, which are brute beasts; you shall be able to be reborn out of the judgment of your own soul into the higher beings, which are divine." ❞

of the new learning. Although humanist academies were not open to women, a few women did become educated in the classics. They argued in letters and published writings that reason was not limited to men and that learning was compatible with virtue for women as well as men. (See "Primary Source 12.2: Cassandra Fedele on Humanist Learning," page 364.)

No book on education had broader influence than Baldassare Castiglione's *The Courtier* (1528). This treatise sought to train, discipline, and fashion the young man into the courtly ideal, the gentleman. According to Castiglione (kahs-teel-YOH-nay), himself a courtier serving several different rulers, the educated man should have a broad background in many academic subjects, and should train his spiritual and physical faculties as well as intellect. Castiglione envisioned a man who could compose a sonnet, wrestle, sing a song while accompanying himself on an instrument, ride expertly, solve difficult mathematical problems, and, above all, speak and write eloquently. Castiglione also included discussion of the perfect court lady, who, like the courtier, was to be well educated and able to play a

O sublime generosity of God the Father! O highest and most wonderful felicity of man! To him it was granted to have what he chooses, to be what he wills. At the moment when they are born, beasts bring with them from their mother's womb, as Lucilius [the classical Roman author] says, whatever they shall possess. From the beginning or soon afterwards, the highest spiritual beings have been what they are to be for all eternity. When man came into life, the Father endowed him with all kinds of seeds and the germs of every way of life. Whatever seeds each man cultivates will grow and bear fruit in him. If these seeds are vegetative, he will be like a plant; if they are sensitive, he will become like the beasts; if they are rational, he will become like a heavenly creature; if intellectual, he will be an angel and a son of God. And if, content with the lot of no created being, he withdraws into the centre of his own oneness, his spirit, made one with God in the solitary darkness of the Father, which is above all things, will surpass all things.

Who then will not wonder at this chameleon of ours, or who could wonder more greatly at anything else? **"**

EVALUATE THE EVIDENCE

1. Why, in Pico's view, does man have great dignity and capacity?
2. What does Pico see as the purpose of human life?
3. Renaissance humanism has sometimes been viewed as opposed to religion, and especially to the teachings of the Catholic Church at the time. Do Pico's words support this idea? What do you find in them that fits with Christian teachings, and what stands in opposition to Christian teachings?

Source: "On the Dignity of Man" by Giovanni Pico della Mirandola, translated by Mary M. McLaughlin, from *The Portable Renaissance Reader* by James B. Ross and Mary M. McLaughlin, editors, copyright 1953, renewed © 1981 by Viking Penguin Inc. Used by permission of Viking Penguin, a division of Penguin Group (USA) Inc.

musical instrument, to paint, and to dance. Physical beauty, delicacy, affability, and modesty were also important qualities for court ladies.

In the sixteenth and seventeenth centuries *The Courtier* was translated into most European languages and widely read. It influenced the social mores and patterns of conduct of elite groups in Renaissance and early modern Europe and became a how-to manual for people seeking to improve themselves and rise in the social hierarchy as well. Echoes of its ideal for women have perhaps had an even longer life.

Political Thought

Ideal courtiers should preferably serve an ideal ruler, and biographies written by humanists often described rulers who were just, wise, pious, dignified, learned, brave, kind, and distinguished. In return for such flattering portraits of living rulers or their ancestors, authors sometimes received positions at court, or at least substantial payments. Particularly in Italian cities, however, which often were divided by political factions, taken over by homegrown or regional despots, and attacked by foreign armies, such ideal rulers were hard to find. Humanists thus looked to the classical past for their models. Some, such as Bruni, argued that republicanism was the best form of government. Others used the model of Plato's philosopher-king in the *Republic* to argue that rule by an enlightened individual might be best. Both sides agreed that educated men should be active in the political affairs of their city, a position historians have since termed "civic humanism."

The most famous (or infamous) civic humanist, and ultimately the best-known political theorist of this era, was Niccolò Machiavelli (1469–1527). After the ouster of the Medici with the French invasion of 1494, Machiavelli was secretary to one of the governing bodies in the city of Florence; he was responsible for diplomatic missions and organizing a citizen army. Almost two decades later, power struggles in Florence between rival factions brought the Medici family back to power, and Machiavelli was arrested, tortured, and imprisoned on suspicion of plotting against them. He was released but had no government position, and he spent the rest of his life writing—political theory, poetry, prose works, plays, and a multivolume history of Florence—and making fruitless attempts to regain employment.

The first work Machiavelli finished—though not the first to be published—is his most famous: *The Prince* (1513), which uses the examples of classical and contemporary rulers to argue that the function of a ruler (or any government) is to preserve order and security. Weakness only leads to disorder, which might end in civil war or conquest by an outsider, situations clearly detrimental to any people's well-being. To preserve the state, a ruler should use whatever means he needs—brutality, lying, manipulation—but should not do anything that would make the populace turn against him; stealing or cruel actions done for a ruler's own pleasure would lead to resentment and destroy the popular support needed for a strong, stable realm. "It is much safer for the prince to be feared than loved," Machiavelli advised, "but he ought to avoid making himself hated."[4]

Like the good humanist he was, Machiavelli knew that effective rulers exhibited the quality of virtù. He presented examples from the classical past of just the type of ruler he was describing, but also wrote about

What makes a genius? A deep curiosity about an extensive variety of subjects? A divine spark that emerges in talents that far exceed the norm? Or is it just "one percent inspiration and ninety-nine percent perspiration," as Thomas Edison said? However it is defined, Leonardo da Vinci counts as a genius. In fact, Leonardo was one of the individuals whom the Renaissance label "genius" was designed to describe: a special kind of human being with exceptional creative powers. Leonardo (who, despite the title of a popular novel and film, is always called by his first name) was born in Vinci, near Florence, the illegitimate son of Caterina, a local peasant girl, and Ser Piero da Vinci, a notary public. When Ser Piero's marriage to Donna Albrussia produced no children, he and his wife took in Leonardo, whose mother had married another man. Ser Piero secured Leonardo an apprenticeship with the painter and sculptor Andrea del Verrocchio in Florence. In 1472, when Leonardo was just twenty years old, he was already listed as a master in Florence's "Company of Artists."

Leonardo's most famous portrait, *Mona Lisa*, shows a woman with an enigmatic smile that Giorgio Vasari described as "so pleasing that it seemed divine rather than human." The portrait, probably of the young wife of a rich Florentine merchant (her exact identity is hotly debated), may be the best-known painting in the history of art. One of its competitors for that designation would be another work of Leonardo, *The Last Supper*, which has been called "the most revered painting in the world."

Leonardo's reputation as a genius does not rest on his paintings, however, which are actually few in number, but rather on the breadth of his abilities and interests. He is considered by many the first "Renaissance man," a phrase still used for a multitalented individual. Hoping to reproduce what the eye can see, he drew everything he saw around him, including executed criminals hanging on gallows as well as the beauties of nature. Trying to understand how the human body worked, Leonardo studied live and dead bodies, doing autopsies and dissections to investigate muscles and circulation. He carefully analyzed the effects of light, and he experimented with perspective.

Leonardo used his drawings not only as the basis for his paintings but also as a tool of scientific investigation. He drew plans for hundreds of inventions, many of which would be-

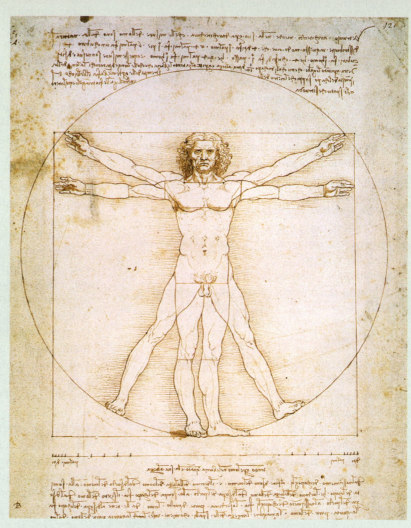

Vitruvian Man, a drawing by Leonardo showing correlations between the ideal human proportions and the geometric shapes of the circle and square, is based on the ideas of the ancient Roman architect Vitruvius, whose works Leonardo read. (Galleria dell' Accademia, Venice, Italy/The Bridgeman Art Library)

ONLINE DOCUMENT ASSIGNMENT

How did the needs and desires of Leonardo's patrons influence his work? Go to the Integrated Media and examine letters and visual evidence that shed light on the dynamic between the artist and his employers, and then complete a writing assignment based on the evidence and details from this chapter.

come reality centuries later, such as the helicopter, tank, machine gun, and parachute. He was hired by one of the powerful new rulers in Italy, Duke Ludovico Sforza of Milan, to design weapons, fortresses, and water systems, as well as to produce works of art. Leonardo left Milan when Sforza was overthrown, and spent the last years of his life painting, drawing, and designing for the pope and the French king.

Leonardo experimented with new materials for painting and sculpture, not all of which worked. The experimental method he used to paint *The Last Supper* caused the picture to deteriorate rapidly, and it began to flake off the wall as soon as it was finished. Leonardo regarded it as never quite completed, for he could not find a model for the face of Christ who would evoke the spiritual depth he felt the figure deserved. His gigantic equestrian statue in honor of Ludovico's father, Duke Francesco Sforza, was never made, and the clay model collapsed. He planned to write books on many subjects but never finished any of them, leaving only notebooks. Leonardo once said that "a painter is not admirable unless he is universal." The patrons who supported him — and he was supported very well — perhaps wished that his inspirations would have been a bit less universal in scope, or at least accompanied by more perspiration.

QUESTIONS FOR ANALYSIS

1. In what ways do the notions of a "genius" and of a "Renaissance man" both support and contradict each other? Which better fits Leonardo?
2. Has the idea of artistic genius changed since the Renaissance? How?

Sources: Giorgio Vasari, *Lives of the Artists*, vol. 1, trans. G. Bull (London: Penguin Books, 1965); S. B. Nuland, *Leonardo da Vinci* (New York: Lipper/Viking, 2000).

contemporary leaders. Cesare Borgia (1475?–1507), Machiavelli's primary example, was the son of Rodrigo Borgia, a Spanish nobleman who later became Pope Alexander VI. Cesare Borgia combined his father's power and his own ruthlessness to build up a state of his own in central Italy. He made good use of new military equipment and tactics, hiring Leonardo da Vinci (1452–1519) as a military engineer, and murdered his political enemies, including the second husband of his sister, Lucrezia. Despite Borgia's efforts, his state fell apart after his father's death, which Machiavelli ascribed not to weakness, but to the operations of fate (*fortuna*, for-TOO-nah, in Italian), whose power even the best-prepared and most merciless ruler could not fully escape, though he should try. Fortuna was personified and portrayed as a goddess in ancient Rome and Renaissance Italy, and Machiavelli's last words about fortune are expressed in gendered terms: "It is better to be impetuous than cautious, for fortune is a woman, and if one wishes to keep her down, it is necessary to beat her and knock her down."[5]

The Prince is often seen as the first modern guide to politics, though Machiavelli was denounced for writing it, and people later came to use the word *Machiavellian* to mean cunning and ruthless. Medieval political philosophers had debated the proper relation between church and state, but they regarded the standards by which all governments were to be judged as emanating from moral principles established by God. Machiavelli argued that governments should instead be judged by how well they provided security, order, and safety to their populace. A ruler's moral code in maintaining these was not the same as a private individual's, for a leader could — indeed, should — use any means necessary. Machiavelli put a new spin on the Renaissance search for perfection, arguing that ideals needed to be measured in the cold light of the real world. This more pragmatic view of the purposes of government, along with Machiavelli's discussion of the role of force and cruelty, was unacceptable to many.

Even today, when Machiavelli's more secular view of the purposes of government is widely shared, scholars debate whether Machiavelli actually meant what he wrote. Most regard him as realistic or even cynical, but some suggest that he was being ironic or satirical, showing princely government in the worst possible light to contrast it with republicanism. He dedicated *The Prince* to the new Medici ruler of Florence, however, so any criticism was deeply buried within what was, in that era of patronage, essentially a job application.

Christian Humanism

In the last quarter of the fifteenth century, students from the Low Countries, France, Germany, and England flocked to Italy, absorbed the "new learning,"

Thomas More, *Utopia*

Published in 1516, Utopia is written as a dialogue between Thomas More and Raphael Hythloday, a character More invented who has, in More's telling, recently returned from the newly discovered land of Utopia somewhere in the New World. More and Hythloday first discuss the problems in Europe, and then Hythloday describes how these have been solved in Utopia, ending with a long discussion of the Utopians' ban on private property.

❝ Well, that's the most accurate account I can give you of the Utopian Republic. To my mind, it's not only the best country in the world, but the only one that has the right to call itself a republic. Elsewhere, people are always talking about the public interest, but all they really care about is private property. In Utopia, where there's no private property, people take their duty to the public seriously. And both attitudes are perfectly reasonable. In other "republics" practically everyone knows that, if he doesn't look out for himself, he'll starve to death, however prosperous his country may be. He's therefore compelled to give his own interests priority over those of the public; that is, of other people. But in Utopia, where everything's under public ownership, no one has any fear of going short, as long as the public storehouses are full. Everyone gets a fair share, so there are never any poor men or beggars. Nobody owns anything, but everyone is rich — for what greater wealth can there be than cheerfulness, peace of mind, and freedom from anxiety? Instead of being worried about his food supply, upset by the plaintive demands of his wife, afraid of poverty for his son, and baffled by the problem of finding a dowry for his daughter, the Utopian can feel absolutely sure that he, his wife, his children, his grandchildren, his great-grandchildren, and as long a line of descendants as the proudest peer could wish to look forward to, will always have enough to eat and enough to make them happy. There's also the further point that those who are too old to work are just as well provided for as those who are still working.

Now, will anyone venture to compare these fair arrangements in Utopia with the so-called justice of other countries? — in which I'm damned if I can see the slightest trace of justice or fairness. For what sort of justice do you call this? People like aristocrats, goldsmiths, or money-lenders, who either do no work at all, or do work that's really not essential, are rewarded for their laziness or their unnecessary activities by a splendid life of luxury. But labourers, coachmen, carpenters, and farmhands, who never stop working like cart-horses, at jobs so essential that, if they *did* stop working, they'd bring any country to a standstill within twelve months — what happens to them? They get so little to eat, and have such a wretched time, that they'd be almost better off if they *were* cart-horses. Then at least, they wouldn't work quite such long hours, their food wouldn't be very much worse, they'd enjoy it more, and they'd have no fears for the future. As it is, they're not only ground down by unrewarding toil in the present, but also worried to death by the prospect of a poverty-stricken old age. ❞

EVALUATE THE EVIDENCE

1. How does the Utopians' economic system compare with that of Europe, in Hythloday's opinion?
2. Hythloday's comments about wealth have been seen by some scholars as More's criticism of his own society, and by others as proof that More wrote this as a satire, describing a place that could never be. Which view seems most persuasive to you?

Source: Thomas More, *Utopia*, trans. Paul Turner (London: Penguin Books, 1965), pp. 128–129. Reproduced by permission of Penguin Books Ltd.

---

and carried it back to their own countries. Northern humanists shared the ideas of Ficino and Pico about the wisdom of ancient texts, but they went beyond Italian efforts to synthesize the Christian and classical traditions to see humanist learning as a way to bring about reform of the church and deepen people's spiritual lives. These **Christian humanists**, as they were later called, thought that the best elements of classical and Christian cultures should be combined. For example, the classical ideals of calmness, stoical patience, and broad-mindedness should be joined in human conduct with the Christian virtues of love, faith, and hope.

The English humanist Thomas More (1478–1535) began life as a lawyer, studied the classics, and entered government service. Despite his official duties, he had time to write, and he became most famous for his controversial dialogue *Utopia* (1516), a word More invented from the Greek words for "nowhere." *Utopia* describes a community on an island somewhere beyond Europe where all children receive a good education, primarily in the Greco-Roman classics, and adults divide their days between manual labor or business

Christian humanists
Northern humanists who interpreted Italian ideas about and attitudes toward classical antiquity and humanism in terms of their own religious traditions.

pursuits and intellectual activities. The problems that plagued More's fellow citizens, such as poverty and hunger, have been solved by a beneficent government. (See "Primary Source 12.4: Thomas More, *Utopia*," at left.) There is religious toleration, and order and reason prevail. Because Utopian institutions are perfect, however, dissent and disagreement are not acceptable.

More's purposes in writing *Utopia* have been debated just as much as have Machiavelli's in penning *The Prince*. Some view it as a revolutionary critique of More's own hierarchical and violent society, some as a call for an even firmer hierarchy, and others as part of the humanist tradition of satire. It was widely read by learned Europeans in the Latin in which More wrote it, and later in vernacular translations, and its title quickly became the standard word for any imaginary society.

Better known by contemporaries than Thomas More was the Dutch humanist Desiderius Erasmus (dehz-ih-DARE-ee-us ih-RAZ-muhs) (1466?–1536) of Rotterdam. His fame rested on both scholarly editions and translations and popular works. Erasmus's long list of publications includes *The Education of a Christian Prince* (1504), a book combining idealistic and practical suggestions for the formation of a ruler's character through the careful study of the Bible and classical authors; *The Praise of Folly* (1509), a witty satire poking fun at political, social, and especially religious institutions; and, most important, a new Latin translation of the New Testament alongside the first printed edition of the Greek text (1516). In the preface to the New Testament, Erasmus expressed his ideas about Bible translations: "I wish that even the weakest woman should read the Gospel—should read the epistles of Paul. And I wish these were translated into all languages, so that they might be read and understood, not only by Scots and Irishmen, but also by Turks and Saracens."[6]

Two fundamental themes run through all of Erasmus's work. First, education in the Bible and the classics is the means to reform, the key to moral and intellectual improvement. Erasmus called for a renaissance of the ideals of the early church to accompany the renaissance in classical education that was already going on, and criticized the church of his day for having strayed from these ideals. Second, renewal should

be based on what he termed "the philosophy of Christ," an emphasis on inner spirituality and personal morality rather than Scholastic theology or outward observances such as pilgrimages or venerating relics. His ideas, and Christian humanism in general, were important roots of the Protestant Reformation, although Erasmus himself denied this and never became a follower of Luther (see Chapter 13).

The Printed Word

The fourteenth-century humanist Petrarch and the sixteenth-century humanist Erasmus had similar ideas on many topics, but the immediate impact of their ideas was very different because of one thing: the invention of the printing press with movable metal type. The ideas of Petrarch were spread slowly from person to person by hand copying. The ideas of Erasmus were spread quickly through print, allowing hundreds or thousands of identical copies to be made in a short time.

Printing with movable metal type developed in Germany in the 1440s as a combination of existing technologies. Several metal-smiths, most prominently Johann Gutenberg, recognized that the metal stamps used to mark signs on jewelry could be covered with ink and used to mark symbols onto a surface in the same way that other craftsmen were using carved wood stamps to print books. (This woodblock printing tech-

Printing Press In this reproduction of Gutenberg's printing press, metal type sits in a frame (left) ready to be placed in the bottom part of the press, with a leather-covered ink ball for spreading ink on the type ready nearby. Once the type was in place, paper was placed over the frame and a heavy metal plate (right) was lowered onto the paper with a firm pull of the large wooden handle, a technology adapted from winepresses.
(Erich Lessing/Art Resource, NY)

Printing centers with date of establishment
- ◆ 15th century
- ▲ 16th century
- — Political boundaries in 1490

NORWAY
SWEDEN
Stockholm 1483
SCOTLAND
Edinburgh 1507
IRELAND
Dublin 1551
North Sea
DENMARK
Copenhagen 1493
Baltic Sea
ENGLAND
Oxford 1478
London 1480
Amsterdam 1523
Emden 1554
Lübeck 1475
Hamburg 1491
HOLY ROMAN EMPIRE
Deventer 1477
Utrecht 1472
Berlin 1540
POLAND
Bruges 1474
Antwerp 1470
Brussels 1474
Cologne 1466
Bonn 1543
Leipzig 1481
ATLANTIC OCEAN
Gutenberg establishes first printing press, 1448
Mainz
Frankfurt 1478
Bamberg 1460
Nuremberg 1470
Wrocław 1475
Prague 1478
Kraków 1474
Paris 1470
Strasbourg 1460
FRANCE
Basel 1462
Augsburg 1468
Munich 1482
Cluny 1483
Bern 1525
Zürich 1508
Vienna 1482
Buda 1473
HUNGARY
MOLDAVIA
Lyons 1473
Geneva 1478
Milan 1470
Venice 1469
VENICE
Belgrade 1552
Danube R.
PORTUGAL
NAVARRE
Madrid 1499
ARAGON
Florence 1471
PAPAL STATES
OTTOMAN EMPIRE
Constantinople 1488
Lisbon 1489
CASTILE
Barcelona 1475
Rome 1467
Subiaco 1465
Thessalonica 1515
Valencia 1473
Naples 1471
NAPLES
GRANADA
Mediterranean Sea
Reggio di Calabria 1480
AFRICA

MAPPING THE PAST

Map 12.2 The Growth of Printing in Europe, 1448–1552

The speed with which artisans spread printing technology across Europe provides strong evidence for the growing demand for reading material. Presses in the Ottoman Empire were first established by Jewish immigrants who printed works in Hebrew, Greek, and Spanish.

ANALYZING THE MAP What part of Europe had the greatest number of printing presses by 1550? What explains this?

CONNECTIONS Printing was developed in response to a market for reading materials. Use Maps 10.2 and 10.3 (pages 302 and 310) to help explain why printing spread the way it did.

nique originated in China and Korea centuries earlier.) Gutenberg and his assistants made metal stamps—later called *type*—for every letter of the alphabet and built racks that held the type in rows. This type could be rearranged for every page and so used over and over.

The printing revolution was also made possible by the ready availability of paper, which was also produced using techniques that had originated in China, though, unlike the printing press, this technology had

been brought into Europe through Muslim Spain rather than developing independently.

By the fifteenth century the increase in urban literacy, the development of primary schools, and the opening of more universities had created an expanding market for reading materials (see Chapter 11). When Gutenberg developed what he saw at first as a faster way to copy, professional copyists writing by hand and block-book makers, along with monks and nuns, were already churning out reading materials on paper as fast as they could for the growing number of people who could read.

Gutenberg was not the only one to recognize the huge market for books, and his invention was quickly copied. Other craftsmen made their own type, built their own presses, and bought their own paper, setting themselves up in business (Map 12.2). Historians estimate that, within a half century of the publication of Gutenberg's Bible in 1456, somewhere between 8 million and 20 million books were printed in Europe. Whatever the actual figure, the number is far greater than the number of books produced in all of Western history up to that point.

The effects of the invention of movable-type printing were not felt overnight. Nevertheless, movable type radically transformed both the private and the public lives of Europeans by the dawn of the sixteenth century. Print shops became gathering places for people interested in new ideas. Though printers were trained through apprenticeships just like blacksmiths or butchers were, they had connections to the world of politics, art, and scholarship that other craftsmen did not.

Printing gave hundreds or even thousands of people identical books, allowing them to more easily discuss the ideas that the books contained with one another in person or through letters. Printed materials reached an invisible public, allowing silent individuals to join causes and groups of individuals widely separated by geography to form a common identity; this new group consciousness could compete with and transcend older, localized loyalties.

Government and church leaders both used and worried about printing. They printed laws, declarations of war, battle accounts, and propaganda, and they also attempted to censor books and authors whose ideas they thought challenged their authority or were incorrect. Officials developed lists of prohibited books and authors, enforcing their prohibitions by confiscating books, arresting printers and booksellers, or destroying the presses of printers who disobeyed. None of this was very effective, and books were printed secretly, with fake title pages, authors, and places of publication, and smuggled all over Europe.

Printing also stimulated the literacy of laypeople and eventually came to have a deep effect on their private lives. Although most of the earliest books and pamphlets dealt with religious subjects, printers produced anything that would sell. They printed professional reference sets for lawyers, doctors, and students, and historical romances, biographies, and how-to manuals for the general public. They discovered that illustrations increased a book's sales, so they published books on a wide range of topics—from history to pornography—full of woodcuts and engravings. Single-page broadsides and fly sheets allowed great public events and "wonders" such as comets and two-headed calves to be experienced vicariously by a stay-at-home readership. Since books and other printed materials were read aloud to illiterate listeners, print bridged the gap between the written and oral cultures.

Art and the Artist
How did art reflect new Renaissance ideals?

No feature of the Renaissance evokes greater admiration than its artistic masterpieces. The 1400s (*quattrocento*) and 1500s (*cinquecento*) bore witness to dazzling creativity in painting, architecture, and sculpture. In all the arts, the city of Florence led the way. But Florence was not the only artistic center, for Rome and Venice also became important, and northern Europeans perfected their own styles.

Patronage and Power

In early Renaissance Italy, powerful urban groups often flaunted their wealth by commissioning works of art. The Florentine cloth merchants, for example, delegated Filippo Brunelleschi (broo-nayl-LAYS-kee) to build the magnificent dome on the cathedral of Florence and selected Lorenzo Ghiberti (gee-BEHR-tee) to design the bronze doors of the adjacent Baptistery, a separate building in which baptisms were performed. These works represented the merchants' dominant influence in the community.

Increasingly in the late fifteenth century, wealthy individuals and rulers, rather than corporate groups, sponsored works of art. Patrician merchants and bankers, popes, and princes spent vast sums on the arts to glorify themselves and their families. Writing in about 1470, Florentine ruler Lorenzo de' Medici declared that his family had spent hundreds of thousands of gold florins for artistic and architectural commissions, but commented, "I think it casts a brilliant light on our estate [public reputation] and it seems to me that the monies were well spent and I am very pleased with this."[7]

Patrons varied in their level of involvement as a work progressed; some simply ordered a specific subject or scene, while others oversaw the work of the artist or architect very closely, suggesting themes and styles and demanding changes while the work was in progress. For example, Pope Julius II (pontificate 1503–1513), who commissioned Michelangelo to paint the ceiling of the Vatican's Sistine Chapel in 1508, demanded that the artist work as fast as he could and frequently visited him at his work with suggestions and criticisms.

Michelangelo's *David* (1501–1504) and the *Last Judgment* (detail, 1537–1541)
Like all Renaissance artists, Michelangelo worked largely on commissions from patrons. Officials of the city of Florence contracted the young sculptor to produce a statue of the Old Testament hero David (left) to be displayed on the city's main square. Michelangelo portrayed David anticipating his fight against the giant Goliath, and the statue came to symbolize the republic of Florence standing up to its larger and more powerful enemies. More than thirty years later, Michelangelo was commissioned by the pope to paint a scene of the Last Judgment on the altar wall of the Sistine Chapel, where he had earlier spent four years covering the ceiling with magnificent frescoes. The massive work shows a powerful Christ standing in judgment, with souls ascending into Heaven while others are dragged by demons into Hell (above). The *David* captures ideals of human perfection and has come to be an iconic symbol of Renaissance artistic brilliance, while the dramatic and violent *Last Judgment* conveys both terror and divine power. (sculpture: Scala/ Ministero per i Beni e le Attività Culturali/Art Resource, NY; painting: Alinari/The Bridgeman Art Library)

Michelangelo, a Florentine who had spent his young adulthood at the court of Lorenzo de' Medici, complained in person and by letter about the pope's meddling, but his reputation did not match the power of the pope, and he kept working until the chapel was finished in 1512.

In addition to power, art reveals changing patterns of consumption among the wealthy elite in European society. In the rural world of the Middle Ages, society had been organized for war, and men of wealth spent their money on military gear. As Italian nobles settled in towns (see Chapter 10), they adjusted to an urban culture. Rather than employing knights for warfare, cities hired mercenaries. Accordingly, expenditures

Procession of the Magi This segment of a huge fresco by Bennozzo Gozzoli covering three walls of a chapel in the Medici Palace in Florence shows members of the Medici family and other contemporary individuals in a procession accompanying the biblical three wise men (*magi* in Italian) as they brought gifts to the infant Jesus. The painting was ordered in 1459 by Cosimo and Piero de' Medici, who had just finished building the family palace in the center of the city. The artist places the elderly Cosimo and Piero at the head of the procession, accompanied by their grooms, and includes himself in the group. (Chapel of Palazzo Medici Riccardi, Florence/De Agostini Picture Library/G. Nimatallah/The Bridgeman Art Library)

on military hardware by nobles declined. For the noble recently arrived from the countryside or the rich merchant of the city, a grand urban palace represented the greatest outlay of cash. Wealthy individuals and families ordered gold dishes, embroidered tablecloths, wall tapestries, paintings on canvas (an innovation), and sculptural decorations to adorn these homes. By the late sixteenth century the Strozzi banking family of Florence spent more on household goods than they did on clothing, jewelry, or food, though these were increasingly elaborate as well.

After the palace itself, the private chapel within the palace symbolized the largest expenditure for the wealthy of the sixteenth century. Decorated with religious scenes and equipped with ecclesiastical furniture, the chapel served as the center of the household's religious life and its cult of remembrance of the dead.

Changing Artistic Styles

The content and style of Renaissance art both often differed from those of the Middle Ages. Religious topics, such as the Annunciation of the Virgin and the Nativity, remained popular among both patrons and artists, but frequently the patron had himself and his family portrayed in the scene. As the fifteenth century advanced and humanist ideas spread more widely, classical themes and motifs, such as the lives and loves of pagan gods and goddesses, figured increasingly in painting and sculpture, with the facial features of the gods sometimes modeled on living people.

The individual portrait emerged as a distinct artistic genre in this movement. Rather than reflecting a spir-itual ideal, as medieval painting and sculpture tended to do, Renaissance portraits showed human ideals, often portrayed in the more realistic style increasingly favored by both artists and patrons. The Florentine painter Giotto (JAH-toh) (1276–1337) led the way in the use of realism; his treatment of the human body and face replaced the formal stiffness and artificiality that had long characterized representation of the human body. Piero della Francesca (frahn-CHAY-skah) (1420–1492) and Andrea Mantegna (mahn-TEHN-yuh) (1430/31–1506) pioneered perspective, the linear representation of distance and space on a flat surface, which enhanced the realism of paintings and differentiated them from the flatter and more stylized images of medieval art. The sculptor Donatello (1386–1466) revived the classical figure, with its balance and self-awareness. In architecture, Filippo Brunelleschi (1377–1446) looked to the classical past for inspiration, designing a hospital for orphans and foundlings in which all proportions—of the windows, height, floor plan, and covered walkway with a series of rounded arches—were carefully thought out to achieve a sense of balance and harmony.

Art produced in northern Europe tended to be more religious in orientation than that produced in

Italy. Some Flemish painters, notably Rogier van der Weyden (1399/1400–1464) and Jan van Eyck (1366–1441), were considered the artistic equals of Italian painters and were much admired in Italy. Van Eyck was one of the earliest artists to use oil-based paints successfully, and his religious scenes and portraits all show great realism and remarkable attention to human personality. Albrecht Dürer (1471–1528), from the German city of Nuremberg, studied with artists in Italy, and produced woodcuts, engravings, and etchings that rendered the human form and the natural world in amazing detail. He was fascinated with the theoretical and practical problems of perspective, and designed mechanical devices that could assist artists in solving these. Late in his life he saw the first pieces of Aztec art shipped back to Europe from the New World and commented in his diary about how amazing they were.

In the early sixteenth century the center of the new art shifted from Florence to Rome, where wealthy cardinals and popes wanted visual expression of the church's and their own families' power and piety. Renaissance popes expended enormous enthusiasm and huge sums of money to beautify the city. Pope Julius II tore down the old Saint Peter's Basilica and began work on the present structure in 1506. Michelangelo went to Rome from Florence in about 1500 and began the series of statues, paintings, and architectural projects from which he gained an international reputation: the *Pietà*, *Moses*, the redesigning of the plaza and surrounding palaces on the Capitoline Hill in central Rome, and, most famously, the dome for Saint Peter's and the ceiling and altar wall of the nearby Sistine Chapel.

Raphael Sanzio (1483–1520), another Florentine, got the commission for frescoes in the papal apartments, and in his relatively short life he painted hundreds of portraits and devotional images, becoming the most sought-after artist in Europe. Raphael also oversaw a large workshop with many collaborators and apprentices—who assisted on the less difficult sections of some paintings—and wrote treatises on his philosophy of art in which he emphasized the importance of imitating nature and developing an orderly sequence of design and proportion.

Venice became another artistic center in the sixteenth century. Titian (TIH-shuhn) (1490–1576) produced portraits, religious subjects, and mythological scenes, developing techniques of painting in oil without doing elaborate drawings first, which speeded up the process and pleased patrons eager to display their acquisitions. Titian and other sixteenth-century painters developed an artistic style known in English as "mannerism" (from *maniera* or "style" in

***Descent from the Cross*, ca. 1435**   Taking as his subject the suffering and death of Jesus, a popular theme of Netherlandish piety, Rogier van der Weyden shows Christ's descent from the cross, surrounded by nine sorrowing figures. An appreciation of human anatomy, the rich fabrics of the clothes, and the pierced and bloody hands of Jesus were all intended to touch the viewers' emotions. (Prado, Madrid, Spain/The Bridgeman Art Library)

Villa Capra　Architecture as well as literature and art aimed to re-create classical styles. The Venetian architect Andrea Palladio modeled this country villa, constructed for a papal official in 1566, on the Pantheon of ancient Rome (see Chapter 6). Surrounded by statues of classical deities, it is completely symmetrical, capturing humanist ideals of perfection and balance. This villa and other buildings that Palladio designed influenced later buildings all over the world, including the U.S. Capitol in Washington, D.C., and countless state capitol buildings. (age fotostock/Superstock)

Italian) in which artists sometimes distorted figures, exaggerated musculature, and heightened color to express emotion and drama more intently. (A painting by Titian can be found on pages 380 and 382; this is also the style in which Michelangelo painted the *Last Judgment* in the Sistine Chapel, shown on page 374.)

The Renaissance Artist

Some patrons rewarded certain artists very well, and some artists gained great public acclaim as, in Vasari's words, "rare men of genius." This adulation of the artist has led many historians to view the Renaissance as the beginning of the concept of the artist as having a special talent. In the Middle Ages people believed that only God created, albeit through individuals; the medieval conception recognized no particular value in artistic originality. Renaissance artists and humanists came to think that a work of art was the deliberate creation of a unique personality who transcended traditions, rules, and theories. A genius had a peculiar gift, which ordinary laws should not inhibit. Michelangelo and Leonardo da Vinci perhaps best embody the new concept of the Renaissance artist as genius. (See "Individuals in Society: Leonardo da Vinci," page 368.)

It is important not to overemphasize the Renaissance notion of genius. As certain artists became popular and well known, they could assert their own artistic

styles and pay less attention to the wishes of patrons, but even major artists like Raphael generally worked according to the patron's specific guidelines. Whether in Italy or northern Europe, most Renaissance artists trained in the workshops of older artists; Botticelli, Raphael, Titian, and at times even Michelangelo were known for their large, well-run, and prolific workshops. Though they might be men of genius, artists were still expected to be well trained in proper artistic techniques and stylistic conventions; the notion that artistic genius could show up in the work of an untrained artist did not emerge until the twentieth century. Beginning artists spent years mastering their craft by copying drawings and paintings; learning how to prepare paint and other artistic materials; and, by the sixteenth century, reading books about design and composition. Younger artists gathered together in the evenings for further drawing practice; by the later sixteenth century some of these informal groups had turned into more formal artistic "academies," the first of which was begun in 1563 in Florence by Vasari under the patronage of the Medici.

As Vasari's phrase indicates, the notion of artistic genius that developed in the Renaissance was gendered. All the most famous and most prolific Renaissance artists were male. The types of art in which more women were active, such as textiles, needlework, and painting on porcelain, were not regarded as "major

Botticelli, *Primavera* (Spring), ca. 1482 Framed by a grove of orange trees, Venus, goddess of love, is flanked on the right by Flora, goddess of flowers and fertility, and on the left by the Three Graces, goddesses of banquets, dance, and social occasions. Above, Venus's son Cupid, the god of love, shoots darts of desire, while at the far right the wind-god Zephyrus chases the nymph Chloris. The entire scene rests on classical mythology, though some art historians claim that Venus is an allegory for the Virgin Mary. Botticelli captured the ideal for female beauty in the Renaissance: slender, with pale skin, a high forehead, red-blond hair, and sloping shoulders. (Galleria degli Uffizi, Florence, Italy/The Bridgeman Art Library)

arts," but only as "minor" or "decorative" arts. (The division between "major" and "minor" arts begun in the Renaissance continues to influence the way museums and collections are organized today.) Like painting, embroidery changed in the Renaissance to become more naturalistic, more visually complex, and more classical in its subject matter. Embroiderers were not trained to view their work as products of individual genius, however, so they rarely included their names on the works, and there is no way to discover their identities.

There are no female architects whose names are known and only one female sculptor, though several women did become well known as painters in their day. Stylistically, their works are different from one another, but their careers show many similarities. The majority of female painters were the daughters of painters or of minor noblemen with ties to artistic circles. Many were eldest daughters or came from families in which there were no sons, so their fathers took unusual interest in their careers. Many women painters began their careers before they were twenty and either produced far fewer paintings after they married or stopped

painting entirely. Women were not allowed to study the male nude, a study that was viewed as essential if one wanted to paint large history or biblical paintings with many figures. Women also could not learn the technique of fresco, in which colors are applied directly to wet plaster walls, because such work had to be done in public, which was judged inappropriate for women. Joining a group of male artists for informal practice was also seen as improper, so women had no access to the newly established artistic academies. Like universities, humanist academies, and most craft guild shops, artistic workshops were male-only settings in which men of different ages came together for training and created bonds of friendship, influence, patronage, and sometimes intimacy.

Women were not alone in being excluded from the institutions of Renaissance culture. Though a few rare men of genius such as Leonardo and Michelangelo emerged from artisanal backgrounds, most scholars and artists came from families with at least some money. The ideas of the highly educated humanists did not influence the lives of most people in cities and did not affect life in the villages at all. For rural people and for

***The Chess Game*, 1555**   In this oil painting, the Italian artist Sofonisba Anguissola (1532–1625) shows her three younger sisters playing chess, a game that was growing in popularity in the sixteenth century. Each sister looks at the one immediately older than herself, with the girl on the left looking out at her sister, the artist. Anguissola's father, a minor nobleman, recognized his daughter's talent and arranged for her to study with several painters. She became a court painter at the Spanish royal court, where she painted many portraits. Returning to Italy, she continued to be active, painting her last portrait when she was over eighty. (Museum Narodowe, Poznan, Poland/The Bridgeman Art Library)

less well-off town residents, work and play continued much as they had in the High Middle Ages: religious festivals and family celebrations provided people's main amusements, and learning came from one's parents, not through formal schooling (see Chapter 10).

Social Hierarchies

What were the key social hierarchies in Renaissance Europe?

The division between educated and uneducated people was only one of many social hierarchies evident in the Renaissance. Every society has social hierarchies; in ancient Rome, for example, there were patricians and plebeians (see Chapter 5). Such hierarchies are to some degree descriptions of social reality, but they are also idealizations—that is, they describe how people imagined their society to be, without all the messy reality of social-climbing plebeians or groups that did not fit the standard categories. Social hierarchies in the Renaissance were built on those of the Middle Ages that divided nobles from commoners, but they also developed new concepts that contributed to modern social hierarchies, such as those of race, class, and gender.

Race and Slavery

Renaissance people did not use the word *race* the way we do, but often used *race*, *people*, and *nation* interchangeably for ethnic, national, religious, or other groups—the French race, the Jewish nation, the Irish people, "the race of learned gentlemen," and so on. They did make distinctions based on skin color that provide some of the background for later conceptualizations of race, but these distinctions were interwoven with other characteristics when people thought about human differences.

Ever since the time of the Roman Republic, a small number of black Africans had lived in western Europe. They had come, along with white slaves, as the spoils of war. Even after the collapse of the Roman Empire, Muslim and Christian merchants continued to import them. Unstable political conditions in many parts of Africa enabled enterprising merchants to seize people and sell them into slavery. Local authorities afforded these Africans no protection. Long tradition, moreover, sanctioned the practice of slavery. The evidence of medieval art attests to the continued presence of Africans in Europe throughout the Middle Ages and to Europeans' awareness of them.

Beginning in the fifteenth century sizable numbers of black slaves entered Europe. Portuguese sailors brought perhaps a thousand Africans a year to the markets of Seville, Barcelona, Marseilles, and Genoa. In the late fifteenth century this flow increased, with thousands of people taken from the west coast of Africa. By 1530 between four thousand and five thousand were sold to the Portuguese each year. By the mid-sixteenth century blacks, both slave and free, constituted about 10 percent of the population of the Portuguese cities of Lisbon and Évora and roughly 3 percent of the Portuguese population overall. Cities such as Lisbon also had significant numbers of people of mixed African and European descent, as African slaves intermingled

***Laura de Dianti*, 1523** The Venetian artist Titian portrays a young Italian woman with a gorgeous blue dress and an elaborate pearl and feather headdress, accompanied by a young black page with a gold earring. Both the African page and the headdress connect the portrait's subject with the exotic, though slaves from Africa and the Ottoman Empire were actually common in wealthy Venetian households. (Courtesy, Friedrich Kisters, Heinz Kisters Collection)

with the people they lived among and sometimes intermarried.

Although blacks were concentrated in the Iberian Peninsula, some Africans must have lived in northern Europe as well. In the 1580s, for example, Queen Elizabeth I of England complained that there were too many "blackamoores" competing with needy English people for places as domestic servants. Black servants were much sought after; the medieval interest in curiosities, the exotic, and the marvelous continued in the Renaissance. Italian aristocrats had their portraits painted with their black page boys to indicate their wealth (as in the painting above). Blacks were so greatly in demand at the Renaissance courts of northern Italy, in fact, that the Venetians defied papal threats of excommunication to secure them. In 1491 Isabella d'Este, the duchess of Mantua and a major patron of the arts, instructed her agent to secure a black girl between four and eight years old, "shapely and as black as possible." She hoped the girl would become "the best buffoon in

the world," noting that "we shall make her very happy and shall have great fun with her."[8] The girl would join musicians, acrobats, and dancers at Isabella's court as a source of entertainment, her status similar to that of the dwarves who could be found at many Renaissance courts.

Africans were not simply amusements at court. In Portugal, Spain, and Italy slaves supplemented the labor force in virtually all occupations—as servants, agricultural laborers, craftsmen, and seamen on ships going to Lisbon and Africa. Agriculture in Europe did not involve large plantations, so large-scale agricultural slavery did not develop there as it would in the late fifteenth century in the New World.

Until the voyages down the African coast in the late fifteenth century, Europeans had little concrete knowledge of Africans and their cultures. They perceived Africa as a remote place, the home of strange people isolated by heresy and Islam from superior European civilization. Africans' contact, even as slaves, with Christian Europeans could only "improve" the blacks, they thought. The expanding slave trade reinforced negative preconceptions about the inferiority of black Africans.

Wealth and the Nobility

The word *class*—as in working class, middle class, and upper class—was not used in the Renaissance to describe social divisions, but by the thirteenth century, and even more so by the fifteenth, the idea of a hierarchy based on wealth was emerging. This was particularly true in cities, where wealthy merchants who oversaw vast trading empires lived in splendor that rivaled the richest nobles. As we saw earlier, in many cities these merchants had gained political power to match their economic might, becoming merchant oligarchs who ruled through city councils. This hierarchy of wealth was more fluid than the older divisions into noble and commoner, allowing individuals and families to rise—and fall—within one generation.

The development of a hierarchy of wealth did not mean an end to the prominence of nobles, however, and even poorer nobility still had higher status than wealthy commoners. Thus wealthy Italian merchants enthusiastically bought noble titles and country villas in the fifteenth century, and wealthy English or Spanish merchants eagerly married their daughters and sons into often-impoverished noble families. The nobility maintained its status in most parts of Europe not by maintaining rigid boundaries, but by taking in and integrating the new social elite of wealth.

Along with being tied to hierarchies of wealth and family standing, social status was linked to considerations of honor. Among the nobility, for example, certain weapons and battle tactics were favored because they were viewed as more honorable. Among urban dwellers, certain occupations, such as city executioner or manager of the municipal brothel, might be well paid but were understood to be dishonorable and so of low status. In cities, sumptuary laws reflected both wealth and honor (see Chapter 10); merchants were specifically allowed fur and jewels, while prostitutes were ordered to wear yellow bands that would remind potential customers of the flames of Hell.

Gender Roles

Renaissance people would not have understood the word *gender* to refer to categories of people, but they would have easily grasped the concept. Toward the end of the fourteenth century, learned men (and a few women) began what was termed the **debate about women** (*querelle des femmes*), a debate about women's character and nature that would last for centuries. Misogynist (muh-SAH-juh-nihst) critiques of women from both clerical and secular authors denounced females as devious, domineering, and demanding. In answer, several authors compiled long lists of famous and praiseworthy women exemplary for their loyalty, bravery, and morality. Christine de Pizan was among the writers who were interested not only in defending women, but also in exploring the reasons behind women's secondary status — that is, why the great philosophers, statesmen, and poets had generally been men. In this they were anticipating discussions about the "social construction of gender" by six hundred years. (See "Primary Source 11.5: Christine de Pizan, Advice to the Wives of Artisans," page 347, and "Primary Source 12.2: Cassandra Fedele on Humanist Learning," page 364.)

With the development of the printing press, popular interest in the debate about women grew, and works were translated, reprinted, and shared around Europe. Prints that juxtaposed female virtues and vices were also very popular, with the virtuous women depicted as those of the classical or biblical past and the vice-ridden dressed in contemporary clothes. The favorite metaphor for the virtuous wife was either the snail or the tortoise, both animals that never leave their "houses" and are totally silent, although such images were never as widespread as those depicting wives beating their husbands or hiding their lovers from them.

Beginning in the sixteenth century, the debate about women also became a debate about female rulers, sparked primarily by dynastic accidents in many countries, including Spain, England, Scotland, and France, which led to women ruling in their own right or serving as advisers to child kings. The questions were vigorously and at times viciously argued. They directly concerned the social construction of gender: could a woman's being born into a royal family and educated to rule allow her to overcome the limitations of her sex? Should it? Or stated another way: which was (or should be) the stronger determinant of character and social role, gender or rank? Despite a prevailing sentiment that women were not as fit to rule as men, there were no successful rebellions against female rulers simply because they were women, but in part this was because female rulers, especially Queen Elizabeth I of England, emphasized qualities regarded as masculine — physical bravery, stamina, wisdom, duty — whenever they appeared in public.

Ideas about women's and men's proper roles determined the actions of ordinary men and women even more forcefully. The dominant notion of the "true" man was that of the married head of household, so men whose social status and age would have normally conferred political power but who remained unmarried did not participate in politics to the same

debate about women Debate among writers and thinkers in the Renaissance about women's qualities and proper role in society.

Phyllis Riding Aristotle   Among the many scenes that expressed the debate about women visually were woodcuts, engravings, paintings, and even cups and plates that showed the classical philosopher Aristotle as an old man being ridden by the young, beautiful Phyllis (shown here in a German woodcut). The origins of the story are uncertain, but in the Renaissance everyone knew the tale of how Aristotle's infatuation with Phyllis led to his ridicule. Male moralists used it as a warning about the power of women's sexual allure, though women may have interpreted it differently. (Réunion des Musées Nationaux/Art Resource, NY)

In the Renaissance wealthy people displayed their power and prosperity on their bodies as well as in their houses and household furnishings. Expanded trade brought in silks, pearls, gemstones, feathers, dyes, and furs, which tailors, goldsmiths, seamstresses, furriers, and hatmakers turned into magnificent clothing and jewelry. Nowhere was fashion more evident than on the men in Renaissance cities and courts. Young men favored multicolored garments that fit tightly, often topping the ensemble with a matching hat on carefully combed long hair. The close-cut garments emphasized the male form, which was further accentuated by tight hose stylishly split to reveal a brightly colored codpiece. Older men favored more subdued colors but with multiple padded shirts, vests, and coats that emphasized real or simulated upper-body strength and that allowed the display of many layers of expensive fabrics. Golden rings, earrings, pins, and necklaces provided additional glamour.

Padded leather jerkin embroidered with silk and metal thread from the late sixteenth century. There are eyelets for tying up hose inside. (Museo Stibbert, Florence)

The Venetian painter Titian's portrait of Emperor Charles V with one of his hunting dogs. (Prado, Madrid, Spain/Giraudon/The Bridgeman Art Library)

level as their married brothers. Unmarried men in Venice, for example, could not be part of the ruling council. (See "Living in the Past: Male Clothing and Masculinity," above.)

Women were also understood as either "married or to be married," even if the actual marriage patterns in Europe left many women (and men) unmarried until quite late in life (see Chapter 11). This meant that women's work was not viewed as financially supporting a family—even if it did—and was valued less than men's. If they worked for wages, and many women did, women

earned about half to two-thirds of what men did, even for the same work. Regulations for vineyard workers in the early sixteenth century, for example, specified:

Men who work in the vineyards, doing work that is skilled, are to be paid 16 pence per day; in addition, they are to receive soup and wine in the morning, at midday beer, vegetables and meat, and in the evening soup, vegetables and wine. Young boys are to be paid 10 pence per day. Women who work as haymakers are to be given 6 pence a day. If the

Two young men, who are side figures in *The Adoration of the Magi,* **by Luca Signorelli** (1445–1523). (Scala/Art Resource, NY)

QUESTIONS FOR ANALYSIS

1. Male clothing in any era communicates social values and ideas about masculinity. What does Renaissance fashion suggest about notions of manhood in this era?

2. In *The Prince*, Machiavelli used the word *effeminate* to describe the worst kind of ruler, though the word carried different connotations than it does today. Strong heterosexual passion was not a sign of manliness but could make one "effeminate"—that is, dominated by women as well as similar to them. Look at the portrait of Charles V here and at the other portraits in this chapter. How did male rulers visually symbolize their masculinity?

> employer wants to have them doing other work, he may make an agreement with them to pay them 7 or 8 pence. He may also give them soup and vegetables to eat in the morning—but no wine—milk and bread at midday, but nothing in the evening.[9]

The maintenance of appropriate power relationships between men and women, with men dominant and women subordinate, served as a symbol of the proper functioning of society as a whole. Disorder in the proper gender hierarchy was linked with social upheaval and was viewed as threatening. Of all the ways in which Renaissance society was hierarchically arranged—social rank, age, level of education, race, occupation—gender was regarded as the most "natural" and therefore the most important to defend.

Politics and the State in Western Europe

How did nation-states develop in this period?

The High Middle Ages had witnessed the origins of many of the basic institutions of the modern state. Sheriffs, inquests, juries, circuit judges, professional bureaucracies, and representative assemblies all trace their origins to the twelfth and thirteenth centuries. The linchpin for the development of states, however, was strong monarchy, and during the period of the Hundred Years' War, no ruler in western Europe was able to provide effective leadership. The resurgent power of feudal nobilities weakened the centralizing work begun earlier.

Beginning in the fifteenth century, however, rulers utilized aggressive methods to rebuild their governments. First in the regional states of Italy, then in the expanding monarchies of France, England, and Spain, rulers began the work of reducing violence, curbing unruly nobles, and establishing domestic order. They attempted to secure their borders and enhanced methods of raising revenue. The monarchs of western Europe emphasized royal majesty and royal sovereignty and insisted on the respect and loyalty of all subjects, including the nobility. In central Europe the Holy Roman emperors attempted to do the same, but they were not able to overcome the power of local interests to create a unified state (see Chapter 13).

France

The Black Death and the Hundred Years' War left France drastically depopulated, commercially ruined, and agriculturally weak. Nonetheless, the ruler whom Joan of Arc had seen crowned at Reims, Charles VII (r. 1422–1461), revived the monarchy and France. He seemed an unlikely person to do so. Frail, indecisive, and burdened with questions about his paternity (his father had been deranged; his mother, notoriously promiscuous), Charles VII nevertheless began France's long recovery.

Charles reconciled the Burgundians and Armagnacs (ahr-muhn-YAKZ), who had been waging civil war for thirty years. By 1453 French armies had expelled the English from French soil except in Calais. Charles reorganized the royal council, giving increased influence to lawyers and bankers, and strengthened royal finances through taxes on certain products and on land, which remained the Crown's chief sources of income until the Revolution of 1789.

By establishing regular companies of cavalry and archers—recruited, paid, and inspected by the state—Charles created the first permanent royal army anywhere in Europe. His son Louis XI (r. 1461–1483), called the "Spider King" because of his treacherous character, improved upon Charles's army and used it to control the nobles' separate militias and to curb urban independence. The army was also employed in 1477 when Louis conquered Burgundy upon the death of its ruler Charles the Bold. Three years later, the extinction of the house of Anjou with the death of its last legitimate male heir brought Louis the counties of Anjou, Bar, Maine, and Provence.

Two further developments strengthened the French monarchy. The marriage of Louis XII (r. 1498–1515) and Anne of Brittany added the large western duchy of Brittany to the state. Then King Francis I and Pope Leo X reached a mutually satisfactory agreement about church and state powers in 1516. The new treaty, the Concordat of Bologna, approved the pope's right to receive the first year's income of newly named bishops and abbots in France. In return, Leo X recognized the French ruler's right to select French bishops and abbots. French kings thereafter effectively controlled the appointment and thus the policies of church officials in the kingdom.

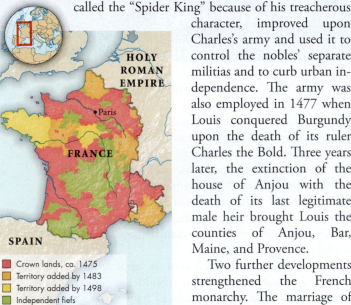

The Expansion of France, 1475–1500

- Crown lands, ca. 1475
- Territory added by 1483
- Territory added by 1498
- Independent fiefs
- Boundary of France, ca. 1500

England

English society also suffered severely from the disorders of the fifteenth century. The aristocracy dominated the government of Henry IV (r. 1399–1413) and indulged in disruptive violence at the local level, fighting each other, seizing wealthy travelers for ransom, and plundering merchant caravans (see Chapter 11). Population continued to decline. Between 1455 and 1471 adherents of the ducal houses of York and Lancaster contended for control of the Crown in a civil war, commonly called the Wars of the Roses because the symbol of the Yorkists was a white rose and that of the Lancastrians a red one. The chronic disorder hurt trade, agriculture, and domestic industry. Under the pious but mentally disturbed Henry VI (r. 1422–1461), the authority of the monarchy sank lower than it had been in centuries.

The Yorkist Edward IV (r. 1461–1483) began establishing domestic tranquillity. He succeeded in defeating the Lancastrian forces and after 1471 began to reconstruct the monarchy. Edward, his brother Richard III (r. 1483–1485), and Henry VII (r. 1485–1509) of the Welsh house of Tudor worked to restore royal prestige, to crush the power of the nobility, and to establish order and law at the local level. All three rulers used methods that Machiavelli himself would have praised—ruthlessness, efficiency, and secrecy.

Edward IV and subsequently the Tudors, except Henry VIII, conducted foreign policy on the basis of diplomacy, avoiding expensive wars. Thus the English monarchy did not have to depend on Parliament for money, and the Crown undercut that source of aristocratic influence.

Henry VII did summon several meetings of Parliament in the early years of his reign, primarily to confirm laws, but the center of royal authority was the royal council, which governed at the national level. There Henry VII revealed his distrust of the nobility: though not completely excluded, very few great lords were among the king's closest advisers. Instead he chose men from among the smaller landowners and urban residents trained in law. The council conducted negotiations with foreign governments and secured international recognition of the Tudor dynasty through the marriage in 1501 of Henry VII's eldest son, Arthur, to Catherine of Aragon, the daughter of Ferdinand and Isabella of Spain. The council dealt with real or potential aristocratic threats through a judicial offshoot, the Court of Star Chamber, so called because of the stars painted on the ceiling of the room. The court applied methods that were sometimes terrifying: accused persons were not entitled to see evidence against them; sessions were secret; juries were not called; and torture could be applied to extract confessions. These procedures ran directly counter to English common-law precedents, but they effectively reduced aristocratic troublemaking.

When Henry VII died in 1509, he left a country at peace both domestically and internationally, a substantially augmented treasury, an expanding wool trade, and a crown with its dignity and role much enhanced. He was greatly missed after he died "by all his subjects," wrote the historian Polydore Vergil, "who had been able to conduct their lives peaceably, far removed from the assaults and evildoings of scoundrels."[10]

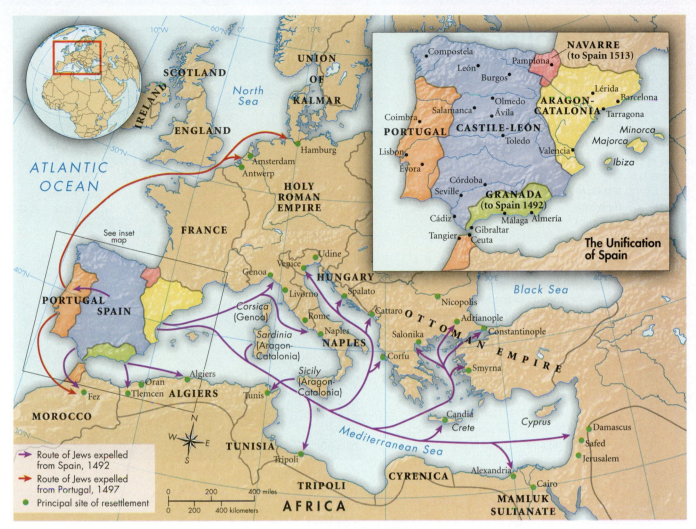

Map 12.3 The Unification of Spain and the Expulsion of the Jews, Fifteenth Century The marriage of Ferdinand of Aragon and Isabella of Castile in 1469 brought most of the Iberian Peninsula under one monarchy, although different parts of Spain retained distinct cultures, languages, and legal systems. In 1492 Ferdinand and Isabella conquered Granada, where most people were Muslim, and expelled the Jews from all of Spain. Spanish Jews resettled in cities of Europe and the Mediterranean that allowed them in, including Muslim states such as the Ottoman Empire. Muslims were also expelled from Spain over the course of the sixteenth and early seventeenth centuries.

Spain

While England and France laid the foundations of unified nation-states during the Middle Ages, Spain remained a conglomerate of independent kingdoms. By the middle of the fifteenth century, the kingdoms of Castile and Aragon dominated the weaker Navarre, Portugal, and Granada; and the Iberian Peninsula, with the exception of Granada, had been won for Christianity (Map 12.3). But even the wedding in 1469 of the dynamic and aggressive Isabella of Castile and the crafty and persistent Ferdinand of Aragon did not bring about administrative unity. Rather, their marriage constituted a dynastic union of two royal houses, not the political union of two peoples. Although Ferdinand

and Isabella (r. 1474–1516) pursued a common foreign policy, until about 1700 Spain existed as a loose confederation of separate kingdoms, each maintaining its own cortes (parliament), laws, courts, and systems of coinage and taxation.

Ferdinand and Isabella were able to exert their authority in ways similar to the rulers of France and England, however. They curbed aristocratic power by excluding high nobles from the royal council, which had full executive, judicial, and legislative powers under the monarchy, instead appointing lesser landowners. The council and various government boards recruited men trained in Roman law, which exalted the power of the Crown. They also secured from the Spanish

Tax Collectors

New types of taxes and more effective methods of tax collection were essential to the growth of Renaissance states, but both were often highly unpopular. In this painting from about 1540, the Dutch artist Marinus van Reymerswaele depicts two tax collectors as they count their take and record it in a ledger. Tax collectors were of middling status, but the men shown here wear clothing more appropriate for nobles.

(Erich Lessing/Art Resource, NY)

EVALUATE THE EVIDENCE

1. What elements of the men's clothing suggest wealth? How would you describe the expressions on their faces? What does the painting suggest about the artist's opinion of tax collectors?
2. In Spain, converso tax collectors were widely resented. What were some of the reasons behind this resentment? How did this hatred shape political developments in Spain?

Borgia pope Alexander VI—Cesare Borgia's father—the right to appoint bishops in Spain and in the Hispanic territories in America, enabling them to establish the equivalent of a national church. With the revenues from ecclesiastical estates, they were able to expand their territories to include the remaining land held by Arabs in southern Spain. The victorious entry of Ferdinand and Isabella into Granada on January 6, 1492, signaled the conclusion of the reconquista (see Map 9.3, page 260). Granada was incorporated into the Spanish kingdom, and in 1512 Ferdinand conquered Navarre in the north.

There still remained a sizable and, in the view of the majority of the Spanish people, potentially dangerous minority, the Jews. When the kings of France and England had expelled the Jews from their kingdoms (see Chapter 9), many had sought refuge in Spain. During the long centuries of the reconquista, Christian kings had recognized Jewish rights and privileges; in fact, Jewish industry, intelli-

New Christians A term for Jews and Muslims in the Iberian Peninsula who accepted Christianity; in many cases they included Christians whose families had converted centuries earlier.

gence, and money had supported royal power. While Christians borrowed from Jewish moneylenders and while all who could afford them sought Jewish physicians, a strong undercurrent of resentment of Jewish influence and wealth festered.

In the fourteenth century anti-Semitism in Spain was aggravated by fiery anti-Jewish preaching, by economic dislocation, and by the search for a scapegoat during the Black Death. Anti-Semitic pogroms swept the towns of Spain, and perhaps 40 percent of the Jewish population was killed or forced to convert. Those converted were called *conversos* or **New Christians**. Conversos were often well educated and held prominent positions in government, the church, medicine, law, and business. Numbering perhaps two hundred thousand in a total Spanish population of about 7.5 million, New Christians and Jews in fifteenth-century Spain exercised influence disproportionate to their numbers.

Such successes bred resentment. Aristocratic grandees resented the conversos' financial dependence; the poor hated the converso tax collectors; and churchmen doubted the sincerity of their conversions. (See "Primary Source 12.5: Tax Collectors," at left.) Queen Isabella shared these suspicions, and she and Ferdinand had received permission from Pope Sixtus IV in 1478 to establish their own Inquisition to "search out and punish converts from Judaism who had transgressed against Christianity by secretly adhering to Jewish beliefs and performing rites of the Jews."[11] Investigations and trials began immediately, as officials of the Inquisition looked for conversos who showed any sign of incomplete conversion, such as not eating pork.

Recent scholarship has carefully analyzed documents of the Inquisition. Most conversos identified themselves as sincere Christians; many came from families that had received baptism generations before. In response to conversos' statements, officials of the Inquisition developed a new type of anti-Semitism. A person's status as a Jew, they argued, could not be changed by religious conversion, but was in the person's blood and was heritable, so Jews could never be true Christians. In what were known as "purity of blood" laws, having pure Christian blood became a requirement for noble status. Ideas about Jews developed in Spain were important components in European concepts of race, and discussions of "Jewish blood" later expanded into notions of the "Jewish race."

In 1492, shortly after the conquest of Granada, Isabella and Ferdinand issued an edict expelling all practicing Jews from Spain. Of the community of perhaps 200,000 Jews, 150,000 fled. Many Muslims in Granada were forcibly baptized and became another type of New Christian investigated by the Inquisition. Absolute religious orthodoxy and purity of blood served as the theoretical foundation of the Spanish national state.

The Spanish national state rested on marital politics as well as military victories and religious courts. In 1496 Ferdinand and Isabella married their second daughter, Joanna, heiress to Castile, to the archduke Philip, heir to the Burgundian Netherlands and the Holy Roman Empire. Philip and Joanna's son Charles V (r. 1519–1556) thus succeeded to a vast inheritance. When Charles's son Philip II joined Portugal to the Spanish crown in 1580, the Iberian Peninsula was at last politically united.

Notes

1. In Gertrude R. B. Richards, *Florentine Merchants in the Age of the Medici* (Cambridge: Harvard University Press, 1932).
2. From *The Portable Renaissance Reader*, p. 27, by James B. Ross and Mary Martin McLaughlin, editors, copyright 1953, renewed © 1981 by Viking Penguin Inc. Used by permission of Viking Penguin, a division of Penguin Group (USA) Inc.
3. Ibid., pp. 480–481, 482, 492.
4. Niccolò Machiavelli, *The Prince*, trans. Leo Paul S. de Alvarez (Prospect Heights, Ill.: Waveland Press, 1980), p. 101.
5. Ibid., p. 149.
6. Quoted in F. Seebohm, *The Oxford Reformers* (London: J. M. Dent & Sons, 1867), p. 256.
7. Quoted in Lauro Martines, *Power and Imagination: City-States in Renaissance Italy* (New York: Vintage Books, 1980), p. 253.
8. Quoted in J. Devisse and M. Mollat, *The Image of the Black in Western Art*, vol. 2, trans. W. G. Ryan (New York: William Morrow, 1979), pt. 2, pp. 187–188.
9. Stuttgart, Württembergische Hauptstaatsarchiv, Generalreskripta, A38, Bü. 2, 1550; trans. Merry Wiesner-Hanks.
10. Denys Hay, ed. and trans., *The Anglia Historia of Polydore Vergil, AD 1485–1537*, book 74 (London: Camden Society, 1950), p. 147.
11. Quoted in Benzion Netanyahu, *The Origins of the Inquisition in Fifteenth Century Spain* (New York: Random House, 1995), p. 921.

 **LOOKING BACK LOOKING AHEAD** The art historian Giorgio Vasari, who first called this era the Renaissance, thought that his contemporaries had both revived the classical past and gone beyond it. Vasari's judgment was echoed for centuries as historians sharply contrasted the art, architecture, educational ideas, social structures, and attitude toward life of the Renaissance with those of the Middle Ages: in this view, whereas the Middle Ages were corporate and religious, the Renaissance was individualistic and secular. More recently, historians and other scholars have stressed continuity as well as change. Families, kin networks, guilds, and other corporate groups remained important in the Renaissance, and religious belief remained firm. This re-evaluation changes our view of the relationship between the Middle Ages and the Renaissance. It may also change our view of the relationship between the Renaissance and the dramatic changes in religion that occurred in Europe in the sixteenth century. Those religious changes, the Reformation, used to be viewed as a rejection of the values of the Renaissance and a return to the intense concern with religion of the Middle Ages. This idea of the Reformation as a sort of counter-Renaissance may be true to some degree, but there are powerful continuities as well. Both movements looked back to a time people regarded as purer and better than their own, and both offered opportunities for strong individuals to shape their world in unexpected ways.

REVIEW and EXPLORE

MAKE IT STICK

> ✓ **LearningCurve**
> After reading the chapter, go online and use LearningCurve to retain what you've read.

Identify Key Terms

Identify and explain the significance of each item below.

Renaissance (p. 358)

patronage (p. 358)

communes (p. 358)

popolo (p. 359)

signori (p. 360)

courts (p. 360)

humanism (p. 363)

virtù (p. 363)

Christian humanists (p. 370)

debate about women (p. 381)

New Christians (p. 386)

Review the Main Ideas

Answer the focus questions from each section of the chapter.

◆ How did politics and economics shape the Renaissance? (p. 358)

◆ What new ideas were associated with the Renaissance? (p. 362)

◆ How did art reflect new Renaissance ideals? (p. 373)

◆ What were the key social hierarchies in Renaissance Europe? (p. 379)

◆ How did nation-states develop in this period? (p. 383)

Make Connections

Think about the larger developments and continuities within and across chapters.

1. The word *Renaissance*, invented to describe the cultural flowering in Italy that began in the fifteenth century, has often been used for other periods of advances in learning and the arts, such as the "Carolingian Renaissance" that you read about in Chapter 8. Can you think of other, more recent "Renaissances"? How else is the word used today?

2. Many artists in the Renaissance consciously modeled their works on those of ancient Greece (Chapters 3 and 4) and Rome (Chapters 5 and 6). Comparing the art and architecture shown in those chapters with those in this chapter, what similarities do you see? Are there aspects of classical art and architecture that were *not* emulated in the Renaissance? Why do you think this might be?

3. The Renaissance was clearly a period of cultural change for educated men. Given what you have read about women's lives and ideas about women in this and earlier chapters, did women have a Renaissance? (This question was posed first by the historian Joan Kelly in 1977 and remains a topic of great debate.) Why or why not?

ONLINE DOCUMENT ASSIGNMENT
Leonardo da Vinci

How did the needs and desires of Leonardo's patrons influence his work?

You encountered Leonardo da Vinci's story on page 368. Keeping the question above in mind, go to the Integrated Media and examine written and visual evidence that shed light on the dynamic between the artist and his employers. Then complete a writing assignment based on the evidence and details from this chapter.

Suggested Reading and Media Resources

BOOKS

- Earle, T. F., and K. J. P. Lowe, eds. *Black Africans in Renaissance Europe.* 2005. Includes essays discussing many aspects of ideas about race and the experience of Africans in Europe.

- Eisenstein, Elizabeth. *The Printing Press as an Agent of Change: Communications and Cultural Transformations in Early Modern Europe.* 1979. The definitive study of the impact of printing.

- Ertman, Thomas. *The Birth of Leviathan: Building States and Regimes in Medieval and Early Modern Europe.* 1997. A good introduction to the creation of nation-states.

- Hartt, Frederick, and David Wilkins. *History of Italian Renaissance Art,* 7th ed. 2010. A comprehensive survey of painting, sculpture, and architecture in Italy.

- Jardine, Lisa. *Worldly Goods: A New History of the Renaissance.* 1998. Discusses changing notions of social status, artistic patronage, and consumer goods.

- Johnson, Geraldine. *Renaissance Art: A Very Short Introduction.* 2005. An excellent brief survey that includes male and female artists, and sets the art in its cultural and historical context.

- King, Ross. *Machiavelli: Philosopher of Power.* 2006. A brief biography that explores Machiavelli's thought in its social and political context.

- Man, John. *Gutenberg Revolution: The Story of a Genius and an Invention That Changed the World.* 2002. Presents a rather idealized view of Gutenberg, but has good discussions of his milieu and excellent illustrations.

- Najemy, John M. *A History of Florence, 1200–1575.* 2008. A comprehensive survey of cultural, political, and social developments, based on the newest research.

- Nauert, Charles. *Humanism and the Culture of Renaissance Europe,* 2d ed. 2006. A thorough introduction to humanism throughout Europe.

- Rummel, Erica. *Desiderius Erasmus.* 2006. An excellent short introduction to Erasmus as a scholar and Christian thinker.

- Waley, Daniel, and Trevor Dean. *The Italian City States,* 4th ed. 2004. Analyzes the rise of independent city-states in northern Italy, including discussion of the artistic and social lives of their inhabitants.

- Wiesner-Hanks, Merry E. *Women and Gender in Early Modern Europe,* 3d ed. 2008. Discusses all aspects of women's lives and ideas about gender.

DOCUMENTARIES

- *Leonardo da Vinci* (BBC, 2004). A three-part documentary telling the life story of Leonardo as an artist, inventor, and engineer. Features tests of his designs for the parachute, tank, diving suit, and glider, and an investigation of the *Mona Lisa*.

- *The Medici: Godfathers of the Renaissance* (PBS, 2004). A four-part documentary examining the power and patronage of the Medici family, shot on location, with extensive coverage of art and architecture.

FEATURE FILMS AND TELEVISION

- *The Agony and the Ecstasy* (Carol Reed, 1965). A classic film highlighting the conflict between Michelangelo and Pope Julius II over the painting of the Sistine Chapel, with Charlton Heston as the artist and Rex Harrison as the pope.

- *The Borgias* (Showtime, 2011). A fictionalized docudrama of the rise of the Borgia family to power in the church and in Italy, with Jeremy Irons as Pope Alexander VI.

- *Dangerous Beauty* (Marshall Herskovitz, 1998). A biographical drama about the life of Veronica Franco, a well-educated courtesan in sixteenth-century Venice, based on the biography of Franco written by Margaret Rosenthal.

WEB SITES

- *Medici Archive Project.* A database for researching the nearly three million letters held by the archives on the Medici Grand Dukes of Tuscany, who ruled Florence from 1537 to 1743. Includes topical "document highlights" in English and Italian, accompanied by illustrations. **www.medici.org/**

- *Other Women's Voices: Translations of Women's Writing Before 1700.* Created and maintained by Dorothy Disse with substantial excerpts from more than 120 authors, about half of whom come from the Renaissance era. **home.infionline.net/~ddisse/**

- *Timeline of Art History.* A chronological, geographical, and thematic exploration of the history of art from around the world, run by the Metropolitan Museum of Art. Includes numerous special topics sections on nearly every aspect of Renaissance art, and also on book production, musical instruments, clothing, household furnishings, and political and economic developments. **www.metmuseum.org/toah/**

13

Reformations and Religious Wars

1500–1600

Calls for reform of the Christian Church began very early in its history. Throughout the centuries, many Christians believed that the early Christian Church represented a golden age, akin to the golden age of the classical past celebrated by Renaissance humanists. When Christianity became the official religion of the Roman Empire in the fourth century, many believers thought that the church had abandoned its original mission, and they called for a return to a church that was not linked to the state. Throughout the Middle Ages, individuals and groups argued that the church had become too wealthy and powerful and urged monasteries, convents, bishoprics, and the papacy to give up their property and focus on service to the poor. Some asserted that basic teachings of the church were not truly Christian and that changes were needed in theology as well as in institutional structures and practices. The Christian humanists of the late fifteenth and early sixteenth centuries such as Erasmus urged reform, primarily through educational and social change. What was new in the sixteenth century was the breadth of acceptance and the ultimate impact of the calls for reform. This acceptance was due not only to religious issues and problems within the church, but also to political and social factors. In 1500 there was one Christian Church in western Europe to which all Christians at least nominally belonged. One hundred years later there were many, a situation that continues today. ■

Religious Violence in Urban Life.   This 1590 painting shows Catholic military forces, including friars in their robes, processing through one of the many towns affected by the French religious wars that followed the Reformation. (Musée des Beaux-Arts, Valenciennes, France/Giraudon/The Bridgeman Art Library)

CHAPTER PREVIEW

 LearningCurve
After reading the chapter, go online and use LearningCurve to retain what you've read.

The Early Reformation

What were the central ideas of the reformers, and why were they appealing to different social groups?

The Reformation and German Politics

How did the political situation in Germany shape the course of the Reformation?

The Spread of Protestant Ideas

How did Protestant ideas and institutions spread beyond German-speaking lands?

The Catholic Reformation

What reforms did the Catholic Church make, and how did it respond to Protestant reform movements?

Religious Violence

What were the causes and consequences of religious violence, including riots, wars, and witch-hunts?

The Early Reformation

What were the central ideas of the reformers, and why were they appealing to different social groups?

In early-sixteenth-century Europe a wide range of people had grievances with the church. Educated laypeople such as Christian humanists and urban residents, villagers and artisans, and church officials themselves called for reform. This widespread dissatisfaction helps explain why the ideas of Martin Luther, an obscure professor from a new and not very prestigious German university, found a ready audience. Within a decade of his first publishing his ideas (using the new technology of the printing press), much of central Europe and Scandinavia had broken with the Catholic Church, and even more radical concepts of the Christian message were being developed and linked to calls for social change.

The Christian Church in the Early Sixteenth Century

If external religious observances are an indication of conviction, Europeans in the early sixteenth century were deeply pious. Villagers participated in processions honoring the local saints. Merchants and guild members made pilgrimages to the great shrines, such as Saint Peter's in Rome, and paid for altars in local churches. Men and women continued to remember the church in their wills. People of all social groups devoted an enormous amount of their time and income to religious causes and foundations.

Despite—or perhaps because of—the depth of their piety, many people were also highly critical of the Roman Catholic Church and its clergy. The papal conflict with the German emperor Frederick II in the thirteenth century, followed by the Babylonian Captivity and the Great Schism, badly damaged the prestige of church leaders, and the fifteenth-century popes' concentration on artistic patronage and building up family power did not help matters. Papal tax collection methods were attacked orally and in print. Some criticized the papacy itself as an institution, and even the great wealth and powerful courts of the entire church hierarchy. Some groups and individuals argued that certain doctrines taught by the church, such as the veneration of saints and the centrality of the sacraments, were incorrect. They suggested measures to reform institutions, improve clerical education and

anticlericalism Opposition to the clergy.

indulgence A document issued by the Catholic Church lessening penance or time in purgatory, widely believed to bring forgiveness of all sins.

behavior, and alter basic doctrines. Occasionally these reform efforts had some success, and in at least one area, Bohemia (the modern-day Czech Republic), they led to the formation of a church independent of Rome a century before Luther (see Chapter 11).

In the early sixteenth century, court records, bishops' visitations of parishes, and popular songs and printed images show widespread **anticlericalism**, or opposition to the clergy. The critics concentrated primarily on three problems: clerical immorality, clerical ignorance, and clerical pluralism (the practice of holding more than one church office at a time), with the related problem of absenteeism. Charges of clerical immorality were aimed at a number of priests who were drunkards, neglected the rule of celibacy, gambled, or indulged in fancy dress. Charges of clerical ignorance were motivated by barely literate priests who simply mumbled the Latin words of the Mass by rote without understanding their meaning. Many priests, monks, and nuns lived pious lives of devotion, learning, and service and had strong support from the laypeople in their areas, but everyone also knew (and repeated) stories about lecherous monks, lustful nuns, and greedy priests.

In regard to absenteeism and pluralism, many clerics held several benefices, or offices, simultaneously, but they seldom visited the benefices, let alone performed the spiritual responsibilities those offices entailed. Instead, they collected revenues from all of them and hired a poor priest, paying him just a fraction of the income to fulfill the spiritual duties of a particular local church. Many Italian officials in the papal curia, the pope's court in Rome, held benefices in England, Spain, and Germany. Revenues from those countries paid the Italian clerics' salaries, provoking not only charges of absenteeism but also nationalistic resentment aimed at the upper levels of the church hierarchy, which was increasingly viewed as foreign. This was particularly the case in Germany, where the lack of a strong central government to negotiate with the papacy meant that demands for revenue were especially high.

There was also local resentment of clerical privileges and immunities. Priests, monks, and nuns were exempt from civic responsibilities, such as defending the city and paying taxes. Yet religious orders frequently held large amounts of urban property, in some cities as much as one-third. City governments were increasingly determined to integrate the clergy into civic life by reducing their privileges and giving them public responsibilities. Urban leaders wanted some say in who would be appointed to high church offices, rather than having this decided far away in Rome. This brought city leaders into opposition with bishops and the papacy, which for centuries had stressed the independence of the church from lay control and the distinction between members of the clergy and laypeople.

Martin Luther

By itself, widespread criticism of the church did not lead to the dramatic changes of the sixteenth century. Instead, the personal religious struggle of a German university professor and priest, Martin Luther (1483–1546), propelled the wave of movements we now call the Reformation. Luther was born at Eisleben in Saxony. At considerable sacrifice, his father sent him to school and then to the University of Erfurt, where he earned a master's degree with distinction. Luther was to proceed to the study of law and a legal career, which for centuries had been the stepping-stone to public office and material success. Instead, however, a sense of religious calling led him to join the Augustinian friars, a religious order whose members often preached to, taught, and assisted the poor. (Religious orders were groups whose members took vows and followed a particular set of rules.) Luther was ordained a priest in 1507 and after additional study earned a doctorate of theology. From 1512 until his death in 1546, he served as professor of the Scriptures at the new University of Wittenberg. Throughout his life, he frequently cited his professorship as justification for his reforming work.

Martin Luther was a very conscientious friar, but his scrupulous observance of religious routine, frequent confessions, and fasting gave him only temporary relief from anxieties about sin and his ability to meet God's demands. Through his study of Saint Paul's letters in the New Testament, he gradually arrived at a new understanding of Christian doctrine. His understanding is often summarized as "faith alone, grace alone, Scripture alone." He believed that salvation and justification come through faith. Faith is a free gift of God's grace, not the result of human effort. God's word is revealed only in Scripture, not in the traditions of the church.

At the same time that Luther was engaged in scholarly reflections and professorial lecturing, Pope Leo X authorized the sale of a special Saint Peter's indulgence to finance his building plans in Rome. The archbishop who controlled the area in which Wittenberg was located, Albert of Mainz, was an enthusiastic promoter of this indulgence sale. For his efforts, he received a share of the profits so that he could pay off a debt he had incurred in order to purchase a papal dispensation allowing him to become the bishop of several other territories as well.

What exactly was an **indulgence**? According to Catholic theology, individuals who sin could be reconciled to God by confessing their sins to a priest and by doing an assigned penance, such as praying or fasting. But beginning in the twelfth century learned theologians increasingly emphasized the idea of purgatory, a place where souls on their way to Heaven went to make further amends for their earthly sins. Both earthly penance and time in purgatory could be shortened by drawing on what was termed the "treasury of merits." This was a collection of all the virtuous acts that Christ, the apostles, and the saints had done during their lives. People thought of it as a sort of strongbox, like those in

Chronology

1517	Martin Luther writes "Ninety-five Theses on the Power of Indulgences"
1521	Diet of Worms
1521–1559	Habsburg-Valois wars
1525	German Peasants' War
1526	Turkish victory at Mohács, which allows spread of Protestantism in Hungary
1530s	Henry VIII ends the authority of the pope in England
1535	Angela Merici establishes the Ursulines as first women's teaching order
1536	John Calvin publishes *The Institutes of the Christian Religion*
1540	Papal approval of Society of Jesus (Jesuits)
1542	Pope Paul III establishes the Supreme Sacred Congregation of the Roman and Universal Inquisition
1545–1563	Council of Trent
1553–1558	Reign of Mary Tudor and temporary restoration of Catholicism in England
1555	Peace of Augsburg; official recognition of Lutheranism
1558–1603	Reign of Elizabeth in England
1560–1660	Height of the European witch-hunt
1568–1578	Civil war in the Netherlands
1572	Saint Bartholomew's Day massacre
1588	England defeats Spanish Armada
1598	Edict of Nantes

Selling Indulgences A German single-page pamphlet shows a monk offering an indulgence, with the official seals of the pope attached, as people run to put their money in the box in exchange for his promise of heavenly bliss, symbolized by the dove above his head. Indulgences were sold widely in Germany and became the first Catholic practice that Luther criticized openly. This pamphlet also attacks the sale of indulgences, calling this practice devilish and deceitful. Indulgences were often printed fill-in-the-blank forms. This indulgence (upper left), purchased in 1521, has space for the indulgence seller's name at the top, the buyer's name in the middle, and the date at the bottom. (pamphlet: akg-images; indulgence: Visual Connection Archive)

which merchants carried coins. An indulgence was a piece of parchment (later, paper), signed by the pope or another church official, that substituted a virtuous act from the treasury of merits for penance or time in purgatory. The papacy and bishops had given Crusaders such indulgences, and by the later Middle Ages they were offered for making pilgrimages or other pious activities and also sold outright (see Chapter 9).

Archbishop Albert's indulgence sale, run by a Dominican friar named Johann Tetzel who mounted an advertising blitz, promised that the purchase of indulgences would bring full forgiveness for one's own sins or release from purgatory for a loved one. One of the slogans—"As soon as coin in coffer rings, the soul from purgatory springs"—brought phenomenal success, and people traveled from miles around to buy indulgences.

Luther was severely troubled that many people believed they had no further need for repentance once they had purchased indulgences. In 1517 he wrote a letter to Archbishop Albert on the subject and enclosed in Latin his "Ninety-five Theses on the Power of Indulgences." His argument was that indulgences undermined the seriousness of the sacrament of penance, competed with the preaching of the Gospel, and downplayed the importance of charity in Christian life. After Luther's death, biographies reported that the theses were also nailed to the door of the church at

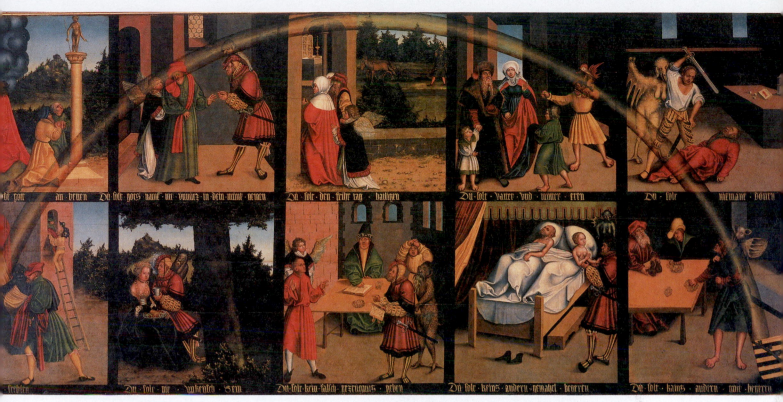

The Ten Commandments Lucas Cranach the Elder, the court painter for the elector of Saxony, painted this giant illustration of the Ten Commandments (more than 5 feet by 11 feet) for the city hall in Wittenberg in 1516, just at the point that Luther was beginning to question Catholic doctrine. Cranach was an early supporter of Luther, and many of his later works depict the reformer and his ideas. Paintings were used by both Protestants and Catholics to teach religious ideas. (Lutherhalle, Wittenberg/The Bridgeman Art Library)

Wittenberg Castle on October 31, 1517. Such an act would have been very strange — they were in Latin and written for those learned in theology, not for ordinary churchgoers — but it has become a standard part of Luther lore.

Whether the theses were posted or not, they were quickly printed, first in Latin and then in German translation. Luther was ordered to come to Rome, although because of the political situation in the empire, he was able instead to engage in formal scholarly debate with a representative of the church, Johann Eck, at Leipzig in 1519. He refused to take back his ideas and continued to develop his calls for reform, publicizing them in a series of pamphlets in which he moved further and further away from Catholic theology. Both popes and church councils could err, he wrote, and secular leaders should reform the church if the pope and clerical hierarchy did not. There was no distinction between clergy and laypeople, and requiring clergy to be celibate was a fruitless attempt to control a natural human drive. Luther clearly understood the power of the new medium of print, so he authorized the publication of his works.

The papacy responded with a letter condemning some of Luther's propositions, ordering that his books be burned, and giving him two months to recant or be excommunicated. Luther retaliated by publicly burning the letter. By 1521, when the excommunication was supposed to become final, Luther's theological issues had become interwoven with public controversies about the church's wealth, power, and basic structure. The papal legate wrote of the growing furor, "All Germany is in revolution. Nine-tenths shout 'Luther' as their war cry; and the other tenth cares nothing about Luther, and cries 'Death to the court of Rome.'"[1] In this highly charged atmosphere, the twenty-one-year-old emperor Charles V held his first diet (assembly of the nobility, clergy, and cities of the Holy Roman Empire) in the German city of Worms and summoned Luther to appear. Luther refused to give in to demands that he take back his ideas. "Unless I am convinced by the evidence of Scripture or by plain reason," he said, "I cannot and will not recant anything, for it is neither safe nor right to go against conscience."[2] His appearance at the Diet of Worms in 1521 created an even broader audience for reform ideas, and throughout central Europe other individuals began to preach and publish against the existing doctrines and practices of the church, drawing on the long tradition of calls for change as well as on Luther.

Martin Luther, *On Christian Liberty*

The idea of liberty has played a powerful role in the history of Western society and culture, but the meaning and understanding of liberty has undergone continual change and interpretation. In the Roman world, where slavery was a basic institution, liberty meant the condition of being a free man. In the Middle Ages, possessing liberty meant having special privileges or rights that other persons or institutions did not have. Citizens in London, for example, were said to possess the "freedom of the city," which allowed them to practice trades and own property without interference.

The idea of liberty also has a religious dimension, and the reformer Martin Luther formulated a classic interpretation of liberty in his treatise On Christian Liberty *(sometimes translated as* On the Freedom of a Christian*), arguably his finest piece. Written in Latin for the pope but translated immediately into German and published widely, it contains the main themes of Luther's theology: the importance of faith, the relationship between Christian faith and good works, the dual nature of human beings, and the fundamental importance of scripture. Luther writes that Christians were freed from sin and death through Christ, not through their own actions.*

" A Christian man is the most free lord of all, and subject to none; a Christian man is the most dutiful servant of all, and subject to everyone. Although these statements appear contradictory, yet, when they are found to agree together, they will do excellently for my purpose. They are both the statements of Paul himself, who says, "Though I be free from all men, yet have I made myself a servant unto all" (I Corinthians 9:19) and "Owe no man anything but to love one another" (Romans 13:8). Now love is by its own nature dutiful and obedient to the beloved object. Thus even Christ, though Lord of all things, was yet made of a woman; made under the law; at once free and a servant; at once in the form of God and in the form of a servant.

Let us examine the subject on a deeper and less simple principle. Man is composed of a twofold nature, a spiritual and a bodily. As regards the spiritual nature, which they name the soul, he is called the spiritual, inward, new man; as regards the bodily nature, which they name the flesh, he is called the fleshly, outward, old man. The Apostle speaks of this: "Though our outward man perish, yet the inward man is renewed day by day" (II Corinthians 4:16). The result of this diversity is that in the Scriptures opposing statements are made concerning the same man, the fact being that in the same man these two men are opposed to one another; the flesh lusting against the spirit, and the spirit against the flesh (Galatians 5:17).

We first approach the subject of the inward man, that we may see by what means a man becomes justified, free, and a true Christian; that is, a spiritual, new, and inward man. It is certain that absolutely none among outward things, under whatever name they may be reckoned, has any influence in producing Christian righteousness or liberty, nor, on the other hand, unrighteousness or slavery. This can be shown by an easy argument. What can it profit to the soul that the body should be in good condition, free, and full of life, that it should eat, drink, and act according to its pleasure, when even the most impious slaves of every kind of vice are prosperous in these matters? Again, what harm can ill health, bondage, hunger, thirst, or any other outward evil, do to the soul, when even the most pious of men, and the freest in the purity of their conscience, are harassed by these things? Neither of these states of things has to do with the liberty or the slavery of the soul.

And so it will profit nothing that the body should be adorned with sacred vestment, or dwell in holy places, or be occupied in sacred offices, or pray, fast, and abstain from certain meats, or do whatever works can be done through the body and in the body. Something widely different will be necessary for the justification and liberty of the soul, since the things I have spoken of can be done by an impious person, and only hypocrites are produced by devotion to these things. On the other hand, it will not at all injure the soul that the body should be clothed in profane raiment, should dwell in profane places, should eat and drink in the ordinary fashion, should not pray aloud, and should leave undone all the things above mentioned, which may be done by hypocrites. . . .

One thing, and one alone, is necessary for life, justification, and Christian liberty; and that is the most Holy Word of God, the Gospel of Christ, as He says, "I am the resurrection and the life; he that believeth in me shall not die eternally" (John 9:25), and also, "If the Son shall make you free, ye shall be free indeed" (John 8:36), and "Man shall not live by bread alone, but by every word that proceedeth out of the mouth of God" (Matthew 4:4).

Let us therefore hold it for certain and firmly established that the soul can do without everything except the Word of God, without which none at all of its wants is provided for. But, having the Word, it is rich and wants for nothing, since that is the Word of life, of truth, of light, of peace, of justification, of salvation, of joy, of liberty, of wisdom, of virtue, of grace, of glory, and of every good thing. . . .

But you will ask, "What is this Word, and by what means is it to be used, since there are so many words of God?" I answer, "The Apostle Paul (Romans 1) explains what it is, namely the Gospel of God, concerning His Son, incarnate, suffering, risen, and glorified through the Spirit, the Sanctifier." To preach Christ is to feed the soul, to justify it, to set it free, and to save it, if it believes the preaching. For faith alone, and the efficacious use of the Word of God, bring salvation. "If thou shalt confess with thy mouth the Lord Jesus, and shalt believe in thine heart that God hath raised Him from the dead, thou shalt be saved" (Romans 9:9); . . . and "The just shall live by faith" (Romans 1:17). . . .

But this faith cannot consist of all with works; that is, if you imagine that you can be justified by those works, whatever they are, along with it. . . . Therefore, when you begin to believe, you learn at the same time that all that is in you is utterly guilty, sinful, and damnable, according to that saying, "All have sinned, and come short of the glory of God" (Romans 3:23). . . . When you have learned this, you will know that Christ is necessary for you, since He has suffered and risen again for you, that, believing on Him, you might by this faith become another man, all your sins being remitted, and you being justified by the merits of another, namely Christ alone. . . .

And since it [faith] alone justifies, it is evident that by no outward work or labour can the inward man be at all justified, made free, and saved; and that no works whatever have any relation to him. . . . Therefore the first care of every Christian ought to be to lay aside all reliance on works, and strengthen his faith alone more and more, and by it grow in knowledge, not of works, but of Christ Jesus, who has suffered and risen again for him, as Peter teaches (I Peter 5). **"**

EVALUATE THE EVIDENCE

1. What did Luther mean by liberty?
2. Why, for Luther, was Scripture basic to Christian life?

Source: *Luther's Primary Works*, ed. H. Wace and C. A. Buchheim (London: Holder and Stoughton, 1896). Reprinted in *The Portable Renaissance Reader*, ed. James Bruce Ross and Mary Martin McLaughlin (New York: Penguin Books, 1981), pp. 721–726.

Protestant Thought

The most important early reformer other than Luther was the Swiss humanist, priest, and admirer of Erasmus, Ulrich Zwingli (ZWIHNG-lee) (1484–1531). Zwingli announced in 1519 that he would not preach from the church's prescribed readings but, relying on Erasmus's New Testament, go right through the New Testament "from A to Z," that is, from Matthew to Revelation. Zwingli was convinced that Christian life rested on the Scriptures, which were the pure words of God and the sole basis of religious truth. He went on to attack indulgences, the Mass, the institution of monasticism, and clerical celibacy. In his gradual reform of the church in Zurich, he had the strong support of the city authorities, who had long resented the privileges of the clergy.

The followers of Luther, Zwingli, and others who called for a break with Rome came to be called Protestants. The word **Protestant** derives from the protest drawn up by a small group of reforming German princes at the Diet of Speyer in 1529. The princes "protested" the decisions of the Catholic majority, and the word gradually became a general term applied to all non-Catholic western European Christians.

> **Protestant** The name originally given to followers of Luther, which came to mean all non-Catholic Western Christian groups.

Luther, Zwingli, and other early Protestants agreed on many things. First, how is a person to be saved? Traditional Catholic teaching held that salvation is achieved by both faith and good works. Protestants held that salvation comes by faith alone, irrespective of good works or the sacraments. God, not people, initiates salvation. (See "Primary Source 13.1: Martin Luther, *On Christian Liberty*," at left.) Second, where does religious authority reside? Christian doctrine had long maintained that authority rests both in the Bible and in the traditional teaching of the church. For Protestants, authority rested in the Bible alone. For a doctrine or issue to be valid, it had to have a scriptural basis. Because of this, most Protestants rejected Catholic teachings about the sacraments—the rituals that the church had defined as imparting God's benefits on the believer (see Chapter 10)—holding that only baptism and the Eucharist have scriptural support.

Third, what is the church? Protestants held that the church is a spiritual priesthood of all believers, an invisible fellowship not fixed in any place or person, which differed markedly from the Roman Catholic practice of a hierarchical clerical institution headed by the pope in Rome. Fourth, what is the highest form of Christian life? The medieval church had stressed the superiority of the monastic and religious life over the secular. Protestants disagreed and argued that every person should serve God in his or her individual calling.

In the Reformation era, controversy raged over the purpose and function of art. Protestants and Catholics disagreed, and Protestant groups disagreed with one another. Some Protestant leaders, including Ulrich Zwingli and John Calvin, stressed that "the Word of God" should be the only instrument used in the work of evangelization. Swiss Protestants and Calvinists in many parts of Europe stripped statues, images, and decoration out of many formerly Catholic churches or redesigned them with a stark, bare simplicity. Martin Luther, by contrast, believed that painting and sculpture had value in spreading the Gospel message because "children and simple folk are more apt to retain the divine stories when taught by pictures and parables than merely by words or instruction." He collaborated with artists such as Lucas Cranach the Elder (1472–1553), who conveyed Protestant ideas in woodcuts and paintings. (See Cranach's *The Ten Commandments*, page 395.)

Both Protestants and Catholics used pictures for propaganda purposes. In *The True and False Churches*, Lucas Cranach the Younger (1515–1586) shows Luther standing in a pulpit, preaching the word of God from an open Bible. At the right, a flaming open mouth symbolizing the jaws of Hell engulfs the pope, cardinals, and friars, one kind of "false church." At the left, Cranach shows a crucified Christ emerging out of the "lamb of God" on the altar as people are receiving communion. This image of the "true church" represents the Lutheran understanding of the Lord's Supper, in which Christ is really present in the bread and wine, in contrast to the view of other Protestants such as Zwingli, who saw the ceremony as a symbol or memorial.

The Catholic Church officially addressed the subject of art at the Council of Trent in 1563. The church declared that honor and veneration should be given to likenesses of Christ, the Virgin Mary, and the saints; that images should

Lucas Cranach the Younger, *The True and False Churches.* (© akg/Newscom)

Jesuit Priest Distributing Holy Pictures. (From Pierre Chenu, *The Reformation* [New York: St. Martin's Press, 1986])

remind people of the saints' virtues in order to encourage imitation; and that pictorial art should promote piety and the love of God. Consider the anonymous painting *Jesuit Priest Distributing Holy Pictures.* Parish priests and Jesuits often distributed such pictures to laypeople, including children, to help educate them in matters of doctrine. Church leaders also sponsored the building of lavishly decorated churches that appealed to the senses and proclaimed the power of the reformed Catholic Church. (See Church of the Gesù, page 417.)

QUESTIONS FOR ANALYSIS

1. What does Cranach's woodcut suggest about Protestants who had a different interpretation than Luther's about the Lord's Supper?
2. Cranach's woodcut could be easily reproduced through the technology of the printing press. How would this have enhanced its impact?
3. In what way does the artist of the Jesuit image suggest that people are eager for the Catholic message? How might this painting itself have aroused piety?

Protestants did not agree on everything, and one important area of dispute was the ritual of the Eucharist (also called communion, the Lord's Supper, and, in Catholicism, the Mass). Catholicism holds the dogma of transubstantiation: by the consecrating words of the priest during the Mass, the bread and wine become the actual body and blood of Christ. In opposition, Luther believed that Christ is really present in the consecrated bread and wine, but this is the result of God's mystery, not the actions of a priest. Zwingli understood the Eucharist as a memorial in which Christ was present in spirit among the faithful, but not in the bread and wine. The Colloquy of Marburg, summoned in 1529 to unite Protestants, failed to resolve these differences, though Protestants reached agreement on almost everything else.

The Appeal of Protestant Ideas

Pulpits and printing presses spread the Protestant message all over Germany, and by the middle of the sixteenth century people of all social classes had rejected Catholic teachings and had become Protestant. What was the immense appeal of Luther's religious ideas and those of other Protestants?

Educated people and many humanists were much attracted by Luther's teachings. He advocated a simpler personal religion based on faith, a return to the spirit of the early church, the centrality of the Scriptures in the liturgy and in Christian life, and the abolition of elaborate ceremonies—precisely the reforms the Christian humanists had been calling for. The Protestant insistence that everyone should read and reflect on the Scriptures attracted literate and thoughtful city residents. This included many priests and monks who left the Catholic Church to become clergy in the new Protestant churches. In addition, townspeople who envied the church's wealth and resented paying for it were attracted by the notion that the clergy should also pay taxes and should not have special legal privileges. After Zurich became Protestant, the city council taxed the clergy and placed them under the jurisdiction of civil courts.

Scholars in many disciplines have attributed Luther's fame and success to the invention of the printing press, which rapidly reproduced and made known his ideas. Many printed works included woodcuts and other illustrations, so that even those who could not read could grasp the main ideas. (See "Living in the Past: Uses of Art in the Reformation," at left.) Equally important was Luther's incredible skill with language, as seen in his two catechisms (compendiums of basic religious knowledge) and in hymns that he wrote for congregations to sing. Luther's linguistic skill, together with his translation of the New Testament into German in 1523, led to the acceptance of his dialect of

German as the standard written version of the German language.

Both Luther and Zwingli recognized that for reforms to be permanent, political authorities as well as concerned individuals and religious leaders would have to accept them. Zwingli worked closely with the city council of Zurich, and city councils themselves took the lead in other cities and towns of Switzerland and south Germany. They appointed pastors who they knew had accepted Protestant ideas, required them to swear an oath of loyalty to the council, and oversaw their preaching and teaching.

Luther lived in a territory ruled by a noble—the elector of Saxony—and he also worked closely with political authorities, viewing them as fully justified in asserting control over the church in their territories. Indeed, he demanded that German rulers reform the papacy and its institutions, and he instructed all Christians to obey their secular rulers, whom he saw as divinely ordained to maintain order. Individuals may have been convinced of the truth of Protestant teachings by hearing sermons, listening to hymns, or reading pamphlets, but a territory became Protestant when its ruler, whether a noble or a city council, brought in a reformer or two to re-educate the territory's clergy, sponsored public sermons, and confiscated church property. This happened in many of the states of the Holy Roman Empire during the 1520s.

The Radical Reformation and the German Peasants' War

While Luther and Zwingli worked with political authorities, some individuals and groups rejected the idea that church and state needed to be united. Beginning in the 1520s groups in Switzerland, Germany, and the Netherlands sought instead to create a voluntary community of believers separate from the state, as they understood it to have existed in New Testament times. In terms of theology and spiritual practices, these individuals and groups varied widely, though they are generally termed "radicals" for their insistence on a more extensive break with prevailing ideas. Some adopted the baptism of adult believers, for which they were called by their enemies "Anabaptists," which means "rebaptizers." (Early Christians had practiced adult baptism, but infant baptism became the norm, which meant that adults undergoing baptism were repeating the ritual.) Some groups attempted communal ownership of property, living very simply and rejecting anything they thought unbiblical. Some reacted harshly to members who deviated, but others argued for complete religious toleration and individualism.

Some religious radicals thought the end of the world was coming soon, and in the 1530s a group took over the German city of Münster, which they predicted would be the site of a New Jerusalem that would survive God's final judgment. They called for communal ownership of property and expelled those who refused to be rebaptized. Combined armies of Catholics and Protestants besieged the city and executed its leaders. The insurrection at Münster and the radicals' unwillingness to accept a state church marked them as societal outcasts and invited hatred and persecution, for both Protestant and Catholic authorities saw a state church as key to maintaining order. Anabaptists and other radicals were banished or cruelly executed by burning, beating, or drowning. (See "Individuals in Society: Anna Jansz of Rotterdam," at right.) Their community spirit and heroism in the face of martyrdom, however, contributed to the survival of radical ideas. Later, the Quakers, with their pacifism; the Baptists, with their emphasis on inner spiritual light; the Congregationalists, with their democratic church organization; and in 1787 the authors of the U.S. Constitution, with their opposition to the "establishment of religion" (state churches), would all trace their origins, in part, to the radicals of the sixteenth century.

Radical reformers sometimes called for social as well as religious change, a message that resonated with the increasingly struggling German peasantry. In the early sixteenth century the economic condition of the peasantry varied from place to place but was generally worse than it had been in the fifteenth century and was deteriorating. Crop failures in 1523 and 1524 aggravated an explosive situation. Nobles had aggrieved peasants by seizing village common lands, by imposing new rents and requiring additional services, and by taking the peasants' best horses or cows whenever a head of household died. The peasants made demands that they believed conformed to the Scriptures, and they cited radical thinkers as well as Luther as proof that they did.

Luther wanted to prevent rebellion. Initially he sided with the peasants, blasting the lords for robbing their subjects. But when rebellion broke out, peasants who expected Luther's support were soon disillusioned. Freedom for Luther meant independence from the authority of the Roman Church; it did not mean opposition to legally established secular powers. As for biblical support for the peasants' demands, he maintained that Scripture had nothing to do with earthly justice or material gain, a position that Zwingli supported. Firmly convinced that rebellion would hasten the end of civilized society, Luther wrote the tract *Against the Murderous, Thieving Hordes of the Peasants:* "Let everyone who can smite, slay, and stab [the peasants], secretly and openly, remembering that nothing can be more poisonous, hurtful or devilish than a rebel."[3] The nobility ferociously crushed the revolt. Historians estimate that more than seventy-five thousand peasants were killed in 1525.

Anna Jansz (1509–1539) was born into a well-to-do family in the small city of Briel in the Netherlands. She married, and when she was in her early twenties she and her husband came to accept Anabaptism after listening to a traveling preacher. They were baptized in 1534 and became part of a group who believed that God would soon come to bring judgment on the wicked and deliver his true followers. Jansz wrote a hymn conveying these apocalyptic beliefs and foretelling vengeance on those who persecuted Anabaptists: "I hear the Trumpet sounding, From far off I hear her blast! . . . O murderous seed, what will you do? Offspring of Cain, you put to death The lambs of the Lord, without just cause— It will be doubly repaid to you! Death now comes riding on horseback, We have seen your fate! The sword is passing over the land, With which you will be killed and slain, And you will not escape from Hell!"

An etching of Anna Jansz on the way to her execution, from a 1685 Anabaptist martyrology. (Used by permission of the Mennonite Historical Library, Goshen College, Indiana)

Jansz and her husband traveled to England, where she had a child, but in November 1538 she and her infant son, Isaiah, returned to the Netherlands, along with another woman. As the story was later told, the two women were recognized as Anabaptists by another traveler because of songs they were singing, perhaps her "Trumpet Song" among them. They were arrested and interrogated in the city of Rotterdam, and sentenced to death by drowning. The day she was executed— January 24, 1539— Anna Jansz wrote a long testament to her son, providing him with spiritual advice: "My son, hear the instruction of your mother, and open your ears to hear the words of my mouth. Watch, today I am travelling the path of the Prophets, Apostles, and Martyrs, and drink from the cup from which they have all tasted. . . . But if you hear of the existence of a poor, lowly, cast-out little company, that has been despised and rejected by the World, go join it. . . . Honor the Lord through the works of your hands. Let the light of Scripture shine in you. Love your Neighbor; with an effusive, passionate heart deal your bread to the hungry."

Anabaptists later compiled accounts of trials and executions, along with letters and other records, into martyrologies designed to inspire deeper faith. One of the most widely read of these describes Jansz on her way to the execution. She offered a certain amount of money to anyone who would care for her son; a poor baker with six children agreed, and she passed the child to him. The martyrology reports that the baker later became quite wealthy, and that her son, Isaiah, became mayor of the city of Rotterdam. As such, he would have easily been able to read the court records of his mother's trial.

Anna Jansz was one of thousands of people executed for their religious beliefs in sixteenth-century Europe. A few of these were high-profile individuals such as Thomas More, the Catholic former chancellor of England executed by King Henry VIII, but most were quite ordinary people. Many were women. Women's and men's experiences of martyrdom were similar in many ways, but women also confronted additional challenges. Some were pregnant while in prison—execution was delayed until the baby was born—or, like Jansz, had infants with them. They faced procedures of questioning, torture, and execution that brought dishonor as well as pain. Eventually many Anabaptists, as well as others whose religion put them in opposition to their rulers, migrated to parts of Europe that were more tolerant. By the seventeenth century the Netherlands had become one of the most tolerant places in Europe, and Rotterdam was no longer the site of executions for religious reasons.

QUESTIONS FOR ANALYSIS

1. How did religion, gender, and social class all shape Jansz's experiences and the writings that she left behind?
2. Why might Jansz's hymn and her Anabaptist beliefs have seemed threatening to those who did not share her beliefs?

Source: Quotations are from *Elisabeth's Manly Courage: Testimonials and Songs of Martyred Anabaptist Women in the Low Countries*, ed. and trans. Hermina Joldersma and Louis Peter Grijp (Milwaukee: Marquette University Press, 2001).

ONLINE DOCUMENT ASSIGNMENT

What might have led Jansz and thousands like her to die for their religious convictions? Go to the Integrated Media and learn more about Anna Jansz and other Anabaptist martyrs by analyzing images and hymns, and then complete a writing assignment based on the evidence and details from this chapter.

The German Peasants' War of 1525 greatly strengthened the authority of lay rulers. Not surprisingly, the Reformation lost much of its popular appeal after 1525, though peasants and urban rebels sometimes found a place for their social and religious ideas in radical groups. Peasants' economic conditions did moderately improve, however. For example, in many parts of Germany, enclosed fields, meadows, and forests were returned to common use.

Marriage, Sexuality, and the Role of Women

Luther and Zwingli both believed that a priest's or nun's vows of celibacy went against human nature and God's commandments, and that marriage brought spiritual advantages and so was the ideal state for nearly all human beings. Luther married a former nun, Katharina von Bora (1499–1532), and Zwingli married a Zurich widow, Anna Reinhart (1491–1538). Both women quickly had several children. Most other Protestant reformers also married, and their wives had to create a new and respectable role for themselves—pastor's wife—to overcome being viewed as simply a new type of priest's concubine. They were living demonstrations of their husband's convictions about the superiority of marriage to celibacy, and they were expected to be models of wifely obedience and Christian charity.

Though they denied that marriage was a sacrament, Protestant reformers stressed that it had been ordained by God when he presented Eve to Adam, served as a "remedy" for the unavoidable sin of lust, provided a site for the pious rearing of the next generation of God-fearing Christians, and offered husbands and wives companionship and consolation. (See "Primary Source 13.2: Domestic Scene," at right.) A proper marriage was one that reflected both the spiritual equality of men and women and the proper social hierarchy of husbandly authority and wifely obedience.

Protestants did not break with medieval scholastic theologians in their idea that women were to be sub-

Martin Luther and Katharina von Bora   Lucas Cranach the Elder painted this double marriage portrait to celebrate Luther's wedding in 1525 to Katharina von Bora, a former nun. The artist was one of the witnesses at the wedding and, in fact, had presented Luther's marriage proposal to Katharina. Using a go-between for proposals was very common, as was having a double wedding portrait painted. This particular couple quickly became a model of the ideal marriage, and many churches wanted their portraits. More than sixty similar paintings, with slight variations, were produced by Cranach's workshop and hung in churches and wealthy homes. (Galleria degli Uffizi, Florence, Italy/Alinari/The Bridgeman Art Library)

Domestic Scene

The Protestant notion that the best form of Christian life was marriage and a family helps explain the appeal of Protestantism to middle-class urban men and women, such as those shown in this domestic scene. The engraving, titled "Concordia" (Harmony), includes the biblical inscription of what Jesus called the greatest commandment — "You shall love the Lord your God with all your heart and all your soul and your neighbor as yourself" (Deuteronomy 6; Matthew 22) — on tablets at the back. The large covered bed at the back was both a standard piece of furniture in urban homes and a symbol of proper marital sexual relations.

(Mary Evans Picture Library/The Image Works)

EVALUATE THE EVIDENCE

1. What are the different family members doing? What elements of this image suggest that this is a pious, Christian family?
2. How do the various family roles shown here support the Protestant ideal of marriage and family?

ject to men. Women were advised to be cheerful rather than grudging in their obedience, for in doing so they demonstrated their willingness to follow God's plan. Men were urged to treat their wives kindly and considerately, but also to enforce their authority, through physical coercion if necessary. European marriage manuals used the metaphor of breaking a horse for teaching a wife obedience, though laws did set limits on the husband's power to do so.

Protestants saw marriage as a contract in which each partner promised the other support, companionship, and the sharing of mutual goods. Because, in Protestant eyes, marriage was created by God as a remedy for human weakness, marriages in which spouses did not comfort or support one another physically, materially, or emotionally endangered their own souls and the surrounding community. The only solution might be divorce and remarriage, which most Protestants came to allow. Protestant allowance of divorce differed markedly from Catholic doctrine, which viewed marriage as a sacramental union that, if validly entered into, could not be dissolved (Catholic canon law allowed only separation with no remarriage). Although permitting divorce was a dramatic legal change, it did not have a dramatic impact on newly Protestant areas. Because marriage was the cornerstone of society socially and economically, divorce was a desperate last resort. In many Protestant jurisdictions the annual divorce rate hovered around 0.02 to 0.06 per thousand people. (By contrast, in 2010 the U.S. divorce rate was 3.6 per thousand people.)

As Protestants believed marriage was the only proper remedy for lust, they uniformly condemned prostitution. The licensed brothels that were a common feature of late medieval urban life (see Chapter 11) were closed in Protestant cities, and harsh punishments were set for prostitution. Many Catholic cities soon closed their brothels as well, although Italian cities favored stricter regulations rather than closure. Selling sex was couched in moral rather than economic terms, as simply one type of "whoredom," a term that also included premarital sex, adultery, and other unacceptable sexual activities. "Whore" was also a term that reformers used for their theological opponents; Protestants compared the pope to the biblical whore of Babylon, a symbol of the end of the world, while Catholics called Luther's wife a whore because she had first been married to Christ as a nun before her marriage to Luther. Closing brothels did not end the exchange of sex for money, of course, but simply reshaped it. Smaller illegal brothels were established, or women selling sex moved to areas right outside city walls.

The Protestant Reformation clearly had a positive impact on marriage, but its impact on women was more mixed. Many nuns were in convents not out of a strong sense of religious calling, but because their parents placed them there. Convents nevertheless provided women of the upper classes with an opportunity to use their literary, artistic, medical, or administrative talents if they could not or would not marry. The Reformation generally brought the closing of monasteries and convents, and marriage became virtually the only occupation for upper-class Protestant women. Women in some convents recognized this and fought the Reformation, or argued that they could still be pious Protestants within convent walls. Most nuns left, however, and we do not know what happened to them. The Protestant emphasis on marriage made unmarried women (and men) suspect, for they did not belong to the type of household regarded as the cornerstone of a proper, godly society.

A few women took Luther's idea about the priesthood of all believers to heart and wrote religious works. Argula von Grumbach, a German noblewoman, supported Protestant ideas in print, asserting, "I am not unfamiliar with Paul's words that women should be silent in church but when I see that no man will or can speak, I am driven by the word of God when he said, he who confesses me on earth, him will I confess, and he who denies me, him will I deny."[4] No sixteenth-century Protestants allowed women to be members of the clergy, however, though monarchs such as Elizabeth I of England and female territorial rulers of the states of the Holy Roman Empire did determine religious policies just as male rulers did.

The Reformation and German Politics

How did the political situation in Germany shape the course of the Reformation?

Although criticism of the church was widespread in Europe in the early sixteenth century, reform movements could be more easily squelched by the strong central governments that had evolved in Spain and France. England, too, had a strong monarchy, but the king broke from the Catholic Church for other reasons (see page 407). The Holy Roman Empire, in contrast, included hundreds of largely independent states. Against this background of decentralization and strong local power, Martin Luther had launched a movement to reform the church. Two years after he published the "Ninety-five Theses," the electors of the Holy Roman Empire chose as emperor a nineteen-year-old Habsburg prince who ruled as Charles V (r. 1519–1556). The course of the Reformation was shaped by this election and by the political relationships surrounding it.

The Rise of the Habsburg Dynasty

War and diplomacy were important ways that states increased their power in sixteenth-century Europe, but so was marriage. Royal and noble sons and daughters were important tools of state policy. The benefits of an advantageous marriage stretched across generations, a process that can be seen most dramatically with the Habsburgs. The Holy Roman emperor Frederick III, a Habsburg who was the ruler of most of Austria, acquired only a small amount of territory—but a great deal of money—with his marriage to Princess Eleonore of Portugal in 1452. He arranged for his son Maximilian to marry Europe's most prominent heiress, Mary of Burgundy, in 1477; she inherited the Netherlands, Luxembourg, and the County of Burgundy in what is now eastern France. Through this union with the rich and powerful duchy of Burgundy, the Austrian house of Habsburg, already the strongest ruling family in the empire, became an international power. The marriage of Maximilian and Mary angered the French, however, who considered Burgundy French territory, and inaugurated centuries of conflict between the Austrian house of Habsburg and the kings of France.

Maximilian learned the lesson of marital politics well, marrying his son and daughter to the children of Ferdinand and Isabella, the rulers of Spain, much of southern Italy, and eventually the Spanish New World empire. His grandson Charles V (1500–1558) fell heir to a vast and incredibly diverse collection of states and peoples, each governed in a different manner and held together only by the person of the emperor (Map 13.1). Charles's Italian adviser, the grand chancellor Gattinara, told the young ruler, "God has set

you on the path toward world monarchy." Charles, a Catholic, not only believed this but also was convinced that it was his duty to maintain the political and religious unity of Western Christendom.

Religious Wars in Switzerland and Germany

In the sixteenth century the practice of religion remained a public matter. The ruler determined the official form of religious practice in his (or occasionally her) jurisdiction. Almost everyone believed that the presence of a faith different from that of the majority represented a political threat to the security of the state, and few believed in religious liberty.

Luther's ideas appealed to German rulers for a variety of reasons. Though Germany was not a nation,

Map 13.1 The Global Empire of Charles V, ca. 1556 Charles V exercised theoretical jurisdiction over more European territory than anyone since Charlemagne. He also claimed authority over large parts of North and South America (see Map 14.2, page 436), though actual Spanish control was weak in much of the area.

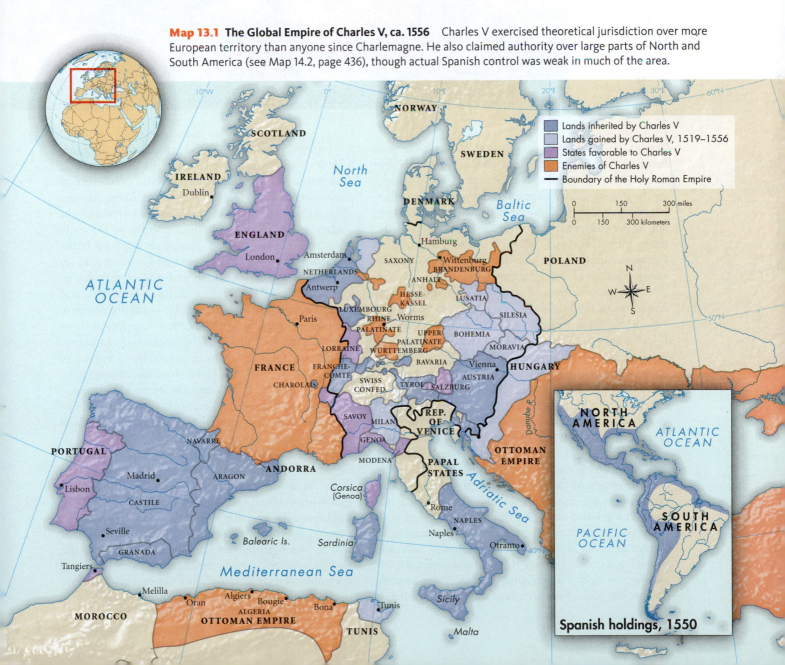

Fresco of Pope Clement VII and Emperor Charles V In this double portrait, artist Giorgio Vasari uses matching hand gestures to indicate agreement between the pope and the emperor, though the pope's red hat and cape make him the dominant figure. Charles V remained loyal to Catholicism, though the political situation and religious wars in Germany eventually required him to compromise with Protestants. (Palazzo Vecchio, Florence/Scala/Art Resource, NY)

people did have an understanding of being German because of their language and traditions. Luther frequently used the phrase "we Germans" in his attacks on the papacy. Luther's appeal to national feeling influenced many rulers otherwise confused by or indifferent to the complexities of the religious matters of the time. Some German rulers were sincerely attracted to Lutheran ideas, but material considerations swayed many others to embrace the new faith. The rejection of Roman Catholicism and adoption of Protestantism would mean the legal confiscation of lush farmlands, rich monasteries, and wealthy shrines. Thus many political authorities in the empire became Protestant in part to extend their financial and political power and to enhance their independence from the emperor.

Charles V was a vigorous defender of Catholicism, so it is not surprising that the Reformation led to religious wars. The first battleground was Switzerland, which was officially part of the Holy Roman Empire, though it was really a loose confederation of thirteen largely autonomous territories called cantons. Some cantons remained Catholic, and some became Protestant, and in the late 1520s the two sides went to war. Zwingli was killed on the battlefield in 1531, and both sides quickly decided that a treaty was preferable to further fighting. The treaty basically allowed each canton to determine its own religion and ordered each side to give up its foreign alliances, a policy of neutrality that has been characteristic of modern Switzerland.

Trying to halt the spread of religious division, Charles V called an Imperial Diet in 1530, to meet at Augsburg. The Lutherans developed a statement of faith, later called the Augsburg Confession, and the Protestant princes presented this to the emperor. (The Augsburg Confession remains an authoritative statement of belief for many Lutheran churches.) Charles refused to accept it and ordered all Protestants to return to the Catholic Church and give up any confiscated church property. This demand backfired, and Protestant territories in the empire—mostly northern German principalities and southern German cities—formed a military alliance. The emperor could not respond militarily, as he was in the midst of a series of wars with the French: the Habsburg-Valois wars (1521–1559), fought in Italy along the eastern and southern borders of France and eventually in Germany. The Ottoman Turks had also taken much of Hungary and in 1529 were besieging Vienna.

The 1530s and early 1540s saw complicated political maneuvering among many of the powers of Europe. Various attempts were made to heal the religious split with a church council, but stubbornness on both sides made it increasingly clear that this would not be possible and that war was inevitable. Charles V realized that he was fighting not only for religious unity, but also for a more unified state, against territorial rulers who wanted to maintain their independence. He was thus defending both church and empire.

Fighting began in 1546, and initially the emperor was very successful. This success alarmed both France and the pope, however, who did not want Charles to become even more powerful. The pope withdrew papal troops, and the Catholic king of France sent money and troops to the Lutheran princes. Finally, in 1555 Charles agreed to the Peace of Augsburg, which, "in order to bring peace into the holy empire," officially recognized Lutheranism. The political authority in each territory was permitted to decide whether the territory would be Catholic or Lutheran and was ordered to let other territories "enjoy their religious beliefs, liturgy, and ceremonies as well as their estates in peace." Most of northern and central Germany became Lutheran, while the south remained Roman Catholic. There was no freedom of religion within the territories, however. Princes or town councils established state churches to which all subjects of the area had to belong. Dissidents had to convert or leave, although the treaty did order that "they shall neither be hindered in the sale of their estates after due payment of the local taxes nor injured in their honor."[5] Religious refugees became a common feature on the roads of the empire, though rulers did not always let their subjects leave as easily as the treaty stipulated.

The Peace of Augsburg ended religious war in Germany for many decades. His hope of uniting his empire under a single church dashed, Charles V abdicated in 1556 and moved to a monastery, transferring power over his holdings in Spain and the Netherlands to his son Philip and his imperial power to his brother Ferdinand.

The Spread of Protestant Ideas

How did Protestant ideas and institutions spread beyond German-speaking lands?

States within the Holy Roman Empire were the earliest territories to accept the Protestant Reformation, but by the later 1520s and 1530s religious change came to Denmark-Norway, Sweden, England, France, and eastern Europe. In most of these areas, a second generation of reformers built on Lutheran and Zwinglian ideas to develop their own theology and plans for institutional change. The most important of the second-generation reformers was John Calvin, whose ideas would profoundly influence the social thought and attitudes of European peoples and their descendants all over the world.

Scandinavia

The first area outside the empire to officially accept the Reformation was the kingdom of Denmark-Norway under King Christian III (r. 1536–1559). Danish scholars studied at the University of Wittenberg, and Lutheran ideas spread into Denmark very quickly. In the 1530s the king officially broke with the Catholic Church, and most clergy followed. The process went smoothly in Denmark, but in northern Norway and Iceland (which Christian also ruled) there were violent reactions, and Lutheranism was only gradually imposed on a largely unwilling populace.

In Sweden, Gustavus Vasa (r. 1523–1560), who came to the throne during a civil war with Denmark, also took over control of church personnel and income. Protestant ideas spread, though the Swedish Church did not officially accept Lutheran theology until later in the century.

Henry VIII and the Reformation in England

As on the continent, the Reformation in England had economic and political as well as religious causes. The impetus for England's break with Rome was the desire of King Henry VIII (r. 1509–1547) for a new wife, though his own motives also included political, social, and economic elements.

Henry VIII was married to Catherine of Aragon, the daughter of Ferdinand and Isabella and widow of Henry's older brother, Arthur. Marriage to a brother's widow went against canon law, and Henry had been required to obtain a special papal dispensation to marry Catherine. The marriage had produced only one living heir, a daughter, Mary. By 1527 Henry decided that God was showing his displeasure with the marriage by denying him a son, and he appealed to the pope to have the marriage annulled. He was also in love with a court lady in waiting, Anne Boleyn, and assumed that she would give him the son he wanted. Normally an annulment would not have been a problem, but the troops of Emperor Charles V were in Rome at that point, and Pope Clement VII was essentially their prisoner. Charles V was the nephew of Catherine of Aragon and thus was vigorously opposed to an annulment, which would have declared his aunt a fornicator and his cousin Mary a bastard. The pope stalled.

With Rome thwarting his matrimonial plans, Henry decided to remove the English Church from papal jurisdiction. In a series of measures during the 1530s, Henry used Parliament to end the authority of the pope and make himself the supreme head of the church in England. Some opposed the king and were beheaded, among them Thomas More, the king's chan-

Allegory of the Tudor Dynasty   The unknown creator of this work intended to glorify the virtues of the Protestant succession; the painting has no historical reality. Henry VIII (seated) hands the sword of justice to his Protestant son Edward VI. The Catholic Queen Mary and her husband Philip of Spain (left) are followed by Mars, god of war, signifying violence and civil disorder. At right the figures of Peace and Plenty accompany the Protestant Elizabeth I, symbolizing England's happy fate under her rule. (Yale Center for British Art, Paul Mellon Collection/The Bridgeman Art Library)

cellor and author of *Utopia* (see Chapter 12). When Anne Boleyn failed twice to produce a male child, Henry VIII charged her with adulterous incest and in 1536 had her beheaded. His third wife, Jane Seymour, gave Henry the desired son, Edward, but she died in childbirth. Henry went on to three more wives.

Theologically, Henry was conservative, and the English Church retained such traditional Catholic practices and doctrines as confession, clerical celibacy, and transubstantiation. Under the influence of his chief minister, Thomas Cromwell, and the man he had appointed archbishop of Canterbury, Thomas Cranmer, he did agree to place an English Bible in every church. He also decided to dissolve the English monasteries, primarily because he wanted their wealth. Working through Parliament, between 1535 and 1539 the king ended nine hundred years of English monastic life, dispersing the monks and nuns and confiscating their lands. Their proceeds enriched the royal treasury, and hundreds of properties were sold to the middle and

upper classes, the very groups represented in Parliament. The dissolution of the monasteries did not achieve a more equitable distribution of land and wealth; rather, the redistribution of land strengthened the upper classes and tied them to both the Tudor dynasty and the new Protestant Church.

The nationalization of the church and the dissolution of the monasteries led to important changes in government administration. Vast tracts of formerly monastic land came temporarily under the Crown's jurisdiction, and new bureaucratic machinery had to be developed to manage those properties. Cromwell reformed and centralized the king's household, the council, the secretariats, and the Exchequer. New departments of state were set up. Surplus funds from all departments went into a liquid fund to be applied to areas where there were deficits. This balancing resulted in greater efficiency and economy, and Henry VIII's reign saw the growth of the modern centralized bureaucratic state.

Did the religious changes under Henry VIII have broad popular support? Historians disagree about this. Some English people had been dissatisfied with the existing Christian Church before Henry's measures, and Protestant literature circulated. Traditional Catholicism exerted an enormously strong and vigorous hold over the imagination and loyalty of the people, however. Most clergy and officials accepted Henry's moves, but all did not quietly acquiesce. In 1536 popular opposition in the north to the religious changes led to the Pilgrimage of Grace, a massive rebellion that proved the largest in English history. The "pilgrims" accepted a truce, but their leaders were arrested, tried, and executed. Recent scholarship points out that people rarely "converted" from Catholicism to Protestantism overnight. People responded to an action of the Crown that was played out in their own neighborhood—the closing of a monastery, the ending of Masses for the dead—with a combination of resistance, acceptance, and collaboration. Some enthusiastically changed to Protestant forms of prayer, for example, while others recited Protestant prayers in church while keeping pictures of the Catholic saints at home.

Loyalty to the Catholic Church was particularly strong in Ireland. Ireland had been claimed by English kings since the twelfth century, but in reality the English had firm control of only the area around Dublin, known as the Pale. In 1536, on orders from London, the Irish parliament, which represented only the English landlords and the people of the Pale, approved the English laws severing the church from Rome. The Church of Ireland was established on the English pattern, and the (English) ruling class adopted the new reformed faith. Most of the Irish people remained Roman Catholic, thus adding religious antagonism to the ethnic hostility that had been a feature of English policy toward Ireland for centuries (see Chapter 11). Irish armed opposition to the Reformation led to harsh repression by the English. Catholic property was confiscated and sold, and the profits were shipped to England. The Roman Church was essentially driven underground, and the Catholic clergy acted as national as well as religious leaders.

Upholding Protestantism in England

In the short reign of Henry's sickly son, Edward VI (r. 1547–1553), Protestant ideas exerted a significant influence on the religious life of the country. Archbishop Thomas Cranmer simplified the liturgy, invited Protestant theologians to England, and prepared the first *Book of Common Prayer* (1549), which was later approved by Parliament. In stately and dignified English, the *Book of Common Prayer* included the order for all services and prayers of the Church of England.

The equally brief reign of Mary Tudor (r. 1553–1558) witnessed a sharp move back to Catholicism. The devoutly Catholic daughter of Catherine of Aragon, Mary rescinded the Reformation legislation of her father's reign and restored Roman Catholicism. Mary's marriage to her cousin Philip II of Spain (r. 1556–1598), son of the emperor Charles V, proved highly unpopular in England, and her execution of several hundred Protestants further alienated her subjects. During her reign, about a thousand Protestants fled to the continent. Mary's death raised to the throne her half-sister Elizabeth, Henry's daughter with Anne Boleyn, who had been raised a Protestant. Elizabeth's reign from 1558 to 1603 inaugurated the beginnings of religious stability.

At the start of Elizabeth's reign, sharp differences existed in England. On the one hand, Catholics wanted a Roman Catholic ruler. On the other hand, a vocal number of returning exiles wanted all Catholic elements in the Church of England eliminated. The latter, because they wanted to "purify" the church, were called "Puritans."

Shrewdly, Elizabeth chose a middle course between Catholic and Puritan extremes. Working through Parliament, she ordered church and government officials to swear that she was supreme in matters of religion as well as politics, required her subjects to attend services in the Church of England or risk a fine, and called for frequent preaching of Protestant ideas. (See "Primary Source 13.3: Elizabethan Injunctions About Religion," page 411.) She did not interfere with people's privately held beliefs, however. As she put it, she did not "want to make windows into men's souls." The Anglican Church, as the Church of England was called, moved in a moderately Protestant direction. Services were conducted in English, monasteries were not re-established, and clergymen were allowed to marry. But the church remained hierarchical, with archbishops and bishops, and services continued to be elaborate, with the clergy in distinctive robes, in contrast to the simpler services favored by many continental Protestants.

Toward the end of the sixteenth century Elizabeth's reign was threatened by European powers attempting to re-establish Catholicism. Philip II of Spain had hoped that his marriage to Mary Tudor would reunite England with Catholic Europe, but Mary's death ended those plans. Another Mary—Mary, Queen of Scots (r. 1560–1567)—provided a new opportunity. Mary was Elizabeth's cousin, but she was Catholic. Mary was next in line to the English throne, and Elizabeth imprisoned her because she worried—quite rightly—that Mary would become the center of Catholic plots to overthrow her. In 1587 Mary became implicated in a plot to assassinate Elizabeth, a conspiracy that had Philip II's full backing. When the English executed Mary, the Catholic pope urged Philip to retaliate.

Philip prepared a vast fleet to sail from Lisbon to Flanders, where a large army of Spanish troops was stationed because of religious wars in the Netherlands (see page 419). The Spanish ships were to escort barges carrying some of the troops across the English Channel to attack England. On May 9, 1588, *la felicissima armada*—"the most fortunate fleet," as it was ironically called in official documents—composed of more than 130 vessels, sailed from Lisbon harbor. The **Spanish Armada** met an English fleet in the Channel before it reached Flanders. The English ships were smaller, faster, and more maneuverable, and many of them had greater firing power than their Spanish counterparts. A combination of storms and squalls, spoiled food and rank water, inadequate Spanish ammunition, and, to a lesser extent, English fire ships that caused the Spanish to scatter gave England the victory. On the journey home many Spanish ships went down in the rough seas around Ireland; perhaps sixty-five ships managed to reach home ports.

The Route of the Spanish Armada, 1588

The battle in the English Channel has frequently been described as one of the decisive battles in world history. In fact, it had mixed consequences. Spain soon rebuilt its navy, and after 1588 the quality of the Spanish fleet improved. The war between England and Spain dragged on for years. Yet the defeat of the Spanish Armada prevented Philip II from reimposing Catholicism on England by force. In England the victory contributed to a David and Goliath legend that enhanced English national sentiment.

Calvinism

In 1509, while Luther was preparing for a doctorate at Wittenberg, John Calvin (1509–1564) was born in Noyon in northwestern France. As a young man he studied law, which had a decisive impact on his mind and later his thought. In 1533 he experienced a religious crisis, as a result of which he converted to Protestantism.

Spanish Armada The fleet sent by Philip II of Spain in 1588 against England as a religious crusade against Protestantism. Weather and the English fleet defeated it.

The Institutes of the Christian Religion Calvin's formulation of Christian doctrine, which became a systematic theology for Protestantism.

predestination The teaching that God has determined the salvation or damnation of individuals based on his will and purpose, not on their merit or works.

Calvin believed that God had specifically selected him to reform the church. Accordingly, he accepted an invitation to assist in the reformation of the city of Geneva. There, beginning in 1541, Calvin worked assiduously to establish a well-disciplined Christian society in which church and state acted together.

To understand Calvin's Geneva, it is necessary to understand Calvin's ideas. These he embodied in **The Institutes of the Christian Religion**, published first in 1536 and in its final form in 1559. The cornerstone of Calvin's theology was his belief in the absolute sovereignty and omnipotence of God and the total weakness of humanity. Before the infinite power of God, he asserted, men and women are as insignificant as grains of sand.

Calvin did not ascribe free will to human beings because that would detract from the sovereignty of God. Men and women cannot actively work to achieve salvation; rather, God in his infinite wisdom decided at the beginning of time who would be saved and who damned. This viewpoint constitutes the theological principle called **predestination**. Calvin explained his view:

> Predestination we call the eternal decree of God, by which he has determined in himself, what he would have become of every individual. . . . For they are not all created with a similar destiny; but eternal life is foreordained for some, and eternal damnation for others. . . . To those whom he devotes to condemnation, the gate of life is closed by a just and irreprehensible, but incomprehensible, judgment. How exceedingly presumptuous it is only to inquire into the causes of the Divine will; which is in fact, and is justly entitled to be, the cause of everything that exists. . . . For the will of God is the highest justice; so that what he wills must be considered just, for this very reason, because he wills it.[6]

Many people consider the doctrine of predestination, which dates back to Saint Augustine and Saint Paul, to be a pessimistic view of the nature of God. But "this terrible decree," as even Calvin called it, did not lead to pessimism or fatalism. Instead, many Calvinists came to believe that although one's own actions could do nothing to change one's fate, hard work, thrift, and proper moral conduct could serve as signs that one was among the "elect" chosen for salvation.

Elizabethan Injunctions About Religion

In 1559, acting through Parliament, Queen Elizabeth issued a series of rules governing many aspects of religious life. These prohibited clergy and laypeople from engaging in certain religious practices, and required them to do others.

❝ The first is that all deans, archdeacons, parsons, vicars, and other ecclesiastical persons shall faithfully keep and observe, and as far as in them may be, shall cause to be observed and kept of others, all and singular laws and statutes made for the restoring to the crown the ancient jurisdiction over the state ecclesiastical, and abolishing of all foreign power repugnant to the same. And furthermore, all ecclesiastical persons having cure of soul [that is, clergy who preach], shall to the uttermost of their wit, knowledge, and learning, purely and sincerely, and without any color or dissimulation, declare, manifest and open, four times every year at the least, in their sermons and other collations, that all usurped and foreign power, having no establishment nor ground by the law of God, was of most just causes taken away and abolished, and that therefore no manner of obedience or subjection within her Highness's realms and dominions is due unto any such foreign power. And that the queen's power within her realms and dominions is the highest power under God, to whom all men within the same realms and dominions, by God's laws owe most loyalty and obedience, afore and above all other powers and potentates in earth. . . .

That they, the persons above rehearsed, shall preach in their churches, and every other cure they have, one sermon, every quarter of the year at the least, wherein they shall purely and sincerely declare the Word of God, and in the same, exhort their hearers to the works of faith, mercy, and charity specially prescribed and commanded in Scripture, and that works devised by men's fantasies, besides Scripture, as wandering to pilgrimages, offering of money, candles, or tapers to relics or images, or kissing and licking of the same, praying upon beads, or such like superstition, have not only no promise of reward in Scripture, for doing of them, but contrariwise, great threats and malediction of God, for that they be things tending to idolatry and superstition, which of all other offenses God almighty doth most detest and abhor, for that the same diminish his honor and glory. . . .

Every parson, vicar, and curate shall upon every holy day and every second Sunday in the year, hear and instruct all the youth of the parish for half an hour at the least, before Evening Prayer, in the Ten Commandments, the Articles of the Belief, and in the Lord's Prayer. . . .

Because in all alterations and specially in rites and ceremonies, there happeneth discord among the people, and thereupon slanderous words and railings whereby charity, the knot of all Christian society, is loosed. The queen's Majesty being most desirous of all other earthly things, that her people should live in charity both towards God and man, and therein abound in good works, willeth and straightly commandeth all manner of her subjects to forbear all vain and contentious disputations in matters of religion. ❞

EVALUATE THE EVIDENCE

1. Whose authority in matters of religion do these rules reject, and whose do they declare to be supreme? What religious activities are required, and what religious activities are prohibited?
2. Given what you have read in this chapter, would you expect that the queen's order to end "disputations in matters of religion" was followed?

Source: Denis R. Janz, ed., *A Reformation Reader: Primary Texts with Introductions* (Minneapolis: Fortress Press, 1999), pp. 315, 316.

Calvin transformed Geneva into a community based on his religious principles. The most powerful organization in the city became the Consistory, a group of laymen and pastors charged with investigating and disciplining deviations from proper doctrine and conduct. (See "Primary Source 13.4: 1547 Ordinances in Calvin's Geneva," page 412.)

Serious crimes and heresy were handled by the civil authorities, which, with the Consistory's approval, sometimes used torture to extract confessions. Between 1542 and 1546 alone seventy-six persons were banished from Geneva, and fifty-eight were executed for heresy, adultery, blasphemy, and witchcraft (see page 420). Among them was the Spanish humanist and refugee Michael Servetus, who was burned at the stake for denying the scriptural basis for the Trinity, rejecting child baptism, and insisting that a person under twenty cannot commit a mortal sin, all of which were viewed as threats to society.

Geneva became the model of a Christian community for many Protestant reformers. Religious refugees from France, England, Spain, Scotland, and Italy visited Calvin's Geneva, and many of the most prominent exiles from Mary Tudor's England stayed. Subsequently, the church of Calvin—often termed "Reformed"—served as the model for the Presbyterian Church in

1547 Ordinances in Calvin's Geneva

John Calvin thought that a well-disciplined city, like a well-disciplined individual, might be seen as evidence of God's election. He put his ideas into action in Geneva, encouraging city leaders to issue ordinances that regulated many aspects of life, and establishing the Consistory to enforce them. The following ordinances also applied to the villages that the city controlled in the surrounding territory.

Concerning the Times of Assembling at Church

❝ That the temples [the churches] be closed for the rest of the time [when services are not in session], in order that no one shall enter therein out of hours, impelled thereto by superstition; and if anyone be found engaged in any special act of devotion therein or near by he shall be admonished for it: if it be found to be of a superstitious nature for which simple correction is inadequate then he shall be chastised.

Blasphemy

Whoever shall have blasphemed, swearing by the body or by the blood of our Lord, or in similar manner, he shall be made to kiss the earth for the first offence; for the second to pay 5 sous, and for the third 6 sous, and for the last offence be put in the pillory [a wooden frame set up in a public place, in which a person's head and hands could be locked] for one hour.

Drunkenness

1. That no one shall invite another to drink under penalty of 3 sous.

2. That taverns shall be closed during the sermon, under penalty that the tavern-keeper shall pay 3 sous, and whoever may be found therein shall pay the same amount.

3. If anyone be found intoxicated he shall pay for the first offence 3 sous and shall be remanded to the consistory; for the second offence he shall be held to pay the sum of 6 sous, and for the third 10 sous and be put in prison.

Songs and Dances

If anyone sing immoral, dissolute or outrageous songs, or dance the *virollet* or other dance, he shall be put in prison for three days and then sent to the consistory.

Usury

That no one shall take upon interest or profit [on a loan] more than five percent, upon penalty of confiscation of the principal and of being condemned to make restitution as the case may demand.

Games

That no one shall play at any dissolute game or at any game whatsoever it may be, neither for gold nor silver nor for any excessive stake, upon penalty of 5 sous and forfeiture of stake played for. ❞

EVALUATE THE EVIDENCE

1. Given the actions prohibited in these ordinances, how would you describe ideal Christian behavior, in Calvin's eyes?

2. Other than the punishments set for disobeying these ordinances, what might have motivated Genevans to obey them, particularly given Calvinist beliefs that a person's own behavior had no effect on whether he or she would achieve salvation?

Source: Merrick Whitcomb, ed., *Translations and Reprints from the Original Sources of European History*, vol. 3 (Philadelphia: University of Pennsylvania, 1897), no. 3, pp. 10–11.

Scotland, the Huguenot Church in France (see page 418), and the Puritan churches in England and New England.

Calvinism became the compelling force in international Protestantism. Calvinists believed that any occupation could be a God-given "calling," and should be carried out with diligence and dedication. This doctrine encouraged an aggressive, vigorous activism in both work and religious life, and Calvinism became the most dynamic force in sixteenth- and seventeenth-century Protestantism.

Calvinism spread on the continent of Europe, and also found a ready audience in Scotland. There, as else-where, political authority was the decisive influence in reform. The monarchy was weak, and factions of virtually independent nobles competed for power. King James V and his daughter Mary, Queen of Scots, staunch Catholics and close allies of Catholic France, opposed reform, but the Scottish nobles supported it. One man, John Knox (1505?–1572), dominated the reform movement, which led to the establishment of a state church.

Knox was determined to structure the Scottish Church after the model of Geneva, where he had studied and worked with Calvin. In 1560 Knox persuaded the Scottish parliament, which was dominated by

Young John Calvin   This oil painting of the reformer as a young man captures his spiritual intensity and determination, qualities that the artist clearly viewed as positive. (Bibliothèque de Genève, Département iconographique)

reform-minded barons, to end papal authority and rule by bishops, substituting governance by presbyters, or councils of ministers. The Presbyterian Church of Scotland was strictly Calvinist in doctrine, adopted a simple and dignified service of worship, and laid great emphasis on preaching.

The Reformation in Eastern Europe

While political and economic issues determined the course of the Reformation in western and northern Europe, ethnic factors often proved decisive in eastern Europe, where people of diverse backgrounds had settled in the later Middle Ages. In Bohemia in the fifteenth century, a Czech majority was ruled by Germans. Most Czechs had adopted the ideas of Jan Hus, and the emperor had been forced to recognize a separate Hussite Church (see Chapter 11). Yet Lutheranism appealed to Germans in Bohemia in the 1520s and 1530s, and the nobility embraced Lutheranism in opposition to the Catholic Habsburgs. The forces of the Catholic Reformation (see page 414) promoted a

Catholic spiritual revival in Bohemia, and some areas reconverted. This complicated situation would be one of the causes of the Thirty Years' War in the early seventeenth century.

By 1500 Poland and the Grand Duchy of Lithuania were jointly governed by king, senate, and diet (parliament), but the two territories retained separate officials, judicial systems, armies, and forms of citizenship. The combined realms covered almost five hundred thousand square miles, making Poland-Lithuania the largest European polity, but a population of only about 7.5 million people was very thinly scattered over that land.

The population of Poland-Lithuania was also very diverse; Germans, Italians, Tartars, and Jews lived among Poles and Lithuanians. Such peoples had come as merchants, invited by medieval rulers because of their wealth or to make agricultural improvements. Each group spoke its native language, though all educated people spoke Latin. Luther's ideas took root in Germanized towns but were opposed by King Sigismund I (r. 1506–1548) as well as by ordinary Poles, who held strong anti-German feeling. The Reformed tradition of John Calvin, with its stress on the power of church elders, appealed to the Polish nobility, however. The fact that Calvinism originated in France, not in Germany, also made it more attractive than Lutheranism. But doctrinal differences among Calvinists, Lutherans, and other groups prevented united opposition to Catholicism, and a Counter-Reformation gained momentum. By 1650, due largely to the efforts of the Jesuits (see page 416), Poland was again staunchly Roman Catholic.

Hungary's experience with the Reformation was even more complex. Lutheranism was spread by Hungarian students who had studied at Wittenberg, and sympathy for it developed at the royal court of King Louis II in Buda. But concern about "the German heresy" by the Catholic hierarchy and among the high nobles found expression in a decree of the Hungarian diet in 1523 that "all Lutherans and those favoring them . . . should have their property confiscated and themselves punished with death as heretics."[7]

Before such measures could be acted on, a military event on August 26, 1526, had profound consequences for both the Hungarian state and the Protestant Reformation there. On the plain of Mohács in southern Hungary, the Ottoman sultan Suleiman the Magnificent inflicted a crushing defeat on the Hungarians, killing King Louis II, many of the nobles, and more than sixteen thousand ordinary soldiers. The Hungarian kingdom was then divided into three parts: the Ottoman Turks absorbed the great plains, including the capital, Buda; the Habsburgs ruled the north and west; and Ottoman-supported Janos Zapolya held eastern Hungary and Transylvania.

The Turks were indifferent to the religious conflicts of Christians, whom they regarded as infidels. Christians of all types paid extra taxes to the sultan, but kept their faith. Many Magyar (Hungarian) nobles accepted Lutheranism; Lutheran schools and parishes headed by men educated at Wittenberg multiplied; and peasants welcomed the new faith. The majority of Hungarian people were Protestant until the late seventeenth century, when Hungarian nobles recognized Habsburg (Catholic) rule and Ottoman Turkish withdrawal in 1699 led to Catholic restoration.

The Catholic Reformation

What reforms did the Catholic Church make, and how did it respond to Protestant reform movements?

Between 1517 and 1547 Protestantism made remarkable advances. Nevertheless, the Roman Catholic Church made a significant comeback. After about 1540 no new large areas of Europe, other than the Netherlands, accepted Protestant beliefs (Map 13.2). Many historians see the developments within the Catholic Church after the Protestant Reformation as two interrelated movements: one a drive for internal reform linked to earlier reform efforts, the other a Counter-Reformation that opposed Protestants intellectually, politically, militarily, and institutionally. In both movements, the papacy, new religious orders, and the Council of Trent that met from 1545 to 1563 were important agents.

Papal Reform and the Council of Trent

Renaissance popes and their advisers were not blind to the need for church reforms, but they resisted calls for a general council representing the entire church, and feared that any transformation would mean a loss of power, revenue, and prestige. This changed beginning with Pope Paul III (pontificate 1534–1549), when the papal court became the center of the reform movement rather than its chief opponent. The lives of the pope and his reform-minded cardinals, abbots, and bishops were models of decorum and piety, in contrast to Renaissance popes who concentrated on building churches and enhancing the power of their own families. Paul III and his successors supported improvements in education for the clergy, the end of simony (the selling of church offices), and stricter control of clerical life.

Holy Office The official Roman Catholic agency founded in 1542 to combat international doctrinal heresy.

In 1542 Pope Paul III established the Supreme Sacred Congregation of the Roman and Universal Inquisition, often called the **Holy Office**, with jurisdiction over the Roman Inquisition, a powerful instrument of the Catholic Reformation. The Roman Inquisition was a committee of six cardinals with judicial authority over all Catholics and the power to arrest, imprison, and execute suspected heretics. The Holy Office published the *Index of Prohibited Books*, a catalogue of forbidden reading that included works by Christian humanists such as Erasmus as well as by Protestants. Within the Papal States, the Inquisition effectively destroyed heresy, but outside the papal territories, its influence was slight.

Pope Paul III also called a general council, which met intermittently from 1545 to 1563 at Trent, an imperial city close to Italy. It was called not only to reform the Catholic Church but also to secure reconciliation with the Protestants. Lutherans and Calvinists were invited to participate, but their insistence that the Scriptures be the sole basis for discussion made reconciliation impossible. In addition, the political objectives of Charles V and France both worked against reconciliation: Charles wanted to avoid alienating the Lutheran nobility in the empire, and France wanted the Catholics and Lutherans to remain divided in order to keep Germany decentralized and weak.

Nonetheless, the decrees of the Council of Trent laid a solid basis for the spiritual renewal of the Catholic Church. It gave equal validity to the Scriptures and to tradition as sources of religious truth and authority. It reaffirmed the seven sacraments and the traditional Catholic teaching on transubstantiation. It tackled the disciplinary matters that had disillusioned the faithful, requiring bishops to reside in their own dioceses, suppressing pluralism and simony, and forbidding the sale of indulgences. Clerics who kept concubines were to give them up, and bishops were given greater authority. The council required every diocese to establish a seminary for the education and training of the clergy. Seminary professors were to determine whether candidates for ordination had vocations, genuine callings to the priesthood. This was a novel idea, since from the time of the early church, parents had determined their sons' (and daughters') religious careers. For the first time, great emphasis was laid on preaching and instructing the laity, especially the uneducated.

One decision had especially important social consequences for laypeople. The Council of Trent stipulated that for a marriage to be valid, the marriage vows had to be made publicly before a priest and witnesses. Trent thereby ended the widespread practice of private marriages in Catholic countries, curtailing the number of denials and conflicts that inevitably resulted from marriages that took place in secret.

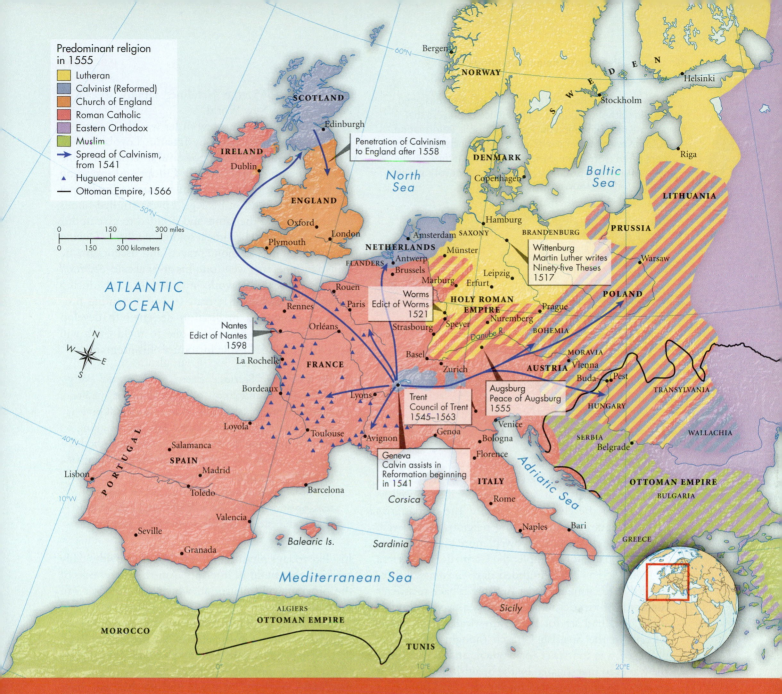

Predominant religion
in 1555
- Lutheran
- Calvinist (Reformed)
- Church of England
- Roman Catholic
- Eastern Orthodox
- Muslim
→ Spread of Calvinism, from 1541
▲ Huguenot center
— Ottoman Empire, 1566

Penetration of Calvinism to England after 1558

Wittenburg
Martin Luther writes Ninety-five Theses
1517

Worms
Edict of Worms
1521

Augsburg
Peace of Augsburg
1555

Nantes
Edict of Nantes
1598

Trent
Council of Trent
1545–1563

Geneva
Calvin assists in Reformation beginning in 1541

MAPPING THE PAST

Map 13.2 Religious Divisions in Europe, ca. 1555

The Reformations shattered the religious unity of Western Christendom. The situation was even more complicated than a map of this scale can show. Many cities within the Holy Roman Empire, for example, accepted a different faith than the surrounding countryside; Augsburg, Basel, and Strasbourg were all Protestant, though surrounded by territory ruled by Catholic nobles.

ANALYZING THE MAP Which countries were the most religiously diverse in Europe? Which were the least diverse?

CONNECTIONS Where was the first arena of religious conflict in sixteenth-century Europe, and why did it develop there and not elsewhere? To what degree can nonreligious factors be used as an explanation for the religious divisions in sixteenth-century Europe?

Rosary Beads Rosaries were loops of beads designed to help Catholics count a set sequence of prayers that became more common during the Catholic Reformation. Rosaries with fancier beads, such as the one shown here, were often worn around the neck or looped through the belt, serving as a fashion item as well as a devotional aid. (Image © Cleveland Museum of Art, acc. # 1952.277)

Although it did not achieve all of its goals, the Council of Trent composed decrees that laid a solid basis for the spiritual renewal of the church. The doctrinal and disciplinary legislation of Trent served as the basis for Roman Catholic faith, organization, and practice through the middle of the twentieth century.

New and Reformed Religious Orders

Just as seminaries provided education, so did religious orders, which aimed at raising the moral and intellectual level of the clergy and people. The monasteries and convents of many existing religious orders were reformed so that they followed more rigorous standards. In Spain, for example, the Carmelite nun Teresa of Ávila (1515–1582) founded new convents and reformed her Carmelite order to bring it back to stricter standards of asceticism and poverty, a task she understood God had set for her in mystical visions. Some officials in the Spanish Church thought the life she proposed was too strict for women, and at one point she was even investigated by the Spanish Inquisition in an effort to make sure her inspiration came from God and not the Devil. The process was dropped, and she founded many new convents, which she saw as answers to the Protestant takeover of Catholic churches elsewhere in Europe. (See "Primary Source 13.5: Saint Teresa of Ávila, *The Life*," page 418.)

New religious orders were founded, some of which focused on education. The Ursuline order of nuns, for example, founded by Angela Merici (1474–1540), focused on the education of women. The daughter of a country gentleman, Angela Merici worked for many years among the poor, sick, and uneducated around her native Brescia in northern Italy. In 1535 she established the first women's religious order concentrating exclusively on teaching young girls, with the goal of re-Christianizing society by training future wives and mothers. After receiving papal approval in 1565, the Ursulines rapidly spread to France and the New World.

The most significant new order was the Society of Jesus, or **Jesuits**. Founded by Ignatius Loyola (1491–1556), the Jesuits played a powerful international role in strengthening Catholicism in Europe and spreading the faith around the world. While recuperating from a severe battle wound in his legs, Loyola studied books about Christ and the saints and decided to give up his military career and become a soldier of Christ. During a year spent in seclusion, prayer, and asceticism, he gained insights that went into his great classic, *Spiritual Exercises* (1548). This work, intended for study during a four-week period of retreat, set out a training program of structured meditation designed to develop spiritual discipline and allow one to meld one's will with that of God. Loyola introduces his program:

> By the term "Spiritual Exercises" is meant every method of examination of conscience, of meditation, of contemplation, of vocal and mental prayer, and of other spiritual activities. For just as taking a walk, journeying on foot, and running are bodily exercises, so we call Spiritual Exercises every way of preparing and disposing the soul to rid itself of all inordinate attachments, and, after their removal, of seeking and finding the will of God in the disposition of our life for the salvation of our soul.[8]

Just like today's physical trainers, Loyola provides daily exercises that build in intensity over the four weeks of the program, and charts on which the exerciser can track his progress.

Loyola was a man of considerable personal magnetism. After study at universities in Salamanca and Paris, he gathered a group of six companions and in 1540 secured papal approval of the new Society of Jesus. The first Jesuits, recruited primarily from wealthy merchant and professional families, saw their mission as improving people's spiritual condition rather than altering doctrine. Their goal was not to reform the church, but "to help souls."

The Society of Jesus developed into a highly centralized, tightly knit organization. In addition to the traditional vows of poverty, chastity, and obedience, professed members vowed special obedience to the pope. Flexibility and the willingness to respond to the needs of time and circumstance formed the Jesuit tradition, which proved attractive to many young men. The Jesuits achieved phenomenal success for the papacy and the reformed Catholic Church, carrying Christianity to India and Japan before 1550 and to Brazil, North America, and the Congo in the seventeenth century. Within Europe the Jesuits brought southern Germany and much of eastern Europe back to Catholicism. Jesuit schools adopted the modern humanist curricula

Jesuits Members of the Society of Jesus, founded by Ignatius Loyola, whose goal was the spread of the Roman Catholic faith.

Church of the Gesù   Begun in 1568 as the mother church for the Jesuit order, the Church of the Gesù in Rome conveyed a sense of drama, motion, and power through its lavish decorations and shimmering frescoes. Gesù served as a model for Catholic churches elsewhere in Europe and the New World, their triumphant and elaborate style reflecting the dynamic and proselytizing spirit of the Catholic Reformation. (The Art Archive/Corbis)

and methods, educating the sons of the nobility as well as the poor. As confessors and spiritual directors to kings, Jesuits exerted great political influence.

Religious Violence

What were the causes and consequences of religious violence, including riots, wars, and witch-hunts?

In 1559 France and Spain signed the Treaty of Cateau-Cambrésis (CAH-toh kam-BRAY-sees), which ended the long conflict known as the Habsburg-Valois wars. Spain was the victor. France, exhausted by the struggle, had to acknowledge Spanish dominance in Italy, where much of the fighting had taken place. However, true peace was elusive, and over the next century religious differences led to riots, civil wars, and international conflicts. Especially in France and the Netherlands, Protestants and Catholics used violent actions as well as preaching and teaching against each other, for each side regarded the other as a poison in the community that would provoke the wrath of God. Catholics continued to believe that Calvinists and Lutherans could be reconverted; Protestants persisted in thinking that

the Roman Church should be destroyed. Catholics and Protestants alike feared people of other faiths, whom they often saw as agents of Satan. Even more, they feared those who were explicitly identified with Satan: witches living in their midst. This era was the time of the most virulent witch persecutions in European history, as both Protestants and Catholics tried to make their cities and states more godly.

French Religious Wars

The costs of the Habsburg-Valois wars, waged intermittently through the first half of the sixteenth century, forced the French to increase taxes and borrow heavily. King Francis I (r. 1515–1547) also tried two new devices to raise revenue: the sale of public offices and a treaty with the papacy. The former proved to be only a temporary source of money: once a man bought an office, he and his heirs were exempt from taxation. But the latter, known as the Concordat of Bologna (see Chapter 12), gave the French crown the right to appoint all French bishops and abbots, ensuring a rich supplement of money and offices. Because French rulers possessed control over appointments and had a vested financial interest in Catholicism, they had no need to revolt against Rome.

Significant numbers of those ruled, however, were attracted to the Reformed religion of Calvinism.

Saint Teresa of Ávila, *The Life*

Teresa entered the Carmelite convent in Ávila when she was a teenager, and lived quietly until she was in her late thirties, when she began to have profound mystical experiences—visions and voices in which Christ chastised her for her worldly concerns. She responded with great energy, eventually traveling throughout Spain to form reformed convents, writing hundreds of letters seeking support for her plans, and writing a number of works. The following selection is from The Life, *a long spiritual autobiography in which Teresa describes many of her visions.*

❝ It pleased the Lord that I should sometimes see the following vision. I would see beside me, on my left hand, an angel in bodily form. . . . In his hands I saw a long golden spear and at the end of the iron tip I seemed to see a point of fire. With this he seemed to pierce my heart several times so that it penetrated to my entrails. When he drew it out, I thought he was drawing them out with it and he left me completely afire with a great love of God. . . .

One night, when I was so unwell that I meant to excuse myself from mental prayer, I took a rosary, so as to occupy myself in vocal prayer. . . . I had been in that condition only a very short time when there came to me a spiritual impulse of such vehemence that resistance to it was impossible. I thought I was being carried up to Heaven: the first persons I saw there were my father and mother. . . .

With the great progress of time, the Lord continued to show me further great secrets: sometimes He does so still. The soul may wish to see more than is pictured to it, but there is no way in which it may do so, nor is it possible that it should; and so I never on any occasion saw more than the Lord was pleased to show me. What I saw was so great that the smallest part of it was sufficient to leave my soul amazed and to do it so much good that it esteemed and considered all the things of this life as of little worth. . . .

Once, when I had been for more than an hour in this state, and the Lord had shown me wonderful things, and it seemed as if He were not going to leave me, He said to me: "See, daughter, what those who are against Me lose: do not fail to tell them of it." Ah, my Lord, how little will my words profit those who are blinded by their own actions unless Thy Majesty gives them light! . . .

The soul that feels like this has great dominion over itself—so great that I do not know if it can be understood by anyone who does not possess it, for it is a real, natural detachment, achieved without labour of our own. It is all effected by God, for, when His Majesty reveals these truths, they are so deeply impressed upon our souls as to show us clearly that we could not in so short a time acquire them ourselves. ❞

EVALUATE THE EVIDENCE

1. How does Teresa describe her visions and their effects on her?
2. How would you compare Teresa's understanding of the role of God's power and human efforts with that of Luther and Calvin?

Source: *The Complete Works of St. Teresa of Jesus*, vol. 1, ed. and trans. E. Allison Peers (London: Sheed & Ward, 1972), pp. 192–193, 267–268, 269. Used by permission of Sheed & Ward.

Initially, Calvinism drew converts from among reform-minded members of the Catholic clergy, industrious city dwellers, and artisan groups. Most French Calvinists, called **Huguenots**, lived in major cities, such as Paris, Lyon, and Rouen. By the time King Henry II (r. 1547–1559) died in 1559—accidentally shot in the face at a tournament celebrating the Treaty of Cateau-Cambrésis—perhaps one-tenth of the population had become Calvinist.

The feebleness of the French monarchy was the seed from which the weeds of civil violence sprang. The three weak sons of Henry II who occupied the throne could not provide the necessary leadership, and they were often dominated by their mother, Catherine de' Medici. The French nobility took advantage of this monarchical weakness. Just as German princes in the Holy Roman Empire had adopted Lutheranism as a means of opposition to Emperor Charles V, so French nobles frequently adopted Protestantism as a religious cloak for their independence. Armed clashes between Catholic royalist lords and Calvinist antimonarchical lords occurred in many parts of France. Both Calvinists and Catholics believed that the others' books, services, and ministers polluted the community. Preachers incited violence, and religious ceremonies such as baptisms, marriages, and funerals triggered it.

Calvinist teachings called the power of sacred images into question, and mobs in many cities took down and smashed statues, stained-glass windows, and paintings, viewing this as a way to purify the church. Though it was often inspired by fiery Protestant sermons, this iconoclasm, or destruction of religious images, is an example of ordinary men and women carrying out the Reformation themselves. Catholic mobs responded by defending images, and crowds on both sides killed their opponents, often in gruesome ways.

A savage Catholic attack on Calvinists in Paris on Saint Bartholomew's Day, August 24, 1572, followed the usual pattern. The occasion was the marriage ceremony of the king's sister Margaret of Valois to the Protestant Henry of Navarre, which was intended to help reconcile Catholics and Huguenots. Instead, Huguenot wedding guests in Paris were massacred, and other Protestants were slaughtered by mobs. Religious violence spread to the provinces, where thousands were killed. This Saint Bartholomew's Day massacre led to a civil war that dragged on for fifteen years. Agriculture in many areas was destroyed; commercial life declined severely; and starvation and death haunted the land.

What ultimately saved France was a small group of moderates of both faiths, called **politiques**, who believed that only the restoration of strong monarchy could reverse the trend toward collapse. The politiques also favored accepting the Huguenots as an officially recognized and organized group. The death of Catherine de' Medici, followed by the assassination of King Henry III, paved the way for the accession of Henry of Navarre (the unfortunate bridegroom of the Saint Bartholomew's Day massacre), a politique who became Henry IV (r. 1589–1610).

Henry's willingness to sacrifice religious principles to political necessity saved France. He converted to Catholicism but also issued the **Edict of Nantes** in 1598, which granted liberty of conscience and liberty of public worship to Huguenots in 150 fortified towns. The reign of Henry IV and the Edict of Nantes prepared the way for French absolutism in the seventeenth century by helping restore internal peace in France.

The Netherlands Under Charles V

In the Netherlands, what began as a movement for the reformation of the church developed into a struggle for Dutch independence. Emperor Charles V had inherited the seventeen provinces that compose present-day Belgium and the Netherlands (see page 405). Each was self-governing and enjoyed the right to make its own laws and collect its own taxes. The provinces were united politically only in recognition of a common ruler, the emperor. The cities of the Netherlands made their living by trade and industry.

In the Low Countries as elsewhere, corruption in the Roman Church and the critical spirit of the Renaissance provoked pressure for reform, and Lutheran ideas took root. Charles V had grown up in the Netherlands, however, and he was able to limit their impact. But Charles V abdicated in 1556 and transferred power over the Netherlands to his son Philip II, who had grown up in Spain. Protestant ideas spread.

By the 1560s Protestants in the Netherlands were primarily Calvinists. Calvinism's intellectual serious-ness, moral gravity, and emphasis on any form of labor well done appealed to urban merchants, financiers, and artisans. Whereas Lutherans taught respect for the powers that be, Calvinism tended to encourage opposition to political authorities who were judged to be ungodly.

When Spanish authorities attempted to suppress Calvinist worship and raised taxes in the 1560s, rioting ensued. Calvinists sacked thirty Catholic churches in Antwerp, destroying the religious images in them in a wave of iconoclasm. From Antwerp the destruction spread. Philip II sent twenty thousand Spanish troops under the duke of Alva to pacify the Low Countries. Alva interpreted "pacification" to mean ruthless extermination of religious and political dissidents. On top of the Inquisition, he opened his own tribunal, soon called the "Council of Blood." On March 3, 1568, fifteen hundred men were executed. To Calvinists, all this was clear indication that Spanish rule was ungodly and should be overthrown.

Huguenots French Calvinists.

politiques Catholic and Protestant moderates who held that only a strong monarchy could save France from total collapse.

Edict of Nantes A document issued by Henry IV of France in 1598, granting liberty of conscience and of public worship to Calvinists, which helped restore peace in France.

Iconoclasm in the Netherlands Calvinist men and women break stained-glass windows, remove statues, and carry off devotional altarpieces. Iconoclasm, or the destruction of religious images, is often described as a "riot," but here the participants seem very purposeful. Calvinist Protestants regarded pictures and statues as sacrilegious and saw removing them as a way to purify the church. (The Fotomas Index/The Bridgeman Art Library)

United Provinces
Spanish Netherlands
Treaty line, 1609

North Sea
Amsterdam
Utrecht
Bruges
Ghent
Antwerp
Brussels
HOLY ROMAN EMPIRE
FRANCE

The Netherlands, 1609

Between 1568 and 1578 civil war raged in the Netherlands between Catholics and Protestants and between the seventeen provinces and Spain. Eventually the ten southern provinces, the Spanish Netherlands (the future Belgium), came under the control of the Spanish Habsburg forces. The seven northern provinces, led by Holland, formed the **Union of Utrecht** and in 1581 declared their independence from Spain. The north was Protestant; the south remained Catholic. Philip did not accept this, and war continued. England was even drawn into the conflict, supplying money and troops to the northern United Provinces. (Spain launched an unsuccessful invasion of England in response; see page 410.) Hostilities ended in 1609 when Spain agreed to a truce that recognized the independence of the United Provinces.

The Great European Witch-Hunt

The relationship between the Reformation and the upsurge in trials for witchcraft that occurred at roughly the same time is complex. Increasing persecution for witchcraft actually began before the Reformation in the 1480s, but it became especially common about 1560, and the mania continued until roughly 1660. Religious reformers' extreme notions of the Devil's powers and the insecurity created by the religious wars contributed to this increase. Both Protestants and Catholics tried and executed witches, with church officials and secular authorities acting together.

The heightened sense of God's power and divine wrath in the Reformation era was an important factor in the witch-hunts, but so was a change in the idea of what a witch was. Nearly all premodern societies believe in witchcraft and make some attempts to control witches, who are understood to be people who use magical forces. In the later Middle Ages, however, many educated Christian theologians, canon lawyers, and officials added a demonological component to this notion of what a witch was. For them, the essence of witchcraft was making a pact with the Devil. Witches were no longer simply people who used magical power to get what they wanted, but rather people used by

the Devil to do what he wanted. Witches were thought to engage in wild sexual orgies with the Devil, fly through the night to meetings called sabbats that parodied Christian services, and steal communion wafers and unbaptized babies to use in their rituals. Some demonological theorists also claimed that witches were organized in an international conspiracy to overthrow Christianity. Witchcraft was thus spiritualized, and witches became the ultimate heretics, enemies of God.

Trials involving this new notion of witchcraft as diabolical heresy began in Switzerland and southern Germany in the late fifteenth century, became less numerous in the early decades of the Reformation when Protestants and Catholics were busy fighting each other, and then picked up again in about 1560. Scholars estimate that during the sixteenth and seventeenth centuries between 100,000 and 200,000 people were officially tried for witchcraft and between 40,000 and 60,000 were executed.

Though the gender balance varied widely in different parts of Europe, between 75 and 85 percent of those tried and executed were women. Ideas about women and the roles women actually played in society were thus important factors shaping the witch-hunts. Some demonologists expressed virulent misogyny, or hatred of women, and particularly emphasized women's powerful sexual desire, which could be satisfied only by a demonic lover. Most people viewed women as weaker and so more likely to give in to an offer by the Devil. In both classical and Christian traditions, women were associated with nature, disorder, and the body, all of which were linked with the demonic. Women's actual lack of power in society and gender norms about the use of violence meant that they were more likely to use scolding and cursing to get what they wanted instead of taking people to court or beating them up. Curses were generally expressed (as they often are today) in religious terms; "go to Hell" was calling on the powers of Satan.

Legal changes also played a role in causing, or at least allowing for, massive witch trials. One of these was a change from an accusatorial legal procedure to an inquisitorial procedure. In the former, a suspect knew the accusers and the charges they had brought, and an accuser could in turn be liable for trial if the charges were not proven. In the latter, legal authorities themselves brought the case. This change made people much more willing to accuse others, for they never had to take personal responsibility for the accusation or face the accused person's relatives. Areas in Europe that did not make this legal change saw very few trials. Inquisitorial procedure involved intense questioning of the suspect, often with torture. Torture was also used to get the names of additional suspects, as most lawyers firmly believed that no witch could act alone.

Union of Utrecht The alliance of seven northern provinces (led by Holland) that declared its independence from Spain and formed the United Provinces of the Netherlands.

The use of inquisitorial procedure did not always lead to witch-hunts. The most famous inquisitions in early modern Europe, those in Spain, Portugal, and Italy, were in fact very lenient in their treatment of people accused of witchcraft. The Inquisition in Spain executed only a handful of witches, the Portuguese Inquisition only one, and the Roman Inquisition none, though in each of these there were hundreds of cases. Inquisitors believed in the power of the Devil and were no less misogynist than other judges, but they doubted very much whether the people accused of witchcraft had actually made pacts with the Devil that gave them special powers. They viewed such people not as diabolical Devil worshippers but as superstitious and ignorant peasants who should be educated rather than executed. Thus most people brought up before the Inquisition for witchcraft were sent home with a warning and a penance.

Most witch trials began with a single accusation in a village or town. Individuals accused someone they knew of using magic to spoil food, make children ill, kill animals, raise a hailstorm, or do other types of harm. Tensions within families, households, and neighborhoods often played a role in these accusations. Women number very prominently among accusers and witnesses as well as among those accused of witchcraft because the actions witches were initially charged with, such as harming children or curdling milk, were

generally part of women's sphere. A woman also gained economic and social security by conforming to the standard of the good wife and mother and by confronting women who deviated from it.

Once a charge was made, the suspect was brought in for questioning. One German witch pamphlet from 1587 described a typical case:

> Walpurga Hausmännin . . . upon kindly questioning and also torture . . . confessed . . . that the Evil One indulged in fornication with her . . . and made her many promises to help her in her poverty and need. . . . She promised herself body and soul to him and disowned God in heaven. . . . She destroyed a number of cattle, pigs, and geese . . . and dug up [the bodies] of one or two innocent children. With her devil-paramour and other playfellows she has eaten these and used their hair and their little bones for witchcraft.

Confession was generally followed by execution. In this case, Hausmännin was "dispatched from life to death by burning at the stake . . . her body first to be torn five times with red-hot irons."[9]

Detailed records of witch trials survive for many parts of Europe. They have been used by historians to study many aspects of witchcraft, but they cannot directly answer what seems to us an important question: did people really practice witchcraft and think they were witches? They certainly confessed to evil deeds and demonic practices, sometimes without torture, but where would we draw the line between reality and fantasy? Clearly people were not riding through the air on pitchforks, but did they think they did? Did they actually invoke the Devil when they were angry at a neighbor, or was this simply in the minds of their accusers? Trial records cannot tell us, and historians have answered these questions very differently, often using insights from psychoanalysis or the study of more recent victims of torture in their explanations.

After the initial suspect had been questioned, and particularly if he or she had been tortured, the people who had been implicated were brought in for questioning. This might lead to a small hunt, involving from five to ten suspects, and it sometimes grew into a much

Witch Pamphlet   This printed pamphlet presents the confession of "Mother Waterhouse," a woman convicted of witchcraft in England in 1566, who describes her "many abominable deeds" and "execrable sorcery" committed over fifteen years, and asks for forgiveness right before her execution. Enterprising printers often produced cheap, short pamphlets during witch trials, knowing they would sell, sometimes based on the actual trial proceedings and sometimes just made up. They both reflected and helped create stereotypes about what witches were and did. (The Granger Collection, New York)

larger hunt, which historians have called a "witch panic." Panics were most common in the part of Europe that saw the most witch accusations in general: the Holy Roman Empire, Switzerland, and parts of France. Most of this area consisted of very small governmental units that were jealous of each other and, after the Reformation, were divided by religion. The rulers of these small territories often felt more threatened than did the monarchs of western Europe, and they saw persecuting witches as a way to demonstrate their piety and concern for order. Moreover, witch panics often occurred after some type of climatic disaster, such as an unusually cold and wet summer, and they came in waves.

In large-scale panics a wider variety of suspects were taken in—wealthier people, children, a greater proportion of men. Mass panics tended to end when it became clear to legal authorities, or to the community itself, that the people being questioned or executed were not what they understood witches to be, or that the scope of accusations was beyond belief.

As the seventeenth century ushered in new ideas about science and reason, many began to question whether witches could make pacts with the Devil or engage in the wild activities attributed to them. Doubts about whether secret denunciations were valid or whether torture would ever yield truthful confessions gradually spread among the same type of religious and legal authorities who had so vigorously persecuted witches. Prosecutions for witchcraft became less common and were gradually outlawed. The last official execution for witchcraft in England was in 1682, though the last one in the Holy Roman Empire was not until 1775.

Notes

1. Quoted in Owen Chadwick, *The Reformation* (Baltimore: Penguin Books, 1976), p. 55.
2. Quoted in E. H. Harbison, *The Age of Reformation* (Ithaca, N.Y.: Cornell University Press, 1963), p. 52.
3. Quoted in S. E. Ozment, *The Age of Reform, 1250–1550: An Intellectual and Religious History of Late Medieval and Reformation Europe* (New Haven, Conn.: Yale University Press, 1980), p. 284.
4. Ludwig Rabus, *Historien der heyligen Außerwolten Gottes Zeugen, Bekennern und Martyrern* (n.p., 1557), fol. 41. Trans. Merry Wiesner-Hanks.
5. From Henry Bettenson, ed., *Documents of the Christian Church*, 2d ed. (London: Oxford University Press, 1963), pp. 301–302. Used by permission of Oxford University Press.
6. J. Allen, trans., *John Calvin: The Institutes of the Christian Religion* (Philadelphia: Westminster Press, 1930), bk. 3, chap. 21, para. 5, 7.
7. Quoted in David P. Daniel, "Hungary," in *The Oxford Encyclopedia of the Reformation*, vol. 2, ed. H. J. Hillerbrand (New York: Oxford University Press, 1996), p. 273.
8. *The Spiritual Exercises of St. Ignatius of Loyola*, trans. Louis J. Puhl, S.J. (Chicago: Loyola University, 1951), p. 1.
9. From *The Fugger News-Letters*, ed. Victor von Klarwell, trans. P. de Chary (London: John Lane, The Bodley Head Ltd., 1924), quoted in James Bruce Ross and Mary Martin McLaughlin, *The Portable Renaissance Reader* (New York: Penguin, 1968), pp. 258, 260, 262.

LOOKING BACK LOOKING AHEAD

The Renaissance and the Reformation are often seen as two of the key elements in the creation of the "modern" world. The radical changes brought by the Reformation contained many aspects of continuity, however. Sixteenth-century reformers looked back to the early Christian Church for their inspiration, and many of their reforming ideas had been advocated for centuries. Most Protestant reformers worked with political leaders to make religious changes, just as early church officials had worked with Emperor Constantine and his successors as Christianity became the official religion of the Roman Empire in the fourth century. The spread of Christianity and the spread of Protestantism were accomplished not only by preaching, persuasion, and teaching, but also by force and violence. The Catholic Reformation was carried out by activist popes, a church council, and new religious orders, like earlier reforms of the church had been.

Just as they linked with earlier developments, the events of the Reformation were also closely connected with what is often seen as the third element in the "modern" world: European exploration and colonization. Only a week after Martin Luther stood in front of Charles V at the Diet of Worms declaring his independence in matters of religion, Ferdinand Magellan, a Portuguese sea captain with Spanish ships, was killed in a group of islands off the coast of Southeast Asia. Charles V had provided the backing for Magellan's voyage, the first to circumnavigate the globe. Magellan viewed the spread of Christianity as one of the purposes of his trip, and later in the sixteenth century institutions created as part of the Catholic Reformation, including the Jesuit order and the Inquisition, would operate in European colonies overseas as well as in Europe itself. The islands where Magellan was killed were later named the Philippines, in honor of Charles's son Philip, who sent the ill-fated Spanish Armada against England. Philip's opponent Queen Elizabeth was similarly honored when English explorers named a huge chunk of territory in North America "Virginia" as a tribute to their "Virgin Queen." The desire for wealth and power was an important motivation in the European voyages and colonial ventures, but so was religious zeal.

REVIEW and EXPLORE

MAKE IT STICK

 LearningCurve
After reading the chapter, go online and use LearningCurve to retain what you've read.

Identify Key Terms

Identify and explain the significance of each item below.

anticlericalism (p. 392)

indulgence (p. 393)

Protestant (p. 397)

Spanish Armada (p. 410)

The Institutes of the Christian Religion (p. 410)

predestination (p. 410)

Holy Office (p. 414)

Jesuits (p. 416)

Huguenots (p. 418)

politiques (p. 419)

Edict of Nantes (p. 419)

Union of Utrecht (p. 420)

Review the Main Ideas

Answer the focus questions from each section of the chapter.

◆ What were the central ideas of the reformers, and why were they appealing to different social groups? (p. 392)

◆ How did the political situation in Germany shape the course of the Reformation? (p. 404)

◆ How did Protestant ideas and institutions spread beyond German-speaking lands? (p. 407)

◆ What reforms did the Catholic Church make, and how did it respond to Protestant reform movements? (p. 414)

◆ What were the causes and consequences of religious violence, including riots, wars, and witch-hunts? (p. 417)

Make Connections

Think about the larger developments and continuities within and across chapters.

1. Martin Luther is always on every list of the one hundred most influential people of all time. Should he be? Why or why not? Who else from this chapter should be on such a list, and why?

2. How did Protestant ideas about gender, marriage, and the role of women break with those developed earlier in the history of the Christian Church (Chapters 6, 7, 9)? What continuities do you see? What factors account for the pattern that you have found?

3. In what ways was the Catholic Reformation of the sixteeenth century similar to earlier efforts to reform the church, including the Gregorian reforms of the twelfth century (Chapter 9) and late medieval reform efforts (Chapter 11)? In what ways was it different?

ONLINE DOCUMENT ASSIGNMENT
Anna Jansz of Rotterdam

What might have led Jansz and thousands like her to die for their religious convictions?

You encountered Anna Jansz's story on page 401. Keeping the question above in mind, go to the Integrated Media and learn more about Jansz and other Anabaptist martyrs by analyzing images and hymns, and then complete a writing assignment based on the evidence and details from this chapter.

Suggested Reading and Media Resources

BOOKS

- Brady, Thomas A. *German Histories in the Age of Reformations, 1400–1650.* 2009. Examines the broad political context of the Holy Roman Empire and the ways in which this shaped both the Reformation and subsequent German history.

- Cameron, Euan. *The European Reformation*, 2d ed. 2012. A thorough analysis of the Protestant and Catholic Reformations throughout Europe.

- Gordon, Bruce. *John Calvin.* 2009. Situates Calvin's theology and life within the context of his relationships and the historical events of his time.

- Hendrix, Scott. *Luther.* 2009. A brief introduction to Luther's thought; part of the Abingdon Pillars of Theology series.

- Holt, Mack P. *The French Wars of Religion, 1562–1629*, 2d ed. 2005. A thorough survey designed for students.

- Hsia, R. Po-Chia. *The World of Catholic Renewal, 1540–1770*, 2d ed. 2005. Situates the Catholic Reformation in a global context and provides coverage of colonial Catholicism.

- Levack, Brian. *The Witch-Hunt in Early Modern Europe*, 3d ed. 2007. A good introduction to the witch-hunts, with helpful bibliographies of the vast literature on witchcraft.

- Levi, Anthony. *Renaissance and Reformation: The Intellectual Genesis.* 2002. Surveys the ideas of major Reformation figures against the background of important political issues.

- Matheson, Peter, ed. *Reformation Christianity.* 2004. This volume in the People's History of Christianity series explores social issues and popular religion.

- O'Malley, John W. *Trent and All That: Renaming Catholicism in the Early Modern Era.* 2000. Provides an excellent historiographical review of the literature, and explains why and how early modern Catholicism influenced early modern European history.

- Shagan, Ethan. *Popular Politics and the English Reformation.* 2003. Analyzes the process of the Reformation in local areas.

DOCUMENTARIES

- *The Protestant Revolution* (BBC, 2007). A four-part documentary series that examines the religious roots and the scientific, cultural, social, economic, and political impact of Protestantism, viewing these as wide ranging and global in scope.

FEATURE FILMS AND TELEVISION

- *Luther* (Eric Till, 2003). A fairly accurate biopic, starring Joseph Fiennes, which traces Martin Luther's life from his becoming a monk through his break with the church, marriage, and the German Peasants' War.

- *A Man for All Seasons* (Fred Zinnemann, 1966). A classic Academy Award–winning film on Thomas More's confrontation with Henry VIII over the king's efforts to obtain a divorce; portrays More as a heroic figure who followed his principles.

- *The Tudors* (Showtime, 2007–2010). A four-season historical fiction extravaganza centering on Henry VIII and his wives, full of sex and intrigue. Great fun, not so great history.

- *Witchcraze* (BBC, 2003). A docudrama examining the Scottish witch trials of 1590–1591, when thirty women and one man were arrested, tortured, and eventually hanged or burned at the stake; based on original documents from the period, including court records.

WEB SITES

- *H. Henry Meeter Center for Calvin Studies.* Resources, including audio and video recordings, on John Calvin and Calvinism, collected by the Meeter Center at Calvin College in Michigan. **www.calvin.edu/meeter/**

- *Project Wittenberg.* Concordia Theological Seminary's site devoted to the life and works of Martin Luther, with the largest online collection of Luther's writings in English, and many of his works in the original German or Latin. **iclnet.org/pub/resources/text/wittenberg/wittenberg-home.html**

- *Tudor History.* Frequently updated site run by Lara E. Eakins with much useful general information on people, chronologies, an image gallery, links, and a Tudor history blog. **www.tudorhistory.org/**

14

European Exploration and Conquest

1450–1650

Before 1450 Europeans were relatively marginal players in a centuries-old trading system that linked Africa, Asia, and Europe. Elites everywhere prized Chinese porcelains and silks, while wealthy members of the Celestial Kingdom, as China called itself, wanted ivory and black slaves from Africa, and exotic goods and peacocks from India. African people wanted textiles from India and cowrie shells from the Maldives in the Indian Ocean. Europeans craved Asian silks and spices, but they had few desirable goods to offer their trading partners.

Europeans' search for better access to Asian trade led to a new empire in the Indian Ocean and the accidental discovery of the Western Hemisphere. Within a few decades European colonies in South and North America would join this worldwide web of commerce. Capitalizing on the goods and riches they found in the Americas, Europeans came to dominate trading networks and built political empires of truly global proportions. The era of globalization had begun.

Global contacts created new forms of cultural exchange, assimilation, conversion, and resistance. Europeans struggled to comprehend the peoples and societies they encountered and sought to impose European cultural values on them. New forms of racial prejudice emerged, but so did new openness and curiosity about different ways of life. Together with the developments of the Renaissance and the Reformation, the Age of Discovery — as the period of European exploration and conquest from 1450 to 1650 is known — laid the foundations for the modern world. ◼

Life in the Age of Discovery. The arrival of the Portuguese in Japan in 1453 inspired a series of artworks depicting the *namban-jin* or southern barbarians, as they were known. This detail from an early-seventeenth-century painted screen shows Portuguese sailors unloading trade goods from a merchant ship. (akg-images/De Agostini Picture Library)

CHAPTER PREVIEW

 LearningCurve
After reading the chapter, go online and use LearningCurve to retain what you've read.

World Contacts Before Columbus
What was the Afroeurasian trading world before Columbus?

The European Voyages of Discovery
How and why did Europeans undertake ambitious voyages of expansion?

The Impact of Conquest
What was the impact of European conquest on the peoples and ecologies of the New World?

Europe and the World After Columbus
How was the era of global contact shaped by new commodities, commercial empires, and forced migrations?

Changing Attitudes and Beliefs
How did new ideas about race and the works of Montaigne and Shakespeare reflect the encounter with new peoples and places?

World Contacts Before Columbus

What was the Afroeurasian trading world before Columbus?

Columbus did not sail west on a whim. To understand his and other Europeans' explorations, we must first understand late medieval trade networks. Historians now recognize that a type of world economy, known as the Afroeurasian trade world, linked the products and people of Asia, Africa, and Europe in the fifteenth century. The West was not the dominant player before Columbus, and the European voyages derived from a desire to share in and control the wealth coming from the Indian Ocean.

The Trade World of the Indian Ocean

The Indian Ocean was the center of the Afroeurasian trade world. Its location made it a crossroads for exchange among China, India, the Middle East, Africa, and Europe (Map 14.1). From the seventh through the fourteenth centuries, the volume of this trade steadily increased, declining only during the years of the Black Death.

Merchants congregated in a series of cosmopolitan port cities strung around the Indian Ocean. Most of these cities had some form of autonomous self-government. Mutual self-interest had largely limited violence and attempts to monopolize trade. The most developed area of this commercial web was in the South China Sea. In the fifteenth century the port of Malacca became a great commercial entrepôt (AHN-truh-poh), a trading post to which goods were shipped for storage while awaiting redistribution. To Malacca came Chinese porcelains, silks, and camphor (used in the manufacture of many medications); pepper, cloves, nutmeg, and raw materials such as sandalwood from the Moluccas; sugar from the Philippines; and Indian textiles, copper weapons, incense, dyes, and opium.

The Mongol emperors opened the doors of China to the West, encouraging Europeans like the Venetian trader and explorer Marco Polo to do business there. Marco Polo's tales of his travels from 1271 to 1295 and his encounter with the Great Khan fueled Western fantasies about the exotic Orient. Polo vividly recounted the splendors of the Khan's court and the city of Hangzhou, which he described as "the finest and noblest

The Port of Calicut in India The port of Calicut, located on the west coast of India, was a center of the Indian Ocean spice trade during the Middle Ages. Vasco da Gama arrived in Calicut in 1498 and obtained permission to trade there, leading to hostilities between the Portuguese and the Arab traders who had previously dominated the port. (Private Collection/The Stapleton Collection/The Bridgeman Art Library)

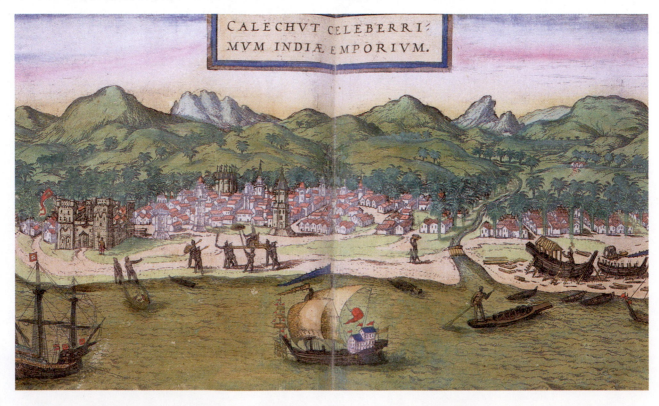

CALECHVT CELEBERRI: MVM INDIÆ EMPORIVM.

in the world" in which "the number and wealth of the merchants, and the amount of goods that passed through their hands, was so enormous that no man could form a just estimate thereof."[1] After the Mongols fell to the Ming Dynasty in 1368, China entered a period of economic expansion, population growth, and urbanization. By the end of the dynasty in 1644, the Chinese population had tripled to between 150 million and 200 million. The city of Nanjing had 1 million inhabitants, making it the largest city in the world, while the new capital, Beijing, had more than 600,000 inhabitants, larger than any European city. Historians agree that China had the most advanced economy in the world until at least the start of the eighteenth century.

China also took the lead in exploration, sending Admiral Zheng He's fleet along the trade web as far west as Egypt. From 1405 to 1433, each of his seven expeditions involved hundreds of ships and tens of thousands of men. In one voyage alone, Zheng He (JEHNG HUH) sailed more than 12,000 miles, compared to Columbus's 2,400 miles on his first voyage some sixty years later.[2] Court conflicts and the need to defend against renewed Mongol encroachment led to the abandonment of the maritime expeditions after the deaths of Zheng He and the emperor. China's turning away from external trade opened new opportunities for European states to claim a decisive role in world trade.

Another center of trade in the Indian Ocean was India. The subcontinent had ancient links with its neighbors to the northwest: trade between South Asia and Mesopotamia dates back to the origins of human civilization. Romans had acquired cotton textiles, exotic animals, and other luxury goods from India. Arab merchants who circumnavigated India on their way to trade in the South China Sea established trading posts along the southern coast of India, where the cities of Calicut and Quilon became thriving commercial centers. India was an important contributor of goods to the world trading system; much of the world's pepper was grown there, and Indian cotton textiles were highly prized.

The Trading States of Africa

By 1450 Africa had a few large empires along with hundreds of smaller states. From 1250 until its defeat by the Ottomans in 1517, the Mamluk Egyptian empire was one of the most powerful on the continent. Its capital, Cairo, was a center of Islamic learning and religious authority as well as a hub for Indian Ocean

Chronology

1271–1295	Marco Polo travels to China
1443	Portuguese establish first African trading post at Arguin
1492	Columbus lands in the Americas
1511	Portuguese capture Malacca from Muslims
1518	Spanish king authorizes slave trade to New World colonies
1519–1522	Magellan's expedition circumnavigates the world
1521	Cortés conquers the Mexica Empire
1533	Pizarro conquers the Inca Empire
1602	Dutch East India Company established

trade goods. Sharing in Cairo's prosperity was the African highland state of Ethiopia, a Christian kingdom with scattered contacts with European rulers. On the east coast of Africa, Swahili-speaking city-states engaged in the Indian Ocean trade, exchanging ivory, rhinoceros horn, tortoise shells, and slaves for textiles, spices, cowrie shells, porcelain, and other goods. Peopled by confident and urbane merchants, cities like Kilwa, Malindi, Mogadishu, and Mombasa were known for their prosperity and culture.

In the fifteenth century most of the gold that reached Europe came from the western part of the Sudan region in West Africa and from the Akan (AH-kahn) peoples living near present-day Ghana. Transported across the Sahara by Arab and African traders on camels, the gold was sold in the ports of North Africa. Other trading routes led to the Egyptian cities of Alexandria and Cairo, where the Venetians held commercial privileges.

Nations inland that sat astride the north-south caravan routes grew wealthy from this trade. In the mid-thirteenth century the kingdom of Mali emerged as an important player on the overland trade route, gaining prestige from its ruler Mansa Musa's fabulous pilgrimage to Mecca in 1324/25. Mansa Musa reportedly came to the throne after the previous king failed to return from a naval expedition he led to explore the Atlantic Ocean. A document by a contemporary scholar, al-Umari, quoted Mansa Musa's description of his predecessor as a man who "did not believe that the ocean was impossible to cross. He wished to reach the other side and was passionately interested in doing so."[3] After only one ship returned from an earlier expedition, the king set out himself at the head of a fleet of two thousand vessels, a voyage from which no one returned. Corroboration of these early expeditions is lacking, but this report underlines the wealth and ambition of Mali in this period. In later centuries the

Map 14.1 The Fifteenth-Century Afroeurasian Trading World   After a period of decline following the Black Death and the Mongol invasions, trade revived in the fifteenth century. Muslim merchants dominated trade, linking ports in East Africa and the Red Sea with those in India and the Malay Archipelago. Chinese admiral Zheng He's voyages (1405–1433) followed the most important Indian Ocean trade routes, in the hope of imposing Ming dominance of trade and tribute.

diversion of gold away from the trans-Sahara routes would weaken the inland states of Africa politically and economically.

Gold was one important object of trade; slaves were another. Slavery was practiced in Africa, as it was virtually everywhere else in the world, before the arrival of Europeans. Arabic and African merchants took West African slaves to the Mediterranean to be sold in European, Egyptian, and Middle Eastern markets and also brought eastern Europeans—a major element of European slavery—to West Africa as slaves. In addition, Indian and Arabic merchants traded slaves in the coastal regions of East Africa.

Legends about Africa played an important role in Europeans' imagination of the outside world. They long cherished the belief in a Christian nation in Africa ruled by a mythical king, Prester John, who was believed to be a descendant of one of the three kings who visited Jesus after his birth.

The Ottoman and Persian Empires

The Middle East served as an intermediary for trade between Asia, Africa, and Europe and was also an important supplier of goods for foreign exchange, especially silk and cotton. Two great rival empires, the Persian Safavids (sah-FAH-vidz) and the Turkish Ottomans, dominated the region. Persian merchants could be found in trading communities as far away as the Indian Ocean. Persia was also a major producer and exporter of silk.

The Persians' Shi'ite Muslim faith clashed with the Ottomans' adherence to Sunnism. Economically, the two competed for control over western trade routes to the East. Under Sultan Mohammed II (r. 1451–1481), the Ottomans captured Europe's largest city, Constantinople, in May 1453. Renamed Istanbul, the city became the capital of the Ottoman Empire. By the

mid-sixteenth century the Ottomans controlled the sea trade in the eastern Mediterranean, Syria, Palestine, Egypt, and the rest of North Africa, and their power extended into Europe as far west as Vienna.

Ottoman expansion frightened Europeans. The Ottoman armies seemed invincible and the empire's desire for expansion limitless. In France in the sixteenth century, only forty books were published on the American discoveries compared to eighty on Turkey and the Turks.[4] The strength of the Ottomans helps explain some of the missionary fervor Christians brought to new territories. It also raised economic concerns. With trade routes to the East dominated by the Ottomans, Europeans wished to find new trade routes free of Ottoman control.

Genoese and Venetian Middlemen

Compared to the riches and vibrancy of the East, Europe constituted a minor outpost of the world trading system. European craftsmen produced few products to rival the fine wares and coveted spices of Asia. In the late Middle Ages, the Italian city-states of Venice and Genoa controlled the European luxury trade with the East.

In 1304 Venice established formal relations with the sultan of Mamluk Egypt, opening operations in Cairo, the gateway to Asian trade. Venetian merchants specialized in goods like spices, silks, and carpets, which they obtained from middlemen in the eastern Mediterranean and Asia Minor. A little went a long way. Venetians purchased no more than five hundred tons of spices a year around 1400, with a profit of about 40 percent. The most important spice was pepper, grown in India and Indonesia, which composed 60 percent of the spices they purchased in 1400.[5]

The Venetians exchanged Eastern luxury goods for European products they could trade abroad, including Spanish and English wool, German metal goods, Flemish textiles, and silk cloth made in their own manufactures with imported raw materials. Eastern demand for such items, however, was low. To make up the difference, the Venetians earned currency in the shipping industry and through trade in firearms and slaves. At least half of what they traded with the East took the form of precious metal, much of it acquired in Egypt and North Africa. When the Portuguese arrived in Asia in the late fifteenth century, they found Venetian coins everywhere.

Venice's ancient rival was Genoa. In the wake of the Crusades, Genoa dominated the northern route to Asia through the Black Sea. Expansion in the thirteenth and fourteenth centuries took the Genoese as far as Persia and the Far East. In 1291 they sponsored an expedition into the Atlantic in search of India. The ships were lost, and their exact destination and motivations remain unknown. This voyage reveals the long roots of Genoese interest in Atlantic exploration.

In the fifteenth century, with Venice claiming victory in the spice trade, the Genoese shifted focus from trade to finance and from the Black Sea to the western Mediterranean. Located on the northwestern coast of Italy, Genoa had always been active in the western Mediterranean, trading with North African ports, southern France, Spain, and even England and Flanders through the Strait of Gibraltar. When Spanish and Portuguese voyages began to explore the western

Atlantic (see pages 435–440), Genoese merchants, navigators, and financiers provided their skills to the Iberian monarchs, whose own subjects had much less commercial experience. The Genoese, for example, ran many of the sugar plantations established on the Atlantic islands colonized by the Portuguese. Genoese merchants would eventually help finance Spanish colonization of the New World.

A major element of Italian trade was slavery. Merchants purchased slaves, many of whom were fellow Christians, in the Balkans. The men were sold to Egypt for the sultan's army or sent to work as agricultural laborers in the Mediterranean. Young girls, who constituted the majority of the trade, were sold in western Mediterranean ports as servants or concubines. After the loss of the Black Sea—and thus the source of slaves—to the Ottomans, the Genoese sought new supplies of slaves in the West, taking the Guanches (indigenous peoples from the Canary Islands), Muslim prisoners and Jewish refugees from Spain, and by the early 1500s both black and Berber Africans. With the growth of Spanish colonies in the New World, Genoese and Venetian merchants would become important players in the Atlantic slave trade.

Italian experience in colonial administration, slaving, and international trade served as a model for the Iberian states as they pushed European expansion to new heights. Mariners, merchants, and financiers from Venice and Genoa—most notably Christopher Columbus—played a crucial role in bringing the fruits of this experience to the Iberian Peninsula and to the New World.

The European Voyages of Discovery

How and why did Europeans undertake ambitious voyages of expansion?

As we have seen, Europe was by no means isolated before the voyages of exploration and its "discovery" of the New World. But because they did not produce many products desired by Eastern elites, Europeans played only a small role in the Indian Ocean trading world. As Europe recovered after the Black Death, new European players entered the scene with novel technology, eager to spread Christianity and to undo Italian and Ottoman domination of trade with the East. A century after the plague, Iberian explorers began the overseas voyages that helped create the modern world, with staggering consequences for their own continent and the rest of the planet.

Causes of European Expansion

European expansion had multiple causes. By the middle of the fifteenth century, Europe was experiencing a revival of population and economic activity after the lows of the Black Death. This revival created demand for luxuries, especially spices, from the East. The fall of Constantinople and subsequent Ottoman control of trade routes created obstacles to fulfilling these demands. Europeans needed to find new sources of precious metal to trade with the Ottomans or trade routes that bypassed the Ottomans.

Why were spices so desirable? Introduced into western Europe by the Crusaders in the twelfth century, pepper, nutmeg, ginger, mace, cinnamon, and cloves added flavor and variety to the monotonous European diet. Not only did spices serve as flavorings for food, but they were also used in anointing oil and as incense for religious rituals, and as perfumes, medicines, and dyes in daily life. Take, for example, cloves, for which Europeans found many uses. If picked green and sugared, the buds could be transformed into jam; if salted and pickled, cloves became a flavoring for vinegar. Cloves sweetened the breath. When added to food or drink, they were thought to stimulate the appetite and clear the intestines and bladder. When crushed and powdered, they were a medicine rubbed on the forehead to relieve head colds and applied to the eyes to strengthen vision. Taken with milk, they were believed to enhance sexual pleasure.

Religious fervor was another important catalyst for expansion. The passion and energy ignited by the Christian reconquista (reconquest) of the Iberian Peninsula encouraged the Portuguese and Spanish to continue the Christian crusade. Just seven months separated Isabella and Ferdinand's conquest of the emirate of Granada, the last remaining Muslim state on the Iberian Peninsula, and Columbus's departure across the Atlantic. Overseas exploration was in some ways a transfer of the crusading spirit to new non-Christian territories. Since the remaining Muslim states, such as the mighty Ottoman Empire, were too strong to defeat, Iberians turned their attention elsewhere.

Combined with eagerness to earn profits and to spread Christianity was the desire for glory and the urge to chart new waters. Scholars have frequently described the European discoveries as a manifestation of Renaissance curiosity about the physical universe—the desire to know more about the geography and peoples of the world. The detailed journals many voyagers kept attest to their wonder and fascination with the new peoples and places they visited.

Individual explorers combined these motivations in unique ways. Christopher Columbus was a devout Christian who was increasingly haunted by messianic obsessions in the last years of his life. As Portuguese explorer Bartholomew Diaz put it, his own motives were "to serve God and His Majesty, to give light to those who were in darkness and to grow rich as all men desire to do." When the Portuguese explorer Vasco da Gama reached the port of Calicut, India, in 1498 and a native asked what he wanted, he replied, "Christians and spices."[6] The bluntest of the Spanish **conquistadors** (kohn-KEES-tuh-dorz), Hernando Cortés, announced as he prepared to conquer Mexico, "I have come to win gold, not to plow the fields like a peasant."[7]

Eagerness for exploration was heightened by a lack of opportunity at home. After the reconquista, young men of the Spanish upper classes found their economic and political opportunities greatly limited. The ambitious turned to the sea to seek their fortunes.

Their voyages were made possible by the growth of government power. The Spanish monarchy was stronger than before and in a position to support foreign ventures. In Portugal explorers also looked to the monarchy, to Prince Henry the Navigator in particular (page 435), for financial support and encouragement. Like voyagers, monarchs shared a mix of motivations, from the desire to please God to the desire to win glory and profit from trade. Competition among European monarchs and between Protestant and Catholic states was an important factor in encouraging the steady stream of expeditions that began in the late fifteenth century.

Ordinary sailors were ill paid, and life at sea meant danger, overcrowding, and hunger. For months at a time, 100 to 120 people lived and worked in a space of 1,600 to 2,000 square feet. A lucky sailor would find enough space on deck to unroll his sleeping mat. Horses, cows, pigs, chickens, rats, and lice accompanied sailors on the voyages. As one scholar concluded, "traveling on a ship must have been one of the most uncomfortable and oppressive experiences in the world."[8]

Men chose to join these miserable crews to escape poverty at home, to continue a family trade, or to find better lives as illegal immigrants in the colonies. Many orphans and poor boys were placed on board as young pages and had little say in the decision. Women also paid a price for the voyages of exploration. Left alone for months or years at a time, and frequently widowed, sailors' wives struggled to feed their families. The widow of a sailor lost on a voyage in 1519 had to wait almost thirty years to collect her husband's salary from the Spanish crown.[9]

The people who stayed at home had a powerful impact on the process. Royal ministers and factions at court influenced monarchs to provide or deny support for exploration. The small number of people who could read served as a rapt audience for tales of fantastic places and unknown peoples. Cosmography, natural history, and geography aroused enormous interest among educated people in the fifteenth and sixteenth centuries. One of the most popular books of the time was the fourteenth-century text *The Travels of Sir John Mandeville*, which purported to be a firsthand account of the author's travels in the Holy Land, Egypt, Ethiopia, the Middle East, and India and his service to the Mamluk sultan of Egypt and the Mongol Great Khan of China. Although we now know the stories were fictional, these fantastic tales of cannibals, one-eyed giants, men with the heads of dogs, and other marvels convinced audiences through their vividly and persuasively described details. Christopher Columbus took a copy of Mandeville and the equally popular and more reliable *The Travels of Marco Polo* on his voyage in 1492.

Technology and the Rise of Exploration

Technological developments in shipbuilding, weaponry, and navigation also paved the way for European expansion. Since ancient times, most seagoing vessels had been narrow, open boats called galleys, propelled largely by slaves or convicts manning the oars. Though well suited to the placid waters of the Mediterranean, galleys could not withstand the rough winds and uncharted shoals of the Atlantic. The need for sturdier craft, as well as population losses caused by the Black Death, forced the development of a new style of ship that would not require much manpower to sail. In the course of the fifteenth century, the Portuguese developed the **caravel**, a small, light, three-mast sailing ship. Though somewhat slower than the galley, the caravel held more cargo. Its triangular lateen sails and sternpost rudder also made the caravel a much more maneuverable vessel. When fitted with cannon, it could dominate larger vessels.

Great strides in cartography and navigational aids were also made during this period. Around 1410 Arab scholars reintroduced Europeans to **Ptolemy's Geography**. Written in the second century c.e. by a Hellenized Egyptian, the work synthesized the geographical knowledge of the classical world. Ptolemy's work provided significant improvements over medieval cartography, clearly depicting the world as round and introducing the idea of latitude and longitude to plot position accurately. It

conquistador Spanish for "conqueror"; Spanish soldier-explorers, such as Hernando Cortés and Francisco Pizarro, who sought to conquer the New World for the Spanish crown.

caravel A small, maneuverable, three-mast sailing ship developed by the Portuguese in the fifteenth century that gave the Portuguese a distinct advantage in exploration and trade.

Ptolemy's Geography A second-century-c.e. work that synthesized the classical knowledge of geography and introduced the concepts of longitude and latitude. Reintroduced to Europeans about 1410 by Arab scholars, its ideas allowed cartographers to create more accurate maps.

also contained crucial errors. Unaware of the Americas, Ptolemy showed the world as much smaller than it is, so that Asia appeared not very distant from Europe to the west. Based on this work, cartographers fashioned new maps that combined classical knowledge with the latest information from mariners. First the Genoese and Venetians, and then the Portuguese and Spanish, took the lead in these advances.

The magnetic compass enabled sailors to determine their direction and position at sea. The astrolabe, an instrument invented by the ancient Greeks and perfected by Muslim navigators, was used to determine the altitude of the sun and other celestial bodies. It permitted mariners to plot their latitude, that is, their precise position north or south of the equator.

Like the astrolabe, much of the new technology that Europeans used on their voyages was borrowed from the East. Gunpowder, the compass, and the sternpost rudder were Chinese inventions. The lateen sail, which allowed European ships to tack against the wind, was a product of the Indian Ocean trade world. Advances in cartography drew on the rich tradition of Judeo-Arabic mathematical and astronomical learning in Iberia. Sometimes assistance to Europeans came from humans rather than instruments. The famed explorer Vasco da Gama employed a local Indian pilot to guide his expedition from the East African coast to India. In exploring new territories, European sailors thus called on techniques and knowledge developed over centuries in China, the Muslim world, and the Indian Ocean.

Brass Astrolabe   Between 1500 and 1635 over nine hundred ships sailed from Portugal to ports on the Indian Ocean, in annual fleets composed of five to ten ships. Portuguese sailors used astrolabes, such as the one shown here, to accurately plot their position. (© The Trustees of the British Museum)

Ptolemy's *Geography*   The recovery of Ptolemy's *Geography* in the early fifteenth century gave Europeans new access to ancient geographical knowledge. This 1486 world map, based on Ptolemy, is a great advance over medieval maps but contains errors with significant consequences for future exploration. It shows a single continent watered by a single ocean, with land covering three-quarters of the world's surface. Africa and Asia are joined with Europe, making the Indian Ocean a landlocked sea and rendering the circumnavigation of Africa impossible. Australia and the Americas are nonexistent, and the continent of Asia is stretched far to the east, greatly shortening the distance from Europe to Asia via the Atlantic. (Bibliothèque nationale de France/Giraudon/The Bridgeman Art Library)

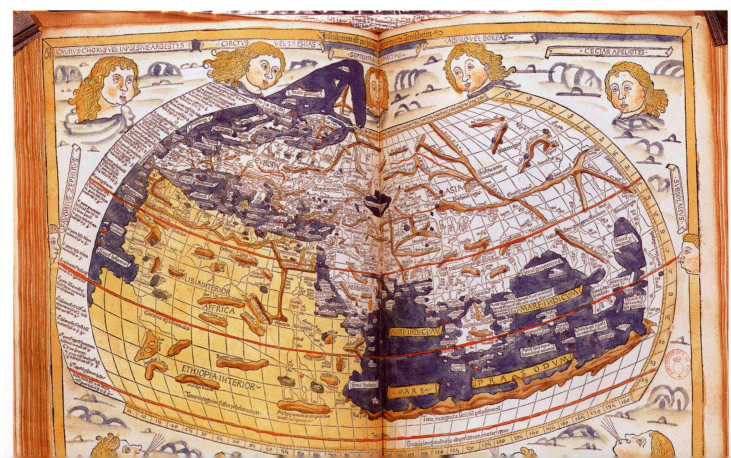

The Portuguese Overseas Empire

For centuries Portugal was a small, poor nation on the margins of European life whose principal activities were fishing and subsistence farming. It would have been hard for a European to predict Portugal's phenomenal success overseas after 1450. Yet Portugal had a long history of seafaring and navigation. Blocked from access to western Europe by Spain, the Portuguese turned to the Atlantic and North Africa, whose waters they knew better than other Europeans. Nature favored the Portuguese: winds blowing along their coast offered passage to Africa, its Atlantic islands, and, ultimately, Brazil.

In the early phases of Portuguese exploration, Prince Henry (1394–1460), a younger son of the king, played a leading role. A nineteenth-century scholar dubbed Henry "the Navigator" because of his support for the study of geography and navigation and for the annual expeditions he sponsored down the western coast of Africa. Although he never personally participated in voyages of exploration, Henry's involvement ensured that Portugal did not abandon the effort despite early disappointments.

The objectives of Portuguese exploration policy included military glory; the conversion of Muslims; and a quest to find gold, slaves, and an overseas route to the spice markets of India. Portugal's conquest of Ceuta, an Arab city in northern Morocco, in 1415 marked the beginning of European overseas expansion. In the 1420s, under Henry's direction, the Portuguese began to settle the Atlantic islands of Madeira (ca. 1420) and the Azores (1427). In 1443 they founded their first African commercial settlement at Arguin in North Africa. By the time of Henry's death in 1460, his support for exploration was vindicated by thriving sugar plantations on the Atlantic islands, the first arrival of enslaved Africans in Portugal (see page 450), and new access to African gold.

The Portuguese next established trading posts and forts on the gold-rich Guinea coast and penetrated into the African continent all the way to Timbuktu (Map 14.2). By 1500 Portugal controlled the flow of African gold to Europe. The golden century of Portuguese prosperity had begun.

The Portuguese then pushed farther south down the west coast of Africa. In 1487 Bartholomew Diaz rounded the Cape of Good Hope at the southern tip, but storms and a threatened mutiny forced him to turn back. A decade later Vasco da Gama succeeded in rounding the Cape while commanding a fleet of four ships in search of a sea route to India. With the help of an Indian guide, da Gama reached the port of Calicut in India. Overcoming local hostility, he returned to Lisbon loaded with spices and samples of Indian cloth. He had failed to forge any trading alliances with local powers, and Portuguese arrogance ensured the future hostility of Muslim merchants who dominated the trading system. Nonetheless, da Gama proved the possibility of lucrative trade with the East via the Cape route. Thereafter, a Portuguese convoy set out for passage around the Cape every March.

Lisbon became the entrance port for Asian goods into Europe, but this was not accomplished without a fight. Muslim-controlled port city-states had long controlled the rich spice trade of the Indian Ocean, and they did not surrender their dominance willingly. From 1500 to 1511 the Portuguese used a combination of bombardment and diplomatic treaties to establish trading forts at Calicut, Malacca, Hormuz, and Goa, thereby laying the foundation for Portuguese imperialism in the sixteenth and seventeenth centuries. (See "Primary Source 14.1: A Portuguese Traveler Describes Swahili City-States of East Africa," page 437.)

In March 1493, between the voyages of Diaz and da Gama, Spanish ships under a triumphant Genoese mariner named Christopher Columbus (1451–1506), in the service of the Spanish crown, entered Lisbon harbor. Spain also had begun the quest for an empire.

The Problem of Christopher Columbus

Christopher Columbus is a controversial figure in history—glorified by some as a courageous explorer, vilified by others as a cruel exploiter of Native Americans. Many have questioned how he could "discover" the Americas, given the millennia of indigenous population prior to his arrival and earlier transatlantic crossings of the Vikings. Rather than judging Columbus by debates and standards of our time, it is more important to understand him in the context of his own time. First, what kind of man was Columbus, and what forces or influences shaped him? Second, in sailing westward from Europe, what were his goals? Third, did he achieve his goals, and what did he make of his discoveries?

In his dream of a westward passage to the Indies, Columbus embodied a long-standing Genoese ambition to circumvent Venetian domination of eastward trade, which was now being claimed by the Portuguese. Columbus was very knowledgeable about the sea. He had worked as a mapmaker, and he was familiar with fifteenth-century Portuguese navigational developments and the use of the compass as a nautical instrument. As he asserted in his journal: "I have spent twenty-three years at sea and have not left it for any length of time worth mentioning, and I have seen every thing from east to west [meaning he had been to

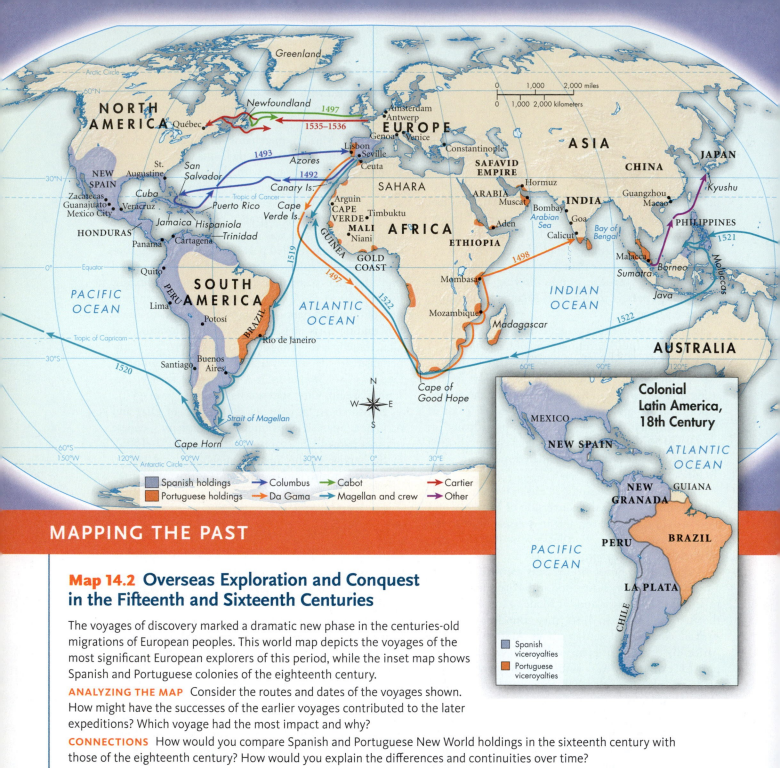

MAPPING THE PAST

Map 14.2 Overseas Exploration and Conquest in the Fifteenth and Sixteenth Centuries

The voyages of discovery marked a dramatic new phase in the centuries-old migrations of European peoples. This world map depicts the voyages of the most significant European explorers of this period, while the inset map shows Spanish and Portuguese colonies of the eighteenth century.

ANALYZING THE MAP Consider the routes and dates of the voyages shown. How might have the successes of the earlier voyages contributed to the later expeditions? Which voyage had the most impact and why?

CONNECTIONS How would you compare Spanish and Portuguese New World holdings in the sixteenth century with those of the eighteenth century? How would you explain the differences and continuities over time?

England] and I have been to Guinea [North and West Africa]."[10] His successful thirty-three-day voyage to the Caribbean owed a great deal to his seamanship.

Columbus was also a deeply religious man. He had witnessed the Spanish conquest of Granada and shared fully in the religious and nationalistic fervor surrounding that event. Like the Spanish rulers and most Europeans of his age, Columbus understood Christianity as a missionary religion that should be carried to all places of the earth. He viewed himself as a divine agent: "God made me the messenger of the new heaven and the new earth of which he spoke in

the Apocalypse of St. John . . . and he showed me the post where to find it."[11]

What was the object of this first voyage? Columbus gave the answer in the very title of the expedition, "The Enterprise of the Indies." He wanted to find a direct ocean trading route to Asia. Rejected for funding by the Portuguese in 1483 and by Ferdinand and Isabella in 1486, the project finally won the backing of the Spanish monarchy in 1492. The Spanish crown named Columbus viceroy over any territory he might discover and promised him one-tenth of the material rewards of the journey. Inspired by the stories of Mandeville and

A Portuguese Traveler Describes Swahili City-States of East Africa

Duarte Barbosa traveled to India as an interpreter and scribe for the Portuguese government and ultimately perished as a member of Magellan's expedition in 1521. Before embarking with Magellan, he published a book of his observations of the people, lands, and commerce of the Indian Ocean trade world, from which the excerpt below is taken.

❝ Going along the coast from this town of Mozambique, there is an island hard by the mainland which is called Kilwa, in which is a Moorish [Muslim] town with many fair houses of stone and mortar, with many windows after our fashion, very well arranged in streets, with many flat roofs. . . . From this place they trade with Sofala, whence they bring back gold, and from here they spread all over . . . the sea-coast [which] is well-peopled with villages and abodes of Moors. Before the King our Lord [the Portuguese king] sent out his expedition to discover India the Moors of Sofala, Cuama, Angoya and Mozambique were all subject to the King of Kilwa, who was the most mighty king among them. And in this town was great plenty of gold, as no ships passed towards Sofala without first coming to this island. Of the Moors there are some fair and some black, they are finely clad in many rich garments of gold and silk and cotton, and the women as well. . . .

This town was taken by force from its king by the Portuguese, as, moved by arrogance, he refused to obey the King our Lord. There they took many prisoners and the king fled from the island, and His Highness [the Portuguese king] ordered that a fort should be built there, and kept it under his rule and governance. . . .

Journeying along the coast towards India, there is a fair town on the mainland lying along a strand, which is named Malindi. It pertains to the Moors and has a Moorish king over it; the which place has many fair stone and mortar houses of many storeys, with great plenty of windows and flat roofs, after our fashion. The place is well laid out in streets. The folk are both black and white; they go naked, covering only their private parts with cotton and silk cloths. Others of them wear cloths folded like cloaks and waist-bands, and turbans of many rich stuffs on their heads.

They are great barterers, and deal in cloth, gold, ivory, and divers other wares with the Moors and Heathen of the great kingdom of Cambaya; and to their haven come every year many ships with cargoes of merchandise, from which they get great store of gold, ivory and wax. In this traffic the Cambay merchants make great profits, and thus, on one side and the other, they earn much money. There is great plenty of food in this city (rice, millet and some wheat which they bring from Cambaya), and divers sorts of fruit, inasmuch as there is here abundance of fruit-gardens and orchards. Here too are plenty of round-tailed sheep, cows and other cattle and great store of oranges, also of hens.

The king and people of this place ever were and are friends of the King of Portugal, and the Portuguese always find in them great comfort and friendship and perfect peace. ❞

EVALUATE THE EVIDENCE

1. What impressed Barbosa in the city-states he visited? What was his attitude toward the various peoples and places he saw? Do you detect any Portuguese or Western prejudices?

2. How does this document help explain Portuguese ambitions in the Indian Ocean trade world and the relationship between the Portuguese and the Swahili city-states at the time Duarte Barbosa visited them?

Source: Mansel Longworth Dames, trans., *The Book of Duarte Barbosa*, vol. 1 (London: Bedford Press, 1918), 17–18, 22–23.

Marco Polo, Columbus dreamed of reaching the court of the Mongol emperor, the Great Khan (not realizing that the Ming Dynasty had overthrown the Mongols in 1368). Based on Ptolemy's *Geography* and other texts, he expected to pass the islands of Japan and then land on the east coast of China.

How did Columbus interpret what he had found, and in his mind did he achieve what he had set out to do? Columbus's small fleet left Spain on August 3, 1492. He landed in the Bahamas, which he christened

San Salvador, on October 12, 1492. Columbus believed he had found some small islands off the east coast of Japan. On encountering natives of the islands, he gave them some beads and "many other trifles of small value," pronouncing them delighted with these gifts and eager to trade. In a letter he wrote to Ferdinand and Isabella on his return to Spain, Columbus described the natives as handsome, peaceful, and primitive people whose body painting reminded him of that of the Canary Islands natives. Believing he was in the

Columbus Describes His First Voyage

On his return voyage to Spain in February 1493, Christopher Columbus composed a letter intended for wide circulation and had copies of it sent ahead to Queen Isabella and King Ferdinand. Because the letter sums up Columbus's understanding of his achievements, it is considered the most important document of his first voyage. Remember that his knowledge of Asia rested heavily on Marco Polo's Travels, published around 1298.

" Since I know that you will be pleased at the great success with which the Lord has crowned my voyage, I write to inform you how in thirty-three days I crossed from the Canary Islands to the Indies, with the fleet which our most illustrious sovereigns gave me. I found very many islands with large populations and took possession of them all for their Highnesses; this I did by proclamation and unfurled the royal standard. No opposition was offered.

I named the first island that I found "San Salvador," in honour of our Lord and Saviour who has granted me this miracle. . . . When I reached Cuba, I followed its north coast westwards, and found it so extensive that I thought this must be the mainland, the province of Cathay. . . .* From there I saw another island eighteen leagues eastwards which I then named "Hispaniola." . . .†

Hispaniola is a wonder. The mountains and hills, the plains and meadow lands are both fertile and beautiful. They are most suitable for planting crops and for raising cattle of all kinds, and there are good sites for building towns and villages. The harbours are incredibly fine and there are many great rivers with broad channels and the majority contain gold.‡ The trees, fruits and plants are very different from those of Cuba. In Hispaniola there are many spices and large mines of gold and other metals. . . .§

The inhabitants of this island, and all the rest that I discovered or heard of, go naked, as their mothers bore them, men and women alike. A few of the women, however, cover a single place with a leaf of a plant or piece of cotton which they weave for the purpose. They have no iron or steel or arms and are not capable of using them, not because they are not strong and well built but because they are amazingly timid. All the weapons they have are canes cut at seeding time, at the end of which they fix a sharpened stick, but they have not the courage to make use of these, for very often when I have sent two or three men to a village to have conversation with them a great number of them have come out. But as soon as they saw my men all fled immediately, a father not even waiting for his son. And this is not because we have harmed any of them; on the contrary, wherever I have gone and been able to have conversation with them, I have given them some of the various things I had, a cloth and other articles, and received nothing in exchange. But they have still remained incurably timid.

True, when they have been reassured and lost their fear, they are so ingenuous and so liberal with all their possessions that no one who has not seen them would believe it. If one asks for anything they have they never say no. On the contrary, they offer a share to anyone with demonstrations of heartfelt affection, and they are immediately content with any small thing, valuable or valueless, that is given them. I forbade the men to give them bits of broken crockery, fragments of glass or tags of laces, though if they could get them they fancied them the finest jewels in the world. . . .

I hoped to win them to the love and service of their Highnesses and of the whole Spanish nation and to persuade them to collect and give us of the things which they possessed in abundance and which we needed. They have no religion and are not idolaters; but all believe that power and goodness dwell in the sky and they are firmly convinced that I have come from the sky with these ships and people. In this belief they gave me a good reception everywhere, once they had overcome their fear; and this is not because they are stupid — far from it, they are men of great intelligence, for they navigate all those seas, and give a marvellously good account of every thing — but because they have never before seen men clothed or ships like these. . . .

In all these islands the men are seemingly content with one woman, but their chief or king is allowed more than twenty. The women appear to work more than the men and I have not been able to find out if they have private property. As far as I could see whatever a man had was shared among all the rest and this particularly applies to food. . . . In another island, which I am told is larger than Hispaniola, the people have no hair. Here there is a vast quantity of gold, and from here and the other islands I bring Indians as evidence.

*Cathay is the old name for China. In the logbook and later in this letter, Columbus accepts the native story that Cuba is an island that can be circumnavigated in something more than twenty-one days, yet he insists here and during the second voyage that it is part of the Asiatic mainland.

†Hispaniola is the second-largest island of the West Indies. Haiti occupies the western third of the island, the Dominican Republic the rest.

‡This did not prove to be true.

§These statements are also inaccurate.

In conclusion, to speak only of the results of this very hasty voyage, their Highnesses can see that I will give them as much gold as they require, if they will render me some very slight assistance; also I will give them all the spices and cotton they want. . . . I will also bring them as much aloes as they ask and as many slaves, who will be taken from the idolaters. I believe also that I have found rhubarb and cinnamon and there will be countless other things in addition. . . .

So all Christendom will be delighted that our Redeemer has given victory to our most illustrious King and Queen and their renowned kingdoms, in this great matter. They should hold great celebrations and render solemn thanks to the Holy Trinity with many solemn prayers, for the great triumph which they will have, by the conversion of so many peoples to our holy faith and for the temporal benefits which will follow, for not only Spain, but all Christendom will receive encouragement and profit.

This is a brief account of the facts. Written in the caravel off the Canary Islands.**

15 February 1493

At your orders   THE ADMIRAL 〞

EVALUATE THE EVIDENCE

1. How did Columbus explain the success of his voyage?
2. What was Columbus's view of the Native Americans he met?
3. In what ways does he exaggerate about the Caribbean islands possessing gold, cotton, and spices?

Source: Approximately 1,109 words from *The Four Voyages of Christopher Columbus*, pp. 115–123, ed. and trans. J. M. Cohen (Penguin Classics, 1969). Copyright © J. M. Cohen, 1969. Reproduced by permission of Penguin Books Ltd.

**Actually, Columbus was off Santa Maria in the Azores.

Indies, he called them "Indians," a name later applied to all inhabitants of the Americas. Columbus concluded that they would make good slaves and could easily be converted to Christianity. (See "Primary Source 14.2: Columbus Describes His First Voyage," at left.)

Scholars have identified the inhabitants of the islands as the Taino people, speakers of the Arawak language, who inhabited Hispaniola (modern-day Haiti and Dominican Republic) and other islands in the Caribbean. Columbus received reassuring reports from Taino villagers—via hand gestures and mime—of the presence of gold and of a great king in the vicinity. From San Salvador, Columbus sailed southwest, believing that this course would take him to Japan or the coast of China. He landed instead on Cuba on October 28. Deciding that he must be on the mainland near the coastal city of Quinsay (now Hangzhou), he sent a small embassy inland with letters from Ferdinand and Isabella and instructions to locate the grand city.

Columbus's First Voyage to the New World, 1492–1493

The landing party found only small villages. Confronted with this disappointment, Columbus apparently gave up on his aim to meet the Great Khan. Instead, he focused on trying to find gold or other valuables among the peoples he had discovered. The sight of Taino people wearing gold ornaments on Hispaniola seemed to prove that gold was available in the region. In January, confident that its source would soon be found, he headed back to Spain to report on his discovery. News of his voyage spread rapidly across Europe.[12]

Over the next decades, the Spanish would follow a policy of conquest and colonization in the New World, rather than one of exchange with equals (as envisaged for the Mongol khan). On his second voyage, Columbus forcibly subjugated the island of Hispaniola and enslaved its indigenous peoples. On this and subsequent voyages, Columbus brought with him settlers for the new Spanish territories, along with agricultural seed and livestock. Columbus himself, however, had limited skills in governing. Revolt soon broke out against him and his brother on Hispaniola. A royal expedition sent to investigate returned the brothers to Spain in chains. Columbus was cleared of wrongdoing, but the territories remained under royal control.

Columbus was very much a man of his times. To the end of his life in 1506, he believed that he had found small islands off the coast of Asia. He never realized the scope of his achievement: to have found a vast continent unknown to Europeans, except for a fleeting Viking presence centuries earlier. He could not know that the scale of his discoveries would revolutionize world power, raising issues of trade, settlement, government bureaucracy, and the rights of native and African peoples.

Later Explorers

The Florentine navigator Amerigo Vespucci (veh-SPOO-chee) (1454–1512) realized what Columbus had not. Writing about his discoveries on the coast of modern-day Venezuela, Vespucci stated: "Those new regions which we found and explored with the fleet . . . we may rightly call a New World." This letter, titled *Mundus Novus* (The New World), was the first document to describe America as a continent separate from Asia. In recognition of Amerigo's bold claim, the continent was named for him.

To settle competing claims to the Atlantic discoveries, Spain and Portugal turned to Pope Alexander VI. The resulting **Treaty of Tordesillas** (tor-duh-SEE-yuhs) in 1494 gave Spain everything to the west of an imaginary line drawn down the Atlantic and Portugal everything to the east. This arbitrary division worked in Portugal's favor when in 1500 an expedition led by Pedro Alvares Cabral, en route to India, landed on the coast of Brazil, which Cabral claimed as Portuguese territory.

The search for profits determined the direction of Spanish exploration. With insignificant profits from the Caribbean compared to the enormous riches that the Portuguese were reaping in Asia, Spain renewed the search for a western passage to Asia. In 1519 Charles V of Spain sent the Portuguese mariner Ferdinand Magellan (1480–1521) to find a sea route to the spices of the Moluccas off the southeast coast of Asia. Magellan sailed southwest across the Atlantic to Brazil, and after a long search along the coast he located the treacherous straits that now bear his name (see Map 14.2). The new ocean he sailed into after a rough passage through the straits seemed so calm that Magellan dubbed it the Pacific, from the Latin word for peaceful. He soon realized his mistake. His fleet sailed north up the west coast of South America and then headed west into the immense expanse of the Pacific toward the Malay Archipelago. (Some of these islands were conquered later, in the 1560s, and named the "Philippines" for Philip II of Spain.)

Terrible storms, disease, starvation, and violence devastated the expedition. Magellan had set out with a fleet of five ships and around 270 men. Sailors on two of the ships attempted mutiny on the South American coast; one ship was lost, and another ship deserted and returned to Spain before even traversing the straits. The trip across the Pacific took ninety-eight days, and the men survived on rats and sawdust. Magellan himself died in a skirmish in the islands known today as the Philippines. Only one ship, with eighteen men aboard, returned to Spain from the east by way of the Indian Ocean, the Cape of Good Hope, and the Atlantic in 1522. The voyage—the first to circumnavigate the globe—had taken close to three years.

This voyage revolutionized Europeans' understanding of the world by demonstrating the vastness of the Pacific. The earth was clearly much larger than Columbus had believed. Although the voyage made a small profit in spices, it also demonstrated that the westward passage to the Indies was too long and dangerous for commercial purposes. Spain soon abandoned the attempt to oust Portugal from the Eastern spice trade and concentrated on exploiting her New World territories.

Spain's European rivals also set sail across the Atlantic during the early days of exploration in search of a northwest passage to the Indies. In 1497 John Cabot, a Genoese merchant living in London, undertook a voyage to Brazil, but discovered Newfoundland instead. The next year he returned and reconnoitered the New England coast. These forays proved futile, and the English established no permanent colonies in the territories they explored. News of the riches of Mexico and Peru later inspired the English to renew their efforts, this time in the extreme north. Between 1576 and 1578 Martin Frobisher made three voyages in and around the Canadian bay that now bears his name. Frobisher hopefully brought a quantity of ore back to England with him, but it proved to be worthless.

Early French exploration of the Atlantic was equally frustrating. Between 1534 and 1541 Frenchman Jacques Cartier made several voyages and explored the St. Lawrence region of Canada, searching for a passage to the wealth of Asia. His exploration of the St. Lawrence was halted at the great rapids west of the present-day island of Montreal; he named the rapids "La Chine" in the optimistic belief that China lay just beyond. When this hope proved vain, the French turned to a new source of profit within Canada itself: trade in beavers and other furs. As had the Portuguese in Asia, French traders bartered with local peoples, who maintained control over their trade goods. French fishermen also competed with Spanish and English ships for the teeming schools of cod they found in the Atlantic waters around Newfoundland. Fishing vessels salted the catch

Treaty of Tordesillas The 1494 agreement giving Spain everything to the west of an imaginary line drawn down the Atlantic and giving Portugal everything to the east.

Mexica Empire Also known as the Aztec Empire, a large and complex Native American civilization in modern Mexico and Central America that possessed advanced mathematical, astronomical, and engineering technology.

on board and brought it back to Europe, where a thriving market for fish was created by the Catholic prohibition on eating meat on Fridays and during Lent.

Spanish Conquest in the New World

In 1519, the year Magellan departed on his worldwide expedition, the Spanish sent an exploratory expedition from their post in Cuba to the mainland under the command of the brash and determined conquistador Hernando Cortés (1485–1547). Accompanied by six hundred men, sixteen horses, and ten cannon, Cortés was to launch the conquest of the **Mexica Empire**. Its people were later called the Aztecs, but now most scholars prefer to use the term *Mexica* to refer to them and their empire.

The Mexica Empire was ruled by Montezuma II (r. 1502–1520) from his capital at Tenochtitlán (tay-nawch-teet-LAHN), now Mexico City. Larger than any European city of the time, it was the heart of a sophisticated civilization with advanced mathematics,

astronomy, and engineering; a complex social system; and oral poetry and historical traditions.

Cortés landed on the coast of the Gulf of Mexico on April 21, 1519. The Spanish camp was soon visited by delegations of unarmed Mexica leaders bearing lavish gifts and news of their great emperor. (See "Primary Source 14.3: Doña Marina Translating for Hernando Cortés During His Meeting with Montezuma," page 442.) Impressed with the wealth of the local people, Cortés soon began to exploit internal dissension within the empire to his own advantage. The Mexica state religion necessitated constant warfare against neighboring peoples to secure captives for religious sacrifices and laborers for agricultural and building projects. Conquered peoples were required

Invasion of Tenochtitlán, 1519–1521

→ Cortés's original route, 1519
→ Cortés's retreat, 1520
→ Cortés's return route, 1520–1521

The Mexica Capital of Tenochtitlán   This woodcut map was published in 1524 along with Cortés's letters describing the conquest of the Mexica. As it shows, Tenochtitlán occupied an island and was laid out in concentric circles. The administrative and religious buildings were at the heart of the city, which was surrounded by residential quarters. Cortés himself marveled at the city in his letters: "The city is as large as Seville or Cordoba. . . . There are bridges, very large, strong, and well constructed, so that, over many, ten horsemen can ride abreast. . . . The city has many squares where markets are held. . . . There is one square . . . where there are daily more than sixty thousand souls, buying and selling. In the service and manners of its people, their fashion of living was almost the same as in Spain, with just as much harmony and order." (Newberry Library, Chicago, Illinois, USA/The Bridgeman Library)

Doña Marina Translating for Hernando Cortés During His Meeting with Montezuma

(The Granger Collection, New York)

In April 1519 Doña Marina (or Malintzin as she is known in Nahuatl) was among twenty women given to the Spanish as slaves. Fluent in Nahuatl (NAH-wah-tuhl) and Yucatec Mayan (spoken by a Spanish priest accompanying Cortés), she acted as an interpreter and diplomatic guide for the Spanish. She had a close relationship with Cortés and bore his son, Don Martín Cortés, in 1522. This image was created by Tlaxcalan artists shortly after the conquest of Mexico and represents one indigenous perspective on the events.

EVALUATE THE EVIDENCE

1. What role does Doña Marina (far right) appear to be playing in this image? Does she appear to be subservient or equal to Cortés (right, seated)? How did the painter indicate her identity as non-Spanish?

2. How do you think the native rulers negotiating with Cortés might have viewed her? What about a Spanish viewer of this image? What does the absence of other women here suggest about the role of women in these societies?

to relinquish products of their agriculture and craftsmanship to pay tribute to the Mexica state through their local chiefs.

Cortés quickly forged an alliance with the Tlaxcalas (Tlah-scalas) and other subject kingdoms, which chafed under the tribute demanded by the Mexica. In October a combined Spanish-Tlaxcalan force occupied the city of Cholula, the second largest in the empire and its religious capital, and massacred many thousands of inhabitants. Strengthened by this display of power, Cortés made alliances with other native king-

doms. In November 1519, with a few hundred Spanish men and some six thousand indigenous warriors, Cortés marched on Tenochtitlán.

Montezuma refrained from attacking the Spaniards as they advanced toward his capital and welcomed Cortés and his men into Tenochtitlán. Historians have often condemned the Mexica ruler for vacillation and weakness. Certainly other native leaders did attack the Spanish. But Montezuma relied on the advice of his state council, itself divided, and on the dubious loyalty of tributary communities. Historians have questioned one long-standing explanation, that he feared the Spaniards as living gods. This idea is mostly found in texts written after the fact by Spanish missionaries and their converts, who used it to justify and explain the conquest. Montezuma's hesitation proved disastrous. When Cortés took Montezuma hostage and tried to rule the Mexica through the emperor's authority, Montezuma's influence over his people crumbled.

In May 1520 Spanish forces massacred Mexica warriors dancing at an indigenous festival. This act provoked an uprising within Tenochtitlán, during which Montezuma was killed. The Spaniards and their allies escaped from the city and began gathering forces against the Mexica. One year later, in May 1521, Cortés laid siege to Tenochtitlán at the head of an army of approximately 1,000 Spanish and 75,000 native warriors.[13] Spanish victory in August 1521 resulted from its superior technology and the effects of the siege and smallpox. After the defeat of Tenochtitlán, Cortés and other conquistadors began the systematic conquest of Mexico. Over time, a series of indigenous kingdoms gradually fell under Spanish domination, although not without decades of resistance.

More surprising than the defeat of the Mexica was the fall of the remote **Inca Empire**. Perched more than 9,800 feet above sea level, the Incas were isolated from North American indigenous cultures and knew nothing of the Mexica civilization or its collapse. Like the Mexica, the Incas had created a civilization that rivaled that of the Europeans in population and complexity. To unite their vast and well-fortified empire, the Incas built an extensive network of roads, along which traveled a highly efficient postal service. The imperial government, with its capital in the city of Cuzco, taxed, fed, and protected its subjects.

At the time of the Spanish invasion the Inca Empire had been weakened by an epidemic of disease, possibly smallpox. Even worse, the empire had been embroiled in a civil war over succession. Francisco Pizarro (ca. 1475–1541), a conquistador of modest Spanish origins, landed on the northern coast of Peru on May 13, 1532, the very day Atahualpa (ah-tuh-WAHL-puh) won control of the empire after five years of fighting. As Pizarro advanced across the steep Andes toward Cuzco, Atahualpa was proceeding to the capital for his coronation.

Like Montezuma in Mexico, Atahualpa was aware of the Spaniards' movements. He sent envoys to invite the Spanish to meet him in the provincial town of Cajamarca. His plan was to lure the Spanish into a trap, seize their horses and ablest men for his army, and execute the rest. With an army of some forty thousand men stationed nearby, Atahualpa felt he had little to fear. Instead, the Spaniards ambushed and captured him, collected an enormous ransom in gold, and then executed him in 1533 on trumped-up charges. The

Spanish now marched on the capital of the empire itself, profiting once again from internal conflicts to form alliances with local peoples. When Cuzco fell in 1533, the Spanish plundered immense riches in gold and silver.

As with the Mexica, decades of violence and resistance followed the defeat of the Incan capital. Struggles also broke out among the Spanish for the spoils of empire. Nevertheless, Spanish conquest opened a new chapter in European relations with the New World. It was not long before rival European nations attempted to forge their own overseas empires.

Early French and English Settlement in the New World

For over a hundred years, the Spanish and the Portuguese dominated settlement in the New World. The first English colony was founded at Roanoke (in what is now North Carolina) in 1585. After a three-year loss of contact with England, the settlers were found to have disappeared; their fate remains a mystery. (See "Primary Source 14.4: Interpreting the Spread of Disease Among Natives," page 444.) The colony of Virginia, founded by a private company of investors at Jamestown in 1607, also struggled in its first years and relied on food from the Powhatan Confederacy. Over time, the colony gained a steady hold by producing tobacco for a growing European market.

Settlement on the coast of New England was undertaken for different reasons. There, radical Protestants sought to escape Anglican repression in England and begin new lives. The small and struggling outpost of Plymouth (1620), founded by the Pilgrims who arrived on the *Mayflower*, was followed by Massachusetts (1630), a colony of Puritans that grew into a prosperous settlement. Religious disputes in Massachusetts itself led to the dispersion of settlers into the new communities of Providence, Connecticut, Rhode Island, and New Haven. Catholics acquired their own settlement in Maryland (1632) and Quakers in Pennsylvania (1681).

Whereas the Spanish conquered indigenous empires and established large-scale dominance over Mexico and Peru, English settlements merely hugged the Atlantic coastline. This did not prevent conflict with the indigenous inhabitants over land and resources, however. At Jamestown, for example, English expansion undermined prior cooperation with the Powhatan Confederacy; disease and warfare with the English led to drastic population losses among the Powhatans. The haphazard nature of English colonization also led to conflicts of authority within the colonies. As the English crown grew more interested in colonial

> **Inca Empire** The vast and sophisticated Peruvian empire centered at the capital city of Cuzco that was at its peak from 1438 until 1532.

Interpreting the Spread of Disease Among Natives

Thomas Hariot participated in the 1585 expedition to Roanoke, the short-lived English colony. After his return, he wrote A Briefe and True Report of the New Found Land of Virginia, *which describes the natural environment and the indigenous peoples he encountered. Although biased by his Christian faith and European way of life, Hariot strove to present an accurate, detailed, and balanced viewpoint, making his work a precious source on Native American life and early contacts with Europeans. In this passage, he describes the disastrous effects on the Carolina Algonquins of contagious disease, perhaps measles, smallpox, or influenza.*

" There was no town where we had any subtle device [cunning maneuvers] practiced against us, we leaving it unpunished or not revenged (because we sought by all means possible to win them by gentleness) but that within a few days after our departure from every such town, the people began to die very fast, and many in short space; in some towns about twenty, in some forty, in some sixty, & in one six score, which in truth was very many in respect of their numbers. This happened in no place that we could learn but where we had been, where they used some practice against us, and after such time; The disease also so strange, that they neither knew what it was, nor how to cure it; the like by report of the oldest men in the country never happened before, time out of mind. A thing specially observed by us as also by the natural inhabitants themselves.

Insomuch that when some of the inhabitants which were our friends . . . had observed such effects in four or five towns to follow their wicked practices [of harming the Englishmen], they were persuaded that it was the work of our God through our means, and that we by him might kill and slay whom we would without weapons and not come near them.

And thereupon when it had happened that they had understanding that any of their enemies had abused us in our journeys, hearing that we had wrought no revenge with our weapons, . . . [they] did come and entreat us that we would be a means to our God that [their enemies] as others that had dealt with us might in like sort die; alleging how much it would be for our credit and profit, as also theirs; and hoping furthermore that we would do so much at their requests in respect of the friendship we profess them.

Whose entreaties although we showed that they were ungodly, affirming that our God would not subject himself to any such prayers and requests of me: that indeed all things have been and were to be done according to his good pleasure as he had ordained: and that we to show ourselves his true servants ought rather to make petition for the contrary, that they with them might live together with us, be made partakers of his truth & serve him in righteousness; but notwithstanding in such sort, that we refer that as all other things, to be done according to his divine will & pleasure, and as by his wisdom he had ordained to be best. "

EVALUATE THE EVIDENCE

1. According to Hariot, how did the Native Americans allied with the English interpret the epidemics of disease that struck indigenous villages? How do they seem to have viewed their relations with the English?

2. This document sheds light on how one group of indigenous people experienced the suffering and death brought by European diseases. Based on your reading in this chapter, could you imagine differing responses among other groups?

Source: Thomas Hariot, *A Briefe and True Report of the New Found Land of Virginia* (1590; New York: J. Sabin & Sons, 1871), p. 28. Spelling modernized.

expansion, efforts were made to acquire the territory between New England in the north and Virginia in the south. This would allow the English to unify their holdings and overcome French and Dutch competition on the North American mainland.

French navigator and explorer Samuel de Champlain founded the first permanent French settlement, at Quebec, in 1608, a year after the English founding of Jamestown. Ville-Marie, latter-day Montreal, was founded in 1642. Although the population of New France was small compared to that of the English and Spanish colonies, the French were energetic traders and explorers. Following the waterways of the St. Lawrence, the Great Lakes, and the Mississippi, they ventured into much of modern-day Canada and at least thirty-five of the fifty states of the United States. French traders forged relations with the Huron Confederacy, a league of four indigenous nations that dominated a large region north of Lake Erie, as a means of gaining access to hunting grounds and trade routes for beaver and other animals. In 1682 French explorer René-Robert Cavelier LaSalle descended the Mississippi to the Gulf of Mexico, opening the way for French occupation of Louisiana.

While establishing their foothold in the north, the French slowly acquired new territories in the West Indies, including Cayenne (1604), St. Christophe (1625), Martinique, Guadeloupe, and Saint-Domingue (1697) on the western side of the island of Hispaniola. These islands became centers of tobacco and then sugar production. French ambitions on the mainland and in the Caribbean sparked a century-long competition with the English.

European involvement in the Americas led to profound transformation of pre-existing indigenous societies and the rise of a transatlantic slave trade. It also led to an acceleration of global trade and cultural exchange. Over time, the combination of indigenous, European, and African cultures gave birth to new societies in the New World. In turn, the profits of trade and the impact of cultural exchange greatly influenced European society.

The Impact of Conquest

What was the impact of European conquest on the peoples and ecologies of the New World?

The growing European presence in the New World transformed its land and its peoples forever. Violence and disease wrought devastating losses, while surviving peoples encountered new political, social, and economic organizations imposed by Europeans. The Columbian exchange brought infectious diseases to the Americas, but also gave new crops to the Old World that altered consumption patterns in Europe and across the globe (see pages 448–449).

Colonial Administration

Spanish conquistadors had claimed the lands they had "discovered" for the Spanish crown. As the wealth of the new territories became apparent, the Spanish government acted to impose its authority and remove that of the original conquerors. The House of Trade, located in Seville, controlled the flow of goods and people to and from the colonies, while the Council of the Indies guided royal policy and served as the highest court for colonial affairs.

The crown divided its New World possessions into two **viceroyalties**, or administrative divisions: New Spain, with the capital at Mexico City, and Peru, with the capital at Lima. Two new viceroyalties added in the eighteenth century were New Granada, with Bogotá as its administrative center, and La Plata, with Buenos Aires as the capital (see Map 14.2).

Within each territory, the viceroy, or imperial governor, exercised broad military and civil authority as the direct representative of Spain. The viceroy presided over the *audiencia* (ow-dee-EHN-see-ah), a board of twelve to fifteen judges that served as his advisory council and court of appeal. At the local level, officials called *corregidores* (kuh-REH-gih-dawr-ays) held judicial and administrative powers.

The Portuguese adopted similar patterns of rule, with India House in Lisbon functioning much like the Spanish House of Trade and royal representatives overseeing its possessions in West Africa and Asia. To secure the vast expanse of Brazil, the Portuguese implemented the system of captaincies, hereditary grants of land given to nobles and loyal officials who bore the costs of settling and administering their territories. Over time, the Crown secured greater power over the captaincies, appointing royal governors to act as administrators. The captaincy of Bahia was the site of the capital, Salvador, home to the governor general and other royal officials.

Like their European neighbors, France and England initially entrusted their overseas colonies to individual explorers and monopoly trading companies. By the end of the seventeenth century, the French crown had successfully imposed direct rule over New France and other colonies. The king appointed military governors to rule alongside intendants, royal officials possessed of broad administrative and financial authority within their intendancies. In the mid-1700s, reform-minded Spanish king Charles III (r. 1759–1788) adopted the intendant system for the Spanish colonies.

England's colonies followed a distinctive path. Drawing on English traditions of representative government (see Chapter 15), its colonists established their own proudly autonomous assemblies to regulate local affairs. Wealthy merchants and landowners dominated the assemblies, although even common men had more say in politics than was the case in England. Up to the mid-eighteenth century, the Crown found little reason to dispute colonial liberties in the north, but it did acquire greater control over the wealthy plantation colonies of the Caribbean and tobacco-rich Virginia.

Impact of European Settlement on Indigenous Peoples

Before Columbus's arrival, the Americas were inhabited by thousands of groups of indigenous peoples, each with distinct cultures and languages. Their patterns of life varied widely, from hunter-gatherer tribes organized into tribal confederations on the North American plains to two large-scale agriculture-based empires connecting bustling cities and towns, the Mexica (Aztec) Empire centered in modern-day Mexico and the Inca Empire in the Andean highlands. The history of human

viceroyalties The name for the four administrative units of Spanish possessions in the Americas: New Spain, Peru, New Granada, and La Plata.

settlement in the Americas was so long and complex that many cultures had risen and fallen by the time of Columbus's voyage. These included the abandoned city of Cahokia (near modern-day St. Louis, Missouri) that at its peak in the twelfth century held a population of up to 10,000 people and the palaces and cities of ancestors of the Maya in the Yucatán peninsula, whose regional capital of Chichén Itzá thrived around the same period. Although historians continue to debate the numbers, the best estimate is that in 1492 the peoples of the Americas numbered around 50 million.

Their lives were radically transformed by the arrival of Europeans. In the sixteenth century perhaps two hundred thousand Spaniards immigrated to the New World. After assisting in the conquest of the Mexica and the Incas, these men carved out vast estates called haciendas in temperate grazing areas and imported Spanish livestock. In coastal tropical areas, the Spanish erected huge plantations to supply sugar to the European market. Around 1550 silver was discovered in present-day Bolivia and Mexico. To work the cattle ranches, sugar plantations, and silver mines, the conquistadors first turned to the indigenous peoples.

The Spanish quickly established the **encomienda system**, in which the Crown granted the conquerors the right to employ groups of Native Americans as laborers or to demand tribute from them in exchange for providing food and shelter. Theoretically, the Spanish were supposed to care for the indigenous people under their command and teach them Christianity; in actuality, the system was a brutal form of exploitation only one level removed from slavery.

encomienda system
A system whereby the Spanish crown granted the conquerors the right to forcibly employ groups of Indians in exchange for providing food, shelter, and Christian teaching.

The new conditions and hardships imposed by conquest and colonization resulted in enormous native population losses. The major cause of death was disease. Having little or no resistance to diseases brought from the Old World, the inhabitants of the New World fell victim to smallpox, typhus, influenza, and other illnesses. Another factor was overwork. Unaccustomed to forced labor, especially in the blistering heat of tropical cane fields or in dank and dangerous mines, native workers died in staggering numbers. Moreover, forced labor diverted local people from agricultural work, leading to malnutrition, reduced fertility rates, and starvation. Women forced to work were separated from their infants, leading to high infant mortality rates in a population with no livestock to supply alternatives to breast milk. Malnutrition and hunger in turn lowered resistance to disease. Finally, many indigenous peoples also died through outright violence in warfare.[14]

The Franciscan Bartolomé de Las Casas (1474–1566) was one of the most outspoken critics of Spanish brutality against indigenous peoples. Las Casas documented their treatment at the hands of the Spanish:

> To these quiet Lambs . . . came the Spaniards like most c(r)uel Tygres, Wolves and Lions, enrag'd with a sharp and tedious hunger; for these forty years past, minding nothing else but the slaughter of these unfortunate wretches, whom with divers kinds of torments neither seen nor heard of before, they have so cruelly and inhumanely butchered, that of three millions of people which Hispaniola itself did contain, there are left remaining alive scarce three hundred persons.[15]

Las Casas and other missionaries asserted that the Indians had human rights, and through their persistent pressure the Spanish emperor Charles V abolished the worst abuses of the encomienda system in 1531.

Franciscan, Dominican, and Jesuit missionaries who accompanied the conquistadors and other European settlers played an important role in converting indigenous peoples to Christianity, teaching them European methods of agriculture, and instilling loyalty to their colonial masters. In areas with small Spanish populations, the friars set up missions for a period of ten years, after which established churches and priests would take over and they could move on to new areas. Jesuits in New France also established missions far distant from the centers of French settlement. Behind its wooden palisades, a mission might contain a chapel, a hospital, a mill, stables, barns, workshops, and residences from which the Jesuits traveled to spread the word of God.

Missionaries' success in conversion varied over time and space. In Central and South America, large-scale conversion forged enduring Catholic cultures in Portuguese and Spanish colonies. One Franciscan missionary estimated that he and his colleagues had baptized between 4 and 9 million indigenous people in New Spain by 1536. Although these figures must be significantly inflated (both by the exaggeration of zealous missionaries and by multiple baptism of the same individuals), they suggest the extensive Christianization under way among the native population. Galvanized by their opposition to Catholicism and fueled by their own religious fervor, English colonizers also made efforts to convert indigenous peoples. On the whole, however, these attempts were less successful, in part because the English did not establish wholesale dominance over large native populations as did the Spanish.

Rather than a straightforward imposition of Christianity, conversion entailed a complex process of cultural exchange. (See "Primary Source 14.5: Tenochtitlán Leaders Respond to Spanish Missionaries," at right.) Catholic friars were among the first Europeans to seek understanding of native cultures and languages as part

Tenochtitlán Leaders Respond to Spanish Missionaries

For the conquered peoples of the New World, the imposition of Christianity and repression of their pre-existing religions represented yet another form of loss. This document describes the response of the vanquished leaders of Tenochtitlán to Franciscan missionaries seeking to convert them in 1524. The account was written down in the 1560s by or for Bernardino de Sahagún, a Franciscan missionary. Sahagún is well known for his General History of the Things of New Spain *(also known as the* Florentine Codex*), a multivolume account of Mexica history, culture, and society he produced in collaboration with indigenous artists and informants.*

You have told us that we do not know the One who gives us life and being, who is Lord of the heavens and of the earth. You also say that those we worship are not gods. This way of speaking is entirely new to us, and very scandalous. We are frightened by this way of speaking because our forebears who engendered and governed us never said anything like this. On the contrary, they left us this our custom of worshiping our gods, in which they believed and which they worshiped all the time that they lived here on earth. They taught us how to honor them. And they taught us all the ceremonies and sacrifices that we make. They told us that through them [our gods] we live and are, and that we were beholden to them, to be theirs and to serve countless centuries before the sun began to shine and before there was daytime. They said that these gods that we worship give us everything we need for our physical existence: maize, beans, chia seeds, etc. We appeal to them for the rain to make the things of the earth grow.

These our gods are the source of great riches and delights, all of which belong to them. They live in very delightful places where there are always flowers, vegetation, and great freshness, a place unknown to mere mortals, called Tlalocan, where there is never hunger, poverty, or illness. It is they who bestow honors, property, titles, and kingdoms, gold and silver, precious feathers, and gemstones.

There has never been a time remembered when they were not worshiped, honored, and esteemed. Perhaps it is a century or two since this began; it is a time beyond counting. . . .

It is best, our lords, to act on this matter very slowly, with great deliberation. We are not satisfied or convinced by what you have told us, nor do we understand or give credit to what has been said of our gods. . . . All of us together feel that it is enough to have lost, enough that the power and royal jurisdiction have been taken from us. As for our gods, we will die before giving up serving and worshiping them.

EVALUATE THE EVIDENCE

1. What reasons do the leaders of Tenochtitlán offer for rejecting the missionaries' teachings? In their view, what elements of their lives will be affected by abandoning the worship of their gods?
2. What insight does this document provide into the mind-set of Mexica people shortly following conquest?

Source: *Coloquios y doctrina Cristiana*, ed. Miguel León-Portilla, in *Colonial Spanish America: A Documentary History*, ed. Kenneth Mills and William B. Taylor (Wilmington, Del.: SR Books, 1998), pp. 21–22. Used by permission of Rowan & Littlefield.

---

of their effort to render Christianity comprehensible to indigenous people. In turn, Christian ideas and practices in the New World took on a distinctive character. For example, a sixteenth-century apparition of the Virgin Mary in Mexico City, known as the Virgin of Guadalupe, became a central icon of Spanish-American Catholicism.

The pattern of devastating disease and population loss occurred everywhere Europeans settled. The best estimate of native population loss is a decline from roughly 50 million people in 1492 to around 9 million by 1700. It is important to note, however, that native populations and cultures did survive the conquest period, sometimes by blending with European incomers and sometimes by maintaining cultural autonomy.

For colonial administrators, the main problem posed by the astronomically high death rate was the loss of a subjugated labor force to work the mines and sugar plantations. As early as 1511 King Ferdinand of Spain observed that the Indians seemed to be "very frail" and that "one black could do the work of four Indians."[16] Thus was born an absurd myth, and the new tragedy of the transatlantic slave trade would soon follow (see page 452).

Life in the Colonies

Many factors helped to shape life in European colonies, including geographical location, religion, indigenous cultures and practices, patterns of European settlement, and the cultural attitudes and official policies of the European nations that claimed them as empire. Throughout the New World, colonial settlements were hedged by immense borderlands where European power was weak and Europeans and non-Europeans interacted on a more equal basis.

Women played a crucial role in the creation of new identities and the continuation of old ones. The first explorers formed unions with native women, through coercion or choice, and relied on them as translators and guides and to form alliances with indigenous powers. As settlement developed, the character of each colony was influenced by the presence or absence of European women. Where women and children accompanied men, as in the British colonies and the Spanish mainland colonies, new settlements took on European languages, religion, and ways of life that have endured, with input from local cultures, to this day. Where European women did not accompany men, as on the west coast of Africa and most European outposts in Asia, local populations largely retained their own cultures, to which male Europeans acclimatized themselves. The scarcity of women in all colonies, at least initially, opened up opportunities for those who did arrive, leading one cynic to comment that even "a whore, if handsome, makes a wife for some rich planter."[17]

Columbian exchange The exchange of animals, plants, and diseases between the Old and the New Worlds.

It was not just the availability of Englishwomen that prevented Englishmen from forming unions with indigenous women. English cultural attitudes drew strict boundaries between "civilized" and "savage," and even settlements of Christianized native peoples were segregated from the English. This was in strong contrast with the situation in New France, where royal officials initially encouraged French traders to form ties with indigenous people, including marrying local women. Assimilation of the native population was seen as one solution to the low levels of immigration from France.

Most women who crossed the Atlantic were Africans, constituting four-fifths of the female newcomers before 1800.[18] Wherever slavery existed, masters profited from their power to engage in sexual relations with enslaved women. One important difference among European colonies was in the status of children born from such unions. In some colonies, mostly those dominated by the Portuguese, Spanish, or French, substantial populations of free people of color descended from the freed children of such unions. In English colonies, masters were less likely to free children they fathered with female slaves.

The mixing of indigenous peoples with Europeans and Africans created whole new populations and ethnicities and complex self-identities. In Spanish America the word *mestizo* — *métis* in French — described people of mixed Native American and European descent. The blanket terms "mulatto" and "people of color" were used for those of mixed African and European origin. With its immense slave-based plantation agriculture system, large indigenous population, and relatively low Portuguese immigration, Brazil developed a particularly complex racial and ethnic mosaic.

The Columbian Exchange

The migration of peoples to the New World led to an exchange of animals, plants, and disease, a complex process known as the **Columbian exchange**. European immigrants to the Americas wanted a familiar diet, so they searched for climatic zones favorable to those crops. Columbus had brought sugar plants on his second voyage; Spaniards also introduced rice and bananas from the Canary Islands, and the Portuguese carried these items to Brazil. Everywhere they settled, the Spanish and Portuguese brought and raised wheat with labor

A Mixed Race Procession   Incas used drinking vessels, known as keros, for the ritual consumption of maize beer at feasts. This kero from the early colonial period depicts a multiracial procession: an Incan dignitary is preceded by a Spanish trumpet player and an African drummer. This is believed to be one of the earliest visual representations of an African in the Americas. (akg-images/Werner Forman)

provided by the encomienda system. Grapes and olives brought over from Spain did well in parts of Peru and Chile. Not all plants arrived intentionally. In clumps of mud on shoes and in the folds of textiles came the seeds of immigrant grasses, including the common dandelion.

Apart from wild turkeys and game, Native Americans had no animals for food. Moreover, they did not domesticate animals for travel or use as beasts of burden, except for alpacas and llamas in the Inca Empire. On his second voyage in 1493 Columbus introduced horses, cattle, sheep, dogs, pigs, chickens, and goats. The multiplication of these animals proved spectacular. The horse enabled the Spanish conquerors and native populations to travel faster and farther and to transport heavy loads. In turn, Europeans returned home with many food crops that became central elements of their diet. (See "Living in the Past: Foods of the Columbian Exchange," page 450.)

Disease brought by European people and animals was perhaps the most important form of exchange. The wave of catastrophic epidemic disease that swept the Western Hemisphere after 1492 can be seen as an extension of the swath of devastation wreaked by the Black Death in the 1300s, first on Asia and then on Europe. The world after Columbus was thus unified by disease as well as by trade and colonization.

Europe and the World After Columbus

How was the era of global contact shaped by new commodities, commercial empires, and forced migrations?

The centuries-old Afroeurasian trade world was forever changed by the European voyages of discovery and their aftermath. For the first time, a truly global economy emerged in the sixteenth and seventeenth centuries, and it forged new links among far-flung peoples, cultures, and societies. The ancient civilizations of Europe, Africa, the Americas, and Asia confronted one another in new and rapidly evolving ways. Those confrontations often led to conquest and exploitation, but they also contributed to cultural exchange and renewal.

Sugar and Slavery

Throughout the Middle Ages slavery was deeply entrenched in the Mediterranean, but it was not based on race; many slaves were white. How, then, did black African slavery enter the European picture and take

A New World Sugar Refinery, Brazil　Sugar was the most important and most profitable plantation crop in the New World. This image shows the processing and refinement of sugar on a Brazilian plantation. Sugarcane was grown, harvested, and processed by African slaves who labored under brutal and ruthless conditions to generate enormous profits for plantation owners. (The Bridgeman Art Library/Getty Images)

Foods of the Columbian Exchange

Many people are aware of the devastating effects of European diseases on peoples of the New World and of the role of gunpowder and horses in the conquest of native civilizations. They may be less aware of how New World foodstuffs transformed Europeans' daily life.

Prior to Christopher Columbus's voyages, many common elements of today's European diet were unknown in Europe. It's hard to imagine Italian pizza without tomato sauce or Irish stew without potatoes, yet tomatoes and potatoes were both unknown in Europe before 1492. Additional crops originating in the Americas included many varieties of beans, squash, pumpkins, avocados, and peppers.

One of the most important of such crops was maize (corn), first introduced to Europe by Columbus in 1493. Because maize gives a high yield per unit of land, has a short growing season, and thrives in climates too dry for rice and too wet for wheat, it proved an especially important crop for Europeans. By the late seventeenth century the crop had become a staple in Spain, Portugal, southern France, and Italy, and in the eighteenth century it became one of the chief

Incan women milking goats, from a collection of illustrations by a Spanish bishop that offers a valuable view of life in Peru in the 1780s. (Oronoz)

foods of southeastern Europe. Even more valuable was the nutritious white potato, which slowly spread from west to east — to Ireland, England, and France in the seventeenth century, and to Germany, Poland, Hungary, and Russia in the eighteenth, contributing everywhere to a rise in population. Ironically, the white potato reached New England from old England in the early eighteenth century.

Europeans' initial reaction to these crops was often fear or hostility. Adoption of the tomato and the potato was long hampered by the belief that they were unfit for human consumption and potentially poisonous. Both plants belong to the deadly nightshade family, and both contain poison in their leaves and stems. It took time and persuasion for these plants to win over tradition-minded European peasants, who used potatoes mostly as livestock feed. During the eighteenth-century Enlightenment, scientists and doctors played an important role in popularizing the nutritive benefits of the potato.

Columbus himself contributed to misconceptions about New World foods when he mistook the chili pepper for black pepper, one of the spices he had hoped to find in the Indies. The Portuguese quickly began exporting chili peppers from Brazil to Africa, India, and Southeast Asia along the trade routes they dominated. The chili pepper arrived in North America through its place in the diet of enslaved Africans.

root in the Americas? In 1453 the Ottoman capture of Constantinople halted the flow of white slaves from the eastern Mediterranean to western Europe. The successes of the Iberian reconquista also meant that the supply of Muslim captives had drastically diminished. Cut off from its traditional sources of slaves, Mediterranean Europe then turned to sub-Saharan Africa, which had a long history of internal slave trading. (See "Individuals in Society: Juan de Pareja," page 453.) As Portuguese explorers began their voyages along the

western coast of Africa, one of the first commodities they sought was slaves. In 1444 the first ship returned to Lisbon with a cargo of enslaved Africans; the Crown was delighted, and more shipments followed.

While the first slaves were simply seized by small raiding parties, Portuguese merchants soon found that it was easier to trade with local leaders, who were accustomed to dealing in slaves captured through warfare with neighboring powers. From 1490 to 1530 Portuguese traders brought hundreds of enslaved Africans to

The first European scientific illustration of maize appeared in 1542, a half century after it was introduced to the continent. (The LuEsther T. Mertz Library, NYBG/Art Resource, NY)

Saint Diego of Alcala Feeding the Poor (1645–1646), by Bartolome Esteban Murillo, the first dated European depiction of the potato in art. (Joseph Martin/akg-images)

European settlers introduced various foods to the native peoples of the New World, including rice, wheat, lettuce, and onions. Perhaps the most significant introduction to the diet of Native Americans came via the meat and milk of the livestock that the early conquistadors brought with them, including cattle, sheep, and goats.

The foods of the Columbian exchange traveled a truly global path. They provided important new sources of nutrition to people all over the world, as well as creating new and beloved culinary traditions. French fries with ketchup, anyone?

QUESTIONS FOR ANALYSIS

1. Why do you think it was so difficult for Europeans to accept new types of food, even when they were high in nutritional quality?
2. What do the painting and illustrations shown here suggest about the importance of the Columbian exchange?
3. List the foods you typically eat in a day. How many of them originated in the New World, and how many in the Old World? How does your own life exemplify the outcome of the Columbian exchange?

Lisbon each year (Map 14.3), where they eventually constituted 10 percent of the city's population.

In this stage of European expansion, the history of slavery became intertwined with the history of sugar. Originally sugar was an expensive luxury that only the very affluent could afford, but population increases and monetary expansion in the fifteenth century led to increasing demand. Native to the South Pacific, sugar was taken in ancient times to India, where farmers learned to preserve cane juice as granules that could be stored and shipped. From there, sugar crops traveled to China and the Mediterranean, where islands like Crete and Sicily had the warm and wet climate needed for growing sugarcane. When Genoese and other Italians colonized the Canary Islands and the Portuguese settled on the Madeira Islands, sugar plantations came to the Atlantic.

Sugar was a particularly difficult and demanding crop to produce for profit. Seed-stems were planted by hand, thousands to the acre. When mature, the cane

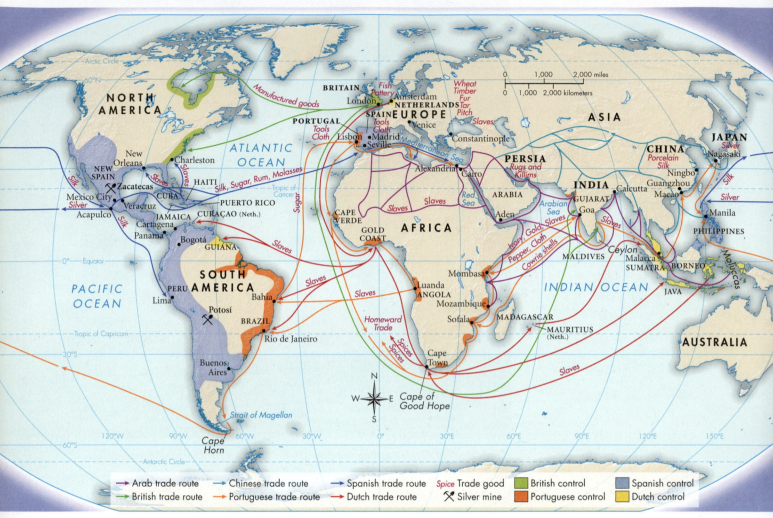

Map 14.3 Seaborne Trading Empires in the Sixteenth and Seventeenth Centuries   By the mid-seventeenth century, trade linked all parts of the world except for Australia. Notice that trade in slaves was not confined to the Atlantic but involved almost all parts of the world.

had to be harvested and processed rapidly to avoid spoiling, requiring days and nights of work with little rest. Moreover, sugar's growing season is virtually constant, meaning that there is no fallow period when workers could recuperate from the arduous labor. The demands of sugar production only increased with the invention of roller mills to crush the cane more efficiently. Yields could be augmented, but only if a sufficient labor force was found to supply the mills. Europeans solved the labor problem by forcing first native islanders and then enslaved Africans to provide the backbreaking work.

Sugar gave New World slavery its distinctive shape. Columbus himself, who spent a decade in Madeira, brought the first sugar plants to the New World. The transatlantic slave trade began in 1518 when the Spanish emperor Charles V authorized traders to bring enslaved Africans to the Americas. The Portuguese brought slaves to Brazil around 1550; by 1600 four thousand

were being imported annually. After its founding in 1621, the Dutch West India Company, with the full support of the United Provinces, transported thousands of Africans to Brazil and the Caribbean, mostly to work on sugar plantations. In the mid-seventeenth century the English got involved. From 1660 to 1698 the Royal African Company held a monopoly over the slave trade from the English crown.

European sailors found the Atlantic passage cramped and uncomfortable, but conditions for enslaved Africans were lethal. Before 1700, when slavers decided it was better business to improve conditions, some 20 percent of slaves died on the voyage.[19] The most common cause of death was from dysentery induced by poor-quality food and water, crowding, and lack of sanitation. Men were often kept in irons during the passage, while women and girls were considered fair game for sailors. To increase profits, slave traders packed several hundred captives on each ship. One slaver explained that

During the long wars of the reconquista, Muslims and Christians captured each other in battle and used the defeated as slaves. As the Muslims were gradually eliminated from Iberia in the fifteenth and sixteenth centuries, the Spanish and Portuguese turned to the west coast of Africa for a new supply of slaves. Most slaves worked as domestic servants, rather than in the fields. Some received specialized training as artisans.

Not all people of African descent were slaves, and some experienced both freedom and slavery in a single lifetime. The life and career of Juan de Pareja (pah-REH-huh) illustrates the complexities of the Iberian slave system and the heights of achievement possible for those who gained freedom.

Pareja was born in Antequera, an agricultural region and the old center of Muslim culture near Seville in southern Spain. Of his parents we know nothing. Because a rare surviving document calls him a "mulatto," one of his parents must have been white and the other must have had some African blood. In 1630 Pareja applied to the mayor of Seville for permission to

Velázquez, *Juan de Pareja*, 1650. (Private Collection/Photo © Christie's Images/The Bridgeman Art Library)

travel to Madrid to visit his brother and "to perfect his art." The document lists his occupation as "a painter in Seville." Since it mentions no other name, it is reasonable to assume that Pareja arrived in Madrid a free man. Sometime between 1630 and 1648, however, he came into the possession of the artist Diego Velázquez (1599–1660); Pareja became a slave.

How did Velázquez acquire Pareja? By purchase? As a gift? Had Pareja fallen into debt or committed some crime and thereby lost his freedom? We do not know. Velázquez, the greatest Spanish painter of the seventeenth century, had a large studio with many assistants. Pareja was set to grinding powders to make colors and to preparing canvases. He must have demonstrated ability because when Velázquez went to Rome in 1648, he chose Pareja to accompany him.

In 1650, as practice for a portrait of Pope Innocent X, Velázquez painted Pareja. The portrait shows Pareja dressed in fine clothing and gazing self-confidently at the viewer. Displayed in Rome in a public exhibition of Velázquez's work, the painting won acclaim from his contemporaries. That same year, Velázquez signed the document that gave Pareja his freedom, to become effective in 1654. Pareja lived out the rest of his life as an independent painter.

What does the public career of Pareja tell us about the man and his world? Pareja's career suggests that a person of African descent might fall into slavery and yet still acquire professional training and work alongside his master in a position of confidence. Moreover, if lucky enough to be freed, a former slave could exercise a profession and live his own life in Madrid. Pareja's experience was far from typical for a slave in the seventeenth century, but it reminds us of the myriad forms that slavery took in this period.

QUESTIONS FOR ANALYSIS

1. Since slavery was an established institution in Spain, speculate on Velázquez's possible reasons for giving Pareja his freedom.
2. In what ways does Pareja represent Europe's increasing participation in global commerce and exploration?

ONLINE DOCUMENT ASSIGNMENT

How could an individual like Pareja experience both slavery and freedom in a single lifetime? Go to the Integrated Media and analyze sources from Pareja's contemporaries that reflect changing ideas about racial identity and slavery, and then complete a writing assignment based on the evidence and details from this chapter.

Sources: Jonathan Brown, *Velázquez: Painter and Courtier* (New Haven, Conn.: Yale University Press, 1986); *Grove Dictionary of Art* (New York: Macmillan, 2000); Sister Wendy Beckett, *Sister Wendy's American Collection* (New York: Harper Collins Publishers, 2000), p. 15.

he removed his boots before entering the slave hold because he had to crawl over the slaves' packed bodies.[20] On sugar plantations, death rates from the brutal pace of labor were extremely high, leading to a constant stream of new shipments of slaves from Africa.

In total, scholars estimate that European traders embarked over 10 million enslaved Africans across the Atlantic from 1518 to 1800 (of whom roughly 8.5 million disembarked), with the peak of the trade occurring in the eighteenth century.[21] By comparison, only 2 to 2.5 million Europeans migrated to the New World during the same period. Slaves worked in an infinite variety of occupations: as miners, soldiers, sailors, servants, and artisans and in the production of sugar, cotton, rum, indigo, tobacco, wheat, and corn.

Philip II, ca. 1533   This portrait of Philip II as a young man and crown prince of Spain is by the celebrated artist Titian, court painter to Philip's father, Charles V. After taking the throne, Philip became another great patron of the artist. (Palazzo Pitti, Florence, Italy/The Bridgeman Art Library)

Spanish Silver and Its Economic Effects

The sixteenth century has often been called Spain's golden century, but silver mined in the Americas was the true source of Spain's wealth. In 1545, at an altitude of fifteen thousand feet, the Spanish discovered an extraordinary source of silver at Potosí (poh-toh-SEE) (in present-day Bolivia) in territory conquered from the Inca Empire. The frigid place where nothing grew had been unsettled. A half century later 160,000 people lived there, making it about as populous as the city of London. By 1550 Potosí yielded perhaps 60 percent of all the silver mined in the world. From Potosí and the mines at Zacatecas (za-kuh-TAY-kuhhs) and Guanajuato (gwah-nah-HWAH-toh) in Mexico, huge quantities of precious metals poured forth. To protect this treasure from French and English pirates, armed convoys transported it to Spain each year. Between 1503 and 1650, 35 million pounds of silver and over 600,000 pounds of gold entered Seville's port. Spanish predominance, however, proved temporary.

In the sixteenth century Spain experienced a steady population increase, creating a sharp rise in the demand for food and goods. Spanish colonies in the Americas also demanded consumer goods, such as cloth and luxury goods. Since Spain had expelled some of its best farmers and businessmen — the Muslims and Jews — in the fifteenth century, the Spanish economy was suffering and could not meet the new demands. The excess of demand over supply led to widespread inflation. The result was a rise in production costs and a further decline in Spain's productive capacity.

Did the flood of silver bullion from America cause the inflation? Prices rose most steeply before 1565, but bullion imports reached their peak between 1580 and 1620. Thus silver did not cause the initial inflation. It did, however, exacerbate the situation, and, along with the ensuing rise in population, the influx of silver significantly contributed to the upward spiral of prices. Inflation severely strained government budgets. Several times between 1557 and 1647, Spain's King Philip II and his successors wrote off the state debt, thereby undermining confidence in the government and leaving the economy in shambles. After 1600, when the population declined, prices gradually stabilized.

As Philip II paid his armies and foreign debts with silver bullion, Spanish inflation was transmitted to the rest of Europe. Between 1560 and 1600 much of Europe experienced large price increases. Prices doubled and in some cases quadrupled. Spain suffered most severely, but all European countries were affected. Because money bought less, people who lived on fixed incomes, such as nobles, were badly hurt. Those who owed fixed sums of money, such as the middle class, prospered because in a time of rising prices, debts lessened in value each year. Food costs rose most sharply, and the poor fared worst of all.

In many ways, though, it was not Spain but China that controlled the world trade in silver. The Chinese demanded silver for their products and for the payment of imperial taxes. China was thus the main buyer of world silver, absorbing half the world's production. The silver market drove world trade, with New Spain and Japan being mainstays on the supply side and China dominating the demand side. The world trade in silver is one of the best examples of the new global economy that emerged in this period.

The Birth of the Global Economy

With the Europeans' discovery of the Americas and their exploration of the Pacific, the entire world was linked for the first time in history by seaborne trade. The opening of that trade brought into being three

successive commercial empires: the Portuguese, the Spanish, and the Dutch.

The Portuguese were the first worldwide traders. In the sixteenth century they controlled the sea route to India (see Map 14.3). From their fortified bases at Goa on the Arabian Sea and at Malacca on the Malay Peninsula, ships carried goods to the Portuguese settlement at Macao in the South China Sea. From Macao Portuguese ships loaded with Chinese silks and porcelains sailed to the Japanese port of Nagasaki and to the Philippine port of Manila, where Chinese goods were exchanged for Spanish silver from New Spain. Throughout Asia the Portuguese traded in slaves— sub-Saharan Africans, Chinese, and Japanese. The Portuguese exported horses from Mesopotamia and copper from Arabia to India; from India they exported hawks and peacocks for the Chinese and Japanese markets. Back to Portugal they brought Asian spices that had been purchased with textiles produced in India and

Goods from the Global Economy   Spices from Southeast Asia were a driving force behind the new global economy, and among the most treasured European luxury goods. They were used not only for cooking but also as medicines and health tonics. This fresco (below right) shows a fifteenth-century Italian pharmacist measuring out spices for a customer. After the discovery of the Americas, a wave of new items entered European markets, silver foremost among them. The incredibly rich silver mines at Potosí (modern-day Bolivia) were the source of this eight-reale coin (right) struck at the mine during the reign of Charles II. Such coins were the original "pieces of eight" prized by pirates and adventurers. Soon Asian and American goods were mixed together by enterprising tradesmen. This mid-seventeenth-century Chinese teapot (below left) was made of porcelain with the traditional Chinese design prized in the West, but with a silver handle added to suit European tastes.

(Spice shop: Alfredo Dagli Orti/The Art Archive at Art Resource, NY; teapot: Private Collection/Paul Freeman/The Bridgeman Art Library; coin: Hoberman Collection/SuperStock)

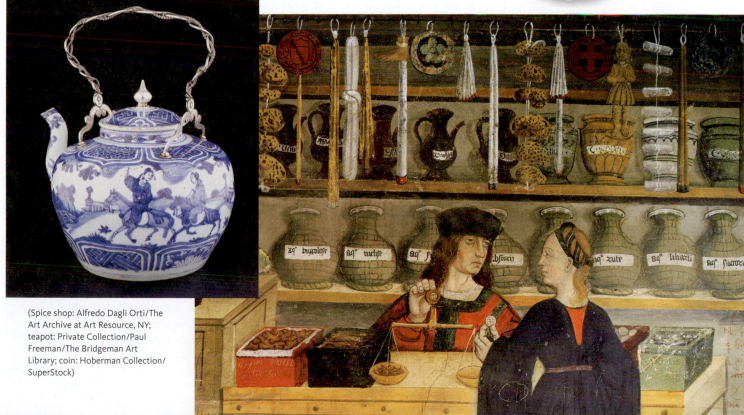

with gold and ivory from East Africa. They also shipped back sugar from their colony in Brazil, produced by enslaved Africans whom they had transported across the Atlantic.

Coming to empire a few decades later than the Portuguese, the Spanish were determined to claim their place in world trade. The Spanish Empire in the New World was basically a land empire, but across the Pacific the Spaniards built a seaborne empire centered at Manila in the Philippines. The city of Manila served as the transpacific bridge between Spanish America and China. In Manila, Spanish traders used silver from American mines to purchase Chinese silk for European markets. The European demand for silk was so huge that in 1597, for example, 12 million pesos of silver, almost the total value of the transatlantic trade, moved from Acapulco in New Spain to Manila (see Map 14.3). After 1640 the Spanish silk trade declined in the face of stiff competition from Dutch imports.

In the late sixteenth century the Protestant Dutch were engaged in a long war of independence from their Spanish Catholic overlords (see Chapter 15). The joining of the Portuguese crown to Spain in 1580 gave the Dutch a strategic incentive to attack Portugal, a major economic competitor for the Dutch. Drawing on their commercial wealth and determined use of force, the Dutch emerged by the end of the seventeenth century as both a free nation and a worldwide seaborne trading power. The Dutch Empire was initially built on spices. In 1599 a Dutch fleet returned to Amsterdam carrying 600,000 pounds of pepper and 250,000 pounds of cloves and nutmeg. Those who had invested in the expedition received a 100 percent profit. The voyage led to the establishment in 1602 of the Dutch East India Company, founded with the stated intention of capturing the spice trade from the Portuguese.

The Dutch set their sights on gaining direct access to and control of the Indonesian sources of spices. The Dutch fleet sailed from the Dutch Republic to the Cape of Good Hope in Africa and, avoiding the Portuguese forts in India, steered directly for the Sunda Strait in Indonesia (see Map 14.3). In return for assisting Indonesian princes in local squabbles and disputes with the Portuguese, the Dutch won broad commercial concessions. Through agreements, seizures, and outright military aggression, they gained control of the western access to the Indonesian archipelago in the first half of the seventeenth century. Gradually, they acquired political domination over the archipelago itself. By the 1660s the Dutch had managed to expel the Portuguese from Ceylon and other East Indian islands, thereby establishing control of the lucrative spice trade.

Not content with challenging the Portuguese in the Indian Ocean, the Dutch also aspired to a role in the Americas. Founded in 1621, when the Dutch were at war with the Spanish, the Dutch West India Company aggressively sought to open trade with North and South America and capture Spanish territories there. The company captured or destroyed hundreds of Spanish ships, seized the Spanish silver fleet in 1628, and captured portions of Brazil and the Caribbean. The Dutch also successfully interceded in the transatlantic slave trade, establishing a large number of trading stations on the west coast of Africa. Ironically, the nation that was known throughout Europe as a bastion of tolerance and freedom came to be one of the principal operators of the slave trade starting in the 1640s.

Dutch efforts to colonize North America were less successful. The colony of New Netherland, governed from New Amsterdam (modern-day New York City), was hampered by lack of settlement and weak governance and was easily captured by the British in 1664.

Changing Attitudes and Beliefs

How did new ideas about race and the works of Montaigne and Shakespeare reflect the encounter with new peoples and places?

The age of overseas expansion heightened Europeans' contacts with the rest of the world. These contacts gave birth to new ideas about the inherent superiority or inferiority of different races, in part to justify European participation in the slave trade. Cultural encounters also inspired more positive views. The essays of Michel de Montaigne epitomized a new spirit of skepticism and cultural relativism, while the plays of William Shakespeare reflected the efforts of one great writer to come to terms with the cultural complexity of his day.

New Ideas About Race

At the beginning of the transatlantic slave trade, most Europeans would have thought of Africans, if they thought of them at all, as savages because of their eating habits, morals, clothing, and social customs and as barbarians because of their language and methods of war. Despite lingering belief in a Christian Ethiopia under the legendary Prester John, they grouped Africans into the despised categories of pagan heathens and Muslim infidels. Africans were certainly not the only peoples subject to such dehumanizing attitudes. Jews were also viewed as alien people who, like Africans, were naturally sinful and depraved. More generally, elite Europeans were accustomed to viewing the peasant masses as a lower form of humanity. They scornfully compared rustic peasants to dogs, pigs, and donkeys and even reviled the dark skin color peasants acquired while laboring in the sun.[22]

As Europeans turned to Africa for new sources of slaves, they drew on and developed ideas about Africans' primitiveness and barbarity to defend slavery and even argue that enslavement benefited Africans by bringing the light of Christianity to heathen peoples. In 1444 an observer defended the enslavement of the first Africans by Portuguese explorers as necessary for their salvation "because they lived like beasts, without any of the customs of rational creatures, since they did not even know what were bread and wine, nor garments of cloth, nor life in the shelter of a house; and worse still was their ignorance, which deprived them of knowledge of good, and permitted them only a life of brutish idleness."[23] Compare this with an early-seventeenth-century Englishman's complaint that the Irish "be so beastly that they are better like beasts than Christians."[24]

Over time, the institution of slavery fostered a new level of racial inequality. In contrast to peasants, Jews, and the Irish, Africans gradually became seen as utterly distinct from and wholly inferior to Europeans. From rather vague assumptions about non-Christian religious beliefs and a general lack of civilization, Europeans developed increasingly rigid ideas of racial superiority and inferiority to safeguard the growing profits gained from plantation slavery. Black skin became equated with slavery itself as Europeans at home and in the colonies convinced themselves that blacks were destined by God to serve them as slaves in perpetuity.

Support for this belief went back to the Greek philosopher Aristotle's argument that some people are naturally destined for slavery and to biblical associations between darkness and sin. A more explicit justification was found in the story of Noah's curse upon Canaan, the son of his own son Ham. According to the Bible, Ham defied Noah's ban on sexual relations on the ark and further enraged his father by entering his tent and viewing him unclothed. To punish Ham, Noah cursed his son Canaan and all his descendants to be the "servant of servants." Biblical genealogies listing Ham's sons as those who peopled North Africa and Cush were read to mean that all inhabitants of those regions bore Noah's curse. From the sixteenth century onward, defenders of slavery often cited this story as justification for their actions.

After 1700 the emergence of new methods of observing and describing nature led to the use of science to define race. Although the term originally referred to a nation or an ethnic group, henceforth "race" would mean biologically distinct groups of people, whose physical differences produced differences in culture, character, and intelligence. Biblical justifications for inequality thereby gave way to supposedly scientific ones.

Michel de Montaigne and Cultural Curiosity

Racism was not the only possible reaction to the new worlds emerging in the sixteenth century. Decades of religious fanaticism, bringing civil anarchy and war, led some Catholics and Protestants to doubt that any one faith contained absolute truth. Added to these doubts was the discovery of peoples in the New World who had radically different ways of life. These shocks helped produce ideas of skepticism and cultural relativism. Skepticism is a school of thought founded on doubt that total certainty or definitive knowledge is ever attainable. The skeptic is cautious and critical and suspends judgment. Cultural relativism suggests that one culture is not necessarily superior to another, just different. Both notions found expression in the work of Frenchman Michel de Montaigne (duh mahn-TAYN) (1533–1592).

Montaigne developed a new literary genre, the essay—from the French *essayer*, meaning "to test or try"— to express his ideas. Published in 1580, Montaigne's *Essays* consisted of short reflections drawing on his extensive reading in ancient texts, his experience as a government official, and his own moral judgment. Intending his works to be accessible to ordinary people, Montaigne wrote in French rather than Latin and in an engaging conversational style. His essays were quickly translated into other European languages and became some of the most widely read texts of the early modern period.

Montaigne's essay "Of Cannibals" reveals the impact of overseas discoveries on one thoughtful European. In contrast to the prevailing views of his day, he rejected the notion that one culture is superior to another. Speaking of native Brazilians, he wrote:

> I find that there is nothing barbarous and savage in this nation [Brazil], . . . except, that everyone gives the title of barbarism to everything that is not according to his usage; as, indeed, we have no other criterion of truth and reason, than the example and pattern of the opinions and customs of the place wherein we live. . . . They are savages in the same way that we say fruits are wild, which nature produces of herself and by her ordinary course; whereas, in truth, we ought rather to call those wild whose natures we have changed by our artifice and diverted from the common order.[25]

In his own time, few would have agreed with Montaigne's challenge to ideas of European superiority or his even more radical questioning of the superiority of humans over animals. Nevertheless, his popular essays contributed to a basic shift in attitudes. "Wonder," he said, "is the foundation of all philosophy, research is the means of all learning, and ignorance is the end."[26] Montaigne thus inaugurated an era of doubt.

William Shakespeare and His Influence

In addition to the essay as a literary genre, the period fostered remarkable creativity in other branches of literature. England—especially in the latter part of Queen Elizabeth I's reign and in the first years of her successor, James I (r. 1603–1625)—witnessed remarkable literary expression. The undisputed master of the period was the dramatist William Shakespeare, whose genius lay in the originality of his characterizations, the diversity of his plots, his understanding of human psychology, and his unsurpassed gift for language. Born in 1564 to a successful glove manufacturer in Stratford-upon-Avon, Shakespeare grew into a Renaissance man with a deep appreciation of classical culture, individualism, and humanism. Although he wrote sparkling comedies and stirring historical plays, his greatest masterpieces were his later tragedies, including *Hamlet*, *Othello*, and *Macbeth*, which explore an enormous range of human problems and are open to an almost infinite variety of interpretations.

Like Montaigne's essays, Shakespeare's work reveals the impact of the new discoveries and contacts of his day. The title character of *Othello* is described as a "Moor of Venice." In Shakespeare's day, the term "Moor" referred to Muslims of North African origin, including those who had migrated to the Iberian Peninsula. It could also be applied, though, to natives of the Iberian Peninsula who converted to Islam or to non-Muslim Berbers in North Africa. To complicate things even more, references in the play to Othello as "black" in skin color have led many to believe that Shakespeare intended him to be a sub-Saharan African. This confusion in the play aptly reflects the uncertainty in Shakespeare's own time about racial and religious classifications. In contrast to the prevailing view of Moors as inferior, Shakespeare presents Othello as a complex human figure, whose only crime is to have "loved [his wife] not wisely, but too well."

Shakespeare's last play, *The Tempest*, also highlights the issue of race and race relations. The plot involves the stranding on an island of sorcerer Prospero and his daughter Miranda. There Prospero finds and raises Caliban, a native of the island, whom he instructs in his own language and religion. After Caliban's attempted rape of Miranda, Prospero enslaves him, earning the hatred of his erstwhile pupil. Modern scholars often note the echoes between this play and the realities of imperial conquest and settlement in Shakespeare's day. It is no accident, they argue, that the poet portrayed Caliban as a monstrous dark-skinned island native who was best suited for slavery. Shakespeare himself borrows words from Montaigne's essay "Of Cannibals," suggesting that he may have intended to criticize, rather than endorse, racial intolerance. Shakespeare's work shows us one of the finest minds of the age grasping to come to terms with the racial and religious complexities around him.

Titus Andronicus   With classical allusions, fifteen murders and executions, a Gothic queen who takes a black lover, and incredible violence, this early Shakespearean tragedy (1594) was a melodramatic thriller that enjoyed enormous popularity with the London audience. The shock value of a dark-skinned character on the English stage is clearly shown in this illustration. (Bibliothèque nationale de France/Giraudon/The Bridgeman Art Library)

Notes

1. Marco Polo, *The Book of Ser Marco Polo, the Venetian: Concerning the Kingdoms and Marvels of the East*, vol. 2, trans. and ed. Colonel Sir Henry Yule (London: John Murray, 1903), pp. 185–186.

2. Thomas Benjamin, *The Atlantic World: Europeans, Africans, Indians and Their Shared History, 1400–1900* (Cambridge, U.K.: Cambridge University Press, 2009), p. 56.

3. Quoted in J. Devisse, "Africa in Inter-Continental Relations," in *General History of Africa*, vol. 4, *Africa from the Twelfth to the Sixteenth Century*, ed. D. T. Niane (Berkeley, Calif.: Heinemann Educational Books, 1984), p. 664.

4. Geoffrey Atkinson, *Les nouveaux horizons de la Renaissance française* (Paris: Droz, 1935), pp. 10–12.

5. G. V. Scammell, *The World Encompassed: The First European Maritime Empires, c. 800–1650* (Berkeley: University of California Press, 1981), pp. 101, 104.

6. Quoted in C. M. Cipolla, *Guns, Sails, and Empires: Technological Innovation and the Early Phases of European Expansion, 1400–1700* (New York: Minerva Press, 1965), p. 132.

7. Quoted in F. H. Littell, *The Macmillan Atlas: History of Christianity* (New York: Macmillan, 1976), p. 75.

8. Pablo E. Pérez-Mallaína, *Spain's Men of the Sea: Daily Life on the Indies Fleet in the Sixteenth Century* (Baltimore: Johns Hopkins University Press, 1998), p. 133.

9. Ibid., p. 19.

10. Quoted in F. Maddison, "Tradition and Innovation: Columbus' First Voyage and Portuguese Navigation in the Fifteenth Century," in *Circa 1492: Art in the Age of Exploration*, ed. J. A. Levenson (Washington, D.C.: National Gallery of Art, 1991), p. 69.

11. Quoted in R. L. Kagan, "The Spain of Ferdinand and Isabella," in *Circa 1492: Art in the Age of Exploration*, ed. J. A. Levenson (Washington, D.C.: National Gallery of Art, 1991), p. 60.

12. Peter Hulme, *Colonial Encounters: Europe and the Native Caribbean, 1492–1797* (London: Methuen, 1986), pp. 22–31.

13. Benjamin, *The Atlantic World*, p. 141.

14. Ibid., pp. 35–59.

15. Quoted in C. Gibson, ed., *The Black Legend: Anti-Spanish Attitudes in the Old World and the New* (New York: Knopf, 1971), pp. 74–75.

16. Quoted in L. B. Rout, Jr., *The African Experience in Spanish America* (New York: Cambridge University Press, 1976), p. 23.

17. Cited in Geoffrey Vaughn Scammell, *The First Imperial Age: European Overseas Expansion, c. 1400–1715* (London: Routledge, 2002), p. 62.

18. Ibid., p. 432.

19. Herbert S. Klein, "Profits and the Causes of Mortality," in David Northrup, ed., *The Atlantic Slave Trade* (Lexington, Mass.: D. C. Heath and Co., 1994), p. 116.

20. Malcolm Cowley and Daniel P. Mannix, "The Middle Passage," in David Northrup, ed., *The Atlantic Slave Trade* (Lexington, Mass.: D. C. Heath and Co., 1994), p. 101.

21. Voyages: The Trans-Atlantic Slave Trade Database, http://www.slavevoyages.org/tast/assessment/estimates.faces.

22. Paul Freedman, *Images of the Medieval Peasant* (Stanford, Calif.: Stanford University Press, 1999).

23. Quoted in James H. Sweet, "The Iberian Roots of American Racist Thought," *The William and Mary Quarterly* 54 (1997): 155.

24. Quoted in Sean J. Connolly, *Contested Island: Ireland, 1460–1630* (Oxford: Oxford University Press, 2007), p. 397.

25. C. Cotton, trans., *The Essays of Michel de Montaigne* (New York: A. L. Burt, 1893), pp. 207, 210.

26. Ibid., p. 523.

LOOKING BACK LOOKING AHEAD

In 1517 Martin Luther issued his "Ninety-five Theses," launching the Protestant Reformation; just five years later, Ferdinand Magellan's expedition sailed around the globe, shattering European notions of terrestrial geography. Within a few short years, old medieval certainties about Heaven and earth began to collapse. In the ensuing decades, Europeans struggled to come to terms with religious difference at home and the multitudes of new peoples and places they encountered abroad. These processes were intertwined, as Puritans and Quakers fled religious persecution at home to colonize the New World and the new Jesuit order proved its devotion to the pope by seeking Catholic converts across the globe. While some Europeans were fascinated and inspired by this new diversity, too often the result was violence. Europeans endured decades of civil war between Protestants and Catholics, and indigenous peoples suffered massive population losses as a result of European warfare, disease, and exploitation. Tragically, both Catholic and Protestant religious leaders condoned the African slave trade that was to bring suffering and death to millions of Africans.

Even as the voyages of discovery coincided with the fragmentation of European culture, they also belonged to longer-term processes of state centralization and consolidation. The new monarchies of the Renaissance produced stronger and wealthier governments capable of financing the huge expenses of exploration and colonization. Competition to gain overseas colonies became an integral part of European politics. Spain's investment in conquest proved spectacularly profitable and yet, as we will see in Chapter 15, the ultimate result was a weakening of its power. Other European nations took longer to realize financial gain, yet over time the Netherlands, England, and France reaped tremendous profits from colonial trade, which helped them build modernized, centralized states. The path from medieval Christendom to modern nation-states led through religious warfare and global encounter.

REVIEW and EXPLORE

MAKE IT STICK

> **LearningCurve**
> After reading the chapter, go online and use LearningCurve to retain what you've read.

Identify Key Terms

Identify and explain the significance of each item below.

conquistador (p. 433)

caravel (p. 433)

Ptolemy's *Geography* (p. 433)

Treaty of Tordesillas (p. 440)

Mexica Empire (p. 441)

Inca Empire (p. 443)

viceroyalties (p. 445)

encomienda system (p. 446)

Columbian exchange (p. 448)

Review the Main Ideas

Answer the focus questions from each section of the chapter.

- ◆ What was the Afroeurasian trading world before Columbus? (p. 428)

- ◆ How and why did Europeans undertake ambitious voyages of expansion? (p. 432)

- ◆ What was the impact of European conquest on the peoples and ecologies of the New World? (p. 445)

- ◆ How was the era of global contact shaped by new commodities, commercial empires, and forced migrations? (p. 449)

- ◆ How did new ideas about race and the works of Montaigne and Shakespeare reflect the encounter with new peoples and places? (p. 456)

Make Connections

Think about the larger developments and continuities within and across chapters.

1. Michel de Montaigne argued that people's assessments of what was "barbaric" merely drew on their own habits and customs; based on the earlier sections of this chapter, how widespread was this openness to cultural difference? Was he alone or did others share this view?

2. To what extent did the European voyages of expansion and conquest inaugurate an era of global history? Is it correct to date the beginning of "globalization" from the late fifteenth century? Why or why not?

ONLINE DOCUMENT ASSIGNMENT
Juan de Pareja

How could an individual like Pareja experience both slavery and freedom in a single lifetime?

You encountered Juan de Pareja's story on page 453. Keeping the question above in mind, go to the Integrated Media and examine primary sources from Pareja's time—including visual art, drama, and legal excerpts. Then complete a writing assignment based on the evidence and details from this chapter.

Suggested Reading and Media Resources

BOOKS

- Crosby, Alfred W. *The Columbian Exchange: Biological and Cultural Consequences of 1492,* 30th anniversary ed. 2003. An innovative and highly influential account of the environmental impact of Columbus's voyages.

- Elliot, J. H. *Empires of the Atlantic World: Britain and Spain in America, 1492–1830.* 2006. A masterful account of the differences and similarities between the British and Spanish Empires in the Americas.

- Fernández-Armesto, Felipe. *Columbus.* 1992. An excellent biography of Christopher Columbus.

- Mann, Charles C. *1491: New Revelations on the Americas Before Columbus,* 2d ed. 2011. A highly readable account of the peoples and societies of the Americas before the arrival of Europeans.

- Menard, Russell R. *Sweet Negotiations: Sugar, Slavery, and Plantation Agriculture in Early Barbados.* 2006. Explores the intertwined history of sugar plantations and slavery in seventeenth-century Barbados.

- Northrup, David, ed. *The Atlantic Slave Trade.* 1994. Collected essays by leading scholars on many different aspects of the slave trade.

- Parker, Charles H. *Global Interactions in the Early Modern Age, 1400–1800.* 2010. An examination of the rise of global connections in the early modern period, which situates the European experience in relation to the world's other empires and peoples.

- Pestana, Carla. *Protestant Empire: Religion and the Making of the British Atlantic World.* 2009. Shows the impact of religious conflict between Protestants and Catholics on the emergence of European empires.

- Pomeranz, Kenneth, and Steven Topik. *The World That Trade Created: Society, Culture, and the World Economy, 1400 to the Present.* 1999. The creation of a world market presented through rich and vivid stories of merchants, miners, slaves, and farmers.

- Restall, Matthew. *Seven Myths of Spanish Conquest.* 2003. A re-examination of common ideas about why and how the Spanish conquered native civilizations in the New World.

- Rountree, Helen C. *Pocahontas, Powhatan, Opechancanough: Three Indian Lives Changed by Jamestown.* 2005. Biographies of three important Native Americans involved in the Jamestown settlement, presenting a rich portrait of the life of the Powhatan people and their encounter with the English.

DOCUMENTARIES

- *Columbus: The Lost Voyage* (History Channel, 2007). Recounts the little-known story of Christopher Columbus's fourth and final voyage, featuring interviews with experts and re-creations of important episodes along the route.

- *Conquistadors* (PBS, 2000). Traveling in the footsteps of the Spanish conquistadors, the narrator tells their story while following the paths and rivers they used. Includes discussion of the perspectives and participation of native peoples.

- *1421: The Year China Discovered America?* (PBS, 2004). Investigates the voyages of legendary Chinese admiral Zheng He, exploring the possibility that he and his fleet reached the Americas decades before Columbus.

FEATURE FILMS AND TELEVISION

- *Black Robe* (Bruce Beresford, 1991). A classic film about French Jesuit missionaries among Algonquin and Huron Indians in New France in the seventeenth century.

- *Marco Polo* (Hallmark Channel, 2007). A made-for-television film that follows Italian merchant Marco Polo as he travels to China to establish trade ties with Mongol emperor Kublai Khan.

- *The New World* (Terrence Malick, 2005). Set in 1607 at the founding of the Jamestown settlement, this film retells the story of John Smith and Pocahontas.

WEB SITES

- *The Globalization of Food and Plants.* Hosted by the Yale University Center for the Study of Globalization, this Web site provides information on how various foods and plants—such as spices, coffee, and tomatoes—traveled the world in the Columbian exchange. **yaleglobal.yale.edu/about/food.jsp**

- *Historic Jamestowne.* Showcasing archaeological work at the Jamestown settlement, the first permanent English settlement in America, this site provides details of the latest digs along with biographical information about settlers, historical background, and resources for teachers and students. **www.historicjamestowne.org**

- *Plymouth Colony Archive Project.* A site hosted by the anthropology department at the University of Illinois that contains a collection of searchable primary and secondary sources relating to the Plymouth colony, including court records, laws, seventeenth-century journals and memoirs, wills, maps, and biographies of colonists. **www.histarch.uiuc.edu/Plymouth/index.html**

15

Absolutism and Constitutionalism

ca. 1589–1725

Despite the lavish lifestyles of wealthy nobles and royals, the seventeenth century was a period of crisis and transformation in Europe. Agricultural and manufacturing slumps led to food shortages and shrinking population rates. Religious and dynastic conflicts led to almost constant war, visiting violence and destruction on ordinary people and reshaping European states. With Louis XIV of France taking the lead, armies grew larger than they had been since the time of the Roman Empire, resulting in new government bureaucracies and higher taxes. Yet even with these obstacles, European states succeeded in gathering more power, and by 1680 much of the unrest that originated with the Reformation was resolved.

These crises were not limited to western Europe. Central and eastern Europe experienced even more catastrophic dislocation, with German lands serving as the battleground of the Thirty Years' War and borders constantly vulnerable to attack from the east. In Prussia and in Habsburg Austria absolutist states emerged in the aftermath of this conflict. Russia and the Ottoman Turks also experienced turmoil in the mid-seventeenth century, but maintained their distinctive styles of absolutist government. The Russian and Ottoman Empires seemed foreign and exotic to western Europeans, who saw them as the antithesis of their political, religious, and cultural values.

While absolutism emerged as the solution to crisis in many European states, a small minority adopted a different path, placing sovereignty in the hands of privileged groups rather than the Crown. Historians refer to states where power was limited by law as "constitutional." The two most important seventeenth-century constitutionalist states were England and the Dutch Republic. Constitutionalism should not be confused with democracy. The elite rulers of England and the Dutch Republic pursued familiar policies of increased taxation, government authority, and social control. Nonetheless, they served as influential models to onlookers across Europe as a form of government that checked the power of a single ruler. ■

Life at the French Royal Court. King Louis XIV receives foreign ambassadors to celebrate a peace treaty. The king grandly occupied the center of his court, which in turn served as the pinnacle for the French people and, at the height of his glory, for all of Europe. (Erich Lessing/Art Resource, NY)

CHAPTER PREVIEW

 LearningCurve
After reading the chapter, go online and use LearningCurve to retain what you've read.

Seventeenth-Century Crisis and Rebuilding

What were the common crises and achievements of seventeenth-century European states?

Absolutism in France and Spain

What factors led to the rise of the French absolutist state under Louis XIV, and why did absolutist Spain experience decline in the same period?

Absolutism in Austria and Prussia

What were the social conditions of eastern Europe, and how did the rulers of Austria and Prussia transform their nations into powerful absolutist monarchies?

The Development of Russia and the Ottoman Empire

What were the distinctive features of Russian and Ottoman absolutism?

Alternatives to Absolutism in England and the Dutch Republic

How and why did the constitutional state triumph in the Dutch Republic and England?

Baroque Art and Music

What was the baroque style in art and music, and where was it popular?

Seventeenth-Century Crisis and Rebuilding

What were the common crises and achievements of seventeenth-century European states?

Historians often refer to the seventeenth century as an "age of crisis." After the economic and demographic growth of the sixteenth century, Europe faltered into stagnation and retrenchment. This was partially due to climate changes beyond anyone's control, but it also resulted from bitter religious divides, increased governmental pressures, and war. These challenges overwhelmed the fragile balance of rural villages, leading to hunger and population loss. Overburdened peasants and city dwellers took action to defend themselves from high prices and overtaxation, sometimes profiting from conflicts to obtain relief. In the long run, however, governments proved increasingly able to impose their will on the populace. With France under Louis XIV commanding European leadership, the period witnessed spectacular growth in army size as well as new forms of taxation, government bureaucracies, and increased state sovereignty.

The Social Order and Peasant Life

Peasants occupied the lower tiers of a society organized in hierarchical levels. At the top, the monarch was celebrated as a semidivine being, chosen by God to embody the state. In Catholic countries, the clergy occupied the second level, due to their sacred role interceding with God and the saints on behalf of their flocks. Next came nobles, whose privileged status derived from their ancient bloodlines and centuries of sacrifice on the battlefield. Christian prejudices against commerce and money meant that merchants could never lay claim to the highest honors. However, many prosperous mercantile families had bought their way into the nobility through service to the rising monarchies of the fifteenth and sixteenth centuries and constituted a second tier of nobles. Those lower on the social scale, the peasants and artisans who constituted the vast majority of the population, were expected to defer to their betters with humble obedience. This was the "Great Chain of Being" that linked God to his creation in a series of ranked social groups.

In addition to being rigidly hierarchical, European societies were patriarchal in nature, with men assuming authority over women as a God-given prerogative. The family thus represented a microcosm of this social order. The father ruled his family like a king ruled his domains. Religious and secular law commanded a man's wife, children, servants, and apprentices to defer to his will. Fathers did not possess the power of life and death, like Roman patriarchs, but they were entitled to use physical violence, imprisonment, and other forceful measures to impose their authority. These powers were balanced by expectations that a good father would provide and care for his dependents.

In the seventeenth century most Europeans lived in the countryside. The hub of the rural world was the small peasant village centered on a church and a manor. Life was in many ways circumscribed by the village, although we should not underestimate the mobility induced by war, food shortage, and the desire to seek one's fortune or embark on a religious pilgrimage.

Estonian Serfs in the 1660s The Estonians were conquered by German military nobility in the Middle Ages and reduced to serfdom. The German-speaking nobles ruled the Estonian peasants with an iron hand, and Peter the Great reaffirmed their domination when Russia annexed Estonia. (Mansell Collection/Time Life Pictures/Getty Images)

In western Europe, a small number of peasants in each village owned enough land to feed themselves and had the livestock and plows necessary to work their land. These independent farmers were leaders of the peasant village. They employed the landless poor, rented out livestock and tools, and served as agents for the noble lord. Below them were small landowners and tenant farmers who did not have enough land to be self-sufficient. These families sold their best produce on the market to earn cash for taxes, rent, and food. At the bottom were villagers who worked as dependent laborers and servants. In eastern Europe, the vast majority of peasants toiled as serfs for noble landowners and did not own land in their own right (see page 479).

Rich or poor, east or west, bread was the primary element of the diet. The richest ate a white loaf, leaving brown bread to those who could not afford better. Peasants paid stiff fees to the local miller for grinding grain into flour and sometimes to the lord for the right to bake bread in his oven. Bread was most often accompanied by a soup made of roots, herbs, beans, and perhaps a small piece of salt pork. An important annual festival in many villages was the killing of the family pig. The whole family gathered to help, sharing a rare abundance of meat with neighbors and carefully salting the extra and putting down the lard. In some areas, menstruating women were careful to stay away from the kitchen for fear they might cause the lard to spoil.

Famine and Economic Crisis

European rural society lived on the edge of subsistence. Because of the crude technology and low crop yield, peasants were constantly threatened by scarcity and famine. In the seventeenth century a period of colder and wetter climate throughout Europe, dubbed the "little ice age" by historians, meant a shorter farming season with lower yields. A bad harvest created food shortages; a series of bad harvests could lead to famine. Recurrent famines significantly reduced the population of early modern Europe. Most people did not die of outright starvation, but through the spread of diseases like smallpox and typhoid, which were facilitated by malnutrition and exhaustion. Outbreaks of bubonic plague continued in Europe until the 1720s.

Chronology

ca. 1500–1650	Consolidation of serfdom in eastern Europe
1533–1584	Reign of Ivan the Terrible in Russia
1589–1610	Reign of Henry IV in France
1598–1613	Time of Troubles in Russia
1620–1740	Growth of absolutism in Austria and Prussia
1642–1649	English civil war, which ends with execution of Charles I
1643–1715	Reign of Louis XIV in France
1653–1658	Military rule in England under Oliver Cromwell (the Protectorate)
1660	Restoration of English monarchy under Charles II
1665–1683	Jean-Baptiste Colbert applies mercantilism to France
1670	Charles II agrees to re-Catholicize England in secret agreement with Louis XIV
1670–1671	Cossack revolt led by Stenka Razin
ca. 1680–1750	Construction of absolutist palaces
1682	Louis XIV moves court to Versailles
1682–1725	Reign of Peter the Great in Russia
1683–1718	Habsburgs push the Ottoman Turks from Hungary
1685	Edict of Nantes revoked in France
1688–1689	Glorious Revolution in England
1701–1713	War of the Spanish Succession

The Estates of Normandy, a provincial assembly, reported on the dire conditions in northern France during an outbreak of plague:

Of the 450 sick persons whom the inhabitants were unable to relieve, 200 were turned out, and these we saw die one by one as they lay on the roadside. A large number still remain, and to each of them it is only possible to dole out the least scrap of bread. We only give bread to those who would otherwise die. The staple dish here consists of mice, which the inhabitants hunt, so desperate are they from hunger. They devour roots which the animals cannot eat; one can, in fact, not put into words the things one sees. . . . We certify to having ourselves seen herds, not of cattle, but of men and women, wandering about the fields between Rheims and Rhétel, turning up the earth like pigs to find a few roots; and as they can only find rotten ones, and not half enough of them, they become so weak that they have not strength left to seek food.[1]

Given the harsh conditions of life, industry also suffered. The output of woolen textiles, one of the most important European manufactures, declined sharply in the first half of the seventeenth century. Food prices were high, wages stagnated, and unemployment soared. This economic crisis was not universal: it struck various regions at different times and to different degrees. In the middle decades of the century, for example, Spain, France, Germany, and England all experienced great economic difficulties, but these years were the golden age of the Netherlands.

The urban poor and peasants were the hardest hit. When the price of bread rose beyond their capacity to pay, they frequently expressed their anger by rioting. In towns they invaded bakers' shops to seize bread and resell it at a "just price." In rural areas they attacked convoys taking grain to the cities. Women often led these actions, since their role as mothers gave them some impunity in authorities' eyes. Historians have used the term "moral economy" for this vision of a world in which community needs predominate over competition and profit.

The Thirty Years' War

In the first half of the seventeenth century, the fragile balance of life was violently upturned by the ravages of the Thirty Years' War (1618–1648). The Holy Roman Empire was a confederation of hundreds of principalities, independent cities, duchies, and other polities loosely united under an elected emperor. The uneasy truce between Catholics and Protestants created by the Peace of Augsburg in 1555 deteriorated as the faiths of various areas shifted. Lutheran princes felt compelled to form the Protestant Union (1608), and Catholics retaliated with the Catholic League (1609). Each alliance was determined that the other should make no religious or territorial advance. Dynastic interests were also involved; the Spanish Habsburgs strongly supported the goals of their Austrian relatives: the unity of the empire and the preservation of Catholicism within it.

Peace of Westphalia The name of a series of treaties that concluded the Thirty Years' War in 1648 and marked the end of large-scale religious violence in Europe.

The war is traditionally divided into four phases. The first, or Bohemian, phase (1618–1625) was characterized by civil war in Bohemia between the Catholic League and the Protestant Union. In 1620 Catholic forces defeated Protestants at the Battle of the White Mountain. The second, or Danish, phase of the war (1625–1629)—so called because of the leadership of the Protestant king Christian IV of Denmark (r. 1588–1648)—witnessed additional Catholic victories. The Catholic imperial army led by Albert of Wallenstein swept through Silesia, north to the Baltic, and east into Pomerania, scoring smashing victories. Under Charles I, England briefly and unsuccessfully intervened in this phase of the conflict by entering alliances against France and Spain. Habsburg power peaked in 1629. The emperor issued the Edict of Restitution, whereby all Catholic properties lost to Protestantism since 1552 were restored, and only Catholics and Lutherans were allowed to practice their faiths.

The third, or Swedish, phase of the war (1630–1635) began with the arrival in Germany of the Swedish king Gustavus Adolphus (r. 1594–1632) and his army. The ablest administrator of his day and a devout Lutheran, he intervened to support the empire's Protestants. The French chief minister, Cardinal Richelieu, subsidized the Swedes, hoping to weaken Habsburg power in Europe. Gustavus Adolphus won two important battles but was fatally wounded in combat. The final, or French, phase of the war (1635–1648) was prompted by Richelieu's concern that the Habsburgs would rebound after the death of Gustavus Adolphus. Richelieu declared war on Spain and sent military as well as financial assistance. Finally, in October 1648 peace was achieved.

The 1648 **Peace of Westphalia** that ended the Thirty Years' War marked a turning point in European history. For the most part, conflicts fought over religious faith receded. The treaties recognized the independent authority of more than three hundred German princes (Map 15.1), reconfirming the emperor's severely limited authority. The Augsburg agreement of 1555 became permanent, adding Calvinism to Catholicism and Lutheranism as legally permissible creeds. The north German states remained Protestant, the south German states Catholic.

The Thirty Years' War was the most destructive event for the central European economy and society prior to the world wars of the twentieth century. Perhaps one-third of urban residents and two-fifths of the rural population died, leaving entire areas depopulated. Trade in southern German cities, such as Augsburg, was virtually destroyed. Agricultural areas suffered catastrophically. Many small farmers lost their land, allowing nobles to enlarge their estates and consolidate their control.[2]

Achievements in State-Building

In the context of war and economic depression, seventeenth-century monarchs began to make new demands on their people. Traditionally, historians have distinguished between the "absolutist" governments of France, Spain, central Europe, and Russia and the constitutionalist governments of England and the Dutch Republic. Whereas absolutist monarchs gathered all power under their personal control, English and Dutch rulers were obliged to respect laws passed by represen-

Map 15.1 Europe After the Thirty Years' War This map shows the political division of Europe after the Treaty of Westphalia (1648) ended the war. France emerged as the strongest power in Europe at the end of the Thirty Years' War. Based on this map, what challenges did the French state still face in dominating Europe after 1648? How does the map represent Swedish gains and Spanish losses in the Treaty of Westphalia?

tative institutions. More recently, historians have emphasized commonalities among these powers. Despite their political differences, all these states shared common projects of protecting and expanding their frontiers, raising new taxes, consolidating central control, and competing for the new colonies opening up in the New and Old Worlds.

Rulers encountered formidable obstacles in achieving these goals. Some were purely material. Without paved roads, telephones, or other modern technology, it took weeks to convey orders from the central government to the provinces. Rulers also suffered from lack of information about their realms, making it impos-

sible to police and tax the population effectively. Local power structures presented another serious obstacle. Nobles, the church, provincial and national assemblies, town councils, guilds, and other bodies held legal privileges, which could not easily be rescinded. In some kingdoms many people spoke a language different from that of the Crown, further diminishing their willingness to obey its commands.

Nonetheless, over the course of the seventeenth century both absolutist and constitutional governments achieved new levels of central control. This increased authority focused on four areas in particular: greater taxation, growth in armed forces, larger and more efficient bureaucracies, and the increased ability to compel obedience from subjects. To meet the demands of running their expanding governments, rulers turned to trusted ministers. Cardinal Richelieu in France and Count-Duke Olivares in Spain each played the role of chief adviser to his king and enabler of state power. Royal favorites acquired power and fortune from their position; however, they were vulnerable to distrust and hostility from others at court. Olivares ended his career in disgrace, while the duke of Buckingham, favorite to James I and Charles I of England, was assassinated.

Over time, centralized power added up to something close to sovereignty. A state may be termed sovereign when it possesses a monopoly over the instruments of justice and the use of force within clearly defined boundaries. In a sovereign state, no system of courts, such as church tribunals, competes with state courts in the dispensation of justice; and private armies, such as those of feudal lords, present no threat to central authority. While seventeenth-century states did not ac-

quire total sovereignty, they made important strides toward that goal.

Warfare and the Growth of Army Size

The driving force of seventeenth-century state-building was warfare. In medieval times, feudal lords had raised armies only for particular wars or campaigns; now monarchs began to recruit their own forces and maintain permanent standing armies. Instead of serving their own interests, army officers were required to be loyal and obedient to those who commanded them. New techniques for training and deploying soldiers meant a rise in the professional standards of the army.

Along with professionalization came an explosive growth in army size. The French took the lead, with the army growing from roughly 125,000 men in the Thirty Years' War to 340,000 at the end of the seventeenth century.[3] Changes in the style of armies encouraged this growth. Mustering a royal army took longer than simply hiring a mercenary band, giving enemies time to form coalitions. For example, the large coalitions Louis XIV confronted (see pages 475–476) required him to fight on multiple fronts with huge armies. In turn, the relative size and wealth of France among European nations allowed Louis to field enormous armies and thereby to pursue the ambitious foreign policies that caused his alarmed neighbors to form coalitions against him.

Noble values of glory and honor outshone concerns for safety or material benefit. Because they personally led their men in battle, noble officers experienced high death rates on the battlefield. Nobles also fell into debt because they had to purchase their positions in the army and the units they commanded, which meant that they were obliged to assume many of the costs involved in creating and maintaining their units. It was not until the 1760s that the French government assumed the full cost of equipping troops.

Other European powers were quick to follow the French example. The rise of absolutism in central and eastern Europe led to a vast expansion in the size of armies. Great Britain followed a similar, albeit distinctive pattern. Instead of building a land army, the British focused on naval forces and eventually built the largest navy in the world.

The Professionalization of the Swedish Army Swedish king Gustavus Adolphus, surrounded by his generals, gives thanks to God for the safe arrival of his troops in Germany during the Thirty Years' War. A renowned military leader, the king imposed constant training drills and rigorous discipline on his troops, which contributed to their remarkable success in the war. (Military Academy of Karlberg)

Popular Political Action

As governments continuously raised taxes to meet the costs of war, neighborhood riots over the cost of bread turned into armed uprisings. Popular revolts were extremely common in England, France, Spain, Portugal, and Italy during the Thirty Years' War. In 1640 Philip IV of Spain faced revolt in Catalonia, the economic center of his realm. At the same time he struggled to put down uprisings in Portugal and in the northern provinces of the Netherlands. In 1647 the city of Palermo, in Spanish-occupied Sicily, exploded in protest over food shortages caused by a series of bad harvests. Fearing public unrest, the city government subsidized the price of bread, attracting even more starving peasants from the countryside. When Madrid ordered an end to subsidies, municipal leaders decided to lighten the loaf rather than raise prices. Not fooled by this change, local women led a bread riot, shouting "Long live the king and down with the taxes and the bad government!" Insurgency spread to the rest of the island and eventually to Naples on the mainland. Apart from affordable food, rebels demanded the suppression of extraordinary taxes and participation in municipal government. Some dreamed of a republic that would abolish noble tax exemptions. Despite initial successes, the revolt lacked unity and strong leadership and could not withstand the forces of the state.

In France urban uprisings became a frequent aspect of the social and political landscape. Beginning in 1630 and continuing on and off through the early 1700s, major insurrections occurred at Dijon, Bordeaux (bor-DOH), Montpellier, Lyons, and Amiens. All were characterized by deep popular anger and violence directed at outside officials sent to collect taxes. These officials were sometimes seized, beaten, and hacked to death. For example, in 1673 Louis XIV's imposition of new taxes on legal transactions, tobacco, and pewter ware provoked an uprising in Bordeaux.

Municipal and royal authorities often struggled to overcome popular revolt. They feared that stern repressive measures, such as sending in troops to fire on crowds, would create martyrs and further inflame the situation, while full-scale occupation of a city would be very expensive and detract from military efforts elsewhere. The limitations of royal authority gave some leverage to rebels. To quell riots, royal edicts were sometimes suspended, prisoners released, and discussions initiated.

By the beginning of the eighteenth century, this leverage had largely disappeared. Municipal governments were better integrated into the national structure, and local authorities had prompt military support from the central government. People who publicly opposed royal policies and taxes received swift and severe punishment.

Absolutism in France and Spain

What factors led to the rise of the French absolutist state under Louis XIV, and why did absolutist Spain experience decline in the same period?

In the Middle Ages jurists held that as a consequence of monarchs' coronation and anointment with sacred oil, they ruled "by the grace of God." Law was given by God; kings "found" the law and acknowledged that they must respect and obey it. Kings in absolutist states amplified these claims, asserting that they were responsible to God alone. They claimed exclusive power to make and enforce laws, denying any other institution or group the authority to check their power. In France the founder of the Bourbon monarchy, Henry IV, established foundations upon which his successors Louis XIII and Louis XIV built a stronger, more centralized French state. Louis XIV is often seen as the epitome of an "absolute" monarch, with his endless wars, increased taxes and economic regulation, and glorious palace at Versailles. In truth, his success relied on collaboration with nobles, and thus his example illustrates both the achievements and the compromises of absolutist rule.

As French power rose in the seventeenth century, the glory of Spain faded. Once the fabulous revenue from American silver declined, Spain's economic stagnation could no longer be disguised, and the country faltered under weak leadership.

The Foundations of Absolutism

Louis XIV's absolutism had long roots. In 1589 his grandfather Henry IV (r. 1589–1610), the founder of the Bourbon dynasty, acquired a devastated country. Civil wars between Protestants and Catholics had wracked France since 1561. Poor harvests had reduced peasants to starvation, and commercial activity had declined drastically. "Henri le Grand" (Henry the Great), as the king was called, promised "a chicken in every pot" and inaugurated a remarkable recovery.

He did so by keeping France at peace during most of his reign. Although he had converted to Catholicism, he issued the Edict of Nantes, allowing Protestants the right to worship in 150 traditionally Protestant towns throughout France. He sharply lowered taxes and instead charged royal officials an annual fee to guarantee the right to pass their positions down to their heirs. He also improved the infrastructure of the country, building new roads and canals and repairing the ravages of years of civil war. Despite his efforts at peace, Henry was murdered in 1610 by a Catholic zealot, setting off a national crisis.

After the death of Henry IV, his wife, the queen-regent Marie de' Medici, headed the government for the nine-year-old Louis XIII (r. 1610–1643). In 1628 Armand Jean du Plessis—Cardinal Richelieu (1585–1642)—became first minister of the French crown. Richelieu's maneuvers allowed the monarchy to maintain power within Europe and within its own borders despite the turmoil of the Thirty Years' War.

Cardinal Richelieu's political genius is best reflected in the administrative system he established to strengthen royal control. He extended the use of intendants, commissioners for each of France's thirty-two districts who were appointed directly by the monarch, to whom they were solely responsible. They recruited men for the army, supervised the collection of taxes, presided over the administration of local law, checked up on the local nobility, and regulated economic activities in their districts. As the intendants' power increased under Richelieu, so did the power of the centralized French state.

Under Richelieu, the French monarchy also acted to repress Protestantism. Louis personally supervised the siege of La Rochelle, an important port city and a major commercial center with strong ties to Protestant Holland and England. After the city fell in October 1628, its municipal government was suppressed. Protestants retained the right of public worship, but the Catholic liturgy was restored. The fall of La Rochelle was one step in the removal of Protestantism as a strong force in French life.

Richelieu did not aim to wipe out Protestantism in the rest of Europe, however. His main foreign policy goal was to destroy the Catholic Habsburgs' grip on territories that surrounded France. Consequently, Richelieu supported Habsburg enemies, including Protestants. In 1631 he signed a treaty with the Lutheran king Gustavus Adolphus promising French support against the Habsburgs in the Thirty Years' War. For the French cardinal, interests of state outweighed religious considerations.

Richelieu's successor as chief minister for the next child-king, the four-year-old Louis XIV, was Cardinal Jules Mazarin (1602–1661). Along with the regent, Queen Mother Anne of Austria, Mazarin continued Richelieu's centralizing policies. His struggle to increase royal revenues to meet the costs of war led to the uprisings of 1648–1653 known as the **Fronde**. A *frondeur* was originally a street urchin who threw mud at the passing carriages of the rich, but the word came to be applied to the many individuals and groups who opposed the policies of the government. In Paris, magistrates of the Parlement of Paris, the na-

Fronde A series of violent uprisings during the early reign of Louis XIV triggered by growing royal control and increased taxation.

tion's most important court, were outraged by the Crown's autocratic measures. These so-called robe nobles (named for the robes they wore in court) encouraged violent protest by the common people. During the first of several riots, the queen mother fled Paris with Louis XIV. As rebellion spread outside Paris and to the sword nobles (the traditional warrior nobility), civil order broke down completely. In 1651 Anne's regency ended with the declaration of Louis as king in his own right. Much of the rebellion died away, and its leaders came to terms with the government.

The violence of the Fronde had significant results for the future. The twin evils of noble rebellion and popular riots left the French wishing for peace and for a strong monarch to reimpose order. This was the legacy that Louis XIV inherited in 1661 when he assumed personal rule of the largest and most populous country in western Europe at the age of twenty-three. Humiliated by his flight from Paris, he was determined to avoid any recurrence of rebellion.

Louis XIV and Absolutism

In the reign of Louis XIV (r. 1643–1715), the longest in European history, the French monarchy reached the peak of absolutist development. In the magnificence of his court and the brilliance of the culture that he presided over, Louis dominated his age. (See "Primary Source 15.1: *Louis XIV, King of France and Navarre, 1701*," at right.) Religion, Anne, and Mazarin all taught Louis the doctrine of the divine right of kings: God had established kings as his rulers on earth, and they were answerable ultimately to him alone. Kings were divinely anointed and shared in the sacred nature of divinity, but they could not simply do as they pleased. They had to obey God's laws and rule for the good of the people. To symbolize his central role in the divine order, when he was fifteen years old Louis danced at a court ballet dressed as the sun, thereby acquiring the title of the "Sun King."

In addition to parading his power before the court, Louis worked very hard at the business of governing. He ruled his realm through several councils of state and insisted on taking a personal role in many of their decisions. He selected councilors from the recently ennobled or the upper middle class because he believed "that the public should know, from the rank of those whom I chose to serve me, that I had no intention of sharing power with them."[4] Despite increasing financial problems, Louis never called a meeting of the Estates General, thereby depriving nobles of united expression or action. Nor did Louis have a first minister. In this way he avoided the inordinate power of a Richelieu.

Although personally tolerant, Louis hated division within the realm and insisted that religious unity was essential to his royal dignity and to the security of the

Louis XIV, King of France and Navarre, 1701

This was one of Louis XIV's favorite portraits of himself. He liked it so much that he had many copies of the portrait made, in full and half-size format.

EVALUATE THE EVIDENCE

1. Why do you think the king liked the portrait so much? What image of the king does it present to the viewer? What details does the painter include, and what impression do they convey?

2. How does this representation of royal power compare with the images of Peter the Great (page 485) and Charles I (page 490)? Which do you find the most impressive, and why?

(Louvre, Paris, France/Giraudon/The Bridgeman Art Library)

state. He thus pursued the policy of Protestant repression launched by Richelieu. In 1685 Louis revoked the Edict of Nantes. The new law ordered the Catholic baptism of Huguenots (French Calvinists), the destruction of Huguenot churches, the closing of schools, and the exile of Huguenot pastors who refused to renounce their faith. The result was the departure of some of the king's most loyal and industrially skilled subjects.

Despite his claims to absolute authority, multiple constraints existed on Louis's power. As a representative of divine power, he was obliged to rule in a manner consistent with virtue and benevolence. He had to uphold the laws issued by his royal predecessors. More-over, he also relied on the collaboration of nobles, who maintained tremendous prestige and authority in their ancestral lands. Without their cooperation, it would have been impossible to extend his power throughout France or wage his many foreign wars. Louis's need to elicit noble cooperation led him to revolutionize court life at his spectacular palace at Versailles.

Life at Versailles

Through most of the seventeenth century, the French court had no fixed home, following the monarch to his numerous palaces and country residences. In 1682

LIVING IN THE PAST
The Absolutist Palace

By 1700 palace building had become a veritable obsession for European rulers. Their dramatic palaces symbolized the age of absolutist power, just as soaring Gothic cathedrals had expressed the idealized spirit of the High Middle Ages. With its classically harmonious, symmetrical, and geometric design, Versailles served as the model for the wave of palace building that began in the last decade of the seventeenth century. Royal palaces like Versailles were intended to overawe the people and proclaim their owners' authority and power.

Located ten miles southwest of Paris, Versailles began as a modest hunting lodge built by Louis XIII in 1623. His son Louis XIV spent decades enlarging and decorating the original structure. Between 1668 and 1670, architect Louis Le Vau (luh VOH) enveloped the old building within a much larger one that still exists today. In 1682 the new palace became the official residence of the Sun King and his court, although construction continued until 1710, when the royal chapel was completed. At any one time, several thousand people occupied the bustling and crowded palace. The awesome splendor of the eighty-yard Hall of Mirrors, replete with floor-to-ceiling mirrors and ceiling murals illustrating the king's triumphs, contrasted with the strong odors from the courtiers who commonly relieved themselves in discreet corners.

In 1693 Charles XI of Sweden, having reduced the power of the aristocracy, ordered the construction of his Royal Palace, which dominates the center of Stockholm to this day. Another such palace was Schönbrunn, an enormous Viennese Versailles begun in 1695 by Emperor Leopold to celebrate Austrian military victories and Habsburg might. Shown at lower right is architect Joseph Bernhard Fischer von Erlach's ambitious plan for Schönbrunn palace. Fischer's plan emphasizes the palace's vast size and its role as a site for military demonstrations. Ultimately, financial constraints resulted in a more modest building.

In central and eastern Europe, the favorite noble servants of royalty became extremely rich and powerful, and they, too, built grandiose palaces in the capital cities. These palaces were in part an extension of the monarch, for they surpassed the buildings of less-favored nobles and showed all the high road to fame and fortune. Take, for example, the palaces of Prince Eugene of Savoy, a French nobleman who became Austria's most famous military hero. It was Eugene who led the Austrian army, smashed the Turks, fought Louis XIV to a standstill, and generally guided the triumph of absolutism in

Prince Eugene's Summer Palace in Vienna. (Erich Lessing/Art Resource, NY)

Louis moved his court and government to the newly renovated palace at Versailles, a former hunting lodge. The palace quickly became the center of political, social, and cultural life. The king required all great nobles to spend at least part of the year in attendance on him there, so he could keep an eye on their activities. Since he controlled the distribution of state power and wealth, nobles had no choice but to obey and compete with each other for his favor at Versailles.

The glorious palace, with its sumptuous interiors and extensive formal gardens, was a mirror to the world of French glory, soon copied by would-be absolutist

Austria. Rewarded with great wealth by his grateful king, Eugene called on the leading architects of the day, Fischer von Erlach and Johann Lukas von Hildebrandt, to consecrate his glory in stone and fresco. Fischer built Eugene's Winter (or Town) Palace in Vienna, and he and Hildebrandt collaborated on the prince's Summer Palace on the city's outskirts. The prince's summer residence featured two baroque gems, the Lower Belvedere and the Upper Belvedere, completed in 1722 and at left. The building's interior is equally stunning, with crouching giants serving as pillars and a magnificent great staircase.

QUESTIONS FOR ANALYSIS

1. Compare these images. What did concrete objects and the manipulation of space accomplish for these rulers that mere words could not?
2. What disadvantages might stem from using architecture as a political tool?
3. Is the use of space and monumental architecture still a political tool in today's world?

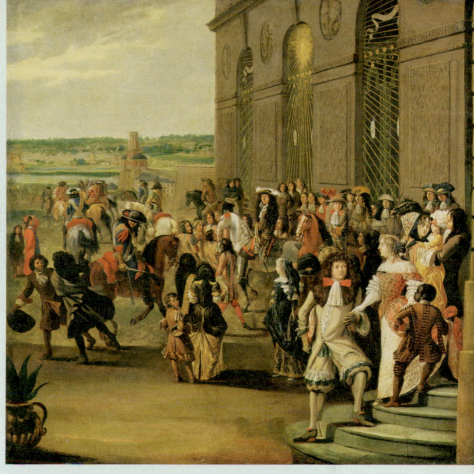

Louis XIV leading a tour of the extensive grounds at Versailles. (Chateau de Versailles, France/Giraudon/The Bridgeman Art Library)

Plans for the Palace at Schönbrunn, ca. 1700. (ONB/Vienna, Picture Archive, L 8001-D)

monarchs across Europe. (See "Living in the Past: The Absolutist Palace," above.) The reality of daily life in the palace was less glamorous. Versailles served as government offices for royal bureaucrats, as living quarters for the royal family and nobles, and as a place of work for hundreds of domestic servants. It was also open to the public at certain hours of the day. As a result, it was crowded with three thousand to ten thousand people every day. Even high nobles had to put up with cramped living space, and many visitors complained of the noise, smell, and crowds. (See "Primary Source 15.2: Letter from Versailles," page 475.)

Louis further revolutionized court life by establishing an elaborate set of etiquette rituals to mark every moment of his day, from waking up and dressing in the morning to removing his clothing and retiring at night. Courtiers vied for the honor of participating in these ceremonies, with the highest in rank claiming the privilege of handing the king his shirt. Endless squabbles broke out over what type of chair one could sit on at court and the order in which great nobles entered and were seated in the chapel for Mass.

These rituals may seem absurd, but they were far from trivial. The king controlled immense resources and privileges; access to him meant favored treatment for government offices, military and religious posts, state pensions, honorary titles, and a host of other benefits. The duke of Saint-Simon wrote of the king's power at court in his memoirs:

> No one understood better than Louis XIV the art of enhancing the value of a favour by his manner of bestowing it; he knew how to make the most of a word, a smile, even of a glance. If he addressed any one, were it but to ask a trifling question or make some commonplace remark, all eyes were turned on the person so honored; it was a mark of favour which always gave rise to comment.[5]

Courtiers sought these rewards for themselves and their family members and followers. A system of patronage—in which a higher-ranked individual protected a lower-ranked one in return for loyalty and services—flowed from the court to the provinces. Through this mechanism Louis gained cooperation from powerful nobles.

Although they could not hold public offices or posts, women played a central role in the patronage system. At court the king's wife, mistresses, and other female relatives recommended individuals for honors, advocated policy decisions, and brokered alliances between factions. Noblewomen played a similar role, bringing their family connections to marriage to form powerful social networks. Onlookers sometimes resented the influence of powerful women at court. The duke of Saint-Simon said of Madame de Maintenon, Louis XIV's mistress and secret second wife, "Many people have been ruined by her, without having been able to discover the author of the ruin, search as they might."

Louis XIV was also an enthusiastic patron of the arts, commissioning many sculptures and paintings for Versailles as well as performances of dance and music. Scholars characterize the art and literature of the age of Louis XIV as French classicism. By this they mean that

mercantilism A system of economic regulations aimed at increasing the power of the state based on the belief that a nation's international power was based on its wealth, specifically its supply of gold and silver.

the artists and writers of the late seventeenth century imitated the subject matter and style of classical antiquity, that their work resembled that of Renaissance Italy, and that French art possessed the classical qualities of discipline, balance, and restraint. Louis XIV also loved the stage, and in the plays of Molière and Racine his court witnessed the finest achievements in the history of the French theater. In this period, aristocratic ladies wrote many genres of literature and held salons in their Parisian mansions where they engaged in witty and cultured discussions of poetry, art, theater, and the latest worldly events. Their refined conversational style led Molière and other observers to mock them as "*précieuses*" (PREH-see-ooz; literally "precious"), or affected and pretentious. Despite this mockery, the *précieuses* represented an important cultural force ruled by elite women.

With Versailles as the center of European politics, French culture grew in international prestige. French became the language of polite society and international diplomacy, gradually replacing Latin as the language of scholarship and learning. Royal courts across Europe spoke French, and the great aristocrats of Russia, Sweden, Germany, and elsewhere were often more fluent in French than in the tongues of their homelands. France inspired a cosmopolitan European culture in the late seventeenth century that looked to Versailles as its center.

French Financial Management Under Colbert

France's ability to build armies and fight wars depended on a strong economy. Fortunately for Louis, his controller general, Jean-Baptiste Colbert (1619–1683), proved to be a financial genius. Colbert's central principle was that the wealth and the economy of France should serve the state. To this end, from 1665 to his death in 1683, Colbert rigorously applied mercantilist policies to France.

Mercantilism is a collection of governmental policies for the regulation of economic activities by and for the state. It derives from the idea that a nation's international power is based on its wealth, specifically its supply of gold and silver. To accumulate wealth, a country always had to sell more goods abroad than it bought. To decrease the purchase of goods outside France, Colbert insisted that French industry should produce everything needed by the French people.

To increase exports, Colbert supported old industries and created new ones, focusing especially on textiles, which were the most important sector of the economy. Colbert enacted new production regulations, created guilds to boost quality standards, and encouraged foreign craftsmen to immigrate to France. To encourage the purchase of French goods, he abolished many do-

Letter from Versailles

Born in 1652, the German princess Elisabeth-Charlotte was the daughter of the elector of the Palatinate, one of the many small states of the Holy Roman Empire. In 1671 she married the duke of Orléans, brother of Louis XIV. When Louis's wife died in 1683, Elisabeth-Charlotte became the highest-ranked woman at the French court. Despite the considerable pride she took in her position, her correspondence reveals her unhappiness and boredom with court life and her longing for home, as shown in the letter to her sister excerpted below.

❝ I have nothing new to tell you; I walk and read and write; sometimes the king drives me to the hunt in his calèche. There are hunts every day; Sundays and Wednesdays are my son's days; the king hunts Mondays and Thursdays; Wednesdays and Saturdays Monseigneur [heir to the throne] hunts the wolf; M. le Comte de Toulouse, Mondays and Wednesdays; the Duc du Maine, Tuesdays; and M. le Duc, Fridays. They say if all the hunting kennels were united there would be from 900 to 1000 dogs. Twice a week there is a comedy. But you know, of course, that I go nowhere [due to mourning for her recently deceased husband]; which vexes me, for I must own that the theatre is the greatest amusement I have in the world, and the only pleasure that remains to me. . . .

If the Court of France was what it used to be one might learn here how to behave in society; but — excepting the king and Monsieur [the king's brother, her deceased husband] — no one any longer knows what politeness is. The young men think only of horrible debauchery. I do not advise any one to send their children here; for instead of learning good things, they will only take lessons in misconduct. You are right in blaming Germans who send their sons to France; how I wish that you and I were men and could go to the wars! — but that's a completely useless wish to have. . . . If I could with propriety return to Germany you would see me there quickly. I love that country; I think it more agreeable than all others, because there is less of luxury that I do not care for, and more of the frankness and integrity which I seek. But, be it said between ourselves, I was placed here against my will, and here I must stay till I die. There is no likelihood that we shall see each other again in this life; and what will become of us after that God only knows. ❞

EVALUATE THE EVIDENCE

1. What are the principal amusements of court life, according to Elisabeth-Charlotte? What comparison does she draw between life in Germany and France?

2. How does the image of Versailles conveyed by Elisabeth-Charlotte contrast with the images of the palace found elsewhere in this chapter? How do you explain this contrast? If courtiers like her found life so dreary at court, why would they stay?

Source: *The Correspondence of Madame, Princess Palatine, Marie-Adélaïde de Savoie, and Madame de Maintenon*, ed. and trans. Katharine Prescott Wormeley (Boston: Hardy, Pratt, 1902), pp. 50–52.

---

mestic tariffs and raised tariffs on foreign products. In 1664 Colbert founded the Company of the East Indies with (unfulfilled) hopes of competing with the Dutch for Asian trade.

Colbert also hoped to make Canada — rich in untapped minerals and some of the best agricultural land in the world — part of a vast French empire. He sent four thousand colonists to Quebec, whose capital had been founded in 1608 under Henry IV. Subsequently, the Jesuit Jacques Marquette and the merchant Louis Joliet sailed down the Mississippi River, which they named Colbert in honor of their sponsor (the name soon reverted to the original Native American one). Marquette and Joliet claimed possession of the land on both sides of the river as far south as present-day Arkansas. In 1684 French explorers continued down the Mississippi to its mouth and claimed vast territories for Louis XIV. The area was called, naturally, "Louisiana."

During Colbert's tenure as controller general, Louis was able to pursue his goals without massive tax increases and without creating a stream of new offices. The constant pressure of warfare after Colbert's death, however, undid many of his economic achievements.

Louis XIV's Wars

Louis XIV wrote that "the character of a conqueror is regarded as the noblest and highest of titles." In pursuit of the title of conqueror, he kept France at war for thirty-three of the fifty-four years of his personal rule. François le Tellier, marquis de Louvois, Louis's secretary of state for war, equaled Colbert's achievements in the economic realm. Louvois created a professional army in which the French state, rather than private nobles, employed the soldiers. Uniforms and weapons were standardized, and a rational system of training and promotion was devised. Many historians believe that the new loyalty, professionalism, and growth of the French army represented the peak of Louis's success in reforming government. As in so many other matters, his model was followed across Europe.

Louis's goal was to expand France to what he considered its natural borders. His armies managed to extend French borders to include important commercial centers in the Spanish Netherlands and Flanders as well as the entire province of Franche-Comté between 1667 and 1678. In 1681 Louis seized the city of Strasbourg, and three years later he sent his armies into the province of Lorraine. At that moment the king seemed invincible. In fact, Louis had reached the limit of his expansion. The wars of the 1680s and 1690s brought no additional territories but placed unbearable strains on French resources. Colbert's successors resorted to desperate measures to finance these wars, including devaluation of the currency and new taxes.

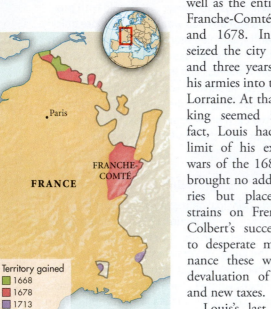

The Acquisitions of Louis XIV, 1668–1713

Territory gained
- 1668
- 1678
- 1713

Louis's last war was endured by a French people suffering high taxes, crop failure, and widespread malnutrition and death. In 1700 the childless Spanish king Charles II (r. 1665–1700) died, opening a struggle for control of Spain and its colonies. His will bequeathed the Spanish crown and its empire to Philip of Anjou, Louis XIV's grandson (Louis's wife, Maria-Theresa, had been Charles's sister). The will violated a prior treaty by which the European powers had agreed to divide the Spanish possessions between the king of France and the Holy Roman emperor, both brothers-in-law of Charles II. Claiming that he was following both Spanish and French interests, Louis broke with the treaty and accepted the will, thereby triggering the War of the Spanish Succession (1701–1713).

In 1701 the English, Dutch, Austrians, and Prussians formed the Grand Alliance against Louis XIV. War dragged on until 1713. The **Peace of Utrecht**, which ended the war, allowed Louis's grandson Philip to remain king of Spain on the understanding that the French and Spanish crowns would never be united. France surrendered Nova Scotia, Newfoundland, and the Hudson Bay territory to England, which also acquired Gibraltar, Minorca, and control of the African slave trade from Spain (Map 15.2).

The Peace of Utrecht represented the balance-of-power principle in operation, setting limits on the extent to which any one power — in this case, France — could expand. It also marked the end of French expansion. Thirty-five years of war had given France the rights to all of Alsace and some commercial centers in the north. But at what price? In 1714 an exhausted France hovered on the brink of bankruptcy. It is no wonder that when Louis XIV died on September 1, 1715, many subjects felt as much relief as they did sorrow.

The Decline of Absolutist Spain in the Seventeenth Century

At the beginning of the seventeenth century, France's position appeared extremely weak. Struggling to recover from decades of religious civil war that had destroyed its infrastructure and economy, France could not dare to compete with Spain's European and overseas empire or its mighty military. Yet by the end of the century their positions were reversed, and France had surpassed all expectations to attain European dominance.

By the early seventeenth century the seeds of Spanish disaster were sprouting. Between 1610 and 1650 Spanish trade with the colonies in the New World fell 60 percent due to competition from local industries in the colonies and from Dutch and English traders. At the same time, the native Indian and African slaves who toiled in the South American silver mines suffered frightful epidemics of disease. Ultimately, the mines that filled the empire's treasury started to run dry, and the quantity of metal produced steadily declined after 1620.

In Madrid, however, royal expenditures constantly exceeded income. To meet mountainous state debt, the Crown repeatedly devalued the coinage and declared bankruptcy, which resulted in the collapse of national credit. Meanwhile, manufacturing and commerce shrank. In contrast to the other countries of western Europe, Spain had a tiny middle class. The elite condemned moneymaking as vulgar and undignified. Thousands entered economically unproductive professions: there were said to be nine thousand monasteries in the province of Castile alone. To make matters worse, the Crown expelled some three hundred thousand *Moriscos*, or former Muslims, in 1609, significantly reducing the pool of skilled workers and merchants. Those working in the textile industry were forced out of business by steep inflation that pushed their production costs to the point where they could not compete in colonial and international markets.[6]

Peace of Utrecht A series of treaties, from 1713 to 1715, that ended the War of the Spanish Succession, ended French expansion in Europe, and marked the rise of the British Empire.

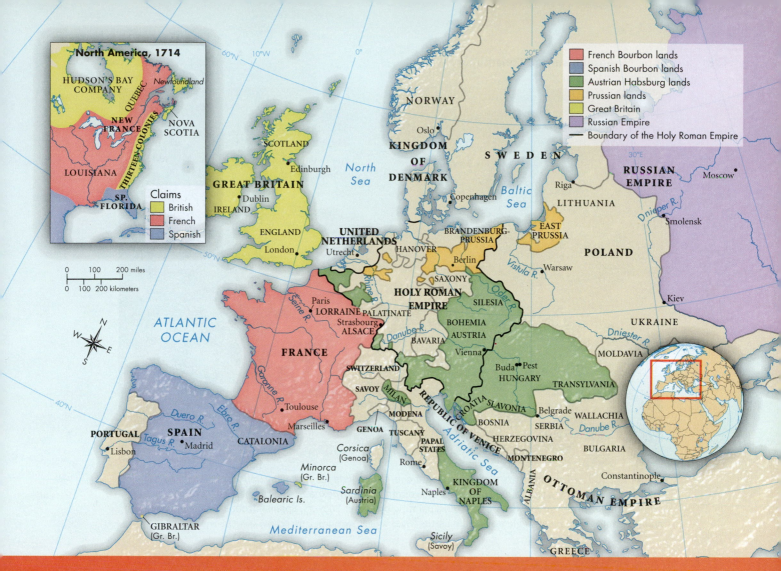

Map 15.2 Europe After the Peace of Utrecht, 1715

The series of treaties commonly called the Peace of Utrecht ended the War of the Spanish Succession and redrew the map of Europe. A French Bourbon king succeeded to the Spanish throne. France surrendered the Spanish Netherlands (later Belgium), then in French hands, to Austria, and recognized the Hohenzollern rulers of Prussia. Spain ceded Gibraltar to Great Britain, for which it has been a strategic naval station ever since. Spain also granted Britain the *asiento*, the contract for supplying African slaves to the Americas.

ANALYZING THE MAP Identify the areas on the map that changed hands as a result of the Peace of Utrecht. How did these changes affect the balance of power in Europe?

CONNECTIONS How and why did so many European countries possess scattered or noncontiguous territories? What does this suggest about European politics in this period? Does this map suggest potential for future conflict?

Spanish aristocrats, attempting to maintain an extravagant lifestyle they could no longer afford, increased the rents on their estates. High rents and heavy taxes in turn drove the peasants from the land, leading to a decline in agricultural productivity. In cities wages and production stagnated. Spain also ignored new scientific methods that might have improved agricultural or manufacturing techniques because they came from the heretical nations of Holland and England.

The Spanish crown had no solutions to these dire problems. Philip III (r. 1598–1621), a melancholy and deeply pious man, handed the running of the government over to the duke of Lerma, who used it to advance his personal and familial wealth. Philip IV (r. 1621–1665)

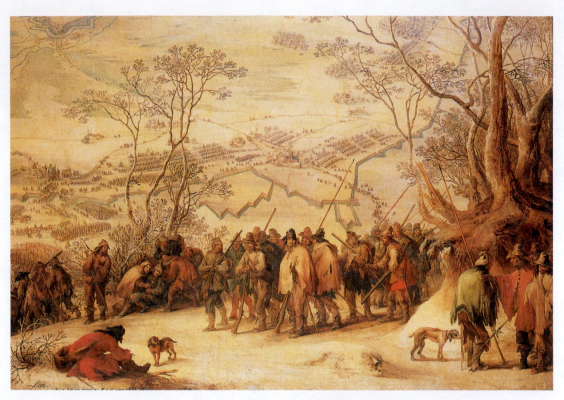

Spanish Troops   The long wars that Spain fought over Dutch independence, in support of Habsburg interests in Germany, and against France left the country militarily exhausted and financially drained by the mid-seventeenth century. In this detail from a painting by Peeter Snayers, Spanish troops — thin, emaciated, and probably unpaid — straggle away from battle. (Prado, Madrid, Spain/Index/The Bridgeman Art Library)

left the management of his several kingdoms to Gaspar de Guzmán, Count-Duke of Olivares. Olivares was an able administrator who has often been compared to Richelieu. He did not lack energy and ideas, and he succeeded in devising new sources of revenue. But he clung to the grandiose belief that the solution to Spain's difficulties rested in a return to the imperial tradition of the sixteenth century. Unfortunately, the imperial tradition demanded the revival of war with the Dutch at the expiration of a twelve-year truce in 1622 and a long war with France over Mantua (1628–1659). Spain thus became embroiled in the Thirty Years' War. These conflicts, on top of an empty treasury, brought disaster.

Spain's situation worsened with internal conflicts and fresh military defeats through the remainder of the seventeenth century. In 1640 Spain faced serious revolts in Catalonia and Portugal. In 1643 the French inflicted a crushing defeat on a Spanish army at Rocroi in what is now Belgium. By the Treaty of the Pyrenees of 1659, which ended the French-Spanish conflict, Spain was compelled to surrender extensive territories to France. In 1688 the Spanish crown reluctantly recognized the independence of Portugal, almost a century after the two crowns were joined. The era of Spanish dominance in Europe had ended.

Absolutism in Austria and Prussia

What were the social conditions of eastern Europe, and how did the rulers of Austria and Prussia transform their nations into powerful absolutist monarchies?

The rulers of eastern Europe also labored to build strong absolutist states in the seventeenth century. But they built on social and economic foundations far different from those in western Europe, namely serfdom and the strong nobility who benefited from it. The endless wars of the seventeenth century allowed monarchs to increase their power by building large armies, increasing taxation, and suppressing representative institutions. In exchange for their growing political authority, monarchs allowed nobles to remain as unchallenged masters of their peasants, a deal that appeased both king and nobility, but left serfs at the mercy of the lords. The most successful states were Austria and Prussia, which witnessed the rise of absolutism between 1620 and 1740.

The Return of Serfdom in the East

While economic and social hardship was common across Europe, important differences existed between east and west. In the west the demographic losses of the Black Death allowed peasants to escape from serfdom as they acquired enough land to feed themselves. In eastern Europe seventeenth-century peasants had largely lost their ability to own land independently. Eastern lords dealt with the labor shortages caused by the Black Death by restricting the right of their peasants to move to take advantage of better opportunities elsewhere. In Prussian territories by 1500 the law required that runaway peasants be hunted down and returned to their lords. Moreover, lords steadily took more and more of their peasants' land and arbitrarily imposed heavier labor obligations. By the early 1500s lords in many eastern territories could command their peasants to work for them without pay for as many as six days a week.

The gradual erosion of the peasantry's economic position was bound up with manipulation of the legal system. The local lord was also the local prosecutor, judge, and jailer. There were no independent royal officials to provide justice or uphold the common law. The power of the lord reached far into serfs' everyday lives. Not only was their freedom of movement restricted, but they also required permission to marry or could be forced to marry. Lords could reallocate the lands worked by their serfs at will or sell serfs apart from their families. These conditions applied even on lands owned by the church.

Between 1500 and 1650 the consolidation of serfdom in eastern Europe was accompanied by the growth of commercial agriculture, particularly in Poland and eastern Germany. As economic expansion and population growth resumed after 1500, eastern lords increased the production of their estates by squeezing sizable surpluses out of the impoverished peasants. They then sold these surpluses to foreign merchants, who exported them to the growing cities of wealthier western Europe. The Netherlands and England benefited the most from inexpensive grain from the east.

It was not only the peasants who suffered in eastern Europe. With the approval of kings, landlords systematically undermined the medieval privileges of the towns and the power of the urban classes. Instead of selling products to local merchants, landlords sold directly to foreigners, bypassing local towns. Eastern towns also lost their medieval right of refuge and were compelled to return runaways to their lords. The population of the towns and the urban middle classes declined greatly. This development both reflected and promoted the supremacy of noble landlords in most of eastern Europe in the sixteenth century.

The Austrian Habsburgs

Like all of central Europe, the Habsburgs emerged from the Thirty Years' War impoverished and exhausted. Their efforts to destroy Protestantism in the German lands and to turn the weak Holy Roman Empire into a real state had failed. Although the Habsburgs remained the hereditary emperors, real power lay in the hands of a bewildering variety of separate political jurisdictions. Defeat in central Europe encouraged the Habsburgs to turn away from a quest for imperial dominance and to focus inward and eastward in an attempt to unify their diverse holdings. If they could not impose Catholicism in the empire, at least they could do so in their own domains.

Habsburg victory over Bohemia during the Thirty Years' War was an important step in this direction. Ferdinand II (r. 1619–1637) drastically reduced the power of the Bohemian Estates, the largely Protestant representative assembly. He also confiscated the landholdings of Protestant nobles and gave them to loyal Catholic nobles and to the foreign aristocratic mercenaries who led his armies. After 1650 a large portion of the Bohemian nobility was of recent origin and owed its success to the Habsburgs.

With the support of this new nobility, the Habsburgs established direct rule over Bohemia. Under their rule the condition of the enserfed peasantry worsened substantially: three days per week of unpaid labor became the norm. Protestantism was also stamped out. These changes were important steps in creating absolutist rule in Bohemia.

Ferdinand III (r. 1637–1657) continued to build state power. He centralized the government in the empire's German-speaking provinces, which formed the core Habsburg holdings. For the first time, a permanent standing army was ready to put down any internal opposition. The Habsburg monarchy then turned east toward the plains of Hungary, which had been divided between the Ottomans and the Habsburgs in the early sixteenth century. Between 1683 and 1699 the Habsburgs pushed the Ottomans from most of Hungary and Transylvania. The recovery of all the former kingdom of Hungary was completed in 1718.

The Hungarian nobility, despite its reduced strength, effectively thwarted the full development of Habsburg absolutism. Throughout the seventeenth century Hungarian nobles rose in revolt against attempts to impose absolute rule. They never triumphed decisively, but neither were they crushed the way the nobility in Bohemia had been in 1620. In 1703, with the Habsburgs bogged down in the War of the Spanish Succession, the Hungarians rose in one last patriotic rebellion under Prince Francis Rákóczy. The prince and his forces were eventually defeated, but the Habsburgs agreed to restore many of the traditional privileges of the aristocracy in return for Hungarian acceptance of hereditary Habsburg rule. Thus Hungary, unlike Austria and Bohemia, was never fully integrated into a centralized, absolute Habsburg state.

Despite checks on their ambitions in Hungary, the Habsburgs made significant achievements in state-building elsewhere by forging consensus with the church and the nobility. A sense of common identity and loyalty to the monarchy grew among elites in Habsburg lands, even to a certain extent in Hungary. German became the language of the state, and zealous Catholicism helped fuse a collective identity.

Vienna became the political and cultural center of the empire. By 1700 it was a thriving city with a population of one hundred thousand and its own version of Versailles, the royal palace of Schönbrunn.

Prussia in the Seventeenth Century

In the fifteenth and sixteenth centuries, the Hohenzollern family had ruled parts of eastern Germany as the imperial electors of Brandenburg and the dukes of Prussia. The title of "elector" gave its holder the privilege of being one of only seven princes or archbishops entitled to elect the Holy Roman emperor, but the electors had little real power. When he came to power in 1640, the twenty-year-old Frederick William, later known as the "Great Elector," was determined to unify his three provinces and enlarge his holdings. These provinces were Brandenburg; Prussia, inherited in 1618; and scattered territories along the Rhine inherited in 1614 (Map 15.3). Each was inhabited by German-speakers, but each had its own estates. Although the estates had not met regularly during the chaotic Thirty Years' War, taxes could not be levied without their consent. The estates of Brandenburg and Prussia were dominated by the nobility and the landowning classes, known as the **Junkers**.

Frederick William profited from ongoing European war and the threat of invasion from Russia when he argued for the need for a permanent standing army. In 1660 he persuaded Junkers in the estates to accept taxation without consent in order to fund an army.

Map 15.3 The Growth of Austria and Brandenburg-Prussia to 1748   Austria expanded to the southwest into Hungary and Transylvania at the expense of the Ottoman Empire. It was unable to hold the rich German province of Silesia, however, which was conquered by Brandenburg-Prussia.

They agreed to do so in exchange for reconfirmation of their own privileges, including authority over the serfs. Having won over the Junkers, the king crushed potential opposition to his power from the towns. One by one, Prussian cities were eliminated from the estates and subjected to new taxes on goods and services.

Thereafter, the estates' power declined rapidly, for the Great Elector had both financial independence and superior force. He revealed his strategy toward managing the estates in the written instructions he left his son:

> Always regulate the expenditures according to the revenues, and have officials diligently render receipts every year. When the finances are in a good state again, then you will have enough means, and you will not have to request money from the estates or address them. Then it is also not necessary to hold the many and expensive parliaments, because the more parliaments you hold, the more authority is taken from you, because the estates always try something that is detrimental to the majesty of the ruler.[7]

By following his own sage advice, Frederick William tripled state revenue during his reign and expanded the army drastically. In 1688 a population of 1 million supported a peacetime standing army of 30,000. In 1701 the elector's son, Frederick I, received the elevated title of king of Prussia (instead of elector) as a reward for aiding the Holy Roman emperor in the War of the Spanish Succession.

The Consolidation of Prussian Absolutism

Frederick William I, "the Soldiers' King" (r. 1713–1740), completed his grandfather's work, eliminating the last traces of parliamentary estates and local self-government. It was he who truly established Prussian absolutism and transformed Prussia into a military state. Frederick William was intensely attached to military life. He always wore an army uniform, and he lived the highly disciplined life of the professional soldier. Years later he followed the family tradition by leaving his own written instructions to his son: "A formidable army and a war chest large enough to make this army mobile in times of need can create great respect for you in the world, so that you can speak a word like the other powers."[8]

Penny-pinching and hard-working, Frederick William achieved results. The king and his ministers built an exceptionally honest and conscientious bureaucracy to administer the country and foster economic development. Twelfth in Europe in population, Prussia had the fourth-largest army by 1740. The Prussian army was the best in Europe, astonishing foreign observers with its precision, skill, and discipline. As one Western traveler put it: "There is no theatre in Berlin whatsoever, diversion is understood to be the handsome troops who parade daily. A special attraction is the great Potsdam Grenadier Regiment . . . when they practice drill, when they fire and when they parade up and down, it is as if they form a single body."[9]

Nevertheless, Prussians paid a heavy and lasting price for the obsessions of their royal drillmaster. Army expansion was achieved in part through forced conscription, which was declared lifelong in 1713.

Junkers The nobility of Brandenburg and Prussia, they were reluctant allies of Frederick William in his consolidation of the Prussian state.

A Prussian Giant Grenadier   Frederick William I wanted tall, handsome soldiers. He dressed them in tight, bright uniforms to distinguish them from the peasant population from which most soldiers came. He also ordered several portraits of his favorites, such as this one, from his court painter, J. C. Merk. Grenadiers (greh-nuh-DEERZ) wore the miter cap instead of an ordinary hat so that they could hurl their heavy grenades unimpeded by a broad brim. (The Royal Collection © 2013, Her Majesty Queen Elizabeth II)

Desperate draftees fled the country or injured themselves to avoid service. Finally, in 1733 Frederick William I ordered that all Prussian men would undergo military training and serve as reservists in the army, allowing him to preserve both agricultural production and army size. To appease the Junkers, the king enlisted them to lead his growing army. The proud nobility thus commanded the peasantry in the army as well as on the estates.

With all men harnessed to the war machine, Prussian civil society became rigid and highly disciplined. As a Prussian minister later summed up, "To keep quiet is the first civic duty."[10] Thus the policies of Frederick William I, combined with harsh peasant bondage and Junker tyranny, laid the foundations for a highly militaristic country.

boyars The highest-ranking members of the Russian nobility.

The Development of Russia and the Ottoman Empire

What were the distinctive features of Russian and Ottoman absolutism?

A favorite parlor game of nineteenth-century intellectuals was debating whether Russia was a Western (European) or non-Western (Asian) society. This question was particularly fascinating because it was unanswerable. To this day, Russia differs from the West in some fundamental ways, though its history has paralleled that of the West in other aspects.

There was no question in the minds of Europeans, however, that the Ottomans were outsiders. Even absolutist rulers disdained Ottoman sultans as cruel and tyrannical despots. Despite stereotypes, however, the Ottoman Empire was in many ways more tolerant than its Western counterparts, providing protection and security to other religions while steadfastly maintaining the Muslim faith. The Ottoman state combined the Byzantine heritage of the territory it had conquered with Persian and Arab traditions. Flexibility and openness to other ideas and practices were sources of strength for the empire.

The Mongol Yoke and the Rise of Moscow

The two-hundred-year period of rule by the Mongol khan (king) set the stage for the rise of absolutist Russia. The Mongols, a group of nomadic tribes from present-day Mongolia, established an empire that, at its height, stretched from Korea to eastern Europe. In the thirteenth century the Mongols conquered the Slavic princes and forced them to render payments of goods, money, and slaves. The princes of Moscow became particularly adept at serving the Mongols and were awarded the title of "great prince." Ivan III (r. 1462–1505), known as Ivan the Great, successfully expanded the principality of Moscow toward the Baltic Sea.

By 1480 Ivan III was strong enough to defy Mongol control and declare the autonomy of Moscow. To legitimize their new position, the princes of Moscow modeled themselves on the Mongol khans. Like the khans, the Muscovite state forced weaker Slavic principalities to render tribute previously paid to Mongols and borrowed Mongol institutions such as the tax system, postal routes, and census. Loyalty from the highest-ranking nobles, or **boyars**, helped the Muscovite princes consolidate their power.

Another source of legitimacy for Moscow was its claim to the political and religious legacy of the Byzantine Empire. After the fall of Constantinople to the Turks in 1453, the princes of Moscow saw themselves as the heirs of both the caesars (or emperors) and Orthodox Christianity. The title "tsar," first taken by Ivan IV in 1547, is in fact a contraction of *caesar*. The tsars considered themselves rightful and holy rulers, an idea promoted by Orthodox churchmen who spoke of "holy Russia" as the "Third Rome." The marriage of Ivan III to the daughter of the last Byzantine emperor further enhanced Moscow's assertion of imperial authority.

The Tsar and His People

Developments in Russia took a chaotic turn with the reign of Ivan IV (r. 1533–1584), the famous "Ivan the Terrible," who rose to the throne at age three. At age sixteen Ivan pushed aside his advisers and in an awe-inspiring ceremony, with gold coins pouring down on his head, he majestically crowned himself tsar.

Ivan's reign was successful in defeating the remnants of Mongol power, adding vast new territories to the realm, and laying the foundations for the huge, multiethnic Russian empire. After the sudden death of his wife, however, Ivan began a campaign of persecution against those he suspected of opposing him. He executed members of leading boyar families, along with their families, friends, servants, and peasants. To replace them, Ivan created a new service nobility, whose loyalty was guaranteed by their dependence on the state for land and titles.

As landlords demanded more from the serfs who survived the persecutions, growing numbers of peasants fled toward wild, recently conquered territories to the east and south. There they joined free groups and warrior bands known as **Cossacks**. Ivan responded by tying peasants ever more firmly to the land and to noble landholders. Simultaneously, he ordered that urban dwellers be bound to their towns and jobs so that he could tax them more heavily. The urban classes had no security in their property, and even the wealthiest merchants were dependent agents of the tsar. These restrictions checked the growth of the Russian middle classes and stood in sharp contrast to economic and social developments in western Europe.

After the death of Ivan and his successor, Russia entered a chaotic period known as the "Time of Troubles" (1598–1613). While Ivan's relatives struggled for power, ordinary people suffered drought, crop failure, and plague. The Cossacks and peasants rebelled against nobles and officials, demanding fairer treatment. This social explosion from below brought the nobles, big and small, together. They crushed the Cossack rebellion and brought Ivan's sixteen-year-old grandnephew, Michael Romanov, to the throne (r. 1613–1645). (See "Primary Source 15.3: A German Account of Russian Life," page 484.)

Although the new tsar successfully reconsolidated central authority, he and his successors did not improve the lot of the common people. In 1649 a law extended serfdom to all peasants in the realm, giving lords unrestricted rights over their serfs and establishing penalties

The Expansion of Russia to 1725

Map legend:
- Moscow, ca. 1300
- Gains by 1505
- Gains by 1584
- Gains by 1725
- Major battle

for harboring runaways. Social and religious uprisings among the poor and oppressed continued through the seventeenth century. One of the largest rebellions was led by the Cossack Stenka Razin, who in 1670 attracted a great army of urban poor and peasants. He and his followers killed landlords and government officials and proclaimed freedom from oppression, but their rebellion was defeated in 1671.

Despite the turbulence of the period, the Romanov tsars, like their Western counterparts, made several important achievements during the second half of the seventeenth century. After a long war, Russia gained land in Ukraine from Poland in 1667 and completed the conquest of Siberia by the end of the century. Territorial expansion was accompanied by growth of the bureaucracy and the army. The tsars employed foreign experts to reform the Russian army, and enlisted Cossack warriors to fight Siberian campaigns. The great profits from Siberia's natural resources, especially furs, funded the Romanovs' bid for Great Power status. Russian imperialist expansion to the east paralleled the Western powers' exploration and conquest of the Atlantic world in the same period.

Cossacks Free groups and outlaw armies originally comprising runaway peasants living on the borders of Russian territory from the fourteenth century onward. By the end of the sixteenth century they had formed an alliance with the Russian state.

Russian Peasant An eighteenth-century French artist visiting Russia recorded his impressions of the daily life of the Russian people in this etching of a fish merchant pulling his wares through a snowy village on a sleigh. Two caviar vendors behind him make a sale to a young mother standing at her doorstep with her baby in her arms. (From Jean-Baptiste Le Prince's second set of Russian etchings, 1765. Private Collection/www.amis-paris-petersbourg.org)

A German Account of Russian Life

Seventeenth-century Russia remained a remote and mysterious land for western and even central Europeans, who had few direct contacts with the tsar's dominion. Westerners portrayed eastern Europe as more "barbaric" and less "civilized" than their homelands. Thus they expanded eastern Europe's undeniably harsher social and economic conditions to encompass a very debatable cultural and moral inferiority.

Knowledge of Russia came mainly from occasional travelers who had visited Russia and sometimes wrote accounts of what they saw. The most famous of these accounts was by the German Adam Olearius (ca. 1599–1671), who was sent to Moscow on three diplomatic missions in the 1630s. These missions ultimately proved unsuccessful, but they provided Olearius with a rich store of information for his Travels in Muscovy, *from which the following excerpts are taken. Published in German in 1647 and soon translated into several languages (but not Russian), Olearius's unflattering but well-informed study played a major role in shaping European ideas about Russia.*

 The government of the Russians is what political theorists call a "dominating and despotic monarchy," where the sovereign, that is, the tsar or the grand prince who has obtained the crown by right of succession, rules the entire land alone, and all the people are his subjects, and where the nobles and princes no less than the common folk — townspeople and peasants — are his serfs and slaves, whom he rules and treats as a master treats his servants. . . .

If the Russians be considered in respect to their character, customs, and way of life, they are justly to be counted among the barbarians. . . . The vice of drunkenness is so common in this nation, among people of every station, clergy and laity, high and low, men and women, old and young, that when they are seen now and then lying about in the streets, wallowing in the mud, no attention is paid to it, as something habitual. If a cart driver comes upon such a drunken pig whom he happens to know, he shoves him onto his cart and drives him home, where he is paid his fare. No one ever refuses an opportunity to drink and to get drunk, at any time and in any place, and usually it is done with vodka. . . .

The Russians being naturally tough and born, as it were, for slavery, they must be kept under a harsh and strict yoke and must be driven to do their work with clubs and whips, which they suffer without impatience, because such is their station, and they are accustomed to it. Young and half-grown fellows sometimes come together on certain days and train themselves in fisticuffs, to accustom themselves to receiving blows, and, since habit is second

nature, this makes blows given as punishment easier to bear. Each and all, they are slaves and serfs. . . .

Because of slavery and their rough and hard life, the Russians accept war readily and are well suited to it. On certain occasions, if need be, they reveal themselves as courageous and daring soldiers. . . .

Although the Russians, especially the common populace, living as slaves under a harsh yoke, can bear and endure a great deal out of love for their masters, yet if the pressure is beyond measure, then it can be said of them: "Patience, often wounded, finally turned into fury." A dangerous indignation results, turned not so much against their sovereign as against the lower authorities, especially if the people have been much oppressed by them and by their supporters and have not been protected by the higher authorities. And once they are aroused and enraged, it is not easy to appease them. Then, disregarding all dangers that may ensue, they resort to every kind of violence and behave like madmen. . . . They own little; most of them have no feather beds; they lie on cushions, straw, mats, or their clothes; they sleep on benches and, in winter, like the non-Germans [natives] in Livonia, upon the oven, which serves them for cooking and is flat on the top; here husband, wife, children, servants, and maids huddle together. In some houses in the countryside we saw chickens and pigs under the benches and the ovens. . . . Russians are not used to delicate food and dainties; their daily food consists of porridge, turnips, cabbage, and cucumbers, fresh and pickled, and in Moscow mostly of big salt fish which stink badly, because of the thrifty use of salt, yet are eaten with relish. . . .

The Russians can endure extreme heat. In the bathhouse they stretch out on benches and let themselves be beaten and rubbed with bunches of birch twigs and wisps of bast (which I could not stand); and when they are hot and red all over and so exhausted that they can bear it no longer in the bathhouse, men and women rush outdoors naked and pour cold water over their bodies; in winter they even wallow in the snow and rub their skin with it as if it were soap; then they go back into the hot bathhouse. And since bathhouses are usually near rivers and brooks, they can throw themselves straight from the hot into the cold bath. . . .

Generally noble families, even the small nobility, rear their daughters in secluded chambers, keeping them hidden from outsiders; and a bridegroom is not allowed to have a look at his bride until he receives her in the bridal chamber. Therefore some happen to be deceived, being given a misshapen and sickly one instead of a fair one, and sometimes a kinswoman or even a maidservant instead of a daughter; of which there have been examples even among the highborn. No wonder therefore that often they live together like cats and dogs and that wife-beating is so common among Russians. . . .

In the Kremlin and in the city there are a great many churches, chapels, and monasteries, both within and without the city walls, over two thousand in all. This is so because every nobleman who has some fortune has a chapel built for himself, and most of them are of stone. The stone churches are round and vaulted inside. . . . They allow neither organs nor any other musical instruments in their churches, saying: Instruments that have neither souls nor life cannot praise God. . . .

In their churches there hang many bells, sometimes five or six, the largest not over two hundred-weights. They ring these bells to summon people to church, and also when the priest during mass raises the chalice. In Moscow, because of the multitude of churches and chapels, there are several thousand bells, which during the divine service create such a clang and din that one unaccustomed to it listens in amazement. **"**

EVALUATE THE EVIDENCE

1. How did Olearius characterize the Russians in general? What supporting evidence did he offer for his judgment? What biases can you detect in his account of Russian people?
2. How might Olearius's account help explain Stenka Razin's rebellion (page 483)?
3. On the basis of these representative passages, why do you think Olearius's book was so popular and influential in central and western Europe?

Source: "A Foreign Traveler in Russia," excerpt from pp. 249–251 in *A Source Book for Russian History from Early Times to 1917*, volume 1, *Early Times to the Late Seventeenth Century*, edited by George Vernadsky, Ralph T. Fisher, Jr., Alan D. Ferguson, Andrew Lossky, and Sergei Pushkarev, compiler. Copyright © 1972 by Yale University Press. Used with permission of the publisher.

The Reforms of Peter the Great

Heir to Romanov efforts at state-building, Peter the Great (r. 1682–1725) embarked on a tremendous campaign to accelerate and complete these processes. A giant for his time at six feet seven inches, and possessing enormous energy and willpower, Peter was determined to build the army and to continue Russian territorial expansion. Fascinated by weapons and foreign technology and eager to gain support against the powerful Ottoman Empire, the tsar led a group of 250 Russian officials and young nobles on an eighteen-month tour of western European capitals. Traveling unofficially to avoid lengthy diplomatic ceremonies, Peter met with foreign kings, toured the sites, and learned shipbuilding and other technical skills from local artisans and experts. He was particularly impressed with the growing economic power of the Dutch and the English, and he considered how Russia could profit from their example.

Returning to Russia, Peter entered into a secret alliance with Denmark and Poland to wage a sudden war of aggression against Sweden with the goal of securing access to the Baltic Sea and opportunities for westward expansion. Peter and his allies believed that their combined forces could win easy victories because Sweden was in the hands of a new and inexperienced king.

Eighteen-year-old Charles XII of Sweden (1697–1718) surprised Peter. He defeated Denmark quickly

Peter the Great   This compelling portrait by Grigory Musikiysky captures the strength and determination of the warrior-tsar in 1723, after more than three decades of personal rule. In his hand Peter holds the scepter, symbol of royal sovereignty, and across his breastplate is draped an ermine fur, a mark of honor. In the background are the battleships of Russia's new Baltic fleet and the famous St. Peter and St. Paul Fortress that Peter built in St. Petersburg. (Hermitage/St. Petersburg, Russia/Bridgeman Art Library)

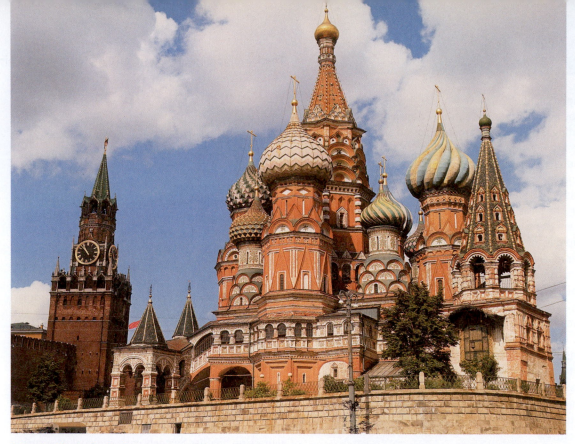

Saint Basil's Cathedral, Moscow With its sloping roofs and colorful onion-shaped domes, Saint Basil's is a striking example of powerful Byzantine influences on Russian culture. According to tradition, an enchanted Ivan the Terrible blinded the cathedral's architects to ensure that they would never duplicate their fantastic achievement, which still dazzles the beholder in today's Red Square. (George Holton/Photo Researchers)

in 1700, then turned on Russia. In a blinding snowstorm, his well-trained professional army attacked and routed unsuspecting Russians besieging the Swedish fortress of Narva on the Baltic coast. It was, for the Russians, a grim beginning to the long and brutal Great Northern War, which lasted from 1700 to 1721.

Peter responded to this defeat with measures designed to increase state power, strengthen his armies, and gain victory. He required all nobles to serve in the army or in the civil administration—for life. Since a more modern army and government required skilled experts, Peter created new schools and universities and required every young nobleman to spend five years in education away from home. Peter established an interlocking military-civilian bureaucracy with fourteen ranks, and he decreed that all had to start at the bottom and work toward the top. The system allowed some people of non-noble origins to rise to high positions, a rarity in Europe at the time. Drawing on his experience abroad, Peter sought talented foreigners and placed them in his service. These measures gradually combined to make the army and government more powerful and efficient.

Peter also greatly increased the service requirements of commoners. In the wake of the Narva disaster, he established a regular standing army of more than two hundred thousand peasant-soldiers, drafted for life and commanded by noble officers. He added an additional hundred thousand men in special regiments of Cossacks and foreign mercenaries. To fund the army, taxes on peasants increased threefold during Peter's reign. Serfs were also arbitrarily assigned to work in the growing number of factories and mines that supplied the military.

Peter's new war machine was able to crush the small army of Sweden in Ukraine at Poltava in 1709, one of the most significant battles in Russian history. Russia's victory against Sweden was conclusive in 1721, and Estonia and present-day Latvia came under Russian rule for the first time. After his victory at Poltava, Peter channeled enormous resources into building a new Western-style capital on the Baltic to rival the great cities of Europe. Originally a desolate and swampy Swedish outpost, the magnificent city of St. Petersburg was designed to reflect modern urban planning, with wide, straight avenues, buildings set in a uniform line, and large parks.

The government drafted twenty-five thousand to forty thousand men each summer to labor in St. Petersburg, many of whom died from hunger, sickness, and accidents. Nobles were ordered to build costly palaces in St. Petersburg and to live in them most of the year. Merchants and artisans were required to settle and build in the new capital. The building of St. Petersburg was, in truth, an enormous direct tax levied on the

Map 15.4 The Ottoman Empire at Its Height, 1566   The Ottomans, like their great rivals the Habsburgs, rose to rule a vast dynastic empire encompassing many different peoples and ethnic groups. The army and the bureaucracy served to unite the disparate territories into a single state under an absolutist ruler.

wealthy, with the peasantry forced to do the manual labor.

There were other important consequences of Peter's reign. For Peter, modernization meant westernization, and both Westerners and Western ideas flowed into Russia for the first time. He required nobles to shave their heavy beards and wear Western clothing, previously banned in Russia. He also ordered them to attend parties where young men and women would mix together and freely choose their own spouses. From these efforts a new elite class of Western-oriented Russians began to emerge.

Peter's reforms were unpopular with many Russians. For nobles, one of Peter's most detested reforms was the imposition of unigeniture—inheritance of land by one son alone—cutting daughters and other sons from family property. For peasants, the reign of the tsar saw a significant increase in the bonds of serfdom, and the gulf between the enserfed peasantry and the educated nobility increased. Despite the unpopularity of Peter's reforms, his modernizing and westernizing of Russia paved the way for it to move somewhat closer to the European mainstream in its thought and institutions during the Enlightenment, especially under Catherine the Great.

The Growth of the Ottoman Empire

Most Christian Europeans perceived the Ottomans as the antithesis of their own values and traditions and viewed the empire as driven by an insatiable lust for warfare and conquest. In their view the fall of Constantinople was considered a historic catastrophe and the taking of the Balkans a form of despotic imprisonment. To Ottoman eyes, the world looked very different. The siege of Constantinople liberated a glorious city from its long decline under the Byzantines. Rather than being a despoiled captive, the Balkans became a haven for refugees fleeing the growing intolerance of Western Christian powers. The Ottoman Empire provided Jews, Muslims, and even some Christians safety from the Inquisition and religious war.

The Ottomans came out of Central Asia as conquering warriors, settled in Anatolia (present-day Turkey), and, at their peak in the mid-sixteenth century, ruled one of the most powerful empires in the world (see Chapter 14). Their possessions stretched from western Persia across North Africa and into the heart of central Europe (Map 15.4).

INDIVIDUALS IN SOCIETY
Hürrem

Hürrem and her ladies in the harem. (Bibliothèque nationale de France)

In Muslim culture, *harem* means a sacred place or a sanctuary. The term was applied to the part of the household occupied by women and children and forbidden to men outside the family. The most famous harem member in Ottoman history was Hürrem, wife of Suleiman the Magnificent.

Like many of the sultan's concubines, Hürrem (1505?–1558) was of foreign birth. Tradition holds that she was born Aleksandra Lisowska in the kingdom of Poland (present-day Ukraine). Captured during a Tartar raid and enslaved, she entered the imperial harem between 1517 and 1520, when she was about fifteen years old. Reports from Venetian visitors claimed that she was not outstandingly beautiful, but was possessed of wonderful grace, charm, and good humor, earning her the Turkish nickname Hürrem, or "joyful one." Soon after her arrival, Hürrem became the imperial favorite.

Suleiman's love for Hürrem led him to set aside all precedents for the role of a concubine, including the rule that concubines must cease having children once they gave birth to a male heir. By 1531 Hürrem had given Suleiman one daughter and five sons. In 1533 or 1534 Suleiman entered formal marriage with his consort—an unprecedented and scandalous honor for a concubine. Suleiman reportedly lavished attention on his wife and defied convention by allowing her to remain in the palace throughout her life instead of accompanying her son to a provincial governorship.

Contemporaries were shocked by Hürrem's influence over the sultan and resentful of the apparent role she played in politics and diplomacy. The Venetian ambassador Bassano wrote that "the Janissaries and the entire court hate her and her children likewise, but because the Sultan loves her, no one dares to speak."* Court rumors circulated that Hürrem used witchcraft to control the sultan and ordered the sultan's execution of his first-born son by another mother.

The correspondence between Suleiman and Hürrem, unavailable until the nineteenth century, along with Suleiman's own diaries, confirms her status as the sultan's most trusted confidant and adviser. During his frequent absences, the pair exchanged passionate love letters. Hürrem included political information and warned of potential uprisings. She also intervened in affairs between the empire and her former home, apparently helping Poland attain its privileged diplomatic status. She brought a feminine touch to diplomatic relations, sending personally embroidered articles to foreign leaders.

Hürrem used her enormous pension to contribute a mosque, two schools, a hospital, a fountain, and two public baths to Istanbul. In Jerusalem, Mecca, and Istanbul, she provided soup kitchens and hospices for pilgrims and the poor. She died in 1558, eight years before her husband. Her son Selim II (r. 1566–1574) inherited the throne.

Relying on Western observers' reports, historians traditionally depicted Hürrem as a manipulative and power-hungry social climber. They portrayed her career as the beginning of a "sultanate of women" in which strong imperial leadership gave way to court intrigue and debauchery. More recent historians have emphasized the intelligence and courage Hürrem demonstrated in navigating the ruthlessly competitive world of the harem.

Hürrem's journey from Ukrainian maiden to concubine to sultan's wife captured enormous public attention. She is the subject of numerous paintings, plays, and novels, as well as an opera, a ballet, and a symphony by the composer Haydn. Interest in and suspicion of Hürrem continues. In 2003 a Turkish miniseries once more depicted her as a scheming intriguer.

QUESTIONS FOR ANALYSIS

1. What types of power did Hürrem exercise during her lifetime? How did her gender enable her to attain certain kinds of power and also constrain her ability to exercise it?
2. What can an exceptional woman like Hürrem reveal about the broader political and social world in which she lived?

Source: Leslie P. Pierce, *The Imperial Harem: Women and Sovereignty in the Ottoman Empire* (New York: Oxford University Press, 1993).

ONLINE DOCUMENT ASSIGNMENT

What forces shaped Western views of Hürrem? Go to the Integrated Media and examine characterizations of Hürrem as seen through the eyes of a Habsburg diplomat, and then complete a writing assignment based on the evidence and details from this chapter.

*Quoted in Galina Yermolenko, "Roxolana: The Greatest Empresse of the East," *The Muslim World* 95 (2005): 235.

The Ottoman Empire was built on a unique model of state and society. Agricultural land was the personal hereditary property of the **sultan**, and peasants paid taxes to use the land. There was therefore an almost complete absence of private landed property and no hereditary nobility.

The Ottomans also employed a distinctive form of government administration. The top ranks of the bureaucracy were staffed by the sultan's slave corps. Because Muslim law prohibited enslaving other Muslims, the sultan's agents purchased slaves along the borders of the empire. Within the realm, the sultan levied a "tax" of one thousand to three thousand male children on the conquered Christian populations in the Balkans every year. These young slaves were raised in Turkey as Muslims and were trained to fight and to administer. Unlike enslaved Africans in European colonies, who faced a dire fate, the most talented Ottoman slaves rose to the top of the bureaucracy, where they might acquire wealth and power. The less fortunate formed the core of the sultan's army, the **janissary corps**. These highly organized and efficient troops gave the Ottomans a formidable advantage in war with western Europeans. By 1683 service in the janissary corps had become so prestigious that the sultan ceased recruitment by force, and it became a volunteer army open to Christians and Muslims.

The Ottomans divided their subjects into religious communities, and each *millet*, or "nation," enjoyed autonomous self-government under its religious leaders. The Ottoman Empire recognized Orthodox Christians, Jews, Armenian Christians, and Muslims as distinct millets, but despite its tolerance, the empire was an explicitly Islamic state. The **millet system** created a powerful bond between the Ottoman ruling class and religious leaders, who supported the sultan's rule in return for extensive authority over their own communities. Each millet collected taxes for the state, regulated group behavior, and maintained law courts, schools, houses of worship, and hospitals for its people.

Istanbul (known outside the empire by its original name, Constantinople) was the capital of the empire. The "old palace" was for the sultan's female family members, who lived in isolation under the care of eunuchs, men who were castrated to prevent sexual relations with women. The newer Topkapi palace was where officials worked and young slaves trained for future administrative or military careers. Sultans married women of the highest social standing, while keeping many concubines of low rank. To prevent the elite families into which they married from acquiring influence over the government, sultans procreated only with their concubines and not with official wives. They also adopted a policy of allowing each concubine to produce only one male heir. At a young age, each son went to govern a province of the empire accompanied by his mother. These practices were intended to stabilize power and prevent a recurrence of the civil wars of the late fourteenth and early fifteenth centuries.

Sultan Suleiman undid these policies when he boldly married his concubine, a former slave of Polish origin named Hürrem, and had several children with her. (See "Individuals in Society: Hürrem," at left.) Starting with Suleiman, imperial wives began to take on more power. Marriages were arranged between sultans' daughters and high-ranking servants, creating powerful new members of the imperial household. Over time, the sultan's exclusive authority waned in favor of a more bureaucratic administration.

sultan The ruler of the Ottoman Empire; he owned all the agricultural land of the empire and was served by an army and bureaucracy composed of highly trained slaves.

janissary corps The core of the sultan's army, composed of slave conscripts from non-Muslim parts of the empire; after 1683 it became a volunteer force.

millet system A system used by the Ottomans whereby subjects were divided into religious communities, with each millet (nation) enjoying autonomous self-government under its religious leaders.

Alternatives to Absolutism in England and the Dutch Republic

How and why did the constitutional state triumph in the Dutch Republic and England?

While France, Prussia, Russia, and Austria developed absolutist states, England and the Netherlands evolved toward **constitutionalism**, which is the limitation of government by law. Constitutionalism also implies a balance between the authority and power of the government, on the one hand, and the rights and liberties of the subjects, on the other. By definition, all constitutionalist governments have a constitution, be it written or unwritten. A nation's constitution may be embodied in one basic document and occasionally revised by amendment, like the Constitution of the United States. Or it may be only partly formalized and include parliamentary statutes, judicial decisions, and a body of traditional procedures and practices, like the English and Dutch constitutions.

Despite their common commitment to constitutional

constitutionalism A form of government in which power is limited by law and balanced between the authority and power of the government, on the one hand, and the rights and liberties of the subjects or citizens on the other hand; could include constitutional monarchies or republics.

government, England and the Dutch Republic represented significantly different alternatives to absolute rule. After decades of civil war and an experiment with **republicanism**, the English opted for a constitutional monarchy in 1688. This settlement, which has endured to this day, retained a monarch as the titular head of government but vested sovereignty in an elected parliament. Upon gaining independence from Spain in 1648, the Dutch rejected monarchical rule, adopting a republican form of government in which elected estates held supreme power. Neither was democratic by any standard, but to other Europeans they were shining examples of the restraint of arbitrary power and the rule of law.

Absolutist Claims in England

In 1588 Queen Elizabeth I of England (r. 1558–1603) exercised very great personal power; by 1689 the English monarchy was severely circumscribed. A rare female monarch, Elizabeth was able to maintain control over her realm in part by refusing to marry and submit to a husband. She was immensely popular with her people, but left no immediate heir to continue her legacy.

In 1603 Elizabeth's Scottish cousin James Stuart succeeded her as James I (r. 1603–1625). King James was well educated and had thirty-five years' experience as king of Scotland. But he was not as interested in displaying the majesty of monarchy as Elizabeth had been. Urged to wave at the crowds who waited to greet their new ruler, James complained that he was tired and threatened to drop his breeches "so they can cheer at my arse."[11]

James's greatest problem, however, stemmed from his absolutist belief that a monarch has a divine right to his authority and is responsible only to God. James went so far as to lecture the House of Commons: "There are no privileges and immunities which can stand against a divinely appointed King." Such a view ran directly counter to English traditions that a person's property could not be taken away without due process of law. James I and his son Charles I (r. 1625–1649) considered such constraints intolerable and a threat to their divine-right prerogative. Consequently, bitter squabbles erupted between the Crown and the House of Commons. The expenses of England's intervention in the Thirty Years' War, through hostilities with Spain (1625–1630) and France (1627–1629), only exacerbated tensions. Charles I's response was to refuse to summon Parliament from 1629 onward.

republicanism A form of government in which there is no monarch and power rests in the hands of the people as exercised through elected representatives.

Puritans Members of a sixteenth- and seventeenth-century reform movement within the Church of England that advocated purifying it of Roman Catholic elements, like bishops, elaborate ceremonials, and wedding rings.

Van Dyck, *Charles I at the Hunt*, ca. 1635   Anthony Van Dyck was the greatest of Rubens's many students. In 1633 he became court painter to Charles I. This portrait of Charles just dismounted from a horse emphasizes the aristocratic bearing, elegance, and innate authority of the king. Van Dyck's success led to innumerable commissions by members of the court and aristocratic society. He had a profound influence on portraiture in England and beyond; some scholars believe that this portrait influenced Rigaud's 1701 portrayal of Louis XIV (see page 471). (Louvre, Paris, France/Giraudon/The Bridgeman Art Library)

Religious Divides and the English Civil War

Relations between the king and the House of Commons were also embittered by religious issues. In the early seventeenth century growing numbers of English people felt dissatisfied with the Church of England established by Henry VIII (r. 1509–1547). Many **Puritans** believed that the Protestant Reformation of the sixteenth century had not gone far enough. They wanted to "purify" the Anglican Church of lingering Roman

Catholic elements—elaborate vestments and ceremonials, bishops, and even the giving and wearing of wedding rings.

James I responded to such ideas by declaring, "No bishop, no king." For James, bishops were among the chief supporters of the throne. His son and successor, Charles I, further antagonized religious sentiments. Not only did he marry a Catholic princess, but he also supported the heavy-handed policies of the archbishop of Canterbury William Laud (1573–1645). In 1637 Laud attempted to impose two new elements on church organization in Scotland: a new prayer book, modeled on the Anglican *Book of Common Prayer*, and bishoprics. The Presbyterian Scots rejected these elements and revolted. To finance an army to put down the Scots, King Charles was compelled to call a meeting of Parliament in November 1640.

Charles had ruled from 1629 to 1640 without Parliament, financing his government through extraordinary stopgap levies considered illegal by most English people. For example, the king revived a medieval law requiring coastal districts to help pay the cost of ships for defense, but he levied the tax, called "ship money," on inland as well as coastal counties. Most members of Parliament were not willing to trust such a despotic king with an army. Moreover, many supported the Scots' resistance to Charles's religious innovations. Accordingly, this Parliament, called the "Long Parliament" because it sat from 1640 to 1660, enacted legislation that limited the power of the monarch and made government without Parliament impossible.

In 1641 the Commons passed the Triennial Act, which compelled the king to summon Parliament every three years. The Commons impeached Archbishop Laud and then threatened to abolish bishops. King Charles, fearful of a Scottish invasion—the original reason for summoning Parliament—reluctantly accepted these measures.

The next act in the conflict was precipitated by the outbreak of rebellion in Ireland, where English governors and landlords had long exploited the people. In 1641 the Catholic gentry of Ireland led an uprising in

Puritan Occupations These twelve engravings depict typical Puritan occupations and show that the Puritans came primarily from the artisan and lower middle classes. The governing classes and peasants made up a much smaller percentage of the Puritans and generally adhered to the traditions of the Church of England. (Visual Connection Archive)

response to a feared invasion by anti-Catholic forces of the British Long Parliament.

Without an army, Charles I could neither come to terms with the Scots nor respond to the Irish rebellion. After a failed attempt to arrest parliamentary leaders, Charles left London for the north of England. There, he recruited an army drawn from the nobility and its cavalry staff, the rural gentry, and mercenaries. In response, Parliament formed its own army, the New Model Army, composed of the militia of the city of London and country squires with business connections. During the spring of 1642 both sides prepared for war. In July a linen weaver became the first casualty of the civil war during a skirmish between royal and parliamentary forces in Manchester.

The English civil war (1642–1649) pitted the power of the king against that of the Parliament. After three years of fighting, Parliament's New Model Army defeated the king's armies at the Battles of Naseby and Langport in the summer of 1645. Charles, though, refused to concede defeat. Both sides jockeyed for position, waiting for a decisive event. This arrived in the form of the army under the leadership of Oliver Cromwell, a member of the House of Commons and a devout Puritan. In 1647 Cromwell's forces captured the king and dismissed anti-Cromwell members of the Parliament. In 1649 the remaining representatives, known as the "Rump Parliament," put Charles on trial for high treason. Charles was found guilty and beheaded on January 30, 1649, an act that sent shock waves around Europe.

The English Civil War, 1642–1649

- Parliamentarians
- Royalists
- ✷ Major battle

Cromwell and Puritanical Absolutism in England

With the execution of Charles, kingship was abolished. The question remained of how the country would be governed. One answer was provided by philosopher Thomas Hobbes (1588–1679). Hobbes held a pessimistic view of human nature and believed that, left to themselves, humans would compete violently for power and wealth. The only solution, as he outlined in his 1651 treatise *Leviathan*, was a social contract in which all members of society placed themselves under the absolute rule of the sovereign, who would maintain peace and order. Hobbes imagined society as a human body in which the monarch served as head and individual subjects together made up the body. Just as the body cannot sever its own head, so Hobbes believed that society could not, having accepted the contract, rise up against its king.

Hobbes's longing for a benevolent absolute monarch was not widely shared in England. Instead, Oliver Cromwell and his supporters enshrined a commonwealth, or republican government, known as the **Protectorate**. Theoretically, legislative power rested in the surviving members of Parliament, and executive power was lodged in a council of state. In fact, the army controlled the government, and Oliver Cromwell controlled the army, ruling what was essentially a military dictatorship.

The army prepared a constitution, the Instrument of Government (1653), that invested executive power in a lord protector (Cromwell) and a council of state. It provided for triennial parliaments and gave Parliament the sole power to raise taxes. But after repeated disputes, Cromwell dismissed Parliament in 1655, and the instrument was never formally endorsed. Cromwell continued the standing army and proclaimed quasi-martial law. He divided England into twelve military districts, each governed by a major general. Reflecting Puritan ideas of morality, Cromwell's state forbade sports, closed the theaters, and rigorously censored the press.

On the issue of religion, Cromwell favored some degree of toleration, and the Instrument of Government gave all Christians except Roman Catholics the right to practice their faith. Cromwell had long associated Catholicism in Ireland with sedition and heresy, and led an army there to reconquer the country in August 1649. One month later, his forces crushed a rebellion at Drogheda and massacred the garrison. After Cromwell's departure for England, atrocities worsened. The English banned Catholicism in Ireland, executed priests, and confiscated land from Catholics for English and Scottish settlers. These brutal acts left a legacy of Irish hatred for England.

Cromwell adopted mercantilist policies similar to those of absolutist France. He enforced a Navigation Act (1651) requiring that English goods be transported on English ships. The act was a great boost to the development of an English merchant marine and brought about a short but successful war with the commercially threatened Dutch. While mercantilist legislation ultimately benefited English commerce, for ordinary people the turmoil of foreign war only added to the harsh conditions of life induced by years of civil war. (See "Primary Source 15.4: Diary of an English Villager," at right.) Cromwell also welcomed the immigration of Jews because of their skills in business, and they began to return to England after four centuries of absence.

Protectorate The English military dictatorship (1653–1658) established by Oliver Cromwell following the execution of Charles I.

Diary of an English Villager

Ralph Josselin was a vicar and prosperous farmer in the village of Earls Colne in the southeast of England. In 1643 he began a diary that he maintained until his death in 1683. Remarkable in its range, it includes intimate details of Josselin's personal life and business activities as well as reflections on national and foreign affairs. The following passage contains entries recorded over one week in June 1651, during the period of Cromwell's Protectorate.

" June 9, 1651. The state of England although worn with civil wars, and scarcity and ill trading for many years, being but in bad terms with Holland, and not altogether sure of Spain, proclaimed open war with Portugal, and is in open war with France, our fleets being in the midland sea: we at the same time are endeavouring to conquer Scotland, and Ireland, attempt Silly [an archipelago off the Cornish coast] with a fleet, and yet send a fleet also to reduce the islands of Barbados in America: and yet the nation is much discontent and divided, yet feared to name not the attempts of any foreigner against them.

June 10. Lent Mr. Litle this day 20 pounds. Received of Goodwife Day 3 pounds. This day my wife went to my Lady Honywood, where unexpectedly we had a mess of peas for which my wife longed very much, this was a good providence of god, a mercy laid out that we were not aware of.

June 12. Heard Goodwife Mole had the small pox, the lord in mercy spare me and mine, lent Goodman Mathew 4 pounds for 3 weeks.

June 15. This week past the lord was good and merciful to me and mine in many outward mercies the lord knows my heart was in a very dead cold frame, for the Sabbath and I was very unprepared for it, carelessness eats up my spirit, and I do not stir up my heart within to gods service, and yet my god [did not] fail me, my navel moist and my belly in a part on my left side as it were sore, my wife ill, my daughter Jane this day ill, oh my lord quicken me and do me good by all, I preached twice, the day very hot, grass burns away, the lord in mercy hear prayer for a comfortable rain. "

EVALUATE THE EVIDENCE

1. What are Josselin's chief concerns in life, as reflected in these passages? How would you describe daily life in mid-seventeenth-century England, as it appears in these entries?
2. What elements of the "seventeenth-century crisis" were apparent to Josselin? Based on these excerpts, how did ordinary people make sense of the fragility and the violence of life in this period?

Source: Alan MacFarlane, ed. *The Diary of Ralph Josselin, 1616–1683* (Oxford: Oxford University Press, 1991), pp. 247–248. Spelling modernized.

The Protectorate collapsed when Cromwell died in 1658 and his ineffectual son succeeded him. Fed up with military rule, the English longed for a return to civilian government and, with it, common law and social stability. By 1660 they were ready to restore the monarchy.

The Restoration of the English Monarchy

The Restoration of 1660 brought to the throne Charles II (r. 1660–1685), eldest son of Charles I, who had been living on the continent. Both houses of Parliament were also restored, together with the established Anglican Church. The Restoration failed to resolve two serious problems, however. What was to be the attitude of the state toward Puritans, Catholics, and dissenters from the established church? And what was to be the relationship between the king and Parliament?

To answer the first question, Parliament enacted the **Test Act** of 1673 against those outside the Church of England, denying them the right to vote, hold public office, preach, teach, attend the universities, or even assemble for meetings. But these restrictions could not be enforced. When the Quaker William Penn held a meeting of his Friends and was arrested, the jury refused to convict him.

In politics, Charles II's initial determination to work well with Parliament did not last long. Finding that Parliament did not grant him an adequate income, in 1670 Charles entered into a secret agreement with his cousin Louis XIV. The French king would give Charles £200,000 annually, and in return Charles would relax the laws against Catholics, gradually re-Catholicize

Test Act Legislation, passed by the English Parliament in 1673, to secure the position of the Anglican Church by stripping Puritans, Catholics, and other dissenters of the right to vote, preach, assemble, hold public office, and teach at or attend the universities.

493

"The Royall Oake of Brittayne"   The chopping down of this tree, as shown in a cartoon from 1649, signifies the end of royal authority, stability, and the rule of law. As pigs graze (representing the unconcerned common people), being fattened for slaughter, Oliver Cromwell, with his feet in Hell, quotes Scripture. This is a royalist view of the collapse of Charles I's government and the rule of Cromwell. (© British Library Board)

England, and convert to Catholicism himself. When the details of this treaty leaked out, a great wave of anti-Catholic sentiment swept England.

When Charles died and his Catholic brother James became king, the worst English anti-Catholic fears were realized. In violation of the Test Act, James II (r. 1685–1688) appointed Roman Catholics to positions in the army, the universities, and local government. When these actions were challenged in the courts, the judges, whom James had appointed, decided in favor of the king. James and his supporters opened new Catholic churches and schools and issued tracts promoting Catholicism. Attempting to broaden his base of support with Protestant dissenters and nonconformists, James granted religious freedom to all.

James's opponents, a powerful coalition of eminent persons in Parliament and the Church of England, bitterly resisted James's ambitions. They offered the English throne to James's heir, his Protestant daughter Mary, and her Dutch husband, Prince William of Orange. In December 1688 James II, his queen, and their infant son fled to France and became pensioners of

Louis XIV. Early in 1689 William and Mary were crowned king and queen of England.

Constitutional Monarchy and Cabinet Government

The English call the events of 1688 and 1689 the "Glorious Revolution" because they believe it replaced one king with another with barely any bloodshed. In truth, William's arrival sparked revolutionary riots and violence across the British Isles and in North American cities such as Boston and New York. Uprisings by supporters of James, known as Jacobites, occurred in 1689 in Scotland. In Ireland, the two sides waged outright war from 1689 to 1691. William's victory at the Battle of the Boyne (1690) and the subsequent Treaty of Limerick (1691) sealed his accession to power.

In England, the revolution represented the final destruction of the idea of divine-right monarchy. The men who brought about the revolution framed their intentions in the Bill of Rights, which was formulated in direct response to Stuart absolutism. Law was to be

John Locke, *Two Treatises of Government*

In 1688 opponents of King James II invited his daughter Mary and her husband, the Dutch prince William of Orange, to take the throne of England. James fled for the safety of France. One of the most outspoken proponents of the "Glorious Revolution" that brought William and Mary to the throne was philosopher John Locke. In this passage, Locke argues that sovereign power resides in the people, who may reject a monarch who does not obey the law.

" But government into whosesoever hands it is put, being as I have before shown, entrusted with this condition, and for this end, that men might have and secure their properties, the prince or senate, however it may have power to make laws for the regulation of property between the subjects one amongst another, yet can never have a power to take to themselves the whole, or any part of the subjects' property, without their own consent. For this would be in effect to leave them no property at all. . . .

'Tis true, governments cannot be supported without great charge, and 'tis fit every one who enjoys his share of the protection, should pay, out of this estate, his proportion for the maintenance of it. But still it must be with his own consent, i.e., the consent of the majority, giving it either by themselves, or their representatives chosen by them; for if any one shall claim a power to lay and levy taxes on the people, by his own authority, and without such consent of the people, he thereby invades the fundamental law of property, and subverts the end of government. For what property have I in that which another may be right to take when he pleases to himself. . . .

The constitution of the legislative is the first and fundamental act of society, whereby provision is made for the continuation of their union, under the direction of persons, and bonds of laws, made by persons authorized thereunto, by the consent and appointment of the people, without which no one man, or number of men, amongst them, can have authority of making laws that shall be binding to the rest. When any one, or more, shall take upon them to make laws, whom the people have not appointed so to do, they make laws without authority, which the people are not therefore bound to obey; by which means they come again to be out of subjection, and may constitute to themselves a new legislative, as they think best, being in full liberty to resist the force of those, who, without authority, would impose any thing upon them. "

EVALUATE THE EVIDENCE

1. For what reason do people form a government, according to Locke? What would be the justification for disobeying laws and rejecting the authority of government?
2. In what ways does this document legitimize the events of the Glorious Revolution?

Source: John Locke, *Two Treatises of Government*. Reprinted in *England's Glorious Revolution, 1688–1689*, ed. Steven C. A. Pincus (Boston: Bedford/St. Martin's, 2006), pp. 161–162, 164.

made in Parliament; once made, it could not be suspended by the Crown. Parliament had to be called at least once every three years. The independence of the judiciary was established, and there was to be no standing army in peacetime. Protestants could possess arms, but the Catholic minority could not. No Catholic could ever inherit the throne. Additional legislation granted freedom of worship to Protestant dissenters, but not to Catholics. William and Mary accepted these principles when they took the throne, and the House of Parliament passed the Bill of Rights in December 1689.

The Glorious Revolution and the concept of representative government found its best defense in political philosopher John Locke's *Second Treatise of Civil Government* (1690). Locke (1632–1704) maintained that a government that oversteps its proper function—protecting the natural rights of life, liberty, and property—becomes a tyranny. (See "Primary Source 15.5: John Locke, *Two Treatises of Government*," above.) By "natural" rights Locke meant rights basic to all men because all have the ability to reason. Under a tyrannical government, the people have the natural right to rebellion. On the basis of this link, he justified limiting the vote to property owners. Locke's idea that there are natural or universal rights equally valid for all peoples and societies was especially popular in colonial America. American colonists also appreciated his arguments that Native Americans had no property rights since they did not cultivate the land and, by extension, no political rights because they possessed no property.

The events of 1688 and 1689 did not constitute a democratic revolution. The revolution placed sovereignty in Parliament, and Parliament represented the upper classes. The age of aristocratic government lasted at least until 1832 and in many ways until 1928, when women received full voting rights.

In the course of the eighteenth century, the cabinet system of government evolved. The term *cabinet* derives from the small private room in which English rulers consulted their chief ministers. In a cabinet system, the leading ministers, who must have seats in and the support of a majority of the House of Commons, formulate common policy and conduct the business of the country. During the administration of one royal minister, Sir Robert Walpole, who led the cabinet from 1721 to 1742, the idea developed that the cabinet was responsible to the House of Commons. The Hanoverian king George I (r. 1714–1727) normally presided at cabinet meetings throughout his reign, but his son and heir, George II (r. 1727–1760), discontinued the practice. The influence of the Crown in decision making accordingly declined. Walpole enjoyed the favor of the monarchy and of the House of Commons and came to be called the king's first, or "prime," minister. In the English cabinet system, both legislative power and executive power are held by the leading ministers, who form the government.

England's brief and chaotic experiment with republicanism under Oliver Cromwell convinced its people of the advantages of a monarchy, albeit with strong checks on royal authority. For supporters of Parliament, the tolerant and moderate Dutch Republic had provided a powerful counterexample to Louis XIV's absolutism.

The Dutch Republic in the Seventeenth Century

In the late sixteenth century the seven northern provinces of the Netherlands fought for and won their independence from Spain. The independence of the Republic of the United Provinces of the Netherlands was recognized in 1648 in the treaty that ended the Thirty Years' War. In this period, often called the "golden age of the Netherlands," Dutch ideas and attitudes played a profound role in shaping a new and modern worldview. At the same time, the United Provinces developed its own distinctive model of a constitutional state.

Rejecting the rule of a monarch, the Dutch established a republic, a state in which power rested in the hands of the people and was exercised through elected representatives. Other examples of republics in early modern Europe included the Swiss Confederation and several autonomous city-states of Italy and the Holy Roman Empire. Among the Dutch, an oligarchy of wealthy businessmen called regents handled domestic affairs in each province's Estates (assemblies). The provincial Estates held virtually all the power. A federal

Jan Steen, *The Merry Family*, 1668   In this painting from the Dutch golden age, a happy family enjoys a boisterous song while seated around the dining table. Despite its carefree appearance, the painting was intended to teach a moral lesson. The children are shown drinking wine and smoking, bad habits they have learned from their parents. The inscription hanging over the mantelpiece (upper right) spells out the message clearly: "As the Old Sing, so Pipe the Young." (Gianni Dagli Orti/The Art Archive)

Satire on Tulipmania This painting mocks the speculative boom in tulips that hit the Dutch Republic in the 1630s. The left side of the image depicts a group of monkeys dressed as wealthy investors engaged in buying and selling tulips. On the right side, investors experience the pain of the crash, as one monkey urinates on a worthless tulip and another is brought to trial for debt. (Private Collection/Johnny Van Haeften Ltd., London/The Bridgeman Art Library)

assembly, or States General, handled foreign affairs and war, but it did not possess sovereign authority. All issues had to be referred back to the local Estates for approval, and each of the seven provinces could veto any proposed legislation. Holland, the province with the largest navy and the most wealth, usually dominated the republic and the States General.

In each province, the Estates appointed an executive officer, known as the **stadholder**, who carried out ceremonial functions and was responsible for military defense. Although in theory freely chosen by the Estates and answerable to them, in practice the strong and influential House of Orange usually held the office of stadholder in several of the seven provinces of the republic. This meant that tensions always lingered between supporters of the House of Orange and those of the staunchly republican Estates, who suspected that the princes of Orange harbored monarchical ambitions. When one of them, William III, took the English throne in 1688 with his wife, Mary, the republic simply continued without stadholders for several decades.

The political success of the Dutch rested on their phenomenal commercial prosperity. The moral and ethical bases of that commercial wealth were thrift, frugality, and religious toleration. Although there is scattered evidence of anti-Semitism, Jews enjoyed a level of acceptance and assimilation in Dutch business and general culture unique in early modern Europe. In the Dutch Republic, toleration paid off: it attracted a great deal of foreign capital and investment.

The Dutch came to dominate the shipping business by putting profits from their original industry—herring fishing—into shipbuilding. They boasted the lowest shipping rates and largest merchant marine in Europe, allowing them to undersell foreign competitors (see Chapter 14).

Trade and commerce brought the Dutch the highest standard of living in Europe, perhaps in the world. Salaries were high, and all classes of society ate well. A scholar has described the Netherlands as "an island of plenty in a sea of want." Consequently, the Netherlands experienced very few of the food riots that characterized the rest of Europe.[12]

stadholder The executive officer in each of the United Provinces of the Netherlands, a position often held by the princes of Orange.

Baroque Art and Music

What was the baroque style in art and music, and where was it popular?

Throughout European history, the cultural tastes of one age have often seemed unsatisfactory to the next. So it was with the baroque. The term *baroque* may have come from the Portuguese word for an "odd-shaped, imperfect pearl" and was commonly used by late-eighteenth-century art critics as an expression of scorn for what they considered an overblown, unbalanced style. Specialists now agree that the baroque style marked one of the high points in the history of Western culture.

Rome and the revitalized Catholic Church of the late sixteenth century spurred the early development of the baroque. The papacy and the Jesuits encouraged the growth of an intensely emotional, exuberant art. These patrons wanted artists to go beyond the Renais-sance focus on pleasing a small, wealthy cultural elite. They wanted artists to appeal to the senses and thereby touch the souls and kindle the faith of ordinary church-goers while proclaiming the power and confidence of the reformed Catholic Church. In addition to this underlying religious emotionalism, the baroque drew its sense of drama, motion, and ceaseless striving from the Catholic Reformation. The interior of the famous Jesuit Church of Jesus in Rome—the Gesù—combined all these characteristics in its lavish, wildly active decorations and frescoes.

Taking definite shape in Italy after 1600, the baroque style in the visual arts developed with exceptional vigor in Catholic countries—in Spain and Latin America, Austria, southern Germany, and Poland. Yet baroque art was more than just "Catholic art" in the seventeenth century and the first half of the eighteenth. True, neither Protestant England nor the Netherlands ever came fully under the spell of the baroque, but neither did Catholic France. And Protestants accounted for some of the finest examples of baroque style, espe-

Rubens, *Garden of Love*, 1633–1634   This painting is an outstanding example of the lavishness and richness of baroque art. Born and raised in northern Europe, Peter Paul Rubens trained as a painter in Italy. Upon his return to the Spanish Netherlands, he became a renowned and amazingly prolific artist, patronized by rulers across Europe. Rubens was a devout Catholic, and his work conveys the emotional fervor of the Catholic Reformation. (Prado, Madrid, Spain/Giraudon/The Bridgeman Art Library)

cially in music. The baroque style spread partly because its tension and bombast spoke to an agitated age that was experiencing great violence and controversy in politics and religion.

In painting, the baroque reached maturity early with Peter Paul Rubens (1577–1640), the most outstanding and most representative of baroque painters. Studying in his native Flanders and in Italy, where he was influenced by masters of the High Renaissance such as Michelangelo, Rubens developed his own rich, sensuous, colorful style, which was characterized by animated figures, melodramatic contrasts, and monumental size. Rubens excelled in glorifying monarchs such as Queen Mother Marie de' Medici of France. He was also a devout Catholic; nearly half of his pictures treat Christian subjects. Yet one of Rubens's trademarks was the fleshy, sensual nudes who populate his canvases as Roman goddesses, water nymphs, and remarkably voluptuous saints and angels.

In music, the baroque style reached its culmination almost a century later in the dynamic, soaring lines of the endlessly inventive Johann Sebastian Bach (1685–1750). Organist and choirmaster of several Lutheran churches across Germany, Bach was equally at home writing secular concertos and sublime religious cantatas. Bach's organ music combined the baroque spirit of invention, tension, and emotion in an unforgettable striving toward the infinite. Unlike Rubens, Bach was not fully appreciated in his lifetime, but since the early nineteenth century his reputation has grown steadily.

Notes

1. Quoted in Cecile Hugon, *Social France in the XVII Century* (London: McMilland, 1911), p. 189.
2. H. Kamen, "The Economic and Social Consequences of the Thirty Years' War," *Past and Present* 39 (1968): 44–61.
3. John A. Lynn, "Recalculating French Army Growth," in *The Military Revolution Debate: Readings on the Military Transformation of Early Modern Europe*, ed. Clifford J. Rogers (Boulder, Colo.: Westview Press, 1995), p. 125.
4. Quoted in John A. Lynn, *Giant of the Grand Siècle: The French Army, 1610–1715* (Cambridge, U.K.: Cambridge University Press, 1997), p. 74.
5. F. Arkwright, ed., *The Memoirs of the Duke de Saint-Simon*, vol. 5 (New York: Brentano's, n.d.), p. 276.
6. J. H. Elliott, *Imperial Spain, 1469–1716* (New York: Mentor Books, 1963), pp. 306–308.
7. *German History Documents*, http://germanhistorydocs.ghidc.org/docpage.cfm?docpage_id=3734.
8. H. Rosenberg, *Bureaucracy, Aristocracy, and Autocracy: The Prussian Experience, 1660–1815* (Boston: Beacon Press, 1966), p. 43.
9. Cited in Giles MacDonogh, *Frederick the Great: A Life in Deed and Letters* (New York: St. Martin's, 2001), p. 23.
10. Rosenberg, *Bureaucracy, Aristocracy, and Autocracy*, p. 40.
11. For a revisionist interpretation, see J. Wormald, "James VI and I: Two Kings or One?" *History* 62 (1983): 187–209.
12. S. Schama, *The Embarrassment of Riches: An Interpretation of Dutch Culture in the Golden Age* (New York: Alfred A. Knopf, 1987), pp. 165–170; quotation is on p. 167.

LOOKING BACK LOOKING AHEAD

The seventeenth century represented a difficult passage between two centuries of dynamism and growth. On one side lay the sixteenth century of religious enthusiasm and strife, overseas expansion, rising population, and vigorous commerce. On the other side stretched the eighteenth-century era of renewed population growth, economic development, and cultural flourishing. The first half of the seventeenth century was marked by the spread of religious and dynastic warfare across Europe, resulting in the death and dislocation of many millions. This catastrophe was compounded by recurrent episodes of crop failure, famine, and epidemic disease, all of which contributed to a stagnant economy and population loss. In the middle decades of the seventeenth century, the very survival of the European monarchies established in the Renaissance appeared in doubt.

With the re-establishment of order in the second half of the century, maintaining political and social stability was of paramount importance to European rulers and elites. In western and eastern Europe, a host of monarchs proclaimed their God-given and "absolute" authority to rule in the name of peace, unity, and good order. Rulers' ability to impose such claims in reality depended a great deal on compromise with local elites, who acquiesced to state power in exchange for privileges and payoffs. In this way, absolutism and constitutionalism did not always differ as much as they claimed. Both systems relied on political compromises forged from decades of strife.

The eighteenth century was to see this status quo thrown into question by new Enlightenment aspirations for human society, which themselves derived from the inquisitive and self-confident spirit of the Scientific Revolution. By the end of the century, demands for real popular sovereignty would challenge the foundations of the political order so painfully achieved in the seventeenth century.

REVIEW and EXPLORE

MAKE IT STICK

 LearningCurve
After reading the chapter, go online and use LearningCurve to retain what you've read.

Identify Key Terms

Identify and explain the significance of each item below.

Peace of Westphalia (p. 466)

Fronde (p. 470)

mercantilism (p. 474)

Peace of Utrecht (p. 476)

Junkers (p. 480)

boyars (p. 482)

Cossacks (p. 483)

sultan (p. 489)

janissary corps (p. 489)

millet system (p. 489)

constitutionalism (p. 489)

republicanism (p. 490)

Puritans (p. 490)

Protectorate (p. 492)

Test Act (p. 493)

stadholder (p. 497)

Review the Main Ideas

Answer the focus questions from each section of the chapter.

- ◆ What were the common crises and achievements of seventeenth-century European states? (p. 464)

- ◆ What factors led to the rise of the French absolutist state under Louis XIV, and why did absolutist Spain experience decline in the same period? (p. 469)

- ◆ What were the social conditions of eastern Europe, and how did the rulers of Austria and Prussia transform their nations into powerful absolutist monarchies? (p. 478)

- ◆ What were the distinctive features of Russian and Ottoman absolutism? (p. 482)

- ◆ How and why did the constitutional state triumph in the Dutch Republic and England? (p. 489)

- ◆ What was the baroque style in art and music, and where was it popular? (p. 498)

Make Connections

Think about the larger developments and continuities within and across chapters.

1. This chapter has argued that, despite their political differences, rulers in absolutist and constitutionalist nations faced similar obstacles in the mid-seventeenth century and achieved many of the same goals. Do you agree with this argument? Why or why not?

2. Proponents of absolutism in western Europe believed that their form of monarchical rule was fundamentally different from and superior to what they saw as the "despotism" of Russia and the Ottoman Empire. What was the basis of this belief and how accurate do you think it was?

ONLINE DOCUMENT ASSIGNMENT
Hürrem

What forces shaped Western views of Hürrem?

You encountered Hürrem's story on page 488. Keeping the question above in mind, go to the Integrated Media and examine characterizations of Hürrem as seen through the eyes of a Habsburg diplomat, and then complete a writing assignment based on the evidence and details from this chapter.

Suggested Reading and Media Resources

BOOKS

- Beik, William. *A Social and Cultural History of Early Modern France.* 2009. An overview of early modern French history, by one of the leading authorities on the period.

- Benedict, Philip, and Myron P. Gutmann, eds. *Early Modern Europe: From Crisis to Stability.* 2005. A helpful introduction to the many facets of the seventeenth-century crisis.

- Clark, Christopher. *Iron Kingdom: The Rise and Downfall of Prussia, 1600–1947.* 2006. A fascinating long-term account tracing Prussia's emergence as an international power and the impact of Prussian history on later political developments in Germany.

- Elliott, John H. *Imperial Spain, 1469–1716,* 2d ed. 2002. An authoritative account of Spain's rise to imperial greatness and its slow decline.

- Gaunt, Peter, ed. *The English Civil War: The Essential Readings.* 2000. A collection showcasing leading historians' interpretations of the civil war.

- Goldgard, Anne. *Tulipmania: Money, Honor, and Knowledge in the Dutch Golden Age.* 2007. A fresh look at the speculative fever for tulip bulbs in the early-seventeenth-century Dutch Republic.

- Hagen, William W. *Ordinary Prussians: Brandenburg Junkers and Villagers, 1500–1840.* 2002. Provides a fascinating encounter with the people of a Prussian estate.

- Hughes, Lindsey, ed. *Peter the Great and the West: New Perspectives.* 2001. Essays by leading scholars on the reign of Peter the Great and his opening of Russia to the West.

- Ingrao, Charles W. *The Habsburg Monarchy, 1618–1815,* 2d ed. 2000. An excellent synthesis of the political and social development of the Habsburg empire in the early modern period.

- Kettering, Sharon. *Patronage in Sixteenth- and Seventeenth-Century France.* 2002. A collection of essays on courtly patronage, emphasizing the role of women in noble patronage networks.

- Parker, Geoffrey. *The Thirty Years' War,* 2d ed. 1997. The standard account of the Thirty Years' War.

- Pincus, Steven. *1688: The First Modern Revolution.* 2009. Revisionary account of the Glorious Revolution, emphasizing its toll in bloodshed and destruction of property and its global repercussions.

- Roman, Rolf, ed. *Baroque: Architecture, Sculpture, Painting.* 2007. A beautifully illustrated presentation of multiple facets of the baroque across Europe.

DOCUMENTARIES

- *The Art of Baroque Dance* (Dancetime Publications, 2006). An introduction to baroque dance incorporating images of the architecture and art of the period alongside dance performances and information on major elements of the style.

- *Rubens: Passion, Faith, Sensuality and the Art of the Baroque* (Kultur Studio, 2011). A documentary introducing viewers to the work of Peter Paul Rubens, one of the greatest artists of the baroque style.

FEATURE FILMS AND TELEVISION

- *Alatriste* (Agustín Díaz Yanes, 2006). Set in the declining years of Spain's imperial glory, this film follows the violent adventures of an army captain who takes the son of a fallen comrade under his care.

- *Charles II: The Power and the Passion* (BBC, 2003). An award-winning television miniseries about the son of executed English king Charles I and the Restoration that brought him to the throne in 1660.

- *Cromwell* (Ken Hughes, 1970). The English civil war from its origin to Oliver Cromwell's victory, with battle scenes as well as personal stories of Cromwell and other central figures.

- *The King Is Dancing* (Gérard Corbiau, 2000). A biography of the Sun King's favorite composer, Jean-Baptiste Lully, depicting a young Louis XIV dancing at the French court.

- *Queen Christina* (Rouben Mamoulian, 1933). A film starring legendary actress Greta Garbo as the cross-dressing queen of seventeenth-century Sweden.

WEB SITES

- *The Jesuit Relations.* This site contains the entire English translation of *The Jesuit Relations and Allied Documents,* the reports submitted by Jesuit missionaries in New France to authorities in the home country. **puffin.creighton.edu/jesuit/relations/**

- *Tour of Restoration London.* A Web site offering information on the places, food, and people of Restoration London, inspired by the novel *Invitation to a Funeral* by Molly Brown (1999). **www.okima.com/**

- *Versailles Palace.* The official Web site of the palace of Versailles, built by Louis XIV and inhabited by French royalty until the revolution of 1789. **en.chateauversailles.fr/homepage**

16

Toward a New Worldview

1540–1789

The intellectual developments of the sixteenth and seventeenth centuries created the modern worldview that the West continues to hold — and debate — to this day. In this period, fundamentally new ways of understanding the natural world emerged. Those leading the changes saw themselves as philosophers and referred to their field of study as "natural philosophy." Nineteenth-century scholars hailed these achievements as a "Scientific Revolution" that produced modern science as we know it. The new science entailed the search for precise knowledge of the physical world based on the union of experimental observations with sophisticated mathematics. Whereas medieval scholars looked to authoritative texts like the Bible or the classics, early modern natural philosophers performed experiments and relied on increasingly complex mathematical calculations. The resulting conception of the universe and its laws remained in force until Einstein's discoveries at the beginning of the twentieth century.

In the eighteenth century philosophers extended the use of reason from the study of nature to human society. They sought to bring the light of reason to bear on the darkness of prejudice, outmoded traditions, and ignorance. Self-proclaimed members of an "Enlightenment" movement, they wished to bring the same progress to human affairs as their predecessors had brought to the understanding of the natural world. While the Scientific Revolution ushered in modern science, the Enlightenment created concepts of human rights, equality, progress, universalism, and tolerance that still guide Western societies today. At the same time, some people used their new understanding of nature and reason to proclaim their own superiority, thus rationalizing such attitudes as racism and male chauvinism. ■

Life During the Scientific Revolution. This 1768 painting by Joseph Wright captures the popularization of science and experimentation during the Enlightenment. Here, a scientist demonstrates the creation of a vacuum by withdrawing air from a flask, with the suffocating cockatoo serving as shocking proof of the experiment. (National Gallery, London/The Bridgeman Art Library)

CHAPTER PREVIEW

 LearningCurve
After reading the chapter, go online and use LearningCurve to retain what you've read.

Major Breakthroughs of the Scientific Revolution
What revolutionary discoveries were made in the sixteenth and seventeenth centuries?

Important Changes in Scientific Thinking
What intellectual and social changes occurred as a result of the Scientific Revolution?

The Enlightenment
What new ideas about society and human relations emerged in the Enlightenment, and what new practices and institutions enabled these ideas to take hold?

Enlightened Absolutism
What impact did new ways of thinking have on political developments and monarchical absolutism?

Major Breakthroughs of the Scientific Revolution

What revolutionary discoveries were made in the sixteenth and seventeenth centuries?

Until the middle of the sixteenth century, Europeans relied on an understanding of motion and matter drawn from the ancient Greek philosopher Aristotle and adapted to Christian theology. The rise of the university, along with the intellectual vitality of the Renaissance and technological advancements, inspired scholars to make closer observations and seek better explanations. From the sun-centered universe proposed by the Polish astronomer Nicolaus Copernicus to the great synthesis of physics and astronomy accomplished by the English scientist Isaac Newton, a revolutionary new understanding of the universe had emerged by the end of the seventeenth century. Hailed today as pioneers of a modern worldview, the major figures of the Scientific Revolution were for the most part devout Christians who saw their work as heralding the glory of cre-

natural philosophy

An early modern term for the study of the nature of the universe, its purpose, and how it functioned; it encompassed what we would call "science" today.

ation and who combined older traditions of magic, astrology, and alchemy with their pathbreaking experimentation.

Scientific Thought in 1500

The term *science* as we use it today came into use only in the nineteenth century. Prior to the Scientific Revolution, many different scholars and practitioners were involved in aspects of what came together to form science. One of the most important disciplines was **natural philosophy**, which focused on fundamental questions about the nature of the universe, its purpose, and how it functioned. In the early 1500s natural philosophy was still based primarily on the ideas of Aristotle, the great Greek philosopher of the fourth century B.C.E. Medieval theologians such as Thomas Aquinas brought Aristotelian philosophy into harmony with Christian doctrines. According to the revised Aristotelian view, a motionless earth was fixed at the center of the universe and was encompassed by ten separate concentric crystal spheres that revolved around it. In the first eight spheres were embedded, in turn, the moon, the sun, the five known planets, and the fixed stars. Then followed two spheres added during the Middle Ages to account for slight changes in the positions of the stars over the centuries. Beyond

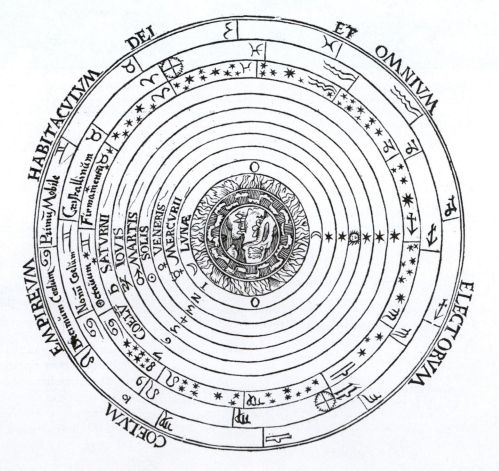

The Aristotelian Universe as Imagined in the Sixteenth Century A round earth is at the center, surrounded by spheres of water, air, and fire. Beyond this small nucleus, the moon, the sun, and the five planets were embedded in their own rotating crystal spheres, with the stars sharing the surface of one enormous sphere. Beyond, the heavens were composed of unchanging ether. (Universal History Archive/UIG/The Bridgeman Art Library)

the tenth sphere was Heaven, with the throne of God and the souls of the saved. Angels kept the spheres moving in perfect circles.

Aristotle's cosmology made intellectual sense, but it could not account for the observed motions of the stars and planets and, in particular, provided no explanation for the apparent backward motion of the planets (which we now know occurs because planets closer to the sun periodically overtake the earth on their faster orbits). The great second-century scholar Ptolemy, a Hellenized Egyptian (see Chapter 14), offered a cunning solution to this dilemma. According to Ptolemy, the planets moved in small circles, called epicycles, each of which moved in turn along a larger circle, or deferent. Ptolemaic astronomy was less elegant than Aristotle's neat nested circles and required complex calculations, but it provided a surprisingly accurate model for predicting planetary motion.

Aristotle's views, revised by medieval philosophers, also dominated thinking about physics and motion on earth. Aristotle had distinguished sharply between the world of the celestial spheres and that of the earth—the sublunar world. The spheres consisted of a perfect, incorruptible "quintessence," or fifth essence. The sublunar world, however, was made up of four imperfect, changeable elements. The "light" elements (air and fire) naturally moved upward, while the "heavy" elements (water and earth) naturally moved downward. These natural directions of motion did not always prevail, however, for elements were often mixed together and could be affected by an outside force such as a human being. Aristotle and his followers also believed that a uniform force moved an object at a constant speed and that the object would stop as soon as that force was removed.

Natural philosophy was considered distinct from and superior to mathematics and mathematical disciplines like astronomy, optics, and mechanics, and Aristotle's ideas about the cosmos were accepted, with revisions, for two thousand years. His views offered a commonsense explanation for what the eye actually saw. Aristotle's science as interpreted by Christian theologians also fit neatly with Christian doctrines. It established a home for God and a place for Christian souls. It put human beings at the center of the universe and made them the critical link in a "great chain of being" that stretched from the throne of God to the lowliest insect on earth. This approach to the natural world was thus a branch of theology, and it reinforced religious thought.

Chronology

ca. 1540–1700	Scientific Revolution
ca. 1690–1789	Enlightenment
ca. 1700–1800	Growth of book publishing
1720–1780	Rococo style in art and decoration
1740–1748	War of the Austrian Succession
1740–1780	Reign of the empress Maria Theresa of Austria
1740–1786	Reign of Frederick the Great of Prussia
ca. 1740–1789	Salons led by Parisian elites
1751–1772	Philosophes publish *Encyclopedia: The Rational Dictionary of the Sciences, the Arts, and the Crafts*
1756–1763	Seven Years' War
1762–1796	Reign of Catherine the Great of Russia
1780–1790	Reign of Joseph II of Austria
1791	Establishment of the Pale of Settlement

Origins of the Scientific Revolution

Why did Aristotelian teachings give way to new views about the universe? The Scientific Revolution drew on long-term developments in European culture, as well as borrowings from Arabic scholars. The first important development was the medieval university. By the thirteenth century permanent universities had been established in western Europe to train the lawyers, doctors, and church leaders society required. By 1300 philosophy—including Aristotelian natural philosophy—had taken its place alongside law, medicine, and theology. Medieval philosophers acquired a limited but real independence from theologians and a sense of free inquiry.

Medieval universities drew on rich traditions of Islamic learning. With the expansion of Islam into lands of the Byzantine Empire in the seventh and eighth centuries, the Muslim world had inherited ancient Greek learning, to which Islamic scholars added their own commentaries and new discoveries. Many Greek texts, including many works of the philosopher Aristotle, which were lost to the West after the fall of the Western Roman Empire in the fifth century, re-entered circulation through translation from the Arabic in the twelfth century; these became the basis for the curriculum of the medieval universities. In the fourteenth and fifteenth centuries leading universities established new professorships of mathematics, astronomy, and optics within their faculties of philosophy. The prestige of the new fields was low, but the stage was set for the union of mathematics with natural philosophy that was to be a hallmark of the Scientific Revolution.

The Renaissance also stimulated scientific progress. Renaissance patrons played a role in funding scientific investigations, as they did for art and literature. Renaissance artists' turn toward realism and their use of geometry to convey three-dimensional perspective encouraged scholars to practice close observation and to use mathematics to describe the natural world. The quest to restore the glories of the ancient past led to the rediscovery of even more classical texts, such as Ptolemy's *Geography* (see Chapter 14), which had been preserved in the Byzantine Empire and was translated into Latin around 1410. The encyclopedic treatise on botany by the ancient Greek philosopher Theophrastus was rediscovered in the 1450s, moldering on the shelves of the Vatican library. The fall of Constantinople to the Muslim Ottomans in 1453 resulted in a great influx of little-known Greek works, as Christian scholars fled to Italy with their precious texts.

Developments in technology also encouraged the emergence of the Scientific Revolution. The rise of printing in the mid-fifteenth century provided a faster and less expensive way to circulate knowledge across Europe. Fascination with the new discoveries being made in Asia and the Americas greatly increased the demand for printed material. Publishers found an eager audience for the books and images they issued about unknown peoples, plants, animals, and other new findings.

The navigational problems of long sea voyages in the age of overseas expansion, along with the rise of trade and colonization, led to their own series of technological innovations. As early as 1484 the king of Portugal appointed a commission of mathematicians to perfect tables to help seamen find their latitude. Navigation and cartography were also critical in the development of many new scientific instruments, such as the telescope, barometer, thermometer, pendulum clock, microscope, and air pump. Better instruments, which permitted more accurate observations, enabled the rise of experimentation as a crucial method of the Scientific Revolution.

Recent historical research has also focused on the contribution to the Scientific Revolution of practices that no longer belong to the realm of science, such as astrology. For most of human history, interest in astronomy was inspired by the belief that the changing relationships between planets and stars influence events on earth. This belief was held in Europe up to and during the Scientific Revolution (and continues among some people today). Many of the most celebrated astronomers were also astrologers and spent much time devising horoscopes for their patrons. Used as a diagnostic

Copernican hypothesis
The idea that the sun, not the earth, was the center of the universe.

tool in medicine, astrology formed a regular part of the curriculum of medical schools.

Centuries-old practices of magic and alchemy also remained important traditions for natural philosophers. Unlike modern-day conjurers, the practitioners of magic strove to understand and control hidden connections they perceived among different elements of the natural world, such as that between a magnet and iron. The idea that objects possessed invisible or "occult" qualities that allowed them to affect other objects through their innate "sympathy" with each other was a particularly important legacy of the magical tradition. Belief in occult qualities—or numerology or cosmic harmony—was not antithetical to belief in God. On the contrary, adherents believed that only a divine creator could infuse the universe with such meaningful mystery.

The Copernican Hypothesis

The desire to explain and thereby glorify God's handiwork led to the first great departure from the medieval system. This was the work of the Polish cleric Nicolaus Copernicus (1473–1543). As a young man Copernicus was drawn to the vitality of the Italian Renaissance. After studies at the University of Kraków, he departed for Italy, where he studied astronomy, medicine, and church law at the famed universities of Bologna, Padua, and Ferrara. Copernicus noted that astronomers still depended on the work of Ptolemy for their most accurate calculations, but he felt that Ptolemy's cumbersome and occasionally inaccurate rules detracted from the majesty of a perfect creator. He preferred an alternative ancient Greek idea: that the sun, rather than the earth, was at the center of the universe.

Finishing his university studies and returning to a position in church administration in East Prussia, Copernicus worked on his hypothesis from 1506 to 1530. Without questioning the Aristotelian belief in crystal spheres or the idea that circular motion was divine, Copernicus theorized that the stars and planets, including the earth, revolved around a fixed sun. Desiring to be certain of his shocking claims before revealing them to the world, Copernicus did not publish his *On the Revolutions of the Heavenly Spheres* until 1543, the year of his death.

The **Copernican hypothesis** had enormous scientific and religious implications, many of which the conservative Copernicus did not anticipate. First, it put the stars at rest, their apparent nightly movement simply a result of the earth's rotation. Thus it destroyed the main reason for believing in crystal spheres capable of moving the stars around the earth. Second, Copernicus's theory suggested a universe of staggering size. If in the course of a year the earth moved around the sun and yet the stars appeared to remain in the same place, then the universe was unthinkably large. Third, by using mathematics, instead of philosophy, to justify his theories, he challenged the traditional hierarchy of the disciplines. Finally, by characterizing the earth as just another planet, Copernicus destroyed the basic idea of Aristotelian physics — that the earthly sphere was quite different from the heavenly one. Where then were Heaven and the throne of God?

Religious leaders varied in their response to Copernicus's theories. A few Protestant scholars became avid Copernicans, while others accepted some elements of his criticism of Ptolemy, but firmly rejected the notion that the earth moved, a doctrine that contradicted the literal reading of some passages of the Bible. Among Catholics, Copernicus's ideas drew little attention prior to 1600. Because the Catholic Church had never held to literal interpretations of the Bible, it did not officially declare the Copernican hypothesis false until 1616.

Other events were almost as influential in creating doubts about traditional astronomy. In 1572 a new star appeared and shone very brightly for almost two years. The new star, which was actually a distant exploding star, made an enormous impression on people. It seemed to contradict the idea that the heavenly spheres were unchanging and therefore perfect. In 1577 a new comet suddenly moved through the sky, cutting a straight path across the supposedly impenetrable crystal spheres. It was time, as a sixteenth-century scientific writer put it, for "the radical renovation of astronomy."[1]

Brahe, Kepler, and Galileo: Proving Copernicus Right

One astronomer who agreed with Copernicus was Tycho Brahe (TEE-koh BRAH-hee) (1546–1601). Born into a Danish noble family, Brahe became passionately interested in astronomy as a young boy and spent many nights gazing at the skies. Completing his studies abroad and returning to Denmark, he established himself as Europe's leading astronomer with his detailed observations of the new star of 1572. Aided by generous grants from the king of Denmark, Brahe built the most sophisticated observatory of his day.

Upon the king's death, Brahe acquired a new patron in the Holy Roman emperor Rudolph II and built a new observatory in Prague. In return for the emperor's support, he pledged to create new and improved tables of planetary motions, dubbed the *Rudolphine Tables*. For twenty years Brahe meticulously observed the stars and planets with the naked eye, compiling much more complete and accurate data than ever before. His limited understanding of mathematics and his sudden death in 1601, however, prevented him from making much sense out of his mass of data. Part Ptolemaic,

Hevelius and His Wife   Portable sextants were used to chart a ship's position at sea by measuring the altitude of celestial bodies above the horizon. Astronomers used much larger sextants to measure the angular distances between two bodies. Here, Johannes Hevelius makes use of the great brass sextant at the Danzig observatory, with the help of his wife, Elisabetha. Six feet in radius, this instrument was closely modeled on the one used by Tycho Brahe. (f Typ 620.73.451, Houghton Library, Harvard College Library)

part Copernican, he believed that all the planets except the earth revolved around the sun and that the entire group of sun and planets revolved in turn around the earth-moon system.

It was left to Brahe's young assistant, Johannes Kepler (1571–1630), to rework Brahe's mountain of observations. From a minor German noble family, Kepler suffered a bout of smallpox as a small child, leaving him with permanently damaged hands and eyesight. A brilliant mathematician, Kepler was inspired by his belief that the universe was built on mystical mathematical relationships and a musical harmony of the heavenly bodies.

Kepler's examination of his predecessor's meticulously recorded findings convinced him that Ptolemy's astronomy could not explain them. Abandoning the notion of epicycles and deferents—which even Copernicus had retained in part—Kepler developed three new and revolutionary laws of planetary motion. First, largely through observations of the planet Mars, he demonstrated that the orbits of the planets around the sun are elliptical rather than circular. Second, he demonstrated that the planets do not move at a uniform speed in their orbits. When a planet is close to the sun it moves more rapidly, and it slows as it moves farther away from the sun. Kepler published the first two laws in his 1609 book, *The New Astronomy*, which heralded the arrival of an entirely new theory of the cosmos. In 1619 Kepler put forth his third law: the time a planet takes to make its complete orbit is precisely related to its distance from the sun.

Kepler's contribution was monumental. Whereas Copernicus had used mathematics to describe planetary movement, Kepler proved mathematically the precise relations of a sun-centered (solar) system. He thus united for the first time the theoretical cosmology of natural philosophy with mathematics. His work demolished the old system of Aristotle and Ptolemy, and with his third law he came close to formulating the idea of universal gravitation (see page 510). In 1627 he also fulfilled Brahe's pledge by completing the *Rudolphine Tables* begun so many years earlier. These tables were used by astronomers for many years.

Kepler was a genius with many talents. Beyond his great contribution to astronomy, he pioneered the field of optics. He was the first to explain the role of refraction within the eye in creating vision, and he invented an improved telescope. He was also a great mathematician whose work furnished the basis for integral calculus and advances in geometry.

Kepler was not, however, the consummate modern scientist that these achievements suggest. His duties as court mathematician included casting horoscopes, and he based his own daily life on astrological principles. He also wrote at length on cosmic harmonies and explained, for example, elliptical motion through ideas about the beautiful music created by the combined motion of the planets. Kepler's fictional account of travel to the moon, written partly to illustrate the idea of a non-earth-centered universe, caused controversy and may have contributed to the arrest and trial of his mother as a witch in 1620. Kepler also suffered deeply as a result of his unorthodox brand of Lutheranism,

experimental method
The approach, pioneered by Galileo, that the proper way to explore the workings of the universe was through repeatable experiments rather than speculation.

law of inertia A law formulated by Galileo that states that motion, not rest, is the natural state of an object, and that an object continues in motion forever unless stopped by some external force.

which led to his rejection by both Lutherans and Catholics. His career exemplifies the complex interweaving of ideas and beliefs in the emerging science of his day.

While Kepler was unraveling planetary motion, a young Florentine named Galileo Galilei (1564–1642) was challenging all the old ideas about motion. Like Kepler and so many early scientists, Galileo was a poor nobleman first marked for a religious career. Instead, his fascination with mathematics led to a professorship in which he examined motion and mechanics in a new way. His great achievement was the elaboration and consolidation of the **experimental method**. That is, rather than speculate about what might or should happen, Galileo conducted controlled experiments to find out what actually did happen.

In his early experiments, Galileo focused on deficiencies in Aristotle's theories of motion. He measured the movement of a rolling ball across a surface, repeating the action again and again to verify his results. In his famous acceleration experiment, he showed that a uniform force—in this case, gravity—produced a uniform acceleration. Through another experiment, he formulated the **law of inertia**. He found that rest was not the natural state of objects. Rather, an object continues in motion forever unless stopped by some external force. His discoveries proved Aristotelian physics wrong.

Galileo then applied the experimental method to astronomy. On hearing details about the invention of the telescope in Holland, Galileo made one for himself and trained it on the heavens. He quickly discovered the first four moons of Jupiter, which clearly suggested that Jupiter could not possibly be embedded in any impenetrable crystal sphere as Aristotle and Ptolemy maintained. This discovery provided new evidence for the Copernican theory, in which Galileo already believed. Galileo then pointed his telescope at the moon. He wrote in 1610 in *The Sidereal Messenger*: "By the aid of a telescope anyone may behold [the Milky Way] in a manner which so distinctly appeals to the senses that all the disputes which have tormented philosophers through so many ages are exploded by the irrefutable evidence of our eyes, and we are freed from wordy disputes upon the subject."[2] (See "Primary Source 16.1: Galileo Galilei, *The Sidereal Messenger*," at right.)

Reading these famous lines, one feels a crucial corner in Western civilization being turned. No longer should one rely on established authority. A new method of learning and investigating was being developed, one that proved useful in any field of inquiry. A historian investigating documents of the past, for example, is not so different from a Galileo studying stars and rolling balls.

In 1597, when Johannes Kepler sent Galileo an early publication defending Copernicus, Galileo replied that it was too dangerous to express his support for helio-

Galileo Galilei, *The Sidereal Messenger*

In this passage from The Sidereal Messenger *(1610), Galileo Galilei recounts his experiments to build a telescope and his observations of the moon. By discovering the irregularity of the moon's surface, Galileo disproved a central tenet of medieval cosmography: that the heavens were composed of perfect, unblemished spheres essentially different from the base matter of earth.*

" About ten months ago a report reached my ears that a Dutchman had constructed a telescope, by the aid of which visible objects, although at a great distance from the eye of the observer, were seen distinctly as if near. . . . A few days after, I received confirmation of the report in a letter written from Paris . . . , which finally determined me to give myself up first to inquire into the principle of the telescope, and then to consider the means by which I might compass [achieve] the invention of a similar instrument, which a little while after I succeeded in doing, through deep study of the theory of refraction; and I prepared a tube, at first of lead, in the ends of which I fitted two glass lenses, both plane on one side, but on the other side one spherically convex, and the other concave. . . . At length, by sparing neither labour nor expense, I succeeded in constructing for myself an instrument so superior that objects seen through it appear magnified nearly a thousand times, and more than thirty times nearer than if viewed by the natural powers of sight alone. . . .

Let me speak first of the surface of the moon, which is turned towards us. For the sake of being understood more easily, I distinguish two parts in it, which I call respectively the brighter and the darker. The brighter part seems to surround and pervade the whole hemisphere, but the darker part, like a sort of cloud, discolours the moon's surface and makes it appear covered with spots. Now these spots . . . are plain to every one, and every age has seen them, wherefore I shall call them *great* or *ancient* spots, to distinguish them from other spots, smaller in size, but so thickly scattered that they sprinkle the whole surface of the moon, but especially the brighter portion of it. These spots have never been observed by any one before me, and from my observations of them, often repeated, I have been led to that opinion which I have expressed, namely, that I feel sure that the surface of the moon is not perfectly smooth, free from inequalities and exactly spherical, as a large school of philosophers considers with regard to the moon and the other heavenly bodies, but that, on the contrary, it is full of inequalities, uneven, full of hollows and protuberances, just like the surface of the earth itself, which is varied everywhere by lofty mountains and deep valleys. "

EVALUATE THE EVIDENCE

1. What did the telescope permit Galileo to see on the moon that was not visible to the naked eye, and how did he interpret his observations?
2. Why were Galileo's observations so important to the destruction of the Ptolemaic universe?

Source: Galileo Galilei, *The Sidereal Messenger* (London: Rivingtons, 1880), pp. 10–11, 14–15.

---

centrism publicly. The rising fervor of the Catholic Reformation increased the church's hostility to such radical ideas, and in 1616 the Holy Office placed the works of Copernicus and his supporters, including Kepler, on a list of books Catholics were forbidden to read. The accompanying decree declared that belief in a heliocentric world was "foolish and absurd, philosophically false and formally heretical."[3]

Galileo was a devout Catholic who sincerely believed that his theories did not detract from the perfection of God. Out of caution he silenced his beliefs for several years, until in 1623 he saw new hope with the ascension of Pope Urban VIII, a man sympathetic to developments in the new science. However, Galileo's 1632 *Dialogue on the Two Chief Systems of the World* went too far. Published in Italian and widely read, this work openly lampooned the traditional views of Aristotle and Ptolemy and defended those of Copernicus. The papal Inquisition placed Galileo on trial for heresy. Imprisoned and threatened with torture, the aging Galileo recanted, "renouncing and cursing" his Copernican errors.

Newton's Synthesis

Despite the efforts of the church, by about 1640 the work of Brahe, Kepler, and Galileo had been largely accepted by the scientific community. The old Aristotelian astronomy and physics were in ruins, and several fundamental breakthroughs had been made. But the new findings failed to explain what forces controlled the movement of the planets and objects on earth. That challenge was taken up by English scientist Isaac Newton (1642–1727).

Newton was born into the lower English gentry in 1642, and he enrolled at Cambridge University in 1661. A genius who spectacularly united the experimental and theoretical-mathematical sides of modern science, Newton was an intensely devout, albeit nonorthodox Christian, who privately rejected the doctrine of the Trinity. Newton was also fascinated by alchemy. He left behind thirty years' worth of encoded journals recording experiments to discover the elixir of life and a way to change base metals into gold and silver. He viewed alchemy as one path, alongside mathematics and astronomy, to the truth of God's creation. Like Kepler and other practitioners of the Scientific Revolution, he studied the natural world not for its own sake, but to understand the divine plan.

Newton arrived at some of his most basic ideas about physics between 1664 and 1666, during a break from studies at Cambridge caused by an outbreak of plague. As he later claimed, during this period he discovered his law of universal gravitation as well as the concepts of centripetal force and acceleration. Not realizing the significance of his findings, the young Newton did not publish them, and upon his return to

law of universal gravitation
Newton's law that all objects are attracted to one another and that the force of attraction is proportional to the objects' quantity of matter and inversely proportional to the square of the distance between them.

Cambridge he took up the study of optics. It was in reference to his experiments in optics that Newton outlined his method of scientific inquiry most clearly, explaining the need for scientists "first to enquire diligently into the properties of things, and to establish these properties by experiment, and then to proceed more slowly to hypotheses for the explanation of them."[4]

In 1684 Newton returned to physics and the preparation of his ideas for publication. The result appeared three years later in *Philosophicae Naturalis Principia Mathematica* (Mathematical Principles of Natural Philosophy). Newton's towering accomplishment was a single explanatory system that could integrate the astronomy of Copernicus, as corrected by Kepler's laws, with the physics of Galileo and his predecessors. *Principia Mathematica* laid down Newton's three laws of motion, using a set of mathematical laws that explain motion and mechanics. These laws of dynamics are complex, and it took scientists and engineers two hundred years to work out all their implications.

The key feature of the Newtonian synthesis was the **law of universal gravitation**. According to this law, every body in the universe attracts every other body in

Galileo's Telescopic Observations of the Moon Among the many mechanical devices Galileo invented was a telescope that could magnify objects thirty times (other contemporary telescopes could magnify objects only three times). Using this telescope, he obtained the empirical evidence that proved the Copernican system. He sketched many illustrations of his observations, including the six phases of the moon shown here. (moons: akg-images/Rabatti–Domingie; telescope: akg-images)

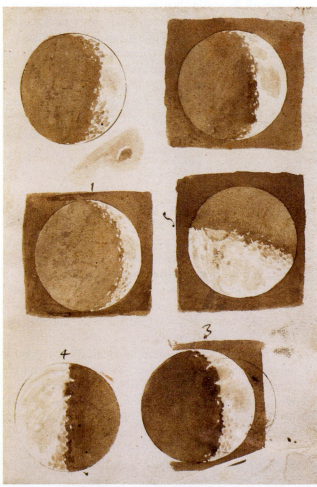

the universe in a precise mathematical relationship, whereby the force of attraction is proportional to the quantity of matter of the objects and inversely proportional to the square of the distance between them. The whole universe—from Kepler's elliptical orbits to Galileo's rolling balls—was unified in one coherent system. The German mathematician and philosopher Gottfried von Leibniz, with whom Newton contested the invention of calculus, was outraged by Newton's claim that the "occult" force of gravity could allow bodies to affect one another at great distances. Newton's religious faith, as well as his alchemical belief in the innate powers of certain objects, allowed him to dismiss such criticism.

Newton's synthesis of mathematics with physics and astronomy prevailed until the twentieth century and established him as one of the most important figures in the history of science. Yet, near the end of his life, this acclaimed figure declared: "I do not know what I may appear to the world; but to myself I seem to have been only like a boy, playing on the seashore, and diverting myself, in now and then finding a smoother pebble or a prettier shell than ordinary, whilst the great ocean of truth lay all undiscovered before me."[5]

Important Changes in Scientific Thinking

What intellectual and social changes occurred as a result of the Scientific Revolution?

The creation of a new science was not accomplished by a handful of brilliant astronomers working alone. Scholars in many fields—medicine, chemistry, and botany, among others—used new methods to seek answers to long-standing problems, sharing their results in a community that spanned Europe. At the same time, monarchs and entrepreneurs launched explorations to uncover and understand the natural riches of newly conquered empires around the globe.

Bacon, Descartes, and the Scientific Method

One of the keys to the achievement of a new worldview in the seventeenth century was the development of better ways of obtaining knowledge about the world. Two important thinkers, Francis Bacon (1561–1626) and René Descartes (day-KAHRT) (1596–1650), were influential in describing and advocating for improved scientific methods based, respectively, on experimentation and mathematical reasoning.

English politician and writer Francis Bacon was the greatest early propagandist for the new experimental method. Rejecting the Aristotelian and medieval method of using speculative reasoning to build general theories, Bacon argued that new knowledge had to be pursued through empirical research. The researcher who wants to learn more about leaves or rocks, for example, should not speculate about the subject but should rather collect a multitude of specimens and then compare and analyze them to derive general principles. Bacon formalized the empirical method, which had already been used by Brahe and Galileo, into the general theory of inductive reasoning known as **empiricism**. Bacon's work, and his prestige as lord chancellor under James I, led to the widespread adoption of what was called "experimental philosophy" in England after his death. In 1660 followers of Bacon created the Royal Society (still in existence), which met weekly to conduct experiments and discuss the latest findings of scholars across Europe.

> **empiricism** A theory of inductive reasoning that calls for acquiring evidence through observation and experimentation rather than deductive reason and speculation.

On the continent, more speculative methods retained support. The French philosopher René Descartes was a multitalented genius who made his first great discovery in mathematics. As a twenty-three-year-old soldier serving in the Thirty Years' War, he experienced a life-changing intellectual vision one night in 1619. Descartes saw that there was a perfect correspondence between geometry and algebra and that geometrical spatial figures could be expressed as algebraic equations and vice versa. A major step forward in the history of mathematics, Descartes's discovery of analytic geometry provided scientists with an important new tool.

Descartes used mathematics to elaborate a highly influential vision of the workings of the cosmos. Accepting Galileo's claim that all elements of the universe are composed of the same matter, Descartes began to investigate the basic nature of matter. Drawing on ancient Greek atomist philosophies, Descartes developed the idea that matter was made up of identical "corpuscles" that collided together in an endless series of motions. All occurrences in nature could be analyzed as matter in motion and, according to Descartes, the total "quantity of motion" in the universe was constant. Descartes's mechanistic view of the universe depended on the idea that a vacuum was impossible, which meant that every action had an equal reaction, continuing in an eternal chain reaction.

Although Descartes's hypothesis about the vacuum was proved wrong, his notion of a mechanistic universe intelligible through the physics of motion proved inspirational. Decades later, Newton rejected Descartes's idea of a full universe and several of his other ideas, but retained the notion of a mechanistic universe as a key element of his own system.

Descartes's greatest achievement was to develop his initial vision into a whole philosophy of knowledge and science. The Aristotelian cosmos was appealing in part because it corresponded with the evidence of the human senses. When the senses were proven to be wrong, Descartes decided it was necessary to doubt them and everything that could reasonably be doubted, and then, as in geometry, to use deductive reasoning from self-evident truths, which he called "first principles," to ascertain scientific laws. Descartes's reasoning ultimately reduced all substances to "matter" and

Cartesian dualism
Descartes's view that all of reality could ultimately be reduced to mind and matter.

"mind"—that is, to the physical and the spiritual. The devout Descartes believed that God had endowed man with reason for a purpose and that rational speculation could provide a path to the truths of creation. His view of the world as consisting of two fundamental entities is known as **Cartesian dualism**. Descartes's thought was highly influential in France and the Netherlands, but less so in England, where experimental philosophy won the day.

Both Bacon's inductive experimentalism and Descartes's deductive mathematical reasoning had their faults. Bacon's inability to appreciate the importance of mathematics and his obsession with practical results clearly showed the limitations of antitheoretical empiricism. Likewise, some of Descartes's positions demonstrated the inadequacy of rigid, dogmatic rationalism. For example, he believed that it was possible to deduce the whole science of medicine from first principles. Although insufficient on their own, Bacon's and Descartes's extreme approaches are combined in the modern scientific method, which began to crystallize in the late seventeenth century.

Medicine, the Body, and Chemistry

The Scientific Revolution soon inspired renewed study of the microcosm of the human body. For many centuries the ancient Greek physician Galen's explanation of the body carried the same authority as Aristotle's account of the universe. According to Galen, the body contained four humors: blood, phlegm, black bile, and yellow bile. Illness was believed to result from an imbalance of humors, which is why doctors frequently prescribed bloodletting to expel excess blood.

Swiss physician and alchemist Paracelsus (1493–1541) was an early proponent of the experimental method in medicine and pioneered the use of chemicals and drugs to address what he saw as chemical, rather than humoral, imbalances. Another experimentalist, Flemish physician Andreas Vesalius (1516–1564), studied anatomy by dissecting human bodies, often those of executed criminals. In 1543, the same year Copernicus published *On the Revolutions*, Vesalius issued his masterpiece, *On the Structure of the Human Body*. Its two hundred precise drawings revolutionized the understanding of human anatomy. The experimen-

Major Contributors to the Scientific Revolution

Nicolaus Copernicus (1473–1543)	*On the Revolutions of the Heavenly Spheres* (1543); theorized that the sun, rather than the earth, was the center of the galaxy
Paracelsus (1493–1541)	Swiss physician and alchemist who pioneered the use of chemicals and drugs to address illness
Andreas Vesalius (1514–1564)	*On the Structure of the Human Body* (1543)
Tycho Brahe (1546–1601)	Built observatory and compiled data for the *Rudolphine Tables*, a new table of planetary data
Francis Bacon (1561–1626)	Advocated experimental method, formalizing theory of inductive reasoning known as empiricism
Galileo Galilei (1564–1642)	Used telescopic observation to provide evidence for Copernican hypothesis; experimented to formulate laws of physics, such as inertia
Johannes Kepler (1571–1630)	Used Brahe's data to mathematically prove the Copernican hypothesis; his new laws of planetary motion united for the first time natural philosophy and mathematics; completed the *Rudolphine Tables* in 1627
William Harvey (1578–1657)	Discovery of circulation of blood (1628)
René Descartes (1596–1650)	Used deductive reasoning to formulate the theory of Cartesian dualism
Robert Boyle (1627–1691)	Boyle's law (1662) governing the pressure of gases
Isaac Newton (1642–1727)	*Principia Mathematica* (1687); set forth the law of universal gravitation, synthesizing previous findings of motion and matter

Frontispiece to *De Humani Corporis Fabrica* (On the Structure of the Human Body)
The frontispiece to Vesalius's pioneering work, published in 1543, shows him dissecting a corpse before a crowd of students. This was a revolutionary new hands-on approach for physicians, who usually worked from a theoretical, rather than a practical, understanding of the body. Based on direct observation, Vesalius replaced ancient ideas drawn from Greek philosophy with a much more accurate account of the structure and function of the body. (© SSPL/Science Museum/The Image Works)

tal approach also led English royal physician William Harvey (1578–1657) to discover the circulation of blood through the veins and arteries in 1628. Harvey was the first to explain that the heart worked like a pump and to explain the function of its muscles and valves.

Some decades later, Irishman Robert Boyle (1627–1691) helped found the modern science of chemistry. Following Paracelsus's lead, he undertook experiments to discover the basic elements of nature, which he believed was composed of infinitely small atoms. Boyle was the first to create a vacuum, thus disproving Descartes's belief that a vacuum could not exist in nature, and he discovered Boyle's law (1662), which states that the pressure of a gas varies inversely with volume.

Empire and Natural History

While the traditional story of the Scientific Revolution focuses exclusively on developments within Europe itself, and in particular on achievements in mathematical astronomy, more recently scholars have emphasized the impact of Europe's overseas empires on the accumu-

lation and transmission of knowledge about the natural world. Thus, moving beyond Ptolemy's *Geography* (see Chapter 14) was as important for the emergence of modern science as overturning his cosmography.

Building on the rediscovery of Theophrastus's botanical treatise (see page 506) and other classical texts, early modern scholars published new works cataloguing forms of life in northern Europe, Asia, and the Americas that were unknown to the ancients. These encyclopedias of natural history included realistic drawings and descriptions that emphasized the usefulness of animal and plant species for trade, medicine, food, and other practical concerns.

Much of the new knowledge contained in such works resulted from scientific expeditions, often sponsored by European governments eager to learn about and profit from their imperial holdings. Spain took an early lead in such voyages, given their early conquests in the Americas (see Chapter 14). The physician of King Philip II of Spain spent seven years in New Spain in the 1560s recording thousands of plant species and interviewing local healers about their medicinal properties. Other countries followed suit as their global em-

"An Account of a Particular Species of Cocoon"

To disseminate its members' work, the Royal Society of England published the results of its meetings in the Philosophical Transactions of the Royal Society. *The passage below is excerpted from a presentation made to the society in the mid-eighteenth century by the Reverend Samuel Pullein, a graduate of Trinity College in Dublin. A relative of the governor of Jamaica, Pullein became fascinated by the idea of introducing silkworm cultivation to the American colonies. His presentation exemplifies the contribution of many minor enthusiasts to the progress of science in this period and the importance of colonialism to the new knowledge.*

❝ Having lately seen the aurelia of a particular species of caterpillar, I judged, from its texture and consistence, that there might be procured from it a silk not inferior to that of the common silk-worm in its quality, and in its quantity much superior. I have made some experiments on this new species of silk-pod, which strengthen this opinion.

This pod is about three inches and a quarter in length, and above one inch in diameter; its outward form not so regular an oval as that of the common silk-worm; its consistence somewhat like that of a dried bladder, when not fully blown; its colour of a reddish brown; its whole weight 21 grains.

Upon cutting open this outer integument, there appeared in the inside a pod completely oval, as that of the silk-worm. It was covered with some floss-silk, by which it was connected to the outer coat, being of the same colour. Its length was two inches; its diameter nearly one inch; and its weight nine grains.

The pod could not be easily unwinded, because it was perforated by the moth: but, upon putting it in hot water, I reeled off so much as sufficed to form a judgment of the strength and staple of its silk.

The single thread winded off the pod in the same manner as that of the common silk-worm; seeming in all respects as fine, and as tough. I doubled this thread so often as to contain twenty in thickness; and the compound thread was as smooth, as elastic, and as glossy, as that of the common silk-worm. I tried what weight it would bear; and it bore fifteen ounces and a half, and broke with somewhat less than sixteen, upon several trials. . . .

The caterpillar which produces this pod is a native of America. It was found in Pennsylvania: the pod was fixed to the small branch of a tree, which seemed to be either of the crab or hawthorn species. . . .

I do not conceive that it will be at all difficult to find out the caterpillar, or the tree it feeds on; or to reel such a quantity of the silk as shall, when woven into ribband, more fully demonstrate whether it be of that value which I judge it. For by comparing it with the *cocoon* of the wild Chinese silk-worm, from which an excellent species of silk is made, I have no doubt of its being the same species; and would be glad if, by this memorial, I could induce the people of America to make trial of it. ❞

EVALUATE THE EVIDENCE

1. What is Pullein's aim in presenting his research to the Royal Society? How does he try to establish the credibility of his claims about the silkworm?
2. In what ways does this document belong to the "Scientific Revolution" as discussed in this chapter? What does Pullein's presentation tell us about the nature of "science" presented to the Royal Society in the mid-eighteenth century?

Source: "An Account of a Particular Species of Cocoon, or Silk-Pod, from America," Reverend Samuel Pullein, M.A., *Philosophical Transactions of the Royal Society* 15 (1759): 54–57.

---

pires expanded. (See "Primary Source 16.2: 'An Account of a Particular Species of Cocoon,'" above.)

Audiences at home eagerly read the accounts of naturalists, who braved the heat, insects, and diseases of tropical jungles to bring home exotic animal, vegetable, and mineral specimens. They heard much less about the many indigenous guides, translators, and practitioners of medicine and science who made these expeditions possible and who contributed rich local knowledge about animal and plant species. In this period the craze for collecting natural history specimens in Europe extended from aristocratic lords to middle-class amateurs. Many public museums, like the British Museum in London, began with the donation of a large private collection.

Science and Society

The rise of modern science had many consequences, some of which are still unfolding. First, it went hand in hand with the rise of a new social group—the international scientific community. Members of this community were linked together by common interests and shared values as well as by journals and the learned scientific societies founded in many countries in the late seventeenth and eighteenth centuries. The personal success of scientists and scholars depended on making new discoveries, and science became competitive. Second, as governments intervened to support and sometimes direct research, the new scientific community became closely tied to the state and its agendas, a development strongly endorsed by Francis Bacon in England. In addition to England's Royal Society, academies of science were created under state sponsorship in Paris in 1666, Berlin in 1700, and later across Europe. At the same time, scientists developed a critical attitude toward established authority that would inspire thinkers to question traditions in other domains as well.

It was long believed that the Scientific Revolution had little relationship to practical concerns and the life of the masses until the late-eighteenth-century Industrial Revolution (see Chapter 20). More recently, historians have emphasized the crossover between the work of artisans and the rise of science, particularly in the development of the experimental method. Many craftsmen developed strong interest in emerging scientific ideas and, in turn, the practice of science in the seventeenth century often relied on artisans' expertise in making instruments and conducting precise experiments.

Some things did not change in the Scientific Revolution. Scholars have noted that nature was often depicted as a female, whose veil of secrecy needed to be stripped away and penetrated by male experts. New "rational" methods for approaching nature did not question traditional inequalities between the sexes— and may have worsened them in some ways. For example, the rise of universities and other professional institutions for science raised new barriers because most of these organizations did not accept women.

There were, however, a number of noteworthy exceptions. In Italy, universities and academies did offer posts to women, attracting some foreigners spurned at home. Women across Europe worked as makers of wax anatomical models and as botanical and zoological illustrators, like Maria Sibylla Merian. They were also very much involved in informal scientific communities, attending salons (see page 522), participating in scientific experiments, and writing learned treatises. Some female intellectuals became full-fledged members of the philosophical dialogue. In England, Margaret Cavendish, Anne Conway, and Mary Astell all contributed to debates about Descartes's mind-body dualism, among other issues. Descartes himself conducted an intellectual correspondence with the princess Elizabeth of Bohemia, of whom he stated: "I attach more weight to her judgment than to those messieurs the Doctors, who take for a rule of truth the opinions of Aristotle rather than the evidence of reason."[6]

Metamorphoses of the Caterpillar and Moth   Maria Sibylla Merian (1647–1717), the stepdaughter of a Dutch painter, became a celebrated scientific illustrator in her own right. Her finely observed pictures of insects in the South American colony of Suriname introduced many new species. For Merian, science was intimately tied with art: she not only painted but also bred caterpillars and performed experiments on them. Her two-year stay in Suriname, accompanied by a teenage daughter, was a daring feat for a seventeenth-century woman. (akg-images)

By the time Louis XIV died in 1715, many of the scientific ideas that would eventually coalesce into a new worldview had been assembled. Yet Christian Europe was still strongly attached to its established political and social structures and its traditional spiritual beliefs. By 1775, however, a large portion of western Europe's educated elite had embraced the new ideas. This was the work of many men and women across Europe who participated in the Enlightenment, either as publishers, writers, and distributors of texts or as members of the eager public that consumed them.

The Enlightenment

What new ideas about society and human relations emerged in the Enlightenment, and what new practices and institutions enabled these ideas to take hold?

The Scientific Revolution was a crucial factor in the creation of the new worldview of the eighteenth-century **Enlightenment**. This worldview, which has played a large role in shaping the modern mind, grew out of a rich mix of diverse and often conflicting ideas that were debated in international networks. Despite the diversity, three central concepts stand at the core of Enlightenment thinking. The first and foremost idea was that the methods of natural science could and should be used to examine and understand all aspects of life. This was what intellectuals meant by *reason*, a favorite word of Enlightenment thinkers. Nothing was to be accepted on faith; everything was to be submitted to **rationalism**, a secular, critical way of thinking. A second important Enlightenment concept was that the scientific method was capable of discovering the laws of human society as well as those of nature. These tenets led to the third key idea, that of progress. Armed with the proper method of discovering the laws of human existence, Enlightenment thinkers believed, it was at least possible for human beings to create better societies and better people.

The Emergence of the Enlightenment

Loosely united by certain key ideas, the European Enlightenment (ca. 1690–1789) was a broad intellectual and cultural movement that gained strength gradually and did not reach its maturity until about 1750. Yet it was the generation that came of age between the publication of Newton's *Principia* in 1687 and the death of Louis XIV in 1715 that tied the crucial knot between the Scientific Revolution and a new outlook on life. Whereas medieval and Reformation thinkers had been concerned primarily with abstract concepts of sin and salvation, and Renaissance humanists had drawn their inspiration from the classical past, Enlightenment thinkers believed that their era had gone far beyond antiquity and that intellectual progress was very possible. Talented writers of that genera-

Enlightenment The influential intellectual and cultural movement of the late seventeenth and eighteenth centuries that introduced a new worldview based on the use of reason, the scientific method, and progress.

rationalism A secular, critical way of thinking in which nothing was to be accepted on faith, and everything was to be submitted to reason.

tion popularized hard-to-understand scientific achievements and set an agenda of human problems to be addressed through the methods of science.

Like the Scientific Revolution, the Enlightenment was also fueled by Europe's increased contacts with the wider world. In the wake of the great discoveries of the fifteenth and sixteenth centuries, the rapidly growing travel literature taught Europeans that the peoples of China, India, Africa, and the Americas all had their own very different beliefs and customs. Europeans shaved their faces and let their hair grow. Turks shaved their heads and let their beards grow. In Europe a man bowed before a woman to show respect. In Siam a man turned his back on a woman when he met her because it was disrespectful to look directly at her. Countless similar examples discussed in travel accounts helped change the perspective of educated Europeans. They began to look at truth and morality in relative, rather than absolute, terms. If anything was possible, who could say what was right or wrong?

The excitement of the Scientific Revolution also generated doubt and uncertainty, contributing to a widespread crisis in late-seventeenth-century European thought. In the wake of the devastation wrought by the Thirty Years' War, some people asked whether ideological conformity in religious matters was really necessary. Others skeptically asked if religious truth could ever be known with absolute certainty and concluded that it could not. The atmosphere of doubt spread from religious to political issues. This was a natural extension, since many rulers viewed religious dissent as a form of political opposition and took harsh measures to stifle unorthodox forms of worship. Thus, questioning religion inevitably led to confrontations with the state.

These concerns combined spectacularly in the career of Pierre Bayle (1647–1706), a French Protestant, or Huguenot, who took refuge from government persecution in the tolerant Dutch Republic. Bayle critically examined the religious beliefs and persecutions of the past in his *Historical and Critical Dictionary* (1697). Demonstrating that human beliefs had been extremely varied and very often mistaken, he concluded that nothing can ever be known beyond all doubt, a view known as skepticism. His very influential *Dictionary* was found in more private libraries of eighteenth-century France than any other book.

Like Bayle, many Huguenots fled France for the Dutch Republic, a center of early Enlightenment thought for people of many faiths. The Dutch Jewish philosopher Baruch Spinoza (1632–1677) borrowed Descartes's emphasis on rationalism and his methods of deductive reasoning, but rejected the French thinker's mind-body dualism. Instead, Spinoza came to believe that mind and body are united in one substance and that God and nature were merely two names for the same thing. He envisioned a deterministic universe in which good and evil were merely relative values and our actions were shaped by outside circumstances, not free will. Spinoza was excommunicated by the relatively large Jewish community of Amsterdam for his controversial religious ideas, but he was heralded by his Enlightenment successors as a model of personal virtue and courageous intellectual autonomy.

The German philosopher and mathematician Gottfried Wilhelm von Leibniz (1646–1716), who had developed calculus independently of Isaac Newton (see page 511), refuted both Cartesian dualism and Spinoza's monism (the idea that there is only one substance in the universe). Instead, he adopted the idea of an infinite number of substances or "monads" from which all matter is composed. His *Theodicy* (1710) declared that ours must be "the best of all possible worlds" because it was created by an omnipotent and benevolent God. Leibniz's optimism was later ridiculed by the French philosopher Voltaire in *Candide or Optimism* (1759).

Out of this period of intellectual turmoil came John Locke's *Essay Concerning Human Understanding* (1690). In this work Locke (1632–1704), a physician and member of the Royal Society, brilliantly set forth a new theory about how human beings learn and form their ideas. Whereas Descartes, Spinoza, and Leibniz based their philosophies on deductive logic, Locke insisted that all ideas are derived from experience. The human mind at birth is like a blank tablet, or tabula rasa, on which the environment writes the individual's understanding and beliefs. Human development is therefore determined by education and social institutions. Locke's essay contributed to the theory of sensationalism, the idea that all human ideas and thoughts are produced as a result of sensory impressions. With his emphasis on the role of perception in the acquisition of knowledge, Locke provided a systematic justification of Bacon's emphasis on the importance of observation and experimentation. The *Essay Concerning Human Understanding* passed through many editions and translations and, along with Newton's *Principia*, was one of the dominant intellectual inspirations of the Enlightenment. Locke's equally important contribution to political theory, *Two Treatises of Civil Government* (1690), insisted on the sovereignty of the elected Parliament against the authority of the Crown (see Chapter 15).

The Influence of the Philosophes

Divergences among the early thinkers of the Enlightenment show that, while they shared many of the same premises and questions, the answers they found differed widely. The spread of this spirit of inquiry and debate owed a great deal to the work of the **philosophes** (fee-luh-ZAWFZ), a group of intellectuals who proudly proclaimed that they, at long last, were bringing the light of reason to their ignorant fellow humans. *Philosophe* is the French word for "philosopher," and in the mid-eighteenth century France became a hub of Enlightenment thought. There were at least three reasons for this. First, French was the international language of the educated classes, and France was the wealthiest and most populous country in Europe. Second, the rising unpopularity of King Louis XV and his mistresses generated growing discontent and calls for reform among the educated elite. Third, the French philosophes made it their goal to reach a larger audience of elites, many of whom were joined together in a concept inherited from the Renaissance known as the Republic of Letters—an imaginary transnational realm of the well educated.

One of the greatest philosophes, the baron de Montesquieu (mahn-tuhs-KYOO) (1689–1755), brilliantly pioneered this approach in *The Persian Letters*, an extremely influential social satire published in 1721 and considered the first major work of the French Enlightenment. It consisted of amusing letters supposedly written by two Persian travelers who as outsiders saw European customs in unique ways, thereby allowing Montesquieu a vantage point for criticizing existing practices and beliefs.

Having gained fame by using wit as a weapon against cruelty and superstition, Montesquieu turned to the study of history and politics. His interest was partly personal, for, like many members of the French robe nobility, he was disturbed by the growth in absolutism under Louis XIV (see Chapter 15). But Montesquieu was also inspired by the example of the physical sciences, and he set out to apply the critical method to the problem of government in *The Spirit of Laws* (1748). The result was a complex, comparative study of republics, monarchies, and despotisms.

Showing that forms of government were shaped by history and geography, Montesquieu focused on the conditions that would promote liberty and prevent tyranny. He argued for a separation of powers, with political power divided and shared by a variety of classes and legal estates. Admiring greatly the English balance of power, Montesquieu believed that in France the thirteen high courts—the *parlements*—were frontline defenders of liberty against royal despotism. Apprehensive about the uneducated poor, Montesquieu was clearly no democrat, but his theory of separation of powers had a great impact on the constitutions

philosophes A group of French intellectuals who proclaimed that they were bringing the light of knowledge to their fellow humans in the Age of Enlightenment.

of the young United States in 1789 and of France in 1791.

The most famous and perhaps most representative philosophe was François Marie Arouet, who was known by the pen name Voltaire (vohl-TAIR) (1694–1778). In his long career, this son of a comfortable middle-class family wrote more than seventy witty volumes, hobnobbed with royalty, and died a millionaire through shrewd speculations. His early career, however, was turbulent, and he was arrested on two occasions for insulting noblemen. Voltaire moved to England for three years in order to avoid a longer prison term in France, and there he came to share Montesquieu's enthusiasm for English liberties and institutions.

Returning to France, Voltaire had the great fortune of meeting Gabrielle-Emilie Le Tonnelier de Breteuil, marquise du Châtelet (SHAH-tuh-lay) (1706–1749), a noblewoman with a passion for science. Inviting

Madame du Châtelet The marquise du Châtelet was fascinated by the new world system of Isaac Newton. She helped spread Newton's ideas in France by translating his *Principia* and by influencing Voltaire, her companion for fifteen years until her death. (Private Collection/The Bridgeman Art Library)

Voltaire to live in her country house at Cirey in Lorraine and becoming his long-time companion (under the eyes of her tolerant husband), Madame du Châtelet studied physics and mathematics and published scientific articles and translations, including the first—and only—translation of Newton's *Principia* into French. (See "Primary Source 16.3: Du Châtelet, *Foundations of Physics*," at right.) Excluded from the Royal Academy of Sciences because she was a woman, Madame du Châtelet had no doubt that women's limited role in science was due to their unequal education. Discussing what she would do if she were a ruler, she wrote, "I would reform an abuse which cuts off, so to speak, half the human race. I would make women participate in all the rights of humankind, and above all in those of the intellect."[7]

While living at Cirey, Voltaire wrote works praising England and popularizing English science. He had witnessed Newton's burial at Westminster Abbey in 1727, and he lauded Newton as history's greatest man, for he had used his genius for the benefit of humanity. In the true style of the Enlightenment, Voltaire mixed the glorification of science and reason with an appeal for better individuals and institutions.

Yet, like almost all of the philosophes, Voltaire was a reformer, not a revolutionary, in politics. He pessimistically concluded that the best one could hope for in the way of government was a good monarch, since human beings "are very rarely worthy to govern themselves." He lavishly praised Louis XIV and conducted an enthusiastic correspondence with King Frederick the Great of Prussia, whom he admired as an enlightened monarch (see page 530). Nor did Voltaire believe in social and economic equality, insisting that the idea of making servants equal to their masters was "absurd and impossible." The only realizable equality, Voltaire thought, was that "by which the citizen only depends on the laws which protect the freedom of the feeble against the ambitions of the strong."[8]

Voltaire's philosophical and religious positions were much more radical than his social and political beliefs. In the tradition of Bayle, his writings challenged the Catholic Church and Christian theology at almost every point. Voltaire clearly believed in God, but, like many eighteenth-century Enlightenment thinkers, he was a deist, envisioning God as akin to a clockmaker

Du Châtelet, *Foundations of Physics*

Gabrielle-Emilie Le Tonnelier de Breteuil, marquise du Châtelet, was a French noblewoman. Frustrated by her limited education as a girl, she befriended philosophes, studied advanced calculus and analytic geometry, and assiduously read the latest scientific publications. Madame du Châtelet translated Newton's Principia *into French and offered her own commentary on his ideas. The passage below is from her* Foundations of Physics *(1740), an overview of natural philosophy that she wrote for her son's education. She died of complications of childbirth at the age of forty-two.*

❝ Descartes appeared in that profound night like a star come to illuminate the universe. The revolution that this great man caused in the sciences is surely more useful, and perhaps even more memorable, than that of the greatest empires, one, it can be said, that human reason owes most to Descartes. For it is very much easier to find the truth, when once one is on the track of it, than to leave those of error. The geometry of this great man, his dioptrics, his method, are masterpieces of sagacity that will make his name immortal, and if he was wrong on some points of physics, that was because he was a man, and it is not given to a single man, nor to a single century, to know all.

We rise to the knowledge of the truth, like those giants who climbed up to the skies by standing on the shoulders of one another.* The Huygenses,† and the Leibnizes learned from Descartes and Galileo, these great men who, so far, are known to you only by name, and with whose works I hope soon to make you acquainted. It is by making the most of the works of Kepler, and using the theorems of Huygens, that M. Newton discovered this universal force spread throughout nature, which makes the planets circle around the Sun, and that operates as gravity on Earth. . . .

Today the systems of Descartes and Newton divide the thinking world, so you should know the one and the other; but so many learned men have taken care to expound and to correct Descartes' system that it will be easy for you to learn from their works. One of my aims in the first part of this work is to put before your eyes the other part of this great process, to make you acquainted with the system of M. Newton, to show you how far making connections and determining probability are pushed, and how the phenomena are explained by the hypothesis of attraction. . . .

Guard yourself, my son, whichever side you take in this dispute among the philosophers, against the inevitable obstinacy to which the spirit of partisanship carries one: this frame of mind is dangerous on all occasions of life; but it is ridiculous in physics. The search for truth is the only thing in which the love of your country must not prevail, and it is surely very unfortunate that the opinions of Newton and of Descartes have become a sort of national affair. About a book of physics one must ask if it is good, not if the author is English, German, or French. ❞

EVALUATE THE EVIDENCE

1. How does Madame du Châtelet explain progress in the physical sciences? What guidance does she offer her son in choosing between Descartes and Newton?
2. What support does this passage provide for the "international" character of the Scientific Revolution? Does this passage suggest any commonalities between the Scientific Revolution and the Enlightenment?

*Here, Madame du Châtelet echoes the famous statement of Newton from a 1676 letter to Robert Hooke, an English scientist.

†Christiaan Huygens (1629–1695) was a Dutch astronomer, physicist, and mathematician who observed the correct shape of the rings of Saturn and patented the first pendulum clock.

Source: Emilie Du Châtelet, *Selected Philosophical and Scientific Writings*, ed. Judith P. Zinsser, trans. Isabelle Bour and Judith P. Zinsser, pp. 118–120. Copyright © 1992 by Cambridge University Press. All rights reserved. Used by permission of University of Chicago Press.

---

who set the universe in motion and then ceased to intervene in human affairs. Above all, Voltaire and most of the philosophes hated all forms of religious intolerance, which they believed led to fanaticism. Simple piety and human kindness—as embodied in Christ's commandments to "love God and your neighbor as yourself"—were religion enough.

The ultimate strength of the philosophes lay in their dedication and organization. The philosophes felt keenly that they were engaged in a common undertaking that transcended individuals. Their greatest and most representative intellectual achievement was, quite fittingly, a group effort—the seventeen-volume *Encyclopedia: The Rational Dictionary of the Sciences, the Arts, and the Crafts*, edited by Denis Diderot (DEE-duh-roh) (1713–1784) and Jean le Rond d'Alembert (dah-luhm-BEHR) (1717–1783). From different circles and with different interests, the two men set out to find coauthors who would examine the rapidly expanding whole of human knowledge. Even more fundamentally, they set out to teach people how to think critically and objectively about all matters. As Diderot said, he wanted the *Encyclopedia* to "change the general way of thinking."[9]

The *Encyclopedia* survived initial resistance from the French government and the Catholic Church. Published between 1751 and 1772, it contained seventy-two thousand articles by leading scientists, writers, skilled workers, and progressive priests, and it treated every aspect of life and knowledge. Not every article was daring or original, but the overall effect was little short of revolutionary. Science and the industrial arts were exalted, religion and immortality questioned. Intolerance, legal injustice, and out-of-date social institutions were openly criticized. The encyclopedists were convinced that greater knowledge would result in greater human happiness, for knowledge was useful and made possible economic, social, and political progress. Summing up the new worldview of the Enlightenment, the *Encyclopedia* was widely read, especially in less-expensive reprint editions, and it was extremely influential.

Jean-Jacques Rousseau

In the early 1740s Jean-Jacques Rousseau (1712–1778), the son of a poor Swiss watchmaker, made his way into the Parisian Enlightenment through his brilliant intellect. He contributed articles on music to the *Encyclopedia* and became friends with its editors. Appealing but neurotic, Rousseau came to believe that the philosophes were plotting against him. In the mid-1750s he broke with them, living thereafter as a lonely outsider with his uneducated common-law wife and going in his own highly original direction.

Like other Enlightenment thinkers, Rousseau was passionately committed to individual freedom. Unlike them, however, he attacked rationalism and civilization as destroying, rather than liberating, the individual. Warm, spontaneous feeling had to complement and correct cold intellect. Moreover, the basic goodness of the individual and the unspoiled child had to be protected from the cruel refinements of civilization. Rousseau's ideals greatly influenced the early romantic movement, which rebelled against the culture of the Enlightenment in the late eighteenth century.

Rousseau also called for a rigid division of gender roles. According to Rousseau, women and men were radically different beings. Destined by nature to assume a passive role in sexual relations, women should also be subordinate in social life. Women's love for displaying themselves in public, attending social gatherings, and pulling the strings of power was unnatural and had a corrupting effect on both politics and society. Rousseau thus rejected the sophisticated way of life of Parisian elite women. His criticism led to calls for privileged women to renounce their frivolous ways and stay at home to care for their children.

Rousseau's contribution to political theory in *The Social Contract* (1762) was based on two fundamental concepts: the general will and popular sovereignty. According to Rousseau, the general will is sacred and absolute, reflecting the common interests of all the people, who have displaced the monarch as the holder of sovereign power. The general will is not necessarily the will of the majority, however. At times the general will may be the authentic, long-term needs of the people as correctly interpreted by a farsighted minority. Little noticed in its day, Rousseau's concept of the general will had a great impact on the political aspirations of the American and French Revolutions. Rousseau was both one of the most influential voices of the Enlightenment and, in his rejection of rationalism and social discourse, a harbinger of reaction against Enlightenment ideas.

The International Enlightenment

The Enlightenment was a movement of international dimensions, with thinkers traversing borders in a constant exchange of visits, letters, and printed materials. Voltaire alone wrote almost eighteen thousand letters to correspondents in France and across Europe. The Republic of Letters was a truly cosmopolitan set of networks stretching from western Europe to its colonies in the Americas, to Russia and eastern Europe, and along the routes of trade and empire to Africa and Asia.

Within this broad international conversation, scholars have identified regional and national particularities. Outside of France, many strains of Enlightenment—Protestant, Catholic, and Jewish—sought to reconcile reason with faith, rather than emphasizing the errors of religious fanaticism and intolerance. Some scholars point to a distinctive "Catholic Enlightenment" that aimed to renew and reform the church from within, looking to divine grace rather than human will as the source of progress.

The Scottish Enlightenment, which was centered in Edinburgh, was marked by an emphasis on common sense and scientific reasoning. After the Act of Union with England in 1707, Scotland was freed from political crisis to experience a vigorous period of intellectual growth. Scottish intellectual revival was also stimulated by the creation of the first public educational system in Europe.

A central figure in Edinburgh was David Hume (1711–1776), whose emphasis on civic morality and religious skepticism had a powerful impact at home and abroad. Building on Locke's teachings on learning, Hume argued that the human mind is really nothing but a bundle of impressions. These impressions originate only in sensory experiences and our habits of joining these experiences together. Since our ideas ultimately reflect only our sensory experiences, our reason cannot tell us anything about questions that cannot be verified by sensory experience (in the form of controlled experiments or mathematics), such as the origin of the universe or the existence of God. Paradoxically, Hume's rationalistic inquiry ended up undermining the Enlightenment's faith in the power of reason.

Another major figure of the Scottish Enlightenment was Adam Smith. His *Theory of Moral Sentiments* (1759) argued that the thriving commercial life of the eighteenth century produced civic virtue through the values of competition, fair play, and individual autonomy. In *An Inquiry into the Nature and Causes of the Wealth of Nations* (1776), Smith attacked the laws and regulations that, he argued, prevented commerce from reaching its full capacity (see Chapter 17).

The Enlightenment in British North America was heavily influenced by English and Scottish thinkers, especially John Locke, and by Montesquieu's arguments for checks and balances in government. Leaders of the American Enlightenment, including Benjamin Franklin and Thomas Jefferson, would play a leading role in the American Revolution (see Chapter 19).

After 1760 Enlightenment ideas were hotly debated in the German-speaking states, often in dialogue with Christian theology. Immanuel Kant (1724–1804), a professor in East Prussia, was the greatest German philosopher of his day. Kant posed the question of the age when he published a pamphlet in 1784 entitled *What Is Enlightenment?* He answered, "*Sapere Aude* [dare to know]! 'Have the courage to use your own understanding' is therefore the motto of enlightenment." He argued that if intellectuals were granted the freedom to exercise their reason publicly in print, enlightenment would almost surely follow. Kant was no revolutionary; he also insisted that in their private lives, individuals must obey all laws, no matter how unreasonable, and should be punished for "impertinent" criticism. Like other Enlightenment figures in central and east-central Europe, Kant thus tried to reconcile absolute monarchical authority and religious faith with a critical public sphere.

Major Figures of the Enlightenment

Baruch Spinoza (1632–1677)	Early Enlightenment thinker excommunicated from the Jewish religion for his concept of a deterministic universe
John Locke (1632–1704)	*Essay Concerning Human Understanding* (1690)
Gottfried Wilhelm von Leibniz (1646–1716)	German philosopher and mathematician known for his optimistic view of the universe
Pierre Bayle (1647–1706)	*Historical and Critical Dictionary* (1697)
Montesquieu (1689–1755)	*The Persian Letters* (1721); *The Spirit of Laws* (1748)
Voltaire (1694–1778)	Renowned French philosophe and author of more than seventy works
David Hume (1711–1776)	Central figure of the Scottish Enlightenment; *Of Natural Characters* (1748)
Jean-Jacques Rousseau (1712–1778)	*The Social Contract* (1762)
Denis Diderot (1713–1784) and Jean le Rond d'Alembert (1717–1783)	Editors of *Encyclopedia: The Rational Dictionary of the Sciences, the Arts, and the Crafts* (1751–1772)
Adam Smith (1723–1790)	*The Theory of Moral Sentiments* (1759); *An Inquiry into the Nature and Causes of the Wealth of Nations* (1776)
Immanuel Kant (1724–1804)	*What Is Enlightenment?* (1784); *On the Different Races of Man* (1775)
Moses Mendelssohn (1729–1786)	Major philosopher of the Haskalah, or Jewish Enlightenment
Cesare Beccaria (1738–1794)	*On Crimes and Punishments* (1764)

Northern Europeans often regarded the Italian states as culturally backward, yet important developments in Enlightenment thought took place in the Italian peninsula. After achieving independence from Habsburg rule (1734), the kingdom of Naples entered a period of intellectual expansion as reformers struggled to lift the heavy weight of church and noble power. In northern Italy a central figure was Cesare Beccaria (1738–1794), a nobleman educated at Jesuit schools and the University of Pavia. His *On Crimes and Punishments* (1764) was a passionate plea for reform of the penal system that decried the use of torture, arbitrary imprisonment, and capital punishment, and advocated the prevention of crime over the reliance on punishment. The text was quickly translated into French and English and made an impact throughout Europe.

Urban Culture and Life in the Public Sphere

Enlightenment ideas did not float on thin air. A series of new institutions and practices encouraged the spread of enlightened ideas in the late seventeenth and eighteenth centuries. First, the European production and consumption of books grew significantly. In Germany, for example, the number of new titles appearing annually rose from roughly six hundred in 1700 to twenty-six hundred in 1780. Moreover, the types of books people read changed dramatically. The proportion of religious and devotional books published in Paris declined after 1750; history and law held constant; the arts and sciences surged.

reading revolution The transition in Europe from a society where literacy consisted of patriarchal and communal reading of religious texts to a society where literacy was commonplace and reading material was broad and diverse.

salon Regular social gathering held by talented and rich Parisians in their homes, where philosophes and their followers met to discuss literature, science, and philosophy.

Reading more books on many more subjects, the educated public approached reading in a new way. The result was what some scholars have called a **reading revolution**. The old style of reading in Europe had been centered on a core of sacred texts that taught earthly duty and obedience to God. Reading had been patriarchal and communal, with the father slowly reading the text aloud to his assembled family. Now reading involved a broader field of books that constantly changed. Reading became individual and silent, and texts could be questioned. Subtle but profound, the reading revolution ushered in new ways of relating to the written word.

Conversation, discussion, and debate also played a critical role in the Enlightenment. Evolving from the gatherings presided over by the *précieuses* in the late seventeenth century (see Chapter 15), the **salon** was a regular meeting held in the elegant private drawing rooms (or salons) of talented, wealthy men and women. There they encouraged the exchange of witty observations on literature, science, and philosophy among great aristocrats, wealthy middle-class finan-

The French Book Trade Book consumption surged in the eighteenth century and, along with it, new bookstores. This appealing bookshop in France with its intriguing ads for the latest works offers to put customers "Under the Protection of Minerva," the Roman goddess of wisdom. Large packets of books sit ready for shipment to foreign countries. (akg-images/De Agostini Picture Library)

Enlightenment Culture

An actor performs the first reading of a new play by Voltaire at the salon of Madame Geoffrin. Voltaire, then in exile, is represented by a bust statue.

(Académie des Sciences, Belles-Lettres, Rouen, France/Giraudon/The Bridgeman Art Library)

EVALUATE THE EVIDENCE

1. Which of these people do you think is the hostess, Madame Geoffrin, and why? Using details from the painting to support your answer, how would you describe the status of the people shown?

2. What does this image suggest about the reach of Enlightenment ideas to common people? To women? Does the painting of the bookstore on page 522 suggest a broader reach? Why?

ciers, high-ranking officials, and noteworthy foreigners. Many of the most celebrated salons were hosted by women, known as *salonnières* (sah-lahn-ee-EHRZ), such as Madame du Deffand, whose weekly Parisian salon included such guests as Montesquieu, d'Alembert, and Benjamin Franklin, then serving as the first U.S. ambassador to France. Invitations to salons were highly coveted; introductions to the rich and powerful could make the career of an ambitious writer, and, in turn, the social elite found amusement and cultural prestige in their ties to up-and-coming artists and men of letters. (See "Primary Source 16.4: Enlightenment Culture," above.)

The salon thus represented an accommodation between the ruling classes and the leaders of Enlightenment thought. Salons were sites in which the philosophes, the French nobility, and the prosperous middle classes intermingled and influenced one another while maintaining due deference to social rank. Critical thought about almost any question became fashionable and flourished alongside hopes for human progress through greater knowledge and enlightened public opinion.

Elite women also exercised great influence on artistic taste. Soft pastels, ornate interiors, sentimental portraits, and starry-eyed lovers protected by hovering cupids were all hallmarks of the style they favored. This style, known as **rococo** (ruh-KOH-koh), was popular throughout Europe in the period from 1720 to 1780. It has been argued that feminine influence in the drawing room went hand in hand with the emergence of polite society and the general attempt to civilize a rough military nobility. Similarly, some philosophes championed greater rights and expanded education for women, claiming that the position and treatment of women were the best indicators of a society's level of civilization and decency.[10] For these male philosophes, greater rights for women did not mean equal rights, and the philosophes were not particularly disturbed by the fact that elite women remained legally subordinate to men in economic and political affairs. Elite women lacked many rights, but so did the majority of European men, who were poor.

While membership at the salons was restricted to the well-born, the well connected, and the exceptionally talented, a number of institutions provided the rest of society with access to Enlightenment ideas. Lending libraries served an important function for people who could not afford their own books. The coffeehouses that first appeared in the late seventeenth century became meccas of philosophical discussion. (See "Living in the Past: Coffeehouse Culture," page 526.) In addition to these institutions, book clubs, debating societies, Masonic lodges (groups of Freemasons, a secret society that accepted craftsmen and shopkeepers as well as middle-class men and nobles), and newspapers all played roles in the creation of a new **public sphere** that celebrated open debate informed by critical reason. The public sphere was an idealized space where members of society came together as individuals to discuss issues relevant to the society, economics, and politics of the day.

What of the common people? Did they participate in the Enlightenment? Enlightenment philosophes did not direct their message to peasants or urban laborers. They believed that the masses had no time or talent for philosophical speculation and that elevating them would be a long and potentially dangerous process. Deluded by superstitions and driven by violent passions, the people, they thought, were like children in need of firm parental guidance. D'Alembert characteristically made a sharp distinction between "the truly

rococo A popular style in Europe in the eighteenth century, known for its soft pastels, ornate interiors, sentimental portraits, and starry-eyed lovers protected by hovering cupids.

public sphere An idealized intellectual space that emerged in Europe during the Enlightenment, where the public came together to discuss important issues relating to society, economics, and politics.

enlightened public" and "the blind and noisy multitude."[11] Despite these prejudices, the ideas of the philosophes did find an audience among some members of the common people. At a time of rising literacy, book prices were dropping and many philosophical ideas were popularized in cheap pamphlets and through public reading. Although they were barred from salons and academies, ordinary people were not immune to the new ideas in circulation.

Race and the Enlightenment

If philosophers did not believe the lower classes qualified for enlightenment, how did they regard individuals of different races? In recent years, historians have found in the Scientific Revolution and the Enlightenment a crucial turning point in European ideas about race. A primary catalyst for new ideas about race was the urge to classify nature unleashed by the Scientific Revolution's insistence on careful empirical observation. In *The System of Nature* (1735), Swedish botanist Carl von Linné argued that nature was organized into a God-given hierarchy. As scientists developed taxonomies of plant and animal species, they also began to classify humans into hierarchically ordered "races" and to investigate the origins of race. The comte de Buffon (komt duh buh-FOHN) argued that humans originated with one species that then developed into distinct races due largely to climatic conditions.

Enlightenment thinkers such as David Hume and Immanuel Kant helped popularize these ideas. In *Of Natural Characters* (1748), Hume wrote:

> I am apt to suspect the negroes and in general all other species of men (for there are four or five different kinds) to be naturally inferior to the whites. There never was a civilized nation of any other complexion than white, nor even any individual eminent amongst them, no arts, no sciences. . . . Such a uniform and constant difference could not happen, in so many countries and ages if nature had not made an original distinction between these breeds of men.[12]

Kant taught and wrote as much about "anthropology" and "geography" as he did about standard philosophical themes such as logic, metaphysics, and moral philosophy. He elaborated his views about race in *On the Different Races of Man* (1775), claiming that there were four human races, each of which had derived from an original race. According to Kant, the closest descendants of the original race were the white inhabitants of northern Germany. (Scientists now believe the human race originated in Africa.)

Using the word *race* to designate biologically distinct groups of humans, akin to distinct animal spe-

***Encyclopedia* Image of the Cotton Industry**   This romanticized image of slavery in the West Indies cotton industry was published in Diderot and d'Alembert's *Encyclopedia*. It shows enslaved men, at right, gathering and picking over cotton bolls, while the woman at left mills the bolls to remove their seeds. The *Encyclopedia* presented mixed views on slavery; one article described it as "indispensable" to economic development, while others argued passionately for the natural right to freedom of all mankind. (Courtesy, Dover Publications)

cies, was new. Previously, Europeans grouped other peoples into "nations" based on their historical, political, and cultural affiliations, rather than on supposedly innate physical differences. Unsurprisingly, when European thinkers drew up a hierarchical classification of human species, their own "race" was placed at the top. Europeans had long believed they were culturally superior to "barbaric" peoples in Africa and, since 1492, the New World. Now emerging ideas about racial difference taught them they were biologically superior as well. In turn, scientific racism helped legitimate and justify the tremendous growth of slavery that occurred during the eighteenth century. If one "race" of humans was fundamentally different and inferior, its members could be seen as particularly fit for enslavement and liable to benefit from tutelage by the superior race.

Racist ideas did not go unchallenged. The abbé Raynal's *History of the Two Indies* (1770) fiercely attacked slavery and the abuses of European colonization. *Encyclopedia* editor Denis Diderot adopted Montesquieu's technique of criticizing European attitudes through the voice of outsiders in his dialogue between Tahitian villagers and their European visitors. (See "Primary Source 16.5: Denis Diderot, 'Supplement to Bougainville's Voyage,'" page 528.) Scottish philosopher James Beattie (1735–1803) responded directly to claims of white superiority by pointing out that Europeans had started out as savage as nonwhites supposedly were and that many non-European peoples in the Americas, Asia, and Africa had achieved high levels of civilization. Former slaves, like Olaudah Equiano (see Chapter 17) and Ottobah Cugoana, published eloquent memoirs testifying to the horrors of slavery and the innate equality of all humans. These challenges to racism, however, were in the minority. Many other Enlightenment voices supporting racial inequality—Thomas Jefferson among them—may be found.

Scholars are only at the beginning of efforts to understand the links between Enlightenment thinkers'

LIVING IN THE PAST
Coffeehouse Culture

Customers in today's coffee shops may be surprised to learn that they are participating in a centuries-old institution that has contributed a great deal to the idea of "modernity." Tradition has it that an Ethiopian goatherd first discovered coffee when he noticed that his goats became frisky and danced after consuming the berries. Botanists agree that coffee probably originated in Ethiopia and then spread to Yemen and across the Arabian peninsula by around 1000 C.E. In 1457 the first public coffeehouse opened in Istanbul, and from there coffeehouses became a popular institution throughout the Muslim world.

European travelers in Istanbul were astonished at its inhabitants' passion for coffee, which one described as "blacke as soote, and tasting not much unlike it."* However, Italian merchants introduced coffee to Europe around 1600, and the first European coffee shop opened in Venice in 1645, soon followed by shops in Oxford, England, in 1650, London in 1652, and Paris in 1672. By the 1730s coffee shops had become so popular in London that one observer noted, "There are some people of moderate Fortunes, that lead their Lives mostly in Coffee-Houses, they eat, drink and sleep (in the Day-time) in them."†

Coffeehouses helped spread the ideas and values of the Scientific Revolution and the Enlightenment. They provided a new public space where urban Europeans could learn about and debate the issues of the day. Within a few years, each political party, philosophical sect, scientific society, and literary circle had its own coffeehouse, which served as

Seventeenth-century English coffeehouse. (The Granger Collection, NY)

*Quoted in Markman Ellis, *The Coffee House: A Cultural History* (London: Phoenix, 2004), p. 8.
†Quoted ibid, p. 198.

a central gathering point for its members and an informal recruiting site for new ones. Coffeehouses self-consciously distinguished themselves from the rowdy atmosphere of the tavern; whereas alcohol dulled the senses, coffee sharpened the mind for discussion.

European coffeehouses also played a key role in the development of modern business, as their proprietors began to provide specialized commercial news to attract customers. Lloyd's of London, the famous insurance company, got its start in the shipping lists published by coffeehouse owner Edward Lloyd in the 1690s. The streets around London's stock exchange were crowded with coffeehouses where merchants and traders congregated to strike deals and hear the latest news.

Coffeehouses succeeded in Europe because they met a need common to politics, business, and intellectual life: the spread and sharing of information. In the late seventeenth century newspapers were rare and expensive, there were few banks to guarantee credit, and politics was limited to a tiny elite. To break through these constraints, people needed reliable information. The coffeehouse was an ideal place to acquire it, along with a new kind of stimulant that provided the energy and attention to fuel a lively discussion.

QUESTIONS FOR ANALYSIS

1. What do the images shown here suggest about the customers of eighteenth-century coffeehouses? Who frequented these establishments? Who was excluded?
2. What limitations on the exchange of information existed in early modern Europe? Why were coffeehouses so useful as sites for exchanging information?
3. What social role do coffeehouses play where you live? Do you see any continuities with the eighteenth-century coffeehouse?

Eighteenth-century Viennese coffeehouse. (Erich Lessing/Art Resource, NY)

Denis Diderot,
"Supplement to Bougainville's Voyage"

Denis Diderot was born in a provincial town in eastern France and educated in Paris. Rejecting careers in the church and the law, he devoted himself to literature and philosophy. In 1749, sixty years before Charles Darwin's birth, Diderot was jailed by Parisian authorities for publishing an essay questioning God's role in creation and suggesting the autonomous evolution of species. Following these difficult beginnings, Diderot's editorial work and writing on the Encyclopedia *were the crowning intellectual achievements of his life and, according to some, of the Enlightenment itself.*

Like other philosophes, Diderot employed numerous genres to disseminate Enlightenment thought, ranging from scholarly articles in the Encyclopedia *to philosophical treatises, novels, plays, book reviews, and erotic stories. His "Supplement to Bougainville's Voyage" (1772) was a fictional account of a European voyage to Tahiti inspired by the writings of traveler Louis-Antoine de Bougainville. In this passage, Diderot expresses his own loathing of colonial conquest and exploitation through the voice of an elderly Tahitian man. The character's praise for his own culture allows Diderot to express his Enlightenment idealization of "natural man," free from the vices of civilized societies.*

❝ He was the father of a large family. When the Europeans arrived he looked upon them with scorn, showing neither astonishment, nor fear, nor curiosity. On their approach he turned his back and retired into his hut. Yet his silence and anxiety revealed his thoughts only too well; he was inwardly lamenting the eclipse of his countrymen's happiness. When Bougainville was leaving the island, as the natives swarmed on the shore, clutching his clothes, clasping his companions in their arms and weeping, the old man made his way forward and proclaimed solemnly, "Weep, wretched natives of Tahiti, weep. But let it be for the coming and not the leaving of these ambitious, wicked men. One day you will know them better. One day they will come back, bearing in one hand the piece of wood you see in that man's belt, and, in the other, the sword hanging by the side of that one, to enslave you, slaughter you, or make you captive

to their follies and vices. One day you will be subject to them, as corrupt, vile and miserable as they are. . . ."

Then turning to Bougainville, he continued, "And you, leader of the ruffians who obey you, pull your ship away swiftly from these shores. We are innocent, we are content, and you can only spoil that happiness. We follow the pure instincts of nature, and you have tried to erase its impression from our hearts. Here, everything belongs to everyone, and you have preached I can't tell what distinction between 'yours' and 'mine'. . . . If a Tahitian should one day land on your shores and engrave on one of your stones or on the bark of one of your trees, *This land belongs to the people of Tahiti*, what would you think then? You are stronger than we are, and what does that mean? When one of the miserable trinkets with which your ship is filled was taken away, what an uproar you made, what revenge you exacted! At that moment, in the depths of your heart, you were plotting the theft of an entire country! You are not a slave, you would rather die than be one, and yet you wish to make slaves of us. Do you suppose, then, that a Tahitian cannot defend his own liberty and die for it as well? This inhabitant of Tahiti, whom you wish to ensnare like an animal, is your brother. You are both children of Nature. What right do you have over him that he does not have over you? You came; did we attack you? Have we plundered your ship? Did we seize you and expose you to the arrows of our enemies? Did we harness you to work with our animals in the fields? We respected our own image in you.

"Leave us our ways; they are wiser and more decent than yours. We have no wish to exchange what you call our ignorance for your useless knowledge. Everything that we need and is good for us we already possess. Do we merit contempt because we have not learnt how to acquire superfluous needs? When we are hungry, we have enough to eat. When we are cold, we have enough to wear. You have entered our huts; what do you suppose we lack? Pursue as far as you wish what you call the comforts of life, but let sensible beings stop when they have no more to gain from their labours than imaginary benefits. If you persuade us to go beyond the strict bounds of necessity, when will we finish our work?

ideas about race and their notions of equality, progress, and reason. There are clear parallels, though, between the use of science to propagate racial hierarchies and its use to defend social inequalities between men and women. French philosopher Jean-Jacques Rousseau used women's "natural" passivity to argue for their subordinate role in society, just as other thinkers used non-Europeans' "natural" inferiority to defend slavery and colonial domination. The new powers of science and reason were thus marshaled to imbue traditional stereotypes with the force of natural law.

When will we enjoy ourselves? We have kept our annual and daily labours within the smallest possible limits, because in our eyes nothing is better than rest. Go back to your own country to agitate and torment yourselves as much as you like. But leave us in peace. Do not fill our heads with your factitious needs and illusory virtues. . . ." **"**

EVALUATE THE EVIDENCE

1. On what grounds does the speaker argue for the Tahitians' basic equality with the Europeans?
2. What is the good life according to the speaker, and how does it contrast with the European way of life? Which do you think is the better path?
3. In what ways could Diderot's thoughts here be seen as representative of Enlightenment ideas? Are there ways in which they are not?
4. How realistic do you think this account is? How might defenders of expansion respond?

Source: Edited excerpts from pp. 41–43 in Denis Diderot, *Political Writings*, translated and edited by John Hope Mason and Robert Wokler. Copyright © 1992 by Cambridge University Press. Reprinted by permission of Cambridge University Press.

Enlightened Absolutism

What impact did new ways of thinking have on political developments and monarchical absolutism?

How did the Enlightenment influence political developments? To this important question there is no easy answer. Most Enlightenment thinkers outside of England and the Netherlands, especially in central and eastern Europe, believed that political change could best come from above—from the ruler—rather than from below. Royal absolutism was a fact of life, and the monarchs of Europe's leading states clearly had no intention of giving up their great power. Therefore, the philosophes and their sympathizers realistically concluded that a benevolent absolutism offered the best opportunities for improving society.

Many government officials were interested in philosophical ideas. They were among the best-educated members of society, and their daily involvement in complex affairs of state made them naturally attracted to ideas for improving human society. Encouraged and instructed by these officials, some absolutist rulers tried to reform their governments in accordance with Enlightenment ideals— what historians have called the **enlightened absolutism** of the later eighteenth century. In both Catholic and Protestant lands, rulers typically fused Enlightenment principles with religion, drawing support for their innovations from reform-minded religious thinkers. The most influential of the new-style monarchs were in Prussia, Russia, and Austria, and their example illustrates both the achievements and the great limitations of enlightened absolutism. France experienced its own brand of enlightened absolutism in

enlightened absolutism
Term coined by historians to describe the rule of eighteenth-century monarchs who, without renouncing their own absolute authority, adopted Enlightenment ideals of rationalism, progress, and tolerance.

the contentious decades prior to the French Revolution (see Chapter 19).

Frederick the Great of Prussia

Frederick II (r. 1740–1786), commonly known as Frederick the Great, built masterfully on the work of his father, Frederick William I (see Chapter 15). Although in his youth he embraced culture and literature rather than the militarism championed by his father, by the time he came to the throne Frederick was determined to use the splendid army he had inherited.

Therefore, when the young empress Maria Theresa of Austria inherited the Habsburg dominions upon the death of her father Charles VI, Frederick pounced. He invaded her rich province of Silesia (sigh-LEE-zhuh), defying solemn Prussian promises to respect the Pragmatic Sanction, a diplomatic agreement that had guaranteed Maria Theresa's succession. In 1742, as other greedy powers vied for her lands in the European War of the Austrian Succession (1740–1748), Maria Theresa was forced to cede almost all of Silesia to Prussia. In one stroke Prussia had doubled its population to 6 million people. Now Prussia unquestionably stood as a European Great Power.

Though successful in 1742, Frederick had to fight against great odds to save Prussia from total destruction after the ongoing competition between Britain and France for colonial empire brought another great conflict in 1756. Maria Theresa, seeking to regain Silesia, formed an alliance with the leaders of France and Russia. The aim of the alliance during the resulting Seven Years' War (1756–1763) was to conquer Prussia and divide up its territory. Despite invasions from all sides, Frederick fought on with stoic courage. In the end he was miraculously saved: Peter III came to the Russian throne in 1762 and called off the attack against Frederick, whom he greatly admired.

The terrible struggle of the Seven Years' War tempered Frederick's interest in territorial expansion and brought him to consider how more humane policies for his subjects might also strengthen the state. Thus Frederick went beyond a superficial commitment to

cameralism View that monarchy was the best form of government, that all elements of society should serve the monarch, and that, in turn, the state should use its resources and authority to increase the public good.

Prussia, 1740
Prussian gains, 1742
Austria, 1740
Boundary of the Holy Roman Empire

Königsberg

Berlin

POLAND

SILESIA

Prague

Vienna

AUSTRIA

HUNGARY

The War of the Austrian Succession, 1740–1748

Enlightenment culture for himself and his circle. He tolerantly allowed his subjects to believe as they wished in religious and philosophical matters. He promoted the advancement of knowledge, improving his country's schools and permitting scholars to publish their findings. Moreover, Frederick tried to improve the lives of his subjects more directly. As he wrote to his friend Voltaire, "I must enlighten my people, cultivate their manners and morals, and make them as happy as human beings can be, or as happy as the means at my disposal permit."

The legal system and the bureaucracy were Frederick's primary tools. Prussia's laws were simplified, torture was abolished, and judges decided cases quickly and impartially. Prussian officials became famous for their hard work and honesty. After the Seven Years' War ended in 1763, Frederick's government energetically promoted the reconstruction of agriculture and industry. Frederick himself set a good example. He worked hard and lived modestly, claiming that he was "only the first servant of the state." Thus Frederick justified monarchy in terms of practical results and said nothing of the divine right of kings.

Frederick's dedication to high-minded government went only so far, however. While he condemned serfdom in the abstract, he accepted it in practice and did not free the serfs on his own estates. He accepted and extended the privileges of the nobility, who remained the backbone of the army and the entire Prussian state.

In reforming Prussia's bureaucracy, Frederick drew on the principles of **cameralism**, the German science of public administration that emerged in the decades following the Thirty Years' War. Influential throughout the German lands, cameralism held that monarchy was the best of all forms of government, that all elements of society should be placed at the service of the state, and that, in turn, the state should make use of its resources and authority to improve society. Predating the Enlightenment, cameralist interest in the public good was usually inspired by the needs of war. Cameralism shared with the Enlightenment an emphasis on rationality, progress, and utilitarianism.

Catherine the Great of Russia

Catherine the Great of Russia (r. 1762–1796) was one of the most remarkable rulers of her age, and the French

philosophes adored her. Catherine was a German princess from Anhalt-Zerbst, an insignificant principality sandwiched between Prussia and Saxony. Her father commanded a regiment of the Prussian army, but her mother was related to the Romanovs of Russia, and that proved to be Catherine's opening to power.

Catherine's Romanov connection made her a suitable bride at the age of fifteen for the heir to the Russian throne. It was a mismatch from the beginning, but her *Memoirs* made her ambitions clear: "I did not care about Peter, but I did care about the crown." When her husband, Peter III, came to power during the Seven Years' War, his decision to withdraw Russian troops from the coalition against Prussia alienated the army. Catherine profited from his unpopularity to form a conspiracy to depose her husband. In 1762 Catherine's lover Gregory Orlov and his three brothers, all army officers, murdered Peter, and the German princess became empress of Russia.

Catherine had drunk deeply at the Enlightenment well. Never questioning that absolute monarchy was

the best form of government, she set out to rule in an enlightened manner. She had three main goals. First, she worked hard to continue Peter the Great's effort to bring the culture of western Europe to Russia (see Chapter 15). To do so, she imported Western architects, musicians, and intellectuals. She bought masterpieces of Western art and patronized the philosophes. An enthusiastic letter writer, she corresponded extensively with Voltaire and praised him as the "champion of the human race." When the French government banned the *Encyclopedia*, she offered to publish it in St. Petersburg, and she sent money to Diderot when he needed it. With these actions, Catherine won good press in the West for herself and for her country. Moreover, this intellectual ruler, who wrote plays and loved good talk, set the tone for the entire Russian nobility. Peter the Great westernized Russian armies, but it was Catherine who westernized the imagination of the Russian nobility.

Catherine's second goal was domestic reform, and she began her reign with sincere and ambitious projects.

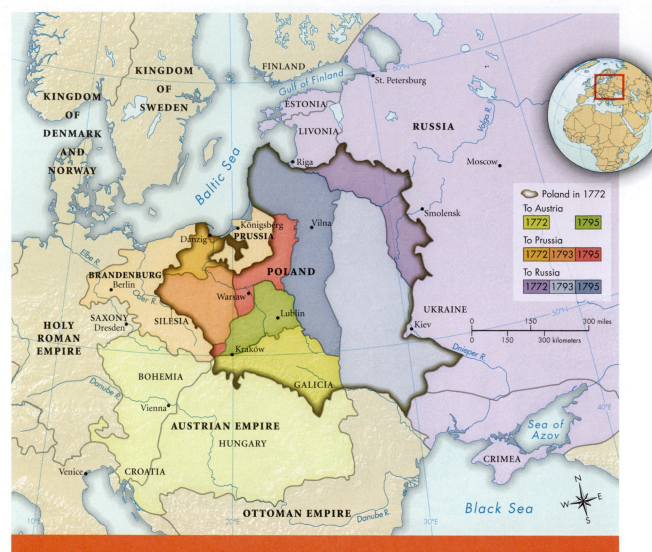

MAPPING THE PAST

Map 16.1 The Partition of Poland, 1772–1795

In 1772 war between Russia and Austria threatened over Russian gains from the Ottoman Empire. To satisfy desires for expansion without fighting, Prussia's Frederick the Great proposed that parts of Poland be divided among Austria, Prussia, and Russia. In 1793 and 1795 the three powers partitioned the remainder, and the republic of Poland ceased to exist.

ANALYZING THE MAP Of the three powers that divided the kingdom of Poland, which gained the most territory? How did the partition affect the geographical boundaries of each state, and what was the significance? What border with the former Poland remained unchanged? Why do you think this was the case?

CONNECTIONS What does it say about European politics at the time that a country could simply cease to exist on the map? Could that happen today?

In 1767 she appointed a legislative commission to prepare a new law code. This project was never completed, but Catherine did restrict the practice of torture and allowed limited religious toleration. She also tried to improve education and strengthen local government. The philosophes applauded these measures and hoped more would follow.

Such was not the case. In 1773 a common Cossack soldier named Emelian Pugachev sparked a gigantic uprising of serfs, very much as Stenka Razin had done a century earlier (see Chapter 15). Proclaiming himself the true tsar, Pugachev issued orders abolishing serfdom, taxes, and army service. Thousands joined his cause, slaughtering landlords and officials over a vast area of southwestern Russia. Pugachev's untrained forces eventually proved no match for Catherine's noble-led army. Betrayed by his own company, Pugachev was captured and savagely executed.

Pugachev's rebellion put an end to any intentions Catherine had about reforming the system. The peasants were clearly dangerous, and her empire rested on the support of the nobility. After 1775 Catherine gave the nobles absolute control of their serfs, and she extended serfdom into new areas, such as Ukraine. In 1785 she freed nobles forever from taxes and state service. Under Catherine the Russian nobility attained its most exalted position, and serfdom entered its most oppressive phase.

Catherine's third goal was territorial expansion, and in this respect she was extremely successful. Her armies subjugated the last descendants of the Mongols and the Crimean Tartars, and began the conquest of the Caucasus (KAW-kuh-suhs). Her greatest coup by far was the partition of Poland (Map 16.1). When, between 1768 and 1772, Catherine's armies scored unprecedented victories against the Ottomans and thereby threatened to disturb the balance of power between Russia and Austria in eastern Europe, Frederick of Prussia obligingly came forward with a deal. He proposed that Turkey be let off easily and that Prussia, Austria, and Russia each compensate itself by taking a gigantic slice of the weakly ruled Polish territory. Catherine jumped at the chance. The first partition of Poland took place in 1772. Subsequent partitions in 1793 and 1795 gave away the rest of Polish territory, and the ancient republic of Poland vanished from the map.

The Austrian Habsburgs

Another female monarch, Maria Theresa (r. 1740–1780) of Austria, set out to reform her nation, although traditional power politics was a more important motivation for her than were Enlightenment teachings. A devoutly Catholic mother and wife who inherited power from her father, Charles VI, Maria Theresa was a remarkable but old-fashioned absolutist. Her more radical son, Joseph II (r. 1780–1790), drew on Enlightenment ideals, earning the title of "revolutionary emperor."

Emerging from the long War of the Austrian Succession in 1748 with the serious loss of Silesia, Maria Theresa was determined to introduce reforms that would make the state stronger and more efficient. First, she initiated church reform, with measures aimed at limiting the papacy's influence, eliminating many religious holidays, and reducing the number of monasteries. Second, a whole series of administrative renovations strengthened the central bureaucracy, smoothed out some provincial differences, and revamped the tax system, taxing even the lands of nobles, previously exempt from taxation. Third, the government sought to improve the lot of the agricultural population, cautiously reducing the power of lords over their hereditary serfs and their partially free peasant tenants.

Coregent with his mother from 1765 onward and a strong supporter of change from above, Joseph II moved forward rapidly when he came to the throne in 1780. Most notably, Joseph abolished serfdom in 1781, and in 1789 he decreed that peasants could pay landlords in cash rather than through labor on their land. This measure was violently rejected not only by the nobility but also by the peasants it was intended to help, because they lacked the necessary cash. When a disillusioned Joseph died prematurely at forty-nine, the entire Habsburg empire was in turmoil. His brother Leopold II (r. 1790–1792) canceled Joseph's radical edicts in order to re-establish order. Peasants once again were required to do forced labor for their lords.

Despite differences in their policies, Joseph II and the other absolutists of the later eighteenth century combined old-fashioned state-building with the culture and critical thinking of the Enlightenment. In doing so, they succeeded in expanding the role of the state in the life of society. They perfected bureaucratic machines that were to prove surprisingly adaptive and enduring. Their failure to implement policies we would recognize as humane and enlightened—such as abolishing serfdom—may reveal inherent limitations in Enlightenment thinking about equality and social justice, rather than deficiencies in their execution of Enlightenment programs. The fact that leading philosophes supported rather than criticized eastern rulers' policies exposes the blind spots of the era.

Jewish Life and the Limits of Enlightened Absolutism

Perhaps the best example of the limitations of enlightened absolutism are the debates surrounding the emancipation of the Jews. Europe's small Jewish

Moses Mendelssohn and the Jewish Enlightenment

In 1743 a small, humpbacked Jewish boy with a stammer left his poor parents in Dessau in central Germany and walked eighty miles to Berlin, the capital of Frederick the Great's Prussia. According to one story, when the boy reached the Rosenthaler (ROH-zuhn-taw-lehr) Gate, the only one through which Jews could pass, he told the inquiring watchman that his name was Moses and that he had come to Berlin "to .learn." The watchman laughed and waved him through. "Go Moses, the sea has opened before you."*

In Berlin the young Mendelssohn studied Jewish law and eked out a living copying Hebrew manuscripts in a beautiful hand. But he was soon fascinated by an intellectual world that had been closed to him in the Dessau ghetto. There, like most Jews throughout central Europe, he had spoken Yiddish—a mixture of German, Polish, and Hebrew. Now, working mainly on his own, he mastered German; learned Latin, Greek, French, and English; and studied mathematics and Enlightenment philosophy. Word of his exceptional abilities spread in Berlin's Jewish community (the dwelling of 1,500 of the city's 100,000 inhabitants). He began tutoring the children of a wealthy Jewish silk merchant, and he soon became the merchant's clerk and later his partner. But his great passion remained the life of the mind and the spirit, which he avidly pursued in his off-hours.

Gentle and unassuming in his personal life, Mendelssohn was a bold thinker. Reading eagerly in Western philosophy since antiquity, he was, as a pious Jew, soon convinced that Enlightenment teachings need not be opposed to Jewish thought and religion. He concluded that reason could complement and strengthen religion, although each would retain its integrity as a separate sphere.† Developing his idea in his first great work, *On the Immortality of the Soul* (1767), Mendelssohn

Lavater (right) attempts to convert Mendelssohn, in a painting by Moritz Oppenheim of an imaginary encounter. (akg-images)

ONLINE DOCUMENT ASSIGNMENT

How did Moses Mendelssohn fit into the larger Enlightenment debate about religious tolerance? Go to the Integrated Media and examine primary sources written by Mendelssohn and his contemporaries, and then complete a writing assignment based on the evidence and details from this chapter.

*H. Kupferberg, *The Mendelssohns: Three Generations of Genius* (New York: Charles Scribner's Sons, 1972), p. 3.

†David Sorkin, *Moses Mendelssohn and the Religious Enlightenment* (Berkeley: University of California Press, 1996), pp. 8ff.

used the neutral setting of a philosophical dialogue between Socrates and his followers in ancient Greece to argue that the human soul lived forever. In refusing to bring religion and critical thinking into conflict, he was strongly influenced by contemporary German philosophers who argued similarly on behalf of Christianity. He reflected the way the German Enlightenment generally supported established religion, in contrast to the French Enlightenment, which attacked it.

Mendelssohn's treatise on the human soul captivated the educated German public, which marveled that a Jew could have written a philosophical masterpiece. In the excitement, a Christian zealot named Lavater challenged Mendelssohn in a pamphlet to accept Christianity or to demonstrate how the Christian faith was not "reasonable." Replying politely but passionately, the Jewish philosopher affirmed that his studies had only strengthened him in his faith, although he did not seek to convert anyone not born into Judaism. Rather, he urged toleration in religious matters and spoke up courageously against Jewish oppression.

Orthodox Jew and German philosophe, Moses Mendelssohn serenely combined two very different worlds. He built a bridge from the ghetto to the dominant culture over which many Jews would pass, including his novelist daughter Dorothea and his famous grandson, the composer Felix Mendelssohn.

QUESTIONS FOR ANALYSIS

1. How did Mendelssohn seek to influence Jewish religious thought in his time?
2. How do Mendelssohn's ideas compare with those of the French Enlightenment?

populations lived under highly discriminatory laws. For the most part, Jews were confined to tiny, overcrowded ghettos, were excluded by law from most professions, and could be ordered out of a kingdom at a moment's notice. Still, a very few did manage to succeed and to obtain the right of permanent settlement, usually by performing some special service for the state. Many rulers relied on Jewish bankers for loans to raise armies and run their kingdoms. Jewish merchants prospered in international trade because they could rely on contacts with colleagues in Jewish communities scattered across Europe.

The Pale of Settlement, 1791

In the eighteenth century an Enlightenment movement known as the **Haskalah** emerged from within the European Jewish community, led by the Prussian philosopher Moses Mendelssohn (1729–1786). (See "Individuals in Society: Moses Mendelssohn and the Jewish Enlightenment," at left.) Christian and Jewish Enlightenment philosophers, including Mendelssohn, began to advocate for freedom and civil rights for European Jews. In an era of reason and progress, they argued, restrictions on religious grounds could not stand. The Haskalah accompanied a period of controversial social change within Jewish communities, in which rabbinic controls loosened and heightened interaction with Christians took place.

Haskalah The Jewish Enlightenment of the second half of the eighteenth century, led by the Prussian philosopher Moses Mendelssohn.

Arguments for tolerance won some ground. The British Parliament passed a law allowing naturalization of Jews in 1753, but later repealed the law due to public outrage. The most progressive reforms took place under Austrian emperor Joseph II. Among his liberal edicts of the 1780s were measures intended to integrate Jews more fully into society, including eligibility for military service, admission to higher education and artisanal trades, and removal of requirements for special clothing or emblems. Welcomed by many Jews, these reforms raised fears among traditionalists of assimilation into the general population.

Many monarchs rejected all ideas of emancipation. Although he permitted freedom of religion to his Christian subjects, Frederick the Great of Prussia firmly opposed any general emancipation for the Jews, as he did for the serfs. Catherine the Great, who acquired most of Poland's large Jewish population when she annexed part of that country in the late eighteenth century, similarly refused. In 1791 she established the Pale of Settlement, a territory including parts of modern-day Poland, Latvia, Lithuania, Ukraine, and Belarus, in which most Jews were required to live. Jewish habitation was restricted to the Pale until the Russian Revolution in 1917.

The first European state to remove all restrictions on the Jews was France under the French Revolution. Over the next hundred years, Jews gradually won full legal and civil rights throughout the rest of western Europe. Emancipation in eastern Europe took even longer and aroused more conflict and violence.

Maria Theresa The empress (see page 533) and her husband pose with twelve of their sixteen children at Schönbrunn palace in this family portrait by court painter Martin Meytens (1695–1770). Joseph, the heir to the throne, stands at the center of the star on the floor. Wealthy women often had very large families, in part because they, unlike poor women, seldom nursed their babies. (Château de Versailles, France, The Bridgeman Art Library)

Notes

1. Quoted in Butterfield, *The Origins of Modern Science*, p. 47.
2. Ibid., p. 120.
3. Quoted in John Freely, *Aladdin's Lamp: How Greek Science Came to Europe Through the Islamic World* (New York: Knopf, 2009), p. 206.
4. Ibid., p. 217.
5. Ibid., p. 225.
6. Jacqueline Broad, *Women Philosophers of the Seventeenth Century* (Cambridge, U.K.: Cambridge University Press, 2003), p. 17.
7. L. Schiebinger, *The Mind Has No Sex? Women in the Origins of Modern Science* (Cambridge, Mass.: Harvard University Press, 1989), p. 64.
8. Quoted in G. L. Mosse et al., eds., *Europe in Review* (Chicago: Rand McNally, 1964), p. 156.
9. Quoted in P. Gay, "The Unity of the Enlightenment," *History* 3 (1960): 25.
10. See E. Fox-Genovese, "Women in the Enlightenment," in *Becoming Visible: Women in European History*, 2d ed., ed. R. Bridenthal, C. Koonz, and S. Stuard (Boston: Houghton Mifflin, 1987), esp. pp. 252–259, 263–265.
11. Jean Le Rond d'Alembert, *Eloges lus dans les séances publiques de l'Académie française* (Paris, 1779), p. ix, quoted in Mona Ozouf, "'Public Opinion' at the End of the Old Regime," *The Journal of Modern History* 60, Supplement: Rethinking French Politics in 1788 (September 1988): S9.
12. Quoted in Emmanuel Chukwudi Eze, ed., *Race and the Enlightenment: A Reader* (Oxford: Blackwell, 1997), p. 33.

LOOKING BACK LOOKING AHEAD

Hailed as the origin of modern thought, the Scientific Revolution must also be seen as a product of its past. Medieval universities gave rise to important new scholarship, and the ambition and wealth of Renaissance patrons nurtured intellectual curiosity. Religious faith also influenced the Scientific Revolution, inspiring thinkers to understand the glory of God's creation, while bringing censure and personal tragedy to others. Natural philosophers following Copernicus pioneered new methods of observing and explaining nature while drawing on centuries-old traditions of mysticism, astrology, alchemy, and magic.

The Enlightenment ideas of the eighteenth century were a similar blend of past and present; they could serve as much to bolster absolutist monarchical regimes as to inspire revolutionaries to fight for individual rights and liberties. Although the Enlightenment fostered critical thinking about everything from science to religion, the majority of Europeans, including many prominent thinkers, remained devout Christians.

The achievements of the Scientific Revolution and the Enlightenment are undeniable. Key Western values of rationalism, human rights, and open-mindedness were born from these movements. With their new notions of progress and social improvement, Europeans would embark on important revolutions in industry and politics in the centuries that followed. Nonetheless, others have seen a darker side. For these critics, the mastery over nature permitted by the Scientific Revolution now threatens to overwhelm the earth's fragile equilibrium, and the Enlightenment belief in the universal application of reason can lead to arrogance and intolerance of other people's spiritual, cultural, and political values. Such vivid debates about the legacy of these intellectual and scientific developments testify to their continuing importance in today's world.

REVIEW and EXPLORE

MAKE IT STICK

LearningCurve
After reading the chapter, go online and use LearningCurve to retain what you've read.

Identify Key Terms

Identify and explain the significance of each item below.

natural philosophy (p. 504)

Copernican hypothesis (p. 506)

experimental method (p. 508)

law of inertia (p. 508)

law of universal gravitation (p. 510)

empiricism (p. 511)

Cartesian dualism (p. 512)

Enlightenment (p. 516)

rationalism (p. 516)

philosophes (p. 517)

reading revolution (p. 522)

salon (p. 522)

rococo (p. 524)

public sphere (p. 524)

enlightened absolutism (p. 529)

cameralism (p. 530)

Haskalah (p. 535)

Review the Main Ideas

Answer the focus questions from each section of the chapter.

◆ What revolutionary discoveries were made in the sixteenth and seventeenth centuries? (p. 504)

◆ What intellectual and social changes occurred as a result of the Scientific Revolution? (p. 511)

◆ What new ideas about society and human relations emerged in the Enlightenment, and what new practices and institutions enabled these ideas to take hold? (p. 516)

◆ What impact did new ways of thinking have on political developments and monarchical absolutism? (p. 529)

Make Connections

Think about the larger developments and continuities within and across chapters.

1. How did the era of European exploration and discovery (Chapter 14) impact the ideas of scientists and philosophers discussed in this chapter? In what ways did contact with new peoples and places stimulate new forms of thought among Europeans?

2. What was the relationship between the Scientific Revolution and the Enlightenment? How did new ways of understanding the natural world influence thinking about human society?

3. Compare the policies and actions of seventeenth-century absolutist rulers (Chapter 15) with their "enlightened" descendants described in this chapter. How accurate is the term *Enlightened absolutism*?

ONLINE DOCUMENT ASSIGNMENT
Moses Mendelssohn

How did Moses Mendelssohn fit into the larger Enlightenment debate about religious tolerance?

You encountered Moses Mendelssohn's story on page 534. Keeping the question above in mind, go to the Integrated Media and examine primary sources from Mendelssohn's time—including a letter to a contemporary, an excerpt from a play, and a philosophical treatise. Then complete a writing assignment based on the evidence and details from this chapter.

● Suggested Reading and Media Resources

BOOKS

◆ Dear, Peter. *Revolutionizing the Sciences: European Knowledge and Its Ambitions, 1500–1700,* 2d ed. 2009. An accessible and well-illustrated introduction to the Scientific Revolution.

◆ Delbourgo, James, and Nicholas Dew, eds. *Science and Empire in the Atlantic World.* 2008. A collection of essays examining the relationship between the Scientific Revolution and the imperial expansion of European powers across the Atlantic.

◆ Ellis, Markman. *The Coffee House: A Cultural History.* 2004. An engaging study of the rise of the coffeehouse and its impact on European cultural and social life.

◆ Eze, Emmanuel Chukwudi, ed. *Race and the Enlightenment: A Reader.* 1997. A pioneering source on the origins of modern racial thinking in the Enlightenment.

◆ Liebersohn, Harry. *The Travelers' World: Europe to the Pacific.* 2008. A beautifully written account of Europeans' voyages to the Pacific and the impact of these voyages on Enlightenment ideas.

◆ Massie, Robert K. *Catherine the Great: Portrait of a Woman.* 2012. Recounts the life story of Catherine from obscure German princess to enlightened ruler of Russia.

◆ McMahon, Darrin M. *Happiness: A History.* 2006. Discusses how worldly pleasure became valued as a duty of individuals and societies in the Enlightenment.

◆ Messbarger, Rebecca. *The Lady Anatomist: The Life and Work of Anna Morandi Manzolini.* 2010. The life of an Italian woman artist and scientist who showed the opportunities and constraints for eighteenth-century women.

◆ Outram, Dorinda. *The Enlightenment,* 2d ed. 2006. An outstanding and accessible introduction to Enlightenment debates that emphasizes the Enlightenment's social context and global reach.

◆ Robertson, John. *The Case for the Enlightenment: Scotland and Naples, 1680–1760.* 2005. A comparative study of Enlightenment movements in Scotland and Naples, emphasizing commonalities between these two small kingdoms on the edges of Europe.

◆ Shapin, Steven. *The Scientific Revolution.* 2001. A concise and well-informed general introduction to the Scientific Revolution.

◆ Sorkin, David. *Moses Mendelssohn and the Religious Enlightenment.* 1996. A brilliant study of the Jewish philosopher and of the role of religion in the Enlightenment.

DOCUMENTARIES

◆ *Galileo's Battle for the Heavens* (PBS, 2002). Recounts the story of Galileo's struggle with the Catholic Church over his astronomical discoveries, featuring re-enactments of key episodes in his life.

◆ *Newton's Dark Secrets* (PBS, 2005). Explores Isaac Newton's fundamental scientific discoveries alongside his religious faith and practice of alchemy.

FEATURE FILMS AND TELEVISION

◆ *Catherine the Great* (A&E, 1995). A made-for-television movie starring Catherine Zeta-Jones as the German princess who becomes Catherine the Great.

◆ *Dangerous Liaisons* (Stephen Frears, 1988). Based on a 1782 novel, the story of two aristocrats who cynically manipulate others, until one of them falls in love with a chaste widow chosen as his victim.

◆ *Longitude* (A&E, 2000). A television miniseries that follows the parallel stories of an eighteenth-century clockmaker striving to find a means to measure longitude at sea and a modern-day veteran who restores the earlier man's clocks.

◆ *Ridicule* (Patrice Leconte, 1996). When a provincial nobleman travels to the French court in the 1780s to present a project to drain a malarial swamp in his district, his naïve Enlightenment ideals incur the ridicule of decadent courtiers.

WEB SITES

◆ *The Encyclopedia of Diderot & d'Alembert Collaborative Translation Project.* A collaborative project to translate the *Encyclopedia* edited by Denis Diderot and Jean le Rond d'Alembert into English, with searchable entries submitted by students and scholars and vetted by experts. **quod.lib.umich.edu/d/did/**

◆ *The Hermitage Museum.* The Web site of the Russian Hermitage Museum founded by Catherine the Great in the Winter Palace in St. Petersburg, with virtual tours of the museum's rich collections. **www.hermitagemuseum.org/html_En/index.html**

◆ *Mapping the Republic of Letters.* A site hosted by Stanford University showcasing projects using mapping software to create spatial visualizations based on correspondence and travel of members of the eighteenth-century Republic of Letters. **republicofletters.stanford.edu/**

17

The Expansion of Europe

1650–1800

Absolutism and aristocracy, a combination of raw power and elegant refinement, were a world apart from the common people. For most people in the eighteenth century, life remained a struggle with poverty and uncertainty, with the landlord and the tax collector. In 1700 peasants on the land and artisans in their shops lived little better than had their ancestors in the Middle Ages, primarily because European societies still could not produce very much as measured by modern standards. Despite the hard work of ordinary men and women, there was seldom enough good food, warm clothing, and decent housing. The idea of progress, of substantial improvement in the lives of great numbers of people, was still the dream of only a small elite in fashionable salons.

Yet the economic basis of European life was beginning to change. In the course of the eighteenth century, the European economy emerged from the long crisis of the seventeenth century, responded to challenges, and began to expand once again. Population resumed its growth, while colonial empires extended and developed. Some areas were more fortunate than others. The rising Atlantic powers — the Dutch Republic, France, and above all England — and their colonies led the way. The expansion of agriculture, industry, trade, and population marked the beginning of a surge comparable to that of the eleventh- and twelfth-century springtime of European civilization. But this time, broadly based expansion was not cut short by plague and famine. This time the response to new challenges led toward one of the most influential developments in human history, the Industrial Revolution, considered in Chapter 20. ■

Life in the Expanding Europe of the Eighteenth Century. The activities of the bustling cosmopolitan port of Marseilles were common to ports across Europe in the eighteenth century. Here a wealthy Frenchwoman greets a group of foreign merchants, while dockhands struggle to shift their heavy loads. (Gianni Dagli Orti/The Art Archive at Art Resource, NY)

CHAPTER PREVIEW

 LearningCurve
After reading the chapter, go online and use LearningCurve to retain what you've read.

Working the Land
What important developments led to increased agricultural production, and how did these changes affect peasants?

The Beginning of the Population Explosion
Why did the European population rise dramatically in the eighteenth century?

The Growth of Rural Industry
How and why did rural industry intensify in the eighteenth century?

The Debate over Urban Guilds
What were guilds, and why did they become controversial in the eighteenth century?

The Atlantic World and Global Trade
How did colonial markets boost Europe's economic and social development, and what conflicts and adversity did world trade entail?

Working the Land

What important developments led to increased agricultural production, and how did these changes affect peasants?

At the end of the seventeenth century the economy of Europe was agrarian. With the exception of the Dutch Republic and England, at least 80 percent of the people of western Europe drew their livelihoods from agriculture. In eastern Europe the percentage was considerably higher. Men and women were tied to the land, plowing fields and sowing seed, reaping harvests and storing grain. Yet even in a rich agricultural region such as the Po Valley in northern Italy, every bushel of wheat seed sown yielded on average only five or six bushels of grain at harvest. By modern standards, output was distressingly low.

In most regions of Europe, climatic conditions produced poor or disastrous harvests every eight or nine years. In famine years the number of deaths soared far above normal. A third of a village's population might disappear in a year or two. But new developments in agricultural technology and methods gradually brought an end to the ravages of hunger in western Europe.

The Legacy of the Open-Field System

Why, in the late seventeenth century, did many areas of Europe produce barely enough food to survive? The answer lies in the pattern of farming that had developed in the Middle Ages, which sustained fairly large numbers of people, but did not produce material abundance. From the Middle Ages up to the seventeenth century, much of Europe was farmed through the open-field system. The land to be cultivated was divided into several large fields, which were in turn cut up into long, narrow strips. The fields were open, and the strips were not enclosed into small plots by fences or hedges. The whole peasant village followed the same pattern of plowing, sowing, and harvesting in accordance with long-standing traditions.

The ever-present problem was soil exhaustion. Wheat planted year after year in a field will deplete nitrogen in the soil. Since the supply of manure for fertilizer was limited, the only way for the land to recover was to lie fallow for a period of time. Clover and other annual grasses that sprang up in unplanted fields restored nutrients to the soil and also provided food for livestock. In the early Middle Ages a year of fallow was alternated with a year of cropping; then three-year rotations were introduced. On each strip of land, a year of wheat or rye was followed by a year of oats or beans and only then by a year of fallow. Peasants staggered

the rotation of crops, so some wheat, legumes, and pastureland were always available. The three-year system was an important achievement because cash crops could be grown two years out of three, rather than only one year in two.

Traditional village rights reinforced communal patterns of farming. In addition to rotating field crops in a uniform way, villages maintained open meadows for hay and natural pasture. After the harvest villagers also pastured their animals on the wheat or rye stubble. In many places such pasturing followed a brief period, also established by tradition, for the gleaning of grain. In this process, poor women would go through the fields picking up the few single grains that had fallen to the ground in the course of the harvest. Many villages were surrounded by woodlands, also held in common, which provided essential firewood, building materials, and nutritional roots and berries.

The state and landlords continued to levy heavy taxes and high rents, thereby stripping peasants of much of their meager earnings. The level of exploitation varied. Generally speaking, the peasants of eastern Europe were worst off. As we saw in Chapter 15, they were serfs bound to their lords in hereditary service. In much of eastern Europe, working several days per week on the lord's land was not uncommon. Well into the nineteenth century, individual Russian serfs and serf families were regularly bought and sold.

Social conditions were better in western Europe, where peasants were generally free from serfdom. In France, western Germany, England, and the Low Countries (modern-day Belgium and the Netherlands), peasants could own land and could pass it on to their children. In years with normal harvests, most people had enough food to fill their bellies. Yet life in the village was hard, and poverty was the reality for most people.

New Methods of Agriculture

The seventeenth century saw important gains in productivity in some regions that would slowly extend to the rest of Europe. By 1700 less than half of the population of Britain and the Dutch Republic worked in agriculture, producing enough to feed the remainder of the population. Many elements combined in this production growth, but the key was new ways of rotating crops that allowed farmers to forgo the unproductive fallow period altogether and maintain their land in continuous cultivation. The secret to eliminating the fallow lay in deliberately alternating grain with crops that restored nutrients to the soil, such as peas and beans, root crops such as turnips and potatoes, and clover and other grasses.

Clover was one of the most important crops, because it restores nitrogen directly to the soil through its roots. Other crops produced additional benefits. Potatoes and many types of beans came to Europe as part of the sixteenth-century Columbian exchange between the New and the Old Worlds (see Chapter 14). Originally perceived by Europeans as fit only for animal feed, potatoes eventually made their way to the human table, where they provided a nutritious supplement to the peasant's meager diet. With more fodder, hay, and root vegetables for the winter months, peasants and larger farmers could build up their herds of cattle and sheep. More animals meant more manure to fertilize and restore the soil. More animals also meant more meat and dairy products as well as more power to pull ploughs in the fields and bring carts to market.

Over time, crop rotation spread to other parts of Europe, and farmers developed increasingly sophisticated patterns of crop rotation to suit different kinds of soils. For example, in the late eighteenth century farmers in French Flanders near Lille alternated a number of grain, root, and hay crops in a given field on a ten-year schedule. Ongoing experimentation, fueled by developments in the Scientific Revolution (see Chapter 16), led to more methodical farming.

Advocates of the new crop rotations, who included an emerging group of experimental scientists, some government officials, and a few big landowners, believed that new methods were scarcely possible within the traditional framework of open fields and common rights. A farmer who wanted to experiment with new methods would have to get all the landholders in the village to agree to the plan. Advocates of improvement argued that innovating agriculturalists needed to enclose and consolidate their scattered holdings into compact, fenced-in fields in order to farm more effectively. In doing so, the innovators also needed to enclose the village's natural pastureland, or common, into individual shares. According to proponents of this movement, known as **enclosure**, the upheaval of village life was the necessary price of technical progress.

That price seemed too high to many rural people who had small, inadequate holdings or very little land at all. Traditional rights were precious to these poor peasants, who used commonly held pastureland to graze livestock, and marshlands or forest outside the village as a source for foraged goods that could make the difference between survival and famine in harsh times. Thus, when the small landholders and the village poor could effectively oppose the enclosure of the open fields

Chronology

1600–1850	Growth in agriculture, pioneered by the Dutch Republic and England
1651–1663	British Navigation Acts
1652–1674	Anglo-Dutch wars
1700–1790	Height of Atlantic slave trade; expansion of rural industry in Europe
1701–1763	British and French mercantilist wars of empire
1720–1722	Last outbreak of bubonic plague in Europe
1720–1789	Growth of European population
1756–1763	Seven Years' War
1760–1815	Height of parliamentary enclosure in England
1763	Treaty of Paris; France cedes its possessions in India and North America
1770	James Cook claims the east coast of Australia for England
1776	Adam Smith publishes *An Inquiry into the Nature and Causes of the Wealth of Nations*
1805	British takeover of India complete
1807	British slave trade abolished

and the common lands, they did so. In many countries they found allies among the larger, predominantly noble landowners who were also wary of enclosure because it required large investments in purchasing and fencing land and thus posed risks for them as well.

The old system of unenclosed open fields and the new system of continuous rotation coexisted in Europe for a long time. Open fields could still be found in much of France and Germany as late as the nineteenth century because peasants there had successfully opposed eighteenth-century efforts to introduce the new techniques. Throughout the end of the eighteenth century, the new system of enclosure was extensively adopted only in the Low Countries and England.

> **enclosure** The movement to fence in fields in order to farm more effectively, at the expense of poor peasants who relied on common fields for farming and pasture.

The Leadership of the Low Countries and England

The seventeenth-century Dutch Republic, already the most advanced country in Europe in many areas of human endeavor (see Chapter 15), pioneered advancements in agriculture. By the middle of the seventeenth century intensive farming was well established, and the innovations of enclosed fields, continuous rotation, heavy manuring, and a wide variety of crops were all present. Agriculture was highly specialized and commercialized, especially in the province of Holland.

One reason for early Dutch leadership in farming was that the area was one of the most densely populated in Europe. In order to feed themselves and provide employment, the Dutch were forced at an early date to seek maximum yields from their land and to increase the cultivated area through the steady draining of marshes and swamps. The pressure of population was connected with the second cause: the growth of towns and cities. Stimulated by commerce and overseas trade, Amsterdam grew from thirty thousand to two hundred thousand inhabitants in its golden seventeenth century. The growing urban population provided Dutch peasants with markets for all they could produce and allowed each region to specialize in what it did best. Thus the Dutch could develop their potential, and the Low Countries became, as one historian wrote, "the Mecca of foreign agricultural experts who came . . . to see Flemish agriculture with their own eyes, to write about it and to propagate its methods in their home lands."[1]

The English were among their best students. In the mid-seventeenth century English farmers borrowed the system of continuous crop rotation from the Dutch. They also drew on Dutch expertise in drainage and water control. Large parts of seventeenth-century Holland had once been sea and sea marsh, and the efforts of centuries had made the Dutch the world's leaders in drainage. In the first half of the seventeenth century, Dutch experts made a great contribution to draining the extensive marshes, or fens, of wet and rainy England. The most famous of these Dutch engineers, Cornelius Vermuyden, directed one large drainage project in Yorkshire and another in Cambridgeshire. In the Cambridge fens, Vermuyden and his Dutch workers eventually reclaimed forty thousand acres, which were then farmed intensively in the Dutch manner. Swampy wilderness was converted into thousands of acres of some of the best land in England.

Based on the seventeenth-century achievements, English agriculture continued to progress during the eighteenth century, growing enough food to satisfy a rapidly growing population. Jethro Tull (1674–1741), part crank and part genius, was an important English

The Vegetable Market, 1662   The wealth and well-being of the industrious, capitalistic Dutch shine forth in this winsome market scene by Dutch artist Hendrick Sorgh. The market woman's baskets are filled with delicious fresh produce that ordinary citizens can afford — eloquent testimony to the responsive, enterprising character of Dutch agriculture. (Rijksmuseum, Amsterdam)

Arthur Young on the Benefits of Enclosure

In the 1760s Arthur Young farmed his family property in Essex, England, devoting himself to experiments in the latest techniques of agriculture and animal husbandry. He traveled through the British Isles and France meeting with farmers and collecting information on their crop yields and methods of cultivation. His published observations — and his optimistic views on progress in agriculture — were widely read and acclaimed in his day. In the passage below, Young expounds on the benefits of enclosing open fields.

❝ Respecting open field lands, the quantity of labour in them is not comparable to that of enclosures; for, not to speak of the great numbers of men that in enclosed countries are constantly employed in winter in hedging and ditching, what comparison can there be between the open field system of one half or a third of the lands being in fallow, receiving only three ploughings; and the same portion now tilled four, five, or six times by Midsummer, then sown with turnips, those hand-hoed twice, and then drawn by hand, and carted to stalls for beasts; or else hurdled out in portions for fatting sheep! What a scarcity of employment in one case, what a variety in the other! And consider the vast tracts of land in the kingdom (no less than the whole upon which turnips are cultivated) that have undergone this change since the last century. I should also remind the reader of other systems of management; beans and peas hand-hoed for a fallow — the culture of potatoes — of carrots, of coleseed, &c. — the hoeing of white corn — with the minuter improvements in every part of the culture of all crops — every article of which is an increase of labour. Then he should remember the vast tracts of country uncultivated in the last century, which have been enclosed and converted into new farms, a much greater tract in 80 years than these writers dream of: all this is the effect of enclosures, and consequently they also have yielded a great increase of employment. . . .

The fact is this; In the central counties of the kingdom, particularly Northamptonshire, Leicestershire, and parts of Warwick, Huntingdon and Buckinghamshires, there have been within 30 years large tracts of the open field arable under that vile course, 1 fallow, 2 wheat, 3 spring corn, enclosed and laid down to grass, being much more suited to the wetness of the soil than corn; and yields in beef, mutton, hides and wool, beyond comparison a greater neat produce than when under corn. . . . Thus the land yields a greater neat produce in food for mankind — the landlord doubles his income, which enables him to employ so many more manufacturers and artisans — the farmer increases his income, by means of which he also does the same — the hides and wool are a creation of so much employment for other manufacturers. ❞

EVALUATE THE EVIDENCE

1. What are the various improvements in agriculture described by Young in this passage? How do they relate to one another?
2. Why does Young think that enclosures produce more employment opportunities than open fields? Based on your reading in the chapter, did everyone perceive the benefits produced by enclosure in the same way as Young?

Source: Arthur Young, *Political Arithmetic: Containing Observations on the Present State of Great Britain; and the Principles of Her Policy in the Encouragement of Agriculture* (London: W. Nicoll, 1774), pp. 72–73, 148.

innovator. A true son of the early Enlightenment, Tull adopted a critical attitude toward accepted ideas about farming and tried to develop better methods through empirical research. He was especially enthusiastic about using horses, rather than slower-moving oxen, for plowing. He also advocated sowing seed with drilling equipment rather than scattering it by hand. Drilling distributed seed in an even manner and at the proper depth. There were also improvements in livestock, inspired in part by the earlier successes of English country gentlemen in breeding ever-faster horses for the races and fox hunts that were their passions. Selective breeding of ordinary livestock was a marked improvement over the haphazard breeding of the past.

One of the most important — and bitterly contested — aspects of agricultural development was the enclosure of open fields and commons. More than half the farmland in England was enclosed through private initiatives prior to 1700; Parliament completed this work in the eighteenth century. From the 1760s to 1815 a series of acts of Parliament enclosed most of the remaining common land. Arthur Young, another agricultural experimentalist, celebrated large-scale enclosure as a necessary means to achieve progress. (See "Primary Source 17.1: Arthur Young on the Benefits of Enclosure," above.) Many of his contemporaries, as well as the historians that followed him, echoed that conviction. More recent research, however, has shown that regions that maintained open-field farming were still able to adopt crop rotation and other innovations, suggesting that enclosures were not a prerequisite for increased production.

Many critics of Arthur Young's day emphasized the social upheaval caused by enclosure. By eliminating common rights and greatly reducing the access of poor men and women to the land, the eighteenth-century enclosure movement marked the completion of two major historical developments in England—the rise of market-oriented estate agriculture and the emergence of a landless rural proletariat. By the early nineteenth century a tiny minority of wealthy English and Scottish landowners held most of the land and pursued profits aggressively, leasing their holdings through agents at competitive prices to middle-size farmers, who relied on landless laborers for their work-

proletarianization The transformation of large numbers of small peasant farmers into landless rural wage earners.

force. These landless laborers worked very long hours, usually following a dawn-to-dusk schedule six days a week all year long. Not only was the small landholder deprived of his land, but improvements in technology meant that fewer laborers were needed to work the large farms, and unemployment spread throughout the countryside. As one observer commented:

> It is no uncommon thing for four or five wealthy graziers to engross a large inclosed lordship, which was before in the hands of twenty or thirty farmers, and as many smaller tenants or proprietors. All these are thereby thrown out of their livings, and many other families, who were chiefly employed and supported by them, such as blacksmiths, carpenters, wheelwrights and other artificers and tradesmen, besides their own labourers and servants.[2]

In no other European country had this **proletarianization**—this transformation of large numbers of small peasant farmers into landless rural wage earners—gone so far. England's village poor found the cost of change heavy and unjust.

The Beginning of the Population Explosion

Why did the European population rise dramatically in the eighteenth century?

Another factor that affected the existing order of life and forced economic changes in the eighteenth century was the beginning of the population explosion. Explosive growth continued in Europe until the twentieth century, by which time it was affecting non-Western areas of the globe. In this section we examine the background and causes of the population growth; the following section considers how the challenge of more

mouths to feed and more hands to employ affected the European economy.

Long-Standing Obstacles to Population Growth

Until 1700 the total population of Europe grew slowly much of the time, and it followed an irregular cyclical pattern (Figure 17.1). This cyclical pattern had a great influence on many aspects of social and economic life. The terrible ravages of the Black Death of 1348–1350 caused a sharp drop in population and food prices after 1350 and also created a labor shortage throughout Europe. Some economic historians calculate that for those common people in western Europe who managed to steer clear of warfare and of power struggles within the ruling class, the later Middle Ages was an era of exceptional well-being.

By the mid-sixteenth century much of Europe had returned to its pre-plague population levels. In this buoyant period, farmers brought new land into cultivation and urban settlements grew significantly. But this well-being eroded in the course of the sixteenth century. The second great surge of population growth outstripped the growth of agricultural production after about 1500. There was less food per person, and food prices rose more rapidly than wages, a development intensified by the inflow of precious metals from the Americas (see Chapter 14) and a general, if uneven, European price revolution. The result was a substantial decline in living standards throughout Europe. By 1600 the pressure of population on resources was severe in much of Europe, and widespread poverty was an undeniable reality.

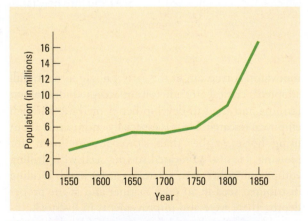

Figure 17.1 The Growth of Population in England, 1550–1850 England is a good example of both the uneven increase of European population before 1700 and the third great surge of growth that began in the eighteenth century.

Source: Data from E. A. Wrigley et al., *English Population History from Family Reconstitution, 1580–1837* (Cambridge: Cambridge University Press, 1997), p. 614.

Births and deaths, fertility and mortality, were in a crude but effective balance. The population grew modestly in normal years at a rate of perhaps 0.5 to 1 percent, or enough to double the population in 70 to 140 years. This is, of course, a generalization encompassing many different patterns. In areas such as Russia and colonial New England, where there was a great deal of frontier to be settled, the annual rate of natural increase, not counting immigration, might well have exceeded 1 percent. In a country such as France, where the land had long been densely settled, the rate of increase might have been less than 0.5 percent.

Although population growth of even 1 percent per year seems fairly modest, it will produce a very large increase over a long period: in three hundred years it will result in sixteen times as many people. Yet such significant increases did not occur in agrarian Europe. In certain abnormal years and tragic periods—the Black Death was only the most extreme example—many more people died than were born, and total population fell sharply, even catastrophically. A number of years of modest growth would then be necessary to make up for those who had died in an abnormal year. Such savage increases in deaths occurred periodically in the seventeenth century on a local and regional scale, and these demographic crises combined to check the growth of population until after 1700.

The grim reapers of demographic crisis were famine, epidemic disease, and war. Episodes of famine were inevitable in all eras of premodern Europe, given low crop yields and unpredictable climatic conditions. In the seventeenth century much of Europe experienced unusually cold and wet weather, which produced even more severe harvest failures and food shortages than usual. Contagious diseases, like typhus, smallpox, syphilis, and the ever-recurring bubonic plague, also continued to ravage Europe's population on a periodic basis. War was another scourge, and its indirect effects were even more harmful than the purposeful killing during military campaigns. Soldiers and camp followers passed all manner of contagious diseases throughout the countryside. Armies requisitioned scarce food supplies and disrupted the agricultural cycle while battles destroyed precious crops, livestock, and farmlands. The Thirty Years' War (1618–1648) witnessed all possible combinations of distress (see Chapter 15). The number of inhabitants in the German states alone declined by more than two-thirds in some large areas and by at least one-third almost everywhere else.

The New Pattern of the Eighteenth Century

In the eighteenth century the population of Europe began to grow markedly. Growth took place unevenly, with Russia growing very quickly after 1700 and France

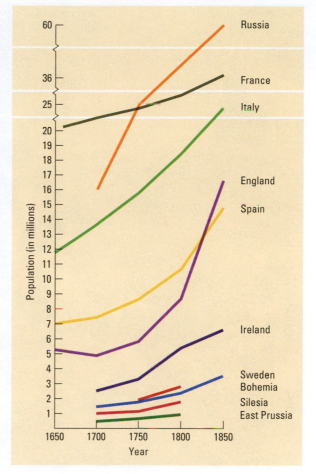

Figure 17.2 **The Increase of Population in Europe, 1650–1850** Population grew across Europe in the eighteenth century, though the most dramatic increases occurred after 1750. Russia experienced the largest increase and emerged as Europe's most populous state, as natural increase was complemented by growth from territorial expansion.
Source: Data from Massimo Livi Bacci, *The Population of Europe* (Wiley-Blackwell, 2000), p. 8.

much more slowly. Nonetheless, the explosion of population was a major phenomenon in all European countries. Europeans grew in numbers steadily from 1720 to 1789, with especially dramatic increases after about 1750 (Figure 17.2). Between 1700 and 1835, the population of Europe doubled in size.

What caused this population growth? In some areas, especially England, women had more babies than before because new opportunities for employment in rural industry (see page 549) allowed them to marry at an earlier age. But the basic cause of European population increase as a whole was a decline in mortality—fewer deaths.

One of the primary reasons behind this decline was the mysterious disappearance of the bubonic plague. Following the Black Death in the fourteenth century, plagues had remained part of the European experience,

The Plague at Marseilles The bishop of Marseilles blesses victims of the plague that over-whelmed Marseilles in 1720. Some one hundred thousand people died in the outbreak, which was the last great episode of plague in western Europe. (Louvre/Réunion des Musée Nationaux/Art Resource, NY)

striking again and again with savage force, particularly in towns. In 1720 a ship from Syria and the Levant brought the disease to Marseilles. As a contemporary account described it, "The Porters employ'd in unloading the Vessel, were immediately seiz'd with violent Pains in the Head . . . soon after they broke out in Blotches and Buboes, and died in three Days."[3] Plague quickly spread within and beyond Marseilles, killing up to one hundred thousand. By 1722 the epidemic had passed, and that was the last time plague fell on western and central Europe. Exactly why plague disappeared is unknown. Stricter measures of quarantine in Mediterranean ports and along the Austrian border with the Ottoman Empire helped by carefully isolating human carriers of plague. Chance and plain good luck were probably just as important.

Advances in medical knowledge did not contribute much to reducing the death rate in the eighteenth century. The most important advance in preventive medicine in this period was inoculation against smallpox, and this great improvement was long confined mainly to England, probably doing little to reduce deaths throughout Europe until the latter part of the century. However, improvements in the water supply and sewage, which were frequently promoted by strong absolutist monarchies, resulted in somewhat better public health and helped reduce such diseases as typhoid and typhus in some urban areas of western Europe. Improvements in water supply and the drainage of swamps also reduced Europe's large insect population. Flies and mosquitoes played a major role in spreading diseases, especially those striking children and young adults. Thus early public health measures helped the decline in mortality that began with the disappearance of plague and continued into the early nineteenth century.

Human beings also became more successful in their efforts to safeguard the supply of food. The eighteenth century was a time of considerable canal and road building in western Europe. These advances in transportation, which were also among the more positive aspects of strong absolutist states, lessened the impact of local crop failure and famine. Emergency supplies could be brought in, and localized starvation became less frequent. Wars became less destructive than in the seventeenth century and spread fewer epidemics. None of the population growth would have been possible if not for the advances in agricultural production in the seventeenth and eighteenth centuries, which increased the food supply and contributed nutritious new foods, particularly the potato from South America. In short, population grew in the eighteenth century primarily because years of higher-than-average death rates were less catastrophic. Famines, epidemics, and wars continued to occur and to affect population growth, but their severity moderated.

Population growth intensified the imbalance between the number of people and the economic opportunities available to them. Deprived of land by the enclosure movement, the rural poor were forced to look for new ways to make a living.

The Growth of Rural Industry

How and why did rural industry intensify in the eighteenth century?

The growth of population increased the number of rural workers with little or no land, and this in turn contributed to the development of industry in rural areas. The poor in the countryside increasingly needed to supplement their agricultural earnings with other types of work, and urban capitalists were eager to employ them, often at lower wages than urban workers received. **Cottage industry**, which consisted of manufacturing with hand tools in peasant cottages and work sheds, grew markedly in the eighteenth century and became a crucial feature of the European economy.

To be sure, peasant communities had always made clothing, processed food, and constructed housing for their own use. But medieval peasants did not produce manufactured goods on a large scale for sale in a market. By the eighteenth century, however, the pressures of rural poverty led many poor villagers to seek additional work, and far-reaching changes for daily rural life were set in motion.

The Putting-Out System

Cottage industry was often organized through the **putting-out system**. The two main participants in the putting-out system were the merchant capitalist and the rural worker. In this system, the merchant loaned, or "put out," raw materials to cottage workers, who processed the raw materials in their own homes and returned the finished products to the merchant. There were endless variations on this basic relationship. Sometimes rural workers bought their own raw materials and worked as independent producers before they sold to the merchant. Sometimes whole families were involved in domestic industry; at other times the tasks were closely associated with one gender. Sometimes several workers toiled together to perform a complicated process in a workshop outside the home. The relative importance of earnings from the land and from industry varied greatly for handicraft workers, although industrial wages usually became more important for a given family with time.

As industries grew in scale and complexity, production was often broken into many stages. For example, a merchant would provide raw wool to one group of workers for spinning into thread. He would then pass the thread to another group of workers to be bleached, to another for dyeing, and to another for weaving into cloth. The merchant paid outworkers by the piece and proceeded to sell the finished product to regional, national, or international markets.

The putting-out system grew because it had competitive advantages. Underemployed labor was abundant, and poor peasants and landless laborers would work for low wages. Since production in the countryside was unregulated, workers and merchants could change procedures and experiment as they saw fit. Because workers did not need to meet rigid guild standards, cottage industry became capable of producing many kinds of goods. Textiles; all manner of knives, forks, and housewares; buttons and gloves; and clocks could be produced quite satisfactorily in the countryside. Although luxury goods for the rich, such as exquisite tapestries and fine porcelain, demanded special training, close supervision, and centralized workshops, the limited skills of rural industry were sufficient for everyday articles.

Rural manufacturing did not spread across Europe at an even rate. It developed most successfully in England, particularly for the spinning and weaving of woolen cloth. By 1500 half of England's textiles were being produced in the countryside. By 1700 English industry was generally more rural than urban and heavily reliant on the putting-out system. Most continental countries, with the exception of Flanders and the Dutch Republic, developed rural industry more slowly. The latter part of the eighteenth century witnessed a

cottage industry A stage of industrial development in which rural workers used hand tools in their homes to manufacture goods on a large scale for sale in a market.

putting-out system The eighteenth-century system of rural industry in which a merchant loaned raw materials to cottage workers, who processed them and returned the finished products to the merchant.

Map 17.1 Industry and Population in Eighteenth-Century Europe

The growth of cottage manufacturing in rural areas helped country people increase their income and contributed to population growth. The putting-out system began in England, and much of the work was in the textile industry. Cottage industry was also strong in the Low Countries — modern-day Belgium and the Netherlands.

ANALYZING THE MAP What does this map suggest about the relationship between population density and the growth of textile production? What geographical characteristics seem to have played a role in encouraging this industry?

CONNECTIONS How would you account for the distribution of each type of cloth across Europe? Did metal production draw on different demographic and geographical conditions? Why do you think this was the case?

remarkable expansion of rural industry in certain densely populated regions of continental Europe (Map 17.1).

The Lives of Rural Textile Workers

Until the nineteenth century, the industry that employed the most people in Europe was textiles. The making of linen, woolen, and eventually cotton cloth was the typical activity of cottage workers engaged in the putting-out system. A look inside the cottage of the

English weaver illustrates a way of life as well as an economic system. The rural worker lived in a small cottage with tiny windows and little space. The cottage was often a single room that served as workshop, kitchen, and bedroom. There were only a few pieces of furniture, of which the weaver's loom was by far the largest and most important. That loom changed somewhat in the early eighteenth century when John Kay's invention of the flying shuttle enabled the weaver to throw the shuttle back and forth between the threads with one hand. Aside from that improvement, however, the loom was as it had been for much of history and as it would remain until the arrival of mechanized looms in the first decades of the nineteenth century.

Handloom weaving was a family enterprise. All members of the family helped in the work, so that "every person from seven to eighty (who retained their sight and who could move their hands) could earn their bread," as one eighteenth-century English observer put it.[4] Operating the loom was usually considered a man's job, reserved for the male head of the family. Women and children worked at auxiliary tasks; they prepared the warp (vertical) threads and mounted them on the loom, wound threads on bobbins for the weft (horizontal) threads, and sometimes operated the warp frame while the father passed the shuttle.

The work of four or five spinners was needed to keep one weaver steadily employed. Since the weaver's family usually could not produce enough thread, merchants hired the wives and daughters of agricultural workers, who took on spinning work in their spare time. In England, many widows and single women also became "spinsters," so many in fact that the word be-

came a synonym for an unmarried woman. In parts of Germany, spinning employed whole families and was not reserved for women.

Relations between workers and employers were often marked by sharp conflict. (See "Primary Source 17.2: Contrasting Views on the Effects of Rural Industry," page 552.) There were constant disputes over the weights of materials and the quality of finished work. Merchants accused workers of stealing raw materials, and weavers complained that merchants delivered underweight bales. Suspicion abounded.

Conditions were particularly hard for female workers. While men could earn decent wages through long hours of arduous labor, women's wages were usually much lower because they were not considered the family's primary wage earner. In England's Yorkshire wool industry, a male wool comber earned a good wage of 12 shillings or more a week, while a female spinner could hope for only 3½ shillings.[5] A single or widowed spinner faced a desperate struggle with poverty. Any period of illness or unemployment could spell disaster for her and any children she might have. In 1788 one

The Weaver's Repose   This painting by Decker Cornelis Gerritz (1594–1637) captures the pleasure of release from long hours of toil in cottage industry. The loom realistically dominates the cramped living space and the family's modest possessions. (Musées Royaux des Beaux-Arts, Brussels. Copyright A.C.I.)

Contrasting Views on the Effects of Rural Industry

English commentators quickly noted the effects of rural industry on families and daily life. Some were greatly impressed by the rise in living standards made possible by the putting-out system, while others noted the rising economic inequality between merchants and workers and the power the former acquired over the latter. In the first excerpt, novelist and economic writer Daniel Defoe enthusiastically praises cottage industry. He notes that the labor of women and children in spinning and weaving brought in as much as or more income than the man's agricultural work, allowing the family to eat well and be warmly clothed. It is interesting to note that Defoe assumes a rural world in which the process of enclosure is complete; poor men do not own their own land, but toil as wage laborers on the land of others. He also offers one explanation for the increasing use of Africans as slaves in British colonies: reliable wages from cottage industry meant that the English poor did not have to "sell themselves to the Plantations," thus leading plantation owners to seek other sources of labor.

The second source is a popular song written around 1700. Couched in the voice of the ruthless cloth merchant, it expresses the bitterness and resentment textile workers felt against their employers. One can imagine a group of weavers gathered together at the local tavern singing their protest on a rare break from work.

Daniel Defoe, *A Plan of the English Commerce*

❝ *Being a compleat prospect of the trade of this nation, as well the home trade as the foreign*, 1728

[A] poor labouring man that goes abroad to his Day Work, and Husbandry, Hedging, Ditching, Threshing, Carting, &c. and brings home his Week's Wages, suppose at eight Pence to twelve Pence a Day, or in some Counties less; if he has a Wife and three or four Children to feed, and who get little or nothing for themselves, must fare hard, and live poorly; 'tis easy to suppose it must be so.

But if this Man's Wife and Children can at the same Time get Employment, if at next Door, or at the next Village there lives a Clothier, or a Bay Maker, or a stuff or Drugget Weaver;* the Manufacturer sends the poor Woman combed Wool, or carded Wool every Week to spin, and she gets eight Pence or nine Pence a day at home; the Weaver sends for her two little Children, and they work by the Loom, winding, filling quills, &c. and the two bigger Girls spin at home with their Mother, and these earn three Pence or four Pence a Day each: So that put it together, the Family at Home gets as much as the Father gets Abroad, and generally more.

*Bay, stuff, and drugget were types of coarse woolen cloth typical of the inexpensive products of rural weaving.

This alters the Case extremely, the Family feels it, they all feed better, are cloth'd warmer, and do not so easily nor so often fall into Misery and Distress; the Father gets them Food, and the Mother gets them Clothes; and as they grow, they do not run away to be Footmen and Soldiers, Thieves and Beggars or sell themselves to the Plantations to avoid the Gaol and the Gallows, but have a Trade at their Hands, and every one can get their Bread.

N.B. I once went through a large populous manufacturing Town in England, and observ'd, that an Officer planted there, with a Serjeant and two Drums, had been beating up a long Time and could get no Recruits, except two or three Sots. . . . Enquiring the Reason of it, an honest Clothier of the Town answered me effectually thus, *The Case is plain*, says he, thus there is at this Time a brisk Demand for Goods, we have 1100 Looms, *added he*, in this Town and the Villages about it and not one of them want Work; and there is not a poor Child in the Town of above four Years old, but can earn his Bread; besides, there being so good a Trade at this Time, causes us to advance Wages a little and the Weaver and the Spinner get more than they used to do; and while it is so, they may beat the Heads of their Drums out, if they will, they'll get no Soldiers here. ❞

Anonymous, "The Clothier's Delight"

❝ *Or the rich Men's Joy, and the poor Men's Sorrow, wherein is exprest the Craftiness and Subtility of many Clothiers in England, by beating down their Workmen's Wages*, ca. 1700

Of all sorts of callings that in England be
There is none that liveth so gallant as we;
Our trading maintains us as brave as a knight,
We live at our pleasure and take our delight;
We heapeth up richest treasure great store
Which we get by griping and grinding the poor.
    And this is a way for to fill up our purse
    Although we do get it with many a curse.

Throughout the whole kingdom, in country and town,
There is no danger of our trade going down,
So long as the Comber can work with his comb,
And also the Weaver weave with his lomb;
The Tucker and Spinner that spins all the year,
We will make them to earn their wages full dear.
    And this is a way, etc.

And first for the Combers, we will bring them down,
From eight groats a score until half a crown;
If at all they murmur and say 'tis too small
We bid them choose whether they will work at all.
We'll make them believe that trading is bad

We care not a pin, though they are n'er so sad.
  And this is a way, etc.

We'll make the poor Weavers work at a low rate,
We'll find fault where there's no fault, and so we will
  bate;
If trading grows dead, we will presently show it,
But if it grows good, they shall never know it;
We'll tell them that cloth beyond sea will not go,
We care not whether we keep clothing or no.
  And this is a way, etc.

Then next for the Spinners we shall ensue;
We'll make them spin three pound instead of two;
When they bring home their work unto us, they
  complain
And say that their wages will not them maintain;
But that if an ounce of weight they do lack,
Then for to bate threepence we will not be slack.
  And this is a way, etc.

But if it holds weight, then their wages they crave,
We have got no money, and what's that you'd have?
We have bread and bacon and butter that's good,
With oatmeal and salt that is wholesome for food;
We have soap and candles whereby to give light,
That you may work by them so long as you have sight.
  And this is a way, etc.

. . .

And thus, we do gain our wealth and estate
By many poor men that work early and late;
If it were not for those that labour so hard,
We might go and hang ourselves without regard;
The combers, the weavers, the tuckers also,
With the spinners that work for wages full low,
By these people's labour we fill up our purse,
Although we do get it with many a curse. **"**

EVALUATE THE EVIDENCE

1. What division of labor in the textile industry does
    Defoe describe? How does this division of labor
    resemble or differ from the household in which you
    grew up?

2. On what basis are wages paid, and what strategies
    do merchants use to keep wages down, according
    to "The Clothier's Delight"? How are they able to
    impose such strategies on workers?

3. How do you reconcile the difference of opinion
    between the two sources? Was one right and the
    other wrong, or was the situation more complex?

Sources: Daniel Defoe, *A Plan of the English Commerce: Being a compleat prospect of the trade of this nation, as well the home trade as the foreign* (London, 1728), pp. 90–91; Paul Mantoux and Marjorie Vernon, eds., *The Industrial Revolution in the Eighteenth Century: An Outline of the Beginnings of the Modern Factory System in England* (1928; Taylor and Francis, 2006), pp. 76–77.

English writer condemned the low wages of spinners in Norwich: "The suffering of thousands of wretched individuals, willing to work, but starving from their ill requited labour; of whole families of honest industrious children offering their little hands to the wheel, and asking bread of the helpless mother, unable through this well regulated manufacture to give it to them."[6]

From the merchant capitalist's point of view, the problem was not low wages but maintaining control over the labor force. Cottage workers were scattered across the countryside and their work depended on the agricultural calendar. In spring and late summer planting and haymaking occupied all hands in the rural village, leading to shortages in the supply of thread. Merchants bitterly resented their lack of control over rural labor because their own livelihood depended on their ability to meet orders on time. They accused workers—especially female spinners—of laziness, drunkenness, and immorality. If workers failed to produce enough thread, they reasoned, it must be because their wages were too high and they had little incentive to work.

Merchants thus insisted on maintaining the lowest possible wages to force the "idle" poor into productive labor. They also lobbied for, and obtained, new police powers over workers. Imprisonment and public whipping became common punishments for pilfering small amounts of yarn or cloth. For poor workers, their right to hold on to the bits and pieces left over in the production process was akin to the traditional peasant right of gleaning in common lands. With progress came the loss of traditional safeguards for the poor.

The Industrious Revolution

One scholar has used the term **industrious revolution** to summarize the social and economic changes taking place in northwestern Europe in the late seventeenth and early eighteenth centuries.[7] This occurred as households reduced leisure time, stepped up the pace of work, and, most important, redirected the labor of women and children away from the production of goods for household consumption and toward wage work. In the countryside, the spread of cottage industry can be seen as one manifestation of the industrious revolution, while in the cities there was a rise in female employment outside the home (see page 556). By working harder and increasing the number of wageworkers, rural and urban households could purchase more goods, even in a time of stagnant or falling wages.

industrious revolution
The shift that occurred as families in northwestern Europe focused on earning wages instead of producing goods for household consumption; this reduced their economic self-sufficiency but increased their ability to purchase consumer goods.

The Linen Industry in Ireland   Many steps went into making textiles. Here the women are beating away the woody part of the flax plant so that the man can comb out the soft part. The combed fibers will then be spun into thread and woven into cloth by this family enterprise. The increased labor of women and girls from the late seventeenth century helped produce a significant expansion in the production of textiles in western Europe. (Private Collection/ The Stapleton Collection/The Bridgeman Art Library)

The effect of these changes is still debated. While some scholars lament the encroachment of longer work hours and stricter discipline, others insist that poor families made decisions based on their own self-interests. With more finished goods becoming available at lower prices, households sought cash income to participate in an emerging consumer economy.

The role of women and girls in this new economy is particularly controversial. When women entered the labor market, they almost always worked at menial, tedious jobs for very low wages. Yet when women earned their own wages, they also seem to have taken on a greater role in household decision making. Most of their scant earnings went for household necessities, items of food and clothing they could no longer produce now that they worked full-time, but sometimes a few shillings were left for a ribbon or a new pair of stockings. Women's use of their surplus income thus helped spur the rapid growth of the textile industries in which they labored so hard.

These new sources and patterns of labor established important foundations for the Industrial Revolution of the late eighteenth and nineteenth centuries (see Chapter 20). They created households in which all members worked for wages rather than in a family business and in which consumption relied on market-produced rather than homemade goods. It was not until the mid-nineteenth century, with rising industrial

wages, that a new model emerged in which the male "breadwinner" was expected to earn enough to support the whole family and women and children were relegated back to the domestic sphere. With women estimated to compose 40 percent of the global workforce, today's world is experiencing a second industrious revolution in a similar climate of stagnant wages and increased demand for consumer goods.[8]

The Debate over Urban Guilds

What were guilds, and why did they become controversial in the eighteenth century?

One consequence of the growth of rural industry was an undermining of the traditional **guild system** that protected urban artisans. Guilds continued to dominate production in towns and cities, providing their masters with economic privileges as well as a proud social identity, but they increasingly struggled against competition from rural workers. Meanwhile, those excluded from guild membership — women, day laborers, Jews, and foreigners — worked on the margins of the urban economy.

In the second half of the eighteenth century, critics attacked the guilds as outmoded institutions that obstructed technical progress and innovation. Until recently, most historians repeated that view. An ongoing reassessment of guilds now emphasizes their ability to adapt to changing economic circumstances.

Urban Guilds

Originating around 1200 during the economic boom of the Middle Ages, the guild system reached its peak in most of Europe in the seventeenth and eighteenth centuries. During this period, urban guilds increased dramatically in cities and towns across Europe. In Louis XIV's France, for example, finance minister Jean-Baptiste Colbert revived the urban guilds and used them to encourage high-quality production and to collect taxes (see Chapter 15). The number of guilds in the city of Paris grew from 60 in 1672 to 129 in 1691.

Guild masters occupied the summit of the world of work. Each guild possessed a detailed set of privileges, including exclusive rights to produce and sell certain goods, access to restricted markets in raw materials, and the rights to train apprentices, hire workers, and open shops. Any individual who violated these monopolies could be prosecuted. Guilds also served social and religious functions, providing a locus of sociability and group identity to the middling classes of European cities.

To ensure there was enough work to go around, guilds jealously restricted their membership to local men who were good Christians, had several years of work experience, paid stiff membership fees, and completed a masterpiece. They also favored family connections. Masters' sons enjoyed automatic access to their fathers' guilds, while outsiders were often barred from

guild system The organization of artisanal production into trade-based associations, or guilds, each of which received a monopoly over its trade and the right to train apprentices and hire workers.

Guild Procession in Seventeenth-Century Brussels Guilds played an important role in the civic life of the early modern city. They collected taxes from their members, imposed quality standards and order on the trades, and represented the interests of commerce and industry to the government. In return, they claimed exclusive monopolies over their trades and the right to govern their own affairs. Guilds marched in processions, like the one shown here, at important city events, proudly displaying their corporate insignia. (Victoria & Albert Museum, London/Art Resource, NY)

Adam Smith on the Division of Labor

In An Inquiry into the Nature and Causes of the Wealth of Nations *(1776), Scottish philosopher Adam Smith argued that commercial society — his term for the early capitalism of his age — was finally freeing the individual from the constraints of tradition, superstition, and cumbersome regulations. The passage below contains Smith's famous description of the division of labor, which permits a small number of men to do the work of many more. Although Smith lauded the gains in efficiency, skilled artisans bitterly resented the loss of control and specialized knowledge imposed by dividing production into isolated, repetitive steps.*

❝ To take an example, therefore, from a very trifling manufacture; but one in which the division of labor has been very often taken notice of, the trade of the pin-maker; a workman not educated to this business . . . nor acquainted with the use of the machinery employed in it . . . could scarce, perhaps, with his utmost industry, make one pin in a day, and certainly could not make twenty. But in the way in which this business is now carried on, not only the whole work is a peculiar trade, but it is divided into a number of branches, of which the greater part are likewise peculiar trades. One man draws out the wire, another straightens it, a third cuts it, a fourth points it, a fifth grinds it at the top for receiving the head; to make the head requires two or three distinct operations; to put it on, is a peculiar business, to whiten the pins is another; it is even a trade by itself to put them into the paper; and the important business of making a pin is, in this manner, divided into about eighteen distinct operations, which, in some manufactories, are all performed by distinct hands, though in others the same man will sometimes perform two or three of them. I have seen a small manufactory of this kind where ten men only were employed, and where some of them consequently performed two or three distinct operations. But though they were very poor, and therefore but indifferently accommodated with the necessary machinery, they could, when they exerted themselves, make among them about twelve pounds of pins in a day. There are in a pound upward of four thousand pins of a middling size. Those ten persons, therefore, could make among them upward of forty-eight thousand pins in a day. Each person, therefore, making a tenth part of forty-eight thousand pins, might be considered as making four thousand eight hundred pins in a day. But if they had all wrought separately and independently, and without any of them having been educated to this peculiar business, they certainly could not each of them have made twenty, perhaps not one pin in a day; that is, certainly not the two hundred and fortieth, perhaps not the four thousand eight hundredth part of what they are at present capable of performing, in consequence of a proper division and combination of their different operations. ❞

EVALUATE THE EVIDENCE

1. Into what steps — what Smith calls "peculiar trades" — is pin making divided? How do these steps make it possible for ten men to do the work of hundreds?
2. Why would skilled craftsmen oppose the division of labor described by Smith? What disadvantages did it create for them? For their guilds?

Source: Adam Smith, *The Wealth of Nations*, part 1 (New York: P. F. Collier & Son, 1902), pp. 44–45.

entering. Most urban men and women worked in non-guild trades as domestic servants, as manual laborers, and as vendors of food, used clothing, and other goods.

The guilds' ability to enforce their rigid barriers varied a great deal across Europe. In England, national regulations superseded guild rules, sapping their importance. In France, the Crown developed an ambiguous attitude toward guilds, relying on them for taxes and enforcement of quality standards, yet allowing non-guild production to flourish in the countryside in the 1760s, and even in some urban neighborhoods. The German guilds were perhaps the most powerful in Europe, and the most conservative. Journeymen in German cities, with their masters' support, violently protested the encroachment of non-guild workers.

While most were hostile to women, a small number of guilds did accept women. Most involved needlework and textile production, occupations that were considered appropriate for women. In 1675 seamstresses gained a new all-female guild in Paris, and soon seamstresses joined tailors' guilds in parts of France, England, and the Dutch Republic. By the mid-eighteenth century male masters began to hire more female workers, often in defiance of their own guild statutes.

Adam Smith and Economic Liberalism

At the same time that cottage industry began to infringe on the livelihoods of urban artisans, new Enlightenment ideals called into question the very existence of the guild system. Eighteenth-century critics derided guilds as outmoded and exclusionary institutions that obstructed technical innovation and progress. One of the best-known critics of government regulation of trade and industry was Adam Smith (1723–1790), a leading figure of the Scottish Enlightenment (see Chapter 16). Smith developed the general idea of freedom of enterprise and established the basis for modern economics in his groundbreaking work *Inquiry into the Nature and Causes of the Wealth of Nations* (1776). Smith criticized guilds for their stifling and outmoded restrictions, a critique he extended to all state monopolies and privileged companies. Far preferable was free competition, which would best protect consumers from price gouging and give all citizens a fair and equal right to do what they did best. Smith advocated a more highly developed "division of labor," which entailed separating craft production into individual tasks to increase workers' speed and efficiency. (See "Primary Source 17.3: Adam Smith on the Division of Labor," at left.)

In keeping with his deep-seated fear of political oppression and with the "system of natural liberty" that he championed, Smith argued that government should limit itself to "only three duties": it should provide a defense against foreign invasion, maintain civil order with courts and police protection, and sponsor certain indispensable public works and institutions that could never adequately profit private investors. He believed that the pursuit of self-interest in a competitive market would be sufficient to improve the living conditions of citizens, a view that quickly emerged as the classic argument for **economic liberalism**.

In the nineteenth and twentieth centuries Smith was often seen as an advocate of unbridled capitalism, but his ideas were considerably more complex. Unlike many disgruntled merchant capitalists, he applauded the modest rise in real wages of British workers in the eighteenth century, stating: "No society can surely be flourishing and happy, of which the far greater part of the members are poor and miserable." Smith also observed that employers were "always and everywhere in a sort of tacit, but constant and uniform combination, not to raise the wages of labor above their actual rate" and sometimes entered "into particular combinations to sink the wages even below this rate." While he celebrated the rise in productivity allowed by the division of labor, he also acknowledged its demoralizing effects on workers and called for government intervention to raise workers' living standards.[9]

Many educated people in France, including government officials, shared Smith's ideas. In 1776 the reform-minded economics minister Anne-Robert-Jacques Turgot issued a law abolishing all French guilds. The law stated:

> We wish to abolish these arbitrary institutions, which do not allow the poor man to earn his living; which reject a sex whose weakness has given it more needs and fewer resources . . . ; which destroy emulation and industry and nullify the talents of those whose circumstances have excluded them from membership of a guild; which deprive the state and the arts of all the knowledge brought to them by foreigners; which retard the progress of these arts . . . ; [and which] burden industry with an oppressive tax, which bears heavily on the people.[10]

Vociferous protests against this measure led to Turgot's disgrace shortly afterward, but the legislators of the French Revolution (see Chapter 19) were of the same liberal mind-set and disbanded the guilds again in 1791. Other European countries followed suit more slowly, with guilds surviving in central Europe and Italy into the second half of the nineteenth century.

Many artisans welcomed the economic liberalization espoused by Smith, but some continued to uphold the ideals of the guilds. In the late eighteenth and early nineteenth centuries, skilled artisans across Europe espoused the values of hand craftsmanship and limited competition in contrast to the proletarianization and loss of skills they endured in mechanized production. Recent scholarship has also challenged some of the criticism of the guilds, emphasizing the flexibility and adaptability of the guild system and the role it played in fostering confidence in quality standards. Nevertheless, by the middle of the nineteenth century economic deregulation was championed by most European governments and elites.

economic liberalism
A belief in free trade and competition based on Adam Smith's argument that the invisible hand of free competition would benefit all individuals, rich and poor.

The Atlantic World and Global Trade

How did colonial markets boost Europe's economic and social development, and what conflicts and adversity did world trade entail?

In addition to agricultural improvement, population pressure, and growing cottage industry, the expansion of Europe in the eighteenth century was characterized by the increase of world trade. Adam Smith himself declared that "the discovery of America and that of a passage to the East Indies by the Cape of Good Hope, are the two greatest and most important events recorded in the history of mankind."[11] In the eighteenth century Spain and Portugal revitalized their empires and began drawing more wealth from renewed colonial development. Yet once again the countries of northwestern Europe—the Dutch Republic, France, and above all Great Britain—benefited most.

The Atlantic economy that these countries developed from 1650 to 1790 would prove crucial in the building of a global economy. Great Britain, which was formed in 1707 by the union of England and Scotland into a single kingdom, gradually became the leading maritime power. Thus the British played the critical role in building a fairly unified Atlantic economy that provided remarkable opportunities for them and their colonists. They also competed ruthlessly with France and the Netherlands for trade and territory in Asia.

Mercantilism and Colonial Competition

Britain's commercial leadership in the eighteenth century had its origins in the mercantilism of the seventeenth century (see Chapter 15). Eventually eliciting criticism from Enlightenment thinker Adam Smith and other proponents of free trade in the late eighteenth century, European mercantilism was a system of economic regulations aimed at increasing the power of the state. As practiced by a leading advocate such as Colbert under Louis XIV, mercantilism aimed particularly at creating a favorable balance of foreign trade in order to increase a country's stock of gold. A country's gold holdings served as an all-important treasure chest that could be opened periodically to pay for war in a violent age.

In England, the desire to increase both military power and private wealth resulted in the mercantile system of the **Navigation Acts**. Oliver Cromwell established the first of these laws in 1651, and the restored monarchy of Charles II extended them in 1660 and 1663. The acts required that most goods imported from Europe into England and Scotland (Great Britain after 1707) be carried on British-owned ships with British crews or on ships of the country producing the article. Moreover, these laws gave British merchants and shipowners a virtual monopoly on trade with British colonies. The colonists were required to ship their products on British (or American) ships and to buy almost all European goods from Britain. It was believed that these economic regulations would eliminate foreign competition, thereby helping British merchants and workers as well as colonial plantation owners and farmers. It was hoped, too,

Navigation Acts A series of English laws that controlled the import of goods to Britain and British colonies.

that the emerging British Empire would develop a shipping industry with a large number of experienced seamen who could serve when necessary in the Royal Navy.

The Navigation Acts were a form of economic warfare. Their initial target was the Dutch, who were far ahead of the English in shipping and foreign trade in the mid-seventeenth century (see Chapter 15). In conjunction with three Anglo-Dutch wars between 1652 and 1674, the Navigation Acts seriously damaged Dutch shipping and commerce. The British seized the thriving Dutch colony of New Amsterdam in 1664 and renamed it New York. By the late seventeenth century the Dutch Republic was falling behind England in shipping, trade, and colonies.

Thereafter France stood clearly as England's most serious rival in the competition for overseas empire. Rich in natural resources, with a population three or four times that of England, and allied with Spain, continental Europe's leading military power was already building a powerful fleet and a worldwide system of rigidly monopolized colonial trade. Thus from 1701 to 1763 Britain and France were locked in a series of wars to decide, in part, which nation would become the leading maritime power and claim the profits of Europe's overseas expansion (Map 17.2).

The first round was the War of the Spanish Succession (see Chapter 15), which started in 1701 when Louis XIV accepted the Spanish crown willed to his grandson. Besides upsetting the continental balance of power, a union of France and Spain threatened to encircle and destroy the British colonies in North America (see Map 17.2). Defeated by a great coalition of states after twelve years of fighting, Louis XIV was forced in the Peace of Utrecht (YOO-trehkt) in 1713 to cede his North American holdings in Newfoundland, Nova Scotia, and the Hudson Bay territory to Britain. Spain was compelled to give Britain control of its West African slave trade—the so-called *asiento* (ah-SYEHN-toh)—and to let Britain send one ship of merchandise into the Spanish colonies annually.

Conflict continued among the European powers over both domestic and colonial affairs. The War of the Austrian Succession (1740–1748), which started when Frederick the Great of Prussia seized Silesia from Austria's Maria Theresa (see Chapter 16), gradually became a world war that included Anglo-French conflicts in India and North America. The war ended with no change in the territorial situation in North America. This inconclusive standoff helped set the stage for the Seven Years' War (1756–1763; see Chapter 19). In central Europe, France aided Austria's Maria Theresa in her quest to win back Silesia from the Prussians, who had formed an alliance with England. In North America, French and British settlers engaged in territorial

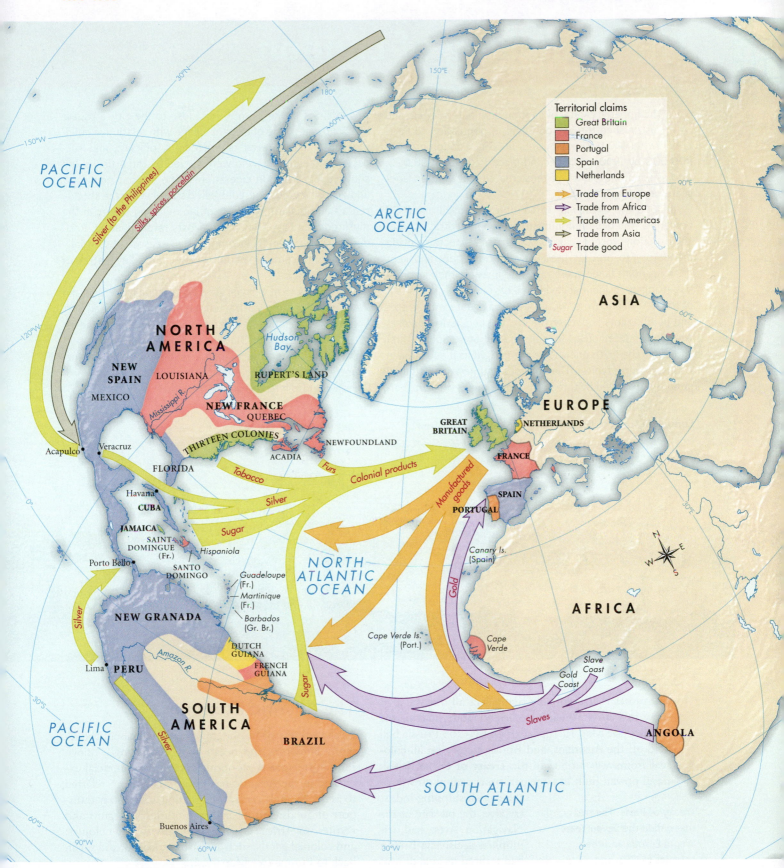

Map 17.2 The Atlantic Economy in 1701   The growth of trade encouraged both economic development and military conflict in the Atlantic basin. Four continents were linked together by the exchange of goods and slaves.

LIVING IN THE PAST
The Remaking of London

The imperial capital of London dominated Britain and astonished the visitor. Equal in population to Paris with 400,000 inhabitants in 1650, London grew to 900,000 by 1800, while second-place Paris had 600,000. And as London grew, its citizens created a new urban landscape and style of living.

In 1666 the Great Fire of London destroyed about 80 percent of the old, predominantly wooden central city. Reconstruction proceeded quickly, with brick structures made mandatory to prevent fires. As London rebuilt and kept growing, noble landowners sought to increase their incomes by setting up residential developments on their estates west of the city. A landowner would lay out a square with streets and building lots and lease the lots to speculative builders who put up fine houses for sale or rent. Soho Square, first laid out in the 1670s and shown at top right as it appeared in 1731, was fairly typical. The spacious square with its gated park is surrounded by three-story row houses on deep, nar-row lots. Set in the country but close to the city, a square like Soho was a kind of elegant village with restrictive building codes that catered to aristocrats, officials, and successful professionals who were served by the artisans and shopkeepers living in side streets. The elegant new area, known as the West End, contrasted sharply with the shoddy rentals and makeshift shacks of laborers and sailors in the mushrooming East End, which artists rarely painted. Residential segregation by income level increased substantially in eighteenth-century London and became a key feature of the modern city.

As the suburban villages grew and gradually merged, the West End increasingly attracted the well-to-do from all over England. Rural landowners and provincial notables came for the social season from October to May. The picture at bottom right of Bloomsbury Square in 1787 and the original country mansion of the enterprising noble developer provides a glimpse into this wellborn culture.

London Before the Great Fire. (Hulton Archive/Getty Images)

skirmishes that eventually resulted in all-out war that drew in Native American allies on both sides of the conflict (see Map 19.1, page 614). By 1763 Prussia had held off the Austrians, and British victory on all colonial fronts was ratified in the **Treaty of Paris**. British naval power, built in large part on the rapid growth of the British shipping industry after the passage of the Navigation Acts, had triumphed decisively: Britain had realized its goal of monopolizing a vast trading and colonial empire.

Treaty of Paris The treaty that ended the Seven Years' War in Europe and the colonies in 1763, and ratified British victory on all colonial fronts.

The Atlantic Economy

As the volume of transatlantic trade increased, the regions bordering the ocean were increasingly drawn into an integrated economic system. Commercial exchange in the Atlantic has traditionally been referred to as the "triangle trade," designating a three-way transport of goods: European commodities, like guns and textiles, to Africa; enslaved Africans to the colonies; and colonial goods, such as cotton, tobacco, and sugar, back to Europe (see Map 17.2).

Across the eighteenth century the economies of European nations bordering the Atlantic Ocean, espe-

Soho Square, 1731.
(Private Collection/The Stapleton Collection/The Bridgeman Art Library)

QUESTIONS FOR ANALYSIS

1. Examining the picture shown at left, how would you characterize London before the Great Fire?
2. Compare the paintings of Soho and Bloomsbury Squares. How are they complementary? Why did the artist choose to include a milkmaid and her cows in the illustration of Bloomsbury Square?

Bloomsbury Square, 1787. (Private Collection/© Look and Learn/Peter Jackson Collection/The Bridgeman Art Library)

cially England, relied more and more on colonial exports. In England, sales to the mainland colonies of North America and the West Indian sugar islands—with an important assist from West Africa and Latin America—soared from £500,000 to £4 million (Figure 17.3). Exports to England's colonies in Ireland and India also rose substantially from 1700 to 1800. By 1800 sales to European countries—England's traditional trading partners—represented only half of exports, down from three-quarters a century earlier. England also benefited from importing colonial products. Colonial monopolies allowed the English to obtain a steady supply of such goods at beneficial prices

and to re-export them to other nations at high profits. Moreover, many colonial goods, like sugar and tobacco, required processing before consumption and thus contributed new manufacturing jobs in England. In the eighteenth century, stimulated by trade and empire building, England's capital city, London, grew into the West's largest and richest city. (See "Living in the Past: The Remaking of London," above.) Thus the mercantilist system achieved remarkable success for England, and by the 1770s the country stood on the threshold of the epoch-making changes that would become known as the Industrial Revolution (see Chapter 20).

Although they lost many possessions to the English in the Seven Years' War, the French still profited enormously from colonial trade. The colonies of Saint-Domingue (modern-day Haiti), Martinique, and Guadeloupe remained in French hands and provided immense fortunes in plantation agriculture and slave trading during the second half of the eighteenth century. By 1789 the population of Saint-Domingue included five hundred thousand slaves whose labor had allowed the colony to become the world's leading producer of coffee and sugar and the most profitable plantation colony in the New World.[12] The wealth generated from colonial trade fostered the confidence of the merchant classes in Paris, Bordeaux, and other large cities, and merchants soon joined other elite groups clamoring for political reforms.

The third major player in the Atlantic economy, Spain, also saw its colonial fortunes improve during the eighteenth century. Not only did it gain Louisiana from France in 1763, but its influence expanded westward all the way to northern California through the efforts of Spanish missionaries and ranchers. Its mercantilist goals were boosted by a recovery in silver production, which had dropped significantly in the seventeenth century.

Silver mining also stimulated food production for the mining camps, and wealthy Spanish landowners developed a system of **debt peonage** to keep indigenous workers on their estates. Under this system, which was similar to serfdom, a planter or rancher would keep workers in perpetual debt bondage by advancing them food, shelter, and a little money.

Although the "triangle trade" model highlights some of the most important flows of commerce across the Atlantic, it significantly oversimplifies the picture. For example, a brisk intercolonial trade also existed, with the Caribbean slave colonies importing food in the form of fish, flour, and livestock from the northern colonies and rice from the south, in exchange for sugar and slaves (see Map 17.2). Many colonial traders violated imperial monopolies to trade with the most profitable partners, regardless of nationality. Moreover, the Atlantic economy was inextricably linked to trade with the Indian and Pacific Oceans (see page 570).

debt peonage A form of serfdom that allowed a planter or rancher to keep his workers or slaves in perpetual debt bondage by periodically advancing food, shelter, and a little money.

Atlantic slave trade The forced migration of Africans across the Atlantic for slave labor on plantations and in other industries; the trade reached its peak in the eighteenth century and ultimately involved more than 12 million Africans.

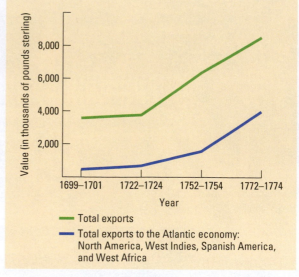

Figure 17.3 **Exports of English Manufactured Goods, 1700–1774** While trade between England and Europe stagnated after 1700, English exports to Africa and the Americas boomed and greatly stimulated English economic development.
(Source: Data from R. Davis, "English Foreign Trade, 1700–1774," *Economic History Review*, 2d ser., 15 [1962]: 302–303.)

The Atlantic Slave Trade

At the core of the Atlantic world were the misery and profit of the **Atlantic slave trade**. The forced migration of millions of Africans—cruel, unjust, and tragic—was a key element in the Atlantic system and western European economic expansion throughout the eighteenth century. The brutal practice intensified dramatically after 1700 and especially after 1750 with the growth of trade and demand for slave-produced goods like sugar and cotton. According to the most authoritative source, European traders purchased and shipped 6.5 million enslaved Africans across the Atlantic between 1701 and 1800—more than half of the estimated total of 12.5 million Africans transported between 1450 and 1900, of whom 15 percent died in procurement and transit.[13] By the peak decade of the 1780s, shipments averaged about eighty thousand individuals per year in an attempt to satisfy the constantly rising demand for labor power—and also for slave owners' profits—in the Americas.

The rise of plantation agriculture was responsible for the tremendous growth of the slave trade. Among all European colonies, the plantations of Portuguese Brazil received by far

Plantation Zones, ca. 1700

the largest number of enslaved Africans over the entire period of the slave trade—45 percent of the total. Another 45 percent were divided among the many Caribbean colonies. The colonies of mainland North America took only 3 percent of slaves arriving from Africa, a little under four hundred thousand, relying mostly on natural growth of the enslaved population.

Eighteenth-century intensification of the slave trade resulted in fundamental changes in its organization. After 1700, as Britain became the undisputed leader in shipping slaves across the Atlantic, European governments and ship captains cut back on fighting among themselves and concentrated on commerce. They generally adopted the shore method of trading, which was less expensive than maintaining fortified trading posts. Under this system, European ships sent boats ashore or invited African dealers to bring traders and slaves out to their ships. This method allowed ships to move easily along the coast from market to market and to depart more quickly for the Americas.

Some African merchants and rulers who controlled exports profited from the greater demand for slaves. With their newfound wealth, some Africans gained access to European and colonial goods, including firearms. But generally such economic returns did not spread very far, and the negative consequences of the expanding slave trade predominated. Wars among African states to obtain salable captives increased, and leaders used slave profits to purchase more arms than

The Atlantic Slave Trade   This engraving from 1814 shows traders leading a group of slaves to the West African coast, where they will board ships to cross the Atlantic. Many slaves died en route or arrived greatly weakened and ill. The newspaper advertisement of the sale of a ship's cargo of slaves in Charleston, South Carolina, promises "fine, healthy negroes," testifying to the dangers of the crossing and to the frequency of epidemic diseases like smallpox. (engraving: Bibliothèque de l'Arsenal, Paris/Archives Charmet/The Bridgeman Art Library; advertisement: The Granger Collection, New York)

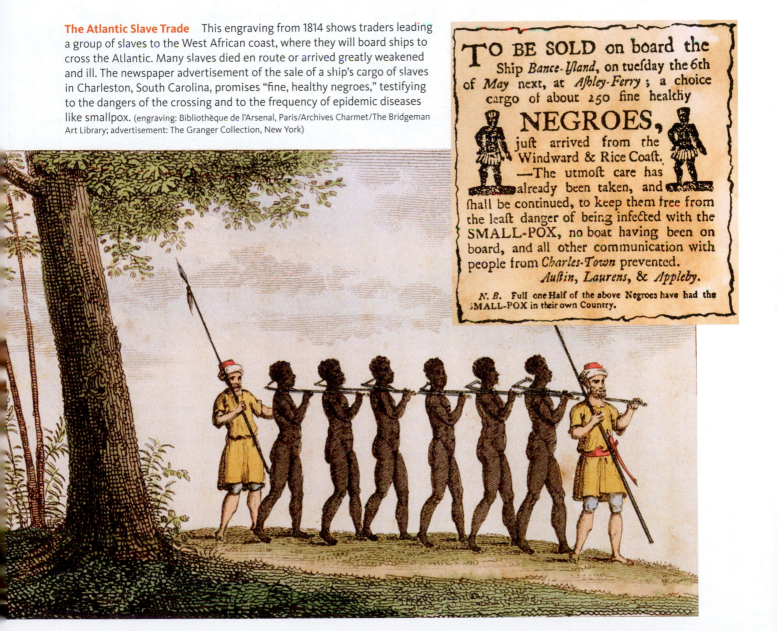

Slaves Harvesting Sugarcane   In this 1828 print, a long line of hard-working slaves systematically harvests the ripe cane on the island of Antigua, while on the right more slaves load cut cane into wagons for refining at the plantation's central crushing mill. The manager on horseback may be ordering the overseer to quicken the work pace, always brutal and unrelenting at harvest time. Slave labor made high-intensity capitalist production of sugar possible in the Americas. (John Carter Brown Library at Brown University)

textiles and consumer goods. While the populations of Europe and Asia grew substantially in the eighteenth century, the population of Africa stagnated or possibly declined. As one contemporary critic observed:

> I do not know if coffee and sugar are essential to the happiness of Europe, but I know that these two products have accounted for the unhappiness of two great regions of the world: America has been depopulated so as to have land on which to plant them; Africa has been depopulated so as to have the people to cultivate them.[14]

Most Europeans did not personally witness the horrors of the slave trade between Africa and the Americas, and until the early part of the eighteenth century they considered the African slave trade a legitimate business. But as details of the plight of enslaved people became known, a campaign to abolish slavery developed in Britain. (See "Primary Source 17.4: Olaudah

Equiano's Economic Arguments for Ending Slavery," at right.) In the late 1780s the abolition campaign grew into a mass movement of public opinion, the first in British history. British women were prominent in this movement, denouncing the immorality of human bondage and stressing the cruel and sadistic treatment of enslaved women and families. These attacks put the defenders of slavery on the defensive. In 1807 Parliament abolished the British slave trade, although slavery continued in British colonies and the Americas for decades.

Identities and Communities of the Atlantic World

Not only slaves and commodities but also cultural ideas and values—as well as free people of European, African, and American descent—circulated through the eighteenth-century Atlantic world. As contacts between the Atlantic coasts of the Americas, Africa, and Europe

Olaudah Equiano's Economic Arguments for Ending Slavery

According to his autobiography, first published in 1789, Olaudah Equiano was born in Benin (modern Nigeria) of Ibo ethnicity and was abducted and transported across the Atlantic as a child. Equiano served a British Royal Navy officer, who educated the boy, but then sold him to a Quaker merchant. Equiano eventually bought his freedom from his master and returned to England, where he worked as a hairdresser and merchant seaman. Having won fame by publishing his life story, Equiano campaigned ardently to end slavery, as documented in the excerpt below.

❝ Tortures, murder, and every other imaginable barbarity and iniquity, are practised upon the poor slaves with impunity. I hope the great slave trade will be abolished. I pray it may be an event at hand. The great body of manufacturers, uniting in the cause, will considerably facilitate and expedite it; and, as I have already stated, it is most substantially their interest and advantage, and as such the nation's at large (except those persons concerned in the manufacturing [of] neck-yokes, collars, chains, handcuffs, leg-bolts, drags, thumbscrews, iron muzzles, and coffins; cats, scourges, and other instruments of torture used in the slave trade). In a short time one sentiment alone will prevail, from motives of interest as well as justice and humanity. Europe contains one hundred and twenty million of inhabitants. Query — How many millions doth Africa contain? Supposing the Africans, collectively and individually, to expend 5£ a head in raiment and furniture yearly when civilized, &c. an immensity beyond the reach of imagination!

This I conceive to be a theory founded upon facts, and therefore an infallible one. If the blacks were permitted to remain in their own country, they would double themselves every fifteen years. In proportion to such increase will be the demand for manufactures. Cotton and indigo grow spontaneously in most parts of Africa; a consideration this of no small consequence to the manufacturing towns of Great Britain. It opens a most immense, glorious, and happy prospect — the clothing, &c. of a continent ten thousand miles in circumference, and immensely rich in productions of every denomination in return for manufactures. **❞**

EVALUATE THE EVIDENCE

1. Why does Equiano believe England will profit more by trading with free Africans than by enslaving them? Who do you think the audience for this document was, and how might the audience affect the message?
2. What broader economic and cultural developments in eighteenth-century England does Equiano's plea reflect?

Source: Olaudah Equiano, *The Interesting Narrative of the Life of Olaudah Equiano*, ed. Robert J. Allison, 2d ed. (Boston: Bedford/St. Martin's, 2007), p. 213.

became more frequent, and as European settlements grew into well-established colonies, new identities and communities emerged.

The term *Creole* referred to people of Spanish ancestry born in the Americas. Wealthy Creoles and their counterparts throughout the Atlantic colonies prided themselves on following European ways of life. In addition to their lavish plantation estates, they maintained townhouses in colonial cities built on the European model, with theaters, central squares, churches, and coffeehouses. They purchased luxury goods made in Europe, and their children were often sent to be educated in the home country.

Over time, however, the colonial elite came to feel that their circumstances gave them different interests and characteristics from those of their home population. As one observer explained, "A turn of mind peculiar to the planter, occasioned by a physical difference of constitution, climate, customs, and education, tends . . . to repress the remains of his former attachment to his native soil."[15] Creole traders and planters increasingly resented the regulations and taxes imposed by colonial bureaucrats, and such resentment would eventually lead to revolution against colonial powers (see Chapter 19).

Not all Europeans in the colonies were wealthy. Numerous poor or middling whites worked as clerks, shopkeepers, craftsmen, and plantation managers. With the exception of British North America, white Europeans made up a minority of the population. Since European migrants were disproportionately male, much of the population of the Atlantic world descended from unions — forced or through choice — of European men and indigenous or African women. (See "Primary

Mulatto Painting

The caption in the upper left-hand corner of this mid-eighteenth-century painting identifies the family as being composed of a Spanish father and a black mother, whose child is described as "mulatto." The painting was number six in a series of sixteen images by the painter Jose de Alcibar, each showing a different racial and ethnic combination. The series belonged to a popular genre in the Spanish Americas known as castas *paintings, which commonly depicted sixteen different forms of racial mixing.*

(Attrib. Jose de Alcibar, 6, *De Espanol y Negra, Mulato*, ca. 1760–1770. Denver Art Museum: Collection of Frederick and Jan Mayer. Photo © James O. Milmoe)

EVALUATE THE EVIDENCE

1. How would you characterize the relations among mother, father, and child as shown in this painting? Does the painter suggest power relations within the family? What attitude does the painter seem to have toward the family?
2. Why do you think such paintings were so popular? Who do you think the audience might have been, and why would viewers be fascinated by such images?

Source 17.5: Mulatto Painting," at left.) Colonial attempts to classify and systematize racial categories greatly influenced developing Enlightenment thought on racial difference (see Chapter 16).

Mixed-race populations sometimes rose to the colonial elite. The Spanish conquistadors often consolidated their power through marriage to the daughters of local rulers, and their descendants were among the most powerful inhabitants of Spanish America. In the Spanish and French Caribbean, as in Brazil, many masters acknowledged and freed their mixed-race children, leading to sizable populations of free people of color. Advantaged by their fathers, some became wealthy land and slave owners in their own right. In the second half of the eighteenth century, the prosperity of some free people of color brought a backlash from the white population of Saint-Domingue in the form of new race laws prohibiting nonwhites from marrying whites and forcing them to adopt distinctive attire.

British colonies followed a distinctive pattern. There, whole families, rather than individual men, migrated, resulting in a rapid increase in the white population. This development was favored by British colonial law, which forbade marriage between English men and women and Africans or Native Americans. In the British colonies of the Caribbean and the southern mainland, masters tended to leave their mixed-race progeny in slavery rather than freeing them, maintaining a stark discrepancy between free whites and enslaved people of color.[16] The identities inspired by racial and ethnic mixing were equally complex. Colonial elites became "Americanized" by adopting native foods, like chocolate and potatoes, and sought relief from tropical disease in native remedies. Some mixed-race people sought to enter Creole society and obtain its many official and unofficial privileges by passing as white. Where they existed in any number, though, free people of color established their own social hierarchies based on wealth, family connections, occupation, and skin color.

Converting indigenous people to Christianity was a key ambition for all European powers in the New World. Galvanized by the Protestant Reformation and the perceived need to protect and spread Catholicism, Catholic powers actively sponsored missionary efforts. Jesuits, Franciscans, Dominicans, and other religious orders established missions throughout Spanish, Portuguese, and French colonies (see Chapter 14). In Central and South America, large-scale conversion forged enduring Catholic cultures in Portuguese and Spanish colonies. Conversion efforts in North America were less effective because indigenous settlements were more scattered and native people were less integrated into colonial communities. On the whole, Protestants were less active as missionaries in this period, although some dissenters, like Moravians, Quakers, and Methodists, did seek converts among indigenous and enslaved

people. (See "Individuals in Society: Rebecca Protten," page 568.)

The practice of slavery reveals important limitations on efforts to spread Christianity. Slave owners often refused to baptize their slaves, fearing that enslaved people would use their Christian status to claim additional rights. In some areas, particularly among the mostly African-born slaves of the Caribbean, elements of African religious belief and practice endured, often incorporated with Christian traditions.

Restricted from owning land and holding many occupations in Europe, Jews were eager participants in the new Atlantic economy and established a network of mercantile communities along its trade routes. As in the Old World, Jews in European colonies faced discrimination; for example, restrictions existed on the number of slaves they could own in Barbados in the early eighteenth century.[17] Jews were considered to be white Europeans and thus ineligible to be slaves, but they did not enjoy equal status with Christians. The status of Jews adds one more element to the complexity of Atlantic identities.

The Colonial Enlightenment

Enlightenment ideas thrived in the colonies, although with as much diversity and disagreement as in Europe (see Chapter 16). The colonies of British North America were deeply influenced by the Scottish Enlightenment, with its emphasis on pragmatic approaches to the problems of life. Following the Scottish model, leaders in the colonies adopted a moderate, "common-sense" version of the Enlightenment that emphasized self-improvement and ethical conduct. In most cases, this version of the Enlightenment was perfectly compatible with religion and was chiefly spread through the growing colleges and universities of the colonies, which remained church-based institutions.

Some thinkers went even further in their admiration for Enlightenment ideas. Benjamin Franklin's writings and political career provide an outstanding example of the combination of the pragmatism and economic interests of the Scottish Enlightenment with the constitutional theories of John Locke, Jean-Jacques Rousseau, and the baron de Montesquieu. Franklin was privately a lifelong deist, meaning that he believed in God but not in organized religion. Nonetheless, he continued to attend church and respect religious proprieties, a cautious pattern followed by fellow deist Thomas Jefferson and other leading thinkers of the American Enlightenment.

Northern Enlightenment thinkers often depicted the Spanish American colonies as the epitome of the superstition and barbarity they contested. The Catholic Church strictly controlled the publication of books there, just as it did on the Iberian Peninsula. None-

Rebecca Protten

In the mid-1720s a young English-speaking girl who came to be known as Rebecca traveled by ship from Antigua to the small Danish sugar colony of St. Thomas, today part of the U.S. Virgin Islands. Eighty-five percent of St. Thomas's four thousand inhabitants were of African descent, almost all enslaved. Sugar plantations demanded backbreaking work, and slave owners used extremely brutal methods to maintain control, including amputations and beheadings for runaways.

Surviving documents refer to Rebecca as a "mulatto," indicating a mixed European and African ancestry. A wealthy Dutch-speaking planter named van Beverhout purchased the girl for his household staff, sparing her a position in the grueling and deadly sugar fields. Rebecca won the family's favor, and they taught her to read, write, and speak Dutch. They also shared with her their Protestant faith and took the unusual step of freeing her.

As a free woman, she continued to work as a servant for the van Beverhouts and to study the Bible and spread its message of spiritual freedom. In 1736 she met some missionaries for the Moravian Church, a German-Protestant sect that emphasized emotion and communal worship and devoted its mission work to the enslaved peoples of the Caribbean. The missionaries were struck by Rebecca's piety and her potential to assist their work. As one wrote: "She researches diligently in the Scriptures, loves the Savior, and does much good for other Negro women because she does not simply walk alone with her good ways but instructs them in the Scriptures as well." A letter Rebecca sent to Moravian women in Germany declared: "Oh how good is the Lord. My heart melts when I think of it. His name is wonderful. Oh! Help me to praise him, who has pulled me out of the darkness. I will take up his cross with all my heart and follow the example of his poor life."*

Rebecca soon took charge of the Moravians' female missionary work. Every Sunday and every evening after work, she would walk for miles to lead meetings with enslaved and free black women. The meetings consisted of reading and writing lessons, prayers, hymns, a sermon, and individual discussions in which she encouraged her new sisters in their spiritual growth.

*Quotations from Jon F. Sensbach, *Rebecca's Revival: Creating Black Christianity in the Atlantic World* (Cambridge, Mass.: Harvard University Press, 2006), pp. 61, 63.

A portrait of Rebecca Protten with her second husband and their daughter, Anna-Maria. (Courtesy of Jon F. Sensbach. Used by permission of the Moravian Archives [Unity Archives, Herrnhut, Germany])

In 1738 Rebecca married a German Moravian missionary, Matthaus Freundlich, a rare but not illegal case of mixed marriage. The same year, her husband bought a plantation, with slaves, to serve as the headquarters of their mission work. The Moravians — and presumably Rebecca herself — wished to spread Christian faith among slaves and improve their treatment, but did not oppose the institution of slavery itself.

Authorities nonetheless feared that baptized and literate slaves would agitate for freedom, and they imprisoned Rebecca and Matthaus and tried to shut down the mission.

ONLINE DOCUMENT ASSIGNMENT

What does Rebecca Protten's story reveal about the complex relationship among slavery, race, and religion in the eighteenth century? Go to the Integrated Media and examine primary sources concerning these interconnected issues, and then complete a writing assignment based on the evidence and details from this chapter.

Only the unexpected arrival on St. Thomas of German aristocrat and Moravian leader Count Zinzendorf saved the couple. Exhausted by their ordeal, they left for Germany in 1741 accompanied by their small daughter, but both father and daughter died soon after their arrival.

In Marienborn, a German center of the Moravian faith, Rebecca encountered other black Moravians, who lived in equality alongside their European brethren. In 1746 she married another missionary, Christian Jacob Protten, son of a Danish sailor and, on his mother's side, grandson of a West African king. She and another female missionary from St. Thomas were ordained as deaconesses, probably making them the first women of color to be ordained in the Western Christian Church.

In 1763 Rebecca and her husband set out for her husband's birthplace, the Danish slave fort at Christiansborg (in what is now Accra, Ghana) to establish a school for mixed-race children. Her husband died in 1769, leaving Rebecca a widow once more. After declining the offer of passage back to the West Indies in 1776, she died in obscurity near Christiansborg in 1780.

QUESTIONS FOR ANALYSIS

1. Why did Moravian missionaries assign such an important leadership role to Rebecca? What particular attributes did she offer?
2. Why did Moravians, including Rebecca, accept the institution of slavery instead of fighting to end it?
3. What does Rebecca's story teach us about the Atlantic world of the mid-eighteenth century?

theless, educated elites were well aware of the new currents of thought, and the universities, newspapers, and salons of Spanish America produced their own reform ideas. The establishment of a mining school in Mexico City in 1792, the first in the Spanish colonies, illuminates the practical achievements of reformers. In all European colonies, one effect of Enlightenment thought was to encourage colonists to criticize the policies of the mother country and aspire toward greater autonomy.

Trade and Empire in Asia and the Pacific

As the Atlantic economy took shape, Europeans continued to vie for dominance in the Asian trade. Between 1500 and 1600 the Portuguese had become major players in the Indian Ocean trading world, eliminating Venice as Europe's chief supplier of spices and other Asian luxury goods. The Portuguese dominated but did not fundamentally alter the age-old pattern of Indian Ocean trade, which involved merchants from many areas as more or less autonomous players. This situation changed radically with the intervention of the Dutch and then the English (see Chapter 14).

Formed in 1602, the Dutch East India Company had taken control of the Portuguese spice trade in the Indian Ocean, with the port of Batavia (Jakarta) in Java as its center of operations. Within a few decades they had expelled the Portuguese from Ceylon and other East Indian islands. Unlike the Portuguese, the Dutch transformed the Indian Ocean trading world. Whereas East Indian states and peoples maintained independence under the Portuguese, who treated them as autonomous business partners, the Dutch established outright control and reduced them to dependents.

After these successes, the Dutch hold in Asia faltered in the eighteenth century due to the company's failure to diversify to meet changing consumption patterns. Spices continued to compose much of its shipping, despite their declining importance in the European diet, probably due to changing fashions in food and luxury consumption. Fierce competition from its main rival, the English East India Company (established 1600), also severely undercut Dutch trade.

Britain initially struggled for a foothold in Asia. With the Dutch monopolizing the Indian Ocean, the British turned to India, the source of lucrative trade in silks, textiles, and pepper. Throughout the seventeenth century the English East India Company relied on trade concessions from the powerful Mughal emperor, who granted only piecemeal access to the subcontinent. Finally, in 1716 the Mughals conceded empire-wide trading privileges. As Mughal power waned, British East India Company agents increasingly intervened in local affairs and made alliances or waged war against Indian princes.

India, 1805

- Mughal Empire, 1707
- British India, 1805

Britain's great rival for influence in India was France. During the War of the Austrian Succession, British and French forces in India supported opposing rulers in local power struggles. In 1757 East India Company forces under Robert Clive conquered the rich northeastern province of Bengal at the Battle of Plassey. French-English rivalry was finally resolved by the Treaty of Paris, which granted all of France's possessions in India to the British with the exception of Pondicherry, an Indian Ocean port city. With the elimination of their rival, British ascendancy in India accelerated. In 1765 the Mughal shah granted the East India Company *diwani*, the right to civil administration and tax collection, in Bengal and neighboring provinces. By the early nineteenth century the company had overcome vigorous Indian resistance to gain economic and political dominance of much of the subcontinent; direct administration by the British government replaced East India Company rule after a large-scale rebellion in 1857.

The late eighteenth century also witnessed the beginning of British settlement of the continent of Australia. The continent was first sighted by Europeans in the early seventeenth century, and thereafter parts of the coast were charted by European ships. Captain James Cook claimed the east coast of Australia for England in 1770, naming it New South Wales. The first colony was established there in the late 1780s, relying on the labor of convicted prisoners forcibly transported from Britain. Settlement of the western portion of the continent followed in the 1790s. The first colonies struggled for survival and, after an initial period of friendly relations, soon aroused the hostility and resistance of aboriginal peoples. Cook himself was killed by islanders in Hawaii in 1779, having charted much of the Pacific Ocean for the first time.

The rising economic and political power of Europeans in this period drew on the connections they established between the Asian and Atlantic trade worlds. An outstanding example is the trade in cowrie shells. These seashells, originating in the Maldive Islands in the Indian Ocean, were used as a form of currency in West

The British in India, ca. 1785 This Indian miniature shows the wife (center) of a British officer attended by many Indian servants. A British merchant (left) awaits her attention. The picture reflects the luxurious lifestyle of the British elite in India, many members of which returned home with colossal fortunes. (Werner Forman/Art Resource, NY)

Africa. European traders obtained them in Asia, packing them alongside porcelains, spices, and silks for the journey home. The cowries were then brought from European ports to the West African coast to be traded for slaves. Indian textiles were also prized in Africa and played a similar role in exchange. Thus the trade of the Atlantic was inseparable from Asian commerce, and Europeans were increasingly found dominating commerce in both worlds.

Notes

1. B. H. Slicher van Bath, *The Agrarian History of Western Europe, A.D. 500–1850* (New York: St. Martin's Press, 1963), p. 240.
2. Cited in Paul Mantoux, *The Industrial Revolution in the Eighteenth Century: An Outline of the Beginnings of the Modern Factory System* (1961; Abingdon, U.K.: Routledge, 2005), p. 175.
3. Thomas Salmon, *Modern History: Or the Present State of All Nations* (London, 1730), p. 406.
4. Quoted in I. Pinchbeck, *Women Workers and the Industrial Revolution, 1750–1850* (New York: F. S. Crofts, 1930), p. 113.
5. Richard J. Soderlund, "'Intended as a Terror to the Idle and Profligate': Embezzlement and the Origins of Policing in the Yorkshire Worsted Industry, c. 1750–1777," *Journal of Social History* 31 (Spring 1998): 658.
6. Cited in Maxine Berg, *The Age of Manufactures, 1700–1820: Industry, Innovation, and Work in Britain* (London: Routledge, 1994), p. 124.
7. Jan de Vries, *The Industrious Revolution: Consumer Behavior and the Household Economy, 1650 to the Present* (Cambridge, U.K.: Cambridge University Press, 2008).
8. Jan de Vries, "The Industrial Revolution and the Industrious Revolution," *The Journal of Economic History* 54, no. 2 (June 1994): 249–270; discusses the industrious revolution of the second half of the twentieth century.
9. R. Heilbroner, *The Essential Adam Smith* (New York: W. W. Norton, 1986), p. 196.
10. S. Pollard and C. Holmes, eds., *Documents of European Economic History*, vol. 1, *The Process of Industrialization, 1750–1870* (New York: St. Martin's Press, 1968), p. 53.
11. Ibid., p. 281.
12. Laurent Dubois and John D. Garrigus, *Slave Revolution in the Caribbean, 1789–1904* (New York: Palgrave, 2006), p. 8.
13. Figures obtained from Voyages: The Trans-Atlantic Slave Trade Database, http://www.slavevoyages.org/tast/assessment/estimates.faces (accessed June 11, 2009).
14. Cited in Thomas Benjamin, *The Atlantic World: Europeans, Africans, Indians and Their Shared History, 1400–1900* (Cambridge, U.K.: Cambridge University Press, 2009), p. 211.
15. Pierre Marie François Paget, *Travels Round the World in the Years 1767, 1768, 1769, 1770, 1771*, vol. 1 (London, 1793), p. 262.
16. Orlando Patterson, *Slavery and Social Death* (Cambridge, Mass.: Harvard University Press, 1982), p. 255.
17. Erik R. Seeman, "Jews in the Early Modern Atlantic: Crossing Boundaries, Keeping Faith," in *The Atlantic in Global History, 1500–2000*, ed. Jorge Cañizares-Esguerra and Erik R. Seeman (Upper Saddle River, N.J.: Pearson Prentice Hall, 2007), p. 43.

LOOKING BACK LOOKING AHEAD

By the turn of the eighteenth century, western Europe had begun to shake off the effects of long decades of famine, disease, warfare, economic depression, and demographic stagnation. The eighteenth century witnessed a breakthrough in agricultural production that, along with improved infrastructure and the retreat of epidemic disease, contributed to a substantial increase in population. One crucial catalyst for agricultural innovation was the Scientific Revolution, which provided new tools of empirical observation and experimentation. The Enlightenment as well, with its emphasis on progress and public welfare, convinced government officials, scientists, and informed landowners to seek better solutions to old problems. By the end of the century, industry and trade had also attracted enlightened commentators who advocated free markets and less government control. Modern ideas of political economy thus constitute one more legacy of the Enlightenment.

As the era of European exploration and conquest gave way to colonial empire building, the eighteenth century witnessed increased consolidation of global markets and bitter competition among Europeans for the spoils of empire. From its slow inception in the mid-fifteenth century, the African slave trade reached brutal heights in the second half of the eighteenth century. The eighteenth-century Atlantic world thus tied the shores of Europe, the Americas, and Africa in a web of commercial and human exchange that also had strong ties with the Pacific and the Indian Oceans.

The new dynamics of the eighteenth century prepared the way for world-shaking changes. Population growth and rural industry began to undermine long-standing traditions of daily life in western Europe. The transformed families of the industrious revolution developed not only new habits of work, but also a new sense of confidence in their abilities. By the 1770s England was approaching an economic transformation fully as significant as the great political upheaval destined to develop shortly in neighboring France. In the same period, the first wave of resistance to European domination rose up in the colonies. The great revolutions of the late eighteenth century would change the world forever.

REVIEW and EXPLORE

MAKE IT STICK

 LearningCurve
After reading the chapter, go online and use LearningCurve to retain what you've read.

Identify Key Terms

Identify and explain the significance of each item below.

enclosure (p. 543)

proletarianization (p. 546)

cottage industry (p. 549)

putting-out system (p. 549)

industrious revolution (p. 553)

guild system (p. 554)

economic liberalism (p. 557)

Navigation Acts (p. 558)

Treaty of Paris (p. 560)

debt peonage (p. 562)

Atlantic slave trade (p. 562)

Review the Main Ideas

Answer the focus questions from each section of the chapter.

◆ What important developments led to increased agricultural production, and how did these changes affect peasants? (p. 542)

◆ Why did the European population rise dramatically in the eighteenth century? (p. 546)

◆ How and why did rural industry intensify in the eighteenth century? (p. 549)

◆ What were guilds, and why did they become controversial in the eighteenth century? (p. 554)

◆ How did colonial markets boost Europe's economic and social development, and what conflicts and adversity did world trade entail? (p. 557)

Make Connections

Think about the larger developments and continuities within and across chapters.

1. What was the relationship among agriculture, industry, and population in the eighteenth century? How and why did developments in one area impact the others?

2. Compare the economic and social situation of western Europe in the mid-eighteenth century with that of the seventeenth century (Chapter 15). What were the achievements of the eighteenth century and what factors allowed for such progress to be made?

3. The eighteenth century was the period of the European Enlightenment, which celebrated tolerance and human liberty (Chapter 16). Paradoxically, it was also the era of a tremendous increase in slavery, which brought suffering and death to millions. How would you reconcile this paradox?

ONLINE DOCUMENT ASSIGNMENT
Rebecca Protten

What does Rebecca Protten's story reveal about the complex relationship among slavery, race, and religion in the eighteenth century?

You encountered Rebecca Protten's story on page 568. Keeping the question above in mind, go to the Integrated Media and examine primary sources concerning these interconnected issues— including an account of early Moravian missionary activity in the West Indies, an essay on the conversion of slaves, and a pamphlet on the same topic. Then complete a writing assignment based on the evidence and details from this chapter.

● Suggested Reading and Media Resources

BOOKS

◆ Allen, Robert, et al., eds. *Living Standards in the Past: New Perspectives on Well-Being in Asia and Europe.* 2004. Offers rich comparative perspectives on population growth and living standards among common people.

◆ Bell, Dean Phillip. *Jews in the Early Modern World.* 2008. A broad examination of Jewish life and relations with non-Jews in the early modern period.

◆ Carpenter, Roger M. *The Renewed, the Destroyed, and the Remade: The Three Thought Worlds of the Iroquois and the Huron, 1609–1650.* 2004. Explores the culture and beliefs of two Native American peoples in the period of European colonization.

◆ Farr, James R. *Artisans in Europe, 1300–1914.* 2000. An overview of guilds and artisanal labor in early modern Europe.

◆ Gullickson, Gary L. *Spinners and Weavers of Auffay: Rural Industry and the Sexual Division of Labor in a French Village, 1750–1850.* 1986. Examines women's labor in cottage industry in northern France.

◆ Harms, Robert W. *The Diligent: A Voyage Through the Worlds of the Slave Trade.* 2002. A deeply moving account of a French slave ship and its victims.

◆ Klein, Herbert S. *The Atlantic Slave Trade.* 1999. An excellent short synthesis on slavery in the Atlantic world.

◆ Morgan, Jennifer Lyle. *Laboring Women: Reproduction and Gender in New World Slavery.* 2004. Focuses on the role of women's labor in the evolution of slavery in Britain's North American colonies.

◆ Ormrod, David. *The Rise of Commercial Empires: England and the Netherlands in the Age of Mercantilism, 1650–1770.* 2003. Examines the battle for commercial and maritime supremacy in the North Sea.

◆ Rothschild, Emma. *Economic Sentiments: Adam Smith, Condorcet, and the Enlightenment.* 2001. A fascinating reconsideration of Smith and the birth of modern economic thought.

◆ Walsh, Lorena S. *Motives of Honor, Pleasure and Profit: Plantation Management in the Colonial Chesapeake, 1607–1763.* 2010. A study of the economic and social rationales at work in the management of tobacco plantations and their enslaved labor force.

DOCUMENTARIES

◆ *Blackbeard: Terror at Sea* (National Geographic, 2006). A documentary recounting the exploits of the most famous eighteenth-century pirate.

◆ *Tales from the Green Valley* (BBC, 2005). A television series exploring life on a British farm in the seventeenth century.

FEATURE FILMS AND TELEVISION

◆ *Amazing Grace* (Michael Apted, 2006). An idealistic Briton's struggle to end his country's involvement in the slave trade alongside allies Olaudah Equiano and a repentant former slave-ship captain.

◆ *The Bounty* (Roger Donaldson, 1984). On a voyage in the South Pacific, the cruelty of Captain Bligh leads to a mutiny among his men.

◆ *The Last of the Mohicans* (Michael Mann, 1992). Set among the battles of the Seven Years' War (known as the French and Indian War in the colonies), a man raised as a Mohican saves the daughter of an English officer.

◆ *Rob Roy* (Michael Caton-Jones, 1995). A Scottish Highlander's effort to better his village by borrowing money to raise and sell cattle is challenged by the treachery of a noble lord and greedy bankers.

WEB SITES

◆ *The Bubble Project.* A Web site presenting historical and modern resources on the South Sea Bubble of 1720, one of the first major international financial crises. **myweb.dal.ca/dmcneil/bubble/bubble.html**

◆ *Common-place: The Interactive Journal of Early American Life.* Aimed at a diverse audience of scholars, teachers, students, and history buffs, with articles, blogs, and other resources on early America. **www.common-place.org**

◆ *Olaudah Equiano, or, Gustavus Vassa, the African.* A Web site featuring material on the movement to abolish slavery and the career of Olaudah Equiano, a former slave who published an autobiography in which he discussed his experience in bondage. **www.brycchancarey.com/equiano**

◆ *The Trans-Atlantic Slave Trade Database.* Presents the results of decades of research into the voyages of the transatlantic slave trade, interpretive articles, and an interactive database including ships, ports of arrival and departure, captains, and information on individuals taken in slavery. **www.slavevoyages.org/tast/index.faces**

18

Life in the Era of Expansion

1650–1800

The discussion of agriculture and industry in the last chapter showed the common people at work, straining to make ends meet within the larger context of population growth, gradual economic expansion, and ferocious political competition at home and overseas. This chapter shows us how that world of work was embedded in a rich complex of family organization, community practices, everyday experiences, and collective attitudes. As with the economy, traditional habits and practices of daily life changed considerably over the eighteenth century. Change was particularly dramatic in the growing cities of northwestern Europe, where traditional social controls were undermined by the anonymity and increased social interaction of the urban setting.

Historians have intensively studied many aspects of popular life, including marriage patterns and family size, childhood and education, nutrition, health care, and religious worship. Uncovering the life of the common people is a formidable challenge because they left few written records and regional variations abounded. Yet imaginative research has resulted in major findings and much greater knowledge. It is now possible to follow the common people into their homes, workshops, churches, and taverns and to ask, "What were the everyday experiences of ordinary people, and how did they change over the eighteenth century?" ■

ONLINE DOCUMENT ASSIGNMENT
The Inner Life of the Individual
How did the increasing emphasis on the inner life and development of the individual in the eighteenth century find expression in the art of the period? Go to the Integrated Media and analyze a series of paintings by Jean-Baptiste-Siméon Chardin that depict various aspects of daily life and reveal the era's increased attention to individual emotion and development. Then complete a writing assignment based on the evidence and details from this chapter.

Life in the Eighteenth Century. The huge fresh-food market known as Les Halles was the pulsing heart of eighteenth-century Paris. Here, peddlers offer food and drink to the men and women of the market, many of whom had arrived in the predawn hours to set up their stalls. (akg-images)

CHAPTER PREVIEW

 LearningCurve
After reading the chapter, go online and use LearningCurve to retain what you've read.

Marriage and the Family
What changes occurred in marriage and the family in the course of the eighteenth century?

Children and Education
What was life like for children, and how did attitudes toward childhood evolve?

Popular Culture and Consumerism
How did increasing literacy and new patterns of consumption affect people's lives?

Religious Authority and Beliefs
What were the patterns of popular religion, and how did they interact with the worldview of the educated public and their Enlightenment ideals?

Medical Practice
How did the practice of medicine evolve in the eighteenth century?

Marriage and the Family

What changes occurred in marriage and the family in the course of the eighteenth century?

The basic unit of social organization is the family. Within the structure of the family human beings love, mate, and reproduce. It is primarily the family that teaches the child, imparting values and customs that condition an individual's behavior for a lifetime. The family is also an institution woven into the web of history. It evolves and changes, assuming different forms in different times and places. The eighteenth century witnessed such an evolution, as patterns of marriage shifted and individuals adapted and conformed to the new and changing realities of the family unit.

Late Marriage and Nuclear Families

Because census data before the modern period are rare, historians have turned to parish registers of births, deaths, and marriages to uncover details of European family life before the nineteenth century. These registers reveal that the three-generation extended family was a rarity in western and central Europe. When young European couples married, they normally established their own households and lived apart from their parents, much like the nuclear families (a family group consisting of parents and their children with no other relatives) common in America today. If a three-generation household came into existence, it was usually because a widowed parent moved into the home of a married child.

Most people did not marry young in the seventeenth and eighteenth centuries. The average person married surprisingly late, many years after reaching adulthood and many more after beginning to work. Studies of western Europe in the seventeenth and eighteenth centuries show that both men and women married for the first time at an average age of twenty-five to twenty-seven. Furthermore, 10 to 20 percent of men and women in western Europe never married at all. Matters were different in eastern Europe, where the multigeneration household was the norm, marriage occurred

Young Serving Girl Increased migration to urban areas in the eighteenth century contributed to a loosening of traditional morals and soaring illegitimacy rates. Young women who worked as servants or shopgirls could not be supervised as closely as those who lived at home. The themes of seduction, fallen virtue, and familial conflict were popular in eighteenth-century art, such as in this painting by Pietro Longhi (1702–1785). (akg-images/Cameraphoto)

around age twenty, and permanent celibacy was much less common.

Why did young people in western Europe delay marriage? The main reason was that couples normally did not marry until they could start an independent household and support themselves and their future children. Peasants often needed to wait until their father's death to inherit land and marry. In the towns, men and women worked to accumulate enough savings to start a small business and establish their own home. As one father stated in an advice book written for his son: "Money is the sinew of love, as well as war; you can do nothing happily in wedlock without it; the other [virtue and beauty] are court-cards, but they are not of the trump-suit and are foiled by every sneaking misadventure."[1]

Laws and tradition also discouraged early marriage. In some areas couples needed permission from the local lord or landowner in order to marry. Poor couples had particular difficulty securing the approval of local officials, who believed that freedom to marry for the lower classes would result in more landless paupers, more abandoned children, and more money for welfare. Village elders often agreed.

The custom of late marriage combined with the nuclear-family household distinguished western European society from other areas of the world. Historians have argued that this late-marriage pattern was responsible for at least part of the economic advantage western Europeans acquired relative to other world regions. Late marriage joined a mature man and a mature woman — two adults who had already accumulated social and economic capital and could transmit self-reliance and skills to the next generation. This marriage pattern also favored a greater degree of equality between husband and wife.

Work Away from Home

Many young people worked within their families until they could start their own households. Boys plowed and wove; girls spun and tended the cows. Many others left home to work elsewhere. In the trades, a lad would enter apprenticeship around age fifteen and finish in his late teens or early twenties. During that time he would not be permitted to marry. An apprentice from a rural village would typically move to a city or town to learn a trade, earning little and working hard. If he was lucky and had connections, he might eventually be admitted to a guild and establish his economic independence. Many poor families could not afford

Chronology

1684	Jean-Baptiste de la Salle founds Brothers of the Christian Schools
1717	Elementary school attendance mandatory in Prussia
1750–1790	John Wesley preaches revival in England
1750–1850	Illegitimacy explosion
1757	Madame du Coudray publishes *Manual on the Art of Childbirth*
1762	Jean-Jacques Rousseau advocates more attentive child care in *Emile*
1763	Louis XV orders Jesuits out of France
1774	Elementary school attendance mandatory in Austria
1776	Thomas Paine publishes *Common Sense*
1796	Edward Jenner performs first smallpox vaccination

apprenticeships for their sons. Without craft skills, these youths drifted from one tough job to another: hired hand for a small farmer, wage laborer on a new road, carrier of water or domestic servant in a nearby town.

Many adolescent girls also left their families to work. The range of opportunities open to them was more limited, however. Apprenticeship was sometimes available with mistresses in traditionally female occupations like seamstress, linen draper, or midwife. With the growth in production of finished goods for the emerging consumer economy during the eighteenth century (see Chapter 17), demand rose for skilled female labor and, with it, greater opportunities for women. Even male guildsmen hired girls and women, despite guild restrictions.

Service in another family's household was by far the most common job for girls, and even middle-class families often sent their daughters into service. The legions of young servant girls worked hard but had little independence. Constantly under the eye of her mistress, the servant girl had many tasks — cleaning, shopping, cooking, child care. Often the work was endless, for there were few laws to limit exploitation. Court records are full of servant girls' complaints of physical mistreatment by their mistresses. There were many like the fifteen-year-old English girl in the early eighteenth century who told the judge that her mistress had not only called her "very opprobrious names, as Bitch, Whore and the like," but also "beat her without provocation and beyond measure."[2]

Male apprentices told similar tales of abuse and they shared the legal status of "servants" with housemaids, but they were far less vulnerable to the sexual exploitation that threatened young girls. In theory, domestic service offered a girl protection and security in a new family. But in practice she was often the easy prey of a lecherous master or his sons or friends. If the girl became pregnant, she could be fired and thrown out in disgrace. Many families could not or would not accept such a girl back into the home. Forced to make their own way, these girls had no choice but to turn to a harsh life of prostitution (see page 580) and petty thievery. "What are we?" exclaimed a bitter Parisian prostitute. "Most of us are unfortunate women, without origins, without education, servants and maids for the most part."[3] Adult women who remained in service, at least in large towns and cities, could gain more autonomy and distressed their employers by changing jobs frequently.

Premarital Sex and Community Controls

Ten years between puberty and marriage was a long time for sexually mature young people to wait. Many unmarried couples satisfied their sexual desires with fondling and petting. Others went further and engaged in premarital intercourse. Those who did so risked pregnancy and the stigma of illegitimate birth. Birth control was not unknown in Europe before the nineteenth century, but it was primitive and unreliable. Condoms, made from sheep intestines, became available in the mid-seventeenth century, replacing uncomfortable earlier versions made from cloth. They were expensive and mainly used by aristocratic libertines and prostitutes. The most common method of contraception was coitus interruptus—withdrawal by the male before ejaculation. The French, who were early leaders in contraception, were using this method extensively by the end of the eighteenth century.

Despite the lack of reliable contraception, premarital sex did not result in a large proportion of illegitimate births in most parts of Europe until 1750. English parish registers seldom listed more than one illegitimate child out of every twenty children baptized. Some French parishes in the seventeenth century had extraordinarily low rates of illegitimacy, with less than 1 percent of babies born out of wedlock. Illegitimate babies were apparently a rarity, at least as far as the official records are concerned.

Where collective control over sexual behavior among youths failed, community pressure to marry often prevailed. A study of seven representative parishes in seventeenth-century England shows that around 20 percent of children were conceived before the couple was married, while only 2 percent were born out of wedlock.[4] Figures for the French village of Auffay in Normandy in the eighteenth century were remarkably similar. No doubt many of these French and English couples were already engaged, or at least in a committed relationship, before they entered into intimate relations, and pregnancy simply set the marriage date once and for all.

The combination of low rates of illegitimate birth with large numbers of pregnant brides reflects the powerful **community controls** of the traditional village, particularly the open-field village, with its pattern of cooperation and common action. An unwed mother with an illegitimate child was inevitably viewed as a grave threat to the economic, social, and moral stability of the community. Irate parents, anxious village elders, indignant priests, and stern landlords all combined to pressure young people who wavered about marriage in the face of unexpected pregnancies. In the countryside these controls meant that premarital sex was not entered into lightly and that it was generally limited to those contemplating marriage.

The concerns of the village and the family weighed heavily on couples' lives after marriage as well. Whereas uninvolved individuals today try to stay out of the domestic disputes of their neighbors, the people in peasant communities gave such affairs loud and unfavorable publicity either at the time or during the carnival season (see page 587). Relying on degrading public rituals, known as **charivari**, the young men of the village would typically gang up on their victim and force him or her to sit astride a donkey facing backward and holding up the donkey's tail. They would parade the overly brutal spouse-beater or the adulterous couple around the village, loudly proclaiming the offenders' misdeeds. The donkey ride and other colorful humiliations ranging from rotten vegetables splattered on the doorstep to obscene and insulting midnight serenades were common punishments throughout much of Europe. They epitomized the community's effort to police personal behavior and maintain moral standards.

New Patterns of Marriage and Illegitimacy

In the second half of the eighteenth century, long-standing patterns of marriage and illegitimacy shifted dramatically. One important change was an increased ability for young people to choose partners for themselves, rather than following the interests of their families. This change occurred because social and economic transformations made it harder for families and communities to supervise their behavior. More youths in the countryside worked for their own wages, rather

community controls A pattern of cooperation and common action in a traditional village that sought to uphold the economic, social, and moral stability of the closely knit community.

charivari Degrading public rituals used by village communities to police personal behavior and maintain moral standards.

The Village Wedding The spirited merrymaking of a peasant wedding was a popular theme of European artists in the eighteenth century. Given the harsh conditions of life, a wedding provided a treasured moment of feasting, dancing, and revelry. With the future of the village at stake, the celebration of marriage was a public event. (Private Collection/The Bridgeman Art Library)

than on a family farm, and their economic autonomy translated into increased freedom of action. Moreover, many youths joined the flood of migrants to the cities, either with their families or in search of work on their own. Urban life provided young people with more social contacts and less social control.

A less positive outcome of loosening social control was an **illegitimacy explosion**, concentrated in England, France, Germany, and Scandinavia. In Frankfurt, Germany, for example, births out of wedlock rose steadily from about 2 percent of all births in the early 1700s to a peak of about 25 percent around 1850. In Bordeaux, France, 36 percent of all babies were being born out of wedlock by 1840. Small towns and villages experienced less startling climbs, but between 1750 and 1850 increases from a range of 1 to 3 percent initially and then 10 to 20 percent were commonplace. The rise in numbers did not alter social disapproval of single mothers and their offspring, leaving them in desperate circumstances.

Why did the number of illegitimate births skyrocket? One reason was a rise in sexual activity among young people. The loosened social controls that gave young people more choice in marriage also provided

them with more opportunities to yield to the attraction of the opposite sex. As in previous generations, many of the young couples who engaged in sexual activity intended to marry. In one medium-size French city in 1787–1788, the great majority of unwed mothers stated that sexual intimacy had followed promises of marriage. Their sisters in rural Normandy frequently reported that they had been "seduced in anticipation of marriage."[5]

The problem for young women who became pregnant was that fewer men followed through on their promises. The second half of the eighteenth century witnessed sharply rising prices for food, homes, and other necessities of life. Many soldiers, day laborers, and male servants were no doubt sincere in their proposals, but their lives were insecure, and they hesitated to take on the burden of a wife and child.

Thus, while some happy couples benefited from matches of love rather than convenience, in many cases the intended marriage did not take place. The romantic yet practical dreams and aspirations of young people were

illegitimacy explosion
The sharp increase in out-of-wedlock births that occurred in Europe between 1750 and 1850, caused by low wages and the breakdown of community controls.

frustrated by low wages, inequality, and changing economic and social conditions. Old patterns of marriage and family were breaking down. Only in the late nineteenth century would more stable patterns reappear.

Sex on the Margins of Society

Not all sex acts took place between men and women hopeful of marriage. Prostitution offered both single and married men an outlet for sexual desire. After a long period of relative tolerance, prostitutes encountered increasingly harsh and repressive laws in the sixteenth and early seventeenth centuries as officials across Europe closed licensed brothels and declared prostitution illegal.

Despite this repression, prostitution continued to flourish in the eighteenth century. Most prostitutes were working women who turned to the sex trade when confronted with unemployment. Such women did not become social pariahs, but retained ties with the communities of laboring poor to which they belonged. If caught by the police, however, they were liable to imprisonment or banishment. Venereal disease was also a constant threat. Prostitutes were subjected to humiliating police examinations for disease, although medical treatments were at best rudimentary. Farther up the social scale were courtesans whose wealthy protectors provided apartments, servants, fashionable clothing, and cash allowances. After a brilliant but brief career, an aging courtesan faced with the loss of her wealthy client could descend once more to streetwalking.

Relations between individuals of the same sex attracted even more condemnation than did prostitution, since they defied the Bible's limitation of sex to the purposes of procreation. Male same-sex relations, described as "sodomy" or "buggery," were prohibited by law in most European states, under pain of death. Such laws, however, were enforced unevenly, most strictly in Spain and far less so in the Scandinavian countries and Russia.[6]

Protected by their status, nobles and royals sometimes openly indulged their same-sex passions, which were accepted as long as they married and produced legitimate heirs. It was common knowledge that King James I, sponsor of the first translation of the Bible into English, had male lovers, but such relations did not prevent him from having seven children with his wife, Anne of Denmark. The duchess of Orléans, sister-in-law of French king Louis XIV, repeated rumors in her letters about the homosexual inclinations of King William of England, hero of the Glorious Revolution (see Chapter 15). She was hardly shocked by the news, given the fortune and favor her own husband lavished on his many *mignons*, as they were called.

In the late seventeenth century new homosexual subcultures began to emerge in Paris, Amsterdam, and London, with their own slang, meeting places, and styles of dress. Unlike the relations described above, which involved men who took both wives and male lovers, these groups included men exclusively oriented toward other men. In London, they called themselves "mollies," a term originally applied to prostitutes, and some began to wear women's clothing and act in effeminate ways. A new self-identity began to form among homosexual men: a belief that their same-sex desire made them fundamentally different from other men. As a character in one late-eighteenth-century fiction declared, he was in "a category of men different from the other, a class Nature has created in order to diminish or minimize propagation."[7]

Same-sex relations existed among women as well, but they attracted less anxiety and condemnation than those among men. Some women were prosecuted for "unnatural" relations; others attempted to escape the narrow confines imposed on them by dressing as men. Cross-dressing women occasionally snuck into the armed forces, such as Ulrika Elenora Stålhammar, who served as a man in the Swedish army for thirteen years and married a woman. After confessing her transgressions, she was sentenced to a lenient one-month imprisonment.[8] The beginnings of a distinctive lesbian subculture appeared in London at the end of the eighteenth century.

Across the early modern period, traditional tolerance for sexual activities outside of heterosexual marriage—be they sex with prostitutes or same-sex relations among male courtiers—faded. This process accelerated in the eighteenth century as Enlightenment critics attacked court immorality and preached virtue and morality for middle-class men, who were expected to prove their worthiness to claim the reins of political power.

Children and Education

What was life like for children, and how did attitudes toward childhood evolve?

On the whole, western European women married late, but then began bearing children rapidly. If a woman married before she was thirty, and if both she and her husband lived to fifty, she would most likely give birth to six or more children. Infant mortality varied across Europe, but was very high by modern standards, and many women died in childbirth due to limited medical knowledge.

For those children who did survive, new Enlightenment ideals in the latter half of the century stressed the importance of parental nurturing. New worldviews also led to an increase in elementary schools throughout Europe, but despite the efforts of enlightened absolutists and religious institutions, formal education reached only a minority of ordinary children.

Child Care and Nursing

Newborns entered a dangerous world. They were vulnerable to infectious diseases, and many babies died of dehydration brought about by bad bouts of ordinary diarrhea. Of those who survived infancy, many more died in childhood. Even in a rich family, little could be done for an ailing child. Childbirth was also dangerous. Women who bore six children faced a cumulative risk of dying in childbirth of 5 to 10 percent, a thousand times as great as the risk in Europe today.[9] They died from blood loss and shock during delivery and from infections caused by unsanitary conditions. The joy of pregnancy was thus shadowed by fear of loss of the mother or her child.

In the countryside, women of the lower classes generally breast-fed their infants for two years or more. Although not a foolproof means of birth control, breast-feeding decreases the likelihood of pregnancy by delaying the resumption of ovulation. By nursing their babies, women limited their fertility and spaced their children two or three years apart. Nursing also saved lives: breast-fed infants received precious immunity-producing substances and were more likely to survive than those who were fed other food.

Areas where babies were not breast-fed—typically in northern France, Scandinavia, and central and eastern Europe—experienced the highest infant mortality rates. In these areas, many people believed that breast-feeding was bad for a woman's health or appearance. Across Europe, women of the aristocracy and upper middle class seldom nursed their own children because they found breast-feeding undignified and it interfered with their social responsibilities. The alternatives to breast-feeding consisted of feeding babies cow's or goat's milk or paying lactating women to provide their milk.

Wealthy women hired live-in wet nurses to suckle their babies (which usually meant sending the nurse's own infant away to be nursed by someone else). Working women in the cities also relied on wet nurses because they needed to earn a living. Unable to afford live-in wet nurses, they often turned to the cheaper services of women in the countryside. Rural **wet-nursing** was a widespread business in the eighteenth century, conducted within the framework of the putting-out system. The traffic was in babies rather than in yarn or cloth, and two or three years often passed before the wet-nurse worker in the countryside finished her task.

Wet-nursing was particularly common in northern France. Toward the end of the century, roughly twenty thousand babies were born in Paris each year. Almost half were placed with rural wet nurses through a government-supervised distribution network; 20 to 25 percent were placed in the homes of Parisian nurses personally selected by their parents; and another 20 to 25 percent were abandoned to foundling hospitals, which would send them to wet nurses in the countryside. The remainder (perhaps 10 percent) were nursed at home by their mothers or live-in nurses.[10]

Reliance on wet nurses raised levels of infant mortality because of the dangers of travel, the lack of supervision of conditions in wet nurses' homes, and the need to share milk between a wet nurse's own baby and the one or more babies she was hired to feed. A study of parish registers in northern France during the late seventeenth and early eighteenth centuries reveals that 35 percent of babies died before their first birthday, and another 20 percent before age ten.[11] In England, where more mothers nursed, only some 30 percent of children did not reach their tenth birthday.

Mortality rates were also higher in overcrowded and dirty cities; in low-lying, marshy regions; and during summer months when rural women were busy in agricultural work and had less time to tend to infants. The corollary of high infant mortality was high fertility. Women who did not breast-feed their babies or whose children died in infancy became pregnant more quickly and bore more children. Thus, on balance, the number of children who survived to adulthood tended to be the same across Europe, with higher births balancing the greater loss of life in areas that relied on wet-nursing.

In the second half of the eighteenth century, critics mounted a harsh attack against wet-nursing. Enlightenment thinkers proclaimed that wet-nursing was robbing European society of reaching its full potential. They were convinced, incorrectly, that the population was declining (in fact it was rising, but they lacked accurate population data) and blamed this decline on women's failure to nurture their children properly. Some also railed against practices of contraception and masturbation, which they believed were robbing their nations of potential children. Despite these complaints, many women continued to rely on wet nurses for convenience or from necessity.

> **wet-nursing** A widespread and flourishing business in the eighteenth century in which women were paid to breast-feed other women's babies.

Foundlings and Infanticide

The young woman who could not provide for an unwanted child had few choices, especially if she had no prospect of marriage. Abortions were illegal, dangerous, and apparently rare. In desperation, some women, particularly in the countryside, hid unwanted pregnancies, delivered in secret, and smothered their newborn infants. If discovered, infanticide was punishable by death.

Women in cities had more choices for disposing of babies they could not support. Foundling homes (orphanages) first took hold in Italy, Spain, and Portugal in the sixteenth century, spreading to France in 1670 and the rest of Europe thereafter. In eighteenth-century England the government acted on a petition calling for a foundling hospital "to prevent the frequent murders of poor, miserable infants at birth" and "to suppress the inhuman custom of exposing newborn children to perish in the streets." By the end of the eighteenth century, European foundling hospitals were admitting annually about one hundred thousand abandoned children, nearly all of them infants. At their best, foundling homes were a good example of Christian charity and social concern in an age of great poverty and inequality. Yet the foundling home was no panacea. By the 1770s one-third of all babies born in Paris were being immediately abandoned to foundling homes by their mothers. Many were the offspring of single women, the result of the illegitimacy explosion of the second half of the eighteenth century. But fully one-third of all the foundlings were abandoned by married couples too poor to feed another child.[12]

Millions of babies entered foundling homes, but few left. Even in the best of these homes, 50 percent of the babies normally died within a year. In the worst, fully 90 percent did not survive, falling victim to infectious disease, malnutrition, and neglect.[13] There appears to have been no differentiation by sex in the numbers of children sent to foundling hospitals.

Attitudes Toward Children

What were the typical circumstances of children's lives? Some scholars have claimed that high mortality rates prevented parents from forming emotional attachments to young children. With a reasonable expectation that a child might die, some scholars believe, parents maintained an attitude of indifference, if not downright negligence. Most historians now believe, however, that seventeenth- and eighteenth-century parents did love their children, suffered anxiously when they fell ill, and experienced extreme anguish when they died.

ONLINE DOCUMENT ASSIGNMENT

The Inner Life of the Individual

How did the increasing emphasis on the inner life and development of the individual in the eighteenth century find expression in the art of the period? Go to the Integrated Media and analyze a series of paintings by Jean-Baptiste-Siméon Chardin that depict various aspects of daily life and reveal the era's increased attention to individual emotion and development.

Parents were well aware of the dangers of infancy and childhood. The great eighteenth-century English historian Edward Gibbon (1737–1794) wrote, with some exaggeration, that "the death of a new born child before that of its parents may seem unnatural but it is a strictly probable event, since of any given number the greater part are extinguished before the ninth year, before they possess the faculties of the mind and the body." Gibbon's father named all his boys Edward after himself, hoping that at least one of them would survive to carry his name. His prudence was not misplaced. Edward the future historian and eldest survived. Five brothers and sisters who followed him all died in infancy.

Emotional prudence could lead to emotional distance. The French essayist Michel de Montaigne, who lost five of his six daughters in infancy, wrote, "I cannot abide that passion for caressing new-born children, which have neither mental activities nor recognisable bodily shape by which to make themselves loveable and I have never willingly suffered them to be fed in my presence."[14] In contrast to this harsh picture, however, historians have drawn ample evidence from diaries, letters, and family portraits that parents of all social classes did cherish their children. This was equally true of mothers and fathers and of attitudes toward sons and daughters. The English poet Ben Jonson wrote movingly in "On My First Son" of the death of his six-year-old son Benjamin, which occurred during a London plague outbreak in 1603:

> Farewell, thou child of my right hand, and joy;
> My sin was too much hope of thee, loved boy.
> Seven years thou wert lent to me, and I thee pay,
> Exacted by thy fate, on the just day.

In a society characterized by much violence and brutality, discipline of children was often severe. The axiom "Spare the rod and spoil the child" seems to have been coined in the mid-seventeenth century. Susannah Wesley (1669–1742), mother of John Wesley, the founder of Methodism (see page 598), agreed. According to her, the first task of a parent toward her children was "to conquer the will, and bring them to an obedient temper." She reported that her babies were "taught to fear the rod, and to cry softly; by which means they escaped the abundance of correction they might otherwise have had, and that most odious noise of the crying of children was rarely heard in the house."[15] They were beaten for lying, stealing, disobeying, and quarreling, and forbidden from playing with other neighbor children. Susannah's methods of disciplining her children were probably extreme even in her own day, but they do reflect a broad consensus that children were born with an innately sinful will that

Parisian Boyhood

The life of Jacques-Louis Ménétra, a Parisian glazier, exemplified many of the social patterns of his day. He lost his mother in infancy, was educated at a parish school, married late, and had four children, two of whom died. Ménétra distinguished himself from other workingmen, however, by writing an autobiography describing his tumultuous childhood, his travels around France as a journeyman, and his settled life as a guild master. Ménétra's father was often violent, but he fiercely defended his son against rumored child abductions in Paris (in reality the police had overstepped orders to arrest children loitering in the streets).

❝ I was born on 13 July 1738 a native of this great city. My father belonged to the class usually called artisans. His profession was that of glazier. Hence it is with him that I begin my family tree and I shall say nothing about my ancestors. My father married and set himself up at the same time and wed a virtuous girl who gave him four children, three daughters and one boy, myself, all of whose little pranks I'm going to write about.

My father became a widower when I was two years old. I had been put out to nurse. My grandmother who always loved me a great deal and even idolized me, knowing that the nurse I was with had her milk gone bad, came to get me and after curing me put me back out to nurse [where] I ended up with a pretty good woman who taught me early on the profession of begging. My [grand]mother and my godfather when they came to see me . . . found me in a church begging charity. They took me home and from then until the age of eleven I lived with my good grandmother. My father wanted me back, afraid that he would have to pay my board. He put me to work in his trade even though several people tried to talk him out of it [but] he wouldn't listen to them. . . .

When I felt a little better, I went back to my usual ways which is to say that my father was always angry with me.

One night when I was lighting the way in a staircase where he was installing a casement and not mounting it the way he wanted with an angry kick [he] knocked out all my teeth. When I got back home my (step)mother took me to a dentist by the name of Ricie who put back the teeth that weren't broken and I went three weeks eating nothing but bouillon and soup.

In those days it was rumored that they were taking young boys and bleeding them and that they were lost forever and that their blood was used to bathe a princess suffering from a disease that could only be cured with human blood. There was plenty of talk about that in Paris. My father came to get me at school as many other fathers did along with seven big coopers armed with crowbars. The rumor was so strong that the windows of the police station were broken and several poor guys were assaulted and one was even burned in the place de Grève because he looked like a police informer. Children weren't allowed to go outside; three poor wretches were hanged in the place de Grève to settle the matter and restore calm in Paris. ❞

EVALUATE THE EVIDENCE

1. What hardships did the young Ménétra face in his childhood? What attitude did he display toward his childhood experiences?
2. What characteristic elements of eighteenth-century family life does Ménétra's childhood reflect? Does his story provide evidence for or against the thesis that parents deeply loved their children?

Source: Jacques-Louis Ménétra, *Journal of My Life*, ed. Daniel Roche, trans. Arthur Goldhammer, pp. 18, 21–22. Copyright © 1986 Columbia University Press. Reprinted with permission of the publisher.

---

parents must overcome. (See "Primary Source 18.1: Parisian Boyhood," above.)

The Enlightenment produced an enthusiastic new discourse about childhood and child rearing. Starting around 1760 critics called for greater tenderness toward children and proposed imaginative new teaching methods. In addition to supporting foundling homes and urging women to nurse their babies, these new voices ridiculed the practice of swaddling babies and using whaleboned corsets to mold children's bones. (See "Primary Source 18.2: The Catechism of Health," page 584.) Instead of dressing children in miniature versions of adult clothing, critics called for comfortable clothing to allow freedom of movement. Rather than emphasizing original sin, these enlightened voices celebrated the child as an innocent product of nature. Since they viewed nature as inherently positive, Enlightenment educators advocated safeguarding and developing children's innate qualities rather than thwarting and suppressing them. Accordingly, they believed the best hopes for a new society, untrammeled by the prejudices of the past, lay in a radical reform of child-rearing techniques.

One of the century's most influential works on child rearing was Jean-Jacques Rousseau's *Emile, or On Education* (1762). Rousseau argued that boys' education

The Catechism of Health

In the second half of the eighteenth century, medical reformers sought to educate children (and through them, their parents) on how to take proper care of their bodies. A popular genre was the health "catechism," which took the form of easy-to-understand questions and answers about issues such as fresh air, cleanliness, proper diet, and exercise. The catechisms often promoted new treatments, like smallpox inoculation, and opposed traditional practices of bloodletting, purging, swaddling infants, and wet-nursing. Bernhard Christoph Faust's The Catechism of Health for the Use of Schools and for Domestic Instruction *(1794), excerpted below, was distributed in schools and reached a wide audience, including Americans, through a 1798 New York edition.*

❝ Q. What does the little helpless infant stand most in need of?

A. The love and care of its mother.

Q. Can this love and care be shewn by other persons?

A. No. Nothing equals maternal love.

Q. Why does a child stand so much in need of the love and care of its mother?

A. Because the attendance and nursing, the tender and affectionate treatment which a child stands in need of, can only be expected from a mother.

Q. How ought infants to be attended and nursed?

A. They ought always to breathe fresh and pure air; be kept dry and clean, and immersed in cold water every day.

Q. Why so?

A. Because children are now, at the time alluded to, more placid, because not being irritable, they grow and thrive better.

Q. Is it good to swathe [swaddle] a child?

A. No. Swathing is a bad custom, and produces in children great anxiety and pains; it is injurious to the growth of the body, and prevents children from being kept clean and dry.

Q. Do children rest and sleep without being rocked?

A. Yes. If they be kept continually dry and clean, and in fresh air, they will rest and sleep well, if not disturbed; the rocking and carrying about of children is quite useless.

Q. It is, therefore, not advisable, I suppose, to frighten children into sleep?

A. By no means; because they may be thrown into convulsions, and get cramps.

Q. Is it necessary or good to give children composing draughts, or other medicines that tend to promote sleep?

A. No. They cause an unnatural, and of course, unwholesome sleep; and are very dangerous and hurtful.

Q. How long must a mother suckle her child?

A. For nine or twelve months.

Q. What food is most suitable for children?

A. Pure unadulterated cow's milk, with a little water and thin gruel; grated crusts of bread, or biscuit boiled with water only, or mixed with milk. . . .

Q. Is it good to cover their heads?

A. By no means; it causes humours to break out. ❞

EVALUATE THE EVIDENCE

1. What practices of child rearing does Faust advocate and what practices does he criticize?

2. In what ways did Faust's advice challenge traditional methods of caring for babies? How would you contrast the message in this passage with ideas and practices of child rearing described in the autobiography of the Parisian boy (see page 583)?

Source: Bernhard Christoph Faust, *The Catechism of Health*, trans. J. H. Basse (Dublin: P. Byrne, 1794), pp. 22–23.

---

should include plenty of fresh air and exercise and that they should be taught practical craft skills in addition to rote book learning. Reacting to what he perceived as the vanity and frivolity of upper-class Parisian women, Rousseau insisted that girls' education focus on their future domestic responsibilities. For Rousseau, women's "nature" destined them solely for a life of marriage and child rearing. The ideas of Rousseau and other reformers were enthusiastically adopted by elite women, some of whom began to nurse their own children.

For all his influence, Rousseau also reveals the occasional hypocrisy of Enlightenment thinkers. Although

a passionate advocate for children's education, Rousseau abandoned the five children he fathered with his common-law wife in foundling hospitals despite their mother's protests. None are known to have survived. For Rousseau, popularizing the idea of creating a natural man was more important than raising real children.

The Spread of Elementary Schools

The availability of education outside the home gradually increased over the early modern period. The wealthy led the way in the sixteenth century with special col-

The First Step of Childhood   This tender snapshot of a baby's first steps toward an adoring mother exemplifies new attitudes toward children and raising them ushered in by the Enlightenment. Authors like Jean-Jacques Rousseau encouraged elite mothers like the one pictured here to take a more personal interest in raising their children, instead of leaving them in the hands of indifferent wet nurses and nannies. Many women responded eagerly to this call, and the period saw a more sentimentalized view of childhood and family life. (Erich Lessing/Art Resource, NY)

leges, often run by Jesuits in Catholic areas. Schools charged specifically with educating children of the common people began to appear in the second half of the seventeenth century. They taught six- to twelve-year-old children basic literacy, religion, and perhaps some arithmetic for the boys and needlework for the girls. The number of such schools expanded in the eighteenth century, although they were never sufficient to educate the majority of the population.

Religion played an important role in the spread of education. From the middle of the seventeenth century, Presbyterian Scotland was convinced that the path to salvation lay in careful study of the Scriptures, and it established an effective network of parish schools for rich and poor alike. The Church of England and the dissenting congregations — Puritans, Presbyterians,

Quakers, and so on — established "charity schools" to instruct poor children. The first proponents of universal education, in Prussia, were inspired by the Protestant idea that every believer should be able to read the Bible and by the new idea of raising a population capable of effectively serving the state. As early as 1717 Prussia made attendance at elementary schools compulsory for boys and girls, albeit only in areas where schools already existed.[16] More Protestant German states, such as Saxony and Württemberg (VUHR-tuhm-burg), followed suit in the eighteenth century.

Catholic states pursued their own programs of popular education. In the 1660s France began setting up charity schools to teach poor children their catechism and prayers as well as reading and writing. These were run by parish priests or by new teaching orders created for this purpose. One of the most famous orders was Jean-Baptiste de la Salle's Brothers of the Christian Schools. Founded in 1684, the schools had thirty-five thousand students across France by the 1780s. Enthusiasm for popular education was even greater in the Habsburg empire. Inspired by the expansion of schools in rival Protestant German states, in 1774 Maria Theresa issued her own compulsory education edict, imposing five hours of school, five days a week, for all children aged six to twelve.[17] Across Europe some elementary education was becoming a reality, and schools became increasingly significant in the life of the child.

Popular Culture and Consumerism

How did increasing literacy and new patterns of consumption affect people's lives?

Because of the new efforts in education, basic literacy was expanding among the popular classes, whose reading habits centered primarily on religious material, but who also began to incorporate more practical and entertaining literature. In addition to reading, people of all classes enjoyed a range of leisure activities including storytelling, fairs, festivals, and sports.

One of the most important developments in European society in the eighteenth century was the emergence of a fledgling consumer culture. Much of the expansion took place among the upper and upper-middle classes, but a boom in cheap reproductions of luxury items also opened doors for people of modest means. From food to ribbons and from coal stoves to umbrellas, the material worlds of city dwellers grew richer and more diverse. This "consumer revolution," as it has been called, created new expectations for comfort, hygiene, and self-expression, thus dramatically changing European daily life in the eighteenth century.

blood sports Events such as bullbaiting and cockfighting that involved inflicting violence and bloodshed on animals and that were popular with the eighteenth-century European masses.

carnival The few days of revelry in Catholic countries that preceded Lent and that included drinking, masquerading, dancing, and rowdy spectacles that upset the established order.

Popular Literature

The surge in childhood education in the eighteenth century led to a remarkable growth in literacy between 1600 and 1800. Whereas in 1600 only one male in six was barely literate in France and Scotland, and one in four in England, by 1800 almost nine out of ten Scottish males, two out of three French males (Map 18.1), and more than half of English males were literate. In all three countries, the bulk of the jump occurred in the eighteenth century. Women were also increasingly literate, although they lagged behind men.

The growth in literacy promoted growth in reading, and historians have carefully examined what the common people read. While the Bible remained the overwhelming favorite, especially in Protestant countries, short pamphlets known as chapbooks were the staple of popular literature. Printed on the cheapest paper, many chapbooks featured Bible stories, prayers, and the lives of saints and exemplary Christians. This pious literature gave believers moral teachings and a faith that helped them endure their daily struggles.

Entertaining, often humorous stories formed a second element of popular literature. Fairy tales, medieval romances, true crime stories, and fantastic adventures were some of the delights that filled the peddler's pack as he approached a village. These tales presented a world of danger and magic, of supernatural powers, fairy godmothers, and evil trolls, that provided a temporary flight from harsh everyday reality. They also contained nuggets of ancient folk wisdom, counseling prudence in a world full of danger and injustice, where wolves dress like grandmothers and eat Little Red Riding Hoods.

Finally, some popular literature was highly practical, dealing with rural crafts, household repairs, useful plants, and similar matters. Much lore was stored in almanacs, where calendars listing secular, religious, and astrological events were mixed with agricultural schedules, arcane facts, and jokes. The almanac was highly appreciated even by many in the comfortable classes. In this way, elites still shared some elements of a common culture with the masses.

While it is safe to say that the vast majority of ordinary people—particularly peasants in isolated villages—did not read the great works of the Enlightenment, they were not immune from the new ideas. Urban working people were exposed to Enlightenment thought through the rumors and gossip that spread across city streets, workshops, markets, and taverns. They also had access to cheap pamphlets that helped translate Enlightenment critiques into ordinary language. Servants, who usually came from rural areas and traveled home periodically, were well situated to transmit ideas from educated employers to the village.

Certainly some ordinary people did assimilate Enlightenment ideals. Thomas Paine, author of some of the most influential texts of the American Revolution, was an English corset-maker's son who left school at age twelve and carried on his father's trade before emigrating to the colonies. His 1776 pamphlet *Common Sense* attacked the weight of custom and the evils of government against the natural society of men. This text, which sold 120,000 copies in its first months of publication, is vivid proof of working people's reception of Enlightenment ideas. Paine's stirring mastery of them was perhaps unique, but his access to them was certainly not.

Leisure and Recreation

Despite the spread of literacy, the culture of the village remained largely oral rather than written. In the cold, dark winter months, peasant families gathered around the fireplace to sing, tell stories, do craftwork, and keep warm. In some parts of Europe, women would gather together in someone's cottage to chat, sew, spin, and laugh. Sometimes a few young men would be invited so that the daughters (and mothers) could size up potential suitors in a supervised atmosphere. A favorite recreation of men was drinking and talking with buddies in public places, and it was a sorry village that had no tavern. In addition to old favorites such as beer and wine, the common people turned with gusto to cheap and potent hard liquor, which fell in price because of improved techniques for distilling grain in the eighteenth century.

Towns and cities offered a wider range of amusements, including pleasure gardens, theaters, and lending libraries. Urban fairs featured prepared foods, acrobats, and conjuring acts. Leisure activities were another form of consumption marked by growing commercialization. For example, commercial, profit-making spectator sports emerged in this period, including horse races, boxing matches, and bullfights. (See "The Past Living Now: The Commercialization of Sports," page 588.) Modern sports heroes, such as brain-bashing heavyweight champions and haughty bullfighting matadors, made their appearance on the historical scene.

Blood sports, such as bullbaiting and cockfighting, also remained popular with the masses. In bullbaiting, the bull, usually staked on a chain in the courtyard of an inn, was attacked by ferocious dogs for the amusement of the innkeeper's clients. Eventually the maimed and tortured animal was slaughtered by a butcher and sold as meat. In cockfighting, two roosters, carefully trained by their owners and armed with razor-sharp steel spurs, slashed and clawed each other in a small ring until the victor won—and the loser died. An added attraction of cockfighting was that the screaming spectators could bet on the lightning-fast combat.

Popular recreation merged with religious celebration in a variety of festivals and processions throughout the year. The most striking display of these religiously inspired events was **carnival**, a time of reveling and excess in Catholic Europe, especially in Mediterranean countries. Carnival preceded Lent—the forty days of fasting and penitence before Easter—and for a few exceptional days in February or March, a wild release of

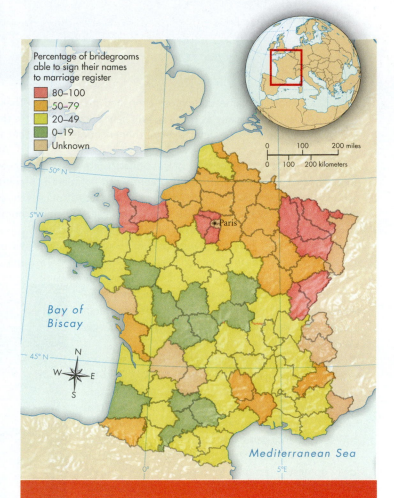

MAPPING THE PAST

Map 18.1 Literacy in France, ca. 1789

Literacy rates increased but still varied widely between and within states in eighteenth-century Europe.

ANALYZING THE MAP　What trends in French literacy rates does this map reveal? Which regions seem to be ahead? How would you explain the regional variations?

CONNECTIONS　Note the highly variable nature of literacy rates across the country. Why might the rate of literacy be higher closer to the capital city of Paris? Why would some areas have low rates?

drinking, masquerading, and dancing reigned. Moreover, a combination of plays, processions, and raucous spectacles turned the established order upside down. Peasants dressed as nobles and men as women, and rich masters waited on their servants at the table. This annual holiday gave people a much-appreciated chance to release their pent-up frustrations and aggressions before life returned to the usual pattern of hierarchy and hard work.

THE PAST LIVING NOW
The Commercialization of Sports

Ask people to name their most cherished memory of school and, as likely as not, you will hear about a victory at football or volleyball or another encounter with organized sport.

Today's world of college and professional sports owes a great deal to the entrepreneurs of seventeenth- and eighteenth-century Europe who produced the first commercialized spectator sports, in which trained athletes, usually male, engaged in organized competitions for the entertainment of ticket-buying fans. These spectacles were part of the array of new leisure-time activities introduced in this era. When they were not strolling in pleasure gardens, debating philosophy in coffeehouses, or perusing fashions in fancy boutiques, crowds of men and women gathered to watch boxing matches and horse races, as well as rowing, walking, and running competitions.

Kings and aristocrats had raced their horses privately for centuries, but first began breeding them for this purpose in the seventeenth and eighteenth centuries, producing the thoroughbred strains still prized today. The first large-scale race meets began in the mid-seventeenth century at Newmarket, still home to today's British racing industry. Originally treated as lowly domestic servants, jockeys gained recognition as independent professionals in the early nineteenth century. Aristocrats also deployed their footmen in pedestrian races, which then grew in popularity and attracted semiprofessional competitors. These races sometimes featured female competitors, including a toddler who in 1749 beat the odds by walking half a mile of a London street in under thirty minutes.*

Professional boxing had less exalted origins in the popular blood sports of the day. In 1719 a London prizefighter named James Figg became the first boxing entrepreneur, opening an "amphitheater" where he staged animal fights and contests among human boxers and swordsmen. With the growing popularity of the sport, the first rules of boxing appeared in the 1740s, calling for fights to include gloves, referees, and judges, and outlawing hitting a man when he was down.

The football and soccer games so central to school spirit in our day arose from the ball games played by peasants across medieval Europe, sometimes taking the form of all-out competitions between rival villages. Elite boarding schools transformed these riotous events into organized and regulated games, because their masters believed that team sports strengthened the body and disciplined the mind. The Rugby School thus produced the first written rules of rugby in 1845.

The games of soccer and football developed from these origins in the nineteenth century, and the first professional leagues began in the 1890s.

Along with commercialization of sports came gambling, cheating, and disorderly crowds, problems that continue to confront professional athletics. A spirit of competition and thirst for victory may be seen as constant elements of the human character; however, historical events profoundly shape the way individuals manifest these qualities. In turn, the way we play and watch sports reveals a great deal about the societies in which we live.

In this early-eighteenth-century painting, two men spar in a boxing match staged in London for the entertainment of the gathered crowd. (Bildarchiv Preussischer Kulturbesitz/Art Resource, NY)

QUESTIONS FOR ANALYSIS

1. In what ways did the commercial sporting events of the eighteenth century reflect the overall "consumer revolution" of this period? How do the professional sports of today's world reflect our own patterns of consumption?

2. What continuities do you see in the social and commercial function of sports between the eighteenth century and today? Conversely, what are the various ways you or those around you "consume" or participate in sports that an eighteenth-century individual might never have dreamed of?

*Allen Guttmann, *Sports: The First Five Millennia* (Amherst: University of Massachusetts Press, 2007), p. 72.

In trying to place the vibrant popular culture of the common people in broad perspective, historians have stressed the growing criticism levied against it by the educated elites in the second half of the eighteenth century. These elites, who had previously shared the popular enthusiasm for religious festivals, carnival, drinking in taverns, blood sports, and the like, now tended to see superstition, sin, disorder, and vulgarity.[18] The resulting attack on popular culture, which was tied to the clergy's efforts to eliminate paganism and superstition, was intensified as an educated public embraced the critical worldview of the Enlightenment.

New Foods and Appetites

At the beginning of the eighteenth century, ordinary men and women depended on grain as fully as they had in the past. Bread was quite literally the staff of life. Peasants in the Beauvais region of France ate two pounds of bread a day, washing it down with water, wine, or beer. Their dark bread was made from roughly ground wheat and rye—the standard flour of the common people. Even peasants normally needed to buy some grain for food, and, in full accord with landless laborers and urban workers, they believed in the moral economy and the **just price**. That is, they believed that prices should be "fair," protecting both consumers and producers, and that just prices should be imposed by government decree if necessary. When

prices rose above this level, they often took action in the form of bread riots (see Chapter 15).

The rural poor also ate a quantity of vegetables. Peas and beans were probably the most common. Grown as field crops in much of Europe since the Middle Ages, they were eaten fresh in late spring and summer. Dried, they became the basic ingredients in the soups and stews of the long winter months. In most regions other vegetables appeared on the tables of the poor in season, primarily cabbages, carrots, and wild greens. Fruit was mostly limited to the summer months. Too precious to drink, milk was used to make cheese and butter, which peasants sold in the market to earn cash for taxes and land rents.

The common people of Europe ate less meat in 1700 than in 1500 because their general standard of living had declined and meat was more expensive. Moreover, harsh laws in most European countries reserved the right to hunt and eat game, such as rabbits, deer, and partridges, to nobles and large landowners. Few laws were more bitterly resented—or more frequently broken—by ordinary people than those governing hunting.

just price The idea that prices should be fair, protecting both consumers and producers, and that they should be imposed by government decree if necessary.

The diet of small traders and artisans—the people of the towns and cities—was less monotonous than that of the peasantry. Bustling markets provided a sub-

Chocolate Drinking These Spanish tiles from 1710 illustrate the new practice of preparing and drinking hot chocolate. Originating in the New World, chocolate was one of the many new foods imported to Europe in the wake of the voyages of discovery. The first Spanish chocolate mills opened in the mid-seventeenth century, and consumption of chocolate rapidly increased. The inclusion of these tiles in the decoration of a nobleman's house testifies to public interest in the new drink. (Courtesy, Museu de Ceramica. Photo: Guillem Fernandez-Huerta)

A Day in the Life of Paris

Louis-Sébastien Mercier (1740–1814) was the best chronicler of everyday life in eighteenth-century Paris. His masterpiece was the Tableau de Paris *(1781–1788), a multivolume work composed of 1,049 chapters that covered subjects ranging from convents to cafés, bankruptcy to booksellers, the latest fashions to royal laws. As this excerpt demonstrates, he aimed to convey the infinite diversity of people, places, and things he saw around him, and in so doing he left future generations a precious record of the changing dynamics of Parisian society in the second half of the eighteenth century.*

Mercier's family belonged to the respectable artisan classes. This middling position ideally situated Mercier to observe the extremes of wealth and poverty around him. Although these volumes contain many wonderful glimpses of daily life, they should not be taken for an objective account. Mercier brought his own moral and political sensibilities, influenced by Jean-Jacques Rousseau, to the task of description.

Chapter 39: How the Day Goes

❝ It is curious to see how, amid what seems perpetual life and movement, certain hours keep their own characteristics, whether of bustle or of leisure. Every round of the clock-hand sets another scene in motion, each different from the last, though all about equal in length. Seven o'clock in the morning sees all the gardeners, mounted on their nags and with their baskets empty, heading back out of town again. No carriages are about, and not a presentable soul, except a few neat clerks hurrying to their offices. Nine o'clock sets all the barbers in motion, covered from head to foot with flour — hence their soubriquet of "whitings"* — wig in one hand, tongs in the other. Waiters from the lemonade-shops are busy with trays of coffee and rolls, breakfast for those who live in furnished rooms. . . . An hour later the Law comes into action; a black cloud of legal practitioners and hangers-on descend upon the Châtelet,† and the other courts; a procession of wigs and gowns and briefbags, with plaintiffs and defendants at their heels. Midday is the stockbrokers' hour, and the idlers'; the former hurry off to the Exchange, the latter to the Palais-Royal.‡ The Saint-Honoré§ quarter, where all the financiers live, is at its busiest now, its streets are crowded with the customers and clients of the great.

At two o'clock those who have invitations to dine set out, dressed in their best, powdered, adjusted, and walking on tiptoe not to soil their stockings. All the cabs are engaged, not one is to be found on the rank; there is a good deal of competition for these vehicles, and you may see two would-be passengers jumping into a cab together from different sides, and furiously disputing which was first. . . .

Three o'clock and the streets are not so full; everyone is at dinner; there is a momentary calm, soon to be broken, for at five fifteen the din is as though the gates of hell were opened, the streets are impassable with traffic going all ways at once, towards the playhouses or the public gardens. Cafés are at their busiest.

Towards seven the din dies down, everywhere and all at once. You can hear the cab-horses' hoofs pawing the stones as they wait — in vain. It is as though the whole town were gagged and bound, suddenly, by an invisible hand. This is the most dangerous time of the whole day for thieves and such, especially towards autumn when the days begin to draw in; for the watch is not yet about, and violence takes its opportunity.

Night falls; and, while scene-shifters set to work at the playhouses, swarms of other workmen, carpenters, masons and the like, make their way towards the poorer quarters. They leave white footprints from the plaster on their shoes, a trail that any eye can follow. They are off home, and to bed, at the hour which finds elegant ladies sitting down to their dressing-tables to prepare for the business of the night.

---

*Small fish typically rolled in flour and fried.

†The main criminal court of Paris.

‡A garden surrounded by arcades with shops and cafés.

§A fashionable quarter for the wealthy.

---

stantial variety of meats, vegetables, and fruits, although bread and beans still formed the bulk of such families' diets. Not surprisingly, the diet of the rich was quite different from that of the poor. The upper classes were rapacious carnivores, and a truly elegant dinner consisted of an abundance of rich meat and fish dishes laced with piquant sauces and complemented with sweets, cheeses, and wine in great quantities. During such dinners, it was common to spend five or more hours at table, eating and drinking and enjoying the witty banter of polite society.

Patterns of food consumption changed markedly as the century progressed. Because of a growth of market gardening, a greater variety of vegetables appeared in towns and cities. This was particularly the case in the Low Countries and England, which pioneered new methods of farming. Introduced into Europe from the Americas — along with corn, squash, tomatoes, and

At nine this begins; they all set off for the play. Houses tremble as the coaches rattle by, but soon the noise ceases; all the fine ladies are making their evening visits, short ones, before supper. Now the prostitutes begin their night parade, breasts uncovered, heads tossing, colour high on their cheeks, and eyes as bold as their hands. These creatures, careless of the light from shop-windows and street lamps, follow and accost you, trailing through the mud in their silk stockings and low shoes, with words and gestures well matched for obscenity. . . .

By eleven, renewed silence. People are at supper, private people, that is; for the cafés begin at this hour to turn out their patrons, and to send the various idlers and workless and poets back to their garrets for the night. A few prostitutes still linger, but they have to use more circumspection, for the watch is about, patrolling the streets, and this is the hour when they "gather 'em in"; that is the traditional expression.

A quarter after midnight, a few carriages make their way home, taking the non–card players back to bed. These lend the town a sort of transitory life; the trades-man wakes out of his first sleep at the sound of them, and turns to his wife, by no means unwilling. More than one young Parisian must owe his existence to this sudden passing rattle of wheels. . . .

At one in the morning six thousand peasants arrive, bringing the town's provision of vegetables and fruits and flowers, and make straight for the Halles.** . . . As for the market itself, it never sleeps. . . . Perpetual noise, perpet-ual motion, the curtain never rings down on the enormous stage; first come the fishmongers, and after these the egg-dealers, and after these the retail buyers; for the Halles keep all the other markets of Paris going; they are the warehouses whence these draw their supplies. The food of the whole city is shifted and sorted in high-piled baskets; you may see eggs, pyramids of eggs, moved here and there, up steps and down, in and out of the throngs, miraculous; not one is ever broken. . . .

**The city's central wholesale food market.

This impenetrable din contrasts oddly with the sleep-ing streets, for at that hour none but thieves and poets are awake.

Twice a week, at six, those distributors of the staff of life, the bakers of Gonesse,†† bring in an enormous quan-tity of loaves to the town, and may take none back through the barriers. And at this same hour workmen take up their tools, and trudge off to their day's labour. Coffee with milk is, unbelievably, the favoured drink among these stalwarts nowadays. . . .

So coffee-drinking has become a habit, and one so deep-rooted that the working classes will start the day on nothing else. It is not costly, and has more flavour to it, and more nourishment too, than anything else they can afford to drink; so they consume immense quantities, and say that if a man can only have coffee for breakfast it will keep him going till nightfall. ❱❱

EVALUATE THE EVIDENCE

1. What different social groups does Mercier describe? Does he approve or disapprove of Parisian society as he describes it?
2. How do the social classes described by Mercier differ in their use of time, and why? Do you think the same distinctions exist today?
3. What evidence of the consumer revolution can you find in Mercier's account? How do the goods used by eighteenth-century Parisians compare to the ones you use in your life today?

Source: Excerpt from *Panorama of Paris: Selections from "Le Tableau de Paris,"* by Louis-Sébastien Mercier, based on the translation by Helen Simpson, edited with a new preface and translations by Jeremy D. Popkin. Copyright © 1999 The Pennsylvania State University. Reprinted by permission of Penn State Press.

††A suburb of Paris, famous for the excellent bread baked there.

many other useful plants—the humble potato pro-vided an excellent new food source. Containing a good supply of carbohydrates, calories, and vitamins A and C, the potato offset the lack of vitamins in the poor person's winter and early-spring diet, and it provided a much higher caloric yield than grain for a given piece of land. After initial resistance, the potato became an important dietary supplement in much of Europe by the end of the century.

The most remarkable dietary change in the eigh-teenth century was in the consumption of commodi-ties imported from abroad. Originally expensive and rare luxury items, goods like tea, sugar, coffee, choco-late, and tobacco became dietary staples for people of all social classes. With the exception of tea—which originated in China—most of the new consumables were produced in European colonies in the Americas. In many cases, the labor of enslaved peoples enabled

Parisian Street Scene   Here a milk seller doubles as a provider of news, reading a hand-printed news sheet to a small gathering. Gossip, rumor, and formal or informal newspapers, like the one pictured here, ensured that information traversed the city at astonishing speeds. (Musée de la Ville de Paris, Musée Carnavalet, Paris/Lauros/Giraudon/The Bridgeman Art Library)

the expansion in production and drop in prices that allowed such items to spread to the masses.

Why were colonial products so popular? Part of the motivation for consuming these products was a desire to emulate the luxurious lifestyles of the elite. Having seen pictures of or read about the fine lady's habit of "teatime" or the gentleman's appreciation for a pipe, common Europeans sought to experience these pleasures for themselves. Moreover, the quickened pace of work in the eighteenth century created new needs for stimulants among working people. (See "Primary Source 18.3: A Day in the Life of Paris," page 590.)

Whereas the gentry took tea as a leisurely and genteel ritual, the lower classes drank tea or coffee at work to fight monotony and fatigue. With the widespread adoption of these products (which both turned out to be mildly to extremely addictive), working people in Europe became increas-

consumer revolution
The wide-ranging growth in consumption and new attitudes toward consumer goods that emerged in the cities of northwestern Europe in the second half of the eighteenth century.

ingly dependent on faraway colonial economies and enslaved labor. Their understanding of daily necessities and how to procure those necessities shifted definitively, linking them to global trade networks they could not comprehend or control.

Toward a Consumer Society

Along with foodstuffs, all manner of other goods increased in variety and number in the eighteenth century. This proliferation led to a growth in consumption and new attitudes toward consumer goods so wide-ranging that some historians have referred to an eighteenth-century **consumer revolution**.[19] The result of this revolution was the birth of a new type of society in which people derived their self-identity as much from their consuming practices as from their working lives and place in the production process. As people gained the opportunity to pick and choose among a new variety of consumer goods, new notions of individuality and self-expression developed. A shopgirl could stand out from

The Fashion Merchant

Well-to-do women spent their mornings preparing their toilettes and receiving visits from close friends and purveyors of various goods and services. In this 1746 painting by François Boucher, a leisured lady has just been coiffed by her hairdresser. Wearing the cape she donned to protect her clothing from the hair powder, she receives a fashion merchant, who displays an array of ribbons and other finery.

(Photos12–ARJ)

EVALUATE THE EVIDENCE

1. In this painting, which woman is the fashion merchant and which is her client? What are they doing at the moment the picture is painted? How would you characterize the relationship between the two women in this painting?

2. In what ways does the fashion merchant's attire provide evidence of the consumer revolution of the eighteenth century? Compare this image to the painting of the serving girl (page 576). What contrasting images of the working woman do these two images present?

her peers by her choice of a striped jacket, a colored parasol, or simply a new ribbon for her hair. The full emergence of a consumer society did not take place until much later, but its roots lie in the eighteenth century.

Increased demand for consumer goods was not merely an innate response to increased supply. Eighteenth-century merchants cleverly pioneered new techniques to incite demand: they initiated marketing campaigns, opened fancy boutiques with large windows, and advertised the patronage of royal princes and princesses. (See "Primary Source 18.4: The Fashion Merchant," page 593.) By diversifying their product lines and greatly accelerating the turnover of styles, they seized the reins of fashion from the courtiers who had earlier controlled it. Instead of setting new styles, duchesses and marquises now bowed to the dictates of fashion merchants. (See "Individuals in Society: Rose Bertin, 'Minister of Fashion,'" at right.) Fashion also extended beyond court circles to touch many more items and social groups.

Clothing was one of the chief indicators of the growth of consumerism. Shrewd entrepreneurs made

fashionable clothing seem more desirable, while legions of women entering the textile and needle trades made it ever cheaper. As a result, eighteenth-century western Europe witnessed a dramatic rise in the consumption of clothing, particularly in large cities. One historian has documented an enormous growth in the size and value of Parisians' wardrobes from 1700 to 1789, as well as a new level of diversity in garments and accessories, colors, and fabrics.[20] Colonial economies again played an important role in lowering the cost of materials, such as cotton and vegetable dyes, largely due to the unpaid toil of enslaved Africans. Cheaper copies of elite styles made it possible for working people to aspire to follow fashion for the first time.

Elite onlookers were sometimes shocked by the sight of lower-class people in stylish outfits. In 1784 Mrs. Fanny Cradock described encountering her milkman during an evening stroll "dressed in a fashionable suit, with an embroidered waistcoat, silk knee-breeches and lace cuffs."[21] The spread of fashion challenged the traditional social order of Europe by blurring the boundaries between social groups and making it harder to distinguish between noble and commoner on the bustling city streets.

Mrs. Cradock's milkman notwithstanding, women took the lead in the spread of fashion. Parisian women significantly out-consumed men, acquiring larger and more expensive wardrobes than those of their husbands, brothers, and fathers. This was true across the social spectrum; in ribbons, shoes, gloves, and lace, European working women reaped in the consumer revolution what they had sown in the industrious revolution (see Chapter 17). There were also new gender distinc-

The Consumer Revolution   From the mid-eighteenth century on, the cities of western Europe witnessed a new proliferation of consumer goods. Items once limited to the wealthy few — such as fans, watches, snuffboxes, umbrellas, ornamental containers, and teapots — were now reproduced in cheaper versions for middling and ordinary people. (fan: Scala/White Images/Art Resource, NY; jar: Victoria & Albert Museum, London/The Bridgeman Art Library)

Rose Bertin, "Minister of Fashion"

One day in 1779, as the French royal family rode in a carriage through the streets of Paris, Queen Marie Antoinette noticed her fashion merchant, Rose Bertin, observing the royal procession. "Ah! there is mademoiselle Bertin," the queen exclaimed, waving her hand. Bertin responded with a curtsy. The king then stood and greeted Bertin, followed by the royal family and their entourage.* The incident shocked the public, for no common merchant had ever received such homage from royalty.

Bertin had come a long way from her humble beginnings. Born in 1747 to a poor family in northern France, she moved to Paris in the 1760s to work as a shop assistant. Bertin eventually opened her own boutique on the fashionable rue Saint-Honoré. In 1775 Bertin received the highest honor of her profession when she was selected by Marie Antoinette as one of her official purveyors.

Based on the queen's patronage, and riding the wave of the new consumer revolution, Bertin became one of the most successful entrepreneurs in Europe. Bertin established not only a large clientele, but also a reputation for pride and arrogance. She refused to work for non-noble customers, claiming that the orders of the queen and the court required all her attention. She astounded courtiers by referring to her "work" with the queen, as though the two were collaborators rather than absolute monarch and lowly subject. Bertin's close relationship with Marie Antoinette and the fortune the queen spent on her wardrobe hurt the royal family's image. One journalist derided Bertin as a "minister of fashion," whose influence outstripped that of all the others in royal government.

In January 1787 rumors spread through Paris that Bertin had filed for bankruptcy with debts of 2 to 3 million livres (a garment worker's annual salary was around 200 livres). Despite her notoriously high prices and rich clients, this news did not shock Parisians, because the nobility's reluctance to pay its debts was equally well known. Bertin somehow held on to her business. Some said she had spread the bankruptcy rumors herself to shame the court into paying her bills.

Bertin remained loyal to the Crown during the tumult of the French Revolution (see Chapter 19) and sent dresses to the queen even after the arrest of the royal family. Fearing for her life, she left France for Germany in 1792 and continued to ply her profession in exile. She returned to France in 1800 and died in 1813, one year before the restoration of the Bourbon monarchy might have renewed her acclaim.†

Rose Bertin scandalized public opinion with her self-aggrandizement and ambition, yet history was on her side. She was the first celebrity fashion stylist and one of the first self-made career women to rise from obscurity to fame and fortune based on her talent, taste, and hard work. Her legacy remains in the exalted status of today's top fashion designers and in the dreams of small-town girls to make it in the big city.

This portrait of Rose Bertin was painted at the height of her popularity in 1780. (Image copyright © The Metropolitan Museum of Art. Image source: Art Resource, NY)

QUESTIONS FOR ANALYSIS

1. Why was the relationship between Queen Marie Antoinette and Rose Bertin so troubling to public opinion? Why would relations between a queen and a fashion merchant have political implications?
2. Why would someone who sold fashionable clothing and accessories rise to such a prominent position in business and society? What makes fashion so important in the social world?

---

*Mémoires secrets pour servir à l'histoire de la république des lettres en France, vol. 13, 299, 5 mars 1779 (London: John Adamson, 1785).

†On Rose Bertin, see Clare Haru Crowston, "The Queen and Her 'Minister of Fashion': Gender, Credit and Politics in Pre-Revolutionary France," Gender and History 14, 1 (April 2002): 92–116.

tions in dress. Previously, noblemen had vied with noblewomen in the magnificence of their apparel; by the end of the eighteenth century men had renounced brilliant colors and voluptuous fabrics to don early versions of the plain dark suit that remains standard male formal wear in the West. This was one more aspect of the increasingly rigid differences drawn between appropriate male and female behavior.

Changes in outward appearances were reflected in inner spaces, as new attitudes about privacy and intimate life also emerged. Historians have used notaries' probate inventories to peer into ordinary people's homes. In 1700 the cramped home of a modest family consisted of a few rooms, each of which had multiple functions. The same room was used for sleeping, receiving friends, and working. In the eighteenth century rents rose sharply, making it impossible to gain more space, but families began attributing specific functions to specific rooms. They also began to erect inner barriers within the home to provide small niches in which individuals could seek privacy.

New levels of comfort and convenience accompanied this trend toward more individualized ways of life. In 1700 a meal might be served in a common dish, with each person dipping his or her spoon into the pot. By the end of the eighteenth century even humble households contained a much greater variety of cutlery and dishes, making it possible for each person to eat from his or her own plate. More books and prints, which also proliferated at lower prices, decorated the shelves and walls. Improvements in glassmaking provided more transparent glass, which allowed daylight to penetrate into gloomy rooms. Cold and smoky hearths were increasingly replaced by more efficient and cleaner coal stoves, which also eliminated the backache of cooking over an open fire. Rooms were warmer, better lit, more comfortable, and more personalized, and the spread of street lighting made it safer to travel in cities at night.

Standards of bodily and public hygiene also improved. Public bathhouses, popular across Europe in the Middle Ages, had gradually closed in the early modern period due to concerns over sexual promiscuity and infectious disease. Many Europeans came to fear that immersing the body in hot water would allow harmful elements to enter the skin. Carefully watched by his physician, Louis XIII of France took his first bath at age seven, while James I of England refused to wash more than his hands. Personal cleanliness consisted of wearing fresh linen and using perfume to mask odors, both expensive practices that bespoke wealth and social status. From the mid-eighteenth century on, enlightened doctors revised their views and began to urge more frequent bathing. Spa towns, like Bath, England, became popular sites for the wealthy

to see and be seen. Officials also took measures to improve the cleaning of city streets in which trash, human soil, and animal carcasses were often left to rot.

The scope of the new consumer economy should not be exaggerated. These developments were concentrated in large cities in northwestern Europe and North America. Even in these centers the elite benefited the most from new modes of life. This was not yet the society of mass consumption that emerged toward the end of the nineteenth century with the full expansion of the Industrial Revolution. The eighteenth century did, however, lay the foundations for one of the most distinctive features of modern Western life: societies based on the consumption of goods and services obtained through the market in which individuals form their identities and self-worth through the goods they consume.

Religious Authority and Beliefs

What were the patterns of popular religion, and how did they interact with the worldview of the educated public and their Enlightenment ideals?

Though the critical spirit of the Enlightenment made great inroads in the eighteenth century, the majority of ordinary men and women, especially those in rural areas, retained strong religious faith. The church promised salvation, and it gave comfort in the face of sorrow and death. Religion also remained strong because it was embedded in local traditions and everyday social experience.

Yet the popular religion of village Europe was also enmeshed in a larger world of church hierarchies and state power. These powerful outside forces sought to regulate religious life at the local level. Their efforts created tensions that helped set the scene for vigorous religious revivals in Protestant Germany and England as well as in Catholic France.

Church Hierarchy

In the eighteenth century religious faith not only endured, but grew in many parts of Europe. The local parish church remained the focal point of religious devotion and community cohesion. Congregants gossiped and swapped stories after services, and neighbors came together in church for baptisms, marriages, funerals, and special events. Priests and parsons kept the community records of births, deaths, and marriages; distributed charity; looked after orphans; and provided primary education to the common people. Thus the parish church was woven into the very fabric of community life.

While the parish church remained central to the community, it was also subject to greater control from the state. In Protestant areas, princes and monarchs headed the official church, and they regulated their "territorial churches" strictly, selecting personnel and imposing detailed rules. Clergy of the official church dominated education, and followers of other faiths suffered religious and civil discrimination. By the eighteenth century the radical ideas of the Reformation had resulted in another version of church bureaucracy.

Catholic monarchs in this period also took greater control of religious matters in their kingdoms, weakening papal authority. In both Spain and Portugal, the Catholic Church was closely associated with the state, a legacy of the long internal reconquista and sixteenth-century imperial conquests overseas. In the eighteenth century the Spanish crown took firm control of ecclesiastical appointments. Papal proclamations could not even be read in Spanish churches without prior approval from the government. In Portugal, religious enthusiasm led to a burst of new churches and monasteries in the early eighteenth century.

France went even further in establishing a national Catholic Church, known as the Gallican Church. Louis XIV's expulsion of Protestants in 1685 was accompanied by an insistence on the king's prerogative to choose and control bishops and issue laws regarding church affairs. Catholicism gained new ground in the Holy Roman Empire with the conversion of a number of Protestant princes and successful missionary work by Catholic orders among the populace. While it could not eradicate Protestantism altogether, the Habsburg monarchy successfully consolidated Catholicism as a pillar of its political control.

The Jesuit order played a key role in fostering the Catholic faith, providing extraordinary teachers, missionaries, and agents of the papacy. In many Catholic countries they exercised tremendous political influence, holding high government positions and educating the nobility in their colleges. By playing politics so effectively, however, the Jesuits elicited a broad coalition of enemies. Bitter controversies led Louis XV to order the Jesuits out of France in 1763 and to confiscate their property. France and Spain then pressured Rome to dissolve the Jesuits completely. In 1773 a reluctant pope caved in, although the order was revived after the French Revolution.

The Jesuit order was not the only Christian group to come under attack in the middle of the eighteenth century. The dominance of the larger Catholic Church and established Protestant churches was also challenged, both by enlightened reformers from above and by the faithful from below. Influenced by Enlightenment ideals, some Catholic rulers believed that the clergy in monasteries and convents should make a more practical contribution to social and religious life. Austria, a leader in controlling the church (see Chapter 16) and promoting primary education, showed how far the process could go. Maria Theresa began by sharply restricting entry into "unproductive" orders. In his Edict on Idle Institutions, her successor, Joseph II, abolished contemplative orders, henceforth permitting only orders that were engaged in teaching, nursing, or other practical work. The state expropriated the dissolved monasteries and used their wealth for charitable purposes and higher salaries for ordinary priests. Joseph II also issued edicts of religious tolerance, including for Jews, making Austria one of the first European states to lift centuries-old restrictions on its Jewish population.

Protestant Revival

Official efforts to reform state churches in the eighteenth century were confronted by a wave of religious enthusiasm from below. By the late seventeenth century the vast transformations of the Protestant Reformation were complete and had been widely adopted in most Protestant churches. Medieval practices of idolatry, saint worship, and pageantry were abolished; stained-glass windows were smashed and murals whitewashed. Yet many official Protestant churches had settled into a smug complacency. This, along with the growth of state power and bureaucracy in local parishes, threatened to eclipse one of the Reformation's main goals—to bring all believers closer to God.

In the Reformation heartland, one concerned German minister wrote that the Lutheran Church "had become paralyzed in forms of dead doctrinal conformity" and badly needed a return to its original inspiration.[22] His voice was one of many that prepared and then guided a Protestant revival that succeeded because it answered the intense but increasingly unsatisfied needs of common people.

The Protestant revival began in Germany in the late seventeenth century. It was known as **Pietism** (PIGH-uh-tih-zum), and three aspects helped explain its powerful appeal. First, Pietism called for a warm, emotional religion that everyone could experience. Enthusiasm—in prayer, in worship, in preaching, in life itself—

Pietism A Protestant revival movement in early-eighteenth-century Germany and Scandinavia that emphasized a warm and emotional religion, the priesthood of all believers, and the power of Christian rebirth in everyday affairs.

was the key concept. "Just as a drunkard becomes full of wine, so must the congregation become filled with spirit," declared one exuberant writer.[23]

Second, Pietism reasserted the earlier radical stress on the priesthood of all believers, thereby reducing the gulf between official clergy and Lutheran laity. Bible reading and study were enthusiastically extended to all classes, and this provided a powerful spur for popular literacy as well as individual religious development. Pietists were largely responsible for the educational reforms implemented by Prussia in the early eighteenth century (see page 585). Finally, Pietists believed in the practical power of Christian rebirth in everyday affairs. Reborn Christians were expected to lead good, moral lives and to come from all social classes.

Pietism soon spread through the German-speaking lands and to Scandinavia. It also had a major impact on John Wesley (1703–1791), who served as the catalyst for popular religious revival in England. (See "Primary Source 18.5: Advice to Methodists," at right.) Wesley came from a long line of ministers, and when he went to Oxford University to prepare for the clergy, he mapped a fanatically earnest "scheme of religion." After becoming a teaching fellow at Oxford, Wesley organized a Holy Club for similarly minded students, who were soon known contemptuously as **Methodists** because they were so methodical in their devotion. Yet like the young Martin Luther, Wesley remained intensely troubled about his own salvation even after his ordination as an Anglican priest in 1728.

Methodists Members of a Protestant revival movement started by John Wesley, so called because they were so methodical in their devotion.

Hogarth's Satirical View of the Church William Hogarth (1697–1764) was one of the foremost satirical artists of his day. This image mocks a London Methodist meeting, where the congregation swoons in enthusiasm over the preacher's sermon. The woman in the foreground giving birth to rabbits refers to a hoax perpetrated in 1726 by a servant named Mary Tofts; the gullibility of those who believed Tofts is likened to that of the Methodist congregation. (The Israel Museum, Jerusalem, Israel/Vera & Arturo Schwarz Collection of Dada and Surrealist Art/The Bridgeman Art Library)

Advice to Methodists

John Wesley (1703–1791) was the fifteenth child of an Angli-can rector and a strict mother. As a small child, he was res-cued from certain death in a house fire; in later years, he saw this moment as a sign of providential grace. Along with his brother Charles, John Wesley is recognized as the founder of Methodism, an evangelical movement that began within the Church of England and was influenced by German Pietism. In the passage below, Wesley offers his advice to followers of the new religious movement he had inspired, who had been dubbed "Methodists" for their scrupulous and methodical approach to religious worship.

By *Methodists* I mean, a People who profess to pursue (in whatsoever Measure they have attained) Holiness of Heart and Life, inward and outward Conformity in all Things to the revealed Will of God: Who place Religion in an uniform Resemblance of the great Object of it; in a steady Imitation of Him they worship, in all his imitable Perfections; more particularly, in Justice, Mercy, and Truth, or universal Love filling the Heart, and governing the Life. . . .

Your *Name* is new, (at least, as used in a religious Sense) not heard of, till a few Years ago, either in our own, or any other Nation. Your *Principles* are new, in this respect, That there is no other Set of People among us (and, possibly, not in the Christian World) who hold them all, in the same Degree and Connection; who so strenu-ously and continually insist on the absolute Necessity of universal Holiness both in Heart and Life; of a peaceful, joyous Love of God; of a supernatural Evidence of Things not seen; of an inward Witness that we are the Children of God, and of the Inspiration of the Holy Ghost, in order to any good Thought, or Word, or Work. And perhaps there is no other Set of People, (at least not visibly united together) who lay *so much*, and yet *no more* Stress than you do, on Rectitude of *Opinions*, on outward *Modes of Worship*, and the Use of those *Ordinances* which you acknowledge to be of God. . . .

Your *Strictness* of Life, taking the whole of it together, may likewise be accounted new. I mean, your making it a Rule, to abstain from fashionable *Diversions*, from *reading* Plays, Romances, or Books of Humour, from *singing* inno-cent Songs, or *talking* in a merry, gay, diverting Manner; your *Plainness* of Dress; your *Manner of Dealing* in Trade; your Exactness in observing the *Lord's Day*; your Scrupu-losity as to Things that have *not paid Custom*; your total Abstinence from *spirituous Liquors* (unless in Cases of Extreme Necessity;) your Rule, "not to mention the Fault of an absent Person, in Particular, of *Ministers*, or of *those in Authority*," may justly be termed new.

EVALUATE THE EVIDENCE

1. What elements of the Methodist faith does Wesley identify as "new" in this document? To what or whom is he comparing Methodists?
2. To what changes under way in English society does this document appear to be responding? What social practices do Methodists oppose according to Wesley?

Source: John Wesley, *Advice to the People Call'd Methodists* (Bristol: Felix Farley, 1745), 3, 5–6.

Wesley's anxieties related to grave problems of the faith in England. The government shamelessly used the Church of England to provide favorites with high-paying jobs. Both church and state officials failed to respond to the spiritual needs of the people, and ser-vices and sermons had settled into an uninspiring rou-tine. The separation of religion from local customs and social life was symbolized by church doors that were customarily locked on weekdays. Moreover, Enlight-enment skepticism was making inroads among the educated classes, and deism—a belief in God but not in organized religion—was becoming popular. Some bishops and church leaders seemed to believe that doc-trines such as the virgin birth were little more than el-egant superstitions.

Wesley's inner search in the 1730s was deeply af-fected by his encounter with Moravian Pietists, whom he first met on a ship as he traveled across the Atlantic to take up a position in Savannah, Georgia. The small Moravian community in Georgia impressed him as a productive, peaceful, and pious world, reflecting the values of the first apostles. (For more on the Mora-vian Church, see Chapter 17, "Individuals in Society: Rebecca Protten," page 568.) After returning to Lon-don, following a disastrous failed engagement and the disappointment of his hopes to convert Native Amer-icans, he sought spiritual counseling from a Pietist minister from Germany. Their conversations prepared Wesley for a mystical, emotional "conversion" in 1738. He described this critical turning point in his *Journal:*

> In the evening I went to a [Christian] society in Aldersgate Street where one was reading Luther's preface to the Epistle to the Romans. About a quarter before nine, while he was describing the change which God works in the heart through faith in Christ, I felt my heart strangely warmed. I felt I did trust in Christ, Christ alone for salvation; and an assurance was given me that he had taken away my sins, even mine, and saved me from the law of sin and death.[24]

Wesley's emotional experience resolved his intellectual doubts about the possibility of his own salvation. Moreover, he was convinced that any person, no matter how poor or uneducated, might have a similarly heartfelt conversion and gain the same blessed assurance. He took the good news to the people, traveling some 225,000 miles by horseback and preaching more than forty thousand sermons between 1750 and 1790. Since existing churches were often overcrowded and the church-state establishment was hostile, Wesley preached in open fields. People came in large numbers. Of critical importance was Wesley's rejection of Calvinist predestination—the doctrine of salvation granted to only a select few. Instead, he preached that all men and women who earnestly sought salvation might be saved. It was a message of hope and joy, of free will and universal salvation.

Jansenism A sect of Catholicism originating with Cornelius Jansen that emphasized the heavy weight of original sin and accepted the doctrine of predestination; it was outlawed as heresy by the pope.

Wesley's ministry won converts, formed Methodist cells, and eventually resulted in a new denomination. And just as Wesley had been inspired by the Pietist revival in Germany, so evangelicals in the Church of England and the old dissenting groups now followed Wesley's example of preaching to all people, giving impetus to an even broader awakening among the lower classes. Thus in Protestant countries religion continued to be a vital force in the lives of the people.

Catholic Piety

Religion also flourished in Catholic Europe around 1700, but there were important differences from Protestant practice. First, the visual contrast was striking; baroque art still lavished rich and emotionally exhilarating figures and images on Catholic churches, just as most Protestants had removed theirs during the Reformation. Moreover, people in Catholic Europe on the whole participated more actively in formal worship than did Protestants. More than 95 percent of the population probably attended church for Easter communion, the climax of the religious year.

The tremendous popular strength of religion in Catholic countries can in part be explained by the church's integral role in community life and popular culture. Thus, although Catholics reluctantly confessed their sins to priests, they enthusiastically came together in religious festivals to celebrate the passage of the liturgical year. In addition to the great processional days—such as Palm Sunday, the joyful reenactment of Jesus's triumphal entry into Jerusalem—each parish had its own saints' days, processions, and pilgrimages. Led by its priest, a congregation might march around the village or across the countryside to a local shrine. Millions of Catholic men and women also joined religious associations, known as confraternities, where they participated in prayer and religious services and collected funds for poor relief and members' funerals. The Reformation had largely eliminated such festivities in Protestant areas.

Catholicism had its own version of the Pietist revivals that shook Protestant Europe. **Jansenism** has been described by one historian as the "illegitimate offspring of the Protestant Reformation and the Catholic Counter-Reformation."[25] It originated with Cornelius Jansen (1585–1638), bishop of Ypres in the Spanish Netherlands, who called for a return to the austere early Christianity of Saint Augustine. In contrast to the worldly Jesuits, Jansen emphasized the heavy weight of original sin and accepted the doctrine of predestination. Although outlawed by papal and royal edicts as Calvinist heresy, Jansenism attracted Catholic followers eager for religious renewal, particularly among the French. Many members of France's urban elite, especially judicial nobles and some parish priests, became known for their Jansenist piety and spiritual devotion. Such stern religious values encouraged the judiciary's increasing opposition to the French monarchy in the second half of the eighteenth century.

Among the urban poor, a different strain of Jansenism took hold. Prayer meetings brought men and women together in ecstatic worship, and some participants fell into convulsions and spoke in tongues. The police of Paris posted spies to report on such gatherings and conducted mass raids and arrests.

Marginal Beliefs and Practices

In the countryside, many peasants continued to hold religious beliefs that were marginal to the Christian faith altogether, often of obscure or even pagan origin. On the Feast of Saint Anthony, for example, priests were expected to bless salt and bread for farm animals to protect them from disease. Catholics believed that saints' relics could bring fortune or attract lovers, and there were healing springs for many ailments. In 1796 the Lutheran villagers of Beutelsbach in southern Germany incurred the ire of local officials when they buried a live bull at a crossroads to ward off an epidemic of hoof-and-mouth disease.[26] The ordinary person combined strong Christian faith with a wealth of time-honored superstitions.

Inspired initially by the fervor of the Reformation era, then by the critical rationalism of the Enlightenment, religious and secular authorities sought increasingly to "purify" popular spirituality. Thus one parish priest in France lashed out at his parishioners, claiming that they were "more superstitious than devout . . . and sometimes appear as baptized idolators."[27] French priests particularly denounced the "various remnants of paganism" found in popular bonfire ceremonies during Lent, in which young men, "yelling and screaming like madmen," tried to jump over the bonfires in order to help the crops grow and protect themselves from illness. One priest saw rational Christians regressing into pagan animals — "the triumph of Hell and the shame of Christianity."[28]

The severity of the attack on popular belief varied widely by country and region. Where authorities pursued purification vigorously, as in Austria under Joseph II, pious peasants saw only an incomprehensible attack on age-old faith and drew back in anger. Their reaction dramatized the growing tension between the attitudes of educated elites and the common people.

It was in this era of growing intellectual disdain for popular beliefs that the persecution of witches slowly came to an end across Europe. Common people in the countryside continued to fear the Devil and his helpers, but the elite increasingly dismissed such fears and refused to prosecute suspected witches. The last witch was executed in England in 1682, the same year France prohibited witchcraft trials. By the late eighteenth century most European states and their colonies had followed suit.

Medical Practice

How did the practice of medicine evolve in the eighteenth century?

Although significant breakthroughs in medical science would not come until the middle and late nineteenth century, the Enlightenment's inherent optimism and its focus on improving human life through understanding of the laws of nature produced a great deal of research and experimentation in the 1700s. Medical practitioners greatly increased in number, although

their techniques did not differ much from those of previous generations. Care of the sick in this era was the domain of several competing groups: traditional healers, apothecaries (pharmacists), physicians, surgeons, and midwives. From the Middle Ages through the seventeenth century, both men and women were medical practitioners. However, since women were generally denied admission to medical colleges and lacked the diplomas necessary to practice, the range of medical activities open to them was restricted. In the eighteenth century women's traditional roles as midwives and healers eroded even further.

Faith Healing and General Practice

In the course of the eighteenth century, traditional healers remained active, drawing on centuries of folk knowledge about the curative properties of roots, herbs, and other plants. Faith healing also remained popular, especially in the countryside. Faith healers and their patients believed that evil spirits caused illness by lodging in people and that the proper treatment was to exorcise, or drive out, the offending devil. Religious and secular officials did their best to stamp out such practices, but with little success.

In the larger towns and cities, apothecaries sold a vast number of herbs, drugs, and patent medicines for every conceivable "temperament and distemper." Some of the drugs and herbs undoubtedly worked. For example, strong laxatives were given to the rich for their constipated bowels, and regular purging of the bowels was considered essential for good health and the treatment of illness. Like all varieties of medical practitioners, apothecaries advertised their wares, their high-class customers, and their miraculous cures in newspapers and commercial circulars. Medicine, like food and fashionable clothing, thus joined the era's new and loosely regulated commercial culture.

Physicians, who were invariably men, were apprenticed in their teens to practicing physicians for several years of on-the-job training. This training was then rounded out with hospital work or some university courses. Seen as gentlemen who did not labor with their hands, many physicians diagnosed and treated patients by correspondence or through oral dialogue, without conducting a physical examination. Because their training was expensive, physicians came mainly from prosperous families and they usually concentrated on urban patients from similar social backgrounds. Nevertheless, even poor people spent hard-won resources to seek treatment for their loved ones.

Physicians in the eighteenth century were increasingly willing to experiment with new methods, but time-honored practices lay heavily on them. Like

LIVING IN THE PAST
Improvements in Childbirth

Most women in eighteenth-century Europe gave birth to at least five or six children over their lifetimes. They were assisted in the arduous, often dangerous process of childbirth by friends, relatives, and, in many cases, professional midwives. Birth took place at home, sometimes with the aid of a birthing chair, such as the folding chair from Sicily shown here.

The training and competency of midwives were often rudimentary, especially in the countryside. Enlightenment interest in education and public health helped inspire a movement across Europe to raise standards. One of its pioneers was Madame Angelique Marguerite Le Boursier du Coudray. Du Coudray herself had undergone a rigorous three-year apprenticeship and was a member of the Parisian surgeons' guild. She set off on a mission to teach rural midwives in the French province of Auvergne.

Du Coudray saw that her unlettered pupils learned through the senses, not through books. Thus she made, possibly for the first time in history, a life-size obstetrical model—a "machine"—out of fabric and stuffing for use in her classes. "I had . . . the students maneuver in front of me on a machine . . . which represented the pelvis of a woman, the womb, its opening, its ligaments, the conduit called the vagina, the bladder, and *rectum intestine*. I added [an artificial] child of natural size, whose joints were flexible enough to be able to be put in different positions."* Now

du Coudray could demonstrate the problems of childbirth, and each student could practice on the model in the "lab session."

As her reputation grew, du Coudray sought to reach a national audience. In 1757 she published her *Manual on the Art of Childbirth*. The *Manual* incorporated her hands-on teaching method and served as a reference for students and graduates. In 1759 the government authorized du Coudray to carry her instruction "throughout the realm" and promised financial support.

Her classes brought women from surrounding villages to meet mornings and afternoons six days a week, with ample time to practice on the mannequin. After two to three months of instruction, Madame du Coudray and her entourage moved on. Teaching thousands of midwives, Madame du Coudray and her model may well have contributed to the

Eighteenth-century birthing chair from Sicily.
(Science & Society Picture Library)

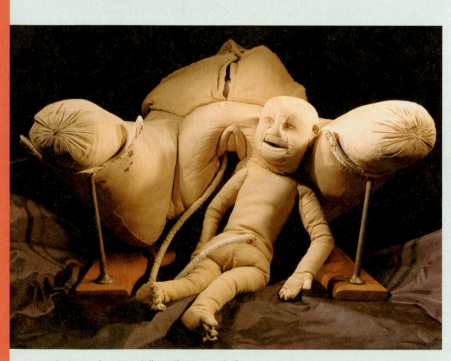

Du Coudray's life-size model for simulating childbirth.
(Musée Flaubert d'histoire de la médecine, Rouen)

*Quotes are from Nina Gelbart, *The King's Midwife: A History and Mystery of Madame du Coudray* (Berkeley: University of California Press, 1998), pp. 60–61.

Childbirth was traditionally a woman's world that brought female relatives, friends, and the midwife to the laboring woman's bedside, as shown in this Dutch painting from the late seventeenth century. (Image copyright © The Metropolitan Museum of Art/Art Resource, NY)

decline in infant mortality and to the increase in population occurring in France in the eighteenth century — an increase she and her royal supporters fervently desired. Certainly she spread better knowledge about childbirth from the educated elite to the common people.

QUESTIONS FOR ANALYSIS

1. How do you account for du Coudray's remarkable success? What does her story suggest about women's lives in this period, both within their families and in the economic realm? What kind of opportunities were available to women?
2. What is painted on the Italian birthing chair where a woman's head would rest during labor? What might this suggest about childbirth in this period?
3. How might the Dutch painting of childbirth shown here differ if painted by a Western artist today?

"Incorrect method of delivery" from du Coudray's *Manual*. (Rare Books Division, Countway [Francis A.] Library of Medicine)

apothecaries, they laid great stress on purging, and bloodletting was still considered a medical cure-all. It was the way "bad blood," the cause of illness, was removed and the balance of humors necessary for good health was restored.

Improvements in Surgery

Long considered to be craftsmen comparable to butchers and barbers, surgeons began studying anatomy seriously and improved their art in the eighteenth century. With endless opportunities to practice, army surgeons on gory battlefields led the way. They learned that a soldier with an extensive wound, such as a shattered leg or arm, could perhaps be saved if the surgeon could obtain a flat surface above the wound that could be cauterized with fire. Thus if a soldier had a broken limb and the bone stuck out, the surgeon amputated so that the remaining stump could be cauterized and the likelihood of death reduced.

The eighteenth-century surgeon (and patient) labored in the face of incredible difficulties. Almost all operations were performed without painkillers, for the anesthesia of the day was hard to control and too dangerous for general use. Many patients died from the agony and shock of such operations. Surgery was also performed in utterly unsanitary conditions, for there was no knowledge of bacteriology and the nature of infection. The simplest wound treated by a surgeon could fester and lead to death.

Midwifery

Midwives continued to deliver the overwhelming majority of babies throughout the eighteenth century. Trained initially by another woman practitioner—and regulated by a guild in many cities—the midwife primarily assisted in labor and delivering babies. She also treated female problems, such as irregular menstrual cycles, breast-feeding difficulties, infertility, and venereal disease, and ministered to small children.

The midwife orchestrated labor and birth in a woman's world, where friends and relatives assisted the pregnant woman in the familiar surroundings of her own home. The male surgeon (and the husband) rarely entered this female world, because most births, then as now, were normal and spontaneous. After the invention of forceps became publicized in 1734, surgeon-physicians used their monopoly over this and other instruments to seek lucrative new business. Attacking midwives as ignorant and dangerous, they sought to undermine faith in midwives and persuaded growing numbers of wealthy women of the superiority of their services. As one male expert proclaimed:

> A midwife is usually a creature of the lowest class of human beings, and of course utterly destitute of education, who from indigence, and that she is incapable of everything else, has been compelled to follow, as the last and sole resources a profession which people fondly imagine no very difficult one, never dreaming that the least glimpse of previous instruction is required for that purpose. . . . Midwives are universally ignorant. For where or how should she come by any thing deserving the name of knowledge.[29]

Research suggests that women practitioners successfully defended much but not all of their practice in the eighteenth century. One enterprising French midwife, Madame du Coudray, wrote a widely used textbook, *Manual on the Art of Childbirth* (1757), in order to address complaints about incompetent midwives. She then secured royal financing for her campaign to teach birthing techniques. Du Coudray traveled all over France using a life-size model of the female torso and fetus to help teach illiterate women. (See "Living in the Past: Improvements in Childbirth," page 602.) Despite criticism, it appears that midwives generally lost no more babies than did male doctors, who were still summoned to treat non-elite women only when life-threatening situations required surgery.

Women also continued to perform almost all nursing. Female religious orders ran many hospitals, and at-home nursing was almost exclusively the province of women. Thus, although they were excluded from the growing ranks of formally trained and authorized practitioners, women continued to perform the bulk of informal medical care. Nursing as a secular profession did not emerge until the nineteenth century.

The Conquest of Smallpox

Experimentation and the intensified search for solutions to human problems led to some real advances in medicine after 1750. The eighteenth century's greatest medical triumph was the eradication of smallpox. With the progressive decline of bubonic plague, smallpox became the most terrible of the infectious diseases, and it is estimated that 60 million Europeans died of it in the eighteenth century.

The first step in the conquest of this killer in Europe came in the early eighteenth century. An English aristocrat whose beauty had been marred by the pox, Lady Mary Wortley Montagu, learned about the long-established practice of smallpox inoculation in the Muslim lands of western Asia while her husband was serving as British ambassador to the Ottoman Empire.

The Wonderful Effects of the New Inoculation!   The talented caricaturist James Gillray satirized widespread anxieties about the smallpox vaccination in this lively image. The discoveries of Edward Jenner a few years prior to Gillray's caricature had led to the adoption of a safer vaccine derived from cowpox. The artist mocks this breakthrough by showing cows bursting from the boils supposedly brought on by the vaccine. (Private Collection/The Bridgeman Art Library)

She had her own son successfully inoculated with the pus from a smallpox victim and was instrumental in spreading the practice in England after her return in 1722. But inoculation was risky and was widely condemned because about one person in fifty died from it. In addition, people who had been inoculated were infectious and often spread the disease.

While the practice of inoculation with the smallpox virus was refined over the century, the crucial breakthrough was made by Edward Jenner (1749–1823), a talented country doctor. His starting point was the countryside belief that dairymaids who had contracted cowpox did not get smallpox. Cowpox produces sores that resemble those of smallpox, but the disease is mild and is not contagious.

For eighteen years Jenner practiced a kind of Baconian science, carefully collecting data. Finally, in 1796 he performed his first vaccination on a young boy using matter taken from a milkmaid with cowpox. After performing more successful vaccinations, Jenner published his findings in 1798. The new method of treatment spread rapidly, and smallpox soon declined to the point of disappearance in Europe and then throughout the world.

Notes

1. Archibald Campbell, Marquis of Argyll, *Instructions to a Son, Containing Rules of Conduct in Publick and Private Life* (Glasgow: E. Foulis, 1743), p. 33.
2. Quoted in J. M. Beattie, "The Criminality of Women in Eighteenth-Century England," *Journal of Social History* 8 (Summer 1975): 86.
3. Quoted in R. Cobb, *The Police and the People: French Popular Protest, 1789–1820* (Oxford, U.K.: Clarendon Press, 1970), p. 238.
4. Peter Laslett, *Family Life and Illicit Love: Essays in Historical Sociology* (Cambridge, U.K.: Cambridge University Press, 1977).
5. G. Gullickson, *Spinners and Weavers of Auffay: Rural Industry and the Sexual Division of Labor in a French Village, 1750–1850* (Cambridge, U.K.: Cambridge University Press, 1986), p. 186.
6. Louis Crompton, *Homosexuality and Civilization* (Cambridge, Mass.: Belknap Press, 2003), p. 321.
7. D. S. Neff, "Bitches, Mollies, and Tommies: Byron, Masculinity and the History of Sexualities," *Journal of the History of Sexuality* 11, 3 (July 2002): 404.

8. George E. Haggerty, ed., *Encyclopedia of Gay Histories and Cultures* (New York: Garland Publishing, 2000), pp. 1311–1312.

9. Pier Paolo Viazzo, "Mortality, Fertility, and Family," in *Family Life in Early Modern Times, 1500–1789*, ed. David I. Kertzer and Marzio Barbagli (New Haven, Conn.: Yale University Press, 2001), p. 180.

10. George Sussman, *Selling Mother's Milk: The Wet-Nursing Business in France, 1715–1914* (Urbana: University of Illinois Press, 1982), p. 22.

11. Robert Woods, "Did Montaigne Love His Children? Demography and the Hypothesis of Parental Indifference," *Journal of Interdisciplinary History* 33, 3 (2003): 426.

12. P. Viazzo, "Mortality, Fertility, and Family," in *The History of the European Family*, vol. 1, ed. D. Kertzer and M. Barbagli (New Haven, Conn.: Yale University Press, 2001), pp. 176–178.

13. Alysa Levene, "The Estimation of Mortality at the London Foundling Hospital, 1741–99," *Population Studies* 59, 1 (2005): 87–97.

14. Cited in Woods, "Did Montaigne Love His Children?" p. 421.

15. Ibid., pp. 13, 16.

16. James Van Horn Melton, *Absolutism and the Eighteenth-Century Origins of Compulsory Schooling in Prussia and Austria* (Cambridge, U.K.: Cambridge University Press, 2003), p. 46.

17. James Van Horn Melton, "The Theresian School Reform of 1774," in *Early Modern Europe*, ed. James B. Collins and Karen L. Taylor (Oxford, U.K.: Blackwell, 2006).

18. I. Woloch, *Eighteenth-Century Europe: Tradition and Progress, 1715–1789* (New York: W. W. Norton, 1982), pp. 220–221.

19. Neil McKendrik, John Brewer, and J. H. Plumb, *The Birth of a Consumer Society: The Commercialization of Eighteenth-Century England* (Bloomington: Indiana University Press, 1982).

20. Daniel Roche, *The Culture of Clothing: Dress and Fashion in the Ancien Regime*, trans. Jean Birrell (Cambridge, U.K.: Cambridge University Press, 1996).

21. Quoted in Cissie Fairchilds, "The Production and Marketing of Populuxe Goods in Eighteenth-Century Paris," in *Consumption and the World of Goods*, ed. John Brewer and Roy Porter (London: Routledge, 1993), p. 228.

22. Quoted in K. Pinson, *Pietism as a Factor in the Rise of German Nationalism* (New York: Columbia University Press, 1934), p. 13.

23. Ibid., pp. 43–44.

24. Quoted in S. Andrews, *Methodism and Society* (London: Longmans, Green, 1970), p. 327.

25. Dale Van Kley, "The Rejuvenation and Rejection of Jansenism in History and Historiography," *French Historical Studies* 29 (Fall 2006): 649–684.

26. David Sabean, *The Power in the Blood: Popular Culture and Village Discourse in Early Modern Germany* (Cambridge, U.K.: Cambridge University Press, 1984), p. 174.

27. Quoted in Woloch, *Eighteenth-Century Europe*, p. 292.

28. Quoted in T. Tackett, *Priest and Parish in Eighteenth-Century France* (Princeton, N.J.: Princeton University Press, 1977), p. 214.

29. Louis Lapeyre, *An Enquiry into the Merits of These Two Important Questions: I. Whether Women with Child Ought to Prefer the Assistance of Their Own Sex to That of Men-Midwives? II. Whether the Assistance of Men-Midwives Is Contrary to Decency?* (London: S. Bladon, 1772), p. 29.

LOOKING BACK LOOKING AHEAD

The fundamental patterns of life in early modern Europe remained very much the same up to the eighteenth century. The vast majority of people lived in the countryside and followed age-old rhythms of seasonal labor in the fields and farmyard. Community ties were close in small villages, where the struggle to prevail over harsh conditions called on all hands to work together and to pray together. The daily life of a peasant in 1700 would have been familiar to his ancestors in the 1400s. Indeed, the three orders of society enshrined in the medieval social hierarchy — clergy, nobility, peasantry — were binding legal categories in France up to 1789.

And yet, the economic changes inaugurated in the late seventeenth century — intensive agriculture, cottage industry, the industrious revolution, and colonial expansion — contributed to the profound social and cultural transformation of daily life in eighteenth-century Europe. Men and women of the laboring classes, especially in the cities, experienced change in many facets of their daily lives: in loosened community controls over sex and marriage, rising literacy rates, new goods and ways of utilizing space, and a wave of religious piety that challenged traditional orthodoxies. Both their age-old cultural practices and new religious fervor were met with mounting disbelief and ridicule by the educated classes in a period of increased distance between popular and elite culture.

Economic, social, and cultural change would culminate in the late eighteenth century with the outbreak of revolution in the Americas and Europe. Initially led by the elite, political upheavals relied on the enthusiastic participation of the poor and their desire for greater inclusion in the life of the nation. Such movements also encountered resistance from the common people when revolutionaries trampled on their religious faith. For many observers, contemporaries and historians alike, the transformations of the eighteenth century constituted a fulcrum between the old world of hierarchy and tradition and the modern world with its claims to equality and freedom.

REVIEW and EXPLORE

MAKE IT STICK

 LearningCurve
After reading the chapter, go online and use LearningCurve to retain what you've read.

Identify Key Terms

Identify and explain the significance of each item below.

community controls (p. 578)

charivari (p. 578)

illegitimacy explosion (p. 579)

wet-nursing (p. 581)

blood sports (p. 587)

carnival (p. 587)

just price (p. 589)

consumer revolution (p. 592)

Pietism (p. 597)

Methodists (p. 598)

Jansenism (p. 600)

Review the Main Ideas

Answer the focus questions from each section of the chapter.

- What changes occurred in marriage and the family in the course of the eighteenth century? (p. 576)

- What was life like for children, and how did attitudes toward childhood evolve? (p. 580)

- How did increasing literacy and new patterns of consumption affect people's lives? (p. 586)

- What were the patterns of popular religion, and how did they interact with the world-view of the educated public and their Enlightenment ideals? (p. 596)

- How did the practice of medicine evolve in the eighteenth century? (p. 601)

Make Connections

Think about the larger developments and continuities within and across chapters.

1. How did the expansion of agriculture and trade (Chapter 17) contribute to a new way of life in the eighteenth century?

2. What were the main areas of improvement in the lives of the common people in the eighteenth century and what aspects of life remained unchanged or even deteriorated?

3. How did Enlightenment thought (Chapter 16) impact education, child care, medicine, and religion in the eighteenth century?

ONLINE DOCUMENT ASSIGNMENT
The Inner Life of the Individual

How did the increasing emphasis on the inner life and development of the individual in the eighteenth century find expression in the art of the period?

Keeping the question above in mind, go to the Integrated Media and analyze a series of paintings by Jean-Baptiste-Siméon Chardin that depict various aspects of daily life and reveal the era's increased attention to individual emotion and development. Then complete a writing assignment based on the evidence and details from this chapter.

Suggested Reading and Media Resources

BOOKS

- Bergin, Joseph. *Church, Society, and Religious Change in France, 1580–1730.* 2009. A study of changing religious views in France from the wars of religion to the Enlightenment and the interaction of church and society.

- Bongie, Laurence L. *From Rogue to Everyman: A Foundling's Journey to the Bastille.* 2005. The story of an eighteenth-century orphan and, through his eyes, the Parisian underworld of gamblers, prostitutes, and police spies.

- Burke, Peter. *Popular Culture in Early Modern Europe,* 3d ed. 2009. An updated version of a classic introduction to everyday life, mentalities, and leisure pursuits.

- Carrell, Jennifer. *The Speckled Monster: A Historical Tale of Battling Smallpox.* 2003. A lively popular account of the spread of inoculation.

- Crawford, Katherine. *European Sexualities, 1400–1800.* 2007. A broad survey of cultural and social aspects of sex and sexuality in early modern Europe.

- Gawthrop, Richard. *Pietism and the Making of Eighteenth-Century Prussia.* 2006. An examination of the importance of Pietist morality and institutions in the making of the Prussian state.

- Gelbart, Nina. *The King's Midwife: A History and Mystery of Madame du Coudray.* 2002. A vivid and accessible biography of the most famous midwife of eighteenth-century France.

- Harrington, Joel. *The Unwanted Child: The Fate of Foundlings, Orphans, and Juvenile Criminals in Early Modern Germany.* 2009. Examines the fate of abandoned, orphaned, and delinquent children through the life stories of five individuals.

- Kertzer, David I., and Marzio Barbagli, eds. *Family Life in Early Modern Times, 1500–1789.* 2001. A rich collection of essays on the history of the family, women, and children in early modern Europe.

- Mintz, Sidney W. *Sweetness and Power: The Place of Sugar in Modern History.* 1985. A fascinating exploration of the shifting cultural significance of sugar and its transformation from elite luxury good to everyday staple.

- Trentman, Frank, ed. *The Oxford Handbook of the History of Consumption.* 2012. A series of essays presenting the most recent research on the history of consumption, including global perspectives.

DOCUMENTARIES

- *At Home with the Georgians* (BBC, 2011). A documentary examining the new domestic ideals of the eighteenth century, with re-enactments of daily life in British homes in all ranks of society.

FEATURE FILMS AND TELEVISION

- *Barry Lyndon* (Stanley Kubrick, 1975). The adventures of an eighteenth-century Irish rogue who marries a rich widow.

- *Beaumarchais the Scoundrel* (Edouard Molinaro, 1996). The story of French playwright Beaumarchais and his numerous romantic escapades in eighteenth-century Paris.

- *City of Vice* (Channel 4, 2008). A British crime series focusing on Henry Fielding, the eighteenth-century writer and magistrate who founded the first police force of London, the Bow Street Runners.

- *The Fortunes and Misfortunes of Moll Flanders* (PBS, 1996). A lively Masterpiece Theater adaptation of Daniel Defoe's famous novel recounting an orphaned girl's struggle to survive in eighteenth-century London.

WEB SITES

- *18th Century Blog: Fashion and Culture from the 1700s.* A blog devoted to the clothing, art, and literature of eighteenth-century Europe, with reviews of books and historical films and links to other relevant blogs and Web sites.
  18thcenturyblog.com/

- *Colonial Williamsburg.* Click on "Coffeehouse" for a set of short videos that document the archaeological excavation of a mid-eighteenth-century coffeehouse at Colonial Williamsburg and that show re-enactments of life in the coffeehouse.
  www.history.org/media/videoPlayer/index.cfm

- *London Lives.* A collection of almost 250,000 searchable digitized primary sources about ordinary people in eighteenth-century London, including criminal trials, hospital records, and other documents.
  www.londonlives.org/static/Project.jsp

19

Revolutions in Politics

1775–1815

A great wave of revolution rocked both sides of the Atlantic Ocean in the last decades of the eighteenth century. As trade goods, individuals, and ideas circulated in ever-greater numbers across the Atlantic Ocean, debates and events in one locale soon influenced those in another. As changing social realities challenged the old order of life and Enlightenment ideals of freedom and equality flourished, reformers in many places demanded fundamental changes in politics and government. At the same time, wars fought for dominance of the Atlantic economy left European states weakened by crushing debts, making them vulnerable to calls for reform.

The revolutionary era began in North America in 1775. Then in 1789 France, the most populous country in western Europe and a center of culture and intellectual life, became the leading revolutionary nation. It established first a constitutional monarchy, then a radical republic, and finally a new empire under Napoleon that would last until 1815. During this period of constant domestic turmoil, French armies violently exported revolution beyond the nation's borders, eager to establish new governments throughout much of Europe. Inspired both by the ideals of the Revolution on the continent and by their own experiences and desires, the slaves of Saint-Domingue rose up in 1791. Their rebellion would eventually lead to the creation of the new independent nation of Haiti in 1804. In Europe and its colonies abroad, the age of modern politics was born. ∎

Life in Revolutionary France. On the eve of the French Revolution, angry crowds like this one gathered in Paris to protest the high-handed actions of the royal government. Throughout the Revolution, decisive events took place in the street as much as in the chambers of the National Assembly. (Musée de la Ville de Paris, Musée Carnavalet, Paris/Lauros/Giraudon, The Bridgeman Art Library)

CHAPTER PREVIEW

 LearningCurve
After reading the chapter, go online and use LearningCurve to retain what you've read.

Background to Revolution
What were the factors behind the revolutions of the late eighteenth century?

The American Revolutionary Era, 1775–1789
Why and how did American colonists forge a new, independent nation?

Revolution in France, 1789–1791
How did the events of 1789 result in a constitutional monarchy in France, and what were the consequences?

World War and Republican France, 1791–1799
Why and how did the French Revolution take a radical turn entailing terror at home and war with European powers?

The Napoleonic Era, 1799–1815
Why did Napoleon Bonaparte assume control of France and much of Europe, and what factors led to his downfall?

The Haitian Revolution, 1791–1804
How did slave revolt on colonial Saint-Domingue lead to the creation of the independent nation of Haiti in 1804?

Background to Revolution

What were the factors behind the revolutions of the late eighteenth century?

The origins of the late-eighteenth-century revolutions in British North America, France, and Haiti were complex. No one cause lay behind them, nor was revolution inevitable or foreordained. However, certain important factors helped set the stage for reform. Among them were fundamental social and economic changes and political crises that eroded state authority. Another significant cause of revolutionary fervor was the impact of political ideas derived from the Enlightenment. Even though intellectuals of the Enlightenment were usually cautious about political reform themselves, their confidence in reason and progress helped inspire a new generation to fight for greater freedom from repressive governments. Perhaps most important, financial crises generated by war expenses brought European states to their knees and allowed abstract discussions of reform to become pressing realities.

Social Change

As in the Middle Ages, eighteenth-century European society was legally divided into groups with special privileges, such as the nobility and the clergy, and groups with special burdens, such as the peasantry. Nobles were the largest landowners, possessing one-quarter of the agricultural land of France, while constituting less than two percent of the population. They enjoyed exemption from direct taxation as well as exclusive rights to hunt game, bear swords, and wear gold ribbon in their clothing. In most countries, various middle-class groups—professionals, merchants, and guild masters—enjoyed privileges that allowed them to monopolize all sorts of economic activity. Poor peasants and urban laborers, who constituted the vast majority of the population, bore the brunt of taxation and were excluded from the world of privilege.

Traditional prerogatives for elite groups persisted in societies undergoing dramatic and destabilizing change. Europe's population rose rapidly after 1750, and its cities and towns swelled in size. Inflation kept pace with population growth, making it ever more difficult to find affordable food and living space. One way the poor kept up, and even managed to participate in the new consumer revolution (see Chapter 18), was by working harder and for longer hours. More women and children entered the paid labor force, challenging the traditional hierarchies and customs of village life.

Economic growth created new inequalities between rich and poor. While the poor struggled with rising prices, investors grew rich from the spread of manufacture in the countryside and overseas trade, including the trade in enslaved Africans and the products of slave labor. Old distinctions between landed aristocracy and city merchants began to fade as enterprising nobles put money into trade and rising middle-class bureaucrats and merchants purchased landed estates and noble titles. Marriages between proud nobles and wealthy, educated commoners (called the *bourgeoisie* [boor-ZHWAH-zee] in France) served both groups' interests, and a mixed-caste elite began to take shape. In the context of these changes, ancient privileges seemed to pose an intolerable burden to many observers.

Another social change involved the racial regimes established in European colonies to legitimize and protect slavery. By the late eighteenth century European law accepted that only Africans and people of African descent were subject to slavery. Even free people of color—a term for nonslaves of African or mixed African-European descent—were subject to special laws restricting the property they could own, whom they could marry, and what clothes they could wear. Racial privilege conferred a new dimension of entitlement on European settlers in the colonies, and they used extremely brutal methods to enforce it. The contradiction between slavery and the Enlightenment ideals of liberty and equality was all too evident to the enslaved and the free people of color.

Growing Demands for Liberty and Equality

In addition to destabilizing social changes, the ideals of liberty and equality helped fuel revolutions in the Atlantic world. What did these concepts mean to eighteenth-century politicians and other people, and why were they so radical and revolutionary in their day?

The call for liberty was first of all a call for individual human rights. Before the revolutionary period, even the most enlightened monarchs believed they needed to regulate what people wrote and believed. Opposing this long-standing practice, supporters of the cause of individual liberty (who became known as "liberals" in the early nineteenth century) demanded freedom to worship according to the dictates of their consciences, an end to censorship, and freedom from arbitrary laws and from judges who simply obeyed orders from the government. The Declaration of the Rights of Man and of the Citizen, issued at the beginning of the French Revolution, proclaimed that "liberty consists in being able to do anything that does not harm another person." In the context of the monarchical and absolutist forms of government then dominating Europe, this was a truly radical idea.

The call for liberty was also a call for a new kind of government. Reformers believed that the people had sovereignty—that is, that the people alone had the authority to make laws limiting an individual's freedom of action. In practice, this system of government meant choosing legislators who represented the people and were accountable to them. Monarchs might retain their thrones, but their rule should be constrained by the will of the people.

Equality was a more ambiguous idea. Eighteenth-century liberals argued that, in theory, all citizens should have identical rights and liberties and that the nobility had no right to special privileges based on birth. However, they accepted a number of distinctions. First, most eighteenth-century liberals were men of their times, and they generally believed that equality between men and women was neither practical nor desirable. Women played an important political role in the revolutionary movements at several points, but the men who wrote constitutions for the new republics limited formal political rights—the right to vote, to run for office, and to participate in government—to men. Second, few questioned the inequality between blacks and whites. Even those who believed that the slave trade was unjust and should be abolished usually felt that emancipation was so dangerous that it needed to be an extremely gradual process.

Finally, liberals never believed that everyone should be equal economically. Although Thomas Jefferson wrote in an early draft of the American Declaration of Independence that everyone was equal in "the pursuit of property," liberals certainly did not expect equal success in that pursuit. (Jefferson later changed "property" to the more noble-sounding "happiness.") Great differences in fortune between rich and poor were perfectly acceptable. The essential point was that every free white male should have a legally equal chance at economic gain. However limited they appear to modern eyes, these demands for liberty and equality were revolutionary, given that a privileged elite had long existed with little opposition.

The two most important Enlightenment references for late-eighteenth-century liberals were John Locke and the baron de Montesquieu (see Chapter 16). Locke maintained that England's long political tradition rested on "the rights of Englishmen" and on representative government through Parliament. He argued that if a government oversteps its proper function of protecting the natural rights of life, liberty, and private property, it becomes a tyranny. Montesquieu was also inspired by English constitutional history and the Glorious Revolution, which placed sovereignty in Parliament (see Chapter 15). He, too, believed that powerful "intermediary groups"—such as the judicial nobility of which he was a proud member—offered the best defense of liberty against despotism.

The belief that representative institutions could defend their liberty and interests appealed powerfully to the educated middle classes. Yet liberal ideas about individual rights and political freedom also appealed to members of the hereditary nobility, at least in western Europe and as formulated by Montesquieu. Representative government did not mean democracy, which liberal thinkers tended to equate with mob rule. Rather, they envisioned voting for representatives as being restricted to men who owned property—those with "a stake in society." The blurring of practical distinctions between landed aristocrats and wealthy commoners meant that there was no clear-cut opposition between nobles and non-nobles on political issues. The poor themselves usually had little time to plan for reform, given the challenges of earning their daily bread.

Revolutions thus began with aspirations for equality and liberty among the social elite. Soon, however, dissenting voices emerged as some revolutionaries became frustrated with the limitations of liberal notions of equality and liberty and clamored for a fuller realization of these concepts. Depending on location, their

Chronology

1775–1783	American Revolution
1786–1789	Height of French monarchy's financial crisis
1789	Ratification of U.S. Constitution; storming of the Bastille; feudalism abolished in France
1789–1799	French Revolution
1790	Burke publishes *Reflections on the Revolution in France*
1791	Slave insurrection in Saint-Domingue
1792	Wollstonecraft publishes *A Vindication of the Rights of Woman*
1793	Execution of Louis XVI
1793–1794	Robespierre's Reign of Terror
1794	Robespierre deposed and executed; France abolishes slavery in all territories
1794–1799	Thermidorian reaction
1799–1815	Napoleonic era
1804	Haitian republic declares independence
1812	Napoleon invades Russia
1814–1815	Napoleon defeated and exiled

Map 19.1 **European Claims in North America and India Before and After the Seven Years' War, 1755–1763**
As a result of the war, France lost its vast territories in North America and India. In an effort to avoid costly conflicts with Native Americans living in the newly conquered territory, the British government in 1763 prohibited colonists from settling west of the Appalachian Mountains. One of the few remaining French colonies in the Americas, Saint-Domingue (on the island of Hispaniola) was the most profitable plantation colony in the New World.

demands included political rights for women and free people of color, the emancipation of slaves, and government regulations to reduce economic inequality. The age of revolution was thus marked by sharp conflicts over how far reform should go once it was initiated.

The Seven Years' War

The roots of revolutionary ideas could be found in the writings of Locke or Montesquieu, but it was by no means inevitable that their ideas would result in revolution. Many members of the educated elite were satisfied with the status quo or too intimidated to challenge it. Instead, events—political, economic, and military—created crises that opened the door for radical action. One of the most important was the global conflict known as the Seven Years' War (1756–1763).

The war's battlefields stretched from central Europe to India to North America (where the conflict was

known as the French and Indian War), pitting a new alliance of England and Prussia against the French and Austrians. Its origins were in conflicts left unresolved at the end of the War of the Austrian Succession in 1748 (see Chapter 16). In central Europe, Austria's Maria Theresa vowed to win back Silesia, which Prussia took in the war of succession, and to crush Prussia, thereby re-establishing the Habsburgs' traditional leadership in German affairs. By the end of the Seven Years' War, Maria Theresa had almost succeeded, but Prussia survived with its boundaries intact.

Unresolved tensions also lingered in North America, particularly regarding the border between the French and British colonies. The encroachment of English settlers into territory claimed by the French in the Ohio Valley resulted in skirmishes that soon became war. Although the inhabitants of New France were greatly outnumbered—Canada counted 55,000 inhabitants, compared to 1.2 million in the thirteen

English colonies—French forces achieved major victories until 1758. Both sides relied on the participation of Native American tribes with whom they had long-standing trading contacts and actively sought new indigenous allies during the conflict. The tide of the conflict turned when the British diverted resources from the war in Europe, using superior sea power to destroy France's fleet and choke its commerce around the world. In 1759 the British laid siege to Quebec for four long months, finally defeating the French in a battle that sealed the nation's fate in North America.

British victory on all colonial fronts was ratified in the 1763 Treaty of Paris. Canada and all French territory east of the Mississippi River passed to Britain, and France ceded Louisiana to Spain as compensation for Spain's loss of Florida to Britain. France also gave up most of its holdings in India, opening the way to British dominance on the subcontinent (Map 19.1).

By 1763 Britain had become the leading European power in both trade and empire, but at a tremendous cost in war debt. France emerged from the conflict humiliated and broke, but with its profitable Caribbean colonies intact. In the aftermath of war, both British and French governments had to raise taxes to repay loans, raising a storm of protest and demands for fundamental reform. Since the Caribbean colony of Saint-Domingue remained French, political turmoil in the mother country would directly affect its population. The seeds of revolutionary conflict in the Atlantic world were thus sown.

Commemorative Teapot Manufacturers were quick to bring products to the market celebrating weighty political events, like this British teapot heralding "Stamp Act Repeal'd." By purchasing such items, ordinary people could champion political causes of the day and bring public affairs into their private lives. (Peabody Essex Museum, Salem, Massachusetts)

The American Revolutionary Era, 1775–1789

Why and how did American colonists forge a new, independent nation?

Increased taxes were a crucial factor behind colonial protests in the New World, where the era of liberal political revolution began. After revolting against their home country, the thirteen mainland colonies of British North America succeeded in establishing a new unified government. Participants in the revolution believed they were demanding only the traditional rights of English men and women. But those traditional rights were liberal rights, and in the American context they had strong democratic and popular overtones. Thus the American Revolution was fought in the name of ideals that were still quite radical for their time. In founding a government based on liberal principles, the Americans set an example that would have a forceful impact on France and its colonies.

The Origins of the Revolution

The high cost of the Seven Years' War doubled the British national debt. Anticipating further expenses to defend newly conquered territories, the government in London imposed bold new administrative measures. Breaking with a tradition of loose colonial oversight, the British announced that they would maintain a large army in North America and tax the colonies directly. In 1765 Parliament passed the Stamp Act, which levied taxes on a long list of commercial and legal documents, diplomas, newspapers, almanacs, and playing cards. A stamp glued to each article indicated that the tax had been paid.

These measures seemed perfectly reasonable to the British, for a much heavier stamp tax already existed in Britain, and proceeds from the tax were to fund the defense of the colonies. Nonetheless, the colonists vigorously protested the Stamp Act by rioting and by boycotting British goods. Thus Parliament reluctantly repealed it.

This dispute raised important political questions. To what extent could the British government reassert its power while limiting the authority of elected colonial bodies? Who had the right to make laws for Americans? The British government replied that Americans were represented in Parliament, albeit indirectly (like most British people), and that Parliament ruled throughout the empire. Many Americans felt otherwise. In the words of John Adams, a major proponent of colonial independence, "A Parliament of Great Britain can have no more rights to tax the colonies than a Parliament of

Paris." Thus British colonial administration and parliamentary supremacy came to appear as unacceptable threats to existing American liberties.

Americans' resistance to these threats was fed by the great degree of independence they had long enjoyed. In British North America, unlike in England and Europe, no powerful established church existed, and religious freedom was taken for granted. Colonial assemblies made the important laws, which were seldom overturned by the British government. Also, the right to vote was much more widespread than in England. In many parts of colonial Massachusetts, for example, as many as 95 percent of adult males could vote.

Moreover, greater political equality was matched by greater social and economic equality, at least for the free white population. No hereditary nobility exercised privileges over peasants and other social groups. Instead, independent farmers dominated colonial society. This was particularly true in the northern colonies, where the revolution originated.

In 1773 disputes over taxes and representation flared up again. Under the Tea Act of that year, the British government permitted the financially hard-pressed East India Company to ship tea from China directly to its agents in the colonies rather than through London middlemen, who sold to independent merchants in the colonies. Thus the company secured a profitable monopoly on the tea trade, and colonial merchants were excluded. The price on tea was actually lowered for colonists, but the act generated a great deal of opposition because it granted a monopoly to the East India Company.

In protest, Boston men disguised as Native Americans staged a rowdy protest (later called the "Tea Party") by boarding East India Company ships and throwing tea from them into the harbor. In response, the so-called Coercive Acts of 1774 closed the port of Boston, curtailed local elections, and expanded the royal governor's power. County conventions in Massachusetts urged that such measures be "rejected as the attempts of a wicked administration to enslave America." Other colonial assemblies joined in the denunciations. In September 1774 the First Continental Congress—consisting of colonial delegates who sought at first to peacefully resolve conflicts with Britain—met in Philadelphia. The more radical members of this assembly argued successfully against concessions to the English crown. The British Parliament also rejected compromise, and in April 1775 fighting between colonial and British troops began at Lexington and Concord.

Independence from Britain

As fighting spread, the colonists moved slowly toward open calls for independence. The uncompromising attitude of the British government and its use of German mercenaries did much to dissolve loyalties to the home country and to unite the separate colonies. *Common Sense* (1775), a brilliant attack by the recently arrived English radical Thomas Paine (1737–1809), also mobilized public opinion in favor of independence. A runaway bestseller with sales of 120,000 copies in a few months, Paine's tract ridiculed the idea of a small island ruling a great continent. In his call for freedom and republican government, Paine expressed Americans' growing sense of separateness and moral superiority.

On July 4, 1776, the Second Continental Congress adopted the Declaration of Independence. Written by Thomas Jefferson and others, this document boldly listed the tyrannical acts committed by George III (r. 1760–1820) and confidently proclaimed the natural rights of mankind and the sovereignty of the American states. The Declaration of Independence in effect universalized the traditional rights of English people and made them the rights of all mankind. It stated that "all Men are created equal, that they are endowed by their Creator with certain unalienable Rights, that among these are Life, Liberty, and the Pursuit of Happiness." No other American political document has ever caused such excitement, either at home or abroad.

After the Declaration of Independence, the conflict often took the form of a civil war pitting patriots against Loyalists, those who maintained an allegiance to the Crown. The Loyalists, who numbered up to 20 percent of the total white population, tended to be wealthy and politically moderate. They were small in number in New England and Virginia, but more common in the Deep South and on the western frontier. British commanders also recruited Loyalists from enslaved people by promising freedom to any slave who left his master to fight for the mother country.

Many wealthy patriots—such as John Hancock and George Washington—willingly allied themselves with farmers and artisans in a broad coalition. This coalition harassed the Loyalists and confiscated their property to help pay for the war, causing 60,000 to 80,000 of them to flee, mostly to Canada. The broad social base of the revolutionaries tended to make the revolution democratic. State governments extended the right to vote to many more men, including free African American men in many cases, but not to women.

On the international scene, the French wanted revenge against the British for the humiliating defeats of the Seven Years' War. Thus they sympathized with the rebels and supplied guns and gunpowder from the beginning of the conflict. By 1777 French volunteers were arriving in Virginia, and a dashing young nobleman, the marquis de Lafayette (1757–1834), quickly became one of the most trusted generals of George Washington, who was commanding American troops. In 1778 the French government offered a formal alliance to the American ambassador in Paris, Benjamin Franklin, and in 1779 and 1780 the Spanish and Dutch declared war on Britain. Catherine the Great of Russia helped organize the League of Armed Neutrality to protect neutral shipping rights and succeeded in hampering Britain's naval power.

Thus by 1780 Britain was engaged in a war against most of Europe as well as the thirteen colonies. In these circumstances, and in the face of severe reverses in India, in the West Indies, and at Yorktown in Virginia, a new British government decided to cut its losses and end the war. American officials in Paris were receptive to negotiating a deal with England alone, for they feared that France wanted a treaty that would bottle up the new nation east of the Allegheny Mountains and give British holdings west of the Alleghenies to France's ally, Spain. Thus the American negotiators deserted their French allies and accepted the extraordinarily favorable terms Britain offered.

Under the Treaty of Paris of 1783, Britain recognized the independence of the thirteen colonies and ceded all its territory between the Allegheny Mountains and the Mississippi River to the Americans. Out of the bitter rivalries of the Old World, the Americans snatched dominion over a vast territory.

The American Revolution

1765	Britain passes the Stamp Act
1773	Britain passes the Tea Act
1774	Britain passes the Coercive Acts in response to the Tea Party in the colonies; the First Continental Congress refuses concessions to the English crown
April 1775	Fighting begins between colonial and British troops
July 4, 1776	Second Continental Congress adopts the Declaration of Independence
1777–1780	The French, Spanish, and Dutch side with the colonists against Britain
1783	Treaty of Paris recognizes the independence of the American colonies
1787	U.S. Constitution is signed
1791	The first ten amendments to the Constitution (the Bill of Rights) are ratified

Framing the Constitution

The liberal program of the American Revolution was consolidated by the federal Constitution, the Bill of Rights, and the creation of a national republic. Assembling in Philadelphia in the summer of 1787, the delegates to the Constitutional Convention were determined to end the period of economic depression, social uncertainty, and leadership under a weak central government that had followed independence. The delegates thus decided to grant the federal, or central, government important powers: regulation of domestic and foreign trade, the right to tax, and the means to enforce its laws.

Strong rule would be placed squarely in the context of representative self-government. Senators and congressmen would be the lawmaking delegates of the voters, and the president of the republic would be an elected official. The central government would operate in Montesquieu's framework of checks and balances, under which authority was distributed across three different branches—the executive, legislative, and judicial branches—that would systematically balance one another, preventing one interest from gaining too much power. The power of the federal government would in turn be checked by that of the individual states.

When the results of the secret deliberations of the Constitutional Convention were presented to the states for ratification, a great public debate began. The opponents of the proposed Constitution—the Antifederalists—charged that the framers of the new document had taken too much power from the individual states and made the federal government too strong. Moreover, many Antifederalists feared for the individual freedoms for which they had fought. To overcome these objections, the Federalists promised to spell out these basic freedoms as soon as the new Constitution was adopted. The result was the first ten amendments to the Constitution, which the first Congress passed shortly after it met in New York in March 1789. These amendments, ratified in 1791, formed an effective Bill of Rights to safeguard the individual. Most of them—trial by jury, due process of law, the right to assemble, freedom from unreasonable search—had their origins in English law and the English Bill of Rights of 1689. Other rights—the freedoms of speech, the press, and religion—reflected natural-law theory and the strong value colonists had placed on independence from the start.

Limitations of Liberty and Equality

The American Constitution and the Bill of Rights exemplified the strengths and the limits of what came to be called classical liberalism. Liberty meant individual freedoms and political safeguards. Liberty also meant representative government, but it did not

Abigail Adams, "Remember the Ladies"

Abigail Adams wrote many letters to her husband, John Adams, during the long years of separation imposed by his political career. In March 1776 he was serving in the Continental Congress in Philadelphia as Abigail and their children experienced the British siege of Boston and a smallpox epidemic. This letter, written from the family farm in Braintree, Massachusetts, combines news from home with pressing questions about the military and political situation, and a call to "Remember the Ladies" when drafting a new constitution.

❝ March 31, 1776

I wish you would ever write me a Letter half as long as I write you; and tell me if you may where your Fleet are gone? What sort of Defence Virginia can make against our common Enemy? Whether it is so situated as to make an able Defence? . . .

Do not you want to see Boston; I am fearful of the smallpox, or I should have been in before this time. I got Mr. Crane to go to our House and see what state it was in. I find it has been occupied by one of the Doctors of a Regiment, very dirty, but no other damage has been done to it. The few things which were left in it are all gone. . . .

I feel very differently at the approach of spring to what I did a month ago. We knew not then whether we could plant or sow with safety, whether when we had toiled we could reap the fruits of our own industry, whether we could rest in our own Cottages, or whether we should not be driven from the sea coasts to seek shelter in the wilderness, but now we feel as if we might sit under our own vine and eat the good of the land. . . .

I long to hear that you have declared an independency — and by the way in the new Code of Laws which I suppose it will be necessary for you to make I desire you would Remember the Ladies, and be more generous and favorable to them than your ancestors. Do not put such unlimited power in the hands of the Husbands. Remember all men would be tyrants if they could. If particular care and attention is not paid to the Ladies we are determined to foment a Rebellion, and will not hold ourselves bound by any Laws in which we have no voice, or Representation.

That your Sex are Naturally Tyrannical is a Truth so thoroughly established as to admit of no dispute, but such of you as wish to be happy willingly give up the harsh title of Master for the more tender and endearing one of Friend. Why then, not put it out of the power of the vicious and the Lawless to use us with cruelty and indignity with impunity. Men of Sense in all Ages abhor those customs which treat us only as the vassals of your Sex. Regard us then as beings placed by providence under your protection and in imitation of the Supreme Being make use of that power only for our happiness. ❞

EVALUATE THE EVIDENCE

1. What does Adams's letter suggest about her relationship with her husband and the role of women in the family in this period?
2. What does Adams's letter tell us about what it was like to live through the American Revolution and how a woman might perceive the new liberties demanded by colonists?

Source: Letter from Abigail Adams to John Adams, 31 March–5 April 1776 (electronic edition), *Adams Family Papers: An Electronic Archive*, Massachusetts Historical Society, http://www.masshist.org/digitaladams/.

---

mean democracy, with its principle of one person, one vote. Equality meant equality before the law, not equality of political participation or wealth. It did not mean equal rights for slaves, indigenous peoples, or women.

A vigorous abolitionist movement during the 1780s led to the passage of emancipation laws in all northern states, but slavery remained prevalent in the South, and discord between pro- and antislavery delegates roiled the Constitutional Convention of 1787. The result was a compromise stipulating that an enslaved person would count as three-fifths of a person in tallying population numbers for taxation and proportional representation in the House of Representatives. This solution levied higher taxes on the South, but also guaranteed slaveholding states greater representation in Congress, which they used to oppose emancipation.

The young republic also failed to protect the Native American tribes whose lands fell within or alongside the territory ceded by Britain to the United States at the Treaty of Paris. The 1787 Constitution promised protection to Native Americans and guaranteed that their land would not be taken without consent. Nonetheless, the federal government forced tribes to concede their land for meager returns; state governments and the rapidly expanding population paid even less heed to the Constitution and often simply seized Native American land for new settlements.

Although lacking the voting rights enjoyed by so many of their husbands and fathers in the relatively democratic colonial assemblies, women played a vital role in the American Revolution. As household provisioners, women were essential participants in boycotts of British goods, like tea, which squeezed profits from British merchants and fostered the revolutionary spirit. After the outbreak of war, women raised funds for the Continental Army and took care of homesteads, workshops, and other businesses when their men went off to fight. Yet despite Abigail Adams's plea to her husband, John Adams, that the framers of the Declaration of the Independence should "remember the ladies," women did not receive the right to vote in the new Constitution, an omission confirmed by a clause added in 1844. (See "Primary Source 19.1: Abigail Adams, 'Remember the Ladies,'" at left.)

Revolution in France, 1789–1791

How did the events of 1789 result in a constitutional monarchy in France, and what were the consequences?

No country felt the consequences of the American Revolution more deeply than France. Hundreds of French officers served in America and were inspired by the experience. The most famous of these, the young and impressionable marquis de Lafayette, left home as a great aristocrat determined to fight France's traditional foe, England. He returned with a love of liberty and firm republican convictions. French intellectuals and publicists engaged in passionate analysis of the federal Constitution as well as the constitutions of the various states of the new United States. The American Revolution undeniably fueled dissatisfaction with the old monarchical order in France. Yet the French Revolution did not mirror the American example. It was more radical and more complex, more influential and more controversial, more loved and more hated. For Europeans and most of the rest of the world, it was the great revolution of the eighteenth century, the revolution that opened the modern era in politics.

Breakdown of the Old Order

As did the American Revolution, the French Revolution had its immediate origins in the government's financial difficulties. The efforts of the ministers of King Louis XV (r. 1715–1774) to raise taxes to meet the expenses of the War of the Austrian Succession and the Seven Years' War were thwarted by the high courts, known as the parlements. The noble judges of the parlements resented the Crown's threat to their exemption from taxation and decried the government's actions as a form of royal despotism.

When renewed efforts to reform the tax system met a similar fate in 1776, the government was forced to finance its enormous expenditures during the American war with borrowed money. As a result, the national debt soared. In 1786 the finance minister informed the timid king Louis XVI that the nation was on the verge of bankruptcy. Fully 50 percent of France's annual budget went to interest payments on the ever-increasing debt. Another 25 percent went to maintain the military, while 6 percent was absorbed by the royal family and the court at Versailles. Less than 20 percent of the national budget served the productive functions of the state, such as transportation and general administration.

Unlike England, which had a far larger national debt relative to its population, France had no central bank and no paper currency. Therefore, when a depressed economy and a lack of public confidence made it increasingly difficult for the government to obtain new loans, the government could not respond simply by printing more money. It had no alternative but to try increasing taxes. Because France's tax system was unfair and out-of-date, increased revenues were possible only through fundamental reforms. Such reforms, which would affect all groups in France's complex and fragmented society, were guaranteed to create social and political unrest.

These crises struck a monarchy that had lost much of its mantle of royal authority. Kings had always maintained mistresses, who were invariably chosen from the court nobility. Louis XV broke that pattern with Madame de Pompadour, daughter of a disgraced bourgeois financier. As the king's favorite mistress from 1745 to 1750, Pompadour exercised tremendous influence that continued even after their love affair ended. She played a key role, for example, in bringing about France's break with Prussia and its new alliance with Austria in the mid-1750s. Pompadour's low birth and political influence generated a stream of libelous pamphleteering. The king was being stripped of the sacred aura of God's anointed on earth (a process called desacralization) and was being reinvented in the popular imagination as a degenerate. Maneuverings among political factions at court further distracted the king and prevented decisive action from his government.

Despite the progressive desacralization of the monarchy, Louis XV would probably have prevailed had he lived longer, but he died in 1774. The new king, Louis XVI (r. 1774–1792), was a shy twenty-year-old with good intentions. Taking the throne, he is reported to have said, "What I should like most is to be loved."[1] The eager-to-please monarch Louis waffled on political reform and the economy, and proved unable to quell the rising storm of opposition.

The Formation of the National Assembly

Spurred by a depressed economy and falling tax receipts, Louis XVI's minister of finance revived old proposals to impose a general tax on all landed property as well as to form provincial assemblies to help administer the tax, and he convinced the king to call an assembly of notables in 1787 to gain support for the idea. The assembled notables, mainly aristocrats and high-ranking clergy, declared that such sweeping tax changes required the approval of the **Estates General**, the representative body of all three estates, which had not met since 1614.

Facing imminent bankruptcy, the king tried to reassert his authority. He dismissed the notables and established new taxes by decree. The judges of the Parlement of Paris promptly declared the royal initiative null and void. When the king tried to exile the judges, a tremendous wave of protest swept the country. Frightened investors refused to advance more loans to the state. Finally in July 1788, a beaten Louis XVI bowed to public opinion and called for the Estates General. Absolute monarchy was collapsing.

As its name indicates, the Estates General was a legislative body with representatives from the three orders, or **estates**, of society: the clergy, nobility, and everyone else. Following centuries-old tradition, each estate met separately to elect delegates, first at a local and then at a regional level. Results of the elections reveal the mind-set of each estate on the eve of the Revolution. The local assemblies of the clergy, representing the first estate, elected mostly parish priests rather than church leaders, demonstrating their dissatisfaction with the church hierarchy. The nobility, or second estate, voted in a majority of conservatives, primarily from the provinces, where nobles were less wealthy and more numerous. Nonetheless, fully one-third of noble representatives were liberals committed to major changes. Commoners of the third estate, who constituted over 95 percent of the population, elected primarily lawyers and government officials to represent them, with few delegates representing business and the poor.

The petitions for change drafted by the assemblies showed a surprising degree of consensus about the key issues confronting the realm. In all three estates, voices spoke in favor of replacing absolutism with a constitutional monarchy in which laws and taxes would require the consent of the Estates General in regular meetings. There was also the strong feeling that individual liberties would have to be guaranteed by law and that economic regulations should be loosened.

On May 5, 1789, the twelve hundred delegates of the three estates gathered in Versailles for the opening session of the Estates General. Despite widespread hopes for serious reform, the Estates General quickly deadlocked over the issue of voting procedures. Controversy had begun during the electoral process itself, when the government confirmed that, following precedent, each estate should meet and vote separately. During the lead-up to the Estates General, critics had demanded a single assembly dominated by the third estate. In his famous pamphlet *What Is the Third Estate?*

Estates General A legislative body in prerevolutionary France made up of representatives of each of the three classes, or estates. It was called into session in 1789 for the first time since 1614.

estates The three legal categories, or orders, of France's inhabitants: the clergy, the nobility, and everyone else.

A FAUT ESPERER Q'EU JEU LA FINIRA BEN TOT

The Three Estates   In this political cartoon from 1789, a peasant of the third estate struggles under the weight of a happy clergyman and a plumed nobleman. The caption — "Let's hope this game ends soon" — sets forth a program of reform that any peasant could understand. (© RMN-Grand Palais/Art Resource, NY)

The Tennis Court Oath, June 20, 1789 Painted two years after the event shown, this dramatic painting by Jacques-Louis David depicts a crucial turning point in the early days of the Revolution. On June 20 delegates of the third estate arrived at their meeting hall in the Versailles palace to find the doors closed and guarded. Fearing the king was about to dissolve their meeting by force, the deputies reassembled at a nearby indoor tennis court and swore a solemn oath not to disperse until they had been recognized as the National Assembly. (Musée de la Ville de Paris, Musée Carnavalet, Paris/Giraudon/The Bridgeman Art Library)

the abbé Emmanuel Joseph Sieyès (himself a member of the first estate) argued that the nobility was a tiny, overprivileged minority and that the third estate constituted the true strength of the French nation. (See "Primary Source 19.2: Abbé Sieyès, *What Is the Third Estate?*, page 622.) The government conceded that the third estate should have as many delegates as the clergy and the nobility combined, but then upheld a system granting one vote per estate instead of one vote per person. This meant that the two privileged estates could always outvote the third.

In angry response, in June 1789 delegates of the third estate refused to meet until the king ordered the clergy and nobility to sit with them in a single body. On June 17 the third estate, which had been joined by a few parish priests, voted to call itself the **National Assembly**. On June 20, excluded from their hall because of "repairs," the delegates moved to a large in-door tennis court where they swore the famous Tennis Court Oath, pledging not to disband until they had been recognized as a national assembly and had written a new constitution.

The king's response was disastrously ambivalent. On June 23 he made a conciliatory speech urging reforms, and four days later he ordered the three estates to meet together. At the same time, Louis apparently followed the advice of relatives and court nobles who urged him to dissolve the Assembly by force. The king called an army of eighteen thousand troops toward the capital to bring the delegates under control, and on July 11 he dismissed his finance minister and other more liberal ministers. It appeared that the monarchy was prepared to use violence to restore its control.

National Assembly The first French revolutionary legislature, made up primarily of representatives of the third estate and a few from the nobility and clergy, in session from 1789 to 1791.

Abbé Sieyès, *What Is the Third Estate?*

In the flood of pamphlets that appeared after Louis XVI's call for a meeting of the Estates General, the most influential was written in 1789 by a Catholic priest named Emmanuel Joseph Sieyès. In "What Is the Third Estate?" the abbé Sieyès vigorously condemned the system of privilege that lay at the heart of French society. The term "privilege" combined the Latin words for "private" and "law." In Old Regime France, no one set of laws applied to all; over time, the monarchy had issued a series of particular laws, or privileges, that enshrined special rights and entitlements for select individuals and groups. Noble privileges were among the weightiest.

Sieyès rejected this entire system of legal and social inequality. Deriding the nobility as a foreign parasite, he argued that the common people of the third estate, who did most of the work and paid most of the taxes, constituted the true nation. His pamphlet galvanized public opinion and played an important role in convincing representatives of the third estate to proclaim themselves a "National Assembly" in June 1789. Sieyès later helped bring Napoleon Bonaparte to power, abandoning the radicalism of 1789 for an authoritarian regime.

" 1. What is the Third Estate? Everything.

2. What has it been until now in the political order? Nothing.

3. What does it want? To become something.

. . . What is a Nation? A body of associates living under a *common* law and represented by the same *legislature*.

Is it not more than certain that the noble order has privileges, exemptions, and even rights that are distinct from the rights of the great body of citizens? Because of this, it [the noble order] does not belong to the common order, it is not covered by the law common to the rest. Thus its civil rights already make it a people apart inside the great Nation. It is truly *imperium in imperio* [a law unto itself].

As for its *political* rights, the nobility also exercises them separately. It has its own representatives who have no mandate from the people. Its deputies sit separately, and even when they assemble in the same room with the deputies of the ordinary citizens, the nobility's representation still remains essentially distinct and separate: it is foreign to the Nation by its very principle, for its mission does not emanate from the people, and by its purpose, since it consists in defending, not the general interest, but the private interests of the nobility.

The Third Estate therefore contains everything that pertains to the Nation and nobody outside of the Third Estate can claim to be part of the Nation. What is the Third Estate? EVERYTHING. . . .

By Third Estate is meant the collectivity of citizens who belong to the common order. Anybody who holds a legal privilege of any kind leaves that common order, stands as an exception to the common law, and in consequence does not belong to the Third Estate. . . . It is certain that the moment a citizen acquires privileges contrary to common law, he no longer belongs to the common order. His new interest is opposed to the general interest; he has no right to vote in the name of the people. . . .

In vain can anyone's eyes be closed to the revolution that time and the force of things have brought to pass; it is none the less real. Once upon a time the Third Estate was in bondage and the noble order was everything that mattered. Today the Third is everything and nobility but a word. Yet under the cover of this word a new and intolerable aristocracy has slipped in, and the people has every reason to no longer want aristocrats. . . .

What is the will of a Nation? It is the result of individual wills, just as the Nation is the aggregate of the individuals who compose it. It is impossible to conceive of a legitimate association that does not have for its goal the common security, the common liberty, in short, the public good. No doubt each individual also has his own personal aims. He says to himself, "protected by the common security, I will be able to peacefully pursue my own personal projects, I will seek my happiness where I will, assured of encountering only those legal obstacles that society will prescribe for the common interest, in which I have a part, and with which my own personal interest is so usefully allied." . . .

Advantages which differentiate citizens from one another lie outside the purview of citizenship. Inequalities of wealth or ability are like the inequalities of age, sex, size, etc. In no way do they detract from the *equality* of citizenship. These individual advantages no doubt benefit from the protection of the law; but it is not the legislator's task to create them, to give privileges to some and refuse them to others. The law grants nothing; it protects what already exists until such time that what exists begins to harm the common interest. These are the only limits on individual freedom. I imagine the law as being at the center of a large globe; we the citizens without exception, stand equidistant from it on the surface and occupy equal places; all are equally dependent on the law, all present it with their liberty and their property to be protected; and this is what I call the *common rights* of citizens, by which they are all alike. All these individuals communicate with each other, enter into contracts, negotiate, always under the common guarantee of the law. If in this general activity somebody wishes to get control over the person of his neighbor or usurp his property, the common law goes into action to repress this criminal attempt and puts everyone back in their place at the same distance from the law. . . .

It is impossible to say what place the two privileged orders [the clergy and the nobility] ought to occupy in the social order: this is the equivalent of asking what place one wishes to assign to a malignant tumor that torments and undermines the strength of the body of a sick person. It must be *neutralized*. We must re-establish the health and working of all organs so thoroughly that they are no longer susceptible to these fatal schemes that are capable of sapping the most essential principles of vitality. **"**

EVALUATE THE EVIDENCE

1. What criticism of noble privileges does Sieyès offer? Why does he believe nobles are "foreign" to the nation?
2. How does Sieyès define the nation, and why does he believe that the third estate constitutes the nation?
3. What relationship between citizens and the law does Sieyès envision? What limitations on the law does he propose?

Source: Excerpt from pp. 65–70 in *The French Revolution and Human Rights: A Brief Documentary History*, edited, translated, and with an introduction by Lynn Hunt. Copyright © 1996 by Bedford Books of St. Martin's Press. Used by permission of the publisher.

Popular Uprising and the Rights of Man

While delegates at Versailles were pressing for political rights, economic hardship gripped the common people. Conditions were already tough, due to the disastrous financial situation of the Crown. A poor grain harvest in 1788 caused the price of bread to soar, and inflation spread quickly through the economy. As a result, demand for manufactured goods collapsed, and many artisans and small traders lost work. In Paris perhaps 150,000 of the city's 600,000 people were unemployed by July 1789.

Against this background of poverty and political crisis, the people of Paris entered decisively onto the revolutionary stage. They believed that, to survive, they should have steady work and enough bread at fair prices. They also feared that the dismissal of the king's liberal finance minister would put them at the mercy of aristocratic landowners and grain speculators. At the beginning of July, knowledge spread of the massing of troops near Paris. On July 14, 1789, several hundred people stormed the Bastille (ba-STEEL), a royal prison, to obtain weapons for the city's defense. Faced with popular violence, Louis soon announced the reinstatement of his finance minister and the withdrawal of troops from Paris. The National Assembly was now free to continue its work.

Just as the laboring poor of Paris had been roused to a revolutionary fervor, the struggling French peasantry had also reached a boiling point. In the summer of 1789, throughout France peasants began to rise in insurrection against their lords, ransacking manor houses and burning feudal documents that recorded their obligations. In some areas peasants reoccupied common lands enclosed by landowners and seized forests. Fear of marauders and vagabonds hired by vengeful landlords—called the **Great Fear** by contemporaries—seized the rural poor and fanned the flames of rebellion.

Faced with chaos, the National Assembly responded to peasant demands with a surprise maneuver on the night of August 4, 1789. By a decree of the Assembly, all the old noble privileges—peasant serfdom where it still existed, exclusive

The Great Fear, 1789

Area of Great Fear revolts

Revolutionary center

Great Fear The fear of noble reprisals against peasant uprisings that seized the French countryside and led to further revolt.

The Figure of Liberty In this painting, the figure of Liberty bears a copy of the Declaration of the Rights of Man and of the Citizen in one hand and a pike to defend them in the other. The painting, by female artist and ardent revolutionary Nanine Vallain, hung in the Jacobin Club until its fall from power. (Musée de la Revolution Française, Vizille/The Bridgeman Art Library)

hunting rights, fees for having legal cases judged in the lord's court, the right to make peasants work on the roads, and a host of other dues—were abolished along with the tithes paid to the church. From this point on, French peasants would seek mainly to protect and consolidate this victory.

Having granted new rights to the peasantry, the National Assembly moved forward with its reforms. On August 27, 1789, it issued the Declaration of the Rights of Man and of the Citizen. This clarion call of the liberal revolutionary ideal guaranteed equality before the law, representative government for a sovereign people, and individual freedom. This revolutionary

credo, only two pages long, was disseminated throughout France, the rest of Europe, and around the world.

The National Assembly's declaration had little practical effect for the poor and hungry people of Paris. The economic crisis worsened after the fall of the Bastille, as aristocrats fled the country and the luxury market collapsed. Foreign markets also shrank, and unemployment among the working classes grew. In addition, women—the traditional managers of food and resources in poor homes—could no longer look to the church, which had been stripped of its tithes, for aid.

On October 5 some seven thousand women marched the twelve miles from Paris to Versailles to demand action. This great crowd, "armed with scythes, sticks and pikes," invaded the National Assembly. Interrupting a delegate's speech, an old woman defiantly shouted into the debate, "Who's that talking down there? Make the chatterbox shut up. That's not the point: the point is that we want bread."[2] Hers was the genuine voice of the people, essential to any understanding of the French Revolution. The women invaded the royal apartments, killed some of the royal bodyguards, and searched for the queen, Marie Antoinette, who was widely despised for her frivolous and supposedly immoral behavior. It seems likely that only the intervention of Lafayette and the National Guard saved the royal family. But the only way to calm the disorder was for the king to live closer to his people in Paris, as the crowd demanded.

Liberal elites brought the Revolution into being and continued to lead politics. Yet the people of France were now roused and would henceforth play a crucial role in the unfolding of events.

A Constitutional Monarchy and Its Challenges

The day after the women's march on Versailles, the National Assembly followed the king to Paris, and the next two years, until September 1791, saw the consolidation of the liberal revolution. In June 1790 the National Assembly abolished the nobility, and in July the king swore to uphold the as-yet-unwritten constitution, effectively enshrining a constitutional monarchy. The king remained the head of state, but all lawmaking power now resided in the National Assembly, elected by the wealthiest half of French males. The constitution passed in September 1791 was the first in French history. It broadened women's rights to seek divorce, to inherit property, and to obtain financial support for illegitimate children from fathers, but excluded women from political office and voting.

This decision was attacked by a small number of men and women who believed that the rights of man should be extended to all French citizens. Olympe de

The Women of Paris March to Versailles   On October 5, 1789, a large group of poor Parisian women marched to Versailles to protest the price of bread. For the people of Paris, the king was the baker of last resort, responsible for feeding his people during times of scarcity. The angry women forced the royal family to return with them and to live in Paris, rather than remain isolated from their subjects at court. (Musée de la Ville de Paris, Musée Carnavalet, Paris, France/Giraudon/The Bridgeman Art Library)

Gouges (1748–1793), a self-taught writer and woman of the people, protested the evils of slavery as well as the injustices done to women. In September 1791 she published her *Declaration of the Rights of Woman*. This pamphlet echoed its famous predecessor, the Declaration of the Rights of Man and of the Citizen, proclaiming, "Woman is born free and remains equal to man in rights." De Gouges's position found little sympathy among leaders of the Revolution, however.

In addition to ruling on women's rights, the National Assembly replaced the complicated patchwork of historic provinces with eighty-three departments of approximately equal size, a move toward more rational and systematic methods of administration. Guilds, workers' associations, and internal customs fees were abolished in the name of economic liberty. Thus the National Assembly applied the spirit of the Enlightenment in a thorough reform of France's laws and institutions.

The National Assembly also imposed a radical reorganization on religious life. The Assembly granted religious freedom to the small minority of French Protestants and Jews. (See "Primary Source 19.3: Petition

of the French Jews," page 626.) In November 1789 it nationalized the Catholic Church's property and abolished monasteries. The government used all former church property as collateral to guarantee a new paper currency, the assignats (A-sihg-nat), and then sold the property in an attempt to put the state's finances on a solid footing.

Imbued with the rationalism and skepticism of the eighteenth-century philosophes, many delegates distrusted popular piety and "superstitious religion." Thus in July 1790, with the Civil Constitution of the Clergy, they established a national church with priests chosen by voters. The National Assembly then forced the Catholic clergy to take an oath of loyalty to the new government. The pope formally condemned these measures, and only half the priests of France swore the oath. Many sincere Christians, especially those in the countryside, were appalled by these changes in the religious order. The attempt to remake the Catholic Church, like the abolition of guilds and workers' associations, sharpened the conflict between the educated classes and the common people that had been emerging in the eighteenth century.

Petition of the French Jews

In August 1789 the legislators of the French Revolution adopted the Declaration of the Rights of Man and of the Citizen, enshrining full legal equality under the law for French citizens. Who exactly could become a citizen and what rights they might enjoy quickly became contentious issues. After granting civil rights to Protestants in December 1789, the National Assembly began to consider the smaller but more controversial population of French Jews. Eager to become citizens in their own right, the Jews of Paris, Alsace, and Lorraine presented a joint petition to the National Assembly in January 1790.

" A great question is pending before the supreme tribunal of France. *Will the Jews be citizens or not?* . . .

In general, civil rights are entirely independent from religious principles. And all men of whatever religion, whatever sect they belong to, whatever creed they practice, provided that their creed, their sect, their religion does not offend the principles of a pure and severe morality, all these men, we say, equally able to serve the fatherland, defend its interests, contribute to its splendor, should all equally have the title and the rights of citizen. . . .

Reflect, then, on the condition of the Jews. Excluded from all the professions, ineligible for all the positions, deprived even of the capacity to acquire property, not daring and not being able to sell openly the merchandise of their commerce, to what extremity are you reducing them? You do not want them to die, and yet you refuse them the means to live: you refuse them the means, and you crush them with taxes. You leave them therefore really no other resource than usury [lending money with interest]. . . .

Everything is changing; the lot of the Jews must change at the same time; and the people will not be more surprised by this particular change than by all those which they see around them everyday. This is therefore the moment, the true moment to make justice triumph: attach the improvement of the lot of the Jews to the revolution; amalgamate, so to speak, this partial revolution to the general revolution. "

EVALUATE THE EVIDENCE

1. On what basis do the Jews of Paris, Alsace, and Lorraine argue for their inclusion in citizenship rights? How do they describe the constraints of the Jewish population prior to the Revolution?
2. What other groups were excluded from full rights prior to the French Revolution, and how were they treated by the National Assembly?

Source: Excerpt from pp. 93, 95–97 in *The French Revolution and Human Rights: A Brief Documentary History*, edited, translated, and with an introduction by Lynn Hunt. Copyright © 1996 by Bedford Books of St. Martin's Press. Used by permission of the publisher.

World War and Republican France, 1791–1799

Why and how did the French Revolution take a radical turn entailing terror at home and war with European powers?

When Louis XVI accepted the National Assembly's constitution in September 1791, a young provincial lawyer and delegate named Maximilien Robespierre (1758–1794) concluded that "the Revolution is over." Robespierre was right in the sense that the most constructive and lasting reforms were in place. Yet he was wrong in suggesting that turmoil had ended, for a much more radical stage lay ahead, one that would bring war with foreign powers, terror at home, and a transformation in France's government.

The International Response

The outbreak of revolution in France produced great excitement and a sharp division of opinion in Europe and the United States. On the one hand, liberals and radicals saw a mighty triumph of liberty over despotism. On the other hand, conservative leaders such as British statesman Edmund Burke (1729–1797) were intensely troubled. In 1790 Burke published *Reflections on the Revolution in France*, in which he defended inherited privileges. He glorified Britain's unrepresentative Parliament and predicted that reform like that occurring in France would lead only to chaos and tyranny.

One passionate rebuttal came from a young writer in London, Mary Wollstonecraft (1759–1797). Incensed by Burke's book, Wollstonecraft (WOOL-stuhn-kraft) wrote a blistering attack, *A Vindication of the Rights of Man* (1790). Two years later, she published her masterpiece, *A Vindication of the Rights of Woman* (1792). Like de Gouges in France, Wollstonecraft demanded equal rights for women. She also advocated coeducation out of the belief that it would make women better wives and mothers, good citizens, and economically independent. Considered very radical for the time, the book became a founding text of the feminist movement.

The kings and nobles of continental Europe, who had at first welcomed the Revolution in France as weakening a competing power, now feared its impact. In June 1791 the royal family was arrested and returned to Paris after trying to slip out of France. To supporters of the Revolution, the attempted flight was proof that the king was treacherously seeking foreign support for an invasion of France. To the monarchs of Austria and Prussia, the arrest of a crowned monarch was unacceptable. Two months later they issued the Declaration of Pillnitz, which professed their willingness to intervene in France to restore Louis XVI's rule if necessary. It was expected to have a sobering effect on revolutionary France without causing war.

But the crowned heads of Europe misjudged the situation. The new French representative body, called the Legislative Assembly, that convened in October 1791 had new delegates and a different character. Although the delegates were still prosperous, well-educated middle-class men, they were younger and less cautious than their predecessors. Many of them belonged to the political **Jacobin Club**. Such clubs had proliferated in Parisian neighborhoods since the beginning of the Revolution, drawing men and women to debate the political issues of the day.

Jacobins and other deputies reacted with patriotic fury to the Declaration of Pillnitz. They said that if the kings of Europe were attempting to incite war against France, then "we will incite a war of people against kings. . . . Ten million Frenchmen, kindled by the fire of liberty, armed with the sword, with reason, with eloquence would be able to change the face of the world and make the tyrants tremble on their thrones."[3] In April 1792 France declared war on Francis II, the Habsburg monarch.

France's crusade against tyranny went poorly at first. Prussia joined Austria against the French, who broke and fled at their first military encounter with this First Coalition of foreign powers united against the Revolution. The Legislative Assembly declared the country in danger, and volunteers rallied to the capital. In this wartime atmosphere, rumors of treason by the king and queen spread in Paris. On August 10, 1792, a revolutionary crowd attacked the royal palace at the Tuileries (TWEE-luh-reez), while the royal family fled to the Legislative Assembly. Rather than offering refuge, the Assembly suspended the king from all his functions, imprisoned him, and called for a constitutional assembly to be elected by universal male suffrage.

The Second Revolution and the New Republic

The fall of the monarchy marked a radicalization of the Revolution, a phase that historians often call the **second revolution**. Louis's imprisonment was followed by the September Massacres. Fearing invasion by the Prussians and riled up by rumors that counter-revolutionaries would aid the invaders, angry crowds stormed the prisons and killed jailed priests and aristocrats. In late September 1792 the new, popularly elected National Convention, which replaced the Legislative Assembly, proclaimed France a republic, a nation in which the people, instead of a monarch, held sovereign power.

As with the Legislative Assembly, many members of the new National Convention belonged to the Jacobin Club of Paris. But the Jacobins themselves were increasingly divided into two bitterly opposed groups — the **Girondists** (juh-RAHN-dihsts) and **the Mountain**, led by Robespierre and another young lawyer, Georges Jacques Danton.

This division emerged clearly after the National Convention overwhelmingly convicted Louis XVI of treason. The Girondists accepted his guilt but did not wish to put the king to death. By a narrow majority, the Mountain carried the day, and Louis was executed on January 21, 1793, by guillotine, which the French had recently perfected. Marie Antoinette suffered the same fate later that year. But both the Girondists and the Mountain were determined to continue the "war against tyranny." The Prussians had been stopped at the Battle of Valmy on September 20, 1792, one day before the republic was proclaimed. French armies then invaded Savoy and captured Nice, moved into the German Rhineland, and by November 1792 were occupying the entire Austrian Netherlands (modern Belgium).

Everywhere they went, French armies of occupation chased princes, abolished feudalism, and found support among some peasants and middle-class people. But French armies also lived off the land, requisitioning food and supplies and plundering local treasures.

Jacobin Club A political club in revolutionary France whose members were well-educated radical republicans.

second revolution From 1792 to 1795, the second phase of the French Revolution, during which the fall of the French monarchy introduced a rapid radicalization of politics.

Girondists A moderate group that fought for control of the French National Convention in 1793.

the Mountain Led by Robespierre, the French National Convention's radical faction, which seized legislative power in 1793.

The liberators therefore looked increasingly like foreign invaders. Meanwhile, international tensions mounted. In February 1793 the National Convention, at war with Austria and Prussia, declared war on Britain, the Dutch Republic, and Spain as well. Republican France was now at war with almost all of Europe.

Groups within France added to the turmoil. Peasants in western France revolted against being drafted into the army, with the Vendée region of Brittany emerging as the epicenter of revolt. Devout Catholics, royalists, and foreign agents encouraged their rebellion, and the counter-revolutionaries recruited veritable armies to fight for their cause.

In March 1793 the National Convention was locked in a life-and-death political struggle between members of the Mountain and the more moderate Girondists. With the middle-class delegates so bitterly divided, the people of Paris once again emerged as the decisive political factor. The laboring poor and the petty traders were often known as the **sans-culottes** because their men wore trousers instead of the knee breeches of the aristocracy and the solid middle class. (See "Primary Source 19.4: Contrasting Visions of the Sans-Culottes," at right.) They demanded radical political action to defend the Revolution. The Mountain, sensing an opportunity to outmaneuver the Girondists, joined with sans-culottes activists to engineer a popular uprising. On June 2, 1793, armed sans-culottes invaded the Convention and forced its deputies to arrest twenty-nine Girondist deputies for treason. All power passed to the Mountain.

The Convention also formed the Committee of Public Safety in April 1793 to deal with threats from within and outside France. The committee, led by Robespierre, held dictatorial power, allowing it to use whatever force necessary to defend the Revolution. Moderates in leading provincial cities revolted against the committee's power and demanded a decentralized government. Counter-revolutionary forces in the Vendée won significant victories, and the republic's armies were driven back on all

Areas of Insurrection, 1793

(map labels) Caen · Paris · BRITTANY · VENDÉE · FRANCE · Lyons · Bordeaux · Marseilles · SPAIN · Mediterranean Sea

■ Vendée Rebellion
■ Counter-revolutionary insurrections

sans-culottes The laboring poor of Paris, so called because the men wore trousers instead of the knee breeches of the aristocracy and middle class; the word came to refer to the militant radicals of the city.

Reign of Terror The period from 1793 to 1794 during which Robespierre's Committee of Public Safety tried and executed thousands suspected of treason and a new revolutionary culture was imposed.

fronts. By July 1793 only the areas around Paris and on the eastern frontier were firmly held by the central government. Defeat seemed imminent.

Total War and the Terror

A year later, in July 1794, the central government had reasserted control over the provinces, and the Austrian Netherlands and the Rhineland were once again in French hands. This remarkable change of fortune was due to the revolutionary government's success in harnessing the explosive forces of a planned economy, revolutionary terror, and modern nationalism in a total war effort.

Robespierre and the Committee of Public Safety advanced on several fronts in 1793 and 1794, seeking to impose republican unity across the nation. First, they collaborated with the sans-culottes, who continued pressing the common people's case for fair prices and a moral economic order. Thus in September 1793 Robespierre and his coworkers established a planned economy with egalitarian social overtones. Rather than let supply and demand determine prices, the government set maximum prices for key products. Though the state was too weak to enforce all its price regulations, it did fix the price of bread in Paris at levels the poor could afford.

The people were also put to work, mainly producing arms and munitions for the war effort. The government told craftsmen what to produce, nationalized many small workshops, and requisitioned raw materials and grain. Through these economic reforms the second revolution produced an emergency form of socialism, which thoroughly frightened Europe's propertied classes and greatly influenced the subsequent development of socialist ideology.

Second, while radical economic measures supplied the poor with bread and the armies with weapons, the **Reign of Terror** (1793–1794) enforced compliance with republican beliefs and practices. Special revolutionary courts responsible only to Robespierre's Committee of Public Safety tried "enemies of the nation" for political crimes. Some forty thousand French men and women were executed or died in prison, making Robespierre's Reign of Terror one of the most controversial phases of the Revolution. Presented as a necessary measure to save the republic, the Terror was a weapon directed against all suspected of opposing the revolutionary government. As Robespierre himself put it, "Terror is nothing more than prompt, severe inflexible justice."[4] For many Europeans of the time, however, the Reign of Terror represented a frightening perversion of the ideals of 1789.

In their efforts to impose unity, the Jacobins took actions to suppress women's participation in political debate, which they perceived as disorderly and a dis-

Contrasting Visions of the Sans-Culottes

These two images offer profoundly different representations of a sans-culotte woman. The image on the left was created by a French artist, while the image on the right is English. The French words above the image on the right read in part, "Heads! Blood! Death! . . . I am the Goddess of Liberty! . . . Long Live the Guillotine!"

(Bibliothèque nationale de France)

Des Tetes! _ du Sang! _ la Mort! _ à la Lanterne! _ à la Guillotine.
_ point de Reine! _ Je suis la Deésse de la Liberté! _ l'egalité! _ que
Londres soit brulé! _ que Paris soit Libre! _ Vive la Guillotine! _

Miss Mary Stokes del.

A PARIS BELLE.

(Bibliothèque nationale de France)

EVALUATE THE EVIDENCE

1. How would you describe the woman on the left? What qualities does the artist seem to ascribe to her, and how do you think these qualities relate to the sans-culottes and the Revolution? How would you characterize the facial expression and attire of the woman on the right? How does the inclusion of the text contribute to your impressions of her?

2. What does the contrast between these two images suggest about differences between French and English perceptions of the sans-culottes and of the French Revolution? Why do you think the artists have chosen to depict women?

traction from women's proper place in the home. On October 30, 1793, the National Convention declared that "the clubs and popular societies of women, under whatever denomination are prohibited." Among those convicted of sedition was writer Olympe de Gouges, who was sent to the guillotine in November 1793.

The Terror also sought to bring the Revolution into all aspects of everyday life. The government sponsored revolutionary art and songs as well as a new series of secular festivals to celebrate republican virtue and patriotism. Moreover, the government attempted to rationalize French daily life by adopting the decimal system for weights and measures and a new calendar based on ten-day weeks. (See "Living in the Past: A Revolution of Culture and Daily Life," page 632.) Another important element of this cultural revolution was the campaign of de-Christianization, which aimed to eliminate Catholic symbols and beliefs. Fearful of the

The Guillotine Prior to the French Revolution, methods of execution included hanging and being broken at the wheel. Only nobles enjoyed the privilege of a relatively swift and painless death by decapitation, delivered by an executioner's ax. The guillotine, a model of which is shown here, was devised by a French revolutionary doctor named Guillotin as a humane and egalitarian form of execution. Ironically, due to the mass executions under the Terror, it is now seen instead as a symbol of revolutionary cruelty. (Musée de la Ville de Paris, Musée Carnavalet, Paris/Giraudon, The Bridgeman Art Library)

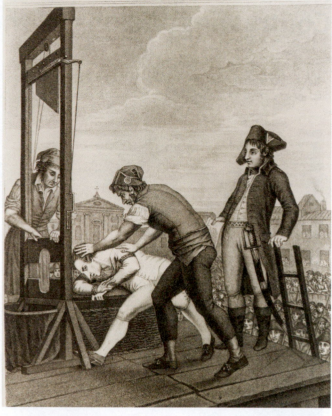

The Execution of Robespierre Completely wooden except for the heavy iron blade, the guillotine was painted red for Robespierre's execution, a detail not captured in this black-and-white engraving of the 1794 event. Large crowds witnessed the execution in a majestic public square in central Paris, then known as the Place de la Revolution and now called the Place de la Concorde (Harmony Square). (Universal History Archive/UIG/The Bridgeman Art Library)

hostility aroused in rural France, however, Robespierre called for a halt to de-Christianization measures in mid-1794.

The third and perhaps most decisive element in the French republic's victory over the First Coalition was its ability to draw on the power of dedication to a national state and a national mission. An essential part of modern nationalism, which would fully emerge throughout Europe in the nineteenth century, this commitment was something new in history. With a common language and a common tradition newly reinforced by the ideas of popular sovereignty and democracy, large numbers of French people were stirred by a common loyalty. They developed an intense emotional commitment to the defense of the nation, and they saw the war against foreign opponents as a life-and-death struggle between good and evil.

Thermidorian reaction
A reaction to the violence of the Reign of Terror in 1794, resulting in the execution of Robespierre and the loosening of economic controls.

The all-out mobilization of French resources under the Terror combined with the fervor of nationalism to create an awesome fighting machine. After August 1793 all unmarried young men were subject to the draft, and by January 1794 French armed forces outnumbered those of their enemies almost four to one.[5] Well trained, well equipped, and constantly indoctrinated, the enormous armies of the republic were led by young, impetuous generals. These generals often had risen from the ranks, and they personified the opportunities the Revolution offered gifted sons of the people. By spring 1794 French armies were victorious on all fronts. The republic was saved.

The Thermidorian Reaction and the Directory

The success of the French armies led Robespierre and the Committee of Public Safety to relax the emergency economic controls, but they extended the political Reign of Terror. In March 1794 Robespierre's Terror wiped out many of his critics. Two weeks later Robespierre sent long-standing collaborators whom he believed had turned against him, including Danton, to the guillotine. A group of radicals and moderates in the Convention, knowing that they might be next, organized a conspiracy. They howled down Robespierre when he tried to speak to the National Convention on July 27, 1794 — a date known as 9 Thermidor according to France's newly adopted republican calendar. The next day it was Robespierre's turn to be guillotined.

As Robespierre's closest supporters followed their leader to the guillotine, the respectable middle-class lawyers and professionals who had led the liberal revolution of 1789 reasserted their authority. This period of **Thermidorian reaction**, as it was called, hearkened back to the beginnings of the Revolution; the middle class rejected the radicalism of the sans-culottes in favor of moderate policies that favored property owners. In 1795 the National Convention abolished many economic controls, let prices rise sharply, and severely restricted the local political organizations through which the sans-culottes exerted their strength.

In 1795 the middle-class members of the National Convention wrote yet another constitution to guarantee their economic position and political supremacy. As in previous elections, the mass of the population could vote only for electors who would in turn elect the legislators, but the new constitution greatly reduced the number of men eligible to become electors by instating a substantial property requirement. It also inaugurated a bicameral legislative system for the first time in the Revolution, with a Council of 500 serving as the lower house that initiated legislation and a Council of Elders (composed of about 250 members aged forty years or older) acting as the upper house that approved new laws. To prevent a new Robespierre from monopolizing power, the new Assembly granted executive power to a five-man body, called the Directory.

The Directory continued to support French military expansion abroad. War was no longer so much a crusade as a response to economic problems. Large, victorious French armies reduced unemployment at home. However, the French people quickly grew weary of the corruption and ineffectiveness that characterized the Directory. This general dissatisfaction revealed itself clearly in the national elections of 1797, which returned a large number of conservative and even monarchist deputies who favored peace at almost any price. Two years later Napoleon Bonaparte ended the Directory in a coup d'état (koo day-TAH) and substituted a strong dictatorship for a weak one.

The French Revolution

■ National Assembly (1789–1791)

May 5, 1789	Estates General meets at Versailles
June 17, 1789	Third estate declares itself the National Assembly
June 20, 1789	Tennis Court Oath
July 14, 1789	Storming of the Bastille
July–August 1789	Great Fear
August 4, 1789	Abolishment of feudal privileges
August 27, 1789	Declaration of the Rights of Man and of the Citizen
October 5, 1789	Women march on Versailles; royal family returns to Paris
November 1789	National Assembly confiscates church land
July 1790	Civil Constitution of the Clergy establishes a national church; Louis XVI agrees to constitutional monarchy
June 1791	Royal family arrested while fleeing France
August 1791	Declaration of Pillnitz

■ Legislative Assembly (1791–1792)

April 1792	France declares war on Austria
August 1792	Mob attacks the palace, and Legislative Assembly takes Louis XVI prisoner

■ National Convention (1792–1795)

September 1792	September Massacres; National Convention abolishes monarchy and declares France a republic
January 1793	Louis XVI executed
February 1793	France declares war on Britain, the Dutch Republic, and Spain; revolts take place in some provinces
March 1793	Struggle between Girondists and the Mountain
April 1793	Creation of the Committee of Public Safety
June 1793	Arrest of Girondist leaders
September 1793	Price controls instituted
October 1793	National Convention bans women's political societies
1793–1794	Reign of Terror
Spring 1794	French armies victorious on all fronts
July 1794	Robespierre executed; Thermidorian reaction begins

■ The Directory (1795–1799)

1795	Economic controls abolished; suppression of the sans-culottes begins
1799	Napoleon seizes power

LIVING IN THE PAST
A Revolution of Culture and Daily Life

The French Revolution brought sweeping political and social change to France, removing one of the oldest monarchies in Europe in favor of broad-based representative government and eliminating age-old distinctions between nobles and commoners. Revolutionaries feared, however, that these measures were not enough to transform the nation. They therefore undertook a parallel revolution of culture intended to purify and regenerate the French people and turn former royal subjects into patriotic citizens capable of realizing the dream of liberty, equality, and fraternity.

To bring about cultural revolution, officials of the new republic targeted the most fundamental elements of daily life: the experience of space and time. Prior to the Revolution, regions of France had their own systems of measurement, meaning that the length of an inch or the weight of a pound differed substantially across the realm. Disgusted with the inefficiency of this state of affairs and determined to impose national unity, the government adopted the decimal-based metric system first proposed in 1670. The length of the meter was scientifically set at one ten-millionth of the distance from the pole to the equator. Henceforth all French citizens would inhabit spaces that were measured and divided in the same way.

The government attempted a similar rationalization of the calendar. Instead of twelve months of varying lengths, each of the twelve months on the new revolutionary calendar was made up of three ten-day weeks, with a five- or six-day interval at the end of each year. To mark the total rebirth of time, the new calendar began at Year 1 on the day of the foundation of the French republic (September 22, 1792). A series of festivals with patriotic themes replaced the traditional Catholic feast days. One of the most important was the festival of the Cult of the Supreme Being (a form of deism promoted by Robespierre as the state religion). There was even a short-lived attempt to put the clock on a decimal system.

Cultural revolution also took on more concrete forms. Every citizen was required to wear a tricolor cockade on his or her hat to symbolize loyalty to the republic. Enterprising merchants sold a plethora of everyday goods with revolutionary themes. One could eat from revolutionary plates, drink from revolutionary mugs, waft revolutionary fans, and even decorate the home with revolutionary wallpaper. Living the French Revolution meant entering a whole new world of sense and experience.

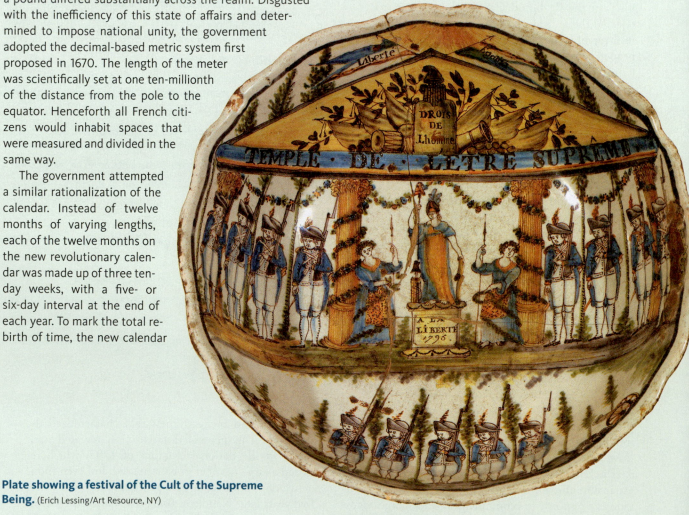

Plate showing a festival of the Cult of the Supreme Being. (Erich Lessing/Art Resource, NY)

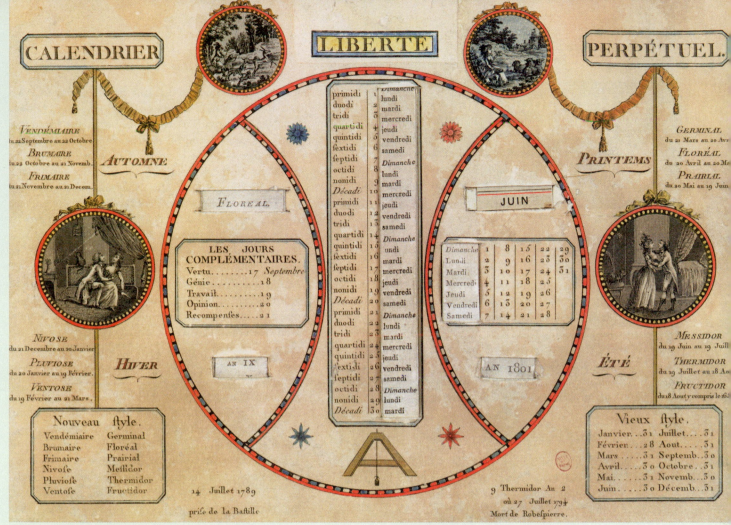

Revolutionary calendar. (Musée de la Ville de Paris, Musée Carnavalet, Paris, France/Giraudon/The Bridgeman Art Library)

QUESTIONS FOR ANALYSIS

1. How easy do you think it would have been to follow the new revolutionary calendar? Why did revolutionaries believe it was necessary to create a new calendar?
2. How would you describe the festival of the Supreme Being as it is shown on the plate? What values of the Revolution does it seem to emphasize?
3. Why were ordinary objects, like plates and playing cards, decorated with symbols of the Revolution? What does this tell you about the ways everyday life was drawn into the experience of revolution?

Revolutionary playing card. (Musée de la Ville de Paris, Musée Carnavalet, Paris, France/Giraudon/ The Bridgeman Art Library)

The Napoleonic Era, 1799–1815

Why did Napoleon Bonaparte assume control of France and much of Europe, and what factors led to his downfall?

For almost fifteen years, from 1799 to 1814, France was in the hands of a keen-minded military dictator of exceptional ability. One of history's most fascinating leaders, Napoleon Bonaparte (1769–1821) realized that he needed to put an end to civil strife in France in order to create unity and consolidate his rule. And he did. But Napoleon saw himself as a man of destiny, and the glory of war and the dream of universal empire proved irresistible. For years he spiraled from victory to victory, but in the end he was destroyed by a mighty coalition united in fear of his restless ambition.

Napoleon's Rule of France

Born in Corsica into an impoverished noble family in 1769, Napoleon left home and became a lieutenant in the French artillery in 1785. Rising rapidly in the new army, Napoleon was placed in command of French forces in Italy and won brilliant victories there in 1796 and 1797. His next campaign, in Egypt, was a failure, but Napoleon returned to France before the fiasco was generally known, and his reputation remained intact.

Napoleon soon learned that some prominent members of the legislature were plotting against the Directory. The plotters' dissatisfaction stemmed not so much from the Directory's ruling dictatorially as from the fact that it was a weak dictatorship. Ten years of upheaval and uncertainty had made firm rule much more appealing than liberty and popular politics to these disillusioned revolutionaries. The abbé Sieyès personified this evolution in thinking. In 1789 he had written that the nobility was grossly overprivileged and that the entire people should rule the French nation. Now Sieyès's motto was "Confidence from below, authority from above."

The flamboyant thirty-year-old Napoleon, nationally revered for his heroism, was an ideal figure of authority. On November 9, 1799, Napoleon and his conspirators ousted the Directors, and the following day soldiers disbanded the legislature at bayonet point. Napoleon was named first consul of the republic, and a new constitution consolidating his position was overwhelmingly approved by a nationwide vote in December 1799. Republican appearances were maintained, but Napoleon became the real ruler of France. (See

The Coronation of Napoleon, 1804   In this detail from a grandiose painting by Jacques-Louis David, Napoleon, instead of the pope, prepares to crown his wife, Josephine, in an elaborate ceremony in Notre Dame Cathedral. Napoleon, the ultimate upstart, also crowned himself. Pope Pius VII, seated glumly behind the emperor, is reduced to being a spectator. (Louvre/Paris, France/The Bridgeman Art Library)

Napoleon's Proclamation to the French People

In his proclamation to the French people, Napoleon justified the coup d'état of November 10, 1799, in which he and co-conspirators overthrew the Directory government. He does not mention the two men named consul alongside him, but takes sole credit for the events, which he presents as a necessary defense of the republic against traitorous legislators.

" On my return to Paris, I found division among all the authorities and agreement only on one truth, that the Constitution was half destroyed and could no longer save liberty.

Every faction came to me, confided their plans in me, and asked me for my support: I refused to be the man of one faction. . . .

The Council of Elders resolved to transfer the Legislative Body to Saint-Cloud; it gave me the responsibility of organizing the force necessary for its independence. I believed it my duty to my fellow citizens, to the soldiers perishing in our armies, and for the national glory acquired at the cost of their blood, to accept the command.

The Councils assembled at Saint-Cloud; republican troops guaranteed their safety from without, but assassins created terror from within. Several deputies from the Council of Five Hundred, armed with stilettos and firearms, circulated death threats. . . .

I took my indignation and grief to the Council of Elders. I asked it to guarantee the execution of its generous plans. I presented it with the evils besetting the fatherland which they were able to imagine. They united with me through new testimony of their steadfast will.

I then went to the Council of Five Hundred; alone, unarmed, head uncovered, just as the Elders had received and applauded me. I came to remind the majority of its wishes, and to assure it of its power.

The stilettos which threatened the deputies were immediately raised against their liberator; twenty assassins threw themselves on me and aimed at my chest. The grenadiers of the Legislative Body, whom I had left at the entrance to the hall, ran to put themselves between me and the assassins. One of the brave grenadiers was struck and had his clothes torn by a stiletto. They carried me out. . . .

They crowded around the president, uttering threats, arms in hand. . . . I ordered that he be snatched from their fury, and six grenadiers of the Legislative Body carried him out. Immediately afterwards, grenadiers from the Legislative Body charged into the hall and had it evacuated.

The factions, thus intimidated, dispersed and fled. The majority, freed from their attacks, returned freely and peaceably to the meeting hall, heard the propositions which were made for public safety, deliberated, and prepared the salutary resolution which is to become the new and provisional law of the Republic.

Frenchmen, you will undoubtedly recognize in this conduct the zeal of a soldier of liberty, of a citizen devoted to the Republic. "

EVALUATE THE EVIDENCE

1. How does Napoleon justify his actions on November 10, 1799, and the dismissal of the existing legislature of France?
2. In what ways does this document illustrate Napoleon's recurrent tactic of presenting his actions as a means to preserve, not destroy, the Revolution and its achievements?

Source: *The French Revolution and Napoleon: A Sourcebook*, ed. Philip G. Dwyer and Peter McPhee (London: Routledge, 2002), p. 138. Used by permission of Taylor & Francis.

"Primary Source 19.5: Napoleon's Proclamation to the French People," above.)

Napoleon's domestic policy centered on using his popularity and charisma to maintain order and end civil strife. He did so by appeasing powerful groups in France by according them favors in return for loyal service. Napoleon's bargain with the solid middle class was codified in the famous Civil Code of March 1804, also known as the **Napoleonic Code**, which reasserted two of the fundamental principles of the Revolution of 1789: equality of all male citizens before the law, and security of wealth and private property. Napoleon and the leading bankers of Paris established the pri-

vately owned Bank of France in 1800, which served the interests of both the state and the financial oligarchy. Napoleon won over peasants by defending the gains in land and status they had won during the Revolution.

At the same time, Napoleon consolidated his rule by recruiting disillusioned revolutionaries to form a network of ministers, prefects, and centrally appointed mayors. Nor were members of the old nobility slighted. In 1800 and

Napoleonic Code French civil code promulgated in 1804 that reasserted the 1789 principles of the equality of all male citizens before the law and the absolute security of wealth and private property, as well as restricting rights accorded to women by previous revolutionary laws.

again in 1802 Napoleon granted amnesty to one hundred thousand émigrés on the condition that they return to France and take a loyalty oath. Members of this returning elite soon ably occupied many high posts in the expanding centralized state. Napoleon also created a new imperial nobility in order to reward his most talented generals and officials.

Napoleon applied his diplomatic skills to healing the Catholic Church in France so that it could serve as a bulwark of social stability. After arduous negotiations, Napoleon and Pope Pius VII (pontificate 1800–1823) signed the Concordat (kuhn-KOHR-dat) of 1801. The pope obtained the right for French Catholics to practice their religion freely, but Napoleon gained political power: his government now nominated bishops, paid the clergy, and exerted great influence over the church.

The domestic reforms of Napoleon's early years were his greatest achievement. Much of his legal and administrative reorganization has survived in France to this day, but order and unity had a price: authoritarian rule. Women lost many of the gains they had made in the 1790s. Under the Napoleonic Code, women were dependents of either their fathers or their husbands, and they could not make contracts or have bank accounts in their own names. Napoleon and his advisers aimed at re-establishing a family monarchy, where the power of the husband and father was as absolute over the wife and the children as that of Napoleon was over his subjects. He also curtailed free speech and freedom of the press and manipulated voting in the occasional elections. After 1810 political suspects were held in state prisons, as they had been during the Terror.

Napoleon's Expansion in Europe

Napoleon was above all a great military man. After coming to power in 1799, he sent peace feelers to Austria and Great Britain, the two remaining members of the Second Coalition that had been formed against France in 1798. When they rejected his overtures, Napoleon's armies decisively defeated the Austrians. In the Treaty of Lunéville (1801), Austria accepted the loss of almost all its Italian possessions, and German territory on the west bank of the Rhine was incorporated into France. The British agreed to the Treaty of Amiens in 1802, allowing France to control the former Dutch Republic (known as the Batavian Republic since 1795),

the Austrian Netherlands, the west bank of the Rhine, and most of the Italian peninsula. The Treaty of Amiens was a diplomatic triumph for Napoleon, and peace with honor and profit increased his popularity at home.

In 1802 Napoleon was secure but driven to expand his power. Aggressively redrawing the map of Germany so as to weaken Austria and encourage the secondary states of southwestern Germany to side with France, Napoleon tried to restrict British trade with all of Europe. He then plotted to attack Great Britain, but his Mediterranean fleet was destroyed by Lord Nelson at the Battle of Trafalgar on October 21, 1805. Invasion of England was henceforth impossible. Renewed fighting had its advantages, however, for the first consul used the wartime atmosphere to have himself proclaimed emperor in late 1804.

Austria, Russia, and Sweden joined with Britain to form the Third Coalition against France shortly before the Battle of Trafalgar. Actions such as Napoleon's assumption of the Italian crown had convinced both Alexander I of Russia and Francis II of Austria that Napoleon was a threat to the European balance of power. Yet they were no match for Napoleon, who scored a brilliant victory over them at the Battle of Austerlitz in December 1805. Alexander I decided to pull back, and Austria accepted large territorial losses in return for peace as the Third Coalition collapsed.

German Confederation of the Rhine, 1806

Napoleon then proceeded to reorganize the German states. In 1806 he abolished many of the tiny German states as well as the ancient Holy Roman Empire and established by decree the German Confederation of the Rhine, a union of fifteen German states minus Austria, Prussia, and Saxony. Naming himself "protector" of the confederation, Napoleon firmly controlled western Germany.

Napoleon's intervention in German affairs alarmed the Prussians, who mobilized their armies after more than a decade of peace with France. Napoleon attacked and won two more brilliant victories in October 1806 at Jena and Auerstädt, where the Prussians were outnumbered two to one. The war with Prussia, now joined by Russia, continued into the following spring. After Napoleon's larger armies won another victory, Alexander I of Russia was ready to negotiate the peace. In the subsequent treaties of Tilsit in 1807, Prussia lost half of its population, while Russia accepted Napoleon's reorganization of western and central Europe and promised to enforce Napoleon's economic blockade against British goods.

The Grand Empire and Its End

Increasingly, Napoleon saw himself as the emperor of Europe, not just of France. The so-called **Grand Empire** he built had three parts. The core, or first part, was an ever-expanding France, which by 1810 included today's Belgium and the Netherlands, parts of northern Italy, and German territories on the east bank of the Rhine. The second part consisted of a number of dependent satellite kingdoms, on the thrones of which Napoleon placed members of his large family. The third part comprised the independent but allied states of Austria, Prussia, and Russia. After 1806 Napoleon expected both satellites and allies to support his **Continental System**, a blockade in which no ship coming from Britain or her colonies could dock at a port controlled by the French. It was intended to halt all trade between Britain and continental Europe, thereby destroying the British economy and its military force.

The impact of the Grand Empire on the peoples of Europe was considerable. In the areas incorporated into France and in the satellites (Map 19.2), Napoleon abolished feudal dues and serfdom to the benefit of the peasants and middle class. Yet Napoleon had to put the prosperity and special interests of France first in order to safeguard his power base. Levying heavy taxes in money and men for his armies, he came to be regarded more as a conquering tyrant than as an enlightened liberator. Thus French rule sparked patriotic upheavals and encouraged the growth of reactive nationalism, for individuals in different lands learned to identify emotionally with their own embattled national families as the French had done earlier.

The first great revolt occurred in Spain. In 1808 a coalition of Catholics, monarchists, and patriots rebelled against Napoleon's attempts to make Spain a French satellite. French armies occupied Madrid, but the foes of Napoleon fled to the hills and waged uncompromising guerrilla warfare. Spain was a clear warning: resistance to French imperialism was growing.

Yet Napoleon pushed on. In 1810, when the Grand Empire was at its height, Britain still remained at war with France, helping the guerrillas in Spain and Portugal. The Continental System was a failure. Instead of harming Britain, the system provoked the British to set up a counterblockade, which created hard times in France. Perhaps looking for a scapegoat, Napoleon turned on Alexander I of Russia, who in 1811 openly repudiated Napoleon's war of prohibitions against British goods.

Napoleon's invasion of Russia began in June 1812 with a force that eventually numbered 600,000, probably the largest force yet assembled in a single army. Only one-third of this army was French, however; nationals of all the satellites and allies were drafted into the operation. Originally planning to winter in the Russian city of Smolensk, Napoleon recklessly pressed on toward Moscow. The great Battle of Borodino that followed was a draw. Alexander

Grand Empire The empire over which Napoleon and his allies ruled, encompassing virtually all of Europe except Great Britain and Russia.

Continental System A blockade imposed by Napoleon to halt all trade between continental Europe and Britain, thereby weakening the British economy and military.

The Napoleonic Era

November 1799	Napoleon overthrows the Directory
December 1799	Napoleon's new constitution approved
1800	Foundation of the Bank of France
1801	France defeats Austria and acquires Italian and German territories in the Treaty of Lunéville; Napoleon signs papal Concordat
1802	Treaty of Amiens
March 1804	Napoleonic Code
December 1804	Napoleon crowned emperor
October 1805	Britain defeats the French fleet at the Battle of Trafalgar
December 1805	Napoleon defeats Austria and Russia at the Battle of Austerlitz
1807	Napoleon redraws map of Europe in the treaties of Tilsit
1808	Spanish revolt against French occupation
1810	Height of the Grand Empire
June 1812	Napoleon invades Russia
Fall–Winter 1812	Napoleon makes a disastrous retreat from Russia
March 1814	Russia, Prussia, Austria, and Britain sign the Treaty of Chaumont, pledging alliance to defeat Napoleon
April 1814	Napoleon abdicates and is exiled to Elba; Louis XVIII restored to constitutional monarchy
February–June 1815	Napoleon escapes from Elba but is defeated at the Battle of Waterloo; Louis XVIII restored to throne for second time

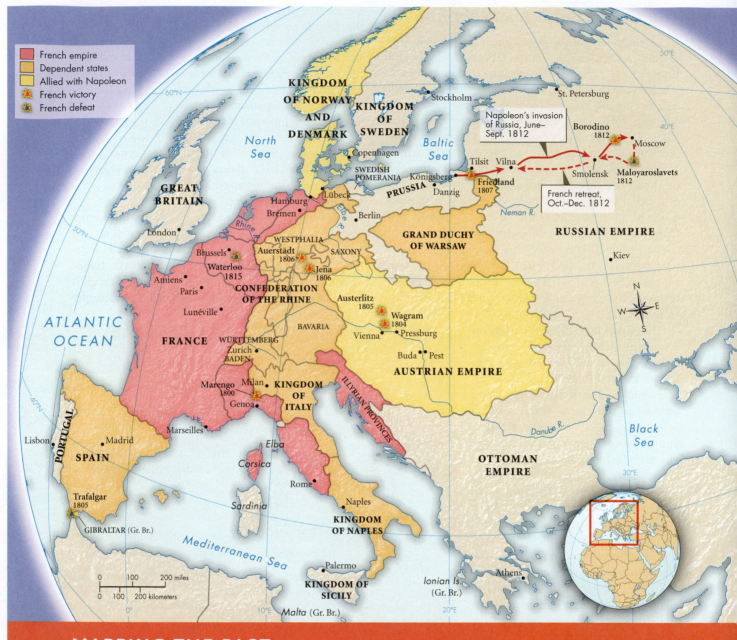

Legend:
- French empire
- Dependent states
- Allied with Napoleon
- ★ French victory
- ★ French defeat

Map labels:
KINGDOM OF NORWAY AND DENMARK · KINGDOM OF SWEDEN · Stockholm · St. Petersburg · Napoleon's invasion of Russia, June–Sept. 1812 · Borodino 1812 · Moscow · North Sea · Baltic Sea · Copenhagen · Tilsit · Vilna · Smolensk · Maloyaroslavets 1812 · SWEDISH POMERANIA · Königsberg · Friedland 1807 · Danzig · French retreat, Oct.–Dec. 1812 · GREAT BRITAIN · Lübeck · Hamburg · Bremen · Berlin · PRUSSIA · Neman R. · RUSSIAN EMPIRE · London · Rhine · Elbe · WESTPHALIA · Auerstädt 1806 · SAXONY · GRAND DUCHY OF WARSAW · Kiev · Brussels · Waterloo 1815 · Jena 1806 · Amiens · Paris · CONFEDERATION OF THE RHINE · Austerlitz 1805 · Lunéville · Wagram 1804 · ATLANTIC OCEAN · BAVARIA · Vienna · Pressburg · FRANCE · WÜRTTEMBERG · Zurich · BADEN · Buda · Pest · AUSTRIAN EMPIRE · Marengo 1800 · Milan · KINGDOM OF ITALY · ILLYRIAN PROVINCES · Genoa · Danube R. · Black Sea · Marseilles · Lisbon · PORTUGAL · Madrid · SPAIN · Elba · Corsica · Rome · OTTOMAN EMPIRE · Naples · Trafalgar 1805 · Sardinia · KINGDOM OF NAPLES · GIBRALTAR (Gr. Br.) · Mediterranean Sea · Palermo · Ionian Is. (Gr. Br.) · Athens · KINGDOM OF SICILY · Malta (Gr. Br.)

Scale: 0 100 200 miles / 0 100 200 kilometers

MAPPING THE PAST

Map 19.2 Napoleonic Europe in 1812

At the height of the Grand Empire in 1810, Napoleon had conquered or allied with every major European power except Britain. But in 1812, angered by Russian repudiation of his ban on trade with Britain, Napoleon invaded Russia with disastrous results. Compare this map with Map 15.2 (page 477), which shows the division of Europe in 1715.

ANALYZING THE MAP How had the balance of power shifted in Europe from 1715 to 1812? What changed, and what remained the same? What was the impact of Napoleon's wars on Germany and the Italian peninsula?

CONNECTIONS Why did Napoleon succeed in achieving vast territorial gains where Louis XIV did not?

Francisco Goya, *The Third of May 1808* Spanish master Francisco Goya created a passionate and moving indictment of the brutality of war in this painting from 1814, which depicts the close-range execution of Spanish rebels by Napoleon's forces in May 1808. Goya's painting evoked the bitterness and despair of many Europeans who suffered through Napoleon's invasions. (Prado, Madrid, Spain/The Bridgeman Art Library)

ordered the evacuation of Moscow, which the Russians then burned in part, and he refused to negotiate. Finally, after five weeks in the scorched and abandoned city, Napoleon ordered a retreat, one of the greatest military disasters in history. The Russian army, the Russian winter, and starvation cut Napoleon's army to pieces. When the frozen remnants staggered into Poland and Prussia in December, 370,000 men had died and another 200,000 had been taken prisoner.[6]

Leaving his troops to their fate, Napoleon raced to Paris to raise yet another army. Possibly he might still have saved his throne if he had been willing to accept a France reduced to its historical size—the proposal offered by Austria's foreign minister, Prince Klemens von Metternich. But Napoleon refused. Austria and Prussia deserted Napoleon and joined Russia and Great Britain in the Treaty of Chaumont in March 1814, by which the four powers pledged allegiance to defeat the French emperor.

All across Europe patriots called for a "war of liberation" against Napoleon's oppression. Less than a month later, on April 4, 1814, a defeated Napoleon abdicated his throne. After this unconditional abdication, the victorious allies granted Napoleon the island of Elba off the coast of Italy as his own tiny state. Napoleon was allowed to keep his imperial title, and France was required to pay him a yearly income of 2 million francs.

The allies also agreed to the restoration of the Bourbon dynasty under Louis XVIII (r. 1814–1824) and promised to treat France with leniency in a peace settlement. The new monarch sought support among the people by issuing the Constitutional Charter, which accepted many of France's revolutionary changes and guaranteed civil liberties.

Yet Louis XVIII lacked the magnetism of Napoleon. Hearing of political unrest in France and diplomatic tensions in Vienna, Napoleon staged a daring escape from Elba in February 1815 and marched on Paris with a small band of followers. French officers and soldiers who had fought so long for their emperor responded to the call. Louis XVIII fled, and once more Napoleon took command. But Napoleon's gamble was a desperate long shot, for the allies were united against him. At the end of a frantic period known as the Hundred Days, they crushed his forces at Waterloo on June 18, 1815, and imprisoned him on the rocky island of St. Helena, off the western coast of Africa. Louis XVIII returned to the throne, and the allies dealt more harshly with the French. As for Napoleon, he took revenge by writing his memoirs, nurturing the myth that he had been Europe's revolutionary liberator, a romantic hero whose lofty work had been undone by oppressive reactionaries.

The Haitian Revolution, 1791–1804

How did slave revolt on colonial Saint-Domingue lead to the creation of the independent nation of Haiti in 1804?

The events that led to the creation of the independent nation of Haiti constitute the third, and perhaps most extraordinary, chapter of the revolutionary era in the late eighteenth century. Prior to 1789 Saint-Domingue, the French colony that was to become Haiti, reaped huge profits through a ruthless system of slave-based plantation agriculture. News of revolution in France lit a powder keg of contradictory aspirations among white planters, free people of color, and slaves. While revolutionary authorities debated how far to extend the rights of man on Saint-Domingue, first free people of color then enslaved people took matters into their own hands, rising up to claim their freedom. A massive slave revolt of 1791 ultimately succeeded in ending slavery and winning independence from France, despite invasion by the British and Spanish and Napoleon Bonaparte's bid to reimpose French control. In 1804 Haiti became the first nation in history to claim its freedom through slave revolt.

Revolutionary Aspirations in Saint-Domingue

On the eve of the French Revolution, Saint-Domingue—the most profitable of all Caribbean colonies—was even more rife with social tensions than France itself. The colony, which occupied the western third of the island of Hispaniola, was inhabited by a variety of social groups who resented and mistrusted one another. The European population included French colonial officials, wealthy plantation owners and merchants, and poor immigrants. Individuals of French or European descent born in the colonies were called "Creoles," and over time they had developed

their own interests, at times distinct from those of metropolitan France. Vastly outnumbering the white population were the colony's five hundred thousand enslaved people alongside a sizable population of some forty thousand free people of African and mixed African and European descent. Members of this last group referred to themselves as free people of color.

Legal and economic conditions on Saint-Domingue vastly favored the white population. Most of the island's enslaved population performed grueling toil in the island's sugar plantations. The highly outnumbered planters used extremely brutal methods, such as beating, maiming, and executing slaves, to maintain their control. The 1685 Code Noir (Black Code) that set the parameters of slavery was intended to provide minimal standards of humane treatment, but its tenets were rarely enforced. Masters calculated that they could earn more by working slaves ruthlessly and purchasing new ones when they died, than by providing the food, rest, and medical care needed to allow the enslaved population to reproduce naturally. This meant a constant inflow of newly enslaved people from Africa was necessary to work the plantations.

Despite their brutality, slaveholders on Saint-Domingue freed a surprising number of their slaves, mostly their own mixed-race children, thereby producing one of the largest populations of free people of color in any slaveholding colony. The Code Noir had originally granted free people of color the same legal status as whites: they could own property, live where they wished, and pursue any education or career they desired. From the 1760s on, however, the rising prosperity and visibility of this group provoked resentment from the white population. In response, colonial administrators began rescinding the rights of free people of color, and by the time of the French Revolution myriad aspects of their lives were subject to discriminatory laws.

The political and intellectual turmoil of the 1780s, with its growing rhetoric of liberty, equality, and fraternity, raised new challenges and possibilities for each of Saint-Domingue's social groups. For enslaved people, who constituted approximately 90 percent of the population, news of abolitionist movements in France led to hopes that the mother country might grant them freedom. Free people of color looked to reforms in Paris as a means of gaining political enfranchisement and reasserting equal status with whites. The Creole elite, not surprisingly, saw matters very differently. Infuriated by talk of abolition and determined to protect their way of life, they looked to revolutionary ideals of representative government for the chance to gain control of their own affairs, as had the American colonists before them.

The National Assembly frustrated the hopes of all these groups. Cowed by colonial representatives who claimed that support for free people of color would result in slave insurrection and independence, the Assembly refused to extend French constitutional safeguards to the colonies. After dealing this blow to the aspirations of slaves and free people of color, the Assembly also reaffirmed French monopolies over colonial trade, thereby angering Creole planters as well. Like the American settlers did earlier, the colonists chafed under the rule of the mother country.

In July 1790 Vincent Ogé (aw-ZHAY) (ca. 1750–1791), a free man of color, returned to Saint-Domingue from Paris determined to win rights for his people. He raised an army of several hundred and sent letters to the new Provincial Assembly of Saint-Domingue demanding political rights for all free citizens. But Ogé's demands were refused, so he and his followers turned to armed insurrection. After initial victories, his army was defeated, and Ogé was tortured and executed by colonial officials. Revolutionary leaders in Paris were more sympathetic to Ogé's cause. In May 1791, responding to what it perceived as partly justified grievances, the National Assembly granted political rights to free people of color born to two free parents who possessed sufficient property. When news of this legis-

lation arrived in Saint-Domingue, the white elite was furious, and the colonial governor refused to enact it. Violence now erupted between groups of whites and free people of color in parts of the colony.

The Outbreak of Revolt

Just as the sans-culottes helped push forward more radical reforms in France, the second stage of revolution in Saint-Domingue also resulted from decisive action from below. In August 1791 slaves, who had witnessed the confrontation between whites and free people of color for over a year, took events into their own hands. Groups of slaves held a series of nighttime meetings to plan a mass insurrection. In doing so, they drew on their own considerable military experience; the majority of slaves had been born in Africa, and many had served in the civil wars of the kingdom of Congo and other conflicts before being taken into slavery.[7] They also drew on a long tradition of slave resistance prior to 1791, which had ranged from work slowdowns, to running away, to taking part in African-derived religious rituals and dances known as *vodou* (or voodoo). According to some

Saint-Domingue Slave Life　Although the brutal conditions of plantation slavery left little time or energy for leisure, slaves on Saint-Domingue took advantage of their day of rest on Sunday to engage in social and religious activities. The law officially prohibited slaves of different masters from mingling together, but such gatherings were often tolerated if they remained peaceful. This image depicts a fight between two slaves, precisely the type of unrest and violence feared by authorities. (Musée du Nouveau Monde, La Rochelle/Photos12.com — ARJ)

Slave Revolt on Saint-Domingue   This illustration, from the proslavery perspective, emphasizes the violence and destructiveness of the slave rebellion in Saint-Domingue. Many white settlers fled to the United States and other Caribbean islands with as much of their property, including slaves, as they could take with them. (The Library Company of Philadelphia)

sources, the August 1791 pact to take up arms was sealed by such a voodoo ritual.[8]

Revolts began on a few plantations on the night of August 22. Within a few days the uprising had swept much of the northern plain, creating a slave army estimated at around 2,000 individuals. By August 27 it was described by one observer as "10,000 strong, divided into 3 armies, of whom 700 or 800 are on horseback, and tolerably well-armed."[9] During the next month enslaved combatants attacked and destroyed hundreds of sugar and coffee plantations.

On April 4, 1792, as war loomed with the European states, the National Assembly issued a decree extending full citizenship rights to free people of color, including the right to vote for men. As in France, voting rights and the ability to hold public office applied to men only. The Assembly hoped this measure would win the loyalty of free people of color and their aid in defeating the slave rebellion.

Warfare in Europe soon spread to Saint-Domingue (Map 19.3). Since the beginning of the slave insurrection, the Spanish colony of Santo Domingo, just to the east of Saint-Domingue, had supported rebel slaves. In early 1793 the Spanish began to bring slave leaders and their soldiers into the Spanish army. Toussaint L'Ouverture (TOO-sahn LOO-vair-toor) (1743–1803),

a freed slave who had joined the revolt, was named a Spanish officer. In September the British navy blockaded the colony, and invading British troops captured French territory on the island. For the Spanish and British, revolutionary chaos provided a tempting opportunity to capture a profitable colony.

Desperate for forces to oppose France's enemies, commissioners sent by the newly elected National Convention promised to emancipate all those who fought for France. By October 1793 they had abolished slavery throughout the colony. On February 4, 1794, the Convention ratified the abolition of slavery and extended it to all French territories, including the Caribbean colonies of Martinique and Guadeloupe. In some ways this act merely acknowledged the achievements already won by the slave insurrection itself.

The tide of battle began to turn when Toussaint L'Ouverture switched sides, bringing his military and political skills, along with four thousand well-trained soldiers, to support the French war effort. By 1796 the French had regained control of the colony, and L'Ouverture had emerged as a key military leader. (See "Individuals in Society: Toussaint L'Ouverture," page 644.) In May 1796 he was named commander of the western province of Saint-Domingue (see Map 19.3). The increasingly conservative nature of the French government during the Thermidorian reaction, however, threatened to undo the gains made by former slaves and free people of color.

The War of Haitian Independence

With Toussaint L'Ouverture acting increasingly as an independent ruler of the western province of Saint-Domingue, another general, André Rigaud (1761–1811), set up his own government in the southern peninsula. Tensions mounted between L'Ouverture and Rigaud. While L'Ouverture was a freed slave of African descent, Rigaud belonged to the free colored elite. This elite resented the growing power of former slaves like L'Ouverture, who in turn accused them of adopting the racism of white settlers. Civil war broke out between the two sides in 1799, when L'Ouverture's forces, led by his lieutenant, Jean Jacques Dessalines (1758–1806), invaded the south. Victory over Rigaud in 1800 gave L'Ouverture control of the entire colony.

This victory was soon challenged by Napoleon, who had his own plans for re-establishing slavery and using the profits as a basis for expanding French power. Napoleon ordered his brother-in-law, General Charles-Victor-Emmanuel Leclerc (1772–1802), to lead an expedition to the island to crush the new regime. In 1802 Leclerc landed in Saint-Domingue and ordered the arrest of Toussaint L'Ouverture. The rebel leader, along with his family, was deported to France, where he died in 1803.

It was left to L'Ouverture's lieutenant, Jean Jacques Dessalines, to unite the resistance, and he led it to a crushing victory over French forces. On January 1, 1804, Dessalines formally declared the independence of Saint-Domingue and the creation of the new sovereign nation of Haiti, the name used by the pre-Columbian inhabitants of the island. The Haitian constitution was ratified in 1805.

Haiti, the second independent state in the Americas and the first in Latin America, was born from the first successful large-scale slave revolt in history. This event spread shock and fear through slaveholding societies in the Caribbean and the United States, bringing their worst nightmares of the utter reversal of their power

Map 19.3 The War of Haitian Independence, 1791–1804 Neighbored by the Spanish colony of Santo Domingo, Saint-Domingue was the most profitable European colony in the Caribbean. In 1770 the French transferred the capital from Le Cap to Port-au-Prince. Slave revolts erupted in the north near Le Cap in 1791. Port-au-Prince became the capital of the newly independent Haiti in 1804.

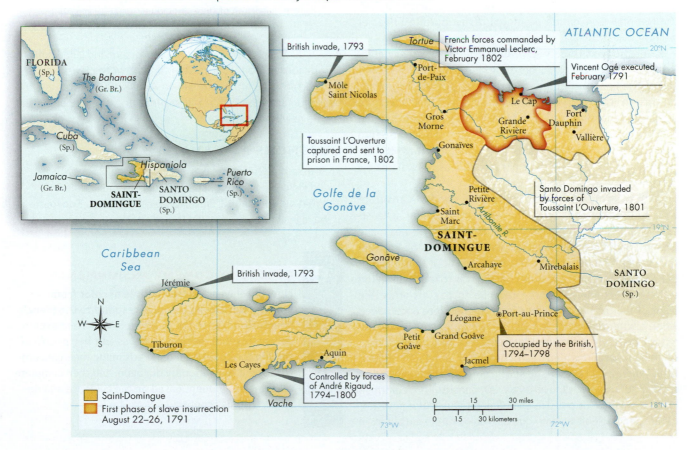

INDIVIDUALS IN SOCIETY
Toussaint L'Ouverture

Little is known of the early life of Saint-Domingue's brilliant military and political leader Toussaint L'Ouverture. He was born in 1743 on a plantation outside Le Cap owned by the Count de Bréda. According to tradition, L'Ouverture was the eldest son of a captured African prince from modern-day Benin. Toussaint Bréda, as he was then called, occupied a privileged position among slaves. Instead of performing backbreaking labor in the fields, he served his master as a coachman and livestock keeper. He also learned to read and write French and some Latin, but he was always more comfortable with the Creole dialect.

During the 1770s the plantation manager emancipated L'Ouverture, who subsequently leased his own small coffee plantation and slaves. He married Suzanne Simone, who already had one son, and the couple had another son during their marriage. In 1791 he joined the slave uprisings that swept Saint-Domingue, and he took on the *nom de guerre* (war name) "L'Ouverture," meaning "the opening." L'Ouverture rose to prominence among rebel slaves allied with Spain and by early 1794 controlled his own army. A devout Catholic who led a frugal and ascetic life, L'Ouverture impressed others with his enormous physical energy, intellectual acumen, and air of mystery. In 1794 he defected to the French side and led his troops to a series of victories against the Spanish. In 1795 the National Convention promoted L'Ouverture to brigadier general.

Over the next three years L'Ouverture successively eliminated rivals for authority on the island. First he freed himself of the French commissioners sent to govern the colony. With a firm grip on power in the northern province, L'Ouverture defeated General André Rigaud in 1800 to gain control in the south. His army then marched on the capital of Spanish Santo Domingo on the eastern half of the island, meeting little resistance. The entire island of Hispaniola was now under his command.

With control of Saint-Domingue in his hands, L'Ouverture was confronted with the challenge of building a post-emancipation society, the first of its kind. The task was made even more difficult by the chaos wreaked by war, the destruction of plantations, and bitter social and racial tensions. For L'Ouverture the most pressing concern was to re-establish the plantation economy. Without revenue to pay his army, the gains of the rebellion could be lost. He therefore encouraged white planters to return to reclaim their property. He also adopted harsh policies toward former slaves, forcing them back to their plantations and restricting their ability to acquire land. When they resisted, he sent troops across the island to enforce submission. L'Ouverture's 1801 constitution reaffirmed his draconian labor policies and named L'Ouverture governor for life, leaving Saint-Domingue as a colony in name alone. In

Equestrian portrait of Toussaint L'Ouverture. (© Photos 12/ Alamy)

June 1802 French forces arrested L'Ouverture and jailed him at Fort de Joux in France's Jura Mountains near the Swiss border. L'Ouverture died of pneumonia on April 7, 1803. It was left to his lieutenant, Jean Jacques Dessalines, to win independence for the new Haitian nation.

QUESTIONS FOR ANALYSIS

1. Toussaint L'Ouverture was both slave and slave owner. How did each experience shape his life and actions?
2. What did Toussaint L'Ouverture and Napoleon Bonaparte have in common? How did they differ?

ONLINE DOCUMENT ASSIGNMENT

How did slaves and free people of color from France's Caribbean colonies respond to the French Revolution? Go to the Integrated Media and explore documents that reveal how slaves and free people of color in the colonies and in Paris made their concerns part of the revolutionary dialogue, and then complete a writing assignment based on the evidence and details from this chapter.

and privilege to life. Fearing the spread of rebellion to the United States, President Thomas Jefferson refused to recognize Haiti as an independent nation. The liberal proponents of American Revolution thus chose to protect slavery at the expense of revolutionary ideals of universal human rights. The French government imposed crushing indemnity charges on Haiti to recompense the loss of French property, dealing a harsh blow to the fledgling nation's economy.

Yet Haitian independence had fundamental repercussions for world history, helping spread the idea that liberty, equality, and fraternity must apply to all people. The next phase of Atlantic revolution soon opened in the Spanish American colonies.

The Haitian Revolution

May 1791	French National Assembly enfranchises free men of color born of two free parents
August 1791	Slave insurrections in Saint-Domingue
April 1792	French National Assembly grants full citizenship rights to free people of color, including the right to vote for men
September 1793	British troops invade Saint-Domingue
February 1794	Abolition of slavery in all French territories
1796	France regains control of Saint-Domingue under Toussaint L'Ouverture
1803	Death of Toussaint L'Ouverture in France
January 1804	Declaration of Haitian independence
May 1805	First Haitian constitution

Notes

1. Quoted in G. Wright, *France in Modern Times*, 4th ed. (New York: W. W. Norton, 1987), p. 34.
2. G. Pernoud and S. Flaisser, eds., *The French Revolution* (Greenwich, Conn.: Fawcett, 1960), p. 61.
3. Quoted in L. Gershoy, *The Era of the French Revolution, 1789–1799* (New York: Van Nostrand, 1957), p. 150.
4. Cited in Wim Klooster, *Revolutions in the Atlantic World: A Comprehensive History* (New York: New York University Press, 2009), p. 74.
5. T. Blanning, *The French Revolutionary Wars, 1787–1802* (London: Arnold, 1996), pp. 116–128.
6. D. Sutherland, *France, 1789–1815: Revolution and Counterrevolution* (New York: Oxford University Press, 1986), p. 420.
7. John K. Thornton, "'I Am the Subject of the King of Congo': African Political Ideology and the Haitian Revolution," *Journal of World History* 4, no. 2 (Fall 1993): 181–214.
8. Laurent Dubois, *Avengers of the New World: The Story of the Haitian Revolution* (Cambridge, Mass.: Belknap Press, 2004), pp. 43–45, 99–100.
9. Quoted ibid., p. 97.

LOOKING BACK LOOKING AHEAD

A great revolutionary wave swept both sides of the Atlantic Ocean in the late eighteenth century. The revolutions in British North America, France, and Haiti were individual and unique, but they shared common origins and consequences for Western and, indeed, world history. Despite the French monarchy's ongoing claims to the absolutist rule imposed by Louis XIV, the eighteenth century had inaugurated monumental changes, as population grew, urbanization spread, and literacy increased. Enlightenment ideals, especially those of John Locke and the baron de Montesquieu, influenced all orders of society and reformers increasingly championed limitations on monarchical authority in the name of popular sovereignty.

The Atlantic world was an essential context for this age of revolutions. The movement of peoples, commodities, and ideas across the Atlantic Ocean in the eighteenth century created a world of common debates, conflicts, and aspirations. Moreover, the high stakes of colonial empire heightened competition among European states, leading to a series of wars that generated crushing costs for overburdened treasuries. For both the British in their North American colonies and the French at home, the desperate need for new taxes weakened government authority and opened the door to revolution. In turn, the ideals of the French Revolution inspired slaves and free people of color in Saint-Domingue, thus opening the promise of liberty, equality, and fraternity to people of all races.

The chain reaction did not end with the birth of an independent Haiti in 1804. On the European continent throughout the nineteenth and early twentieth centuries, periodic convulsions occurred as successive generations struggled over political rights first proclaimed by the generation of 1789. Meanwhile, as dramatic political events unfolded, a parallel economic revolution was gathering steam. This was the Industrial Revolution, originating around 1780 and accelerating through the end of the eighteenth century (see Chapter 20). After 1815 the twin forces of industrialization and democratization would combine to transform Europe and the world.

EVIEW and EXPLORE

MAKE IT STICK

LearningCurve
After reading the chapter, go online and use LearningCurve to retain what you've read.

Identify Key Terms

Identify and explain the significance of each item below.

Estates General (p. 620)

estates (p. 620)

National Assembly (p. 621)

Great Fear (p. 623)

Jacobin Club (p. 627)

second revolution (p. 627)

Girondists (p. 627)

the Mountain (p. 627)

sans-culottes (p. 628)

Reign of Terror (p. 628)

Thermidorian reaction (p. 631)

Napoleonic Code (p. 635)

Grand Empire (p. 637)

Continental System (p. 637)

Review the Main Ideas

Answer the focus questions from each section of the chapter.

- What were the factors behind the revolutions of the late eighteenth century? (p. 612)
- Why and how did American colonists forge a new, independent nation? (p. 615)
- How did the events of 1789 result in a constitutional monarchy in France, and what were the consequences? (p. 619)
- Why and how did the French Revolution take a radical turn entailing terror at home and war with European powers? (p. 626)
- Why did Napoleon Bonaparte assume control of France and much of Europe, and what factors led to his downfall? (p. 634)
- How did slave revolt on colonial Saint-Domingue lead to the creation of the independent nation of Haiti in 1804? (p. 640)

Make Connections

Think about the larger developments and continuities within and across chapters.

1. What were major differences and similarities among the American, French, and Haitian Revolutions?

2. How did the increased circulation of goods, people, and ideas across the Atlantic in the eighteenth century (Chapter 17) contribute to the outbreak of revolution on both sides of the ocean?

3. To what extent would you characterize the revolutions discussed in this chapter as Enlightenment movements (Chapter 16)?

ONLINE DOCUMENT ASSIGNMENT
Toussaint L'Ouverture

How did slaves and free people of color from France's Caribbean colonies respond to the French Revolution?

You encountered Toussaint L'Ouverture's story on page 644. Keeping the question above in mind, go to the Integrated Media and explore documents that reveal how slaves and free people of color in the colonies and in Paris made their concerns part of the revolutionary dialogue, and then complete a writing assignment based on the evidence and details from this chapter.

Suggested Reading and Media Resources

BOOKS

- Armitage, David, and Sanjay Subrahmanyam, eds. *The Age of Revolutions in Global Context, c. 1760–1840.* 2009. Presents the international causes and consequences of the age of revolutions.

- Auslander, Leora. *Cultural Revolutions: Everyday Life and Politics in Britain, North America, and France.* 2009. An innovative interpretation of the revolutions in England, America, and France as cultural revolutions that politicized daily life.

- Bell, David A. *The First Total War: Napoleon's War and the Birth of Warfare as We Know It.* 2007. Argues that the French Revolution created a new form of "total" war that prefigured the world wars of the twentieth century.

- Broers, Michael. *Europe Under Napoleon.* 2002. Probes Napoleon's impact on the territories he conquered.

- Connelly, Owen. *The French Revolution and Napoleonic Era.* 1991. An excellent introduction to the French Revolution and Napoleon.

- Desan, Suzanne. *The Family on Trial in Revolutionary France.* 2004. Studies the effects of revolutionary law on the family, including the legalization of divorce.

- Dubois, Laurent. *Avengers of the New World: The Story of the Haitian Revolution.* 2004. An excellent and highly readable account of the revolution that transformed the French colony of Saint-Domingue into the independent state of Haiti.

- Klooster, Wim. *Revolutions in the Atlantic World: A Comparative History.* 2009. An accessible and engaging comparison of the revolutions in North America, France, Haiti, and Spanish America.

- Schechter, Ronald. *Obstinate Hebrews: Representations of Jews in France, 1715–1815.* 2003. An illuminating study of Jews and attitudes toward them in France from the Enlightenment to emancipation.

- Sepinwall, Alyssa, ed. *Haitian History: New Perspectives.* 2013. A collection of essays showcasing the most important new scholarship on the Haitian Revolution.

- Wood, Gordon S. *The American Revolution: A History.* 2003. A concise introduction to the American Revolution by a Pulitzer Prize–winning historian.

DOCUMENTARIES

- *Égalité for All: Toussaint Louverture and the Haitian Revolution* (PBS, 2009). Uses music, interviews, voodoo rituals, and dramatic re-enactments to explore the Haitian Revolution and its fascinating leader, Toussaint L'Ouverture.

- *Liberty! The American Revolution* (PBS, 1997). A dramatic documentary about the American Revolution, consisting of six hour-long episodes that cover events from 1763 to 1788.

- *The War That Made America* (PBS, 2006). A miniseries about the French and Indian War that focuses on alliances between Native Americans and the French and British, including George Washington's role in the conflict as a young officer.

FEATURE FILMS AND TELEVISION

- *Colonel Chabert* (Yves Angelo, 1994). A Napoleonic cavalryman severely wounded in battle and left for dead recovers and returns home to find that his wife has remarried an ambitious politician.

- *The Crossing* (A&E, 2000). A television film focusing on George Washington's risky decision to lead the Continental Army across the Delaware River and engage British forces at the Battle of Trenton.

- *Farewell, My Queen* (Benoît Jacquot, 2012). A fictional view of the final days of the French monarchy, from the perspective of a female servant whose job is to read to Queen Marie Antoinette.

- *Master and Commander: The Far Side of the World* (Peter Weir, 2003). A British navy captain pursues a French vessel along the coast of South America during the Napoleonic Wars.

WEB SITES

- *Haiti Digital Library.* A guide to online primary sources, articles, and Web sites related to Haitian history, from the revolution to modern times; sponsored by the Haiti Laboratory at Duke University. **sites.duke.edu/haitilab/english/**

- *Liberty, Equality, Fraternity: Exploring the French Revolution.* Features a large image and document collection from the era of the French Revolution, as well as songs, maps, and thematic essays written by expert scholars in the field. **chnm.gmu.edu/revolution/**

- *The Papers of George Washington.* A site with online versions of many documents pertaining to and written by George Washington, accompanied by articles on themes related to Washington's life and views. **gwpapers.virginia.edu/index.html**

anticlericalism Opposition to the clergy. (p. 392)

Atlantic slave trade The forced migration of Africans across the Atlantic for slave labor on plantations and in other industries; the trade reached its peak in the eighteenth century and ultimately involved more than 12 million Africans. (p. 562)

Babylonian Captivity The period from 1309 to 1376 when the popes resided in Avignon rather than in Rome. The phrase refers to the seventy years when the Hebrews were held captive in Babylon. (p. 339)

Black Death Plague that first struck Europe in 1347 and killed perhaps one-third of the population. (p. 325)

blood sports Events such as bullbaiting and cockfighting that involved inflicting violence and bloodshed on animals and that were popular with the eighteenth-century European masses. (p. 587)

boyars The highest-ranking members of the Russian nobility. (p. 482)

cameralism View that monarchy was the best form of government, that all elements of society should serve the monarch, and that, in turn, the state should use its resources and authority to increase the public good. (p. 530)

caravel A small, maneuverable, three-mast sailing ship developed by the Portuguese in the fifteenth century that gave the Portuguese a distinct advantage in exploration and trade. (p. 433)

carnival The few days of revelry in Catholic countries that preceded Lent and that included drinking, masquerading, dancing, and rowdy spectacles that upset the established order. (p. 587)

Cartesian dualism Descartes's view that all of reality could ultimately be reduced to mind and matter. (p. 512)

charivari Degrading public rituals used by village communities to police personal behavior and maintain moral standards. (p. 578)

Christian humanists Northern humanists who interpreted Italian ideas about and attitudes toward classical antiquity and humanism in terms of their own religious traditions. (p. 370)

Columbian exchange The exchange of animals, plants, and diseases between the Old and the New Worlds. (p. 448)

communes Sworn associations of free men in Italian cities led by merchant guilds that sought political and economic independence from local nobles. (p. 358)

community controls A pattern of cooperation and common action in a traditional village that sought to uphold the economic, social, and moral stability of the closely knit community. (p. 578)

conciliarists People who believed that the authority in the Roman Church should rest in a general council composed of clergy, theologians, and laypeople, rather than in the pope alone. (p. 340)

confraternities Voluntary lay groups organized by occupation, devotional preference, neighborhood, or charitable activity. (p. 343)

conquistador Spanish for "conqueror"; Spanish soldier-explorers, such as Hernando Cortés and Francisco Pizarro, who sought to conquer the New World for the Spanish crown. (p. 433)

constitutionalism A form of government in which power is limited by law and balanced between the authority and power of the government on the one hand, and the rights and liberties of the subjects or citizens on the other hand; could include constitutional monarchies or republics. (p. 489)

consumer revolution The wide-ranging growth in consumption and new attitudes toward consumer goods that emerged in the cities of northwestern Europe in the second half of the eighteenth century. (p. 592)

Continental System A blockade imposed by Napoleon to halt all trade between continental Europe and Britain, thereby weakening the British economy and military. (p. 637)

Copernican hypothesis The idea that the sun, not the earth, was the center of the universe. (p. 506)

Cossacks Free groups and outlaw armies originally comprising runaway peasants living on the borders of Russian territory from the fourteenth century onward. By the end of the sixteenth century they had formed an alliance with the Russian state. (p. 483)

cottage industry A stage of industrial development in which rural workers used hand tools in their homes to manufacture goods on a large scale for sale in a market. (p. 549)

courts Magnificent households and palaces where signori and other rulers lived, conducted business, and supported the arts. (p. 360)

debate about women Debate among writers and thinkers in the Renaissance about women's qualities and proper role in society. (p. 381)

debt peonage A form of serfdom that allowed a planter or rancher to keep his workers or slaves in perpetual debt bondage by periodically advancing food, shelter, and a little money. (p. 562)

economic liberalism A belief in free trade and competition based on Adam Smith's argument that the invisible hand of free competition would benefit all individuals, rich and poor. (p. 557)

Edict of Nantes A document issued by Henry IV of France in 1598, granting liberty of conscience and of public worship to Calvinists, which helped restore peace in France. (p. 419)

empiricism A theory of inductive reasoning that calls for acquiring evidence through observation and experimentation rather than deductive reason and speculation. (p. 511)

enclosure The movement to fence in fields in order to farm more effectively, at the expense of poor peasants who relied on common fields for farming and pasture. (p. 543)

encomienda system A system whereby the Spanish crown granted the conquerors the right to forcibly employ groups of Indians in exchange for providing food, shelter, and Christian teaching. (p. 446)

English Peasants' Revolt Revolt by English peasants in 1381 in response to changing economic conditions. (p. 346)

enlightened absolutism Term coined by historians to describe the rule of eighteenth-century monarchs who, without renouncing their own absolute authority, adopted Enlightenment ideals of rationalism, progress, and tolerance. (p. 529)

Enlightenment The influential intellectual and cultural movement of the late seventeenth and eighteenth centuries that introduced a new worldview based on the use of reason, the scientific method, and progress. (p. 516)

estates The three legal categories, or orders, of France's inhabitants: the clergy, the nobility, and everyone else. (p. 620)

Estates General A legislative body in prerevolutionary France made up of representatives of each of the three classes, or estates. It was called into session in 1789 for the first time since 1614. (p. 620)

experimental method The approach, pioneered by Galileo, that the proper way to explore the workings of the universe was through repeatable experiments rather than speculation. (p. 508)

flagellants People who believed that the plague was God's punishment for sin and sought to do penance by flagellating (whipping) themselves. (p. 331)

Fronde A series of violent uprisings during the early reign of Louis XIV triggered by growing royal control and increased taxation. (p. 470)

Girondists A moderate group that fought for control of the French National Convention in 1793. (p. 627)

Grand Empire The empire over which Napoleon and his allies ruled, encompassing virtually all of Europe except Great Britain and Russia. (p. 637)

Great Famine A terrible famine in 1315–1322 that hit much of Europe after a period of climate change. (p. 324)

Great Fear The fear of noble reprisals against peasant uprisings that seized the French countryside and led to further revolt. (p. 623)

Great Schism The division, or split, in church leadership from 1378 to 1417 when there were two, then three, popes. (p. 340)

guild system The organization of artisanal production into trade-based associations, or guilds, each of which received a monopoly over its trade and the right to train apprentices and hire workers. (p. 554)

Haskalah The Jewish Enlightenment of the second half of the eighteenth century, led by the Prussian philosopher Moses Mendelssohn. (p. 535)

Holy Office The official Roman Catholic agency founded in 1542 to combat international doctrinal heresy. (p. 414)

Huguenots French Calvinists. (p. 418)

humanism A program of study designed by Italians that emphasized the critical study of Latin and Greek literature with the goal of understanding human nature. (p. 363)

Hundred Years' War A war between England and France from 1337 to 1453, with political and economic causes and consequences. (p. 332)

illegitimacy explosion The sharp increase in out-of-wedlock births that occurred in Europe between 1750 and 1850, caused by low wages and the breakdown of community controls. (p. 579)

Inca Empire The vast and sophisticated Peruvian empire centered at the capital city of Cuzco that was at its peak from 1438 until 1532. (p. 443)

indulgence A document issued by the Catholic Church lessening penance or time in purgatory, widely believed to bring forgiveness of all sins. (p. 393)

industrious revolution The shift that occurred as families in northwestern Europe focused on earning wages instead of producing goods for household consumption; this reduced their economic self-sufficiency but increased their ability to purchase consumer goods. (p. 553)

Institutes of the Christian Religion, The Calvin's formulation of Christian doctrine, which became a systematic theology for Protestantism. (p. 410)

Jacobin Club A political club in revolutionary France whose members were well-educated radical republicans. (p. 627)

Jacquerie A massive uprising by French peasants in 1358 protesting heavy taxation. (p. 344)

janissary corps The core of the sultan's army, composed of slave conscripts from non-Muslim parts of the empire; after 1683 it became a volunteer force. (p. 489)

Jansenism A sect of Catholicism originating with Cornelius Jansen that emphasized the heavy weight of original sin and accepted the doctrine of predestination; it was outlawed as heresy by the pope. (p. 600)

Jesuits Members of the Society of Jesus, founded by Ignatius Loyola, whose goal was the spread of the Roman Catholic faith. (p. 416)

Junkers The nobility of Brandenburg and Prussia, they were reluctant allies of Frederick William in his consolidation of the Prussian state. (p. 480)

just price The idea that prices should be fair, protecting both consumers and producers, and that they should be imposed by government decree if necessary. (p. 589)

law of inertia A law formulated by Galileo that states that motion, not rest, is the natural state of an object, and that an object continues in motion forever unless stopped by some external force. (p. 508)

law of universal gravitation Newton's law that all objects are attracted to one another and that the force of attraction is proportional to the objects' quantity of matter and inversely proportional to the square of the distance between them. (p. 510)

mercantilism A system of economic regulations aimed at increasing the power of the state based on the belief that a nation's international power was based on its wealth, specifically its supply of gold and silver. (p. 474)

Methodists Members of a Protestant revival movement started by John Wesley, so called because they were so methodical in their devotion. (p. 598)

Mexica Empire Also known as the Aztec Empire, a large and complex Native American civilization in modern Mexico and Central America that possessed advanced mathematical, astronomical, and engineering technology. (p. 440)

millet system A system used by the Ottomans whereby subjects were divided into religious communities, with each millet (nation) enjoying autonomous self-government under its religious leaders. (p. 489)

Mountain, the Led by Robespierre, the French National Convention's radical faction, which seized legislative power in 1793. (p. 627)

Napoleonic Code French civil code promulgated in 1804 that reasserted the 1789 principles of the equality of all male citizens before the law and the absolute security of wealth and private property, as well as restricting rights accorded to women by previous revolutionary laws. (p. 635)

National Assembly The first French revolutionary legislature, made up primarily of representatives of the third estate and a few from the nobility and clergy, in session from 1789 to 1791. (p. 621)

natural philosophy An early modern term for the study of the nature of the universe, its purpose, and how it functioned; it encompassed what we would call "science" today. (p. 504)

Navigation Acts A series of English laws that controlled the import of goods to Britain and British colonies. (p. 558)

New Christians A term for Jews and Muslims in the Iberian Peninsula who accepted Christianity; in many cases they included Christians whose families had converted centuries earlier. (p. 386)

patronage Financial support of writers and artists by cities, groups, and individuals, often to produce specific works or works in specific styles. (p. 358)

Peace of Utrecht A series of treaties, from 1713 to 1715, that ended the War of the Spanish Succession, ended French expansion in Europe, and marked the rise of the British Empire. (p. 476)

Peace of Westphalia The name of a series of treaties that concluded the Thirty Years' War in 1648 and marked the end of large-scale religious violence in Europe. (p. 466)

philosophes A group of French intellectuals who proclaimed that they were bringing the light of knowledge to their fellow humans in the Age of Enlightenment. (p. 517)

Pietism A Protestant revival movement in early-eighteenth-century Germany and Scandinavia that emphasized a warm and emotional religion, the priesthood of all believers, and the power of Christian rebirth in everyday affairs. (p. 597)

politiques Catholic and Protestant moderates who held that only a strong monarchy could save France from total collapse. (p. 419)

popolo Disenfranchised common people in Italian cities who resented their exclusion from power. (p. 359)

predestination The teaching that God has determined the salvation or damnation of individuals based on his will and purpose, not on their merit or works. (p. 410)

proletarianization The transformation of large numbers of small peasant farmers into landless rural wage earners. (p. 546)

Protectorate The English military dictatorship (1653–1658) established by Oliver Cromwell following the execution of Charles I. (p. 492)

Protestant The name originally given to followers of Luther, which came to mean all non-Catholic Western Christian groups. (p. 397)

Ptolemy's *Geography* A second-century-C.E. work that synthesized the classical knowledge of geography and introduced the concepts of longitude and latitude. Reintroduced to Europeans about 1410 by Arab scholars, its ideas allowed cartographers to create more accurate maps. (p. 433)

public sphere An idealized intellectual space that emerged in Europe during the Enlightenment, where the public came together to discuss important issues relating to society, economics, and politics. (p. 524)

Puritans Members of a sixteenth- and seventeenth-century reform movement within the Church of England that advocated purifying it of Roman Catholic elements, like bishops, elaborate ceremonials, and wedding rings. (p. 490)

putting-out system The eighteenth-century system of rural industry in which a merchant loaned raw materials to cottage workers, who processed them and returned the finished products to the merchant. (p. 549)

rationalism A secular, critical way of thinking in which nothing was to be accepted on faith, and everything was to be submitted to reason. (p. 516)

reading revolution The transition in Europe from a society where literacy consisted of patriarchal and communal reading of religious texts to a society where literacy was commonplace and reading material was broad and diverse. (p. 522)

Reign of Terror The period from 1793 to 1794 during which Robespierre's Committee of Public Safety tried and executed thousands suspected of treason and a new revolutionary culture was imposed. (p. 628)

Renaissance A French word meaning "rebirth," used to describe the rebirth of the culture of classical antiquity in Italy during the fourteenth to sixteenth centuries. (p. 358)

representative assemblies Deliberative meetings of lords and wealthy urban residents that flourished in many European countries between 1250 and 1450. (p. 338)

republicanism A form of government in which there is no monarch and power rests in the hands of the people as exercised through elected representatives. (p. 490)

rococo A popular style in Europe in the eighteenth century, known for its soft pastels, ornate interiors, sentimental portraits, and starry-eyed lovers protected by hovering cupids. (p. 524)

salon Regular social gathering held by talented and rich Parisians in their homes, where philosophes and their followers met to discuss literature, science, and philosophy. (p. 522)

sans-culottes The laboring poor of Paris, so called because the men wore trousers instead of the knee breeches of the aristocracy and middle class; the word came to refer to the militant radicals of the city. (p. 628)

second revolution From 1792 to 1795, the second phase of the French Revolution, during which the fall of the French monarchy introduced a rapid radicalization of politics. (p. 627)

signori Government by one-man rule in Italian cities such as Milan; also refers to these rulers. (p. 360)

Spanish Armada The fleet sent by Philip II of Spain in 1588 against England as a religious crusade against Protestantism. Weather and the English fleet defeated it. (p. 410)

stadholder The executive officer in each of the United Provinces of the Netherlands, a position often held by the princes of Orange. (p. 497)

Statute of Kilkenny Law issued in 1366 that discriminated against the Irish, forbidding marriage between the English and the Irish, requiring the use of the English language, and denying the Irish access to ecclesiastical offices. (p. 351)

sultan The ruler of the Ottoman Empire; he owned all the agricultural land of the empire and was served by an army and bureaucracy composed of highly trained slaves. (p. 489)

Test Act Legislation, passed by the English Parliament in 1673, to secure the position of the Anglican Church by stripping Puritans, Catholics, and other dissenters of the right to vote, preach, assemble, hold public office, and teach at or attend the universities. (p. 493)

Thermidorian reaction A reaction to the violence of the Reign of Terror in 1794, resulting in the execution of Robespierre and the loosening of economic controls. (p. 631)

Treaty of Paris The treaty that ended the Seven Years' War in Europe and the colonies in 1763, and ratified British victory on all colonial fronts. (p. 560)

Treaty of Tordesillas The 1494 agreement giving Spain everything to the west of an imaginary line drawn down the Atlantic and giving Portugal everything to the east. (p. 440)

Union of Utrecht The alliance of seven northern provinces (led by Holland) that declared its independence from Spain and formed the United Provinces of the Netherlands. (p. 420)

viceroyalties The name for the four administrative units of Spanish possessions in the Americas: New Spain, Peru, New Granada, and La Plata. (p. 445)

virtù The quality of being able to shape the world according to one's own will. (p. 363)

wet-nursing A widespread and flourishing business in the eighteenth century in which women were paid to breast-feed other women's babies. (p. 581)

A Note About the Index: Names of individuals appear in boldface. Letters in parentheses following page numbers refer to the following:

(d) documents
(b) boxed features
(i) illustrations, including photographs and artifacts
(m) maps
(f) figures, including charts and graphs

Abbeys. *See* Monasticism; Monks and monasteries
Abolition, of slavery, 564, 618
Absenteeism, clerical, 392
Absolute monarchy and absolutism, 462
    armies and, 468
    in Austria, 478–480
    England and, 490, 492–493
    enlightened, 529–536
    in France, 419, 470–476
    palaces and, 472–473*(d)*, 472*(i)*, 473*(i)*
    in Prussia, 480–482
    in Russia, 482–487
    in Spain, 469, 476–478
    state-building and, 466–468
Academies
    humanist, 365, 366
    Platonic, 363
    scientific, 515
Act of Union (1707), 520, 558
Adams, Abigail, "Remember the Ladies," 618*(d)*, 619
Adams, John, 615–616, 619
Administration. *See* Government
Adoration of the Magi, The (Signorelli), 383*(i)*
"Advice to Methodists" (Wesley), 599*(d)*
Advice to the Wives of Artisans (Christine de Pizan), 347*(d)*
Africa. *See also* North Africa
    Europeans and, 380, 456–457
    gold in, 429
    Jesuits in, 416
    Portugal and, 435
    slavery and, 379–380, 449–451, 476, 563–564
    trading states of, 429–430
African Americans, after American Revolution, 616
Africans. *See also* Africa; Slaves and slavery
    as American settlers, 448, 448*(i)*
    European ideas about, 456–457
    freed, 448, 453*(b)*
    in Saint-Domingue, 640
    as slaves, 379–380, 448, 449–451, 562–563
Afro-Eurasia, trade in, 428–432, 430*(m)*
Against the Murderous, Thieving Hordes of the Peasants (Luther), 400

Age, at marriage, 346–348, 576–577
Age of crisis, 17th century as, 464
Age of Discovery, 426, 427*(i)*
Age of exploration. *See* Age of Discovery; Exploration
Agincourt, battle at, 335
Agriculture. *See also* Farms and farming; Peasant(s)
    in 18th century, 542–549
    in Americas, 445
    Dutch, 543–544
    enclosure and, 543, 545–546, 545*(d)*
    in England, 544–546, 545*(d)*
    experimental scientists in, 543
    plague and, 330
    serfdom and, 479
    in Spain, 477
    after Thirty Years' War, 466
Akan peoples, gold from, 429
Alberti, Leon Battista, 364, 365
Albert of Mainz, 393
Albert of Wallenstein, 466
Alchemy, 506, 510
Alexander I (Russia), 636, 637–639
Alexander VI (Pope), 360, 369, 386, 440
Alexandria, trade in, 429
Algebra, 511
Alliance(s). *See also* specific alliances
    religious, 466
    Seven Years' War and, 530
Almanacs, 586
Alpacas, 449
Alsace, France and, 476
Alva, duke of, 419
Amendments, to U.S. Constitution, 617
American Enlightenment, 567–569
American Indians
    Christianity and, 567
    Columbus and, 439
    diet of, 449
    European unions with, 448
    French and, 444
    lifestyle of, 444*(d)*
    population loss by, 446, 447
    in Seven Years' War, 615
    U.S. Constitution and, 618
American Revolution, 520, 521, 586, 615–619
    Haitian independence and, 645
Americas. *See also* New World
    colonial settlement in, 445–449
    Columbian exchange and, 448–449
    converting indigenous people to Christianity in, 567
    Dutch and, 444, 456
    English colonies in, 495
    Enlightenment in, 521
    French exploration of, 475
    global contact and, 449–456
    gold in, 439
    Indians in, 439

    naming of, 440
    scientific knowledge and, 513–514
    silver from, 446, 469
    trade and, 426
Amiens
    revolt in, 469
    Treaty of, 636
Amsterdam, 544
Anabaptists, 400, 401*(b)(i)*
Anagni, papacy and, 340
Analytic geometry, 511
Anatolia. *See also* Turkey
    Ottomans and, 487
Andes region, 445–446
Anesthesia, in 18th century, 604
Anglican Church, 409. *See also* Church of England
Anglo-Dutch wars, 558
Anguissola, Sofonisba, 379*(i)*
Animals, in Columbian exchange, 449
Anjou, 384
Anne of Austria, 470
Anne of Brittany, 384
Anne of Denmark, 580
Anthropology, 524
Anticlericalism, 392
Antifederalists (U.S.), 617
Antigua, 564*(i)*
Anti-Semitism. *See also* Jews and Judaism
    Dutch religious toleration and, 497
    in Spain, 386, 387
Apothecaries, 601, 604
Apprentices, 577
Aquinas, Thomas, 340, 504
Aquitaine, 332, 333, 335, 338
Arabs and Arab world. *See also* Islam; Muslims
    learning in, 505
Arawak language, 439
Archbishop of Canterbury, 491
Archers, 333
Architecture, Renaissance, 373, 375, 377*(i)*
Aristocracy. *See also* Nobility
    in England, 384
    in later Middle Ages, 323*(i)*
    in Spain, 385, 477
    violence by, 350
Aristotle
    Phyllis and, 381*(i)*
    sciences and, 504
    on slavery, 457
    on universe, 504, 504*(i)*, 507, 508
Armada (Spain), 410, 410*(m)*
Armagnacs (France), 383–384
Armed forces. *See also* Military; Soldiers; specific battles and wars
    17th-century state-building and, 467
    English, 468, 492
    French, 384, 468, 475–476, 627–628, 630
    growth in 17th century, 468
    of Napoleon, 636–640

Armed forces (*continued*)
  Ottoman janissaries and, 489
  professionalization of, 468, 468(*i*)
  in Prussia, 481–482, 481(*i*)
  Russian, 483, 486, 533
Armor, 335(*i*)
Arouet, François Marie. *See* Voltaire
Art(s). *See also* Architecture; Literature; Paint-
    ing; specific arts and artists
  baroque, 498–499, 498(*i*)
  in France, 474
  in Reformation, 398–399(*b*), 398(*i*), 399(*i*)
  in Renaissance, 356, 368(*b*)(*i*), 373–379
  rococo style in, 524
  virtù in, 363
  women, 377–378, 379(*i*)
Arthur (England), 384, 407
Artillery. *See also* Weapons
  in Hundred Years' War, 333
Artisans. *See also* Labor; Workers
  division of labor and, 556(*d*)
  guilds and, 557
  sciences and, 515
Asceticism, 331, 416
Asia
  Dutch and, 569
  Jesuits in, 416
  Portugal and, 445
  sea routes to, 436
  trade and empire in, 569–571
Asiento, 558
Assemblies. *See also* Estates (assemblies);
    National assembly (France)
  representative, 338
Assignats (French paper currency), 625
Astell, Mary, 515
Astrolabe (instrument), 434, 434(*i*)
Astrology, 506
Astronomy, 505. *See also* Scientific revolution;
    Universe
  astrology and, 506
  cartography and, 434
  Hevelius and, 507
  Scientific Revolution and, 506
Atahualpa (Inca), 443
Athletics. *See* Sports
Atlantic Ocean region, 557–571
  economy in, 559(*m*), 560–561
  English colonies in, 443
  exploration in, 435–441
  Genoese exploration in, 431–432
  identities and communities of, 564–567
  Magellan in, 440
  powers of, 540
  slave trade in, 432, 562–567, 563(*i*)
Atom, Boye and, 513
Audiencia, 445
Augsburg, Peace of, 407, 466
Augsburg Confession, 406
Austerlitz, Battle of, 636
Australia, British settlement of, 570
Austria
  absolutism in, 472–473(*d*), 478–480
  Catholic church in, 597
  Enlightenment in, 529, 533–534
  France and, 619, 627, 636
  growth to 1748, 480(*m*)

Habsburgs and, 479–480, 530, 533
Jews in, 535
partition of Poland and, 532(*m*), 533
religious toleration in, 535, 597
in Seven Years' War, 614
state-building in, 479–480
Thirty Years' War and, 466
War of the Austrian Succession and, 530,
    530(*m*), 558
Austrian Netherlands, 627, 636. *See also*
    Belgium
Authority. *See* Power (authority)
Avignon, papacy in, 339–340, 339(*d*), 341
Azores, 435
Aztecs, 441, 445

Babylonian Captivity, of Catholic Church,
    339–340, 392
Bach, Johann Sebastian, 499
Bacon, Francis, 511, 515
Bahamas, 437
Bahía, 445
Balance of power
  in eastern Europe, 533
  in Italian Renaissance, 360–361
Ball, John, 345
Baltic region
  plague in, 326
  Russia and, 482, 485–486, 485(*i*)
  in Thirty Years' War, 466
Banking
  in Florence, 358, 359(*i*)
  in France, 617, 635
Bank of France, 635
Baptism
  adult, 400
  infant, 400
  of slaves, 567
Baptistery (Florence), doors of, 373
Baptists, 400
Bar (province), 384
Barbosa, Duarte, on Swahili city-states, 437(*d*)
Barometer, 506
Baroque period, arts of, 498–499, 498(*i*)
Basilicas, 376
Bastille (Paris), storming of, 623
Batavia (Jakarta), Java, 569
Batavian Republic, 636
Bath, England, 596
Bathhouses, 349(*i*)
Bathing, in 18th century, 596
Battles. *See* specific battles and wars
Bayle, Pierre, 516
Beattie, James, 525
Beaver trade, 440
Beccaria, Cesare, 521
Beijing (Peking), China, 429
Belarus (Belorussia), 536
Belgium, 627. *See also* Flanders; Low Coun-
    tries; Netherlands
  France and, 637
Benefices (offices), clerical, 392
Bengal, 570
Berlin
  Jewish community in, 534
  scientific academy in, 515
Bertin, Rose, 595(*b*)(*i*)

Beutelsbach, peasant beliefs in, 601
Bible. *See also* New Testament
  darkness, sin, and, 457
  in English, 340, 408
  Gutenberg, 373
  Protestants on, 397
  reading of, 586
Bill of Rights
  in England, 494–495, 617
  in United States, 617
Birth control, in 18th century, 578, 581
Births and birthrate
  in 18th century, 579
  illegitimacy and, 579
Bishop(s), Catholic Reformation and, 414
Black, skin color, slavery, and, 379–380, 457
Black Death, 325–332, 449. *See also* Plague
  effects of, 330–332
  labor after, 479
  population and, 547–548
  spread in Europe, 327(*m*)
  treatment of, 329–330
Black people. *See also* Africa; African Americans;
    Africans; Free blacks; Slaves and slavery
  in Moravian Church, 568–569(*b*)
  in Renaissance, 379–380
Black Prince. *See* Edward (Black Prince,
    England)
Black Sea region, Genoese trade and, 431, 432
Blockade(s), by Napoleon, 636
"Blood purity," 351
Blood sports, 587
Boats. *See* Ships and shipping
Boccaccio, Giovanni, 329, 330
Bogotá, 445
Bohemia
  anticlericalism in, 392
  Estates in, 479
  Habsburgs in, 479
  Hussites in, 341, 341(*m*)
  Reformation in, 413
  Wyclif's ideas in, 340–341
Bohemian phase, of Thirty Years' War, 466
Boleyn, Anne, 407, 408, 409
Bolivia, 446, 455(*i*)
Bologna
  Concordat of, 384, 417
  republic in, 359
Bonfires of the vanities, 361
Bonhomme, Jacques, 344
Book of Common Prayer, 409, 491
Book of Revelation, 322
Books. *See also* Literature
  Catholic control of, 567–569
  in Enlightenment, 522, 586
  French trade in, 522(*i*)
  printing and, 371–373
Bora, Katharina von, 402, 402(*i*)
Bordeaux, revolt in, 469
Borders, French-English North American, 614
Borgia family
  Cesare, 360, 369, 386
  Rodrigo (Pope Alexander VI), 369
Borodino, Battle of, 637–639
Boston Tea Party, 616
Botany, 506, 513
Botticelli, Sandro, 377, 378(*i*)

Boucher, François, 593(d)(i)
Bougainville, Louis-Antoine de, 528–529(d)
Bourbon dynasty (France), 469, 595(b)
Bourgeoisie, in France, 612
Boxing, 588(b)(i)
Boyars, 482
Boyle, Robert, and Boyle's law, 513
Boyne, Battle of the, 494
Boys. See also Children; Men
    Rousseau on education of, 583–584
Brahe, Tycho, 507
Brandenburg, 480
Brandenburg-Prussia, growth to 1748, 480(m)
Brazil
    Dutch and, 456
    Portugal and, 440, 456
    racial/ethnic characteristics of, 448, 567
    slavery in, 452, 562–563
    sugar in, 448, 449(i), 456
Bread
    in diet, 465, 466
    in France, 623, 628
    riots over, 466, 469
Breast-feeding
    in 18th century, 581
    in American colonies, 446
Brethren and Sisters of the Common Life, 343
Bridget of Sweden, 343
Briefe and True Report of the New Found Land
    of Virginia, A (Hariot), 444(d)
Britain. See England (Britain)
British East India Company, 569, 570, 616
British Empire. See also Colonies and
    colonization
    India and, 570(i)
    after Seven Years' War, 615
    shipping and, 558
British North America, 616. See also Colonies
    and colonization; North America
Brothels, 348, 349(i), 404. See also
    Prostitution
Brothers of the Christian Schools, 586
Brunelleschi, Filippo, 373, 375
Bruni, Leonardo, 363, 367
Brussels, 555(i)
Bubonic plague, 326, 465, 547–548. See also
    Black Death
Buckingham, duke of, 468
Buda, 413
Buenos Aires, 445
Buffon, Comte de, 524
Bullion, silver, 454
Bureaucracy
    17th-century state-building and, 467
    in Austria, 533
    in England, 408
    Ottoman, 489
    in Prussia, 530
Burgundians (France), 337, 383–384
Burgundy, 337, 384
    dukes of, 333
    Habsburgs and, 405
Burke, Edmund, 626
Byzantine Empire
    Ottomans and, 430–431, 431(i)
    plague in, 327–328
    Russia and, 486(i)

Cabinet system, in England, 495–496
Cabot, John, 440
Cabral, Pedro Alvares, 440
Cahokia, 446
Cairo, 429
Calais, 337
Calculus, 508, 517
Calendars, in France, 629, 632(b), 633(i)
Calicut, India, 429, 433, 435
Calvin, John, and Calvinism, 407, 410–413,
    413(i)
    in eastern Europe, 413
    France and, 413, 417–419, 471
    in Netherlands, 419–420
    religious art and, 398(i)
    Wesley and, 600
Cameralism, in Prussia, 530
Canada. See also New France
    Champlain in, 444
    European exploration of, 440
    France and, 475, 614–615
    Loyalists in, 616
    population of, 614–615
Canary Islands, 437, 448
Candide (Voltaire), 517
Cannon, in Hundred Years' War, 333, 336(i)
Canterbury Tales (Chaucer), 352, 352(i)
Cantons (Switzerland), religion in, 406
Cape of Good Hope, 435, 456
Capetian dynasty (France), 332
Capitalism, urban conflicts and, 346
Capitoline Hill (Rome), 376
Captaincies, in Portuguese colonial govern-
    ment, 445
Caravan trade, 429
Caravel, 433
Caribbean region. See also West Indies
    Dutch and, 456
    European exploration of, 440
    France and, 445, 615
    mixed-race children in, 567
    slaves in, 563
Carmelite nuns, 416
Carnival, 587
Cartesian dualism, 512
Cartier, Jacques, 440
Cartography, 433, 434, 506
Castas paintings, 566(i)
Castiglione, Baldassare, 365(i), 366–367
Casualties, from Black Death, 326, 327
Catalonia, 469, 478
Cateau-Cambrésis, Treaty of, 417, 418
Catechism of Health, The (Faust), 584(d)
Catherine de' Medici, 418, 419
Catherine of Aragon, 384, 407, 409
Catherine the Great (Russia), 530–533,
    531(i), 535–536, 617
Catholic Church. See also Catholic Reforma-
    tion; Christianity; Councils (Chris-
    tian); Counter-Reformation;
    Protestantism; Reformation
    in Austria, 479, 533
    Babylonian Captivity of, 339–340
    baroque arts and, 498
    in Britain, 493, 495
    Catholic League and, 466
    Charles V and, 405

colonial book publications and, 567–569
Copernican hypothesis and, 507
criticisms of, 340–343
divorce and, 403–404
in early 16th century, 392–393
education and, 585–586
in English New World colonies, 443
English Protestantism and, 407–409
in France, 417–419, 469, 470–471, 597,
    625, 636
Great Schism in, 340
hierarchy in, 596–597
in Holy Roman Empire, 597
in Hungary, 414
in Ireland, 491–492
in later Middle Ages, 338–343
in Netherlands, 419–420
piety in, 600
in Poland, 413
printing and, 373
reforms of, 340–343, 390
on religious arts, 398–399(b)
religious wars and, 417–420
schism in, 332
in southern Germany, 407
Thirty Years' War and, 466
Catholic Counter-Reformation. See Counter-
    Reformation
Catholic Enlightenment, 520
Catholic League, 466
Catholic Reformation, 413, 414–417
Caucasus region, 533
Cavendish, Margaret, 515
Cayenne, 445
Celestial Kingdom (China), 426
Celibacy
    in 18th century, 577
    Luther and Zwingli on, 402
Central Asia, plague in, 326
Central Europe, plague in, 327
Centralization, state-building and, 467–468,
    470
Ceuta, Morocco, 435
Ceylon, 456, 569
Champlain, Samuel de, 444
Chapbooks, 586
Charity
    foundlings and, 582
    schools, 585
Charivari (public rituals), 578
Charles I (England), 466, 468, 490, 491–492,
    494(i)
Charles II (England), 493–494, 558
Charles II (Spain), 455(i), 476
Charles III (Spain), 445
Charles IV (France), 332
Charles V (France), 340
Charles V (Holy Roman Empire, Spain), 361,
    387, 404–405, 406(i), 409, 419, 440,
    446, 452
    abdication by, 407
    empire of, 405, 405(m)
    Luther and, 395
    papacy and, 406–407
Charles VI (Austria), 530, 533
Charles VII (France), 335–336, 337, 383
Charles VIII (France), 360, 360(m)

Charles XI (Sweden), 472(d)
Charles XII (Sweden), 485
Charles the Bold (Burgundy), 384
Chaucer, Geoffrey, 352, 352(i)
Chaumont, Treaty of, 639
Chemistry, 513
Chess Game, The (Anguissola), 379(i)
Chichén Itzá, 446
Childbirth. *See also* Midwives
    in 18th century, 580–581, 602–603(d),
        602(i), 603(i), 604
Child care, in 18th century, 581
Children. *See also* Illegitimacy
    in 18th-century, 580–584
    in colonies, 448
    in domestic sphere, 554
    infanticide and, 581–582
    interracial, 448
    Rousseau on, 520
Chili peppers, 450(b)
China
    Columbus and, 439
    economy of, 429
    navigation technology from, 434
    plagues in, 326
    population of, 429
    trade and, 429, 455, 456
Chivalry, 333
Chocolate, 589(i)
Cholula, Mexico, 442
Christian III (Denmark), 407
Christian IV (Denmark), 466
Christian church. *See* Christianity; Protestant
        Reformation
Christian humanists, 369–371
Christianity. *See also* Church(es); Orthodox
        Church; Reformation; specific groups
    in American colonies, 446–447, 447(d)
    Aristotelian philosophy and, 504
    Columbus and, 436
    conversion to, 567
    in early 16th century, 392–393
    European voyages of discovery and, 432
    humanists and, 363
    plague and, 331–332
    Protestant revival and, 597–600
    racial ideas and, 457
    slaves and, 567
Christine de Pizan, 347(d), 381
Church(es). *See also* Religion
    in British North American colonies, 616
    Protestant, 397, 411–412
Church councils. *See* Councils
Church fathers. *See* Christianity
Church of England (Anglican Church), 409,
        490
    James II and, 494
    Puritans and, 490–491, 491(i)
    Wesley and, 598–599
Church of Scotland. *See* Presbyterians
Church of the Gesù, 417(i), 498
Cicero, Marcus Tullius, 363
Circumnavigation of earth, 440
Cities and towns. *See also* City-states; Urban
        areas; Villages
    in 18th century, 544
    in eastern Europe, 479

homosexual subcultures in, 580
infant mortality in, 581
as Italian republics, 359
leisure in, 587–589
plague and, 326–327
prostitution in, 348
in Thirty Years' War, 466
City-states
    of East Africa, 437(d)
    in Italian Renaissance, 360–361, 361(m)
Civic humanism, 367
Civil Code (France, 1804), 635
Civil Constitution of the Clergy (France), 625
Civil service. *See* Bureaucracy
Civil war(s)
    in England, 492
    Hundred Years' War as, 333
    in Netherlands, 420
Class. *See also* Hierarchy; Nobility; Orders
    18th-century revolutions and, 612
    French estates as, 620
Classical culture
    Christian humanism and, 370
    Renaissance and, 362
Classicism, French, 474
Clement VII (Pope), 340, 406(i), 407
Clergy. *See also* Friars; Monasticism; Monks
        and monasteries
    anticlericalism and, 392
    in Catholic Reformation, 414
    education and, 597
    in England, 409
    in France, 620, 625
    plague and, 329
    privileges of, 392
Climate
    in 14th century, 324–325
    in 17th century, 465, 547
    in 18th century, 542
Clive, Robert, 570
Cloth and cloth industry. *See also* Textile
        industry
    in later Middle Ages, 325
Clothier's Delight, The, 552–553(d)
Clothing. *See also* Cloth and cloth industry;
        Fashion; Textile industry
    for children, 583
    consumerism and, 594–595
    gender and, 594–596
    male, and masculinity, 382–383(b), 382(i),
        383(i)
    for prostitutes, 348
Clover, 542–543
Cloves, 432
Code Napoleon. *See* Civil Code (France)
Code Noir (Black Code), in Saint-Domingue,
        640
Codes of law. *See* Law codes
Coercive Acts (1774), 616
Coffeehouses, 524, 526–527(b), 526(i), 527(i)
Coins
    in Spain, 455(i)
    Venetian, 431
Colbert, Jean-Baptiste, 474–475, 476, 555,
        558
Colleges. *See also* Universities
    as elementary schools, 584–585

Colonies and colonization. *See also*
        Imperialism
    in Americas, 445–449
    British population characteristics, 567
    Christianity in, 446–447, 447(d)
    Columbian exchange and, 448–449
    disease in, 446
    Dutch, 456
    English, 440, 443–444, 445, 495,
        614–615
    English law and, 495
    Enlightenment in, 567–569
    French, 444–445, 476, 614–615
    imported consumables from, 591–592
    Jews in, 567
    lifestyle in Americas, 447–448
    mercantilism and, 558–560
    population loss in, 446, 447
    Portuguese, 445
    Spanish, 439, 445–447, 476
    trade in, 558
Columbian exchange, 445, 448–449, 450–
        451(b)(i), 543
Columbus, Christopher
    Europe and world after, 449–456
    exploration by, 428(i), 432, 435–440
    first voyage of, 436, 438–439(d), 439(m)
Commandments. *See* Ten Commandments
Commerce. *See also* Economy; Trade
    Dutch, 497
    in Hundred Years' War, 333
    in Renaissance Italy, 358–359
Commercialization, of sports, 588(b)(i)
Committee of Public Safety (France), 628,
        630–631
Common law, in England, 384
Common people. *See also* Lifestyle; Peasant(s)
    in 18th century, 586–592
    in Enlightenment, 524
    in France, 620, 625, 628
    popular culture of, 586–589
    in Russia, 486
Commons (England), 338, 545–546
Common Sense (Paine), 586–587, 616
Communes, in northern Italian cities,
        358–359
Community
    of Atlantic world, 564–567
    churches in, 596–597
Company of the East Indies (France), 475
Compass, 434
Conciliarists, 340–341
Concordat of Bologna, 384, 417
Concordat of 1801, 636
"Concordia," 403(d)(i)
Concubines, Ottoman, 488(b)(i), 489
Condoms, in 18th century, 578
Condottieri, 360
Conflicts. *See* Violence; Wars and warfare;
        specific battles and wars
Confraternities, 343
Congregationalists, 400
Connecticut, 443
Conquistadors, 433, 441, 445, 567
Conscription. *See* Draft (military)
Consistory (Geneva), 411
Constance, Council of (1414–1418), 341

Constantinople (Istanbul). *See also* Byzantine Empire
 Ottoman Turks in, 430–431, 431(i), 487, 488
Constitution, 489
 in England, 492
 in Haiti, 643
 in United States, 400, 617
Constitutional Charter (France), 639
Constitutional Convention (1787), 617, 618
Constitutionalism, 489–497
Constitutional monarchies, 462, 489–497
 in England, 462, 466–467, 490, 494–496
 in France, 624–627
 in Holland, 462, 466–467
Consumer goods. *See also* Goods and services
 in 18th century, 592–596, 594(i)
Consumer revolution, in 18th century, 586, 592–596, 594(i)
Consumers and consumerism
 consumer economy and, 554
 consumer society and, 592–596
 popular culture and, 586–596
Consumption, food, 590–592
Contagious disease. *See* Disease
Continental Congress, 616
Continental System, of Napoleon, 637
Contraception. *See* Birth control
Convents. *See also* Monasticism (Christian); Monks and monasteries; Nuns
 Protestant Reformation and, 404
 of Teresa of Ávila, 416
Conversion (Christian). *See also* Christianity
 of indigenous people, 567
 of Native Americans, 446, 447(d)
 of slaves, 567
 of Spanish Jews, 386–387
Conversos, 386–387
Conway, Anne, 515
Cook, James, 570
Copernican hypothesis, 506–507, 508
Copernicus, Nicolaus, 504, 506, 509
Corn (maize), 450(b), 451(i)
Coronation, of Napoleon, 634(i)
Corporations. *See* Guilds
Corregidores, 445
Cortes (Spanish parliament), 338
Cortés, Hernando, 433, 441–443
Cortés, Martín, 442(d)
Cosmology, of Aristotle, 504–505
Cossacks (Russia), 483, 533
Cottage industry, 549, 553
 in England, 550–553
 putting-out system in, 549
Cotton industry. *See also* Textile industry
 in India, 429
Coudray, Madame du, 602–603(d), 602(i), 604
"Council of Blood" (Netherlands), 419
Council of Elders (France), 631
Council of 500 (France), 631
Councils (Christian)
 of Constance (1414–1418), 341
 at Pisa (1409), 341
 of Trent, 398(b), 414–416
Councils (political). *See* Assemblies
Counter-Reformation, 413, 414–417

Coup d'état, by Napoleon I, 631
Court (households and palaces), in Italy, 360
Court (legal), in sovereign states, 468
Court (royal), in France, 463(i), 471–474
Courtesans, in 18th century, 580
Courtier, The (Castiglione), 366–367
Courtiers. *See* Nobility
Court of Star Chamber (England), 384
Cowrie shells, 570–571
Cradock, Fanny, 594
Cranach, Lucas
 the Elder, 395(i), 398, 402(i)
 the Younger, 398(i)
Cranmer, Thomas, 408, 409
Crécy, battle at, 333, 338
Creoles, 565
 in Saint-Domingue, 640
 society of, 567
Crime and criminals. *See also* Law(s)
 fur-collar, 350
 sexual, in later Middle Ages, 348–349
Crimean Tartars, in Russia, 533
Cromwell, Oliver, 492, 494(i), 558
Cromwell, Thomas, 408
Crops. *See also* Agriculture; Farms and farming
 in 18th century, 542–543
 in Columbian exchange, 445, 448–449, 450–451(b), 451(i)
 rotation of, 542, 543, 544
 vegetable, 589
Crossbow, 333
Cuba, 439, 441
Cugoana, Ottobah, 525
Cults, of the Supreme Being (France), 632(b), 632(i)
Cultural exchange. *See also* Columbian exchange
 in colonial missionary work, 446–447
Cultural relativism, 457
Culture(s). *See also* Art(s); Intellectual thought; Literature
 books and, 522
 coffeehouse, 526–527(b), 526(i), 527(i)
 curiosity about, 457–458
 in Enlightenment, 522–524, 523(d)(i)
 French, 474
 in French Revolution, 632–633(b), 632(i), 633(i)
 literacy and, 353
 of New World, 445
 plague impacts on, 331–332
Curia, papal, 392
Currency. *See also* Money
 cowrie shells as, 570–571
 in France, 625
Curriculum, humanist, 365
Cuzco, 443
Czech Republic. *See also* Bohemia
 anticlericalism in, 392
 Hus and, 340–341, 341(i), 341(m)
 Wyclif in, 340–341

Da Gama, Vasco, 433, 435
Daily life. *See* Lifestyle
D'Alembert, Jean le Rond, 519, 524, 525(i)
Dance of Death, 331(d)(i), 332
Dante Alighieri, 351–352

Danton, Georges Jacques, 627, 631
Dark ages, 363
Dauphin (France), 335
David (Michelangelo), 374(i)
David, Jacques-Louis, 621(i), 634(i)
Death, from famine, 325
Death rate. *See* Mortality
"Debate about women," 381
Debt
 in France, 619
 in Renaissance, 358
 Spanish, 454–455
Debt peonage, 562
Decameron, The (Boccaccio), 329–330
De-Christianization, in France, 629–630
Decimal system, in France, 629
Declaration of Independence (U.S.), 613, 616
Declaration of Pillnitz, 627
Declaration of the Rights of Man and of the Citizen, The (France), 612, 624(i), 626(d)
"Declaration of the Rights of Woman" (de Gouges), 625
Deductive reasoning, 512
Defensor Pacis (Marsiglio of Padua), 340
Defoe, Daniel, 552(d)
Dei, Benedetto, 358
Deism, 518–519, 567
Democracy, vs. representative government, 613
Demography. *See* Population
Denmark. *See also* Scandinavia
 Russia and, 485
 Thirty Years' War and, 466
Denmark-Norway, Protestantism in, 407
Depressions. *See* Economy
Desacralization, of French monarchy, 619
Descartes, René, 511
Descent from the Cross (Van der Weyden), 376(i)
Dessalines, Jean Jacques, 643, 644
D'Este, Isabella, 380
Determinism, of Spinoza, 517
Devil, in Christianity, 420, 421, 422
Dialogue on the Two Chief Systems of the World (Galileo), 509
"Diary of an English Villager," 493(d)
Diaz, Bartholomew, 433, 435
Dictators and dictatorship, in France, 631
Diderot, Denis, 519, 525, 525(i)
 Catherine the Great and, 531
 "Supplement to Bougainville's Voyage," 528–529(d)
Diego of Alcala (Saint), 451(i)
Diet (food)
 in 17th century, 465, 466
 in 18th century, 589–592
 bread in, 465, 466
 medieval famine and, 324–325
 of Native Americans, 449
Diet (political)
 in Germany, 338
 Imperial (1530), 406
 of Speyer (1529), 397
 of Worms (1521), 395
Dijon, revolt in, 469
Directory (France), 631

Discovery. *See* Age of Discovery; Expansion; Voyages
Discrimination, Jews and, 567
Disease
    in 18th century, 604–605, 605*(i)*
    in American colonies, 446, 476
    Black Death as, 325–332
    in Columbian exchange, 445, 449
    famine and, 325
    in New World, 443, 444*(d)*
    population and, 547
    swamp drainage and, 548
Divine Comedy (Dante), 351–352
Divine right of kings, 470, 490. *See also* Absolute monarchy and absolutism
Division of labor, Smith, Adam, on, 556*(d)*, 557
Divorce, Protestantism and, 403–404
Doctors. *See* Physicians
Domestic service, 577–578
Domestic sphere, 554
Dominican Republic, Taino people in, 439
Dominicans (religious order), 446
Donatello, 375
Draft (military)
    in France, 630
    in Prussia, 481–482
Drainage, Dutch and English, 544, 548
Drama
    French, 474
    by Shakespeare, 458
Drogheda, rebellion at, 492
Dualism
    Cartesian, 512
    legal for ethnic groups, 351
Du Châtelet, marquise, 518, 518*(i)*, 519*(d)*
Duchy, 332
Dürer, Albrecht, 376
Dutch. *See also* Dutch Republic; Holland; Netherlands
    American Revolution and, 617
    Asia and, 569
    England and, 558
    farming and, 543–544
    in Jakarta, 569
    New World and, 444
    slave trade and, 452
    Spain and, 478
    trade by, 456
    water management by, 544
Dutch East India Company, 456, 569
Dutch East Indies. *See* East Indies
Dutch Empire, 456
Dutch Republic. *See also* Dutch; Netherlands
    in 17th century, 543–544
    agriculture in, 543–544
    constitutionalism in, 462, 496–497
    France and, 628, 636
    French Huguenots in, 516
    government of, 496–497
    religious toleration in, 497
    rural industry in, 549
    tulipmania in, 497*(i)*
Dutch West India Company, 452, 456
Duties. *See* Tariffs
Dynasties. *See also* Hundred Years' War; specific dynasties
    Thirty Years' War and, 466

Earth. *See also* Astronomy; Universe
    Aristotle on, 504
    circumnavigation of, 440
East Africa
    slave trade and, 430
    Swahili city-states of, 437*(d)*
Eastern Christian Church. *See* Orthodox Church
Eastern Europe. *See also* Orthodox Church
    balance of power in, 533
    peasants in, 542
    plague in, 327
    Reformation in, 413–414
    serfdom in, 479
Eastern Orthodoxy. *See* Orthodox Church
East India Company
    British, 569, 570, 616
    Dutch, 456, 569
East Indies. *See also* Indonesia
    Dutch and, 456, 569
Eating. *See* Diet (food); Food
Eckhart (Meister), 342*(b)(i)*
Economic liberalism, 556–557
Economic regulation, 557, 558
Economy. *See also* Capitalism; Commerce; Trade
    in 17th century, 465–466
    in 18th century, 540, 542, 612
    in Atlantic region, 559*(m)*, 560–562
    of China, 429
    consumer, 554
    European expansion and, 432
    in Florence, 358
    in France, 474–475, 619, 624, 628, 631
    global, 449–456
    government regulation and, 557
    after Hundred Years' War, 338
    in Hundred Years' War, 333
    plague impacts on, 330–331
    population explosion and, 546–547
    in Prussia, 481
    of Saint-Domingue, 640
    Spanish, 454, 469, 476–477
    Thirty Years' War and, 466
Edict of Nantes, 419, 469, 471
Edict on Idle Institutions (Austria), 597
Edinburgh, Enlightenment in, 520
Education. *See also* Literacy; Schools; Universities
    in Enlightenment, 583–584
    humanist, 365–366
    of physicians, 601
    in Prussia, 585
    religion and, 585–586, 597
    in Russia, 486
    for women, 365
Education of a Christian Prince, The (Erasmus), 371
Edward (Black Prince, England), 333–335
Edward II (England), 325
Edward III (England), 332, 333, 338, 345*(d)*, 358
Edward IV (England), 384
Edward VI (England), 408*(i)*, 409
Egypt
    empire of, 429
    Ottoman Empire and, 429

    Suez Canal and, 560–561
    trade in, 429
Elba, Napoleon at, 639
Eleanor of Aquitaine, 332
"Elect," Calvinists and, 410
Electors, of Brandenburg, 480
Elementary schools, 584–586
Elements, Aristotle on, 505
Eleonore of Portugal, 404
Elisabeth-Charlotte (Germany), "Letter from Versailles," 475*(d)*
Elites. *See also* Aristocracy; Nobility
    18th-century revolutions and, 612
    colonial, 567
    consumer economy and, 596
    in Spain, 476
Elizabeth (Bohemia), 515
Elizabeth I (England), 408*(i)*, 409, 490
    gender and, 381
    literature under, 458
    religion and, 404, 411*(d)*
Emancipation
    of Jews, 535–536
    of slaves, 618
Emigration. *See* Immigrants and immigration; Migration
Emile, or On Education (Rousseau), 583–584
Emperor. *See* Holy Roman Empire; specific emperors
Empire(s). *See also* Colonies and colonization; Imperialism; specific empires
    in Africa, 429
    in Asia and Pacific region, 569–571
    natural history and, 513–514
    in New World, 441–443
    Ottoman, 430–431
    Persian, 430–431
    Portuguese, 435
    seaborne trade, 452*(m)*, 456
Empiricism, 511
Enclosure, 543, 545–546, 545*(d)*
Encomienda system, 446, 449
Encyclopedia (Diderot and d'Alembert), 519–520, 525*(i)*, 531
England (Britain). *See also* British East India Company; London; Parliament (England)
    absolutism and, 490, 492–493
    Act of Union with Scotland and Ireland, 520
    agriculture in, 543, 544–546, 545*(d)*
    American Revolution and, 615–617
    armed forces in, 468, 492
    Asia and, 569–570
    Bill of Rights in, 617
    cabinet system of government in, 495–496
    Catholic Church in, 493–494, 495
    civil war in, 492
    coffeehouse in, 526*(b)(i)*
    colonies of, 440, 445
    constitutional monarchy in, 462, 490, 494–496
    cottage industry in, 550–553
    Elizabeth on religion in, 411*(d)*
    enclosure in, 545–546
    expansion by, 443–444
    exploration by, 440

exports of manufactured goods by, 562(f)
famine in, 325
farming in, 590–591
France and, 384, 476, 558, 614–615, 628, 636
government of, 494–495
Hundred Years' War and, 332–338, 334(m)
imports and, 479
India and, 569–570, 570(i), 570(m)
infant mortality in, 581
Ireland and, 351, 494
Jews in, 492, 535
literacy in, 586
Methodism in, 598–600
Napoleon and, 636, 637
Native Americans and, 448
navy of, 468
peasants in, 345, 345(d), 346
plague in, 326, 327
population in, 546(f)
Protestantism in, 407–409, 490–494
Puritans in, 412
religious conversion of colonists by, 446
in Renaissance, 384
Restoration in, 493–494
Robin Hood in, 350
rural textile production in, 549
scientific societies in, 511, 515
Scotland and, 333
Seven Years' War and, 614, 615
slavery and, 452, 563, 564
smallpox in, 548
Spanish Armada and, 410, 410(m)
Statute of Laborers in, 345(d)
taxation in, 338
Thirty Years' War and, 466
trade of, 558
unemployment in, 546
United Provinces and, 420
white colonial population growth and, 567
English East India Company. See British East India Company
English language, 340, 408
English Peasants' Revolt (1381), 346
Enlightened absolutism, 529–536
Enlightenment, 502, 516–529
    18th-century revolutions and, 612
    in Austria, 529, 533–534
    children and, 520, 580–581, 583–584
    coffeehouses in, 524, 526–527(b), 526(i) 527(i)
    colonial, 567–569
    culture in, 522–524, 523(d)(i)
    in Dutch Republic, 516–517
    English, 517
    in France, 517–520
    German, 517
    international, 520–521
    in Italy, 521
    Jews in, 533–536
    philosophes in, 517–520
    in Prussia, 518, 520, 521, 529, 530
    race and, 524–529
    in Russia, 529, 530–533
    science in, 502, 503(i)
    in Scotland, 520–521, 567

urban culture and, 522–524
    workers and, 586
Enslaved peoples. See Slaves and slavery
Entertainment, literature as, 586
Entrepreneurs, in 18th century, 595(b)
Epidemics. See also Disease
    Columbian exchange and, 449
    population and, 547, 549
Equality. See also Rights; Women
    18th-century demands for, 612–614
    in British North American colonies, 616
    in United States, 617–618
Equiano, Olaudah, 525, 565(d)
Erasmus, Desiderius, 371, 390
Erie, Lake, 444
Essay Concerning Human Understanding (Locke), 517
Essays (Montaigne), 457
Established church, 616
Estates (assemblies)
    in Bohemia, 479
    in Brandenburg and Prussia, 480, 481
    Dutch, 496–497
    of Normandy, 466
Estates (classes), in France, 620–621, 620(i)
Estates (land), in Americas, 446
Estates General (France), 470, 620
Estonia
    Russia and, 486
    serfs in, 464(i)
Ethiopia
    Europeans and, 456
    trade and, 429
Ethnic groups. See also specific groups
    in Middle Ages, 350–351
    mixing of, 567
Etiquette, in court of Louis XIV, 474
Eugene of Savoy, palace of, 472(d)(i)
Eunuchs, Ottoman, 489
Europe
    in 18th century, 541(i)
    American colonies of, 441–449
    Black Death in, 325–332
    Columbian exchange and, 450–451(b)
    after Columbus, 449–456
    expansion of, 432–445, 436(m), 540–571
    exploration and conquest by, 426
    French Revolution and, 626–627
    India and, 614(m)
    industrious revolution in, 553–554
    industry and population in 18th century, 550(m)
    Jesuits in, 416–417
    Jews in, 533–536
    North American claims of, 614(m)
    after Peace of Utrecht, 477(m)
    politics in 1530s and 1540s, 406–407
    printing and, 371–373, 372(m)
    racism and, 524–525
    religious divisions of (ca. 1555), 415(m)
    representative assemblies in, 338
    after Thirty Years' War, 467(m)
    trade in, 431–432
    unions with indigenous peoples and, 448
    voyages of discovery by, 432–445
Évora, black people in, 379
Excommunication, of Luther, 395

Expansion. See also Exploration; Imperialism
    age of, 574–605
    English, 443–444
    European, 432–445, 436(m), 540–570
    French, 332, 384(m), 444, 476, 476(m), 636, 637–640
    Ottoman, 430–431
    of Russia, 483–487, 483(m), 533
Expeditions, scientific, 513–514
Experimental method, 508, 512–513, 515
Experimentation
    medical, 601–604
    in Scientific Revolution, 506, 511
Exploration
    in Atlantic Ocean region, 435–441
    by Columbus, 435–440
    by England, 440
    Enlightenment and, 516
    European, 426
    by France, 440, 444–445, 475
    Genoese, 431–432
    overseas, 436(m)
    by Portugal, 431–432, 435
    reasons for, 432–433
    by Spain, 431–432
    technology and, 433–434
    by Vespucci, 440
Exports. See also Trade
    English, 562(f)

Fairy tales, 586
Faith. See also Religion(s)
    salvation by, 393, 397
Faith healing, 601
Families. See also Marriage
    in 17th century, 464
    in 18th century, 576–577
    in cottage industry, 551
    in guilds, 555–556
    mercantile, 358
    nuclear, 576–577
    Protestant, 403(d)(i)
Famine
    in 17th century, 465
    in later Middle Ages, 324–325, 324(i)
    population and, 547
Far East. See Asia
Farms and farming. See also Agriculture; Peasant(s)
    Dutch, 543–544
    foods and, 590–591
    open-field system and, 542
Farnese, Alexander (Cardinal). See Paul III (Pope)
Fashion
    consumerism and, 592–594
    merchants of, 593(d)(i), 594
Fashion Merchant, The (Boucher), 593(d)(i)
Fathers. See Families
Faust, Bernhard Christoph, Catechism of Health for the Use of Schools and for Domestic Instruction, The (Faust), 584(d)
Feast days, 600
Fedele, Cassandra, on humanist learning, 364(d)
Federalists (U.S.), 617

Ferdinand I (Holy Roman Empire), 407
Ferdinand II (Holy Roman Empire), 479
Ferdinand III (Holy Roman Empire), 479
Ferdinand and Isabella (Spain), 384, 385(m), 387, 447
    Columbus and, 436, 438(d)
    Holy Roman Empire and, 405
    on Indians, 447
Ferrara, as city-state, 360
Feudalism, Hundred Years' War and, 333
Ficino, Marsilio, 363, 370
Finance(s)
    in France, 474–475
    of Hundred Years' War, 338
First Coalition, 627, 630
First Continental Congress (1774), 616
First estate (France), clergy as, 620
Fish and fishing industry, in Canada, 440–441
Flagellants, 330(i), 331–332
Flanders. See also Holland; Low Countries
    agriculture in, 543
    France and, 476
    peasant revolt in, 344
    rural industry in, 549
Flemish language and people. See Flanders
Florence
    arts in, 373
    banks in, 358, 359(i)
    as city-state, 360
    economy in, 358
    Machiavelli in, 367–369
    republic in, 359
    same-sex relations in, 348–349
    Savonarola in, 360–361, 362(d)
Florentine Codex, 447(d)
Florida, 615
Flying shuttle, 550
Food. See also Agriculture; Diet (food); Grain; Spice trade
    in 18th century, 589–592
    of Columbian exchange, 448–449, 450–451(b)(i)
    imports of, 591–592
    for livestock, 542
    medieval famine and, 324–325
    population growth and, 546
    riots over, 466, 469
Football, 588(b)
Forced labor. See also Slaves and slavery
    in American colonies, 446
Foreign policy
    of England, 384
    in France, 470, 475–476
Foundations of Physics (du Châtelet), 518, 519(d)
Foundlings, 581–582
"Four Horsemen of the Apocalypse," 322
France. See also French Revolution; Napoleon I (Napoleon Bonaparte); Paris
    absolutism in, 419, 470–476
    Alsace and, 476
    American Revolution and, 616–617
    armed forces in, 468, 475–476
    Austria and, 619
    book trade in, 522(i)
    Calvinism and, 413, 417–419

Catholic Church in, 417–419, 469, 470–471, 597, 625, 636
    charity schools in, 585–586
    clergy in, 620, 625
    colonial trade and, 562
    Constitutional Charter in, 639
    constitutional monarchy in, 624–627
    de-Christianization in, 629–630
    economy in, 474–475, 619, 624, 631
    England and, 384, 558, 614–615
    enlightened absolutism and, 529–530
    estates in, 620–621, 620(i)
    expansion by, 332, 384(m), 444, 476, 476(m)
    exploration by, 440, 444–445
    female succession in, 332–333
    government of, 470
    during Great Schism, 340
    guild system in, 555, 557
    Habsburgs, Burgundy, and, 405
    Huguenots in, 412, 418–419
    Hundred Years' War and, 332–338, 334(m)
    India and, 570
    infant mortality in, 581
    intermarriage in colonies, 448
    Italy invaded by, 360
    Jacquerie uprising in, 344
    Jesuits in, 597
    Jews in, 536
    literacy in, 586, 587(m)
    monarchy in, 418, 619–622, 624, 626, 627
    nobility in, 470, 471, 620, 623–624, 635–636
    peasants in, 344, 623–624
    plague in, 326
    Protestantism in, 417–419, 469, 470–471, 597
    Prussia and, 619
    religion and, 391(i), 417–419, 446, 469, 470, 471, 625–626, 629–630
    in Renaissance, 383–384
    representative government in, 338
    republic in, 627
    revolutionary era in, 610
    royal court in, 463(i)
    Seven Years' War and, 562, 615
    Spain and, 476, 478
    Thirty Years' War and, 466
    urban uprisings and, 469
    voting in, 621
    wars under Louis XIV, 475–476
    weights and measures in, 629, 632(b)
    West Indies and, 445
    wet-nursing in, 581
    women in, 624–625, 628–629, 629(d)(i), 636
Franche-Comté, 476
Francis I (France), 384, 417
Francis II (Austria), 627
Franciscans, 446
Franklin, Benjamin, 521, 567, 617
Frederick I (Prussia), 481
Frederick II (Holy Roman Empire), 392
Frederick II the Great (Prussia), 530, 533
    Enlightenment and, 518, 530
    Jews and, 535

War of the Austrian Succession and, 530, 530(m), 558
Frederick III ("the Ostentatious") (Elector of Brandenburg). See Frederick I (Prussia)
Frederick III (Holy Roman Empire), 404
Frederick William (Great Elector, Brandenburg), 480–481
Frederick William I (the "Soldiers' King") (Prussia), 481–482
Free blacks, in colonies, 448
Freedom(s)
    18th-century revolutions and, 612
    in France, 636
    Rousseau and, 520
Freemasons, 524
Free people of color
    in 18th-century, 567
    in Saint-Domingue, 640, 641, 642, 643
Free trade, 558
French and Indian War. See Seven Years' War
French language, 474
French phase, of Thirty Years' War, 466
French Revolution, 520, 619–625. See also Guillotine (France)
    American Revolution and, 619
    background to, 619
    de-Christianization in, 629–630
    insurrections during, 628(m)
    international reactions to, 626–627
    Jews and, 536, 626
    lifestyle during, 611(i)
    peasants in, 623–624, 628
    radicalism in, 618, 621(d), 624, 627–633
    Saint-Domingue and, 640
    second revolution in, 627–628
    Thermidorian Reaction in, 630–631
    total war and Reign of Terror in, 628–629
    women in, 624–625, 626–627
Freundlich, Matthaus, 568(b)
Friars, Luther as, 393
Frobisher, Martin, 440
Fronde (France), 470
Fruit, in diet, 589
Fur-collar crime, 350
Fur trade, in Canada, 440

Galen (physician), 512
Galilei, Galileo, 508–509, 510(i)
    Sidereal Messenger and, 508, 509(d)
Gallican Church, 597
Gambling, 588
Garden of Love (Rubens), 498(i)
Gattinara (chancellor), 405
Gays. See Homosexuality
Gender and gender issues. See also Men; Sex and sexuality; Voting and voting rights; Women
    consumerism and, 594–596
    education and, 583–584
    of foundlings, 582
    in marriage, 402–404
    Rousseau on, 520
    same-sex relations and, 348–350, 350(i)
    in social hierarchy, 381–383
    in urban workplace, 346
General History of the Things of New Spain (Florentine Codex), 447

General will, 520
Geneva, Calvin and, 410, 411
Genius, 368, 377
Genoa
    plague in, 326
    republic in, 359
    trade and, 358, 431–432
Geoffrin, Marie-Thérèse, salon of, 523(d)(i)
Geography, Kant on, 524
Geography (Ptolemy), 433–434, 434(i), 437, 506, 513
Geometry
    Descartes and, 511
    Kepler and, 508
George I (England), 496
George II (England), 496
George III (England), 616
German Confederation of the Rhine (1806), 636, 636(m)
German language, 400
    in Austria, 479
German Peasants' War (1525), 402
German people, account of Russian life by, 484–485(d)
Germany. *See also* Holy Roman Empire
    Catholic Church in, 407
    diet (political) in, 338
    Estonia and, 464(i)
    France and, 627
    guilds in, 556
    Hohenzollerns in, 480
    Luther and Lutheranism in, 393–395, 407
    Napoleon and, 637
    peasant rebellion in, 400–402
    plague in, 326
    Protestantism in, 399, 404–407, 597–598
    public administration in, 530
    radical Reformation in, 400
    religious war in, 405–407
    serfdom and, 479
    territory to France, 636
    Thirty Years' War and, 466
Gerritz, Decker Cornelis, 551(i)
Gesù, Church of, 498
Ghettos, for Jews, 535
Ghiberti, Lorenzo, 373
Gibbon, Edward, 582
Gibraltar, England and, 476
Gillray, James, 605(i)
Giotto, 375
Girls. *See also* Children; Women
    in consumer economy, 554
    Rousseau on education of, 583–584
Girondists, 627, 628
Global economy. *See also* Economy
    in Atlantic world, 557–567
    after Columbus, 449–456
    goods from, 455(i)
    silver trade and, 455
Glorious Revolution (England, 1688–1689), 494, 495
Goa, 435, 455
Gold
    in Africa, 429
    in Americas, 439
    balance of trade and, 558
    trade and, 430, 435

Golden age, in Netherlands, 496
Goods and services. *See also* Consumer goods
    consumption of, 592–596
    global economy and, 455(i)
Gouges, Olympe de, 624–625, 628
Government. *See also* Absolute monarchy and
        absolutism; Constitutional monarchies;
        Law(s)
    in 17th century, 464, 466–468
    by 18th century, 469
    of American colonies, 445
    of Austria, 479, 530, 533
    of Bohemia, 479
    clergy and, 392
    constitutional, 489–497
    economic regulation by, 557, 558
    in England, 462, 466–467, 490, 494–495
    enlightened absolutism and, 529–536
    in France, 470–471, 624–631, 634–640
    Hundred Years' War and, 338
    in Italian republics, 359–360
    Machiavelli on, 367–369
    Montesquieu on, 517–518
    Occam on, 340
    in Ottoman Empire, 489
    popular, 612–613
    printing and, 373
    in Prussia, 530
    by Puritans in England, 492–493
    representative, 338
    in Russia, 486, 533
    in United States, 617–619
    urban uprisings and, 469
    women and, 381
Goya, Francisco, 639(i)
Gozzoli, Bennozzo, 375(i)
Grain
    in 18th century, 542
    medieval speculation in, 325
Granada, 432
    Spanish conquest of, 385(m), 387, 436
Grand Alliance, against Louis XIV, 476
Grand Duchy of Lithuania, 413
Grand Duchy of Tuscany, 360
Grand Empire (Napoleon), 637–640, 638(m)
Gravitation, 510–511
Great Britain (England). *See also* England
        (Britain)
    formation of, 558
"Great Chain of Being," 464
Great Elector. *See* Frederick William (Great
        Elector, Brandenburg)
Great Famine, in northern Europe, 324
Great Fear (France), 623, 623(m)
Great Fire of London (1666), 560(b), 560(i),
        561(i)
Great Lakes, France and, 444
Great Northern War, 486
Great Powers
    Prussia as, 530
    Russia as, 483
Great Schism, in Catholic Church, 340, 341,
        392
Greece, Renaissance culture and, 363
Greek language, scholarship and, 506
Greek Orthodox Church. *See* Orthodox
        Church

Greenland, 324
Gregory XI (Pope), 339–340
Grenadiers, in Prussia, 481(i)
Grumbach, Argula von, 404
Guadeloupe, 445, 562
Guanajuato, 454
Guilds
    urban, 346
    women in, 556, 577
Guild system, 555–556, 557
    in Brussels, 555(i)
    Enlightenment ideals and, 556–557
    urban, 346, 554–557
Guillotine (France), 627, 629, 630(i), 631
Guinea, Portugal and, 435
Gulf of Mexico, 441, 444
Gunpowder, 434
Guns. *See* Weapons
Gustavus Adolphus (Sweden), 466, 470
Gustavus Vasa (Sweden), 407
Gutenberg, Johann, 371–373, 371(i)
Guzmán, Gaspar de. *See* Olivares, count-duke
        of (Gaspar de Guzmán)

Habsburg dynasty, 404–405
    in Austria, 479–480, 530, 533, 614
    Bohemian Protestantism and, 413
    Catholicism of, 597
    France and, 470
    in Hungary, 413, 414
    Ottomans and, 479
    in Thirty Years' War, 466
Habsburg-Valois wars, 361, 406, 417
Haciendas, 446
Haiti, 562. *See also* L'Ouverture, Toussaint;
        Saint-Domingue
    independence of, 643–645, 643(m)
    revolution in (1791–1804), 640–645
    Taino people in, 439
Hall of Mirrors (Versailles), 472(d)
Hancock, John, 616
Handloom weaving, 551
Hangzhou, 428–429, 439
Hanover, house of (England), 496
Harem, 488(b)
Hariot, Thomas, on Roanoke colony,
        444(d)
Harvey, William, 513
Haskalah (Jewish movement), 535
Hawaii, 570
Health. *See* Disease; Medicine
Heliocentric theory, 504, 506, 508–509
Henry ("the Navigator," Portugal), 433,
        435
Henry II (England), 332
Henry II (France), 418
Henry III (England), 332
Henry III (France), 419
Henry IV (England), 384
Henry IV (France), 418, 469–470
Henry V (England), 335
Henry VI (England), 384
Henry VII (England), 384
Henry VIII (England), 384, 401(b), 407–409,
        408(i), 490
Heresy, Inquisition and, 414
Hevelius, Johannes and **Elisabetha,** 507(i)

Hierarchy. *See also* Class
    in 17th-century society, 464
    in 18th-century churches, 596–597
    racial, 524, 525, 529
    in Renaissance society, 379–383
    of wealth, 380
Higher education. *See* Education; Schools;
        Universities
Highways. *See* Roads and highways
Hispania. *See* Iberian peninsula
Hispaniola, 439, 445, 640
Historical and Critical Dictionary (Bayle), 516
History, division of, 363
History of the Two Indies (Raynal), 525
Hobbes, Thomas, 492
Hogarth, William, 598*(i)*
Hohenzollern dynasty, 480
Holidays, Catholic celebration of, 600
Holland. *See also* Low Countries; Netherlands
    agriculture in, 544
    Brethren and Sisters of the Common Life
        in, 343
    in Dutch Republic, 497
    in Union of Utrecht, 420, 420*(m)*
Holy Office, 414, 509
Holy Roman Empire. *See also* Germany;
        Habsburg dynasty
    Catholic Church in, 597
    under Charles V, 405, 405*(m)*
    city-states in, 496
    Italy and, 361
    plague in, 327
    Protestantism in, 400
    Prussian electors and, 480
    Spain and, 476
    Thirty Years' War and, 466
Homosexuality. *See also* Same-sex relationships
    in 18th century, 580
    in Middle Ages, 348–350, 350*(i)*
Hormuz, 435
Horses
    in Americas, 449
    for plowing, 545
    Portuguese trade in, 455
    racing, 588*(b)*
Hospitals
    in 18th century, 604
    foundling, 582
Households
    as courts in Italy, 360
    lifestyle in, 596
    after marriage, 576
    wage workers in, 554
House of Commons (England), 490–491, 496
House of Orange, 494, 497
House of Representatives (U.S.), 618
House of Trade (Spain), 445
Housing, in 18th century, 596
Hudson Bay region, 476, 558
Huguenots (France), 412, 418–419, 471, 516.
        See also Protestantism
Human body, 512. *See also* Medicine
Humanism, 362–365
    Christian, 369–371
    education and, 365–367
    Fedele on, 364*(d)*
    in Renaissance, 362–365

Hume, David, 520–521, 524
Hundred Days, of Napoleon, 640
Hundred Years' War, 332–338, 334*(m)*
Hungary. *See also* Magyars
    Austrian Empire and, 479–480
    division of, 413
    Habsburgs in, 413
    Ottomans and, 406, 413, 479
    Reformation in, 413
Hunting, for meat, 589
Huron Confederacy, 444
Hürrem (Ottomans), 488*(b)(i)*, 489
Hus, Jan, 341, 341*(i)*, 413
Hussites, 341, 341*(m)*, 413
Hygiene, in 18th century, 596

Iberian Peninsula. *See also* Portugal; Recon-
        quista; Spain
    black people in, 379–380
    Catholic control of books in, 567
    unification of, 387
Ice age, little ice age and, 324
Iceland, Protestantism in, 407
Iconoclasm, 418, 419*(i)*
Identity, in Atlantic world, 564–567
Ideologies, uniformity of, 516
Ignatius. *See* Loyola, Ignatius
Illegitimacy
    in 18th century, 576*(i)*, 578–580
    foundlings and, 582
    increase of, 579
Illness. *See* Disease; Medicine
Illumination (illustrations), 373
Illustration, scientific, 515, 515*(i)*
Images, Catholic Church on, 398–399*(b)*
Imitation of Christ, The (Thomas à Kempis),
        343
Immigrants and immigration. *See also*
        Migration
    ethnic tensions and, 351
Imperial Diet (Augsburg, 1530), 406
Imperialism. *See also* Empire(s)
    French, 637–639
    Russian, 483
    Shakespeare's plays and, 458
Imports
    colonial, 561
    food, 591–592
Inca Empire, 443, 445, 446
Independence
    Dutch, 456
    of Haiti, 643–645, 643*(m)*
    of United States, 616–617
Index of Prohibited Books, 414
India
    in 1805, 570*(m)*
    Anglo-French conflicts in, 558
    Britain and, 569–570, 570*(i)*, 617
    European claims in, 614*(m)*
    France and, 570
    plague in (1890s), 326
    trade and, 429
India House (Portugal), 445
Indian Ocean region, trade and, 428–429,
        435, 437*(d)*, 562
Indians. *See also* American Indians
    origin of term, 439

Indies, search for water route to, 435
Indonesia, 456. *See also* East Indies
Inductive reasoning, 512
Indulgences, 393–395, 394*(i)*
Industrial Revolution, 561
"Industrious revolution," 553–554
Industry. *See also* Cottage industry
    in 18th-century Europe, 550*(m)*
    rural, 549–554, 552–553*(d)*
Inertia, law of, 508
Infant baptism, 400
Infanticide, in 18th century, 581–582
Infant mortality. *See also* Childbirth; Midwives
    in 18th century, 580, 581, 602–603*(d)*
    in American colonies, 446
    breast-feeding and, 581
    in foundling homes, 581
Infantry. *See* Military
Infectious disease. *See* Disease
Inflation
    18th-century revolutions and, 612
    from Black Death, 330
    in Spain, 454, 476
Infrastructure, in France, 469
Inheritance, in Russia, 487
Inoculation, against smallpox, 548, 604–605,
        605*(i)*
*Inquiry into the Nature and Causes of the Wealth
        of Nations* (Smith), 521, 556*(d)*
Inquisition, 414
    Galileo and, 509
    Spain and, 387
    witchcraft trials and, 420
Institutes of the Christian Religion, The (Calvin),
        410
Instrument of Government (England), 492
Integral calculus, 508
Intellectual thought. *See also* Art(s); Culture(s);
        Enlightenment; Ideologies; Industrial
        Revolution; Literature; Philosophy;
        Religion(s); Renaissance
    in Enlightenment, 502, 516–529
    Islamic, 505
    in Renaissance, 362–373
    Scientific Revolution and, 504–515,
        511–515
    women in, 515
Intendants, in France, 470
Intendant system (Spanish royal officials),
        445
Intermarriage
    in colonies, 448
    prohibition of, 351
International agreements. *See* Alliance(s)
International trade. *See* Trade
Interracial relationships. *See also* Mixed races
    children and, 448
    marriage and, 567
Invasions. *See also* Migration
    by France of Italy, 360
Inventions. *See also* Industrial Revolution;
        Technology
    by Leonardo da Vinci, 368–369*(b)*
Iran. *See* Persia; Persian Empire
Ireland
    Catholicism vs. Protestantism in, 409
    England and, 351, 492, 494

legal pluralism and, 351
linen industry in, 554(i)
Isabella (Castile), 385. *See also* Ferdinand and
Isabella (Spain)
Isabella (France), 332
Isabella d'Este, 380
Islam. *See also* Arabs and Arab world; Muslims
plague in, 327
Istanbul. *See* Constantinople (Istanbul)
Italy. *See also* Rome
agriculture in, 542
Austria and, 636
benefices in, 392
city-states in, 360–361, 361(m), 496
coffeehouse in, 526(b)
communes in, 358–359
Enlightenment in, 521
female academics in, 515
Inquisition in, 421
Napoleon and, 636, 637
plague in, 326
Renaissance in, 358–369, 373–379
republics in, 358–360
slave trade and, 432
unification of, 361
Ivan III the Great (Russia), 482
Ivan IV the Terrible (Russia), 482–483

Jacobin Club (France), 627, 628–629
Jacobites (England), 494
Jacquerie uprising, 344
Jakarta, 569
James I (England), 458, 468, 490, 491, 580,
596
James II (England), 494
James V (Scotland), 412
Jamestown, 443
Janissary corps, Ottoman, 488(b), 489
Jansen, Cornelius, 600
Jansenism, 600
Jansz, Anna (Rotterdam), 401(b)(i)
Japan, Portugal and, 427(i), 455
Java, 569
Jefferson, Thomas, 521, 525, 567, 613, 616,
645
Jena, battle at, 636
Jenner, Edward, 605, 605(i)
Jesuit Priest Distributing Holy Pictures, 399(i)
Jesuits, 416, 417(i), 446
Catholicism extended by, 597
schools run by, 585
Jews and Judaism. *See also* Anti-Semitism
in Austria, 535
in colonies, 567
in England, 492
Enlightenment and, 533–536
in France, 625, 626(d)
Mendelssohn family and, 534–535(b),
534(i), 535
moneylending and, 325
New Christians and, 386–387
in Pale of Settlement, 535(m), 536
religious toleration and, 535
in Russia, 535–536
as scapegoats for plague, 332
in Spain, 385(m), 386–387
Spinoza and, 516–517

Joanna of Castile, 387
Joan of Arc (France), 335–337, 337(d)
John VI Kantakouzenos (Byzantine Empire),
328, 330–331
John of Spoleto, 340
Joliet, Louis, 475
Jonson, Ben, on death of son, 582
Joseph II (Austria), 533
Jews and, 535
religion and, 597, 601
Josephine (France), 634
Josselin, Ralph, 493(d)
Journeymen's guilds, 556
Judaism. *See* Jews and Judaism
Judiciary and judicial system. *See* Law(s)
Julius II (Pope), 373, 376
Junkers, 480–481
Jupiter (planet), Galileo and, 508
Justification by faith alone, Luther on, 393
Just price, 589

Kant, Immanuel, 521, 524
Kay, John, 550
Kepler, Johannes, 507–509
Khan. *See* China; Mongols
Kilwa, 429
Kingdom of Naples, 360, 521
Kings and kingdoms. *See also* Monarchs and
monarchies; specific locations
ban on French female succession and,
332–333
in France, 418, 619–622, 624, 626, 627
Naples as, 360
in Prussia, 481
Knights. *See also* Nobility
armor of, 335(i)
crime by, 350
in Hundred Years' War, 338
Knowledge. *See* Intellectual thought
Knox, John, 412–413

Labor. *See also* Forced labor; Gender; Serfs
and serfdom; Slaves and slavery;
Workers
in 17th century, 465
in 18th century, 577
Black Death and, 479
industrious revolution and, 553
in putting-out system, 549
slaves as, 380
Lafayette, marquis de, 616, 619, 624
Lake Erie, 444
Lancaster, house of, 384
Land. *See also* Agriculture
in 17th century, 465
in 18th century, 542–549
after American Revolution, 617
Jews and, 325
peasant ownership of, 542
in Portuguese colonies, 445
Landlords
in 18th century, 542
in Russia, 482
Landowners
in 17th century, 465
in 18th century, 543
Langport, battle at, 492

Language(s)
French, 474
German, 400, 479
Languedoc, houses of prostitution in, 348
La Plata, 445
La Rochelle, siege of, 470
La Salle, Jean-Baptiste de, 586
La Salle, René-Robert Cavelier, 444
Las Casas, Bartolomé de, 446
Last Judgment (Michelangelo), 374, 377
Last Supper, The (Leonardo da Vinci), 368
Lateen sail, 433
Later Middle Ages, 322, 323(i). *See also*
Middle Ages
Black Death and society during, 325–332
Catholic Church in, 338–343
climate change and famine in, 324–325,
324(i)
Hundred Years' War during, 332–338
revolts in, 343–346, 344(m)
society in, 330–332, 338, 343–353
women in, 346–348
Latin America. *See also* South America
Haitian independence and, 644
trade in, 561
Latin Christianity. *See* Catholic Church;
Christianity
Latin language, Renaissance and, 362–363
Latitude, 433, 506
Latvia, 486, 536
Laud, William, 491
Laura de Dianti (Titian), 380(i)
Lavater, Johann Kaspar, 534(i), 535(b)
Law(s). *See also* Law codes; Natural law;
specific laws
in England, 494–495
in France, 469
marriage ages and, 577
in Saint-Domingue, 640
Law (scientific)
of inertia, 508
of planetary motion (Kepler), 508
of universal gravitation, 510–511
Law codes
English common law and, 384
Napoleonic, 635, 636
in Russia, 533
Salic (Salian Franks), 332
Laypeople, literacy of, 352–353
Lay piety, 343
League of Armed Neutrality, 617
Learning. *See also* Education; Intellectual
thought; Renaissance; Schools;
Universities
Christian humanists and, 369–371
Leclerc, Charles-Victor-Emmanuel, 643
Legal system. *See also* Law(s)
in Prussia, 530
Legislation. *See* Law(s)
Legislative Assembly (France), 627
Legislature. *See* Assemblies
Leibniz, Gottfried Wilhelm von, 511, 517
Leisure, in 18th century, 587–589
Lent, carnival and, 587
Leo X (Pope), 384, 393
Leonardo da Vinci, 368–369(b)(i), 369, 377
Leopold II (Holy Roman Empire), 533

Lerma, duke of, 477
Lesbians. *See also* Homosexuality
    subculture in 18th century, 580
Les Halles (Paris), 575(i)
Le Tellier, François. *See* Louvois, marquis de
"Letter from Versailles" (Elisabeth-Charlotte),
    475(d)
Le Vau, Louis (architect), 472(d)
Leviathan (Hobbes), 492
Liberal arts, 363
Liberals and liberalism, 612, 613
    economic, 557
Liberty(ies)
    18th-century demands for, 612–614
    in United States, 617–618
Liberty, figure of, 624(i)
Libraries, in Enlightenment, 524
Life, The (Saint Teresa of Ávila), 418(d)
Lifestyle. *See also* Children; Families; Marriage;
        Middle class(es)
    in 17th century, 464–466
    in 18th century, 574, 575(i)
    in American colonies, 447–448
    of American Indians, 444(d)
    of British in India, 570(i)
    of children, 582–584
    Christian, 403(d)(i)
    Dutch, 497, 543–544
    Enlightenment and, 522–524
    in French Revolution, 611(i), 629–630,
        632–633(b)
    in French royal court, 471–474
    in later Middle Ages, 323(i)
    in Paris, 590–591(d)
    in private spaces, 596
    in Renaissance, 357(i)
    of rural textile workers, 550–553
    of sailors, 433
    of Saint-Domingue slave, 641–642,
        641(i)
Lima, Spain and, 445
Limerick, Treaty of, 494
Linen industry, in Ireland, 554(i)
Linné, Carl von, 524
Lisbon, 379, 435
Literacy
    in 18th century, 586–587
    Bible reading and, 598
    in England, 586
    exploration and, 433
    in France, 586, 587(m)
    of medieval laypeople, 352–353
    printing and, 372–373
    in Scotland, 586
    vernacular literature and, 351–353
Literature. *See also* Drama
    Dance of Death and, 332
    essays and, 457–458
    in France, 474
    popular, 586–587
    Shakespeare and, 458
    vernacular, 351
Lithuania, 413, 536
"Little ice age," 324, 465
Liturgy, in England, 409
*Lives of the Most Excellent Painters, Sculptors,
    and Architects, The* (Vasari), 363

Livestock, 451(b), 542, 543, 545
Llamas, 449
Lloyds of London, 527(b)
Locke, John, 495, 567, 613
    Essay Concerning Human Understanding,
        517
    Two Treatises of Government, 495, 495(d),
        517
Lollards, 340–341
London, Great Fire of (1666) and, 560(b),
        560(i), 561(i)
Longbow, 333, 335, 336(i)
Longhi, Pietro, 576(i)
Longitude, 433
Long Parliament (England), 491, 492
Lorraine, 476
Lotto, Lorenzo, 357(i)
Louis II (Hungary), 413
Louis IX (France), 332
Louis XI "Spider King" (France), 384
Louis XII (France), 384
Louis XIII (France), 470, 596
Louis XIV (France), 463(i), 464, 470,
        471(d)(i), 516, 558
    absolutism of, 470–471
    acquisitions of, 476, 476(m)
    Charles II (England) and, 493
    revolts against, 469
    Versailles and, 471–474, 473(i)
    wars of, 475–476
Louis XV (France), 597, 619
Louis XVI (France), 619, 620, 621
    constitutional monarchy and, 626
    guillotining of, 627
Louis XVIII (France), 639
Louisiana, 444, 475, 615
L'Ouverture, Toussaint, 642–643,
        644(b)(i)
Louvois, marquis de (François le Tellier),
        475–476
Love. *See also* Marriage; Sex and sexuality
    marriage and, 580
Low Countries. *See also* Belgium; Holland;
        Netherlands
    agriculture in, 543–544
    famine in, 325
    farming in, 590–591
    in Hundred Years' War, 333
Lower Belvedere, 473(d)
Loyalists, in American Revolution, 616
Loyola, Ignatius, 416
Lunéville, Treaty of, 636
Luther, Martin, 392, 393–395. *See also*
        Lutheranism; Protestantism
    on arts in religion, 398
    On Christian Liberty, 396–397(d)
    excommunication of, 395
    German politics and, 405–406
    on indulgences, 393–395
    marriage of, 402, 402(i)
    peasants' rebellion and, 400
    on salvation and faith, 393, 397
Lutheranism
    Augsburg Confession and, 406
    in eastern Europe, 413
    in Germany, 407
    in Hungary, 413, 414

Protestant revival and, 597
Protestant Union and, 466
    in Scandinavia, 407
Luxury goods, trade and, 431–432
Lyons, 469

Machiavelli, Niccolò, 367–369
Madeira Islands, 435
Magellan, Ferdinand, 437(d), 440
Magic, science and, 506
Magnetic compass, 434
Magyars, 414. *See also* Hungary
Maine (French county), 384
Maintenon, Madame de, 474
Maize (corn), 450(b), 451(i)
Malacca, 428, 435, 455
Malay Archipelago, 440
Malay Peninsula, Portuguese and, 455
Maldive Islands, 570–571
Mali, trade and, 429
Malindi (city), 429
Mamluks (Egypt), 429
Mandeville, John, 433
Manila, trade in, 455, 456
Mannerism, as art style, 376–377
Mansa Musa. *See* Musa (Mansa)
Mantegna, Andrea, 375
Mantua, 360, 478
Manual on the Art of Childbirth (Coudray),
        602(d), 603(i), 604
Manufacturing. *See also* Industry
    in England, 562(f)
    rural, 549–550
Manumission. *See* Abolition, of slavery
Margaret of Valois, 419
Maria Theresa (Austria), 533, 536(i), 558,
        614
    Catholic Church and, 597
    education and, 586
    Frederick the Great and, 530
Maria Theresa (wife of Louis XIV), 476
Marie Antoinette (France), 595(b), 624
Marie de' Medici, 470, 499
Marina (Doña, La Malinche), 442(d)(i)
Maritime trade, 558
    in 18th century, 541(i), 558
Market(s). *See also* Trade
    diet and, 589–590
Marquette, Jacques, 475
Marriage
    in 18th century, 576–580, 579(i)
    age at, 346–348, 576–577
    Catholic, 414
    ethnic purity in, 351
    interracial, 567
    in later Middle Ages, 346–348
    Luther and, 402, 403(i)
    men and, 348
    in Ottoman Empire, 489
    population growth and, 547
    Protestantism and, 402–404, 402(i)
    in Renaissance, 381–382
    women and, 346–348, 381–382
Marseilles, 326, 541(i), 548(i)
Marsiglio of Padua, 340
Martin V (Pope), 341
Martinique, 445, 562

Martyrs
    Anabaptist, 401(b)(i)
    Joan of Arc as, 337
Mary I Tudor (England), 407, 408(i), 409
Mary II (England), 494
Mary, Queen of Scots, 409, 412
Maryland, 443
Mary of Burgundy, 404–405
Masculinity, clothing and, 382–383(b), 382(i), 383(i)
Masonic lodges, 524
Massachusetts, 443
Masters, in craft guilds, 346
Masturbation, 581
Mathematical Principles of Natural Philosophy (Newton). See *Principia Mathematica* (Newton)
Mathematics, 505
    cartography and, 434
    Copernicus and, 507
    Descartes and, 511–512
    natural philosophy and, 506, 508
    of Newton, 509–511
    scientific instruments and, 506
Maximilian I (Holy Roman Empire), 404–405
Maya people, 446
Mayflower (ship), 443
Mazarin, Jules, 470
Meat, in diet, 589
Mechanistic universe, 511–512
Medici family, 360, 375(i), 377
    Catherine de', 418, 419
    Cosimo de', 360, 363, 375(i)
    Lorenzo de', 360, 373, 374
    Marie de', 470, 499
    Piero, 360, 375(i)
    Savonarola and, 360–361
Medicine
    in 18th century, 601–605
    population growth and, 548
    Scientific Revolution and, 512–513
    women in, 602–603(d), 604
Medieval period. See Middle Ages
Mediterranean region, Genoese trade and, 431
Men. See also Families; Gender
    age at marriage, 348
    as "breadwinner," 554
    marriage in 18th century, 576–577
    as migrants to North American colonies, 565–566
    recreation of, 587
    same-sex relations among, 348–349, 580
    in service, 577–578
Mendelssohn family
    Dorothea, 535(b)
    Felix, 535(b)
    Moses, 534, 534–535(b), 534(i), 535
Ménétra, Jacques-Louis, autobiography of, 583(d)
Mercantilism, 474
    British, 492
    colonial competition and, 558–560
    French, 474–475
Merchant(s). See also Merchant guilds
    in Afro-Eurasian trade, 428–429
    consumerism and, 594

    fashion and, 593(d)(i), 594, 595(b)
    in Italy, 375
    medieval decline of, 325
    in Renaissance, 358, 375
    rural labor and, 553
Merchant guilds, 358
Mercier, Louis-Sébastien, 590–591(d)
Merian, Maria Sibylla, 515, 515(i)
Merici, Angela, 416
Merk, J. C., 481(i)
Merry Family, The (Steen), 496(i)
Mestizos, 448
Methodists and Methodism, 567, 582, 598–600
    Hogarth on, 598(i)
    Wesley's advice to, 599(d)
Métis, 448
Metric system, in France, 632
Metternich, Klemens von, Napoleon and, 639
Mexica Empire, 441–442, 441(i), 441(m), 445, 446
Mexico, 440, 445
    Cortés in, 433
    silver in, 446, 454
    Spanish conquest of, 441–443
Mexico City, 441, 445, 569
Meytens, Martin, 536(i)
Michael Romanov, 483
Michelangelo, 373, 374(i), 376, 377
Microscope, 506
Middle Ages, 363. See also Later Middle Ages
Middle class(es)
    in Russia, 483
    in Spain, 476
Middle East. See Arabs and Arab world; Islam; Muslims
Midwives, 602–603(d), 603(i), 604
Migration. See also Immigrants and immigration; Invasions
    ethnic tensions and, 350–351
Milan, 358, 360
Militarism, in Prussia, 482
Military. See also Armed forces; Navy; Soldiers
    Dutch, 497
    in England, 492
    in Italian republics, 360
    in Prussia, 481–482, 481(i)
    in Russia, 486
Military technology. See also Weapons
    in Hundred Years' War, 338
Millet system (nations), Ottoman, 489
Mind-body dualism, 515
Mines and mining. See also Gold; Silver; Trade
    in Americas, 476
Ming dynasty (China), 429, 437
Minorca, 476
Missions and missionaries. See also Monks and monasteries
    in American colonies, 446
    Columbus and, 436
    Jesuit, 416–417
    Moravians and, 568–569(b)
    in New World, 567
Mississippi River region, France and, 444, 615
Mixed races, 448, 448(i), 565–567, 566(d)(i), 568(b)(i)

Modena, as city-state, 360
Modernization, of Russia, 485–487
Mogadishu, 429
Mohács, Battle of, 413
Mohammed II (Ottoman Empire), 430
Molière (Jean-Baptiste Poquelin), 474
Moluccas, 440
Mombasa, 429
Mona Lisa (Leonardo da Vinci), 368, 373
Monarchs and monarchies. See also Absolute monarchy and absolutism; Constitutional monarchies; Kings and kingdoms; specific rulers and locations
    in 17th century, 464
    cameralism and, 530
    Catholic, 597
    in England, 384
    enlightened absolutism in, 529
    in France, 418, 619–622, 624, 626, 627, 636
    popular government and, 612
Monasticism (Christian). See also Monks and monasteries
    in Spain, 476
Money. See also Coins; Currency; Economy
    marriage ages and, 577
Moneylending, by Jews, 325
Mongols
    in Russia, 482, 533
    trade and, 428–429
Monks and monasteries. See also Convents; Friars; Missions and missionaries; Monasticism
    in Austria, 533, 597
    English dissolution of, 408
Monopolies, colonial, 561
Montagu, Mary Wortley, 604–605
Montaigne, Michel de, 456, 457–458, 582
Montesquieu, baron de (Charles-Louis de Secondat), 517, 567, 613
Montezuma II (Mexica Empire), 441–443
Montpellier
    prostitution in, 348
    revolt in, 469
Montreal, 440, 444
Moon, Galileo and, 509(d), 510(i)
Moors, 458
Moral economy, 466
Morality
    in 18th century, 578
    Puritan, 492
Moravian Church, 567, 568–569(b), 599
More, Thomas, 365, 370–371, 401(b), 407–408
Moriscos (former Muslims), Spanish expulsion of, 476
Mortagne, siege of Castle, 336(i)
Mortality. See also Death; Infant mortality
    in 18th century, 581
    decline in, 547
    of Native Americans, 446, 447
    from plague, 327, 330
Moscow
    Napoleon at, 637, 639
    princes of, 482
    as Third Rome, 482
Moses (Michelangelo), 376

Mothers. *See* Breast-feeding; Childbirth; Children; Families; Marriage; Wet-nursing
Motion
    Aristotle and, 504
    Descartes and, 511
    Galileo and, 508
    Kepler's laws of, 508
Mountain, the, 627, 628
Movable type, 362, 372, 373
Movement of peoples. *See* Immigrants and immigration; Migration
Mulatto, 448, 453(b), 566(d)(i), 568(b)(i)
Mundus Novus, 440
Municipal government, by 18th century, 469
Munitions. *See* Armed forces; Weapons
Münster, Germany, 400
Murillo, Bartolome Esteban, 451(i)
Musa (Mansa), 429
Music, baroque, 499
Muskets, 336(i)
Muslims. *See also* Arabs and Arab world; Islam
    in Ottoman Empire, 430
    plague and, 331
    Shi'ite (Shi'a), 430
    in Spain, 385(m), 387, 476
    trade by, 429, 430(m)
Mysticism, Christian, 342(b), 343

Nagasaki, Portuguese trade with, 455
Nahuatl language, 442(d)
Nanjing (Nanking), 429
Naples
    kingdom of, 360, 521
    revolts in 17th century, 469
Napoleon I (Napoleon Bonaparte), 631, 634–640
    blockade of Britain by, 636
    coronation of, 634(i)
    exile of, 639
    Grand Empire of, 637–640, 638(m)
    Haitian independence and, 643
    Hundred Days of, 640
    proclamation to the French People, 635(d)
    at Waterloo, 640
Napoleonic Code (France), 635, 636
Narva, battle at, 486
Naseby, battle at, 492
Nation, 379. *See also* State (nation)
National Assembly (France), 621, 623, 624
    changes made by, 623–624
    reforms by, 625
    Saint-Domingue and, 640, 641, 642
National Convention (France), 627, 628, 629, 631, 642
National Guard (France), 624
Nationalism
    in England, 338
    in France, 338, 630
    in Hundred Years' War, 351
Nationality. *See* Ethnic groups; specific groups
Nationalization, of English church, 408
National state. *See* State (nation)
Native Americans. *See* American Indians
Natural history, empire and, 513–514
Natural law, U.S. freedoms and, 617

"Natural man"
    Diderot on, 528(d)
    Rousseau and, 584
Natural philosophy, 504, 505, 506, 508
Natural rights, 495, 616
Nature, race and, 524
Navigation. *See also* Maritime trade; Ships and shipping
    scientific instruments for, 506
    technology and, 433–434
Navigation Acts (England), 558, 560
    of 1651, 492, 558
    of 1660, 558
    of 1663, 558
Navy. *See also* Ships and shipping
    British, 468
    Russian, 485(i)
Nelson, Horatio, at Trafalgar, 636
Netherlands. *See also* Austrian Netherlands; Holland; Low Countries
    in 1609, 420(m)
    Anabaptists in, 401(b)
    Dutch Republic and, 496–497
    France and, 637
    golden age in, 496
    imports of grain to, 479
    radical Reformation in, 400
    religion and, 417, 419–420
    Spanish, 419–420, 420(m)
New Amsterdam, 456, 558
New Astronomy, The (Kepler), 508
New Christians, Jews as, 386–387
New England, 443–444
    Cabot exploration of, 440
    population growth in, 547
    Puritans in, 412, 443
Newfoundland, 440, 476, 558
New France, 444–445, 446, 614–615
New Granada, 445
New Haven, 443
New Model Army, 492
New Netherland, 456
News, distribution of, 592(i)
New South Wales, 570
New Spain, 445
New Testament
    Erasmus on, 371
    in German (Luther), 399
    Zwingli on, 397
Newton, Isaac, 504, 509–511, 516
New World. *See also* Americas; Colonies and colonization
    cultures of, 445
    diseases in, 443, 444(d)
    English settlement in, 443–444
    European "discovery" of, 432
    French settlement in, 444–445
    Spain and, 405, 445–447, 456
New York City, as New Amsterdam, 456
Nice, 627
"Ninety-five Theses on the Power of Indulgences" (Luther), 394–395
Nobility. *See also* Aristocracy
    in 17th century, 464, 468
    before 18th-century revolutions, 612
    Austrian, 533
    as bandits, 350

    in England, 384
    fashion and, 594
    in France, 470, 471, 473, 474, 620, 623–624, 635–636
    Hungarian, 479
    peasants and, 479
    Prussian, 530
    in Renaissance, 374–375, 380–381
    in Russia, 482, 486, 487, 533
    same-sex relationships of, 580
Nomads, Mongols as, 482
Normandy, 334 (m)
    England and, 335
    Estates of (assembly), 465
    France and, 335, 338
    in Hundred Years' War, 335
Normans. *See* Normandy; Vikings
North Africa, trade in, 429
North America. *See also* Americas; New World
    Anglo-French conflicts in, 558–560
    colonial trade in, 561
    Enlightenment in, 521
    European claims in, 614(m)
    Jesuits in, 416
    revolutionary era in, 610
    slaves in mainland of, 563
    War of the Spanish Succession and, 558
    white migrants to, 565–566
North Carolina, Roanoke colony in, 443
Northern Europe. *See also* Christian humanists
    Renaissance art in, 375–376
Northmen. *See* Vikings
Norway. *See also* Scandinavia
    Protestant Reformation in, 407
Nova Scotia, 476, 558
Novels. *See* Literature
Nuclear family, in 18th century, 576–577
Nuns (Christian)
    Carmelite, 416
    Protestant Reformation and, 404
Nursing. *See* Breast-feeding
Nutrition. *See* Diet (food); Food

Occult, astronomy and, 506
Occupations. *See also* Labor
    trades as, in 18th century, 577
Oceans. *See* specific ocean regions
"Of Cannibals" (Montaigne), 457
Of Natural Characters (Hume), 524
Ogé, Vincent, 641
Old Regime (France), 622(d)
Olearius, Adam, 484–485(d)
Oligarchy
    in Dutch Republic, 496
    of merchants, 359, 360
Olivares, Count-Duke of (Gaspar de Guzmán), 468, 478
On Christian Liberty (Luther), 396–397(d)
On Crimes and Punishments (Beccaria), 521
"On My First Son" (Jonson), 582
On the Different Races of Man (Kant), 524
"On the Dignity of Man" (Pico della Mirandola), 366–367(d)
On the Immortality of the Soul (Mendelssohn), 534
On the Revolutions of the Heavenly Spheres (Copernicus), 506, 512

On the Structure of the Human Body (Vesalius), 512–513, 513(i)
Open-field system, 542, 543, 545
Oppenheim, Moritz, 534(i)
Optics, 505
  Kepler and, 508
  Newton and, 510
Orange, House of, 494, 497
Orders. *See also* Clergy; Nobility; Peasant(s);
    Religious orders
  social classes as, 620
Original sin, 583
Orléans, battle at, 335, 338
Orléans, duchess of, 580
Orlov, Gregory, 531
Orthodox Church. *See also* Christianity
  in Russia, 482
Othello (Shakespeare), 458
Ottoman Empire, 430–431. *See also* Ottoman
    Turks; Turkey
  Austria and, 479, 480(m)
  Egypt and, 429
  in 1566, 487(m)
  government of, 489
  growth of, 487–489, 487(m)
  Hungary and, 406, 413, 479
  military in, 489
  religious toleration in, 482
  Transylvania and, 479
Ottoman Turks. *See also* Ottoman Empire;
    Turks
  Constantinople and, 430–431, 431(i)
  Hungary, Vienna, and, 406
Overseas expansion. *See* Expansion;
    Exploration

Pacific Ocean region
  Atlantic trade and, 562
  Magellan in, 440
  trade and empire in, 569–571
Pagans and paganism, Christianity and, 600
Paine, Thomas, 586–587, 616
Painting. *See also* Art(s)
  mulatto, 566(d)(i)
  by women, 378
Palaces
  of absolute monarchs, 472–473(d), 472(i),
    473(i)
  in Italy, 360
  in St. Petersburg, 486
Pale (Dublin), 409
Pale of Settlement, 535(m), 536
Palermo, 469
Palladio, Andrew, 377(i)
Panics, witch, 422
Papacy. *See also* Catholic Church; Protestant
    Reformation; specific popes
  in 15th century, 360
  Anagni and, 340
  Babylonian Captivity of, 339–340
  criticisms of, 392
  German emperor and, 392
  Luther and, 395
  reform of, 340
Papal curia, 392
Papal States, 414
Paper, printing and, 372

Paracelsus, 512
Pareja, Juan de, 453(b)(i)
Paris. *See also* France; French Revolution; Paris,
    Treaty of; Parlement of Paris
  autobiography of boyhood in, 583(d)
  Bastille in, 623
  clothing in, 594
  guilds in, 555
  lifestyle in, 590–591(d)
  news distribution in, 592(i)
  scientific academy in, 515
Paris, Treaty of
  of 1259, 332
  of 1763, 560, 615
  of 1783, 617
Parish churches, 596–597
Parlement of Paris, 470, 620
Parlements (France), 517
Parliament (England), 338, 384. *See also*
    House of Commons (England)
  American Revolution and, 615–616
  Charles I and, 490, 491–492
  constitutional monarchy and, 495
  sovereignty in, 613
  statute of 1341 in, 338
Parma, republic in, 359
Partitions, of Poland, 532(m), 533
Patronage, 358
  in French court, 474
  of Renaissance arts, 358, 373–385
Paul III (Pope), 414
Peace of Augsburg, 407, 466
Peace of Utrecht, 476, 477(m), 558
Peace of Westphalia, 466
Peasant(s). *See also* Agriculture; Land; Peasant
    revolts; Serfs and serfdom
  in 17th century, 464–465
  in Austria, 533
  Dutch, 544
  in England, 345, 345(d), 346
  in France, 344, 623–624
  in French Revolution, 623–624, 628
  land rights of, 543
  in later Middle Ages, 323(i), 343–346
  marriage by, 579(i)
  open-field system and, 542
  in Prussia, 479
  radical Reformation and, 400
  in Russia, 482, 483, 483(i), 533
Peasant revolts, 343–346
Pendulum clock, 506
Penn, William, 493
Pennsylvania, 443
Peonage, debt, 562
People of color, 448
Perfume, 596
Persian Empire, 430–431
Persian Letters, The (Montesquieu), 517
Peru, 440, 443, 445
  in 1780s, 450(i)
Peter III (Russia), 530, 531
Peter the Great (Russia), 464(i), 485–487,
    485(i), 531
"Petition of the French Jews," 626(d)
Petrarch, Francesco, 362–363
Petrograd. *See* St. Petersburg
Pharmacy. *See* Apothecaries

Philip (Burgundy, Holy Roman Empire),
    387
Philip II (Spain), 387, 408(i), 440, 454(i)
  Armada and, 410
  empire of, 407
  Mary Tudor and, 409
  Netherlands and, 419
  scientific knowledge and, 513–514
  state debt, silver trade, and, 454
Philip III (Spain), 477
Philip IV the Fair (France), 325, 332
Philip IV (Spain), 469, 477–478
Philip V (Spain), 476
Philip VI (France), 333
Philippines
  naming of, 440
  trade in, 455
Philosophes, 517–520, 523, 524
Philosophy. *See also* Enlightenment; Intellec-
    tual thought; Science
  in 18th century, 502
  experimental, 511
  natural, 504, 505, 506, 508
Phyllis Riding Aristotle, 381(i)
Physicians. *See also* Medicine
  in 18th century, 601
Physics
  Aristotle and, 507
  Newtonian, 509–511
Pico della Mirandola, Giovanni, 363, 370
  "On the Dignity of Man," 366–367(d)
Piero della Francesca, 375
Pietà (Michelangelo), 376
Pietism, 597–598, 599–600
Pilgrimage of Grace (England), 409
Pilgrims, English settlers as, 443
Pisa, council at (1409), 341
Pius VII (Pope), 634(i), 636
Pizarro, Francisco, 443
Plague, 322. *See also* Black Death
  in China and India (1890s), 326
  in Marseilles, 326, 548(i)
  recurrence of, 329
  scapegoats for, 332
  treatment of, 328–329(b), 328(i), 329–
    330, 329(i)
Planetary motion
  Aristotle and, 504, 504(i)
  Brahe, *Rudolfine Tables,* and, 507
  Kepler's laws of, 508
Plan of the English Commerce, A (Defoe),
    552(d)
Plantations
  agricultural slavery and, 562–564
  in Saint-Domingue, 640
  sugar, 449(i)
  zones of (ca. 1700), 562(m)
Plants. *See also* Agriculture; Crops
  in Columbian exchange, 445, 448–449
  as food, 591–592
Plassey, Battle of, 570
Plato
  Renaissance thinkers and, 363, 365
  on rulers, 367
Platonic Academy, 363
Platonic ideals, 363
Plays. *See* Drama

Plessis, Armand Jean du. *See* Richelieu, Cardinal
Plow, horses for, 545
Pluralism
    in church, 392, 414
    legal, 351
Plymouth colony, 443
Pneumonic transmission (plague), 326. *See also* Black Death
Poets and poetry. *See* Literature; specific writers
Poitiers, battle at (1356), 333, 338
Poland
    Catholic Church in, 413
    Jews in, 535
    Napoleon and, 639
    partitions of, 532(m), 533
    plague in, 326
    Reformation and, 413
    Russia and, 483, 485, 532(m), 533
    serfdom and, 479
Poland-Lithuania, 413
Political thought. *See also* Politics
    in Renaissance, 367–369
Politics. *See also* Government
    in Italy, 360
    Protestantism and, 400, 404–407
    in Renaissance, 383–387
Politiques (France), 419
Polo, Marco, 428
    Travels of Marco Polo, The, 433, 438(d)
Poltava, battle at, 486
Pomerania, 466
Pompadour, Madame de, 619
Pondicherry, 570
Poor people. *See also* Peasant(s); Poverty
    18th-century revolutions and, 612
    diet of, 589
    in rural areas, 546, 549, 553
    schools for, 585
Pope(s). *See* Papacy; specific popes
Popolo, in Italy, 358, 359
Popular culture
    consumerism and, 586–596
    literature and, 586–587
Population
    in 18th century, 547–549, 550(m)
    of American colonies, 446, 447
    of China, 429
    city and town growth and, 544
    in England (1550–1850), 546(f)
    of enslaved Africans, 454
    European expansion and, 432
    of Florence, 358
    growth of, 547
    of Spain, 454
    after Thirty Years' War, 466
Population explosion, 546–549
Poquelin, Jean-Baptiste. *See* Molière
Po River region, 542
Portrait of Baldassare Castiglione (Raphael), 365(i)
Portraits, in Renaissance, 375
Portugal
    Africa and, 435
    Brazil and, 440
    colonies of, 445
    Dutch and, 456

empire of, 435, 558
exploration by, 431–432, 433
independence of, 478
Indian Ocean trade and, 569
Inquisition in, 421
Japan and, 427(i)
Napoleon and, 637
religion in, 597
revolts in, 478
slave trade and, 379–380, 450–451, 452, 455, 562–563
Spain and, 469, 478
trade by, 455–456
Treaty of Tordesillas and, 440
Potatoes, 450(b), 543, 549, 591
Potosí, 454, 455(i)
Poverty. *See also* Poor people
    marriage ages and, 577
    population growth and, 546
    rural, 549
Power (authority). *See also* Absolute monarchy and absolutism; Constitutional monarchies
    of men and women, 383
    after Thirty Years' War, 467–468
Power politics, in Italy, 361
Powhatan Confederacy, 443
Pragmatic Sanction (1713), 530
Prague, 340–341
Praise of Folly, The (Erasmus), 371
Predestination, Calvin on, 410, 600
Pregnancy. *See also* Childbirth; Illegitimacy
    in 18th century, 578, 579–580
    marriage and, 578
Premarital sex, 578–580
Presbyterians, in Scotland, 411–412, 413, 491
Prester John, 430, 456
Price(s). *See also* Silver, from Americas
    just, 466
Primavera (Botticelli), 378(i)
Prime minister (England), 496
Prince, The (Machiavelli), 367, 369
Prince(s), in Russia, 482
Principia Mathematica (Newton), 510, 516
Printing. *See also* Books
    in Enlightenment, 586
    growth in Europe, 372(m)
    of Ninety-five Theses (Luther), 395
    Protestantism and, 399–400
    in Renaissance, 362, 371–373
    Scientific Revolution and, 506
Printing press, 371(i)
Privacy, in 18th century, 596
Procession(s), Catholic, 375(i)
Production, agricultural, 542
Professionalization, of armies, 468, 468(i)
Proletarianization, 546
Property. *See also* Inheritance
    in France, 625, 631
Prosperity
    Dutch, 497
    in Italian Renaissance, 358
Prostitution
    in 18th century, 578, 580
    in later Middle Ages, 348
    Protestants on, 404

Protectorate, in England, 492–493, 493(d)
Protestantism, 397–404. *See also* Christianity; Edict of Nantes; Huguenots; Lutheranism
    appeal of, 399–400
    baroque arts and, 498–499
    in Bohemia, 479
    Calvin and, 410–413, 413(i)
    Christian life in, 403(d)(i)
    church hierarchy and, 596–597
    divorce and, 403–404
    education and, 585
    in England, 409–410, 490–494
    in France, 417–419, 469, 470–471, 597, 625
    in Hungary, 413–414
    Hussites and, 341
    Luther and, 393–395
    marriage in, 402–404
    missionaries and, 567
    in Netherlands, 419–420
    politics and, 404–407
    religious wars and, 417–420
    revival of, 597–600
    spread of, 407–414
    territorial churches of, 597
    Thirty Years' War and, 466
    women in, 402–404
Protestant Reformation
    in Bohemia, 413
    in eastern Europe, 413–414
    in England, 407–409
    Erasmus and, 371
    German politics and, 404–407
Protestant Union, 466
Protten, Christian Jacob, 569(b)
Protten, Rebecca, 568–569(b), 568(i)
Provence, in France, 384
Providence, 443
Prussia. *See also* Brandenburg-Prussia; Germany
    in 17th century, 480–481
    Austria and, 530
    cameralism in, 530
    Enlightenment in, 518, 520, 521, 529
    France and, 619, 627, 628
    under Frederick the Great, 530
    military in, 481–482, 481(i)
    Napoleon and, 636, 637
    nobility in, 530
    partition of Poland and, 532(m), 533
    peasants in, 479
    in Seven Years' War, 614
    Silesia and, 530
    state-building in, 480–482
    universal education in, 585
Ptolemy, Claudius (scientist), 505, 506
    Geography by, 433–434, 434(i), 437, 506, 513
Public administration, in Germany, 530
Public sphere, in Enlightenment, 524
Pugachev, Emelian, 531(i), 533
Purging, medicinal, 601, 604
Purification, religious, 601
Puritans, 490
    absolutism in England, 492–493
    Anglican Church and, 409, 490

Calvin and, 412
in New England, 412, 443
occupations of, 491(i)
"Purity of blood," 351
Putting-out system, 549–550, 581
Pyrenees, Treaty of the, 478

Qinsay (Hangzhou), 439
Quakers, 400, 443, 493–494, 567
Quebec, 444, 475, 615
Queens, 381. See also Monarchs and monarchies; specific rulers
Quilon, India, 429

Race and racism. See also Ethnic groups; Slaves and slavery
in 18th century, 612, 613
challenges to, 525
Enlightenment and, 524–529
European attitudes and, 456–457
as human grouping, 524–525
ideas about, 456–458
Jews and, 387
mixed races and, 448, 448(i), 565–567, 566(d)(i)
in Renaissance society, 379–380
scientific justifications of, 457
Shakespeare and, 458
slavery justified by, 525
Racine, Jean, 474
Racing, 588(b)
Radical Reformation, 400–402
Radicals and radicalism, in French Revolution, 618, 621(d), 624, 627–633
Raimon de Cornet, on Avignon papacy, 339(d)
Rákóczy, Francis, 479–480
Rape, in later Middle Ages, 348
Raphael (Sanzio), 365(i), 377
Rationalism, 516, 521, 601
Raynal, abbé, 525
Razin, Stenka, 483, 533
Reading. See also Education; Literacy
in Enlightenment, 522, 586
Reading revolution, 522
Reason. See Enlightenment; Rationalism
Rebellions. See Revolts and rebellions
Reconquista (reconquest)
exploration and, 432
slavery and, 450
Records, of 18th-century life, 576
Recreation. See also Leisure
in 18th century, 587–589
Re-export trade, 561
Reflections on the Revolution in France (Burke), 626
Reform(s). See also Protestant Reformation; Reformation
in Austria, 533
of Catholic Church, 340–343, 390
in France, 476, 619, 625, 628
radical Protestants and, 400
in Russia, 485–487, 531–533
Reformation, 356, 390. See also Counter-Reformation; Protestant Reformation
art in, 398–399(b), 398(i), 399(i)
Catholic, 414–417

in eastern Europe, 413–414
radical, 400–402
Reformed Church, 411–412, 413
Refraction, Kepler on, 508
Refugees, religious, 407
Regulation, government economic, 557, 558
Reign of Terror, in French Revolution, 628–630, 631
Reinhart, Anna, 402
Relics, of saints, 600
Religion(s). See also Cults; specific groups
in 18th century, 596–601
Copernican hypothesis and, 507
education and, 585–586, 597
Enlightenment principles and, 529
ethnicity and, 351
in Europe (ca. 1555), 415(m)
exploration and, 432–433
in France, 417–419, 469, 470–471, 625, 629–630, 636
ideological doubt and, 516
marginal beliefs and, 600–601
in northern European art, 375–376
plague impacts on, 331–332
Protestant revival and, 597–600
violence over, 391(i), 417–422
witch-hunt and, 420–422
Religious orders. See also Monks and monasteries
in 18th century, 597
in Catholic Reformation, 416
privileges of, 392
teaching orders and, 586
Religious toleration
in Austria, 535, 597
Dutch, 497
in England, 492
in France, 419
for Jews, 535
in Netherlands, 401
in Ottoman Empire, 482, 487, 489
Religious wars
in France, 391(i)
in Germany, 405–407
in Switzerland, 406
"Remember the Ladies" (Abigail Adams), 618(d), 619
Renaissance, 356, 358
art and artists in, 373–379
genius in, 368, 377
intellectual thought in, 362–373
in Italy, 358–369, 373–379
in North, 369–371
politics and state in, 383–387
printing in, 371–373, 371(i)
Scientific Revolution and, 506
society in, 356, 357(i), 379–383
taxation in, 386(i)
trade in, 358
"Renaissance man," 365
Rent, for peasants, 542
Representative assemblies, 338
Representative government
18th-century, 613
American Revolution and, 615–616
English, 445, 495
in United States, 617

Republic. See also Dutch Republic; England (Britain)
in France, 627
in Italy, 358–360
Republic (Plato), 367
Republicanism
Dutch, 490
English, 490
Republic of Belarus. See Belarus
Republic of Letters, in Enlightenment, 520
Resistance, by slaves, 641–642
Restoration
in England, 493–494
of French Bourbon dynasty, 595(b)
Revivals, Protestant, 597–600
Revolts and rebellions. See also Wars and warfare
in 17th century, 469
over food, 466, 469
in France, 469, 470
during French Revolution, 628(m)
in Hungary, 479
in Ireland (1641), 491–492
in later Middle Ages, 343–346, 344(m)
against Napoleon, 637
by peasants, 343–346, 400–402
in Russia, 483, 533
by Saint-Domingue slaves, 641–643, 642(i)
urban, 346
Revolution(s). See also American Revolution; French Revolution
1775–1815, 610, 612–614
in Haiti, 640–645
social change and, 612
Revolutionary War in America. See American Revolution
Reymerswaele, Marinus van, 386(i)
Rhineland, France and, 627
Rhine River region, 480
Rhode Island, 443
Rice and rice industry, 448
Richard II (England), Peasants' Revolt and, 346
Richard III (England), 384
Richelieu, Cardinal (Armand Jean du Plessis), 466, 468, 470
Rigaud, André, 643
Rights
18th-century demands for, 613–614
in American Revolution, 616, 617
English law on, 495
in France, 623–624
to land, 543
natural, 495, 616
for women, 524, 624–625, 627
Riots
in 17th century, 466
bread, 466, 469
food, 466, 469
in France, 470
Roads and highways, in 18th century, 548–549
Roanoke, English colony in, 443, 444(d)
Robe nobility (France), 470
Robert of Geneva. See Clement VII
Robespierre, Maximilien, 626, 627, 628–630, 631

Robin Hood, 350
Rococo style, 524
Rocroi, battle at, 478
Roman Catholic Church. *See* Catholic Church
Roman Empire. *See also* Byzantine Empire;
        Holy Roman Empire; Rome
    Renaissance culture and, 362–363
Romanov family (Russia)
    Catherine the Great and, 531
    Michael, 483
Romantic movement, Rousseau and, 520
Rome
    Renaissance art in, 376
    sack of (1527), 361
Rosaries, 416*(i)*
Rotation of crops. *See* Crops, rotation of
Rousseau, Jean-Jacques, 525, 529, 567
    Emile, or On Education, 583–584
Royal African Company, 452
Royalists, in England, 492*(m)*, 494*(i)*
"Royall Oake of Brittayne, The," 494*(i)*
Royal Society (England), 511, 515, 517, 518
Royalty. *See* Kings and kingdoms
Rubens, Peter Paul, 498*(i)*, 499
Rudolph II (Holy Roman Empire), 507
Rudolphine Tables, 507
Rump Parliament, 492
Runaway serfs, 479
Rural areas. *See also* Agriculture; Farms and
        farming; Peasant(s); Serfs and serfdom
    in 17th century, 464
    conflicts in, 343–346
    industrial growth in, 549–554, 552–553*(d)*
    poor people in, 546, 549
    radical Reformation and, 400
    workers in textile industry, 550–553
Russia. *See also* Russian Revolution (1917)
    American Revolution and, 617
    armed forces in, 483, 486
    Baltic region and, 482, 485–486, 485*(i)*
    Catherine the Great in, 530–533, 531*(i)*
    Cossacks in, 483
    development of, 482–487
    Enlightenment in, 529, 530–533
    Estonia and, 464*(i)*
    expansion of, 483–487, 483*(m)*, 533
    France and, 636
    German account of life in, 484–485*(d)*
    inheritance in, 487
    Mongols in, 482
    Napoleon and, 636, 637–639, 638*(m)*
    nobility in, 482, 486, 487, 533
    partition of Poland and, 532*(m)*, 533
    peasants in, 482, 483, 483*(i)*
    population growth in, 547*(f)*
    princes in, 482
    Prussia and, 480–481, 530
    serfdom in, 542
    as Western or non-Western society, 482
Russian Revolution (1917), Jews after, 536

Sacks, of Rome, in 1527, 361
Sacraments, 414
Safavid Empire, trade and, 430–431
Sahagún, Bernardino de, 447*(d)*
Sahara, trade in, 429–430
Sailors, 433. *See also* Ships and shipping

Saint Bartholomew's Day massacre, 419
Saint Basil's Cathedral (Moscow), 486*(i)*
St. Christophe, West Indies, 445
Saint Diego of Alcala Feeding the Poor
        (Murillo), 451*(i)*
Saint-Domingue, 445, 562, 610, 615
    race laws in, 567
    slave revolt in, 640–643
St. Helena, Napoleon at, 640
St. Lawrence River region, 440, 444
Saint Peter's Basilica, 376
St. Petersburg, 486
    in 1825, 486
Saint-Simon, duke of, 474
Salian Franks, law code of, 332
Salons, 522, 523*(d)(i)*, 524
    women in, 515, 523, 523*(d)(i)*
Salvador, 445
Salvation
    Calvin and, 410
    Luther on, 393, 397
    Wesley on, 598–599, 600
Same-sex relationships. *See also* Homosexuality
    in 18th century, 580
    in later Middle Ages, 348–350, 350*(i)*
Sanitation, surgical, 604
San Salvador (Bahamas), 437, 439, 439*(m)*
Sans-culottes (France), 628, 629*(d)(i)*
Saracens. *See* Muslims
Savages, indigenous peoples as, 448
Savonarola, Girolamo, 360–361, 362*(d)*,
        366*(d)*
Savoy, 627
Scandinavia
    plague in, 326
    Protestant Reformation in, 407
Scapegoats, for plague, 332, 386
Schism. *See also* Reformation
    in Catholic Church, 332, 340, 341
Scholarship. *See* Intellectual thought
Scholastics, 371
Schönbrunn palace, 472*(d)*, 473*(i)*, 536*(i)*
Schools. *See also* Education; Universities
    elementary, 584–586
    humanist, 365
    Jesuit, 585
    religious, 584–586
    teaching in, 583
Science. *See also* Mathematics; Scientific
        Revolution
    in 19th century, 504
    as natural philosophy, 504, 505, 506, 508
    race defined by, 457
    society and, 514–515
    theology and, 505
    women in, 515, 517
Scientific expeditions, 513–514
Scientific method, 512
Scientific Revolution, 502, 503*(i)*
    Enlightenment and, 502
    farming and, 543
    intellectual and social changes from,
        511–515
    intellectual crisis in, 516
    origins of, 505–506
    race and, 524
Scientific societies, 511, 514–515

Scotland
    England and, 333
    Enlightenment in, 520–521, 567
    famine in, 325
    Hundred Years' War and, 333
    literacy in, 586
    Presbyterians in, 411–412, 413, 491
Scriptures
    Luther on, 393
    Protestantism and, 399
    Thomas à Kempis on, 343
    Wyclif on, 340
    Zwingli and, 397
Sculpture, in Renaissance, 374*(i)*, 375, 376
Seaborne trade. *See also* Trade
    Dutch, 456
    Spanish, 456
    trading empires and, 452*(m)*, 456
Second Coalition, 636
Second Continental Congress (1776), 616
Second estate (France), nobility as, 620
Second revolution, in French Revolution,
        627–628
Second Treatise of Civil Government (Locke), 495
Self-government, in United States, 617
Selim II (Ottomans), 488*(b)*
Semites. *See* Arabs and Arab world; Jews and
        Judaism
Sensationalism, Locke on, 517
Senses
    Hume and, 520–521
    Locke and, 517
Separation of powers, 517–518
September Massacres (France), 627
Serfs and serfdom. *See also* Peasant(s)
    in 17th century, 465
    in 18th century, 542
    in Austria, 533
    in eastern Europe, 479
    in England, 346
    in Estonia, 464*(i)*
    in Russia, 482–483, 533
Servants
    in 18th century, 576*(i)*, 577–578
    black, 380
    Enlightenment ideas and, 586
    rape of, 348
Servetus, Michael, 411
Service nobility, in Russia, 482
Service requirements, of Russian commoners,
        486
Settlement(s)
    in Americas, 445–449
    in Australia, 570
Seven Years' War, 530, 558–559
    American Revolution and, 615–616
    European claims before, 614*(m)*
    France and, 562, 619
    Prussia and, 530, 614
    Russia and, 531
Sex and sexuality. *See also* Gender; Homo-
        sexuality; Prostitution
    in 18th century, 578–580
    outside of marriage, 580
    premarital sex and, 578–580
    Protestantism and, 404
    in urban areas, 346–350

Sextant, 507(i)
Sexual division of labor. *See* Gender and gender issues
Seymour, Jane, 408
Sforza family, 360
    Francesco, 369(b)
    Ludovico, 369(b)
Shakespeare, William, 456, 457
Shi'ite (Shi'a) Muslims, 430
"Ship money," 491
Ships and shipping. *See also* Maritime trade; Navy
    British Navigation Acts and, 558
    Dutch, 497
    plague spread by, 325
    in slave trade, 452–454
    technological innovations and, 433–434
    Zheng He, Columbus, and, 428(i)
Siberia, 483
Sicily, riots in, 469
Sidereal Messenger, The (Galileo), 508, 509(b)
Siena, 359, 360
Sieyès, Emmanuel Joseph, 634
    What Is the Third Estate?, 620–621, 622–623(d)
Sigismund (Germany), 341
Sigismund I (Poland), 413
Signorelli, Luca, 383(i)
Signori (rulers), 360
Silesia, 466, 530, 533, 558, 614
Silk trade, 456
Silver
    from Americas, 446, 469, 476
    China as buyer of, 455
    Spain and, 454–455
    trade and, 456
Simony, 414
Sistine Chapel, Michelangelo and, 373, 374(i), 376
Sixtus IV (Pope), 387
Skin color, categorizing people by, 457
Slaves and slavery. *See also* Africa; Africans; Race and racism; Serfs and serfdom; Slave trade
    18th-century revolutions and, 612
    in American colonies, 447
    conversions to Christianity and, 567
    economic arguments for ending, 565(d)
    European defenses of, 524, 529
    in Italian trade, 432
    in Ottoman Empire, 489
    plantation agriculture and, 562–564
    racism and, 457, 525
    in Renaissance society, 379–380
    in Saint-Domingue, 610, 640–643, 642(i)
    sexual relations with masters and, 448
    sugar and, 449–454, 564(i)
    in triangle trade, 560
    in United States, 618
Slave trade. *See also* Slaves and slavery
    African, 430, 563
    Atlantic, 432, 562–567, 563(i)
    Dutch and, 452
    England and, 452, 476, 564
    Portugal and, 379–380, 450–451, 452, 455
    ships in, 452–454
    transatlantic, 445

Slavs. *See also* Russia
    Mongols and, 482
Smallpox
    inoculation against, 548, 604–605, 605(i)
    in New World, 443
Smith, Adam, 521
    on division of labor, 556(d), 557
    economic liberalism and, 556–557
    free trade and, 558
    on government economic regulation, 557
Soccer, 588(b)
Social classes. *See* Class
Social contract, American Revolution and, 520
Social Contract, The (Rousseau), 520
Social hierarchy. *See* Hierarchy
Society. *See also* Families; Orders; Rural areas; Urban areas
    in 17th century, 464–465
    in 18th century, 542, 574, 578, 612
    in British North American colonies, 616
    consumer, 592–596
    enclosure movement and, 546
    famine and, 325
    in France, 632–633
    Hobbes on, 492
    after Hundred Years' War, 338
    in later Middle Ages, 330–332, 338, 343–353
    in Mexico City, 441
    peasant revolts in, 343–346
    plague impact on, 325–332
    population explosion and, 546–549
    prostitution regulated by, 348
    in Renaissance, 356, 357(i), 379–383
    science and, 514–515
    Scientific Revolution and, 511–515
    Smith, Adam, on, 557
    Thirty Years' War and, 466
Society of Friends. *See* Quakers
Society of Jesus. *See* Jesuits
Sodomy, as crime, 348–349, 580
Soho Square (London, 1731), 561(i)
Soil, nutrients in, 542
Solar system, 504, 504(i). *See also* Astronomy; Heliocentric theory; Universe
Soldiers. *See also* Armed forces; Casualties; Military; specific battles and wars
    in Hundred Years' War, 338
    Prussian, 481(i)
Sorgh, Hendrick, 544(i)
South America
    Magellan and, 440
    silver from, 476
South Asia, 429
South China Sea, trade in, 428
Sovereignty
    in 17th century, 468
    of American states, 616
    of people, 612–613
Spain. *See also* Exploration; Silver
    absolutism in, 469, 476–478
    American Revolution and, 617
    in Americas, 441–443
    colonies of, 445–447
    cortes in, 338
    division of, 476
    Dutch and, 456, 478, 496

economy in, 476–477
    exploration by, 431–433
    France and, 478, 628
    Inquisition in, 421
    Jesuits in, 597
    Jews in, 386–387
    Muslims in, 385(m), 387, 476
    Napoleon and, 637
    Netherlands and, 419
    plague in, 326
    religion in, 597
    religious conversion of colonists by, 446
    revolts in, 469
    after Seven Years' War, 615
    silver in, 454–455
    Thirty Years' War and, 466
    trade and, 456
    Treaty of Tordesillas and, 440
    unification and expulsion of Jews, 385(m)
    War of the Spanish Succession and, 476, 479, 558
Spanish America. *See also* Latin America
    China trade and, 456
    Columbian exchange and, 448–449
    mixed races in, 448, 567
Spanish Armada, 410, 410(m)
Spanish Empire, trade and, 456, 558
Spanish Netherlands, 419–420, 420(m), 476
Spa towns, 596
Speculation, medieval, 325
Speyer, Diet of (1529), 397
Spice Islands. *See* Moluccas
Spice trade, 432, 435, 440, 455, 455(i), 456, 569
Spinning
    families and, 551
    by women, 551
Spinoza, Baruch, 516–517
Spinster, origins of term, 551
Spirit of Laws, The (Montesquieu), 517
Spiritual Exercises (Loyola), 416
Sports
    blood sports, 587
    commercialization of, 588(b)(i)
Sri Lanka. *See* Ceylon
Stadholder (Dutch), 497
Stamp Act (1765), 615, 615(i)
Standard of living. *See also* Lifestyle
    population growth and, 546
Starvation. *See* Famine
State (nation). *See also* Government; Nationalism
    in Renaissance, 383–387
State-building
    in 17th century, 466–468
    in Austria, 480, 533
    in Prussia, 480–482
Status. *See* Class; Hierarchy
Statute of Kilkenny (Ireland, 1366), 351
Statute of Laborers (England, 1351), 345(d)
Steen, Jan, 496(i)
Sternpost rudder, 433
Stockholm, Royal Palace in, 472(d)
Straits of Magellan, 440
Strasbourg
    France and, 476
    Jews murdered in, 332

Strozzi family, 375
Subcultures, homosexual, 580
Sub-Saharan Africa. *See also* Africa; Slaves and
    slavery; Slave trade
    slave trade in, 450
Succession. *See also* War of the Austrian Suc-
    cession; War of the Spanish Succession
    female in France, 332–333
Sudan, 429
Suffrage. *See* Voting and voting rights
Sugar and sugar industry
    in Americas, 446, 448
    in Brazil, 448, 449(i)
    Genoa and, 432
    slavery and, 449–454, 564(i)
    trade in, 560
    in West Indies, 445
Suleiman I the Magnificent (Ottoman), 413,
    488(b), 489
Sultan, Ottoman, 489
Summer Palace (Vienna), 472(i), 473(d)
Sun-centered (heliocentric) solar system, 504,
    506
Sunda Strait, Indonesia, 456
"Supplement to Bougainville's Voyage"
    (Diderot), 528–529(d)
Supreme Sacred Congregation of the Roman
    and Universal Inquisition. *See* Holy
    Office
Surgeons and surgery, in 18th century, 604
Swahili city-states, 437(d)
Swahili speakers, 429
Swamps, drainage of, 544, 548
Sweden. *See also* Scandinavia
    army professionalization in, 468(i)
    Napoleon and, 636
    Protestant Reformation in, 407
    Russia and, 485
    Thirty Years' War and, 466
Swedish phase, of Thirty Years' War, 466
Swiss Confederation, 496
Switzerland
    radical Reformation in, 400
    religious wars in, 406
    witchcraft trials in, 420
Sword nobility (France), 470
System of Nature, The (Linné), 524

Tableau de Paris (Mercier), 590–591(d)
Taino people, 439
Tariffs. *See also* Taxation
    in France, 475
Tartars. *See also* Mongols
    in Russia, 533
Taverns, 587
Taxation, 542
    in 17th century, 467, 478
    American Revolution and, 615–616
    in Austria, 533
    in England, 338, 346, 491, 492
    in France, 469, 475, 617, 637
    in Hundred Years' War, 338
    in Ottoman Empire, 489
    in Renaissance, 386(i)
    revolts against, 469
Tea, consumption of, 591
Tea Act (1733), 616

Teaching, 583
Teaching orders, 586
Technology. *See also* Industrial Revolution;
    Military technology; Weapons
    exploration and, 433–434
    Scientific Revolution and, 506
Teenagers. *See* Youth
Telescope, 506, 508, 510(i)
Tempest, The (Shakespeare), 458
Tenant farmers, in 17th century, 465
Ten Commandments, The (Cranach the Elder),
    395(i)
Tennis Court Oath, June 20, 1789, 621,
    621(i)
Tenochtitlán, 441, 441(i), 441(m), 442, 443
    Florentine Codex and, 447(d)
Teresa of Ávila (Saint), 416, 418(d)
Territorial churches, Protestant, 597
Territorial expansion. *See* Expansion
Terror, the, in French Revolution, 628–630
Test Act (England, 1673), 493, 494
Tetzel, Johann, 394
Textile industry. *See also* Cotton industry;
    Woolen industry
    in India, 429
    Irish linen industry and, 554(i)
    in rural areas, 549, 550–553
Theater. *See* Drama
Theodicy (Leibniz), 517
Theology
    Erasmus and, 371
    of Henry VIII, 408
    of Luther, 394–395, 396–397(d)
    Protestant, 397
    science and, 505
Theophrastus, 506, 513
Thermidorian Reaction, 630–631, 643
Thermometer, 506
Third Coalition, 636
Third estate (France), 620, 621
Third of May, The (Goya), 639(i)
Third Rome, Moscow as, 482
Thirty Years' War, 413, 462, 466
    England and, 490
    Europe after, 466, 467(m)
    France and, 490
    Habsburgs and, 479
    phases of, 466
    popular revolts during, 469
    population change and, 547
    Spain and, 490
    state-building after, 466–468
Thomas à Kempis, 343
Thomas Aquinas. *See* Aquinas, Thomas
Thought. *See* Intellectual thought
Three-fifths compromise, in U.S. voting, 618
Timbuktu, 435, 436(m)
"Time of Troubles" (Russia), 483
Titian, 376–377, 380(i), 382(i), 454(i)
Titus Andronicus (Shakespeare), 458(i)
Tlaxcala people, 442, 442(i)
Tobacco, 443, 445
Tofts, Mary, 598(i)
Toleration. *See* Religious toleration
Tomatoes, 450(b)
Tordesillas, Treaty of, 440
Total war, in French Revolution, 628–630

Toussaint L'Ouverture. *See* L'Ouverture,
    Toussaint
Towns. *See* Cities and towns
Trade. *See also* Commerce; Maritime trade;
    Slave trade; Spice trade
    Afro-Eurasian, 428–432, 430(m)
    in Asia and Pacific region, 426, 569–570
    Asian-Atlantic, 570
    in Canadian furs, 440
    caravan, 429
    colonial, 558
    Dutch, 497
    England and, 558
    European power and, 570–571
    French Canadian, 444
    in Indian Ocean, 569
    international, 557–567
    medieval famine and, 325
    mercantilism and, 474–475, 558–560
    Ottoman, 430–431
    Persian, 430–431
    Portuguese, 455–456
    in Renaissance, 358
    seaborne, 452(m), 456
    Spanish, 456, 476
Trading companies
    British East India Company, 569, 570
    Company of the East Indies (France),
        475
    Dutch East India Company, 456, 569
    Dutch West India Company, 452, 456
Trading posts, Portuguese, 435
Trading states, in Africa, 429
Trafalgar, Battle of, 636
Training. *See* Education
Transatlantic trade
    in silk, 456
    in slaves, 445, 447, 456
Translation, of Bible, 371
Transportation. *See also* Roads and highways
    population growth and, 548–549
Trans-Saharan trade, 429–430
Transylvania, 413, 479
Travels (Marco Polo), 433, 438(d)
Travels of Sir John Mandeville, The, 433
Treasure of the City of Ladies, The (Christine
    de Pizan), 347
Treaties. *See* specific treaties and wars
Treatment, for plague, 329–330
Trent, Council of, 398(b), 414–416
Trials
    of Joan of Arc, 336, 337, 337(d)
    for witchcraft, 420, 601
Triangle trade, 560, 562
Tricolor, in France, 632(b)
Triennial Act (England, 1641), 491
True and False Churches, The (Cranach the
    Younger), 398(b), 398(i)
Tsars (Russia), 482. *See also* specific rulers
Tudor dynasty (England), 384, 408, 408(i)
Tuileries palace, 627
Tulipmania, 497(i)
Tull, Jethro, 544–545
Turgot, Anne-Robert-Jacques, 557
Turkey. *See also* Anatolia; Ottoman Empire
    Ottomans and, 487
    Russia and, 533

Turks. *See also* Ottoman Empire; Turkey
  Hungary and, 413–414
Tuscany, Florence as Grand Duchy of, 360
Two Treatises of Government (Locke), 495,
  495(d), 517
Type, 371(i), 372
Typhoid, 548
Typhus, 548

Ukraine
  Jews in, 536
  Russia and, 483
  serfdom in, 533
al-Umari, 429
Unemployment
  in England, 546
  in France, 623, 624
  in later Middle Ages, 325
Unification
  of Italy, 361
  of Spain, 385(m)
Unigeniture, in Russia, 487
Union of Utrecht (1581), 420
United Provinces, 420, 420(m), 452, 496.
  See also Dutch Republic
United States
  abolitionism in, 618
  independence of, 616–617
  radical Protestantism and, 400
Universal gravitation, law of, 508, 510–511
Universe
  Aristotle on, 504, 504(i)
  Copernicus on, 506–507
  Descartes and, 511
  Kepler on, 507–509
  Newton on, 510–511
Universities
  during Black Death years, 332
  Scientific Revolution and, 504, 505
Upper Belvedere, 472(i), 473(d)
Upper classes. *See* Aristocracy; Class; Nobility
Uprisings. *See* Revolts and rebellions; Riots
Urban VI (Pope), 340
Urban areas. *See also* Cities and towns
  in 18th century, 544
  clergy in, 392
  conflicts in, 346
  Enlightenment in, 522–524
  guilds in, 554–557
  literacy in, 372
  poor and peasants in, 466
  sex and sexuality in, 346–350
Ursuline order, 416
Utopia (More), 365, 370–371, 408
Utrecht, Peace of, 476, 477(m), 558

Vaccine, for smallpox, 605
Vacuum, 511, 513
Valois dynasty, Habsburg-Valois wars and,
  361, 406
Van der Weyden, Rogier, 376, 376(i)
Van Eyck, Jan, 376
Vasa family. *See* Gustavus Vasa (Sweden)
Vasari, Giorgio, 356, 362, 363–364, 377,
  406(i)
Vatican. *See also* Catholic Church; Papacy
  Sistine Chapel in, 373, 374(i)

Vegetable Market (Sorgh), 544(i)
Velázquez, Diego, 453(b)(i)
Vendée Rebellion (France), 628
Venice
  as city-state, 360
  coffee house in, 526(b)
  trade and, 358, 431–432
Vergil, Polydore, 384
Vermuyden, Cornelius, 544
Vernacular literature, literacy and, 351–353
Versailles palace, 469, 472(d), 473(i)
  court at, 471–474, 619
  Estates General in, 620–621, 623
  "Letter from Versailles" and, 475(d)
  women's march to, 624
Vesalius, Andreas, 512, 513(i)
Vespucci, Amerigo, 440
Viceroyalties, in Spanish New World, 445
Vienna, 480
  coffeehouse in, 527(i)
  Ottoman siege of, 406
  palaces in, 472(d), 472(i)
Vikings, in Greenland, 324
Villa Capra, 377(i)
Villages. *See also* Cities and towns
  in 17th century, 464
  in 18th century, 542
Ville-Marie. *See* Montreal
Vindication of the Rights of Man, A
  (Wollstonecraft), 626
Vindication of the Rights of Woman, A
  (Wollstonecraft), 626–627
Violence. *See also* Wars and warfare
  aristocratic, 350
  in later Middle Ages, 322, 323(i)
  religious, 391(i), 417–422
Virginia colony, 443
Virgin of Guadalupe, 447
Virtù
  in art(s), 363
  in political thought, 367–369
Vitruvian Man (Leonardo da Vinci), 368(i)
Vodou (voodoo), 641–642
Voltaire, 517, 518–519, 523(d)(i)
Von Erlach, Fischer, 473(d)
Von Hildebrandt, Johann Lukas, 473(d)
Voting and voting rights
  in England, 495
  in France, 621
  for women, 618–619
Voyages
  to Africa, 380
  by Cartier, 440
  by Columbus, 436–439, 438–439(d),
    439(m)
  Dutch, 456
  European voyages of discovery, 432–445,
    436(m)
  by Frobisher, 440
  Genoese, 431
  by Magellan, 440
  by Zheng He, 428(i), 429

Wage earners, 546
Wages, in 18th-century, 554
Waksman, Selman, 329
Walpole, Robert, 496

War of Independence. *See* American
  Revolution
War of the Austrian Succession, 530, 530(m),
  558, 570, 614, 619
War of the Spanish Succession, 476, 479,
  558
Wars and warfare. *See also* Civil war(s); Military; Navy; Weapons; specific battles
  and wars
  in Africa, 563–564
  army size and, 468
  in France, 475–476
  in Italian city-states, 361
  population and, 547
  religious, 417–420
  Spanish, 478
Wars of the Roses (England), 384
Washington, George, 616
Water and water resources, in Dutch Republic
  and England, 544
Waterloo, battle at, 640
Wealth
  in Renaissance, 380–381
  silver trade and, 454–455
Wealth gap, 18th-century revolutions and,
  612
Wealth of Nations (Smith). *See Inquiry into the
  Nature and Causes of the Wealth of
  Nations* (Smith)
Weapons, in Hundred Years' War, 333, 335,
  336(i), 338
Weather. *See* Climate
Weavers and weaving, 550. *See also* Textile
  industry
Weaver's Repose, The (Gerritz), 551(i)
Weddings. *See also* Marriage
  peasant, 579(i)
Weights and measures, in France, 629,
  632(b)
Wesley, John, 582, 598–600, 599(d)
Wesley, Susannah, 582
West, the. *See* Western world
West Africa
  Portugal and, 445
  slave trade and, 430
  trade in, 561, 571
Western Europe
  peasants in, 465, 542
  Renaissance politics in, 383–387
Western Hemisphere. *See* Americas; New
  World
Westernization, of Russia, 487, 531
Western world, Russia and, 482
West Indies
  colonial sugar trade and, 561
  England and, 617
  France and, 445
Westphalia, Peace of, 466
Wet-nursing, 581
What Is Enlightenment? (Kant), 521
What Is the Third Estate? (Sieyès), 620–621,
  622–623(d)
Wheat, 448–449
White Mountain, Battle of the, 466
White people
  in American colonies, 565–566
  race and, 524

White people (*continued*)
in Saint-Domingue, 641
supposed superiority of, 524, 525
Widows. *See also* Women
of sailors, 433
as "spinsters," 551
William III of Orange (king of England), 494, 497, 580
William of Occam, 340
Winter Palace (Vienna), 473(*d*)
Witches and witchcraft, European persecution of, 420–422, 421(*i*), 601
Wittenberg
Luther at, 393, 395
Ten Commandments painting in, 395(*i*)
Wives. *See also* Women
in Renaissance, 381
Wollstonecraft, Mary, 626–627
Women. *See also* Gender; Marriage; Midwives; Nuns
African in colonies, 448
age at marriage, 346–348
in American colonies, 448
in American Revolution, 619
as apprentices, 577
in arts, 377–378, 379(*i*)
in Austria, 536(*i*)
bread riots and, 466, 469
Christine de Pizan on, 347(*d*)
Constitution and, 618(*d*)
in consumer economy, 554
debate about, 381
in domestic sphere, 554
education for, 365
in Enlightenment, 523, 523(*d*)(*i*), 524

foundling homes, infanticide, and, 582
in France, 474, 624–625, 628–629, 629(*d*)(*i*), 636
in guilds, 556, 577
leisure activities of, 587
literacy and, 586
march to Versailles by, 624
marriage in 18th century, 576–577
in Ottoman Empire, 489
Paris salons and, 523
philosophes on rights of, 524
pregnancy and, 580
prostitution and, 578, 580
in Protestantism, 402–404
in revolutionary movements, 613
Rousseau on, 520, 529
as rulers, 332
in salons, 515
same-sex relations among, 580
in sciences, 515, 517
as servants, 576(*i*), 577
in textile industry, 551–552
voting rights for, 618–619
voyages of exploration and, 433
witchcraft and, 421–422, 421(*i*)
as workers, 346, 382–383
Women's rights, 524, 624–625, 627
Woodblock printing, 371–372
Woolen industry. *See also* Textile industry
17th-century decline in, 466
female workers in, 551–552
in later Middle Ages, 325
Work. *See also* Labor; Peasant(s); Workers
social context of, 574

Workday, in 18th-century, 554
Workers. *See also* Labor; Peasant(s); Unemployment
in 18th century, 577
Enlightenment ideas and, 586
in guilds, 555–556
industrious revolution and, 553–554
women as, 382–383
Workplace
gender in, 346
in and out of home, 577–578
World trade, in 18th century, 557–567
Worldview
in Enlightenment, 502, 580–581
in Scientific Revolution, 502, 504
Worms, Diet of (1521), 395
Wright, Joseph, 503(*i*)
Writing. *See* Literature; specific writers
Wyclif, John, 340

Yiddish language, 534
York, house of, 384
Young, Arthur, on benefits of enclosure, 545–546, 545(*d*)
Youth, marriage choices by, 578–579
Yucatán peninsula, 446
Yucatec Mayan language, 442(*i*)

Zacatecas, 454
Zapolya, Janos, 413
Zheng He, voyages of, 428(*i*), 429, 430(*m*)
Zinzendorf, Count, 569(*b*)
Zurich, 397, 399, 400
Zwingli, Ulrich, 397, 398(*b*), 400, 402

	Government	Society and Economy
3000 B.C.E.	Emergence of first cities in Mesopotamia, ca. 3800 Unification of Egypt; Archaic Period, ca. 3100–2600 Old Kingdom of Egypt, ca. 2660–2180 Dominance of Akkadian empire in Mesopotamia, ca. 2331–2200 Middle Kingdom in Egypt, ca. 2080–1640	Neolithic peoples rely on settled agriculture, while others pursue nomadic life, ca. 7000–3000 Expansion of Mesopotamian trade and culture into the modern Middle East and Turkey, ca. 2600
2000 B.C.E.	Babylonian empire, ca. 2000–1595 Code of Hammurabi, ca. 1755 Hyksos invade Egypt, ca. 1640–1570 Hittite Empire, ca. 1600–1200 New Kingdom in Egypt, ca. 1570–1075	First wave of Indo-European migrants, by ca. 2000 Extended commerce in Egypt, by ca. 2000 Horses introduced into Asia and North Africa, by ca. 2500
1500 B.C.E.	Third Intermediate Period in Egypt, ca. 1070–712 Unified Hebrew kingdom under Saul, David, and Solomon, ca. 1025–925	Use of iron increases in western Asia, by ca. 1300–1100 Second wave of Indo-European migrants, by ca. 1200 "Dark Age" in Greece, ca. 1100–800
1000 B.C.E.	Hebrew kingdom divided into Israel and Judah, 925 Assyrian Empire, ca. 900–612 Phoenicians found Carthage, 813 Kingdom of Kush conquers and reunifies Egypt, ca. 800–700 Roman monarchy, ca. 753–509 Medes conquers Persia, 710 Babylon wins independence from Assyria, 626 Dracon issues law code at Athens, 621 Solon's reforms at Athens, ca. 594 Cyrus the Great conquers Medes, founds Persian Empire, 550 Persians complete conquest of ancient Near East, 521–464 Reforms of Cleisthenes in Athens, 508	Phoenician seafaring and trading in the Mediterranean, ca. 900–550 First Olympic games, 776 Concentration of landed wealth in Greece, ca. 750–600 Greek overseas expansion, ca. 750–550 Beginning of coinage in western Asia, ca. 640
500 B.C.E.	Persian wars, 499–479 Struggle of the Orders in Rome, ca. 494–287 Growth of the Athenian Empire, 478–431 Peloponnesian War, 431–404 Rome captures Veii, 396 Gauls sack Rome, 387 Roman expansion in Italy, 390–290 Philip II of Macedonia conquers Greece, 338 Conquests of Alexander the Great, 334–324 Punic Wars, 264–146 Reforms of the Gracchi, 133–121	Growth of Hellenistic trade and cities, ca. 330–100 Beginning of Roman silver coinage, 269 Growth of slavery, decline of small farmers in Rome, ca. 250–100 Agrarian reforms of the Gracchi, 133–121

Religion and Philosophy	Science and Technology	Arts and Letters
Growth of anthropomorphic religion in Mesopotamia, ca. 3000–2000	Development of wheeled transport in Mesopotamia, by ca. 3000	Cuneiform and hieroglyphic writing, ca. 3200
Emergence of Egyptian polytheism and belief in personal immortality, ca. 2660	Use of widespread irrigation in Mesopotamia and Egypt, ca. 3000	
Spread of Mesopotamian and Egyptian religious ideas as far north as modern Turkey and as far south as central Africa, ca. 2600	Construction of Stonehenge monument in England, ca. 2500	
	Construction of first pyramid in Egypt, ca. 2600	
Emergence of Hebrew monotheism, ca. 1700	Construction of first ziggurats in Mesopotamia, ca. 2100	*Epic of Gilgamesh*, ca. 1900
Mixture of Hittite and Near Eastern religious beliefs, ca. 1595	Widespread use of bronze in ancient Near East, ca. 1900	
	Babylonian mathematical advances, ca. 1800	
Exodus of the Hebrews from Egypt into Palestine, ca. 1300–1200	Hittites introduce iron technology, ca. 1400	Phoenicians develop alphabet, ca. 1400
		Naturalistic art in Egypt under Akhenaten, 1367–1350
		Egyptian *Book of the Dead*, ca. 1300
Era of the prophets in Israel, ca. 1100–500	Babylonian astronomical advances, ca. 750–400	Homer, traditional author of *Iliad* and *Odyssey*, ca. 800
Beginning of the Hebrew Bible, ca. 950–800	Construction of Parthenon in Athens begins, 447	Hesiod, author of *Theogony* and *Works and Days*, ca. 800
Intermixture of Etruscan and Roman religious cults, ca. 753–509		Aeschylus, first significant Athenian tragedian, ca. 525–456
Growing popularity of local Greek religious cults, ca. 700 B.C.E.–337 C.E.		
Introduction of Zoroastrianism, ca. 600		
Babylonian Captivity of the Hebrews, 587–538		
Pre-Socratic philosophers, ca. 500–400	Hippocrates, formal founder of medicine, ca. 430	Sophocles, tragedian whose plays explore moral and political problems, ca. 496–406
Socrates executed, 399	Building of the Via Appia begins, 312	Herodotus, "father of history," ca. 485–425
Plato, student of Socrates, 427–347	Aristarchos of Samos, advances in astronomy, ca. 310–230	Euripides, most personal of the Athenian tragedians, ca. 480–406
Diogenes, leading proponent of cynicism, ca. 412–323	Euclid codifies geometry, ca. 300	Thucydides, historian of Peloponnesian War, ca. 460–440
Aristotle, student of Plato, 384–322	Herophilus, discoveries in medicine, ca. 300–250	Aristophanes, greatest Athenian comic playwright, ca. 445–386
Epicurus, founder of Epicurean philosophy, 340–270	Archimedes, works on physics and hydrologics, ca. 287–212	
Zeno, founder of Stoic philosophy, 335–262		
Emergence of Mithraism, ca. 300		
Greek cults brought to Rome, ca. 200		
Spread of Hellenistic mystery religions, ca. 200–100		

	Government	Society and Economy
100 B.C.E.	Dictatorship of Sulla, 88–79 B.C.E. Civil war in Rome, 88–31 B.C.E. Dictatorship of Caesar, 45–44 B.C.E. Principate of Augustus, 31 B.C.E.–14 C.E. "Five Good Emperors" of Rome, 96–180 C.E. "Barracks Emperors'" civil war, 235–284 C.E.	Reform of the Roman calendar, 46 B.C.E. "Golden age" of Roman prosperity and vast increase in trade, 96–180 C.E. Growth of serfdom in Roman Empire, ca. 200–500 C.E. Economic contraction in Roman Empire, ca. 235–284 C.E.
300 C.E.	Constantine removes capital of Roman Empire to Constantinople, ca. 315 Visigoths defeat Roman army at Adrianople, 378 Bishop Ambrose asserts church's independence from the state, 380 Odoacer deposes last Roman emperor in the West, 476 Clovis issues Salic law of the Franks, ca. 490	Barbarian migrations throughout western and northern Europe, ca. 378–600
500	Law code of Justinian, 529 Spread of Islam across Arabia, the Mediterranean region, Spain, North Africa, and Asia as far as India, ca. 630–733	Gallo-Roman aristocracy intermarries with Germanic chieftains, ca. 500–700 Decline of towns and trade in the West; agrarian economy predominates, ca. 500–1800
700	Charles Martel defeats Muslims at Tours, 732 Pippin III anointed king of the Franks, 754 Charlemagne secures Frankish crown, r. 768–814	Height of Muslim commercial activity with western Europe, ca. 700–1300
800	Imperial coronation of Charlemagne, Christmas 800 Treaty of Verdun divides Carolingian kingdom, 843 Viking, Magyar, and Muslim invasions, ca. 850–1000 Establishment of Kievan Rus, ca. 900	Invasions and unstable conditions lead to increase of serfdom in western Europe, ca. 800–900 Height of Byzantine commerce and industry, ca. 800–1000
1000	Seljuk Turks conquer Muslim Baghdad, 1055 Norman conquest of England, 1066 Penance of Henry IV at Canossa, 1077	Decline of Byzantine free peasantry, ca. 1025–1100 Growth of towns and trade in the West, ca. 1050–1300 *Domesday Book* in England, 1086
1100	Henry I of England, r. 1100–1135 Louis VI of France, r. 1108–1137 Frederick I of Germany, r. 1152–1190 Henry II of England, r. 1154–1189	Henry I of England establishes the Exchequer, 1130 Beginnings of the Hanseatic League, 1159

Religion and Philosophy	Science and Technology	Arts and Letters
Mithraism spreads to Rome, 27 B.C.E.–270 C.E. Life of Jesus, ca. 3 B.C.E.–29 C.E.	Engineering advances in Rome, ca. 100 B.C.E.–180 C.E.	Flowering of Latin literature: Virgil, 70–19 B.C.E.; Livy, ca. 59 B.C.E.–17 C.E.; Ovid, 43 B.C.E.–17 C.E.
Constantine legalizes Christianity, 312 Theodosius declares Christianity the official state religion, 380 Donatist heretical movement at its height, ca. 400 St. Augustine, *Confessions*, ca. 390; *The City of God*, ca. 425 Clovis adopts Roman Christianity, 496	Construction of Arch of Constantine, ca. 315	St. Jerome publishes Latin *Vulgate*, late 4th c. Byzantines preserve Greco-Roman culture, ca. 400–1000
Rule of St. Benedict, 529 Life of the Prophet Muhammad, ca. 571–632 Pope Gregory the Great publishes *Dialogues*, *Pastoral Care*, *Moralia*, 590–604 Monasteries established in Anglo-Saxon England, ca. 600–700 Publication of the Qur'an, 651 Synod of Whitby, 664	Using watermills, Benedictine monks exploit energy of fast-flowing rivers and streams, by 600 Heavy plow and improved harness facilitate use of multiple-ox teams; harrow widely used in northern Europe, by 600 Byzantines successfully use "Greek fire" in naval combat against Arab fleets attacking Constantinople, 673, 717	Boethius, *The Consolation of Philosophy*, ca. 520 Justinian constructs church of Santa Sophia, 532–537
Bede, *Ecclesiastical History of the English Nation*, ca. 700 Missionary work of St. Boniface in Germany, ca. 710–750 Iconoclastic controversy in Byzantine Empire, 726–843 Pippin III donates Papal States to the papacy, 756		Lindisfarne Gospel Book, ca. 700 *Beowulf*, ca. 700 Carolingian Renaissance, ca. 780–850
Foundation of abbey of Cluny, 909 Byzantine conversion of Russia, late 10th c.	Stirrup and nailed horseshoes become widespread in combat, 900–1000 Paper (invented in China, ca. 150) enters Europe through Muslim Spain, ca. 900–1000	Byzantines develop Cyrillic script, late 10th c.
Schism between Roman and Greek Orthodox churches, 1054 Lateran Council restricts election of pope to College of Cardinals, 1059 Pope Gregory VII, 1073–1085 Theologian Peter Abelard, 1079–1142 First Crusade, 1095–1099 Founding of Cistercian order, 1098	Arab conquests bring new irrigation methods, cotton cultivation, and manufacture to Spain, Sicily, southern Italy, by 1000 Avicenna, Arab scientist, d. 1037	Muslim musicians introduce lute, rebec (stringed instruments, ancestors of violin), ca. 1000 Romanesque style in architecture and art, ca. 1000–1200 *Song of Roland*, ca. 1095
Universities begin, ca. 1100–1300 Concordat of Worms ends investiture controversy, 1122 Height of Cistercian monasticism, 1125–1175	Europeans, copying Muslim and Byzantine models, construct castles with rounded towers and crenellated walls, by 1100	Troubadour poetry, especially of Chrétien de Troyes, circulates widely, ca. 1100–1200 *Rubaiyat of Umar Khayyam*, ca. 1120 Dedication of abbey church of Saint-Denis launches Gothic style, 1144

Government	Society and Economy

1100 (cont.)

Thomas Becket, archbishop of Canterbury, murdered 1170

Philip Augustus of France, r. 1180–1223

1200

Spanish victory over Muslims at Las Navas de Tolosa, 1212

Frederick II of Germany and Sicily, r. 1212–1250

Magna Carta, charter of English political and civil liberties, 1215

Louis IX of France, r. 1226–1270

Mongols end Abbasid caliphate, 1258

Edward I of England, r. 1272–1307

Philip IV (the Fair) of France, r. 1285–1314

European revival, growth of towns; agricultural expansion leads to population growth, ca. 1200–1300

Crusaders capture Constantinople (Fourth Crusade) and spur Venetian economy, 1204

1300

Philip IV orders arrest of Pope Boniface at Anagni, 1303

Hundred Years' War between England and France, 1337–1453

Political disorder in Germany, ca. 1350–1450

Merchant oligarchies or despots rule Italian city-states, ca. 1350–1550

"Little ice age," European economic depression, ca. 1300–1450

Black Death appears ca. 1347; returns intermittently until ca. 1720

Height of the Hanseatic League, 1350–1450

Peasant and working-class revolts: Flanders, 1328; France, 1358; Florence, 1378; England, 1381

1400

Joan of Arc rallies French monarchy, 1429–1431

Medici domination of Florence begins, 1434

Princes in Germany consolidate power, ca. 1450–1500

Ottoman Turks under Mahomet II capture Constantinople, May 1453

War of the Roses in England, 1455–1471

Establishment of the Inquisition in Spain, 1478

Ferdinand and Isabella complete reconquista in Spain, 1492

French invasion of Italy, 1494

Population decline, peasants' revolts, high labor costs contribute to decline of serfdom in western Europe, ca. 1400–1650

Flow of Balkan slaves into eastern Mediterranean, of African slaves into Iberia and Italy, ca. 1400–1500

Christopher Columbus reaches the Americas, 1492

Portuguese gain control of East Indian spice trade, 1498–1511

1500

Charles V, Holy Roman emperor, 1519–1556

Habsburg-Valois Wars, 1521–1559

Philip II of Spain, r. 1556–1598

Revolt of the Netherlands, 1566–1598

St. Bartholomew's Day massacre in France, 1572

English defeat of the Spanish Armada, 1588

Henry IV of France issues Edict of Nantes, 1598

Consolidation of serfdom in eastern Europe, ca. 1500–1650

Balboa discovers the Pacific, 1513

Magellan's crew circumnavigates the earth, 1519–1522

Spain and Portugal gain control of regions of Central and South America, ca. 1520–1550

Peasants' Revolt in Germany, 1524–1525

"Time of Troubles" in Russia, 1598–1613

Religion and Philosophy	Science and Technology	Arts and Letters
Aristotle's works translated into Latin, ca. 1140–1260 Third Crusade, 1189–1192 Pope Innocent III, height of the medieval papacy, 1198–1216	Underground pipes with running water and indoor latrines installed in some monasteries, such as Clairvaux and Canterbury Cathedral Priory, by 1100; elsewhere rare until 1800 Windmill invented, ca. 1180	
Founding of the Franciscan order, 1210 Fourth Lateran Council accepts seven sacraments, 1215 Founding of Dominican order, 1216 Thomas Aquinas, height of scholasticism, 1225–1274	*Notebooks* of architect Villard de Honnecourt, a major source for Gothic engineering, ca. 1250 Development of double-entry bookkeeping in Florence and Genoa, ca. 1250–1340 Venetians purchase secrets of glass manufacture from Syria, 1277 Mechanical clock invented, ca. 1290	*Parzifal, Roman de la rose, King Arthur and the Round Table* celebrate virtues of knighthood and chivalry, ca. 1200–1300 Height of Gothic style, ca. 1225–1300
Pope Boniface VIII declares all Christians subject to the pope in *Unam Sanctam*, 1302 Babylonian Captivity of the papacy, 1309–1376 Theologian John Wyclif, ca. 1330–1384 Great Schism in the papacy, 1378–1417	Edward III of England uses cannon in siege of Calais, 1346 Clocks in general use throughout Europe, by 1400	Paintings of Giotto mark emergence of Renaissance movement in the arts, ca. 1305–1337 Dante, *Divine Comedy*, ca. 1310 Petrarch develops ideas of humanism, ca. 1350 Boccaccio, *The Decameron*, ca. 1350 Jan van Eyck, Flemish painter, 1366–1441 Brunelleschi, Florentine architect, 1377–1446 Chaucer, *Canterbury Tales*, ca. 1387–1400
Council of Constance ends the schism in the papacy, 1414–1418 Pragmatic Sanction of Bourges affirms special rights of French crown over French church, 1438 Expulsion of Jews from Spain, 1492	Water-powered blast furnaces operative in Sweden, Austria, the Rhine Valley, Liège, ca. 1400 Leonardo Fibonacci's *Liber Abaci* popularizes use of Hindu-Arabic numerals, important in rise of Western science, 1402 Paris and largest Italian cities pave streets, making street cleaning possible, ca. 1450 European printing and movable type, ca. 1450	Height of Renaissance movement: Masaccio, 1401–1428; Botticelli, 1444–1510; Leonardo da Vinci, 1452–1519; Albrecht Dürer, 1471–1528; Michelangelo, 1475–1564; Raphael, 1483–1520
Machiavelli, *The Prince*, 1513 More, *Utopia*, 1516 Luther, *Ninety-five Theses*, 1517 Henry VIII of England breaks with Rome, 1532–1534 Merici establishes Ursuline order for education of women, 1535 Loyola establishes Society of Jesus, 1540 Calvin establishes theocracy in Geneva, 1541 Council of Trent shapes essential character of Catholicism until the 1960s, 1545–1563 Peace of Augsburg, official recognition of Lutheranism, 1555	Scientific revolution in western Europe, ca. 1540–1690: Copernicus, *On the Revolutions of the Heavenly Bodies*, 1543; Galileo, 1564–1642; Kepler, 1571–1630; Harvey, 1578–1657	Erasmus, *The Praise of Folly*, 1509 Castiglione, *The Courtier*, 1528 Baroque movement in arts, ca. 1550–1725: Rubens, 1577–1640; Velasquez, 1599–1660 Shakespeare, West's most enduring and influential playwright, 1564–1616 Montaigne, *Essays*, 1598

Government	Society and Economy
1600	
Thirty Years' War begins, 1618	Chartering of British East India Company, 1600
Richelieu dominates French government, 1624–1643	English Poor Law, 1601
Frederick William, Elector of Brandenburg, r. 1640–1688	Chartering of Dutch East India Company, 1602
English Civil War, 1642–1649	Height of Dutch commercial activity, ca. 1630–1665
Louis XIV, r. 1643–1715	
Peace of Westphalia ends the Thirty Years' War, 1648	
The Fronde in France, 1648–1660	
1650	
Anglo-Dutch wars, 1652–1674	Height of mercantilism in Europe, ca. 1650–1750
Protectorate in England, 1653–1658	Agricultural revolution in Europe, ca. 1650–1850
Leopold I, Habsburg emperor, r. 1658–1705	Principle of peasants' hereditary subjugation to their lords affirmed in Prussia, 1653
English monarchy restored, 1660	Colbert's economic reforms in France, ca. 1663–1683
Ottoman siege of Vienna, 1683	Cossack revolt in Russia, 1670–1671
Glorious Revolution in England, 1688–1689	
Peter the Great of Russia, r. 1689–1725	
1700	
War of the Spanish Succession, 1701–1713	Foundation of St. Petersburg, 1701
Peace of Utrecht redraws political boundaries of Europe, 1713	Last appearance of bubonic plague in western Europe, ca. 1720
Frederick William I of Prussia, r. 1713–1740	Growth of European population, ca. 1720–1789
Louis XV of France, r. 1715–1774	Enclosure movement in England, ca. 1730–1830
Maria Theresa of Austria, r. 1740–1780	
Frederick the Great of Prussia, r. 1740–1786	
1750	
Seven Years' War, 1756–1763	Growth of illegitimate births in Europe, ca. 1750–1850
Catherine the Great of Russia, r. 1762–1796	Industrial Revolution in western Europe, ca. 1780–1850
Partition of Poland, 1772–1795	Serfdom abolished in France, 1789
Louis XVI of France, r. 1774–1792	
American Revolution, 1775–1783	
French Revolution, 1789–1799	
Slave insurrection in Saint-Domingue, 1791	
1800	
Napoleonic era, 1799–1815	British takeover of India complete, 1805
Haitian republic declares independence, 1804	British slave trade abolished, 1807
Congress of Vienna re-establishes political power after defeat of Napoleon, 1814–1815	German Zollverein founded, 1834
Greece wins independence from Ottoman Empire, 1830	European capitalists begin large-scale foreign investment, 1840s
French conquest of Algeria, 1830	Great Famine in Ireland, 1845–1851
Revolution in France, 1830	First public health law in Britain, 1848
Great Britain: Reform Bill of 1832; Poor Law reform, 1834; Chartists, repeal of Corn Laws, 1838–1848	
Revolutions in Europe, 1848	

Religion and Philosophy	Science and Technology	Arts and Letters
Huguenot revolt in France, 1625	Further development of scientific method: Bacon, *The Advancement of Learning*, 1605; Descartes, *Discourse on Method*, 1637	Cervantes, *Don Quixote*, 1605, 1615 Flourishing of French theater: Molière, 1622–1673; Racine, 1639–1699 Golden age of Dutch culture, ca. 1625–1675: Rembrandt van Rijn, 1606–1669; Vermeer, 1632–1675
Social contract theory: Hobbes, *Leviathan*, 1651; Locke, *Second Treatise on Civil Government*, 1690 Patriarch Nikon's reforms split Russian Orthodox Church, 1652 Test Act in England excludes Roman Catholics from public office, 1673 Revocation of Edict of Nantes, 1685 James II tries to restore Catholicism as state religion, 1685–1688	Tull (1674–1741) encourages innovation in English agriculture Newton, *Principia Mathematica*, 1687	Construction of baroque palaces and remodeling of capital cities, central and eastern Europe, ca. 1650–1725 Bach, great late baroque German composer, 1685–1750 Enlightenment begins, ca. 1690: Fontenelle, *Conversations on the Plurality of Worlds*, 1686; Voltaire, French philosopher and writer whose work epitomizes Enlightenment, 1694–1778 Pierre Bayle, *Historical and Critical Dictionary*, 1697
Wesley, founder of Methodism, 1703–1791 Montesquieu, *The Spirit of Laws*, 1748	Newcomen develops steam engine, 1705 Charles Townsend introduces four-year crop rotation, 1730	
Hume, *The Natural History of Religion*, 1755 Rousseau, *The Social Contract* and *Emile*, 1762 Fourier, French utopian socialist, 1772–1837 Papacy dissolves Jesuits, 1773 Smith, *The Wealth of Nations*, 1776 Church reforms of Joseph II in Austria, 1780s Kant, *What Is Enlightenment?*, 1784 Reorganization of church in France, 1790s Wollstonecraft, *A Vindication of the Rights of Women*, 1792 Malthus, *Essay on the Principle of Population*, 1798	Hargreaves's spinning jenny, ca. 1765 Arkwright's water frame, ca. 1765 Watt's steam engine promotes industrial breakthroughs, 1780s Jenner's smallpox vaccine, 1796	*Encyclopedia*, edited by Diderot and d'Alembert, published 1751–1765 Classical style in music, ca. 1770–1830: Mozart, 1756–1791; Beethoven, 1770–1827 Wordsworth, English romantic poet, 1770–1850 Romanticism in art and literature, ca. 1790–1850
Napoleon signs Concordat with Pope Pius VII regulating Catholic Church in France, 1801 Spencer, Social Darwinist, 1820–1903 Comte, *System of Positive Philosophy*, 1830–1842 Height of French utopian socialism, 1830s–1840s List, *National System of Political Economy*, 1841 Nietzsche, radical and highly influential German philosopher, 1844–1900 Marx, *Communist Manifesto*, 1848	First railroad, Great Britain, 1825 Faraday studies electromagnetism, 1830–1840s	Staël, *On Germany*, 1810 Balzac, *The Human Comedy*, 1829–1841 Delacroix, *Liberty Leading the People*, 1830 Hugo, *The Hunchback of Notre Dame*, 1831

Government	Society and Economy
1850	
Second Empire in France, 1852–1870	Crédit Mobilier founded in France, 1852
Crimean War, 1853–1856	Japan opened to European influence, 1853
Britain crushes Great Rebellion in India, 1857–1858	Russian serfs emancipated, 1861
Unification of Italy, 1859–1870	First Socialist International, 1864–1871
U.S. Civil War, 1861–1865	
Bismarck leads Germany, 1862–1890	
Unification of Germany, 1864–1871	
Britain's Second Reform Bill, 1867	
Third Republic in France, 1870–1940	
1875	
Congress of Berlin, 1878	Full property rights for women in Great Britain, 1882
European "scramble for Africa," 1880–1900	Second Industrial Revolution; birthrate steadily declines in Europe, ca. 1880–1913
Britain's Third Reform Bill, 1884	Social welfare legislation, Germany, 1883–1889
Dreyfus affair in France, 1894–1899	Second Socialist International, 1889–1914
Spanish-American War, 1898	Witte directs modernization of Russian economy, 1892–1899
South African War, 1899–1902	
1900	
Russo-Japanese War, 1904–1905	Women's suffrage movement, England, ca. 1900–1914
Revolution in Russia, 1905	Social welfare legislation, France, 1904, 1910; Great Britain, 1906–1914
Balkan wars, 1912–1913	Agrarian reforms in Russia, 1907–1912
1914	
World War I, 1914–1918	Planned economics in Europe, 1914
Armenian genocide, 1915	Auxiliary Service Law in Germany, 1916
Easter Rebellion, 1916	Bread riots in Russia, March 1917
U.S. declares war on Germany, 1917	
Bolshevik Revolution, 1917–1918	
Treaty of Versailles, World War I peace settlement, 1919	
1920	
Mussolini seizes power in Italy, 1922	New Economic Policy in U.S.S.R., 1921
Stalin comes to power in U.S.S.R., 1927	Dawes Plan for reparations and recovery, 1924
Hitler gains power in Germany, 1933	Great Depression, 1929–1939
Rome-Berlin Axis, 1936	Rapid industrialization in U.S.S.R., 1930s
Nazi-Soviet Non-Aggression Pact, 1939	Start of Roosevelt's New Deal in U.S., 1933
World War II, 1939–1945	
1940	
United Nations founded, 1945	Holocaust, 1941–1945
Decolonization of Asia and Africa, 1945–1960s	Marshall Plan enacted, 1947
Cold War begins, 1947	European economic progress, ca. 1950–1970
Founding of Israel, 1948	European Coal and Steel Community founded, 1952
Communist government in China, 1949	European Economic Community founded, 1957
Korean War, 1950–1953	
De-Stalinization of Soviet Union under Khrushchev, 1953–1964	
1960	
Building of Berlin Wall, 1961	Civil rights movement in U.S., 1960s
U.S. involvement in Vietnam War, 1964–1973	Stagflation, 1970s
Student rebellion in France, 1968	Feminist movement, 1970s

Religion and Philosophy	Science and Technology	Arts and Letters
Decline in church attendance among working classes, ca. 1850–1914 Mill, *On Liberty*, 1859 Pope Pius IX, *Syllabus of Errors*, denounces modern thoughts, 1864 Marx, *Das Capital*, 1867 Doctrine of papal infallibility, 1870	Modernization of Paris, ca. 1850–1870 Great Exhibition in London, 1851 Freud, founder of psychoanalysis, 1856–1939 Darwin, *On the Origin of Species*, 1859 Pasteur develops germ theory of disease, 1860s Suez Canal opened, 1869 Mendeleev develops periodic table, 1869	Realism in art and literature, ca. 1850–1870 Flaubert, *Madame Bovary*, 1857 Tolstoy, *War and Peace*, 1869 Impressionism in art, ca. 1870–1900 Eliot (Mary Ann Evans), *Middlemarch*, 1872
Growth of public education in France, ca. 1880–1900 Growth of mission schools in Africa, 1890–1914	Emergence of modern immunology, ca. 1875–1900 Electrical industry: lighting and streetcars, ca. 1880–1900 Trans-Siberian Railroad, 1890s Marie Curie, discovery of radium, 1898	Zola, *Germinal*, 1885 Kipling, "The White Man's Burden," 1899
Separation of church and state in France, 1901–1905 Hobson, *Imperialism*, 1902 Schweitzer, *Quest of the Historical Jesus*, 1906	Planck develops quantum theory, ca. 1900 First airplane flight, 1903 Einstein develops theory of special relativity, 1905–1910	Modernism in art and literature, ca. 1900–1929 Conrad, *Heart of Darkness*, 1902 Cubism in art, ca. 1905–1930 Proust, *Remembrance of Things Past*, 1913–1927
Keynes, *Economic Consequences of the Peace*, 1919	Submarine warfare introduced, 1915 Ernest Rutherford splits atom, 1919	Spengler, *The Decline of the West*, 1918
Emergence of modern existentialism, 1920s Revival of Christianity, 1920s–1930s Wittgenstein, *Essay on Logical Philosophy*, 1922 Heisenberg's principle of uncertainty, 1927	"Heroic age of physics," 1920s First major public radio broadcasts in Great Britain and U.S., 1920 First talking movies, 1930 Radar system in England, 1939	Gropius, Bauhaus, 1920s Dadaism and surrealism, 1920s Woolf, *Jacob's Room*, 1922 Joyce, *Ulysses*, 1922 Eliot, *The Waste Land*, 1922 Remarque, *All Quiet on the Western Front*, 1929 Picasso, *Guernica*, 1937
De Beauvoir, *The Second Sex*, 1949 Communists fail to break Catholic Church in Poland, 1950s	U.S. drops atomic bombs on Japan, 1945 Big Science in U.S., ca. 1945–1965 Watson and Crick discover structure of DNA molecule, 1953 Russian satellite in orbit, 1957	Cultural purge in Soviet Union, 1946–1952 Van der Rohe, Lake Shore Apartments, 1948–1951 Orwell, *1984*, 1949 Pasternak, *Doctor Zhivago*, 1956 "Beat" movement in U.S., late 1950s
Second Vatican Council announces sweeping Catholic reforms, 1962–1965 Pope John II, 1978–2005	European Council for Nuclear Research founded, 1960 Space race, 1960s	The Beatles, 1960s Solzhenitsyn, *One Day in the Life of Ivan Denisovich*, 1962

	Government	Society and Economy
1960 (cont.)	Soviet tanks end Prague Spring, 1968	Collapse of postwar monetary system, 1971
	Détente between U.S. and U.S.S.R., 1970s	OPEC oil price increases, 1973, 1979
	Soviet occupation of Afghanistan, 1979–1989	
1980	U.S. military buildup, 1980s	Growth of debt in the West, 1980s
	Solidarity in Poland, 1980	Economic crisis in Poland, 1988
	Unification of Germany, 1989	Maastricht Treaty proposes monetary union, 1990
	Revolutions in eastern Germany, 1989–1990	European Community becomes European Union, 1993
	Persian Gulf War, 1990–1991	Migration to western Europe increases, 1990s
	Dissolution of Soviet Union, 1991	
	Civil war in Yugoslavia, 1991–2001	
	Separatist war breaks out in Chechnya, 1991	
2000	Terrorist attacks on U.S., Sept. 11, 2001	Same-sex marriage legalized in the Netherlands, 2001
	War in Afghanistan begins, 2001	Euro enters circulation, 2002
	Iraq War, 2003–2011	Voters reject new European Union constitution, 2005
	NATO intervenes in Libyan civil war, 2011	Immigrant riots in France, 2005, 2009
	Al-Qaeda leader Osama bin Laden killed, 2011	Worldwide financial crisis begins, 2008
		European financial crisis intensifies, 2010
		Anti-austerity protests across Europe begin, 2010
		Arab Spring uprisings in the Middle East and North Africa, 2011
		France legalizes same-sex marriage, 2013

Religion and Philosophy	Science and Technology	Arts and Letters
	Russian cosmonaut first to orbit globe, 1961 American astronaut first person on moon, 1969	Carson, *Silent Spring*, 1962 Friedan, *The Feminine Mystique*, 1963 Servan-Schreiber, *The American Challenge*, 1967
Revival of religion in Soviet Union, 1985– Growth of Islam in Europe, 1990s Fukuyama proclaims "end of history," 1991	Reduced spending on Big Science, 1980s Computer revolution continues, 1980s–1990s U.S. Genome Project begins, 1990 First World Wide Web server and browser, 1991 Pentium processor invented, 1993 First genetically cloned sheep, 1996	Solzhenitsyn returns to Russia, 1994; dies 2008 Author Salman Rushdie exiled from Iran, 1989 Gehry, Guggenheim Museum, Bilbao, 1997
Ramadan, *Western Muslims and the Future of Islam*, 2004 Pontificate of Benedict XVI, 2005–2013 Jorge Mario Bergoglio elected as Pope Francis, 2013	Growing concern about global warming, 2000s First hybrid car, 2003 Copenhagen Summit on climate change, 2009	Movies and books exploring clash between immigrants and host cultures popular: *Bend It Like Beckham*, 2002; *The Namesake*, 2003; *White Teeth*, 2003; *The Class*, 2008

ABOUT THE AUTHORS

John P. McKay (Ph.D., University of California, Berkeley) is professor emeritus at the University of Illinois. He has written or edited numerous works, including the Herbert Baxter Adams Prize–winning book *Pioneers for Profit: Foreign Entrepreneurship and Russian Industrialization, 1885–1913*.

Bennett D. Hill (Ph.D., Princeton), late of Georgetown University, published *Church and State in the Middle Ages* and numerous articles and reviews, and was one of the contributing editors to *The Encyclopedia of World History*. He taught for many years at the University of Illinois and was a Benedictine monk of St. Anselm's Abbey in Washington, D.C.

John Buckler (Ph.D., Harvard University), late of the University of Illinois, published numerous works, including *Theban Hegemony, 371–362 B.C.*; *Philip II and the Sacred War*; and *Aegean Greece in the Fourth Century B.C.* With Hans Beck, he published *Central Greece and the Politics of Power in the Fourth Century*.

Clare Haru Crowston (Ph.D., Cornell University) teaches at the University of Illinois, where she is currently associate professor of history. She is the author of *Credit, Fashion, Sex: Economies of Regard in Old Regime France* and *Fabricating Women: The Seamstresses of Old Regime France, 1675–1791*, which won the Berkshire and Hagley Prizes. She edited two special issues of the *Journal of Women's History*, has published numerous journal articles and reviews, and is a past president of the Society for French Historical Studies.

Merry E. Wiesner-Hanks (Ph.D., University of Wisconsin–Madison) taught first at Augustana College in Illinois, and since 1985 at the University of Wisconsin–Milwaukee, where she is currently UWM Distinguished Professor in the department of history. She is the Senior Editor of the *Sixteenth Century Journal*, one of the editors of the *Journal of Global History*, and the author or editor of more than twenty books, including *The Marvelous Hairy Girls: The Gonzales Sisters and Their Worlds* and *Gender in History* (2nd ed.). She is the former Chief Reader for Advanced Placement World History.

Joe Perry (Ph.D., University of Illinois at Urbana-Champaign) is associate professor of modern German and European history at Georgia State University. He has published numerous articles and is author of *Christmas in Germany: A Cultural History*. His current research interests focus on issues of consumption, gender, and popular culture in West Germany and Western Europe after World War II.